PEARSON   ALWAYS LEARNING

Larry DeBoer

MacroPolicy
Learning Macroeconomics with Policy History

Sixth Edition

Pearson Learning Solutions, 501 Boylston Street, Suite 900, Boston, MA 02116
A Pearson Education Company
www.pearsoned.com

Printed in the United States of America

1 2 3 4 5 6 7 8 9 10 V036 16 15 14 13 12 11

000200010270728695

CY

ISBN 10: 1-256-36689-7
ISBN 13: 978-1-256-36689-8

MacroPolicy
Learning Macroeconomics With Policy History
Sixth Edition

Larry DeBoer, 2011

For Melody

Larry DeBoer
Department of Agricultural Economics
Purdue University
Krannert Building, Room 618
403 W. State Street
West Lafayette, Indiana   47907-9176
ldeboer@purdue.edu

What's on the Cover?

It's a collection of economic artifacts.
1. *A one dollar greenback issued in 1862, to pay for the Civil War. Chapter 3.*
2. *A one dollar silver certificate from 1890, issued during the bimetallism debate. Chapter 4.*
3. *A 20 yuan bill from China, worth $3.09 in June 2011, and rising. Chapters 4 and 12.*
4. *A one hundred trillion dollar note from the hyperinflation in Zimbabwe, 2008. Chapter 4.*
5. *A one dollar Federal Reserve note issued in 1918, to pay for World War I. Chapter 5.*
6. *A news magazine with Federal Reserve chair Ben Bernanke on the cover. Chapter 6 and throughout.*
7. *A snapshot of the entrance to the New York Stock Exchange, on Wall Street. Chapters 6, 11 and 12.*
8. *A snapshot of a bank window, advertising deposit insurance. Chapter 6.*
9. *A sticker with the "blue eagle" emblem of the National Recovery Administration, a New Deal agency. Chapter 7.*
10. *A book for keeping track of Social Security earnings, from 1937. Chapter 7.*
11. *A matchbox advertising war bonds, from World War II. Chapter 8.*
12. *A ration book and ration stamps, from World War II. Chapter 8.*
13. *A postcard from the Mt. Washington Hotel in Bretton Woods, New Hampshire. Chapter 9.*
14. *A "Whip Inflation Now" WIN button, from the Ford administration in 1974. Chapter 10.*
15. *A 50 baht note from Thailand, issued during the Asian crisis in 1997. Chapters 9 and 11.*
16. *A snapshot of a highway sign advertising the 2009 stimulus program. Chapter 12.*

Table of Contents

Introduction

I wrote this textbook because I couldn't find a textbook like it. I'm interested in macroeconomics. I'm interested in the history of policy. I've always wanted to use the history to teach the economics. That's what this book does.

But a funny thing happened back in 2008: all heck broke loose. The worst financial crisis since the Great Depression, the deepest recession since 1982 (at least), several years of bank runs, market crashes, credit freezes, rising unemployment, a threat of deflation, oil prices rising then falling then rising again, popping speculative bubbles, expansionary fiscal policy, expansionary monetary policy, undreamed of policy innovations, fears of rising debt, fears of hyperinflation. It's not much of a stretch to say that just about everything that has happened in the history of macroeconomic policy, had its parallel from 2007 to 2011.

It may be the greatest "teachable moment" in the history of macroeconomics.

But how to teach it? Introductory macroeconomics can be taught as geometry. I've done it myself, and I love it. Most of my students don't feel that way. Introductory macroeconomics is a required course at my campus, so almost all of my students are taking the class because they have to. And for almost all of them, it's the only economics class they will ever take. The questions are, how to reach these reluctant students, and what to teach them in this one and only opportunity.

They're not very interested in economics, and not interested in geometry. But lots of them are interested in people, and stories about people. Perhaps the stories behind macroeconomic policymaking can attract their interest. So here are stories of Presidents in conflict with Congress, Presidents in conflict with Federal Reserve chairs, Presidential advisors in conflict with each other. How did they resolve their disagreements, what did they decide and why? Those are the stories in this book.

I've got this one shot at teaching these students. No one from my profession will see most of them ever again. Do I teach the difference between GNP and GDP? Between M1 and M2? Do I focus on shifting curves and moving equilibrium points? To ask is to answer.

Instead, let's tell the story of what's been tried and why. What was the experience of the Great Depression, and why do we really want to avoid that again? What was the experience of the Great Inflation, and why does the Federal Reserve act the way it does? What does war do to an economy? What do stock market (and housing market) booms and crashes do to an economy? Who were (and are) William Jennings Bryan, J. P. Morgan, John Maynard Keynes, Frances Perkins, Marriner Eccles, Harry Dexter White, Milton Friedman, Arthur Laffer, Paul Volcker, Alan Greenspan, Ben Bernanke, and what did they do?

And now, what can we learn from what they did, and how can we apply it to the issues of today? That's what I'd like my students to learn.

There are some terrific books that tell the story of American economic policy. If you're interested in policy, here are some books to read.

- Economic Historian Liaquat Ahamed tells the fascinating story of the collapse of international finance from World War I to the Great Depression, through the lives, friendships and rivalries of four central bankers, in *Lords of Finance: The Bankers Who Broke the World*.
- Historian David Kennedy wrote a wonderful account of the Franklin Roosevelt era, called *Freedom from Fear*. It's about more than just economic policy, but Kennedy brings the economic policy debates to life.
- Economist Herbert Stein wrote *The Fiscal Revolution in America*, which has more about policy during the Eisenhower administration than I thought there was to know. And even better, he wrote *Presidential Economics*, about policy making from Roosevelt to Clinton. He was there when Richard Nixon decided to torpedo fixed exchange rates in 1971, and he tells the eye-witness story.
- Federal Reserve Chair Paul Volcker made policy from the 1960's through the 1980's, and his memoir *Changing Fortunes* tells all.
- Presidential aide Joseph Califano was at Lyndon Johnson's side when he decided not to raise taxes to pay for Vietnam, perhaps the crucial decision of the "Great Inflation" era. He wrote all about it in *The Triumph and Tragedy of Lyndon Johnson*.
- Presidential aide David Stockman gives a vote-by-vote account of the Reagan tax cut battle in 1981, in *The Triumph of Politics*.
- Journalist-supreme Bob Woodward turned his attention to economic policymaking in the 1990s, with two books, one on the Clinton administration (*The Agenda*) and one on Alan Greenspan (*Maestro*).
- The definitive book on the Panic of 2008 hasn't been written. Its effects are still unfolding. But Carmen Reinhart and Kenneth Rogoff wrote *This Time Is Different* about a few centuries worth of financial panics. Their point: it's never different, and it wasn't in 2008 either.

A class could be taught from these books, but the problem would be three-fold. That's ten books and that's a lot of reading. Not all of every book is to the point of an introductory macroeconomics course. None of these books applies a macroeconomic model explicitly. Stein and Volcker certainly have one in mind, but there are no demand and supply graphs. To teach with these books you'd need another text on economic theory. That's eleven books. Students will remind you that they have other classes (and they're not made of money).

So this book tries to boil it all down to a manageable 435 or so pages. It starts with three chapters on measurement and models. Each of these chapters frequently stops talking theory, in order to apply it to a current issue. The remaining nine chapters take an era or an issue, to tell the story of policy and policymakers.

Each chapter starts with a current issue, written from recent news articles, called *MacroPolicy Now*. Then the bulk of the chapter tells a story of people and issues, interrupted once in a while to explain what's going on with a macroeconomic model. Sometimes I sneak some theoretical whistles and bells in there too. After that, there's a section at the end that applies the chapter's lessons to today's news. Chapter 12 differs a little, because it's about events since 2008. The whole chapter is pretty much current issues.

Why learn the history of policy? Because it's a guide to policy today. U.S. economic relations with China today are reminiscent of our relations with Great Britain in the 1890's. The Panic of 1907 and the Panic of 2008 have eerie similarities. Even some of the names are the same. The story of any market crash—like housing or tech stocks in the 2000's—must recall the big one in 1929. And, unfortunately, there are always the economic effects of war. We can learn a lot from the similarities and differences of the Civil War, the World Wars, Korea, Vietnam, the Gulf, Iraq and Afghanistan.

I'm excited to teach with this book. I hope you like learning with it.

This edition of *MacroPolicy* benefitted from the excellent proofing and editing work of Chelsea Koons. Anything left that's wrong is my fault. Thanks Chelsea.

Chapter 1
The Big Picture

MacroPolicy Now: The Recession Is Over, Believe It Or Not

"The United States economy has lost more jobs than it has added since the recovery began over a year ago," began a *New York Times* article on September 20, 2010. But the reporter knew that her readers would be skeptical, so she continued "Yes, you read that correctly. The downturn officially ended, and the recovery officially began, in June 2009."

The beginnings and ends of recessions are marked by a committee of seven macroeconomists who make up the Business Cycle Dating Committee at the National Bureau of Economic Research. The NBER is a nonprofit group based in Cambridge, Massachusetts.

The NBER defines a recession as "a significant decline in economic activity [that] spreads across the economy and can last from a few months to more than a year." "Troughs" mark the ends of recessions; "peaks" the ends of expansions. They use data on the production of goods and services, on employment, on incomes earned, and other indicators.

In December 2008 they had announced that the economy had reached a peak in December 2007. The recession was already a year old at that point. The announcement of the June 2009 trough came in September 2010. What takes so long? The NBER keeps a record of peaks and troughs, recessions and expansions, going back to 1854. The committee members are careful; they want to get it right.

"The declaration of the recession's end confirms what many suspected: The 2007-09 recession was not only the longest post-World War II recession, but also the deepest, in terms of both job losses and at least one measure of output declines," wrote the *Times*. "Adjusted for inflation, output contracted more than in any other postwar period, according to Robert E. Hall, a Stanford economics professor and committee chairman."

And the unemployment rate "peaked last October at 10.1 percent. The postwar high was in 1982, at 10.8 percent. But the composition of the work force was very different in the 1980s — it was younger, and younger people tend to have higher unemployment rates — and so if adjusted for age, unemployment this time around actually looks much worse.

So far the recovery has been slow. "Many forecasters estimate that output needs to grow over the long run by about 2.5 percent to keep the unemployment rate constant. . . .The recovery thus far has been so anemic that the job picture seems likely to stagnate, and perhaps even get worse, in the near future." The *Times* noted that this is not unusual.

The three "most recent recoveries have been known as jobless recoveries, as employment growth has significantly lagged output growth."

That's one reason why many Americans would scoff at the idea that the recession is over. "Nonfarm payrolls are still down 329,000 from their level at the recession's official end 15 months ago, and the slow growth in recent months means that the unemployed still have a long slog ahead," wrote the *Times*.

It's a problem of definition. The NBER, and most economists, use the word "recession" to mean a decline in the economy. When economists say a recession is over, it means we've stopped digging an economic hole, and have started climbing out. But we're still in the hole. The first day of expansion is a lot like the last day of recession. It can take a lot of expansion for the economy to get back to normal.

"In declaring the recession over, we're not at all saying the unemployment rate, or anything else, has returned to normal," said James H. Stock, an economics professor at Harvard and a member of the business cycle committee. "We clearly still have a long ways to go."

Is the recession over or not? Is inflation a problem, or isn't it? We need to know the answers to these questions before we can ask: what policies should we adopt to keep the economy growing, with high employment and low inflation? The experience of individual people or businesses doesn't tell us enough. So, we need to measure, add it all up, average it all out. . . .

The recession that began in December 2007 and ended in June 2009 was the longest, and by some measures the deepest, since the 1930's. What made it so bad? Conversely, the 1990's saw the longest economic expansion in United States history. Why did the economy do so well? Why did that long, long expansion have to end in recession? What makes a deep recession turn to expansion? When will this expansion really get going, and how long will it last?

These are the kinds of questions macroeconomics is meant to answer. We will develop models to explain and even predict changes in the economy. But before we can answer these questions, even before we can *ask* them, we have to know what happened. How do we know that there are expansions and recessions? How do we know that there was an expansion during the 1990's, and between 2001 and 2007? How do we know that 2008 and 2009 were recession years?

People didn't need economists to tell them that the economy was doing badly in 2008 and 2009. People were losing their jobs and watching family members, friends and neighbors lose theirs. Businesses were going bankrupt. Banks were failing. Stock values were down, and pension statements were shocking. School districts were laying off teachers. But, even in hard times, some people were being hired, some people were starting businesses, some banks were profitable, and some stocks were rising.

Relying on the experiences of a few individuals is a haphazard way of knowing what is happening. Pick one group's experience and we'll get one view of the economy. Pick another's, and we'll get a different view.

What's the solution to this problem? *Aggregation.* We'll add up the value of the things that businesses produce, and call it total output. We'll add up people's experiences finding and losing jobs, and call it total employment and unemployment. We'll average the prices that people paid for the things they bought, and call it the price level. We'll miss a lot of detail with aggregate measures. But we'll get a surer sense of what is happening to the economy as a whole.

Then we can ask why output rose, then fell, then rose and fell again. Why were people employed yesterday but unemployed today? Why did prices rise so much in 2008, and why did they fall in 2009? We can create a macroeconomic model to answer these questions. The model will explain and predict changes in aggregate measures of the economy. That's what macroeconomics is: the economics of aggregates, the economics of the big picture.

There are five main measures of the economy which our macroeconomic model will try to explain. They are: the output of goods and services, the prices of goods and services, the share of the labor force which is unemployed, the interest rates charged by lenders, and the international exchange rate of the nation's currency. The rest of this chapter will explain how each of these is measured, and then we'll close with a view of how each measure behaves during recessions. We'll use the NBER's peak and trough dates to do that.

Output

Output is the result of production, cars, houses and hamburgers, roads and missiles, doctors', lawyers' and plumbers' services produced in a year. Output is measured by *gross domestic product*, known by its initials, GDP. GDP is defined as "the total value of final goods and services produced in a year."

> **Gross Domestic Product is the total value of final goods and services produced in a year.**

Why is it called gross domestic product? GDP is *product* because it measures production, the products the economy produces. It's *domestic* because it measures the products produced within the borders of the nation. And it's *gross* (make up your own joke here) because it doesn't subtract depreciation, the equipment and infrastructure that wears out when domestic product is produced.

The basic method for calculating GDP is simple. Take the number of things produced, multiply by the price at which those things sold, and add up the resulting dollar values. GDP is thus the dollar value of cars, hamburgers, doctors' services and everything else that people and businesses in the economy produced during the year. That's what we mean by *value.*

There would be a danger of double and triple-counting some production, though, if we didn't limit the value to *final* goods and services. These are the values of products sold to their final users. A car is a final good, sold to a consumer for transportation. The price of the car includes the price of the steel which the carmaker purchased during production. If we count the value of the steel, and the value of the car, we have counted the value of the steel twice. The steel used to make the car is not a final good. Only the sale of the car is counted in GDP. This does not mean that steel output is ignored. It is counted, as part of the value of the car.

Some sales of final goods are not counted in GDP, because they were not *produced during the year*. The biggest category of such goods is housing. The value of houses built in prior years but sold in the current year is not counted in GDP. Only newly constructed houses are included. The same logic applies to sales of used cars and "used" paintings by Picasso. The values of these things were included in the GDP of the year they were made. We don't want to count them again. The services of the real estate agent, auctioneer or broker are included in GDP, though. Bringing buyer and seller together this year is a service that counts as production.

GDP is not a perfect measure of the value of output. Some output is so hard to measure that it's ignored in the GDP accounts. Housewives and househusbands definitely produce services, but their output isn't sold so there's no receipt for prices and quantities. Clean air is valuable, and we make efforts to "produce" it, with smokestack scrubbers and other pollution control equipment, but air isn't bought or sold. You aren't charged every time you take a breath. The value of clean air isn't included in GDP.

Some products are sold for a price, but the transactions are hidden. Illegal drugs are sold—they have prices and quantities—but the "sales people" take pains to hide the transactions. The GDP accountants don't know about them. These hidden transactions are known as the *underground economy*. Less toxic activities like the unrecorded tips of waiters and waitresses are also underground. Since the prices used to value restaurant meals don't include all the tips, their value in GDP probably is undercounted.

GDP is divided into five major categories: *consumption (C), investment (I), government purchases (G), exports (X) and imports (M)*. An identity that can help keep our thinking straight is

$$GDP = Q = C + I + G + X - M.$$

We'll use Q as the single letter symbol for output. It stands for "quantity," the quantity of all goods and services. The other letters stand for consumption, investment, government purchases, exports and imports, in that order.

Consumption is output purchased by households. We usually call them consumers. Some of this output is "non-durable", like food and clothing; some is "durable", like cars and appliances; and some are services, like haircuts, medical care and legal advice.

Consumption is by far the largest category of GDP. Reporters are fond of writing that "consumers are more than two-thirds of the economy." They mean that consumption is always a bit more than two-thirds of GDP.

Investment is output mostly purchased by businesses. It includes factories, equipment, office buildings, retail stores, warehouses, power lines, railroad tracks— in fact, anything used by business to produce other goods. In our model, investment does not mean financial investment. It is *not* stocks, bonds, land or gold. It is the value of the tangible things which are purchased by businesses to produce other things. Housing is included as investment, even though it is purchased by consumers. This is because it lasts so long. Think of a house as a tangible investment that produces a service called "shelter." Inventories are also included as investment. Inventories are the products intended for sale to customers, but not yet sold. A product produced for sale in one year, but not sold until the next, is counted as inventory investment in the year it's produced.

Government purchases are resources or inputs purchased by government. We can't measure government output—the value of national defense or police protection or elementary education—because it is not sold at a price in a market. Even the quantity of government output is often hard to measure. How much "national defense" do the armed forces produce? Instead, we count the value of inputs: the wages of employees and the value of the buildings and equipment governments buy to produce output. Employees, buildings and equipment are inputs used to produce government output. A local school district pays teachers, constructs classrooms and buys desks in order to produce education for pupils. We can't say for sure how much education is produced, and it isn't sold to pupils for a price, so we have to count the value of inputs instead.

Government purchases do not include *transfer payments*, which is revenue collected from taxpayers and distributed to retired people, disabled people, sick people, unemployed people or poor people. Examples are Social Security, Medicare and Medicaid, unemployment insurance, veterans' pensions, and welfare. These are not purchases by government. They are income of benefit recipients, and they are counted as consumption when the recipients spend the income. If we counted transfer payments as government purchases, and counted the consumer goods that beneficiaries buy with these payments, we'd be counting them twice.

Exports are sales of goods and services to people, businesses and governments of other countries. *Imports* are purchases of goods and services from people, businesses and governments of other countries. Since the value of exported goods and services are produced in the country during the year, we want to add them in with the nation's output. Since the value of imported goods is not produced in the country, we do not want to count them. We subtract M in the equation, rather than just ignoring imports, because imports are counted in C, I and G. Consumption, for example, includes cars made in Japan, shirts made in China, computer services delivered from India, coffee grown in Columbia. Imports are subtracted to remove the value of these items from total GDP. Exports minus imports, together, are called *net exports*. Net exports are a measure of the trade balance. If exports exceed imports, there is a trade surplus; if imports exceed exports, there is a trade deficit.

Real GDP. We want changes in GDP to be a measure of changes in production from year to year. Unfortunately, this measure is clouded by inflation. *Nominal GDP* is output measured in current prices, the prices that existed in the year the output was produced. Even if output is the same from one year to the next, or if it declines, GDP may rise because of increases in the prices used to measure value. That makes it hard to identify recessions with nominal GDP.

We solve this problem by dividing nominal GDP by a *price index* to get real GDP. A price index measures the change in the prices of output, on average. Dividing nominal GDP by the price index gives *real* GDP, which is a measure of the change in output without the influence of price changes. This is called "deflating" GDP, which is why the price index is called the *GDP deflator.* Sometimes real GDP is called "GDP adjusted for inflation," sometimes "GDP at constant prices." In the macroeconomic model, and in this book, when we refer to GDP we mean *real* GDP.

Real GDP growth, or "economic growth," or just "growth", is much talked about in economic policy. These terms all mean the percentage change in real GDP from one year to the next. For example, nominal GDP in 2010 was $14,660 billion (a little more than fourteen and a half trillion dollars). Nominal GDP in 2009 was $14,119 billion. The $367 billion increase between these years shows an increase in output. But since prices increased between 2009 and 2010, the true increase is masked. Part of the increase in output was just a rise in prices, not an increase in production.

> **Real Gross Domestic Product is Nominal GDP divided by a price index. Real GDP growth is the percentage change in real GDP from one year to the next.**

A price index, the GDP deflator, is used to change nominal GDP to real GDP. The deflator in 2009 was 109.6. The deflator in 2010 was 110.7. The fact that the deflator increased means that the prices used to measure value increased from 2009 to 2010. The *base year* of the deflator is 2005, which means the deflator has been set to exactly 100 in that year. To measure real GDP, divide nominal GDP for each year by the deflator for that year:

2009: $14,119 / 1.096 = $12,880.
2010: $14,660 / 1.107 = $13,247

To use the GDP deflators this way we must shift their decimal points two places to the left; that is, dividing it by 100. The results are real GDP for each year- GDP as it would be measured if prices had remained at their 2005 levels. It's called constant price GDP, or GDP at 2005 prices (since the deflator is 100 in the year 2005, nominal and real GDP are the same in that year).

GDP growth for 2010 is the percentage change in real GDP from 2009 to 2010:

(13,247 – 12,880) / 12,880 = 367 / 12,880 = 0.028.

Multiply by 100 to show the result in percentage terms, and GDP growth for 2010 is 2.8%. That's a positive number, so the quantity of goods and services increased between 2009 and 2010, though not by much. Sometimes real GDP declines, as it did in 2008. Then the percentage change is negative. We refer to the measure as "growth" even when it's a decline. It's "negative growth." Economic terminology gets quirky, sometimes.

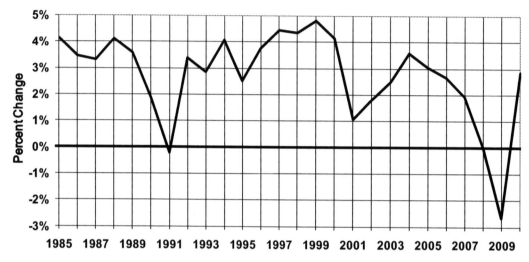

Figure 1-1. Real GDP Growth, 1985-2010. Calculated as the yearly percent change in real Gross Domestic Product. When the U.S. economy is expanding it tends to grow between 2.5% and 4.5% per year. "Negative growth" of real GDP means output fell from one year to the next. That's a recession. There was a recession in 1990-91, and another in 2001. The 2001 recession was mild. Real GDP fell during part of the year, but increased a little for the year as a whole. The 2007-09 recession began in December 2007, but 2008 shows no change in real GDP. That's low enough to call it a recession. The 2.7% drop in real GDP in 2009 was the biggest decline since 1946. A recession, no doubt. The economy began to recover in 2010, but the 2.8% growth rate was slower than was hoped for.

Inflation Rate
We measure the level of prices with a price index. A price index is an average price of the goods and services produced in the economy. The GDP deflator is a price index. The products in the GDP deflator are "weighted" by the importance of each product in GDP. High value items (with high prices, big quantities, or both) are counted more; low value items are counted less. Increases in the price index imply that prices of goods and services have increased, on average. That's *inflation*. Decreases in the price index imply that prices of goods and services have decreased, on average. That's *deflation*.

There are two main price indexes used to measure inflation. One is the GDP deflator, which is the price index used to turn nominal GDP into real GDP. It measures the weighted average price of all the goods and services included in GDP. The other is the *Consumer Price Index,* or CPI, which is the weighted average price of goods and services that a typical household buys.

The GDP deflator includes the prices of more goods and services than the CPI. It averages the prices of the consumer goods and services that are in the CPI, but also investment goods like machinery, government goods and services like police officer wages and missile prices, and the prices of exports and imports. The CPI, though, is a better measure of the prices that households pay. It's also the inflation measure most often reported by the media. We'll use it as our inflation measure most of the time.

Price indexes are weighted averages, because they average the prices of goods and services based on their importance in GDP or in household spending. For example, if households spend twice as much on shoes as they do on shaving cream, the price of shoes will be twice as important as the price of shaving cream in the average price of consumer goods, as measured by the CPI.

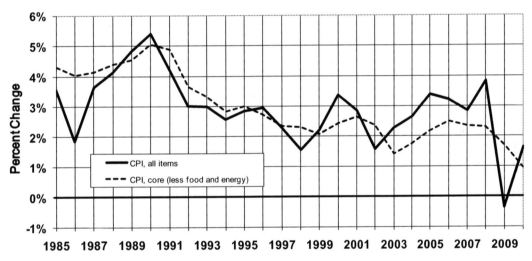

Figure 1-2. Inflation Rates, 1985-2010. Calculated as the yearly percent change in the Consumer Price Index, all items and core. The all items CPI inflation rate is affected by energy prices. When it's above the core inflation rate, oil prices were increasing. When it's below the core inflation rate, oil prices were decreasing. Oil prices surged in 2008 and collapsed in 2009, which explains the extremes in the CPI all items inflation rate. That collapse produced the deflation in 2009, a negative inflation rate. By the end of 2010 oil prices were rising again, and the all items inflation rate was higher than the core rate. Inflation tends to drop in recessions. This is especially evident in the core rate, without the "noise" from oil prices. Core inflation declined during and after the recessions of , as in 1990-91, 2001 and 2007-2009. Likewise, the core rate tends to rise towards the end of expansions, as in 1986-90, 1999-2001, and 2003-2006.

An index takes the value of 100 in an arbitrary year. The GDP deflator equals 100 in the year 2005. The CPI equals 100 for the average of the years 1982-1984. This means that the price index numbers are meaningless by themselves. They take on meaning only when compared over time, only when they are used to measure price changes: inflation and deflation. We measure inflation or deflation as the percentage change in a price index over a period of time, usually a year. The inflation rate for 2010 would be the percentage change in a price index from 2009 to 2010.

For example, the CPI for 2009 was 214.5, the CPI for 2010 was 218.1. The inflation rate for 2010 is

$$(218.1 - 214.5) / 214.5 = 3.6 / 214.5 = 0.017.$$

> **An inflation rate is the percentage change in a price index from one year to the next.**

Multiply by 100 to show the result in percentage terms, and the inflation rate for 2010 is 1.7%. This is a positive number, so it represents inflation. Sometimes—very rarely—the inflation rate is negative. That's deflation. The average price of consumer goods actually fell from 2008 to 2009, mostly because of a huge drop in energy prices. This was the first annual deflation recorded since 1955. We'll still call it an inflation rate though. It's negative inflation.

We want our price index to show what's happening to prices in the economy as a whole. Unfortunately, the CPI often is distorted by big changes in energy prices, especially oil prices, which reflect the state of Middle East politics as much as the state of the U.S. economy. So, sometimes we use a version of the CPI that excludes the prices of energy and food. Food is excluded because its production is influenced by the weather. This is called the *core rate of inflation*, and it's often a more stable measure of price changes than the "all items" CPI.

Unemployment Rate
The *unemployment rate* is the percentage of the labor force that is unemployed. The *labor force* is the number of people age 16 and over who are willing and able to work, whether they are working or not. The labor force is the sum of the number of *employed* people and the number of *unemployed* people. There is also a large group classified as *not in the labor force*. People under age 16 are not classified in any of these categories.

The government surveys about 60,000 people each month to estimate the number of people who are employed, unemployed, and not in the labor force. People are classified as employed if they are working for pay, or working in a family business, on vacation, or otherwise absent from a job to which they expect to return. People are classified as unemployed if they are not working and are actively seeking work, or if they are laid off and expecting recall. People classified as not in the labor force are able to work but not working or looking for work, usually because they are retired, in school or keeping house. A special category of people not in the labor force are the *discouraged workers* who are not working and not seeking work because they do not think they will find a job.

They are not counted as unemployed because they are not seeking work, yet their numbers tend to rise in recessions. The rest of the population couldn't work even if they wanted to. They are mostly children under 16, but also adults in prison or in the hospital. The Bureau of Labor Statistics doesn't count these people.

For example, the average number of employed people each month in 2010 was 139,069,000, and the number of unemployed people was 14,825,000. Numbers are rounded off to the nearest thousand. The labor force is the sum of these two figures, 153,894,000. The number not in the labor force was 83,935,000. The unemployment rate is the number of unemployed as a percentage of the labor force,

> *The unemployment rate is the percentage of unemployed people in the labor force.*

14,825,000 / 153,894,000 = 0.096.

Multiply by 100 to put this figure in percentage terms, and the unemployment rate for 2010 was 9.6%. That's a high rate, the highest since 1983. It's an indicator of the depth of the Great Recession.

Why are people unemployed? It is useful to divide the reasons into three causes: cyclical, frictional and structural. Some unemployment is *cyclical*. When the economy falls into recession, workers are laid off or let go, and people entering the labor force have

> *The three kinds of unemployment are cyclical, frictional and structural.*

difficulty finding jobs. The unemployment rate goes up. When the economy moves back to expansion, workers are recalled to their jobs, firms increase their hiring, and people entering the labor force find it easier to get jobs. The unemployment rate goes down. Cyclical unemployment can drop to zero if the economy is operating at capacity, which simply means that all the economy's resources are in use. This is sometimes called *full employment*.

Some unemployment is *frictional*. Frictional unemployment results from the fact that it takes time for workers to find jobs and for employers to find workers. People must search want ads, post resumes on the internet, and generally "pound the pavement." Employers must sift applications, schedule interviews, and decide who to hire. Frictional unemployment will exist even if the economy is operating at full employment, even if there is a job opening for every unemployed worker. Frictional unemployment is sometimes called "search" unemployment, because it simply takes time for employers and employees to find one another.

Some unemployment is *structural*. There may be a million unemployed people and a million job openings, but if the jobs are for nurses and plumbers, while the unemployed people are programmers and steel workers, the jobs will not be filled and the workers will remain unemployed. Likewise, the job openings may be in Indiana but the unemployed people may be in California, or the job openings may be in the suburbs while the unemployed people are in the central city. Technological change can cause structural unemployment. Film chemists who worked for Kodak found themselves unemployed as the company switched to digital photography, even as Kodak advertised job openings for computer technicians. Structural unemployment is sometimes called *mismatch* unemployment. The skills or locations of the unemployed and the job openings just don't match.

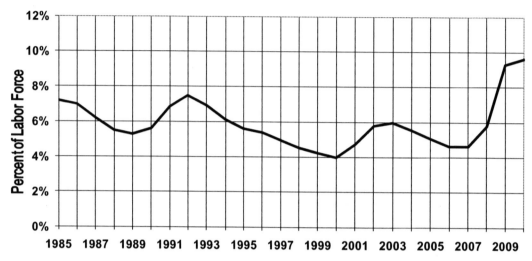

Figure 1-3. Unemployment Rate, 1985-2010. Calculated as the average yearly number of unemployed people as a percentage of the average yearly labor force. The unemployment rate falls in expansions, and rises during and just after recessions. The 1980's expansion brought the unemployment rate down to just above 5%, but after the 1990-91 recession it rose above 7%. The long 1990's expansion brought the unemployment rate down to 4% by 2000, the lowest rate in 30 years. The rate rose to 6% after the 2001 recession. The rate fell back under 5% in the 2000's expansion, but rose to 9.3% in 2009, and 9.6% in 2010, as a result of the 2007-09 recession. Those were the highest rates since the early 1980's. Because of frictional and structural unemployment, the unemployment rate never hits zero.

When cyclical unemployment is zero, the unemployment rate is still positive due to frictional and structural unemployment. This is sometimes called the *natural rate of unemployment*, and sometimes called (really!) the *NAIRU—the non-accelerating inflation rate of unemployment*. Less often it is called the "full employment rate of unemployment," perhaps because that sounds contradictory. Figuring out the level of the NAIRU or natural rate is an important challenge. If the economy's unemployment is primarily cyclical, the actual unemployment rate is higher than the natural rate. Then policies to increase GDP growth can bring unemployment down. If unemployment is mostly frictional and structural, these same policies may only cause inflation, with little effect on unemployment.

Interest Rates

An *interest rate* is an added percentage that a borrower must repay a lender in addition to the amount borrowed. Interest rates are usually measured on an annual basis—the percentage to be paid over a year—even if the loan is for less than or more than a year. Sometimes the interest rate is called "the cost of money" because it is the amount which a borrower must pay to use the lender's money.

Lenders must take account of inflation when setting interest rates. If there is inflation, the money which a borrower pays back to the lender is worth less than when the money was originally lent. With prices higher, a particular amount of money can buy fewer goods and services. The lender must set the interest rate at the rate of return he or she wishes to receive, plus the inflation rate he or she expects. This implies that the *real interest rate* is the interest rate charged by the lender minus the annual inflation rate the lender expects during the length of the loan.

> *The real interest rate is the nominal interest rate charged by lenders minus the expected inflation rate.*

For example, in 2010 the average interest rate on a 30-year mortgage was 4.7%. This is known as the nominal interest rate. The inflation rate for 2010, measured by the core CPI, was 1.0%. The real interest rate was

4.7% - 1.0% = 3.7%.

After the inflation of 2010, the money that a borrower is repaying is worth 1% less to the borrower because prices increased. The lender gained only 3.7% in added purchasing power by earning interest on the loan. Interest rates are set in advance based on the *expected inflation rate,* the rate that the lender expects over the length of the loan. Since measures of expected inflation are scarce, real interest rate calculations usually are made using the inflation rates that actually occurred. These are *ex-post* (after-the-fact), or *realized,* real interest rates—the rate of return that was actually earned during the year.

There are a great many interest rates, because there are a great many kinds of loans. Here are a few of the important interest rates.

- *Federal funds rate.* This is the interest rate charged by banks when they lend to each other over night. At the end of each day, some banks will have excess reserves—more money in the vault than they need—while others will be short of reserves. Those with excess will lend to those that are short, charging the federal funds rate. It is called "federal" even though it is set by banks in private markets. This is because this interest rate is very sensitive to policy decisions of the Federal Reserve. What is the Federal Reserve? It's the United States central bank. Don't worry, we'll get to that.

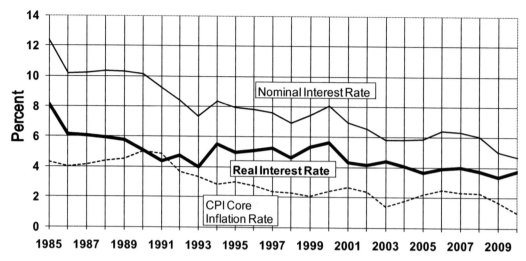

Figure 1-4. Real 30-year Mortgage Interest Rate, 1985-2010. Calculated as the nominal rate paid by homebuyers, less the CPI core inflation rate. The nominal interest rate has trended downward for the past two decades, from very high levels in the early 1980's. The Consumer Price Index core inflation rate is used to deflate the nominal interest rate because it's probably a better measure of the inflation rates that lenders expect. The fluctuations in energy prices are pretty unpredictable, so they aren't always reflected in lenders' rate decisions. The core inflation rate has declined since the mid-80's as well, so the real mortgage rate has not changed very much since the mid-90's.

- *Treasury bond rates.* These are the interest rates paid by the U.S. Treasury when it borrows to finance a budget deficit. A bond is a promise to repay the lender plus interest. The Treasury borrows for shorter and longer periods, ranging from one month to thirty years. These bonds are sold to buyers in the bond market. The buyers are lending money to the government, on the promise of interest and eventual repayment. To buy a Treasury bond is to lend money to the Federal government. Short-term bonds are sometimes called "Treasury bills."

- *Prime rate.* This is the interest rate supposedly charged by banks to their best corporate customers. In fact the prime rate is more of a benchmark for many kinds of lending, including credit card debt and some mortgages. When the prime rate changes, lenders will often adjust these other interest rates too.

- *Commercial paper rates.* These are interest rates on short-term loans that lenders make to businesses for business operations such as stocking inventories or meeting payrolls. The business repays after a few months out of their earnings from the sales of the inventories or the services provided by the employees.

- *Corporate bond rates.* These are the interest rates paid by corporations when they borrow for longer periods of time, usually for business expansion. When a corporation wants to expand its factories, offices, or stores, buy equipment, or buy another company, it will sell bonds in the bond market. Lenders will buy these bonds, the corporation will use the money it receives to expand, and the bond will be repaid from the corporations' added profits.

- *Mortgage rate.* This is the interest rate charged to people borrowing to finance a home purchase. Mortgages vary in length, but a 30-year mortgage is common. This is the interest rate that often concerns consumers the most, because for most people a house is both the largest purchase they make and often represents a large share of their wealth. Home purchases and housing construction can be quite sensitive to variations in the mortgage interest rate.

Exchange Rates

The *exchange rate* of the dollar is the number of foreign currency units that one dollar trades for on international currency markets. The *value of the dollar* is the same thing. There are more than one hundred international currencies that have exchange rates with the dollar. The value of the dollar against most foreign currencies changes every day, even every hour or every minute, depending on how many dollars people want to buy and sell. Prior to 1973, most exchange rates were fixed and often unchanged for years at a time.

In our models and in this book the U.S. exchange rate will be measured as foreign currency units per dollar. That's how much it costs a foreigner to buy a dollar, measured in another currency. This makes sense of the term "value of the dollar," and it means that when the dollar gets "stronger", or it "appreciates" or is "revalued," the exchange rate goes up. When the dollar gets "weaker," "depreciates" or is "devalued," the exchange rate goes down.

> *The exchange rate of the dollar can be measured as the number of foreign currency units per dollar. This is also known as the "value of the dollar."*

On average in 2010, one dollar exchanged for 0.73 European euros (that's the currency used in France, Germany, Italy and many other European countries). It took 73 "eurocents" to buy a dollar. In 2001, a European would have needed 1.12 euros to buy a dollar. The value of the dollar decreased from 2001 to 2008, though it increased a little in 2009 and 2010. The dollar is "weaker" now than it was in 2001. It's depreciated in value.

Exchange rates can be inverted to measure the number of dollars per foreign currency unit. The exchange rate between the dollar and euro is often presented in dollars per euro, not euros per dollar. In 2010 one euro exchanged for $1.37 because 1 / 0.73 = 1.37. In 2001 one euro exchanged for $0.90 (1 / 1.12 = 0.90). When the dollar gets weaker, it costs more dollars to buy a euro. The value of the euro goes up. Since "weaker" sounds more like down than up, we'll measure exchange rates in foreign currency units per dollar.

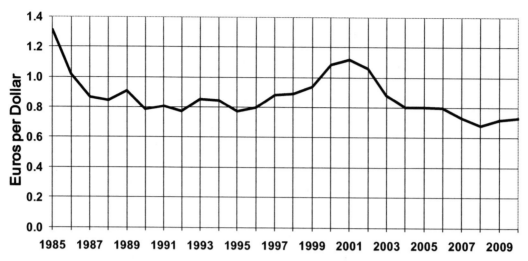

Figure 1-5. Exchange rate, euros per one dollar, 1985-2010 (estimated before 1999). The euro is the European multi-national currency. It replaced the German mark, French franc, Italian lira and several other national currencies in 1999. Prior to 1999 the data here are averages for those currencies. The value of the dollar in euros was high in the mid-1980s. It remained stable around 0.8 euros per dollar from 1990 to 1996. Then the value increased, mostly because there was a world financial crisis. International investors wanted to buy more dollars, in order to invest in nice, safe U.S. Treasury bonds. That pushed the value of the dollar up. Large U.S. trade deficits in the 2000's helped bring the value of the dollar down, but in late 2008 this reversed again as a new financial crisis caused the world to buy dollars. That caused an increase in the value of the dollar in 2009 and 2010.

The value of the dollar is important for imports and exports. When the dollar is stronger, foreign currencies are less expensive. To buy foreign imports, importers must first buy foreign currency, and then use that currency to buy foreign products. If the foreign currency is cheaper, so are the foreign products, as measured in dollars. Likewise, when the dollar is stronger, it costs foreigners more to buy U.S. exports, because the dollars they must buy in order to purchase U.S. goods are more expensive. The value of the dollar influences the amount of goods and services that the U.S. imports and exports.

MacroPolicy Now: The Recession Is Over, Believe It Or Not

The National Bureau of Economic Research marks the beginnings and ends of recessions and expansions. They've been at it since the 1920's, and they've gone back to the 1850's to mark earlier business cycles. We can use our aggregate measures of the economy, along with the NBER's business cycle dates, to see what happens during recessions and expansions. Figure 1-6 shows the quarterly growth rates of real GDP. The figure has dotted lines marking the peak and trough dates (quarters for GDP data). There are three recessions on the chart, and in each real GDP fell during more than one quarter. The peak of our most recent "Great Recession" is marked in the fourth quarter of 2007, and the trough is marked in the second quarter of 2009.

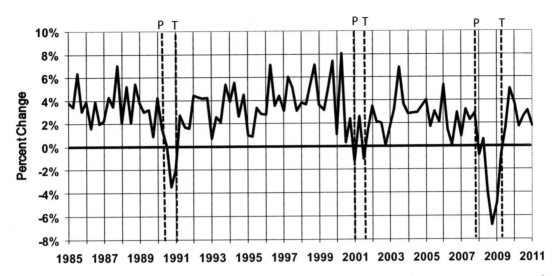

Figure 1-6. Real GDP growth, quarterly. Percent changes are from one quarter to the next, but multiplied by four to make them comparable to annual rates. Vertical gridlines are drawn at the first quarter of each year. Here's one way to use the NBER's peak and trough business cycle dates. The dotted lines labeled P are the peak quarters of three recessions; the T lines are trough quarters. Each recession shows more than one quarter of decline, though they're not necessarily consecutive. The recession that began in December 2007 (the fourth quarter of 2007) got really bad a year later, with drops of 4.0%, 6.8% and 4.9% in the third, fourth and first quarters, 2008-09. One other thing the business cycle dates show, though; trough to peak dates are expansions, and the economy is expanding most of the time.

The percentages in Figure 1-6 are "annual rates." They show what would happen if real GDP grew for a whole year as it did in each quarter. Essentially, it's the quarterly percent change multiplied by four. They quote the numbers that way so they can be compared to past annual figures.

What happens to real GDP during recessions? It goes down; unless it's going up. Real GDP increased in the middle quarter of the 2001 recession, and in the second quarter of 2008. That's one reason why the NBER took so long to call the trough for the recession that began in December 2007. What if the growth in 2009-10 is followed by more declines? Is it a new recession, or a continuation of the old one? Finally, they decided that there had been enough growth since mid-2009, that new declines in real GDP would be marked as a new recession.

Some recessions are more serious than others. The 1990-91 recession had bigger drops in real GDP than the 2001 recession, but both are marked as lasting eight months. The 2007-2009 recession was 18 months long, longer than any recession since the Great Depression of 1929-1933. It had much bigger drops in real GDP than either of the previous two recessions. Sometimes the media uses an easy definition of recession: two consecutive quarters of real GDP decline. The NBER doesn't use that definition. It would have worked for the 1990-91 recession. But in 2001, there were no consecutive quarters of decline. GDP alternated down and up for five quarters. The consecutive quarters definition would not have called 2001 a recession. Likewise, the definition would have marked the 2007-09 recession as starting in the second half of 2008. But employment had been declining for months by then.

Figure 1-6 also shows that the economy is often weak in the year before a recession starts. Each recession saw a quarterly growth rate unusually low within a year before the recession started. A weak quarter shouldn't be taken as a sure sign of a coming recession, though. There were weak quarters in 1993, 1995 and 2002 which were not soon followed by recessions. That's another reason why the NBER waits so long to mark recessions. It would be embarrassing to call a recession that never occurs.

Likewise, the economy has grown slowly in the first few quarters after recession trough dates. The early parts of recoveries have been slow. That was certainly true in 1991 and 2002. Real GDP grew 5.6% in the fourth quarter of 2009, but then slowed quite a bit.

One more observation about figure 1-6: peak to trough dates mark recessions. So trough to peak dates mark expansions. It's clear from the GDP data that most of the time the economy is expanding.

Figure 1-7 makes a different use of the NBER business cycle dates, with monthly data on the unemployment rate. In this figure, the peak month of each recession is numbered zero, and the months after the peak are counted. This lets us compare what happened to the unemployment rate month-by-month as each recession progressed. Six months into each recession, for example, the unemployment rate has risen by a bit less than one percentage point.

The most recent recession tracked those first two for about nine months. But then, in the last two recessions the increase in the unemployment rate slowed down. In 2008, unemployment accelerated. It was in the Fall of 2008 that the 2007-09 recession became "Great."

In the first two recessions, the trough was in month number eight. After that the economy began expanding. Yet the unemployment rate did not come down. It peaked in the 23rd month after the first recession and in the 27th month after the second recession. In the Great Recession the trough was in the 18th month. The unemployment rate didn't peak until month 22. Unemployment rates keep going up even when the economy begins to recover. The reason for this is that the labor force keeps expanding. Young people graduate from high school and college and enter the labor force looking for work. And, when the economy starts expanding, discouraged workers begin to re-enter the labor force, so it grows faster than usual. The number of jobs must increase to employ these added workers. That means the economy must grow, just to keep the unemployment rate from rising. If it doesn't grow fast enough, the unemployment rate will increase.

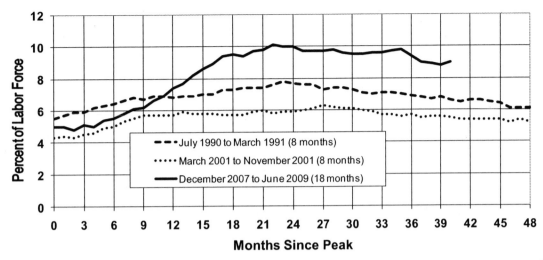

Figure 1-7. Unemployment Rates in Three Recessions. Here's another way to use the NBER's peak and trough business cycle dates: - compare unemployment rates month-by-month during different recessions. The first dotted line shows the unemployment rate starting in July 1990, which was the month that the NBER marks as the peak of the previous expansion, and the start of the 1990-91 recession. The second dotted line does the same thing for the 2001 recession, which started in March 2001. The solid line shows the recession that started in December 2007 and ended in June 2009. The high unemployment rates came 23 and 27 months after the starts of the first two recessions. That means the unemployment rate kept rising after the recessions were marked as over. The unemployment rate rose more rapidly in the most recent recession, but we hope the highest unemployment rate was in the 22nd month. In each case the unemployment rate peaked about two years after the start of the recession.

That's where the phrase "jobless recovery" comes from. It turns out that real GDP has to increase between 2.5% and 3% a year to produce enough jobs to employ the expanding labor force. If it grows less than that, the unemployment rate will increase. Figure 1-6 shows that in all three recessions, it took a year or more after the trough for real GDP to rev up above that growth rate. So the unemployment rate kept increasing, or dropped very slowly.

The recovery since the Great Recession has been a disappointment, because growth has averaged only 2.8% per year. That's not enough to bring the unemployment rate down very fast. The unemployment rate was still at 9.0% in April 2010, down just a point since its peak a year-and-a-half before.

Figure 1-8 plots core CPI inflation in the same way. The inflation rate is measured over twelve months, so each number is the percentage change from the same month a year before. The core rate is appropriate for this purpose because political events were influencing oil prices in different ways during each recession. In 1990-91, during the Gulf War, oil prices rose, then fell. In 2001, oil prices were stable, then dropped after 9-

11. In 2008-09, oil prices rose a lot, then collapsed. Then they began to rise again in 2010. The core rate gives us a picture of prices without the oil politics.

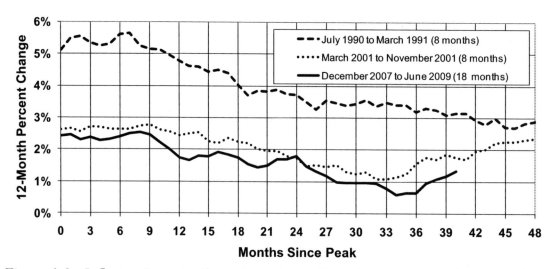

Figure 1-8. Inflation Rates in Three Recessions. This chart compares the core inflation rates month-by-month during different recessions. Inflation is calculated as the percentage change in the core CPI, from the same month one year earlier. Inflation rates tend to hold steady for the first few months of a recession. Then they start to drop. The rates hit their low points 32, 34 and 45 months after the peak. The latest recession looks a lot like the 1990-91 recession. If it continues to follow the earlier pattern, we've already seen the low point for inflation after the Great Recession. . The core rate is a good one to use for comparing inflation rates, because political events were influencing oil prices in different ways during these three periods.

Inflation remained stable in the first nine months in all three recessions, then began to fall. In all three recessions it continued to fall for some time. In the 1990-91 recession, inflation kept falling until the 45th month after the peak. In the 2001 recession, it fell until the 32nd month after the peak. Inflation fell after the 2007-09 recession until the 34th month. Our current inflation rate seems to be tracking the 2001 inflation pattern quite closely.

Sales decline during recessions, and businesses try to hold down price increases and even put their products on sale, trying to attract buyers. But why does inflation keep falling after the recession is over?

When the NBER says a recession is over, that doesn't mean everything is suddenly okay. The "trough" marks the end of a recession, because the aggregate measures have stopped declining. That makes the trough the economy's low point. The months after the trough are pretty close to that low point, too. The economy begins to expand, but full recovery takes years. Sales are still pretty bad in the first year or two of an expansion. Businesses hold off on price increases.

Real interest rates tend to fall in recessions, at least at first. Businesses don't want to borrow as much. They don't see the sense of borrowing to add buildings and equipment when they can't sell what they're producing now. Households don't want to borrow as much, either. They don't want to commit to a mortgage or car payment if their incomes are down or their job prospects are shaky. So, lenders reduce their interest rates, trying to attract customers to borrow their money. Policymakers at the Federal Reserve usually cut interest rates in recession, too, trying to get people to borrow and spend more.

What happens to exchange rates depends. Are net exports near zero, or is there a big trade deficit? Is the recession just in the U.S., or is it worldwide? What's happening to real interest rates? Is there are financial crisis along with the recession?

These are complicated questions. We'd better have a model of the economy if we're going to try to answer them. We'll start developing that model in the next chapter.

Terms in this Chapter, in order of appearance
Aggregation
Gross Domestic Product
Value
Final
Produced during the year
Underground economy
Consumption (C)
Investment (I)
Government purchases (G)
Exports (X)
Imports (M)
Transfer Payments
Net Exports
Real GDP
Nominal GDP
Price index
GDP deflator
GDP growth
Inflation
Deflation
Consumer Price Index
Core rate of inflation
Unemployment rate
Labor force
Employed
Unemployed
Not in the labor force
Discouraged workers
Cyclical unemployment

Frictional unemployment (Search unemployment)
Structural unemployment (Mismatch unemployment)
Natural rate of unemployment
NAIRU--the non-accelerating inflation rate of unemployment
Interest rate
Real interest rate
Expected inflation rate
Ex-post or realized real interest rate
Federal funds rate
Treasury bond rates
Prime rate
Commercial paper rates
Corporate bond rates
Mortgage rate
Exchange rate
Value of the dollar

Notes

Data for GDP, inflation, unemployment, interest rates and exchange rates come from the following websites, all of which I recommend to the interested reader:

GDP. U.S. Department of Commerce, Bureau of Economic Analysis.
www.bea.gov

Inflation (CPI). U.S. Department of Labor, Bureau of Labor Statistics.
stats.bls.gov/cpi/home.htm (no "www")

Unemployment. U.S. Department of Labor, Bureau of Labor Statistics.
stats.bls.gov/cps/home.htm (no "www")

Interest Rates. Federal Reserve Board.
www.federalreserve.gov/releases/h15/update

Exchange Rates. Federal Reserve Board.
www.federalreserve.gov/releases/h10/Current/

For one stop shopping, all of these data and (a lot) more are available at the St. Louis Federal Reserve's website.
research.stlouisfed.org/fred2/ (no "www")

News Articles

National Bureau of Economic Research, Business Cycle Dating Committee. Press Release, September 20, 2010. ," [http://www.nber.org/cycles/sept2010.pdf]

Rampell, Catherine. "Recession May Be Over, but Joblessness Remains," *New York Times*, September 20, 2010.

Chapter 2
Demand and Supply

MacroPolicy Now: The Ups and Downs of Oil and Gasoline

Gasoline prices rose again in the first half of 2011. Consumers coped as best they could. "Online sales boomed in April as shoppers stayed home on weekends, clicking a mouse instead of driving a car," the *New York Times* reported on May 17, 2011. "E-commerce sales grew 19.2 percent in April compared to a year earlier. . . . Car sales have also risen recently as consumers choose smaller cars. In April, vehicle sales rose 18 percent, as shoppers turned toward compact and fuel-efficient models like the Chevrolet Cruze, Ford Fiesta and Focus models, and even electric cars like the Nissan Leaf." Drivers in cities had other options. "In the San Francisco Bay Area, the daily number of cars driving across the Golden Gate Bridge has dropped while passengers on the buses and ferries have risen."

Some consumers made more drastic decisions. The Times interviewed Loraine Greene, a customer relations manager in New York's Hudson Valley, who "spent the weekend packing up to move to a rental house much closer to work. At $4 a gallon, gas is too expensive to justify the 50-mile round-trip commute." Ms. Greene said that "the option was either to sell my truck and get something smaller, or to try to get closer to work,"

"Americans paid an average of nearly $3.99 for a gallon of regular" in April 2011, wrote the *Times* in a May 5 article. "That is still 10 cents higher than a week ago, 30 cents higher than a month ago, and more than $1 more than a year ago." As a result, "a variety of government and private surveys in recent days indicated that gasoline demand declined over last month by between 1.2 percent and 4 percent from the year before."

Why had oil prices increased so much? "The most immediate reason for the oil price spike since January — the turmoil in North Africa and the Middle East — continues to threaten oil supplies. Libya, an OPEC producer that provides high-quality crude that is difficult to replace, remains virtually off the world market. However aside from Libya, unrest has so far not had a significant impact on oil production or deliveries through strategic ports and waterways."

It was not clear how the Organization of Petroleum Exporting Countries, OPEC, would respond. The *Times* reported that "Early in the Libya crisis, Saudi Arabia pledged to expand its production capacity to fill any gaps in the market. But in recent weeks the kingdom has actually decreased production, saying the world market is flush with supplies."

"OPEC spokesmen have given few hints about where the cartel wants prices and production levels to go since the last meeting of the group in December. OPEC meets again June 8, but with tensions high between Saudi Arabia and Iran, oil experts wonder if OPEC members can come up with an acceptable consensus to alter current policies to either cut or add to world supplies."

Meanwhile, in early May, oil prices stopped rising and edged downward. Energy consultant Addison Armstrong said that the drop in price was due to "the beginnings of some demand destruction. The fundamentals have not been strong enough to justify these levels."

Prices rise and fall. Consumers buy less, then more. Businesses produce a lot, then only a little. If we can understand why, we'll know a whole lot about how the economy works. . . .

Economists try to understand what happens to the prices and quantities of goods and services in markets by using *demand and supply*. Consumers demand goods and services, businesses supply them. Over some time period, a quantity of goods or services are bought and sold in the market at a particular price.

Economists use demand and supply to try to figure out how much will be bought or sold, and at what price. More important, they try to understand and even predict how price and quantity will change if businesses or consumers change what they do.

Here's a made-up example: suppose in your community there are lots of consumers who want to buy pizza, and lots of restaurants that want to make and sell pizza. Suppose we, as economists, surveyed the consumers about how much pizza they would want to buy at several different pizza prices during a week. We'd ask each consumer how much he or she would buy at several different prices, and then add up the totals at each price. And, suppose we surveyed restaurants about how much pizza they would want to make and sell at these same prices during a week. Again, we'd add up the numbers of pizzas each restaurant would make and sell at each price.

The result would be a demand and supply *schedule*, and it might look like this.

Price per Pizza	Number of Pizzas Demanded	Number of Pizzas Supplied
$2	12,000	1,000
$6	8,000	2,000
$10	5,000	5,000
$12	3,000	8,000
$14	1,000	11,000

At low prices, people want to buy more pizzas. At higher prices, people want to buy fewer pizzas. Asking why seems a silly question. Of course people would rather pay less for a product than more. It is in their self-interest to spend less money to fill their bellies. They'll have more left over for other purchases.

Economists sometimes point to an idea called *diminishing marginal utility*. Diminishing means getting smaller. Marginal means the extra unit of anything. Utility is the satisfaction people get from the products they buy. The satisfaction people get from each extra unit of anything they buy gets smaller. That first slice of pizza tastes great. The second is almost as good. The third I can take or leave. The fourth—perhaps not. If I eat a fifth I'm going to be sick. Each extra slice brings less added satisfaction.

If I act in my own self-interest, doing the best I can for myself, I'll be willing to pay more for the first slice than the second. The price would have to be pretty low to get me to buy that fifth slice. I'm not interested in getting sick.

> *The Law of Demand says that people will buy less of a product if it costs more, and they'll buy more if it costs less.*

However it's described, we're so sure of the idea that people demand less of a product when its price goes up that we call it the *Law of Demand*.

Businesses set the prices of their products, but we assume they are *price takers*. That means businesses must set their prices in line with what the market will bear. Pizza restaurants can't charge just any price they want. They must set their prices based on what their competitors are doing, and on what people are willing to pay.

No firm wants to make pizza at a loss. We assume they are in business to make profits. They are *profit maximizers*. That's another way of saying that business owners act in their own self-interest (just like consumers).

When the price of pizza is high it will pay to roll out the old oven and hire the slower worker. Profits can be made using less efficient resources when prices are high. And that means that, when prices are high, more is produced. When the price is low only highly efficient resources can be used profitably. When prices are low, less is produced. The quantity supplied increases and decreases with price.

> *When price rises a business can make more profits by increasing production, even if less efficient resources must be used. More products are supplied.*

We're not content with the schedules, though. So we plot demand and supply on a graph, like Figure 2-1. Put the price of pizza on the vertical axis, and the quantity of pizza demanded or supplied on the horizontal axis. Plot the points from the schedule and connect the dots. Label the demand curve with a "D" and the supply curve with an "S".

The demand curve slopes downward. That's because of the Law of Demand. When price is high, people want to buy less. When price is low, people want to buy more. The supply curve slopes upward. That's because businesses are profit maximizers. When price is low, it doesn't pay to supply much. When price is high, it pays to supply more.

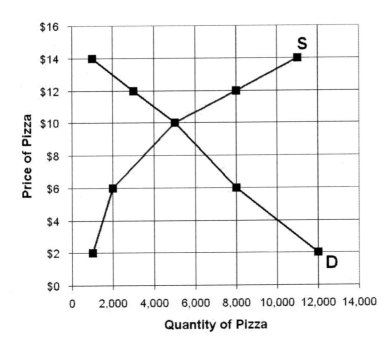

Figure 2-1. Connect the Dots. Each dot shows a pair of price and quantity numbers from the demand or supply schedule. The dot at the lower left, for example, shows that at a price of $2, restaurants will supply 1,000 pizzas. Demand slopes down and supply slopes up. The point where they cross is on both the demand and supply curves. That's the equilibrium price and quantity, $10 and 5,000 pizzas.

There's only one point on this diagram where the amount people want to buy equals the amount businesses want to sell. That's where the two curves cross, at a price of $10 and a quantity of 5,000 pizzas. It's a nice point to be at. Everyone who wants to buy a pizza finds one to buy. Consumers aren't frustrated. Every pizza that a business wants to sell finds a buyer. No flour, tomato paste or pepperoni is wasted.

Is there any reason to think, though, that a market will end up at this point?

The answer is yes. Suppose the price was $14. According to the schedule and the curves, consumers want to buy 1,000 pizzas, but restaurants make 11,000 pizzas for sale. There is a *surplus* of pizza. In such a situation, desperate restaurant owners would try to attract customers by cutting the price of pizza. Some clever consumers might even offer a lower price to the

> **At the equilibrium price the quantity that consumers demand equals the quantity that businesses supply.**

owner to try to take advantage of the surplus. The price falls when there is a surplus, until the surplus is eliminated, at the *equilibrium* price and quantity. Once price equals equilibrium, there is no more surplus, so there's no more reason for price to fall.

Suppose the price is $2. Now there's a *shortage*. Consumers want to buy 12,000 pizzas, but restaurants only make 1,000. Consumers are lined up around the block for a chance to buy pizza. Restaurant owners wouldn't take long to raise their prices in such a situation. Some hungry consumers at the back of the line might offer a higher price, to get into the restaurant. The price rises when there is a shortage, until the shortage is eliminated, at the equilibrium price and quantity. Once price equals equilibrium, there is no more shortage, so there's no more reason for the price to rise.

These ideas were put together first by an 18th century professor from Glasgow, Scotland, named Adam Smith. Smith became famous throughout Europe teaching moral philosophy at the university there. (He was also famous as an absent-minded professor. He once brewed a beverage of bread and butter, and called it a terrible cup of tea.)

Adam Smith was interested in one question in particular: since people (being people) tend to pursue their self-interests before anything else, why does society not fall apart into anarchy? More than that, how do the tasks needed for society's survival get done?

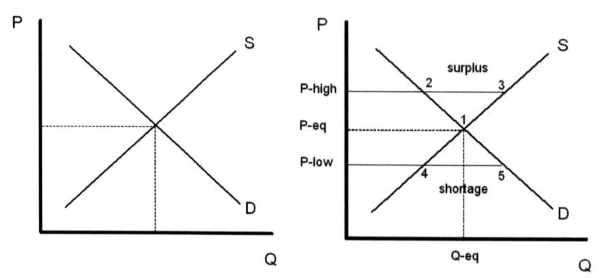

Figure 2-2. The Basics. This is the market for a particular product, like pizza or cars or widgets. P stands for the price of the product, Q for the quantity bought and sold. D stands for demand, S for supply. Demand slopes downward to the right, which means that at higher prices people want to buy less, at lower prices, more. Supply slopes upward, which means that at higher prices businesses want to sell more, at lower prices, less. We call them "curves" even though they usually are drawn as straight lines. Where the demand and supply curves intersect is the "equilibrium" price and quantity, shown by the dotted line. This price and quantity is established by the way people and businesses behave, in a process called the "invisible hand." If price is higher than equilibrium, the amount people want to buy is at 2, the amount businesses want to sell is at 3. There is a surplus of goods on the shelves. Businesses respond by putting their products on sale, consumers by trying to bargain for a better deal. Price falls toward equilibrium at 1. When price is lower than equilibrium, the amount people want to buy is at 5, the amount businesses want to sell is at 4. There is a shortage of goods: the shelves are mostly empty. Businesses realize that they can raise their prices. Desperate consumers are willing to pay more. Price rises toward equilibrium.

In his great work, *The Wealth of Nations*, published in the easy-to-remember year 1776, Smith offered an answer. And offered, and offered—it was a nine hundred page book. *Self-interest* drove men and women to do the tasks that society was willing to pay for. "It is not from the benevolence of the butcher, the brewer, or the baker that we expect our dinner," he wrote, "but from their regard to their self-interest." If more people wanted dinner, they would bid up its price, and butchers, brewers and bakers who wanted that money would respond by making more.

Self-interested trades-people might charge Smith a very high price for his dinner, were it not for a second factor: *competition*. There were lots of people trying to sell dinners. It was in the interest of each to attract customers by undercutting the prices of the others, if they could. Prices would be cut right down to the cost of making the meal. Self-interest and competition combined to deliver the goods that people wanted. And it all happened automatically, in Smith's famous phrase, as if directed by an *"invisible hand."*

Usually we don't put numbers on our demand and supply diagrams, but draw them like Figure 2-2 instead. We can always point to the intersection of the demand and supply curves, though, and call it the equilibrium point. That's where the quantity demanded equals the quantity supplied, and the point where the market will wind up, through the actions of lots of self-interested consumers and profit maximizing suppliers, competing with each other to buy and sell.

Pointing out the equilibrium is just the start. Demand and supply are mainly used to figure out what happens to price and quantity when consumers or businesses change their behavior. When behavior changes, the numbers on the demand and supply schedules change. The quantities that consumers and businesses will buy or sell at every price are different. If demand or supply changes, the equilibrium price and quantity changes. This is shown on the graph as a shift in the demand or supply curve. A shift means that at each price, consumers will demand a different quantity of the product than before, and businesses will supply a different quantity than before.

What can change consumer demand? Here's a list:

- *Income.* If consumer income increases, consumers will demand more of most goods at any price. They can afford to buy more. If income decreases, consumers will demand less. These are called *normal* goods. There are a few *inferior* goods that consumers buy less of when income increases. With higher incomes they can afford better. Macaroni and cheese, ramen noodles and used cars are examples.

- *Prices of other goods.* Some goods are consumed together, like salsa and taco chips. Such goods are known as *complements*. If the price of salsa falls, more salsa will be purchased, and the demand for taco chips will rise too. Demand increases with a fall in the price of a complement, and rises with a rise in the price of a complement. Some goods are consumed instead of one another. Such goods are known as *substitutes*. Pizza and hamburgers are substitutes. If the price of pizza rises, consumers will shift their fast food purchases to hamburgers. Demand increases with a rise in the price of a substitute, and falls with the fall in the price of a substitute.

- *Tastes and preferences.* Sometimes consumers decide that they like a good better than they used to. Fads and fashion or advertising can influence consumers to increase their demand for a good. Sometimes consumers decide that they like a good less. A health warning about a good can influence consumers to decrease their demand for a good.

- *Population.* Demand for a good will increase if there are more consumers in a market, and decrease if there are less.

- *Expectations.* If consumers expect the price to rise in the future, they'll demand more now. If they expect the price to fall, they'll delay their purchases, and demand less now. They'll buy more now if they expect a shortage in the future, too.

> **An increase in demand shifts the demand curve rightward, and increases equilibrium price and quantity. This is also an increase in *quantity supplied*.**

Changes in any of these factors will change demand, and that will change equilibrium price and quantity in the market. For example, when the price of gasoline went up in 2011, many drivers sold their gas guzzlers and bought compact, fuel-efficient or even electric cars. Electric cars are substitutes for gasoline-powered cars. When the price of gasoline went up, the cost of driving a gasoline-powered car increased compared to the cost of buying and driving an electric car. So some drivers bought electrics. A rise in the cost of gasoline increased the demand for a substitute, electric cars.

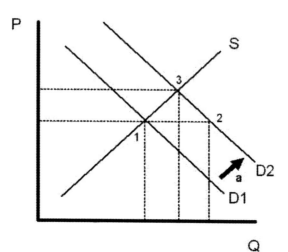

Figure 2-3. Pricey Substitute. Consumers in this market see an increase in the price of a substitute good. They are willing to buy more of the product at every price. Starting equilibrium price and quantity are at 1. Demand increases (a). Because the substitute is more expensive, at the original equilibrium price consumers want to buy more, at 2. If price doesn't change, businesses still want to supply only amount 1. The quantity demanded at 2 is more than the quantity supplied at 1: there's a shortage. Businesses respond to the shortage by raising the price. In some markets consumers may bid up the price trying to buy what they want. The shortage is eliminated at 3, where the amount that consumers want to buy and businesses want to sell is again equal. The movement of the demand curve shown as "a" is an "increase in demand." The movement along the supply curve from 1 to 3 is an effect of the demand increase, and it's called an "increase in quantity supplied" (not an "increase in supply"). The change from equilibrium 1 to equilibrium 2 takes place because of Adam Smith's "invisible hand."

An increase in the price of a substitute increases demand. This creates a shortage at the original equilibrium price. Businesses respond by charging more, and consumers respond to offering more, for the scarce product. Price rises to a new equilibrium. Equilibrium quantity is higher too. This shows up on the graph as a rightward, upward shift in the demand curve, resulting in a new intersection at a new higher equilibrium price and quantity.

We call such a change a *shift in demand* because a change in consumer behavior caused the change in price and quantity. Of course, the amount that businesses supplied also increased as they responded to the change in consumer behavior. Price increased, so businesses could produce and sell more at a profit. The increase in the amount businesses supplied was an effect of the demand increase. To give it a name, we call this a *shift in quantity supplied.*

Supply can change too. Here's a list of what can shift supply.

- *Costs of resources or inputs.* Businesses use employees, machines, land, energy and raw materials to produce goods. Changes in the costs or availability of these resources (also called inputs) will change supply by altering a businesses' profit calculation. If resources become more costly, less can be supplied profitably at every price. If resources become less costly, more can be supplied profitably at every price. This is shown on the graph as a shift in the supply curve. A rise in resource costs shifts the supply curve backwards to the left. That's a decrease in supply. A fall in resource costs shifts the supply curve forward to the right. That's an increase in supply.

- *Technology.* The methods businesses use to combine resources to make their goods is called technology. When technology improves, businesses can produce more goods with the same resources. This reduces the cost of production, and so increases the profitability of supplying the good at every price. Supply increases.

> **An increase in supply shifts the supply curve rightward, and decreases equilibrium price and increases equilibrium quantity. This is also an increase in <u>quantity demanded</u>.**

- *Natural conditions.* Good weather increases the supply of crops; bad weather decreases supply. Natural disasters will reduce supply as well, by damaging and destroying resources. The discovery of new oil or natural gas reserves can be considered an improvement in natural conditions. Depleting those reserves is a deterioration of natural conditions.

- *Number of Firms.* If there are more businesses supplying a good in a market, more of the good will be supplied; fewer businesses mean less supply. More firms might mean more employees, machines, and other resources are being used to produce a good, which would increase supply. Of course, one big business could supply more than many small businesses, so there's another interpretation of this supply determinant. If a market has only a few firms, there is more likely to be collusion among them, an agreement to restrict supply in order to raise the price. If a market has many firms, collusion is more difficult to arrange, and supply is less likely to be restricted.

- *Expectations.* If businesses think the price of their product will rise, they may hold some of their product back from the market for later, decreasing supply now. If businesses think price will fall, they may try to supply more now.

Let's apply these demand and supply ideas by analyzing an issue that's always in the news: oil and gasoline prices.

MacroPolicy Now: The Ups and Downs of Oil and Gasoline

The "Arab Spring" of 2011 resulted in unrest throughout the Arab world. War erupted in Libya. This had an economic effect, because Libya is a supplier of high-quality crude oil. The war took this oil off the world market. The supply of crude oil was reduced. On the list of factors that can change supply, we could say that the number of firms was reduced. One of the oil producing nations had stopped producing.

When supply decreases there is a shortage at the original equilibrium price. Businesses take advantage of the shortage to raise the price. This causes consumers to buy less. The equilibrium price increases, and the equilibrium quantity decreases, with the decrease in supply. This shows up on the graph as a backward, inward, leftward shift in the supply curve. The new intersection is at a higher equilibrium price and a lower equilibrium quantity. We call such a change a *shift in supply* because a change in business behavior caused the change in price and quantity.

Crude oil is an input in the production of gasoline. To produce gasoline refineries must have crude oil. A rise in the price of an input, crude oil, causes a decrease in the supply of a gasoline. And that increases the price of gasoline. That's why the prices of oil and gasoline tend to rise and fall together.

The Organization of Petroleum Exporting Countries (OPEC) is an organization of oil supplying countries—Saudi Arabia, Libya, Iran, Iraq, Venezuela and others—called a *cartel.* A cartel attempts to restrict the supply of a product in order to raise its price and increase its members' profits. Saudi Arabia had pledged to increase production when the Libyan crisis began, but decided later to decrease production. Apparently the higher oil price proved too attractive.

Cartels often have enforcement problems. It's profitable for any one member of the cartel to produce more at the cartel's high price. If all the members do so, though, supply increases and the price falls. The conflict between Saudi Arabia and Iran is not just political or religious. It's also about production and prices.

As the supply of gasoline dropped the amount that consumers demanded also decreased. At a higher price they decided to buy less. We call this a *shift in quantity demanded*, so we know that the change in consumer behavior was an effect of the supply change. This terminology will help us keep cause and effect straight. We reserve the phrase "change in supply" for a shift in the supply curve, caused by a change in business behavior. We reserve the phrase "shift in demand" for a shift in the demand curve, caused by a change in consumer behavior.

Sometimes our analysis of an issue depends not just on the direction price and quantity is changing, but on *how much*. This is the problem of *elasticity*. The elasticity of demand is the amount that quantity changes in response to a change in price. Demand is "elastic" if quantity changes a lot when price changes. Demand is "inelastic" when quantity changes only a little when price changes. Demand is "perfectly inelastic" when quantity doesn't change at all with a price change.

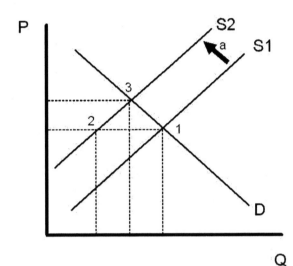

Figure 2-4. Oil and gasoline. Suppose this is the market for gasoline. War in Libya leads to a cut in crude oil production. The price of oil increases. Oil is an input for gasoline production. The higher input price reduces the supply of gasoline (a). The original equilibrium was at 1, but now because gasoline supply is lower, at this price businesses want to sell less, at 2. If price doesn't change, consumers still want to buy the amount at 1. The quantity supplied at 2 is less than the quantity demanded at 1: there's a shortage. Gasoline buyers bid the price up, trying to get their share of scarce gasoline. Sellers ask for higher prices, because they know buyers will pay. The shortage is eliminated at 3, where the amount that businesses want to sell and consumers want to buy are again equal. The movement of the supply curve shown as "a" is a "decrease in supply." The movement along the demand curve from 1 to 3 is an effect of the supply decrease, and it's called a "decrease in quantity demanded" (not a "decrease in demand"). It's another illustration of the invisible hand.

It's convenient to represent demand elasticity with the slope of the demand curve. If the demand curve is flatter, a small change in price will produce a big change in quantity. That's elastic demand. If the demand curve is steep, a big change in price will produce a small change in quantity. That's inelastic demand. Perfectly inelastic demand requires a vertical demand curve—price can vary up and down, but quantity never changes.

What makes demand elastic or inelastic? Whether or not a product is a necessity, for one thing. Some things we can take or leave, so if the price rises, we'll leave. Other things are so essential that we'll move heaven and earth to have them. Price can rise a lot and we'll still buy. I may need a medication to survive. Its price can go up and up and I'll still find a way to buy it. I don't need tacos to survive. If taco prices go up, I'll buy burgers instead. Necessities tend to have inelastic demand.

One definition of a necessity is something that has no substitutes. If there is no substitute for a good, we'll often swallow hard and pay a high price. If there are substitutes, we have the satisfaction of walking out on the seller and buying something else. Products with more substitutes have more elastic demand.

Elasticity measures the size of the response of one variable to another, like the response of quantity demanded to a change in price. If quantity changes a lot, demand is elastic; if it changes only a little, it's inelastic.

When gasoline prices went up in San Francisco the number of cars crossing the Golden Gate Bridge decreased. In a big city, drivers had the option of taking buses and ferries instead. The purchases of gasoline for cars decreased. The availability of substitutes meant a bigger decrease in quantity demanded with the rise in price.

Time matters for elasticity. When the price of a product rises we may pay at first, but if the price hike lasts we'll somehow adjust our lives and buy less. That's what Loraine Greene did. In the Hudson Valley of New York State bus transportation is not available. Over shorter periods of time drivers simply pay the higher gasoline prices. Demand is inelastic. After a while, though, Ms. Greene decided to move closer to work. Her gasoline purchases declined. After longer periods of time demand becomes more elastic.

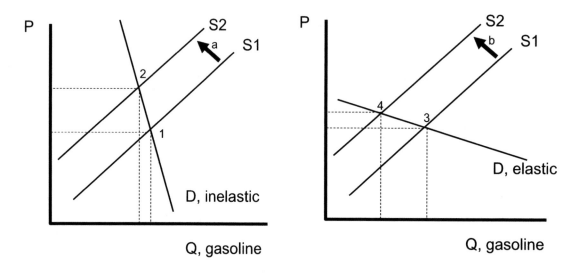

Figure 2-5. Steep or Flat? Suppose the supply of gasoline decreases, shown by a in the left market and b in the right market. In the market on the left, there is no mass transit, so drivers have no choice but to buy gasoline. The quantity of gasoline demanded does not drop very much as price rises, just from 1 to 2. Demand is inelastic. In the market on the right, drivers have the option of taking the bus to work. When the price of gasoline goes up, lots of drivers quit driving, and the quantity of gasoline demanded goes down a lot, from 3 to 4. The decrease in supply is the same, but in a market with inelastic demand price must rise a lot to reach equilibrium. In a market with elastic demand, price only rises a little.

The supply of oil and gasoline decreased. That's a leftward shift of the supply curve. Price increased. Consumers responded by decreasing their purchases, by taking the bus, buying fuel-efficient cars, or moving closer to work. That's a decrease in quantity demanded.

Income matters for elasticities. A rise in the price of bubble gum isn't going to change behavior very much, because the price of gum is such a small share of most consumers' incomes. People with high incomes tend to have lower demand elasticities for everything. For them, price is no object.

There are supply elasticities too, of course. If price rises a little and businesses supply a lot more, supply is elastic. The supply curve is flatter. If price rises and businesses supply only a little bit more, supply is inelastic. The supply curve is steeper. If price rises and nothing happens to the quantity supplied, supply is perfectly inelastic. The supply curve is vertical.

The Times reported that the price of crude oil stopped rising in early May, 2011. One reason was "demand destruction," which meant that consumers were responding to higher prices with bigger reductions in quantity demanded. Gasoline demand was becoming more elastic, and more elastic demand means equilibrium price can't rise as much.

So, demand and supply are useful for analyzing changes in prices and quantities. More than that, though, they are useful for analyzing policy. Here's an example.

MacroPolicy Again: The Minimum Wage Increases

In May 2007 the Congress passed the first increase in the minimum wage in ten years. The rate rose to $5.85 from $5.15 an hour in 2007, then climbed to $6.55 in 2009. The increase to $7.25 in July 2009 was the final step under the legislation.

Even with the raise, the *Washington Post* reported, workers are still behind when inflation is considered: The purchasing power of someone being paid minimum wage is more than 25 percent below what it was in 1968, economists say.

Seven decades after Franklin Roosevelt signed the law creating a minimum wage, each increase still sparks a version of the original debate. The latest increase, which affects about 4.5 million workers among a labor force of 129 million, has renewed the debate over whether the mandate to boost wages will hurt or help the economy.

"Small businesses already have faced employment cuts in the last 12 months -- [and] are projecting more cuts -- and the minimum wage increase will only exacerbate that," National Small Business Association spokeswoman Molly Brogan said. The businesses will "have to make the difficult choice of going under or laying people off."

> But Labor Secretary Hilda L. Solis said the 70-cent hourly increase would have a "minimal" effect on employers but a major impact on the workers. They "will be able to pay their utilities, put food on the table and buy school supplies for their children," Solis said.
>
> The *Atlanta Constitution* reported that economists have studied the issue for decades with varied results. Most studies do not show dramatic job loss because of the wage. But even advocates say that a business at the edge of profitability could be hurt by higher costs.

There's a lot here, but we can handle it. First, there's the claim that even after the increase in 2009, "the purchasing power of someone being paid minimum wage is more than 25 percent below what it was in 1968."

For that we don't need demand and supply, we need the Consumer Price Index from Chapter 1. We need to compare increases in the minimum wage since 1968 to increases in prices since then. We'll measure the price increases with the CPI. If prices have risen faster than the wage, then the wage can buy less now than it could then. The *real minimum wage* is lower.

Here's the data for a few years.

Year	Minimum Wage	CPI	Real Minimum Wage
1968	$1.60 / hour	34.8	$4.60
1976	$2.30 / hour	56.9	$4.04
1983	$3.35 / hour	99.6	$3.36
1989	$3.35 / hour	124.0	$2.70
1997	$5.15 / hour	160.5	$3.04
2006	$5.15 / hour	201.6	$2.55
2008	$6.85 / hour	215.3	$3.18
2009	$7.25 / hour	214.5	$3.38
2010	$7.25 / hour	218.1	$3.32

Back in 1968, when Lyndon Johnson was president, the minimum wage was $1.60 an hour (no kidding!). But prices were a lot lower back then, too. We can tell how much lower from the CPI. The index in 1968 was 34.8, which is about one-sixth of the index now. The average price of the goods and services that consumers buy was about one-sixth of the average price now. Prices have increased more than six-fold since 1968.

To compare the minimum wage and prices we can divide the wage by the CPI (after moving the CPI's decimal place two places to the left).

1968: $1.60 / 0.348 = $4.60
2010: $7.25 / 2.181 = $3.32.

The result is the real minimum wage. This number is the amount needed at 1982-84 prices to buy what $1.60 bought in 1968, or $7.25 bought in 2010. If you had $4.60 in 1982-84, you could buy the same stuff you bought with $1.60 in 1968. If you had $3.32 in 1982-84, you could buy the same stuff you bought with $7.25 in 2010. If we convert wages for all the years to "1982-84 dollars," we can compare the *purchasing power* of the minimum wage over time.

The real minimum wage in 2010 was $3.32, which was 28% lower than the real minimum wage in 1968. The claim that the minimum wage's purchasing power is still well below what it was in 1968 holds up.

It turns out that the purchasing power of the minimum wage was highest in 1968 (which is no doubt why advocates of a higher minimum wage make comparisons to that year). In 1982-84 you would have needed $4.60 to buy what $1.60 bought in 1968. The purchasing power of the minimum wage was lowest in 2006. In 1982-84 you would have needed only $2.55 to buy what $5.15 bought in 2006.

The real minimum wage in 1983 is a special case. Drop that calculation into the above sentence, and it reads, "In 1982-84 you would have needed $3.36 to buy what $3.35 bought in 1983." The *base year* of the CPI is centered on 1983. So, it's already in 1982-84 dollars, and it changes hardly at all when it's deflated. Of course that must be true, because in its base year a price index equals 100, so you're dividing the nominal figure by one when you deflate.

How high would the minimum wage need to be in 2010 to match its purchasing power in 1968? We can provide this policy guidance with the CPI. Prices increased 6.27 times between 1968 and 2010. You get that by dividing the 2010 CPI by the 1968 CPI. So, for the minimum wage to buy now what it bought then, it must rise 6.27 times, too. Here's the calculation.

Price Increase, 1968 to 2010: divide the 2010 index, 218.1, by the 1968 index, 34.8
218.1 / 34.8 = 6.27.

Minimum Wage in 2010 to Match 1968 Purchasing Power: multiply the 1968 minimum wage by the price increase factor to 2010, $1.60 x 6.27 = $10.03.

To match its 1968 purchasing power in 2010, Congress would have had to increase the minimum wage to $10.03. The actual minimum wage is 28% lower than that figure.

It's tempting to say that since the real minimum wage is still low, surely it should be increased some more. We'll help lower income people in less-skilled jobs by raising the minimum.

Not necessarily.

To see why, we must weld a few more gadgets to our demand and supply apparatus.

Gadget #1: The Labor Market. So far we've looked at markets for goods and services that business firms sell to households. In the labor market, buyer and seller are reversed. Households sell labor time, businesses buy it. In the labor market price is the wage paid to employees. The quantity is the number of hours worked or the number of employees hired. Demand shows how many workers that firms will hire at each wage. Supply shows how many workers want to work at each wage. At the equilibrium wage, the number of people seeking jobs equals the number of workers that businesses want to hire.

Gadget #2: A Price Floor. So far we've looked at markets where price is free to find the market's equilibrium. The invisible hand pushes high prices down toward equilibrium and low prices up toward equilibrium. In some markets, though, there are reasons why prices can't adjust. One such reason exists in the labor market. There is a legal minimum wage. It is illegal to pay employees the equilibrium wage if it is below the minimum. At the equilibrium wage, the quantity of labor supplied and the quantity of labor demanded will be equal. If the wage can't fall to equilibrium, the quantity supplied will exceed the quantity demanded. More people will be seeking jobs than businesses want to hire. That's a labor surplus, also known as unemployment.

With these two gadgets, we can see the problem, illustrated in Figure 2-6. Less-skilled workers are earning more at the minimum wage W-min, if they still have their jobs. That's because W-min is above the equilibrium wage, W-eq. *But fewer less-skilled workers have jobs.* With the lower equilibrium wage, the number of jobs businesses offer is L-eq. With the minimum wage, it's only L-D. Those workers who keep their jobs earn more. Those who lose their jobs earn nothing.

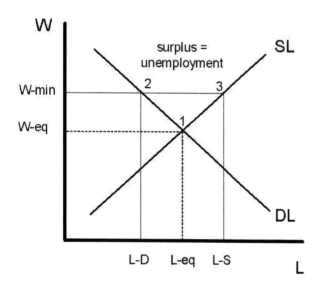

Figure 2-6. The Floor of the Market. This is a diagram of the labor market. The price is the wage paid to labor. The quantity is the number of people working or the number of hours worked. Labor is demanded by business firms—employers. Labor is supplied by households— employees. Equilibrium is at 1, where the quantity of labor demanded equals the quantity of labor supplied. All jobs are filled; all workers find jobs. A legal minimum wage above equilibrium creates a surplus of labor. The quantity of labor demanded is L-D at 2, while the quantity of labor supplied is L-S at 3. This surplus is point 3 less point 2, and it's called unemployment. Households are trying to supply labor that businesses don't want to buy. But those who are working are paid more.

> **The minimum wage is a price floor which keeps the price of labor from falling to equilibrium. Some workers are paid more, but some lose their jobs.**

That's the main thing that everyone argues about. Those who oppose a minimum wage increase point out that firms will hire fewer less-skilled workers if they must pay more. Brogan of the National Small Business Association says the higher minimum wage will exacerbate employment cuts by small business. Obama administration Labor Secretary Solis says workers will be able to take care of basic needs like utilities, food and school supplies when they earn a higher minimum wage.

Demand and supply can take this further. We can compare the effect of the lost jobs to the effect of the higher pay. Just remember a little geometry.

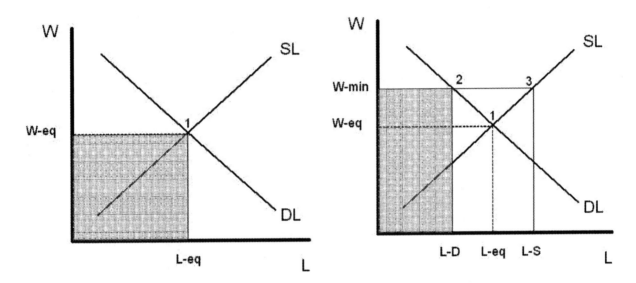

Figure 2-7. Does It Pay? With no minimum wage, the equilibrium is at 1. The wage is W-eq and the number of people employed is L-eq. The wage times the number of people employed is total wages earned. W-eq makes one side of a box, L-eq makes another side, so their product is the area of the box, which is shaded. With a minimum wage, the quantity of labor demanded is at 2, the quantity supplied is at 3. The difference is the surplus of labor, unemployment. The minimum wage (W-min) is higher than the equilibrium wage, so the vertical side of the earnings box is longer. But the horizontal side is shorter, because the number of people that firms hire (L-D) is less than equilibrium employment (L-eq). Less-skilled workers get a higher wage, but fewer are employed. In these two diagrams it's not clear whether less-skilled workers end up earning more or less, in total. Which shaded box is bigger?

Gadget #3. Wage Times Employment Equals Earnings. How do Ms. Brogan's small businesses figure out their payrolls? By multiplying the wage they pay their workers by the number of workers they employ. We can see this on the demand and supply diagram. The equilibrium wage is measured by the distance from the origin (where the two axes meet) and W-eq. The number of employees is measured by the distance from the origin to L-eq. The wage times the number of employees is the total earnings of the workers in this market. Multiply two line segments at right angles together and what do you get? The area of a rectangle! The shaded boxes in Figure 2-7 represent the total earnings of all the employed workers.

When the minimum wage is imposed, the number of workers drops to L-D, but the wage they earn rises to W-min. There's a new shaded box. We can compare the earnings of the workers in this market by comparing the sizes of the boxes. It's hard to tell in Figure 2-7.

So let's make it easier to tell. The change in earnings—in the size of the boxes—caused by the minimum wage depends on the *elasticity of demand for labor.* Remember that the elasticity tells us how much quantity changes with a change in price. When the wage increases, how much does the quantity of labor demanded decrease? How many jobs are lost?

Figure 2-8 shows why it matters. On the left, the demand for labor is inelastic. The curve is steep, and that means that a change in the wage causes just a small decrease in the quantity of labor demanded. Lots more workers earn a higher wage, but only a few lose their jobs. Total earnings increase. The shaded box gets bigger.

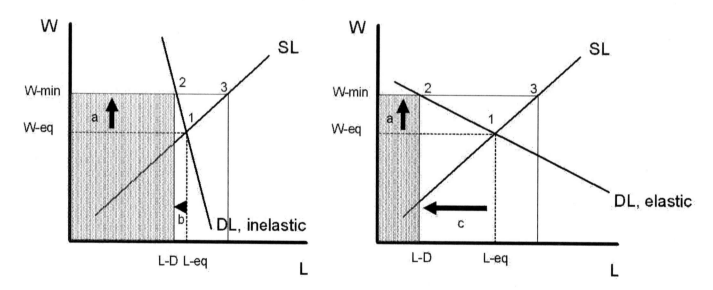

Figure 2-8. How Elastic? The answer to the question of whether less-skilled workers in total earn more or less in total with the minimum wage depends on the elasticity of demand for labor. If demand is inelastic, in the diagram at left, imposing a minimum wage (a) reduces employment only a little (b). The added earnings from the higher wage are greater than the lost earnings from fewer jobs. If demand is elastic, in the diagram at right, imposing a minimum wage (a) reduces employment a lot (c). The added earnings from the higher wage are less than the lost earnings from fewer jobs.

On the right is an elastic demand for labor. The demand curve is drawn flat, which means that a wage increase causes a big drop in the quantity of labor demanded. Lots of jobs are lost, and only a few workers remain employed to earn the higher wage. Total earnings decrease.

Labor Secretary Solis thinks the diagram on the left describes the labor market. She says that the higher minimum wage will have only a minimal effect on employers. Is the demand for labor elastic or inelastic? To figure that out, we need another gadget.

Gadget #4. Measuring Elasticity. We measure the elasticity of demand for a product by gathering data on prices and quantities. When a business increases the price of its product, what happens to sales? When a product's price is slashed, how much more is sold? If we could gather a lot of data about such events, we could calculate an elasticity. We could take the percentage changes in quantity that price changes cause and divide by the percentage change in price. Like this.

Elasticity = (Percentage change in Q) / (Percentage change in P)

If the data we collect show that a 10% rise in price tends to cause a 5% drop in quantity, then the elasticity is -0.5. That's -5% divided by +10%. If the data show that a 20% drop in price causes a 50% rise in quantity, the elasticity is -2.5. Demand elasticities that are more negative than -1 (like -2.5) are called elastic, because the response of quantity to price is big. Elasticities between zero and -1 (like -0.5) are called inelastic, because the response of quantity to price is small.

Knowing the elasticity of a product could be pretty useful to a business. Suppose a shoe store knows from long experience that the elasticity of demand for shoes is -2. The annual sale is coming up, when prices will be cut by 20%. How many more shoes should the store have in stock? The answer is 40% more, because

-20% x -2 = +40%.

The 20% price cut times the -2 elasticity equals a quantity increase of 40%.

There's enough data in the article about oil and gasoline to calculate an elasticity. From May 2010 to May 2011 the price of gasoline increased one dollar, to $3.99. That's an increase from about $3 to about $4, which is a 33% increase. Gasoline purchases decreased by as much as 4 percent over that year, according to the article. So, the elasticity of demand for gasoline is

-4% / 33% = -0.12 .

Demand for gasoline is very inelastic: purchases do not respond very much to changes in price.

Lots of research has been done on the demand for less-skilled labor. The research has produced lots of different results because researchers use different methods on different sets of data. But the consensus seems to be that the elasticity of demand for less-skilled

> *An elasticity is measured as the percentage change in quantity divided by the percentage change in price.*

labor is inelastic. A middle value for the elasticity is around -0.3.

That means the inelastic demand curve on the left in figure 2-8 is the better picture of what actually happens. A minimum wage increase increases the total earnings of less- skilled workers. Economists have not found dramatic job losses from minimum wage increases, the *Journal-Constitution* reports. Most workers remain employed to earn the higher wage.

So can we say that economic analysis supports an increase in the minimum wage? Again; not necessarily.

Can we compare people's experience in this way? The people who lose their jobs pay a very high cost to provide somewhat higher earnings for the rest. Opponents of minimum wage hikes point out research that shows that workers don't earn the minimum for long. After six months or a year, a worker will gain experience and skills and can demonstrate her productivity to her employer. She gets promoted at a wage higher than the minimum.

Some advocates of the minimum wage take the inelastic demand argument one step farther, claiming that a rise in the wage will not reduce employment at all. That implies that the demand for labor is *perfectly inelastic*. Some studies have found that increases in the minimum wage don't cause any job losses at all. That implies a vertical demand curve. Increases or decreases in the wage have no effect on the quantity demanded.

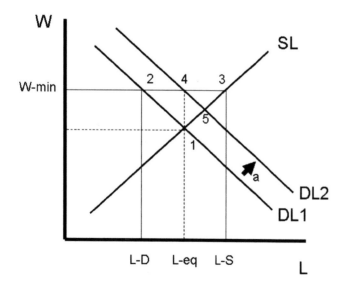

Figure 2-9. All Else is Not Equal. In this labor market, equilibrium without a minimum wage is at 1. A minimum wage W-min is imposed, and a labor surplus would occur between points 2 and 3. But, the economy is growing, so the demand for labor increases (a). At the new minimum wage and the new demand for labor, the number of employees hired is at 4, unchanged from the starting point at 1. If the minimum wage hadn't increased, though, the equilibrium would have been at 5, with a lower wage but more employment.

41

One problem with research on the minimum wage (or just about any economic topic) is that economics has no laboratory. It's not possible to change the minimum wage while holding everything else unchanged, as you would in a laboratory experiment. Other things change, too. Suppose, for example, that demand for less-skilled labor is increasing because the demand for the products of businesses is growing. The growth in demand could offset the higher minimum wage, leaving the number of jobs unchanged. Without the higher minimum, though, employment would have been even higher.

Researchers try to allow for such demand changes, but if they can't they might conclude that the minimum wage increase had no effect on employment. Economists say that, *"all else equal,"* an increase in the minimum wage reduces employment. The phrase "all else equal" does not mean that economists think that nothing else changes. It means, in fact, that economists know that lots of other things change, but if the effect of the rising minimum wage could be isolated, it would reduce employment. Sometimes, when they want to feel smart, economists use the Latin phrase for "all else equal": *ceteris paribus.*

There's more. An increase in the minimum wage increases the costs for businesses that employ less-skilled workers. That decreases the supply of the product. An increase in the minimum wage will raise prices.

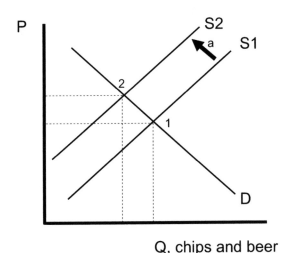

Figure 2-10. Wage up, prices too. Convenience stores often employ minimum wage workers. In the market for convenience store products, like chips and beer, an increase in the minimum wage increases input costs. That's a determinant of supply, which decreases (a). Equilibrium price increases (1 to 2).

Q, chips and beer

That's shown in Figure 2-10. This is the market for convenience store products, like chips and beer. Supply decreases because it depends on input costs. The increase in the minimum wage increases the cost of labor, which is an input to convenience store production. Equilibrium output declines, and equilibrium price increases.

Will the added purchasing power of the minimum wage hike be wiped out by higher prices? Probably not. Here are three reasons:

- Business owners won't be able to pass the whole wage hike on to customers, for fear that they'll stop buying gasoline, chips and beer. The demand curve slopes downward in figure 2-10, so the higher price causes some customers to flee. Owners will take some of the wage hike in lower profits. That's why Small Business spokeswoman Brogan fears that some businesses will go bankrupt. The higher costs from the minimum wage increase will turn their profits into losses.

- Other business costs don't rise. Wholesale product costs stay the same. So do the rents on all those convenience stores. Only part of the cost of selling chips and beer has increased, so their prices won't rise as much as the rise in the wage.

- Most goods and services are produced by workers earning more than the minimum wage. If the minimum wage goes up, the wages of plumbers and lawyers won't rise. The quantity supplied of services by plumbers and lawyers won't decrease, so the prices of their services won't increase. Only a few goods will see price increases.

Since prices won't rise enough to erase the gain from the minimum wage, less-skilled workers who are still employed will have more purchasing power. But what about all those higher wage workers who don't get a pay increase? The added inflation means that the purchasing power of their wages will fall. An increase in the minimum wage shifts real income from more-skilled, higher wage workers to less-skilled, minimum wage workers. It redistributes income.

So, should the minimum wage be increased or not? *Economics can't provide the answer.* What economics can do is analyze the consequences of raising the minimum wage. Here are some:

- The purchasing power of the minimum wage is lower now than it was in the 1960's, even after the recent increases.

- If the minimum wage is increased, most less-skilled workers keep their jobs and earn higher pay. Total earnings of less-skilled workers increase.

- Some less-skilled workers lose their jobs, and they lose the opportunity to advance their careers.

- Businesses that employ less-skilled workers earn lower profits and raise their prices.

- Inflation increases, but not enough to wipe out the increase in the minimum wage's purchasing power.

- Less-skilled minimum wage workers get more purchasing power, while more-skilled higher wage workers get less purchasing power.

Economics provides a lot of information about the consequences of this policy change. But comparing the consequences, the benefits and costs, the pros and cons, requires value judgments. Economists are no more qualified to make those value judgments than are plumbers, lawyers, convenience store workers, or even college students. Economics lays out the issue, and (we hope) raises the quality of the debate. The decision is up to the policymakers, and the public.

Terms in this Chapter, in order of appearance
Demand
Supply
Demand and supply schedule
Diminishing marginal utility
Law of Demand
Price takers
Profit maximizers
Surplus
Shortage
Equilibrium
The Wealth of Nations
Self-interest
Competition
Invisible hand
Income
Normal goods
Inferior goods
Prices of other goods
Complements
Substitutes
Tastes and preferences
Population
Expectations
Shift in demand
Shift in quantity supplied
Costs of resources or inputs
Technology
Natural conditions
Number of firms
Expectations
Shift in supply
Shift in quantity demanded
Elasticity
Real minimum wage
Base year
Labor market
Price Floor

Wage times employment equals earnings
Elasticity of demand for labor
Measuring elasticity
Perfectly inelastic
All else equal
Ceteris paribus

Notes

The first economics book I ever read—and still one of the best—is Robert Heilbroner's *The Worldly Philosophers*. He makes the lives of the great economists exciting, which is no mean feat. There are now later editions, but I used the one I got as a freshman economics student in 1974, the 4th edition. Chapter 3 is about Adam Smith.

The U.S. Department of Labor provides a history of the minimum wage on its website, at www.dol.gov/whd/minwage/chart.htm.

And the U.S. Department of Energy offers data on gasoline prices on its website, at http://tonto.eia.doe.gov/dnav/pet/pet_pri_top.asp   (no   "www").

Sources

Heilbroner, Robert L. 1972. *The Worldly Philosophers*. (4th Edition) New York: Simon and Schuster.

Sasser, Alicia. 2006. "The Potential Economic Impact of Increasing the Minimum Wage in Massachusetts." New England Public Policy Center, Federal Reserve Bank of Boston, No. 06-1, January.

News Articles

Haynes, V. Dion and Emma L. Carew. "Some Attack Timing of Minimum Wage Hike," *Washington Post*, July 24, 2009.

Kanell, Michael E. "Minimum Wage Rises to $6.55 an Hour Starting Thursday," *Atlanta Journal-Constitution*, July 24, 2008.

Krauss, Clifford. "Crude Oil Falls Below $100 a Barrel," New York Times, May 5, 2011.

Rich, Motoko and Stephanie Clifford. "In Consumer Behavior, Signs of Gas Price Pinch," New York Times, May 17, 2011.

Chapter 3
Three Macroeconomic Markets

MacroPolicy Now: It All Goes Wrong

Lehigh Acres is a far suburb of Fort Myers, Florida. Home construction there boomed in the middle of the 2000's. Bill Spikowski, a city planning consultant in Fort Myers, said that from 2004 to the end of 2006, home builders completed 13,183 units in Lehigh Acres. That nearly doubled the total stock of houses that existed in 2000. Housing prices doubled, then tripled, and jobs were plentiful, nearly all of them tied to real estate and home construction. "Sometimes houses would sell three or four times in a few months, and no one would move in," said real estate salesman Bob Elliott. It was a sign of trouble, he thought.

Then in 2007, it all went quiet. Houses stopped selling. Foreclosures multiplied. The median home price in the Fort Myers area dropped from $322,300 in December 2005 to $106,900 in December 2008.

Gloria Chilson lost her house to foreclosure. "I knew it was coming," she said. "You take what you can; you try not to care." She lost her house partly because of the boom (if not for easy credit, she might not have refinanced her mortgage a few years ago), the bust (which led to her husband being laid off from his pest control job), and overspending (which led to more than $20,000 in credit card debt). Some of her neighbors began visiting the local food bank.

A single foreclosure is a tragedy for the homeowner. Lots of foreclosures are a tragedy for the banks that lent the money, too. The Independent Bank of Michigan, in Troy, financed the construction of roads and utilities for the luxurious Whispering Woods Estates subdivision, only to see the developer go belly up before most of the lots were sold. In January 2009 snowdrifts covered the "for sale" signs. "We didn't step back and look at the big picture, asking ourselves, are we really doing the right thing with this loan?" said Keith Lightbody, a vice president of the bank. "Everyone was making a lot of money."

As of the end of September, the bank was burdened by $115 million in bad debts, or nearly 5 percent of its overall loan portfolio, compared with less than 1 percent in 2005. Fearful of repeating past mistakes, the bank made many fewer loans. One manufacturer from western Michigan came to Independent looking for a business loan. The chief lending officer, Stefanie Kimball, examined the company's books. She found that its sales were slipping, and worse: it was having a hard time collecting on bills it had sent to its remaining customers. The bank turned the company down.

Early in 2008, as the recession was beginning, many analysts hoped that growing exports to the rest of the world would give U.S. businesses a reason to hire more workers and produce more goods. But the recession spread to the rest of the world. And, strangely, the resulting anxiety among world investors caused them to want to lend more money to the United States. This increased the exchange value of the dollar.

From March 2008 to March 2009, the dollar rose 13 percent against major foreign currencies. Foreign holdings of Treasury bills rose by $456 billion in 2008. "It's a huge safe haven effect," said economist William R. Cline. "The basic assumption that people are making is that the U.S. government will never default on its debt."

The U.S. central bank, known as the Federal Reserve, responded to the recession by reducing its key interest rate nearly to zero by the end of 2008. Then the central bank began lending money to a wider and wider array of borrowers. The idea was to encourage more economic activity by lowering interest rates, including those on home loans, and to help the financial system as it struggled under the crushing weight of bad loans and poor investments.

There were problems with these policies. For months Fed officials wrestled with the fact that lenders remained unwilling to lend and borrowers were unwilling or unable to borrow. Even though the Fed had been creating money at the fastest rate in its history, much of that money remained dormant.

The Federal Reserve's efforts were only half the story. The new President and the Congress were attempting to stimulate the economy as well. Congress and the administration passed a $787 billion stimulus bill in February 2009. Higher spending and tax cuts were intended to promote economic recovery.

Money for this effort had to be borrowed, from investors in the United States and around the world. The Congressional Budget Office estimated that the stimulus bill would raise real GDP growth through 2014. If borrowing continued, however, it would slightly reduce growth after that. The reason, said the CBO, was that "the increased debt will tend to reduce the stock of productive private capital." Economists call it "crowding out."

Some analysts were skeptical of the whole policy approach. Peter Schiff, president of Euro Pacific Capital, said "Our standard of living must decline to reflect years of reckless consumption and the disintegration of our industrial base. Only by swallowing this tough medicine now will our sick economy ever recover."

The recession was marked at ending in June 2009, but the recovery was sporadic. The economy had turned the corner. Output rose through summer 2010, and then stalled. Growth in the first quarter of 2011 was still slow. It was clear that recovery would take a long, long time.

What happened? We saw events in 2008 and 2009 that hadn't been seen since the Great Depression of the 1930's, events that many economists had consigned to the deep dark past. We need a way to understand it all, maybe a model of how the economy works. . . .

So far we have measures of the aggregate economy, and we have demand and supply. We can combine the two to come up with a model to help us understand the macroeconomy —the bad news from 2008 and 2009, and the somewhat better news since.

We'll call it *the three market model*. Each market stands for a part of the economy that we can measure and uses demand and supply to show what makes each measure change. Here's an overview:

The Goods Market. This is the demand for and supply of the economy's output. We measure output with real Gross Domestic Product, and the price with a price index like the Consumer Price Index or the GDP deflator. Demand is called *aggregate demand*; it depends on spending by households on consumption, by businesses on investment on plant and equipment, by governments for its employees and equipment, by Americans on imports, and by the world on American exports. Supply is called *aggregate supply*; it depends on the production of goods and services by businesses. The equilibrium is the intersection of aggregate demand and aggregate supply, and it determines the price level and the level of output—real GDP. When aggregate demand or aggregate supply change, the equilibrium changes. The resulting increases in real GDP are expansions and decreases in real GDP are recessions. Increases in the price level are inflation and decreases in the price level are deflation.

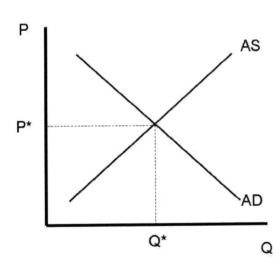

Figure 3-1. The Goods Market. That's output (Q) on the horizontal axis, measured by real Gross Domestic Product, and the price level (P) on the vertical axis, measured by a price index like the Consumer Price Index or the GDP deflator. The demand curve is aggregate demand (AD), which depends on spending, and the supply curve is aggregate supply (AS), which depends on production. The intersection is the equilibrium, where spending equals production. P* shows the price level and Q* shows the level of real GDP.

The Money Market. This is the *demand for money* and the *supply of money*. The important indicator in this market is the real interest rate, which is the price of money. The quantity of money is the amount of cash in circulation plus deposits and reserves in banks. Demand is the demand for money by households and businesses. It is related to income and the price level. Supply is the supply of money, determined by the behavior of private lenders like banks and bond buyers, and by the monetary policy of the Federal Reserve. The equilibrium is the intersection of money demand and money supply. It determines the quantity of money, but more important, it determines the real interest rate. When money demand or money supply changes, the interest rate changes.

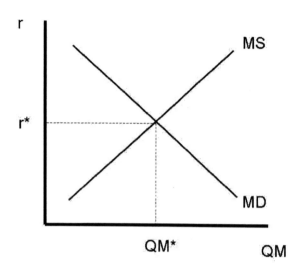

Figure 3-2. The Money Market. The quantity of money in circulation—including cash and reserves and deposits in banks—is on the horizontal axis (QM). The real interest rate (r) is on the vertical axis. That's the price of money. The demand for money (MD) depends on the price level and income, while the supply of money (MS) depends on monetary policy and on bank behavior. The intersection shows the equilibrium quantity of money (QM*) and real interest rate (r*).

The Exchange Market. This is the international *demand for the dollar* and *supply of the dollar*. The important indicator is the exchange rate, which is the value of the dollar in foreign exchange markets measured as foreign currency units (like euros or yen) per dollar. Quantity is the number of dollars traded. Demand is the demand for the dollar by foreigners wishing to buy U.S. goods, lend to U.S. companies or governments, or invest in U.S. assets. Supply is the supply of the dollar by Americans.

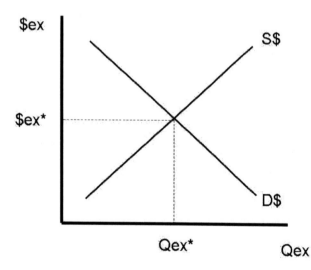

Figure 3-3. The Exchange Market. Quantity (Qex) is the number of dollars traded on foreign exchange markets; price is the exchange rate ($ex), measured as the number of foreign currency units (like euros or yen) that exchange for one dollar. Demand for dollars comes from foreigners wanting to buy, lend or invest in the U.S. Supply comes from Americans supplying their dollars in exchange for foreign currencies. Equilibrium is the intersection, which determines the quantity traded (Qex*) and most importantly, the exchange value of the dollar ($ex*).

Americans supply dollars when they demand foreign currencies, which they do in order to buy foreign goods, lend in foreign countries, or invest in foreign assets. They supply dollars in trade for foreign currencies. The equilibrium is the intersection of dollar demand and dollar supply. It determines the number of dollars traded, but more important, it determines the exchange rate. The exchange rate changes when either dollar demand or dollar supply changes.

The Goods Market

The goods market may be the most important. It's the one that shows us the main things we want to know: what causes recessions and expansions, inflation and deflation, and unemployment?

The goods market looks at what determines spending and production, known as aggregate demand and aggregate supply. The equilibrium shows the price level and real output. When spending or production change, aggregate demand or supply shift. The result is a change in the price level—inflation or deflation—and a change in output—expansion or recession.

> *In the goods market, shifts in aggregate demand and aggregate supply cause changes in output and the price level. That explains recession and expansion, and inflation and deflation.*

Aggregate demand is the sum of spending on consumption, investment, government purchases, and net exports, which are exports minus imports. That's our old friend, C+I+G+X-M. In the following chapters we'll look at what lies behind each kind of spending, but for now, just think of consumers, businesses, governments and the rest of the world making decisions on how much to spend on the nation's output of goods and services.

Aggregate supply is the production of goods and services, mostly by businesses. Its determinants are familiar—the costs of inputs such as labor, capital and land, the level of technology, and natural conditions. These are the same as supply in a single market, discussed in Chapter 2.

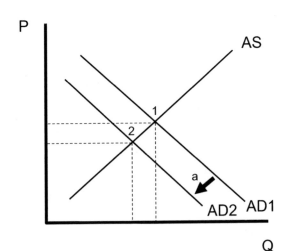

Figure 3-4. Consumers quit spending. In the goods market, start with aggregate demand (AD) and aggregate supply (AS) in equilibrium at 1. The falling value of homes, and the threat of unemployment, causes consumers to cut back on their spending. Consumption declines. Consumption is the most important part of aggregate demand, and the drop in consumption causes aggregate demand to decline (a). The new equilibrium at 2 has lower output and a lower price level. The decline in output is a recession, and the decline in the price level is deflation.

We use the goods market to understand why output and prices change. Consumer spending decreased in 2008 and 2009 for lots of reasons, Home values declined. So did the stock market. People were less wealthy. The unemployment rate went up, so peoples' jobs were less secure. Consumption declined, and so did aggregate demand.

Businesses sell less, so they decide to produce less. Output declines. They lay off workers, who spend less too. That's a recession. Prices of goods and services fall as businesses cut prices to try to unload unsold goods. The price level falls, which is deflation.

Investment Spending in the Goods Market

Like consumption, investment spending by businesses is part of aggregate demand in the goods market. Investment spending is determined in part by the real interest rate. A higher real interest rate reduces investment spending; a lower real interest rate increases it.

Investment spending depends on the real interest rate because money for business investments is often borrowed from banks or from financial investors by selling corporate bonds. Investment decisions are made by comparing the cost of borrowing, which is the real interest rate, to the real expected earnings from the project. A business will make an investment if the project is expected to earn enough to repay the loan with profits left over.

When the real interest rate rises, borrowing becomes more expensive. An investment project must earn more in order to be profitable after the loan is repaid. A rise in the interest rate can make some investment projects unprofitable, causing businesses to cancel them. A higher interest rate reduces business investment in buildings and equipment. When the interest rate falls, borrowing is less expensive, more investment projects look profitable, and investment in buildings and equipment increase.

The Money Market

The real interest rate helps determine investment spending. The real interest rate itself is determined in the money market. Like the goods market, the money market has a demand curve and a supply curve. Equilibrium shows the price of money, which is the real interest rate, and the quantity of money in circulation. Shifts in money demand and money supply change the equilibrium real interest rate and the equilibrium quantity of money.

In the money market, shifts in money demand and money supply cause changes in the real interest rate.

People need money to pay for their purchases of goods and services. Money is demanded because households, businesses, and governments need it to use for *transactions*. The quantity of money in the money market includes cash and coin, but also checking accounts and savings accounts. People keep cash in their pockets to buy lunch. They keep money in their checking accounts to write checks for doctor visits and small appliances. They keep money in savings for they day they'll have to make college tuition payments or buy a car.

And people need money in checking and savings to pay off the credit card bill every month (or at least pay the interest!).

People who have more income make more transactions. That's because most goods and services are normal, meaning the amount purchased increases with income. So, people with more income must keep more cash in their pockets, and bigger balances in checking and savings. When aggregate income rises, lots of people have more income, so the demand for money rises.

Likewise, when prices are higher, people need more cash and bank balances to pay them. Each transaction requires more money. People who face higher prices must keep more cash in their pockets, and bigger balances in checking and savings. When prices rise, so does the demand for money.

> **The Federal Reserve is the U.S. central bank. It conducts monetary policy, which influences the money supply and real interest rates.**

The *Federal Reserve* is the United States' central bank. It's known by its nickname, "The Fed." One of the Fed's important functions is *monetary policy*. Monetary policy is the effort to manipulate the money supply and interest rates to achieve stable prices, high real growth, and low unemployment. How the Fed does this is a topic for later chapters.

When the Fed wishes to reduce interest rates, it increases the money supply. The Fed uses its policy tools to increase the reserves that banks have. Banks respond by lending more and reducing interest rates to attract borrowers. The Federal Reserve can't set bank interest rates, but it can influence bank reserves and lending, therefore influencing interest rates.

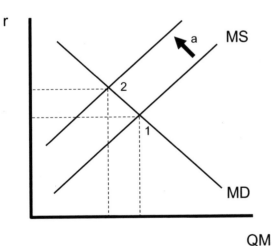

Figure 3-5. It makes the world go around—and stop going around. The money market starts in equilibrium at 1, which defines the equilibrium real interest rate and quantity of money. Banks become pessimistic about lending. This reduces the money supply (a). The equilibrium shifts to 2, at a higher interest rate and smaller quantity of money.

But the Fed's policy is not the only determinant of money supply. What banks do with their reserves also matters. If banks are eager to lend because they are optimistic about the prospect of businesses repaying loans, they will want to lend more. They reduce interest rates to attract more borrowers. More lending puts more money in circulation and increases the money supply.

When banks are pessimistic about potential borrowers because they think businesses will have trouble repaying loans, they lend less. They raise interest rates to chase borrowers away. Less lending reduces the amount of money in circulation, and reduces the money supply. The panic in 2008 caused many banks to lend less, and the reduction in the money supply increased the real interest rate.

Export and Import Spending in the Goods Market

Exports and imports are part of spending and aggregate demand in the goods market. The rest of the world spends on U.S. exports. Americans buy imports from the rest of the world. Export spending adds to aggregate demand for U.S. output. Import spending subtracts from it, because it is not spending on U.S. output.

The exchange rate helps determine export and import spending. When the value of the dollar rises, it exchanges for more yen or pounds or euros. A dollar buys a lot of goods and services sold by Japanese or British or European firms. So, when the value of the dollar rises, Americans buy more imports. A higher value of the dollar implies a lower value of the yen, pound or euro. That makes U.S. exports more expensive for foreigners to buy, so they buy less. A higher value of the dollar increases import spending and decreases export spending. Aggregate demand decreases.

A lower value of the dollar has the opposite effects. Imports are more expensive, so import spending decreases. Exports are less expensive, so export spending increases. Aggregate demand increases.

The Exchange Market

The exchange rate helps determine export and import spending. The exchange rate itself is set in the exchange market.

The dollar and the world's other currencies are traded every day (every minute!) in exchange markets around the world. U.S. currency traders who want yen or pounds or euros offer dollars in exchange. They supply dollars in order to demand other currencies. Japanese or British or European currency traders who want dollars supply their currencies in exchange. They supply their currencies in order to demand dollars.

> *In the exchange market, shifts in the demand for and supply of the dollar cause changes in the dollar's exchange rate.*

But why would a foreigner want dollars? Three reasons: to *buy American goods*, to *lend to Americans*, or to *invest in American assets*. These three motives lie behind the demand for the dollar in the exchange market.

- If foreigners have more income, they'll want to buy more goods from all over the world, including the United States. They'll demand dollars in order to buy U.S. goods.

- If U.S. goods improve in quality relative to goods from other countries, foreigners will want to buy them. They'll demand dollars in order to buy U.S. goods.
- If U.S. goods are produced more efficiently than goods in the rest of the world, they'll have lower prices. Foreigners will demand dollars to buy lower priced U.S. products.
- If U.S. interest rates are higher than interest rates in the rest of the world, foreigners will want to lend in the U.S. They'll demand dollars in order to lend to American businesses and governments.
- If owning businesses in the U.S. is seen as more profitable or less risky than in the rest of the world, foreigners will want to invest in the U.S. They'll want to buy U.S. businesses or build factories or offices in the U.S. And they'll demand dollars in order to make these investments.

So, the demand for the dollar depends on the world's income, U.S. goods quality, U.S. goods prices, U.S. interest rates, and expectations about the U.S. economy. When quality or expectations improve, when goods prices fall or when interest rates rise, the demand for the dollar goes up. The opposite changes make the demand for the dollar go down.

Unlike the goods or money markets, in the exchange market the same factors determine both demand and supply. Dollars are supplied by Americans who want to trade them for other currencies. Americans will supply dollars in order to buy foreign goods, lend to foreigners, or invest in foreign assets.

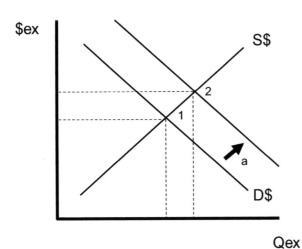

Figure 3-6. Surprise Rise. In the fall of 2008 international investors sought to buy U.S. Treasury bonds as a "safe haven" from world economic turmoil. They demanded dollars in order to lend to the U.S. Federal government. Demand for the dollar increased (a), increasing the equilibrium exchange value of the dollar from 1 to 2.

If American incomes go up, or if foreign goods improve in quality or price relative to U.S. goods, the demand for foreign goods will increase, and the demand for foreign currencies will increase. Americans must offer dollars in trade for foreign currencies, so the *supply* of dollars will increase. Likewise, if foreign interest rates rise relative to U.S. rates, Americans will want to lend to foreigners, so they will demand foreign currencies, so they will supply more dollars. If owning businesses in foreign countries is seen as more profitable or less risky than in the U.S., Americans will want to buy foreign businesses or build in other countries. They'll demand foreign currencies and supply dollars.

This happened in a big way during the panic of 2008. International investors fled from risky investments and loans to private businesses and shaky governments. They tried to lend to the U.S. government instead, which meant buying U.S. Treasury bonds as a *safe haven* for their wealth. This increased the demand for the dollar, and the exchange value of the dollar went up.

Potential Output

Can we spend our way to wealth? So far the goods market says yes. Increase consumption spending, investment spending, government purchases, export spending (or decrease import spending), and aggregate demand will increase. Output will rise. And rise. The more spending rises, the more output rises. Prices rise too, of course, but according to the goods market graph any amount of goods and services can be produced, if only we're willing to spend.

This is wrong.

It's wrong because resources are limited. There's only so much labor, land and capital available at any time, and these resources can only produce so much output with the technology available. We call it *potential output*. It's the amount of output the economy can produce when resources are employed as they normally are. On the goods market diagram it's drawn as a vertical line and labeled Qp, the "quantity" of output that can "potentially" be produced.

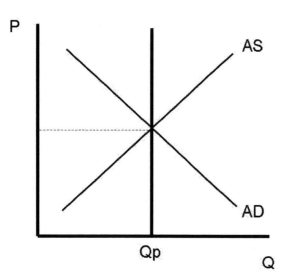

Figure 3-7. Spending won't make it so. Qp is potential output, drawn as a vertical line at a particular output level. Here, it crosses the equilibrium point, where the AD and AS curves intersect. There's a reason for that. Read on.

When the aggregate demand and aggregate supply curves intersect to the left of potential output, there are unemployed resources. Actual output is less than potential because some workers are unemployed, some factories are shut down, and a pile of raw materials is sitting unused in some warehouse. That's called recession. Aggregate demand or aggregate supply has decreased. Policymakers will be called upon to try to increase output back to potential. This is how the three market model represents increases in cyclical unemployment.

> **Potential output is the amount that can be produced when resources are normally employed.**

More difficult to understand, perhaps, is that aggregate demand and aggregate supply can intersect to the *right* of potential output, too. That implies that all the nation's resources are being used, and then some, to produce beyond the supposed limit of potential output.

How can this be? Consider one of the resources: labor. Remember that unemployment has three causes: cyclical, frictional and structural. Potential output is the amount that will be produced when cyclical unemployment is zero. People are still unemployed, because it takes time to find work, or because their skills don't match the open jobs, or because the job openings are in a different place. But not because there are no job openings for all the people who want to work.

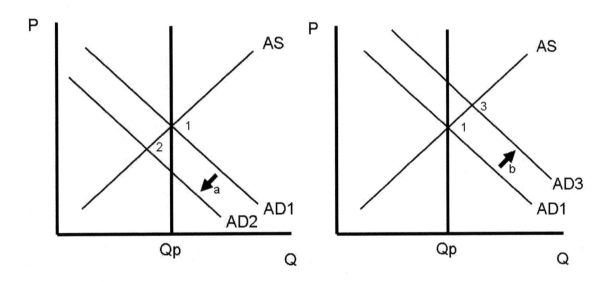

Figure 3-8. A temporary thing. The goods market starts with output at potential (1). Then, perhaps, aggregate demand decreases (a). Consumers or businesses or governments spend less, fewer resources are required to meet this demand, unemployment increases, output drops (2). A recession has pushed output below potential. Or, starting from potential (1), aggregate demand may increase (b). The lure of higher prices, bigger sales, and larger profits causes businesses to hire workers they wouldn't ordinarily hire, and use resources they wouldn't ordinarily use. The lure of higher wages causes workers to accept jobs they wouldn't ordinarily accept. Output increases beyond potential (3). Neither situation (2 nor 3) can last. Ultimately, output will return to potential. We'll see why in coming pages.

The unemployment rate when cyclical unemployment is zero is known as the *natural rate of unemployment*. Suppose, though, that business conditions really improve. Suppose businesses think they can sell all they can produce and more for a high price. They'll want to expand their operations and hire more workers. After a while cyclical unemployment is zero. So many workers have been hired that unemployed workers are hard to find. The businesses raise their wage offers, trying to attract employees.

Workers are excited by these higher-than-usual wages, so they intensify their job searches. Businesses want to hire workers fast, so they accelerate their hiring procedures. Frictional unemployment declines. Workers become willing to move out-of-state to take higher paying jobs or to make long commutes out of the central city to the suburbs. Businesses offer to pay moving expenses or charter transportation from city to suburb. Workers search out training opportunities at community colleges or technical schools. Businesses become willing to hire less-skilled employees and train them. Structural unemployment declines. The unemployment rate drops below the natural rate, more workers are employed, and output rises above potential.

Similar stories can be told about other resources. Farmers may plant pasture land with corn when they expect corn prices to rise. Manufacturers may keep technically obsolete factories open longer because product prices are high.

That's why we define potential output as the amount produced when resources are employed as they normally are. At potential output businesses and employees are not doing anything extraordinary to connect people to jobs.

Output can be above potential. This seems to fly in the face of the potential output idea. What is limiting about potential output, if resources can be used more intensively, pushing output beyond potential? The answer: output above potential can't last.

Second Shifts
We measure five main economic indicators: real output, the price level, the real interest rate, the exchange rate, and the unemployment rate. Understanding how the economy works means we want to know about the relationships among these five indicators. When output rises, what happens to the real interest rate? When the exchange rate falls, what happens to the price level? When the real interest rate, the price level, or the exchange rate changes, what happens to the unemployment rate?

In the three-market model, it's useful to see what happens in one market when one curve shifts. But the model is most useful when it shows what happens when one shift causes another. We'll call these *"second shifts."*

Football coaches and choreographers break down plays or dances into a series of smaller moves that can be learned and practiced one by one. That's what we'll do here. Learn the "second shifts", and when they come up in the "macro policy ballet" you'll understand what's going on.

Second shifts show how a change of one demand or supply curve affects other demand or supply curves in the same market or in other markets. Since there are three markets in our model, there are nine possible combinations of second shifts. Here's a table that summarizes the possibilities.

Table 4-1. Nine Possible Second Shifts

From:	To Goods Market	To Money Market	To Exchange Market
Goods Market	*Goods to Goods*	*Goods to Money*	*Goods to Exchange*
Money Market	*Money to Goods*	*Money to Money*	*Money to Exchange*
Exchange Market	*Exchange to Goods*	*Exchange to Money*	*Exchange to Exchange*

What's a second shift? The "from money to goods" shift is an example. Suppose money supply decreases, increasing the real interest rate. In the goods market, the real interest rate helps determine investment spending. A higher real interest rate reduces investment spending, and that reduces aggregate demand. Output and the price level decline. The change in money supply in the money market caused a change in aggregate demand in the goods market. That's a second shift.

This second shift tells us about the relationship between the real interest rate, real output, and the price level. When the real interest rate goes up, real output and the price level tend to go down. The second shift shows the relationships and tells us why it happens.

> *In our three market model, "second shifts" show how one change in demand or supply causes another change in demand or supply.*

Nine shifts is a lot. We really won't need that many. There are five that we'll use most often. Two more will crop up once in a while. And there are two that we'll never use. Here's the table again, with the five main second shifts numbered, roughly in order of importance. The other two are labeled with letters, and the two we'll never use are blank.

Table 4-2. Second Shifts Used in the Three-Market Model

From:	To Goods Market	To Money Market	To Exchange Market
Goods Market	**1. Goods to Goods**	**3. Goods to Money**	*(a) Goods to Exchange*
Money Market	**2. Money to Goods**		**5. Money to Exchange**
Exchange Market	**4. Exchange to Goods**	*(b) Exchange to Money*	

Second Shift #1: Aggregate Demand to Aggregate Supply
Suppose spending increases. Aggregate demand rises. Firms bring resources into use that would not ordinarily be used. They raise wages to attract workers. Output moves above potential.

But the price level has increased, too. This has eroded the real value of the higher wages. Eventually workers and other resource suppliers discover this fact, and start to demand higher pay and higher prices to compensate. Perhaps it took them a while to demand pay hikes because the price level is made up of hundreds of prices, changing at different times, even in different directions. After a while, though, the trend becomes clear. Or, perhaps labor or supplier contracts had kept wages and costs fixed. Those contracts expire. New contracts are negotiated at higher wages. Input costs increase.

The increase in aggregate demand was the first shift. Now comes the second shift. Increases in input costs cause a decrease in aggregate supply. Output begins to decrease and continues to decrease until it's back at potential output. The price level increases even more.

> **Second Shift #1: In the goods market, when aggregate demand shifts and equilibrium output differs from potential output, aggregate supply will shift to bring output back to potential.**

In the end, the increase in aggregate demand only temporarily increased output. It may take time—months or years—but output eventually returns to potential. The only permanent result is a higher price level. This is why potential output is a limit on equilibrium output. In the short run, before contracts are rewritten or expectations adjust, equilibrium output can be above potential output. But this can't last. Aggregate supply will shift back and equilibrium will return to potential. Potential output limits equilibrium output in the long run.

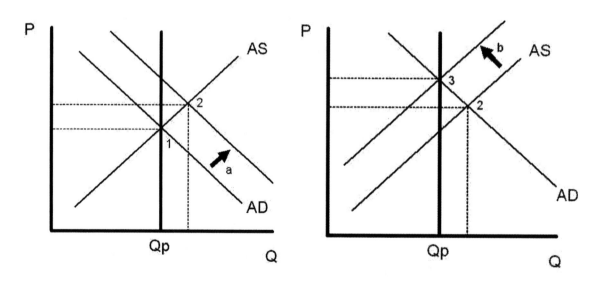

Figure 3-9. Loop. Start with equilibrium at potential output (1). Aggregate demand increases (a). Employees accept wage increases and work more. Product prices have risen even more, so employers want to hire. Output increases (1 to 2). Eventually, workers and other resource suppliers realize that prices have risen, and real pay is down. They demand higher pay. Contracts are rewritten. Resource costs rise, which decreases aggregate supply (b). Output returns to potential (2 to 3).

Second shift #1 works the other way, too. Aggregate demand falls. Businesses cut their prices. Their contracts with their employees fix the wages they must pay so they can't cut wages. Profits are squeezed, and businesses reduce output and lay off workers instead. Or, if there are no contracts, businesses offer lower wages to their employees to stay on, but employees refuse. They haven't adjusted their price expectations; they haven't realized that the price level has fallen. They quit instead. Output declines.

After a while, contracts expire. New contracts are written at new lower wages. Unemployed workers find that they cannot get jobs at the old higher wages. They adjust their price expectations downward and decide that the lower wage offers are acceptable. Wages and other input costs decrease.

Here comes the second shift: lower input costs increase aggregate supply. With resources less costly, firms increase output. Output rises back to potential.

This means that recessions can end on their own. It may not be necessary to print money, increase government spending, or cut taxes. If we wait long enough, people will adjust their expectations about the wages they can earn, the prices they can charge, and the profits they can make.

That's what investor Peter Schiff has in mind when he says that we must swallow tough medicine so our sick economy will recover. Home prices must fall enough so that people can buy them. If this means foreclosure for millions of families, so be it. Prices will fall all the faster. Employees must remain unemployed until they will accept lower wages and benefits. Businesses must go bankrupt, so their buildings and equipment can be sold off at a discount to businesses that survive. That's tough medicine. The increase in aggregate supply is just geometry, but it represents real pain for people.

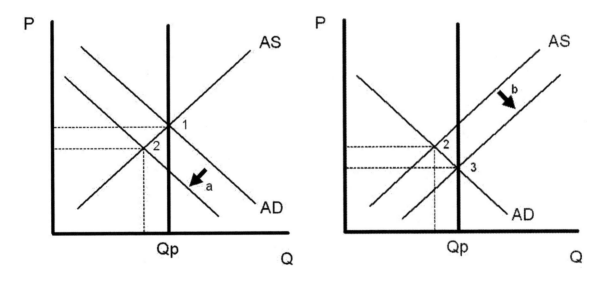

Figure 3-10. de Loop. Start with equilibrium at potential output (1). Aggregate demand decreases (a). Contracts keep wages from falling and employees resist wage cuts, so as prices fall business profits shrink. Output is reduced (1 to 2). Eventually, contracts expire, and workers realize that they must accept lower wages. Resource costs fall, which increases aggregate supply (b). Output returns to potential (2 to 3).

Waiting for wages and prices to fall was the standard advice that economists offered during the Great Depression; at least at first. They thought such adjustments would take place quickly, so the economy would be back at potential output in short order.

In fact, if prices adjust to equilibrium very quickly, even instantly, the aggregate supply curve is effectively vertical at the potential output level. Aggregate demand drops and the aggregate supply shift happens so fast that output never deviates from potential. Recessions would be impossible. Of course, economists knew that recessions happened. Their models predicted that they would be short, though. Then the Great Depression lasted for years and years. What could explain it?

A British economist named *John Maynard Keynes* came up with an answer in his book *The General Theory of Employment, Interest and Money*, published in 1936. It was perhaps the most influential book about economics in the 20th century.

The problem, Keynes said, was consumption, saving and investment. Households would prudently consume less than they earned, saving the rest. Sometimes, businesses would decide that the level of consumption did not justify investment in new plant and equipment. With consumption and investment spending down, output and incomes would fall. In the long run prices might adjust downward to encourage more spending. But, he said, "in the long run we are all dead." Keynes meant that life is what happens in the short run, but economists could only advise people to ignore the short run, because in the long run we all come to a very stable, very still equilibrium. Keynes wanted economists and policymakers to pay attention to the short run, before prices adjusted, when recessions and depressions happened.

By 1965 the economics of John Maynard Keynes reigned supreme. Keynesian economists dominated policymaking in Washington. In December, *Time* magazine put Keynes on its cover, though he had been dead for almost twenty years.

Keynesian economists had decided that there was a tradeoff between inflation and unemployment, which could be used for policy. Engineer an increase in aggregate demand, and a nation could have lower unemployment, but at the cost of higher inflation. Engineer a decrease in aggregate demand, and a nation could have the opposite. Economists in the Kennedy and Johnson administrations in the 1960's engineered an income tax cut to increase consumer spending and bring down unemployment, and that's exactly what happened at first.

Then inflation started rising, and unemployment increased, too. Where was the tradeoff?

University of Chicago economist *Milton Friedman* offered an explanation in a speech to the American Economic Association in 1967. "There is always a temporary tradeoff between inflation and unemployment," Friedman said. But "there is no permanent tradeoff." Why not? Because prices will rise, and "employees will start to reckon on rising prices of the things they buy and to demand higher nominal wages for the future."

Higher wages would eat into employer profits, output would be reduced, and employees would be laid off.

In our three-market model, when output moves beyond potential, prices rise, and aggregate supply decreases. Output returns to potential, and all that results is a higher price level. Inflation is higher, and unemployment is right back where it started. There is no permanent tradeoff.

In a sense, John Maynard Keynes discovered the goods market first shift, the drop in aggregate demand. Milton Friedman discovered the goods market second shift, the increase in aggregate supply.

In 1969, Friedman himself made the cover of *Time*. In 1976 he won the Nobel Prize for Economics. But perhaps his most important legacy is in the macroeconomic model that most economists use every day. The three-market model could be called the Keynes-Friedman model.

Second Shift #2: Money Market to Goods Market

Second shift #1 takes place entirely in the goods market. The other second shifts occur across markets. The three markets interact. A shift of demand or supply in one market can cause another shift in another market. The next four "second shifts" involve the interaction of two of the markets.

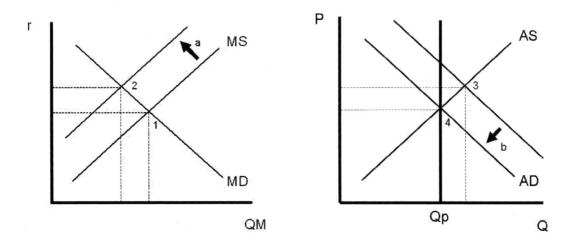

Figure 3-11. Stop inflation before it starts. The Federal Reserve sees output above potential (3), and realizes that inflation is a threat. It decreases the money supply (a), raising the real interest rate (1 to 2). This reduces investment spending, and decreases aggregate demand (b). Output drops back to potential, and the price level does not rise (3 to 4).

The real interest rate is determined in the money market. The interest rate determines investment spending in the goods market. The interest rate changes when the demand for money or the supply of money changes. That changes aggregate demand in the goods market, which changes output and the price level.

Suppose the Federal Reserve changes the money supply.   If the money supply decreases, the interest rate rises. The higher interest rate reduces investment spending, which reduces aggregate demand. Output falls and so does the price level.

> ***Second Shift #2: In the money market, money demand or supply shifts and the equilibrium real interest rate changes. This affects investment in the goods market, causing a shift in aggregate demand.***

The Fed might make such a move when it expects output to rise above potential, or after output has risen above potential. The end result of this excess aggregate demand is inflation. Output can remain above potential only temporarily. Sooner or later, second shift #1 will set in, aggregate supply will fall, and output will drop back to potential. The price level will rise, and that's inflation. To prevent inflation, the Fed might decrease the money supply, raise the interest rate, cut aggregate demand, keep output at potential, and stop inflation before it starts.

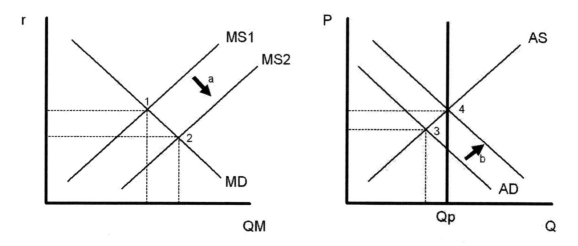

Figure 3-12. Keep that recession mild. The Fed sees the economy in recession (3), with output less than potential. In response, the Fed increases the money supply (a), which reduces the real interest rate (1 to 2). Investment spending increases, which increases aggregate demand (b). Output rises back to potential, and the original price level is restored (3 to 4).

Second shift #2 works the other way, too. If the money supply increases, the interest rate falls. The lower interest rate increases investment spending, which increases aggregate demand. Output rises, and so does the price level.

The Fed might make such a move when it expects output to fall below potential, or after it has fallen below potential. Aggregate demand falls, output drops, unemployment increases, and the economy is in a recession. Of course, the Fed could wait for second shift #1 to work, reducing input costs, increasing aggregate supply, and returning output to potential-ending the recession. That's usually too painful because it takes too long. Too many people have to remain unemployed for too long a time.

Instead, the Fed cuts interest rates to increase aggregate demand. The price level and output rise back to potential. The recession is avoided, or it's shorter and milder than it could have been.

These two Fed moves make up the core of *monetary policy*. That's the effort to manipulate the money supply and interest rates to achieve stable prices, high real growth and low unemployment. The Fed cuts the interest rate when it expects recession, and raises the interest rate when it expects inflation. It aims to keep output at potential, with an unchanged price level.

The monetary policies shown here are *counter-cyclical policy*. Expansions and recessions follow one another in an irregular cycle, known as the business cycle. The Fed tries to change interest rates to "counter" these cyclical changes to make recessions milder and keep inflation from increasing during expansions. As we'll see, sometimes policymakers have made mistakes, or have other priorities, and *pro-cyclical policy* results. Those are policies that "promote" recession and inflation, making them worse.

> *Counter-cyclical policy is an attempt by policymakers to correct the main problems of the economy, or to "counter" the problems of the "business cycle."*

The Federal Reserve used counter-cyclical monetary policy in a big way in 2008 and 2009. It increased its lending to banks so that banks would have more money to lend. It created new money, increasing the money supply. As the news reports said, "The idea was to encourage more economic activity by lowering interest rates." That's second shift #2.

The Fed was having a tough time of it, though. Bank behavior influences the money supply, too. If banks won't lend, less money gets into circulation. The media reported that despite the Fed's efforts, "lenders remained unwilling to lend" and much of the money that the Fed was creating "remained dormant." The money supply didn't increase as much as the Fed hoped it would.

Banks won't hold money dormant forever, though. Once they start lending, will all this new money result in inflation? It could, if the money supply lurches upward, driving down interest rates and rapidly increasing aggregate demand. That's second shift #2 again. If aggregate demand pushes output beyond potential, second shift #1 will produce inflation.

The Fed would have to reverse course and raise interest rates once growth resumes. But knowing when to do so is "more art than science." Timing is everything, and getting it right will be difficult. If the Fed waits too long, we'll get inflation. If it restrains the money supply too fast, we might get a new recession.

Second Shift #3: Goods Market to Money Market
Money demand depends on income and the price level. And income and the price level are determined in the goods market. The price level is right there on the vertical axis. Output is on the horizontal axis, but in the aggregate, output and income are the same thing. That's because businesses sell their products for a price, and the resulting revenue is divided up as income among owners, workers, suppliers, creditors, and landlords. Add up all the businesses, and you've got all the nation's output, but also all of the nation's income.

> *Second Shift #3: In the goods market, aggregate demand or supply shifts and equilibrium price and income changes. This affects money demand in the money market, causing the real interest rate to change.*

When prices and incomes are higher, people need more cash and checking deposits for their transactions. Money demand goes up. That leads to the third "second shift." Suppose spending increases in the goods market. Aggregate demand increases, and this increases output (income) and the price level. A higher price level and income increase money demand in the money market. The interest rate rises.

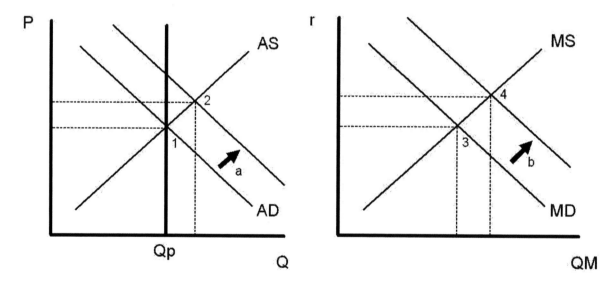

Figure 3-13. Even Without the Fed. Aggregate demand increases (a), raising prices and income (1 to 2). This increases the demand for money (b), because people make more purchases at higher prices. The real interest rate goes up (3 to 4).

This explains why interest rates tend to rise during expansions, even without action by the Federal Reserve. People spend more, aggregate demand increases, and income and prices rise. Money demand increases and the real interest rate goes up.

But second shift #3 also provides an explanation for another phenomenon, called *crowding out*. The rise in the real interest rate creates "feedback" in the goods market. With the interest rate higher, investment spending is lower. An increase in spending started the whole thing, but now the higher interest rate is cutting into that increase in spending. Aggregate demand doesn't increase as much now that the interest rate is higher.

The interest rate won't rise enough to completely offset the initial rise in spending, though. If interest rates rise, second shift #2 implies that investment spending will fall. Aggregate demand will decrease. Now, it can't shift all the way back to the old output and price level (point 1 in Figure 3-14), because then there would be no explanation for the rise in money demand. Instead, aggregate demand and money demand rise at the same time and investment spending falls. Other kinds of spending end up as a larger share of the total and investment ends up as a smaller share.

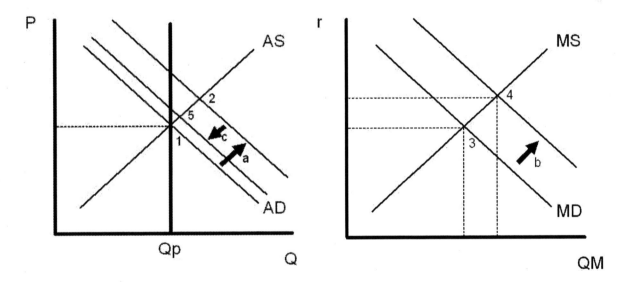

Figure 3-14. Crowding Out. A rise in spending increases aggregate demand (a), which increases money demand (b). The real interest rate rises (3 to 4) and this reduces investment spending as other spending is increasing (c). The reduction in investment spending is "crowding out". Output does not increase as much (1 to 5 instead of 1 to 2), and with less investment, there ultimately will be slower growth in resources and slower growth in potential output.

Crowding out is thought to be a serious problem in the long run. Investment spending creates new capital stock—buildings and equipment—and better technology. These are resources that increase potential output. If fewer new resources accumulate, potential output will increase more slowly. Over many years, the nation will end up poorer than it could have been.

Second Shift #4: Exchange Market to Goods Market.
Exports and imports depend on the exchange rate. And the exchange rate is determined in the exchange market. This leads to second shift #4. The demand for the dollar or supply of the dollar changes in the exchange market. The exchange rate adjusts up or down. Export and import spending are affected in the goods market. Such spending is included in aggregate demand, so aggregate demand shifts. And that changes output and the price level.

Suppose Americans decide to lend more money overseas. Perhaps interest rates in Japan, China, Germany, or Mexico are higher than they are in the U.S., so more profits can be earned by lending in those countries. To lend in Germany, Americans must acquire euros. To acquire euros, Americans must trade dollars. The supply of dollars increases.

> *Second Shift #4: In the exchange market, dollar demand or supply shifts and the equilibrium exchange rate changes. This affects exports and imports in the goods market, causing aggregate demand to change.*

Traders find that they can offer fewer euros for dollars and still make a deal, since so many dollars are being supplied. Americans become a little desperate to get euros, so they accept fewer euros in exchange for their dollars. The value of the dollar falls.

With a lower exchange value of the dollar, U.S. imports become more expensive, and U.S. exports become less expensive. It takes more dollars to buy the euros needed to import goods from Germany. That makes all German imports more expensive, so people buy fewer. Over in the goods market, import spending declines, and Americans spend more on goods produced in the U.S. It takes fewer euros to trade for the dollars needed to buy goods from the U.S. That makes all U.S. exports cheaper. People around the world buy more. Export spending increases.

Aggregate demand is based on spending, and spending is the sum of consumption, investment, government purchases, and exports less imports. If export spending rises and import spending falls, aggregate demand increases. U.S. output rises, and so does the price level.

Second shift #4 can work in reverse, too. Suppose the demand for the dollar increases, which increases the exchange value of the dollar. This happened in 2008 as international investors saw the dollar as a "safe haven" during the financial panic. But this increased the cost of U.S. exports around the world and contributed to the fall in export spending. Aggregate demand went down some more and the recession got worse.

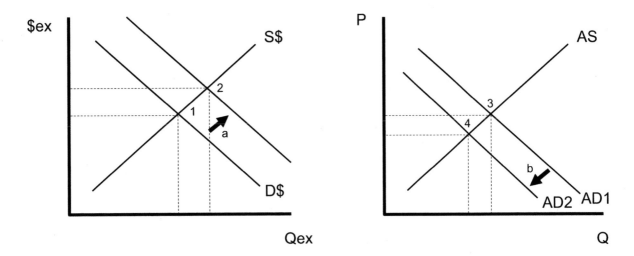

Figure 3-15. Dollar up. The demand for dollars in the exchange market increases (a). The exchange value of the dollar rises (1 to 2). This makes U.S. exports more expensive, so export spending decreases. This also makes U.S. imports less expensive, so import spending increases. Both changes decrease aggregate demand (b). Output falls below potential.

Second Shift #5: Money Market to Exchange Market.
The demand for and supply of the dollar in the exchange market depends in part on the level of the U.S. real interest rate compared to rates in other countries. The higher the U.S. real interest rate, the more attractive it is to lend in the U.S., and the more dollars will be demanded in order to make such loans. The lower the U.S. real interest rate, the less attractive is U.S. lending, so the fewer are the dollars demanded.

The real interest rate is determined in the money market. When money demand rises or money supply falls, the real interest rate goes up. When money demand falls or money supply rises, the real interest rate goes down. These changes affect dollar demand and supply in the exchange market. And that's second shift #5.

> *Second Shift #5: In the money market, money demand or supply shifts and the equilibrium real interest rate changes. This affects dollar demand and supply in the exchange market, causing the equilibrium exchange rate to change.*

Suppose the money supply increases. Perhaps the Federal Reserve is increasing the money supply, trying to encourage borrowing and spending. The real interest rate falls.

The exchange market reacts. Around the world people decide that lending in the U.S. is less profitable than lending in their own countries. They try to convert the dollars they own into other currencies by trading them away in exchange markets. The supply of the dollar rises. And that decreases the exchange value of the dollar.

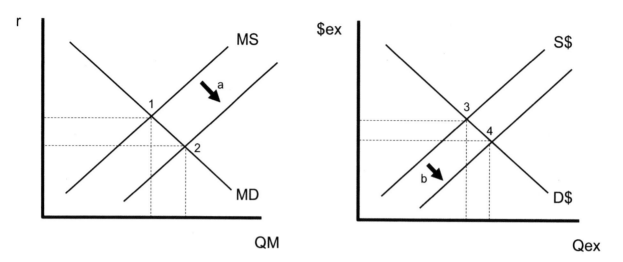

Figure 3-16. Looking elsewhere. The Federal Reserve increases the money supply (a), which decreases the real interest rate (1 to 2). The lower real interest rate makes lending in the U.S. less attractive, so international investors sell their dollars, increasing its supply (b). The exchange value of the dollar falls (3 to 4).

Second Shifts (a) and (b): Goods to Exchange and Exchange to Money
We keep these two shifts in reserve, for the special circumstances when we need them. The goods market can affect the exchange market. That's second shift (a). Suppose consumers decide to buy more imports. In the exchange market, they'll have to supply more dollars in exchange for euros or yen. Dollar supply will rise and this will reduce the exchange rate.

That should be a very useful second shift. The increase in imports may create a trade deficit, with imports exceeding exports. The decline in the exchange rate makes U.S. exports cheaper and imports more expensive. Second shift #4 kicks in, increasing exports and reducing imports. That balances imports and exports again. Second shifts (a) and #4 together could make an equilibrium mechanism, keeping exports and imports in balance.

Second shift (a) is also an explanation for why we say that when a currency's value falls, it gets "weaker." If Americans want more imports from other countries, perhaps it's because other countries are developing better products than are available in the United States (or at least other countries are "catching up"). If U.S. technology or infrastructure growth lags behind, while other countries' leap ahead, the dollar exchange rate will fall. It would be a sign of relative economic weakness. Likewise, if U.S. exports are increasing, maybe the world is beating a path to our door for our superior products. The exchange rate rises, and we say the currency is "stronger."

The trouble is second shift #5 almost always dominates second shift (a). Changes in the interest rate have a more powerful effect on the demand for and supply of the dollar than do changes in exports and imports. This is because the amount of currency trading by people wanting to lend, invest, or speculate is much, much greater than the amount of trading by people wanting to buy or sell goods. Those lenders, investors, and speculators respond to interest rate changes. So, when the two shifts have different effects on the exchange market, #5 dominates. When the two reinforce one another—well, why bother with (a), when #5 already shows the result?

Still, sometimes the effects of second shift (a) sneak through. Over the very long run— like decades--(a) may define the direction in which exchange rates must change. The U.S. trade deficit got big at the end of the 1990's. The dollar began falling in value in 2001, and by mid-decade exports and imports began to respond, and the trade deficit began to close.   But as of 2008 the exchange rate was still not low enough to balance exports and imports. Then the financial crisis made its value rise again.

Second shift (b) is important—sometimes very important—but in a peculiar circumstance that doesn't happen as much as it used to. The exchange market has important effects on the money market when *exchange rates are fixed.*

Like a fixed price in any market (the minimum wage in chapter 2), a fixed exchange rate can create surpluses or shortages. If the exchange rate is fixed above the equilibrium, more of the currency will be supplied than demanded. That's a surplus. If the exchange rate is fixed below the equilibrium, more of the currency will be demanded than supplied. That's a shortage.

These surpluses and shortages can affect a country's money supply, and its real interest rate. How this happens, though, depends on who is fixing the exchange rate, and why. And it depends on international institutions. We'll find second shift (b) useful soon, in chapter 4, which tells the story of an economic crisis in the United States in the 1890's. Back then, exchange rates were fixed because most of the world was on the gold standard. Fixed exchange rates sometimes caused inflows and outflows of gold, which affected a country's money supply.

Today, most exchange rates are flexible. Sometimes, though, nations attempt to hold their exchange rates fixed or nearly fixed. Thailand, Argentina and China are examples from the last decade. When they do, they affect their money supplies, and sometimes those of other countries.

MacroPolicy Now: It All Goes Wrong

As every reporter knows, consumer spending is about two-thirds of total GDP, so what happens to consumers is important for aggregate demand, and so for output and prices. The events in Lehigh Acres show what happened to consumers starting in 2007.

Home prices increased a lot in Florida, and in California, North Carolina, Arizona, Nevada, and several other states. Probably, they started rising for good reason, because populations were increasing in those states, and mortgage interest rates were low. But after a while, people became excited about the financial investment possibilities of buying a house. Buy a house now, wait a few years—or a few months—and sell for a much higher price. That's why real estate agent Bob Elliott called it a sign of trouble that houses would sell more than once without anyone moving in. People were buying houses to speculate on their rising value.

Home builders responded to the rising prices by building more homes. The increase in the price increased the quantity of houses supplied. And, for a while, the houses they built sold at those rising prices. So they built more.

Eventually, though, home prices rose so much that people who wanted to live in those houses couldn't afford them. There was an excess supply at the price home builders expected to receive for all those new houses. Home prices began to fall. Home builders quit building.

Lehigh Acres was full of people who worked construction. As home construction slacked off, construction workers were laid off. Many had taken out mortgage loans to buy their own houses at those high prices. The mortgage payments were high. They couldn't afford them without steady work. Home values fell, and soon many owed more on their mortgages than their houses were worth. That meant they couldn't sell their houses for enough to repay their mortgages.

When they couldn't sell and couldn't pay, the banks foreclosed.

Consumers cut their spending. Gloria Chilson's husband lost his job, and they lost their house. The couple had run up $20,000 in credit card debt. Perhaps they thought that ever-rising home prices would protect them, that they could always borrow against the value of their house to pay off the credit card. After the foreclosure, the Chilsons wouldn't be spending with their credit card very much.

Home prices fall. Households are less wealthy as a result. They spend less. Consumption declines. So does aggregate demand. That's shown in Figure 3-4 above.

With consumers spending less, businesses find they can't sell as many goods and services. They produce less, and they lay off some of the workers they no longer need. These workers spend less, which causes more businesses to cut production some more and lay off more workers. Output falls. That's a recession.

Prices of homes fall as the demand for them dries up. Prices for other goods and services fall too. Businesses cut their prices to try to sell what they can, as their customers melt away. The price cuts are deflation.

Lots of banks and other lenders, like the Independent Bank of Michigan, made loans for home purchases and for housing construction. Some of these loans helped fuel the speculation which drove up house prices. Why did banks do this? As Mr. Lightbody, the bank vice president said, "Everyone was making a lot of money." Rising home prices fooled consumers into spending too much and fooled banks into making unwise loans.

Starting in 2007 these loans started to go sour. Houses failed to sell. Developers couldn't repay their loans. The money Independent lent to the developers of Whispering Woods could not be recovered. Rising unemployment means many homeowners couldn't pay their mortgages. The banks foreclosed, but this presented another problem: they tried to sell the foreclosed houses, but prices had fallen so much that they couldn't recover the amount of the mortgage.

So Independent, and many other lenders, became pessimistic about lending. They had made mistakes that they didn't want to repeat. As the recession began, fewer potential borrowers seemed like good risks. They tightened lending standards, meaning they made fewer loans. They increased interest rates.

In the money market, the reluctance of banks to lend their reserves decreased the money supply. That's in Figure 3-5. The decrease in the money supply increased the equilibrium real interest rate. A higher interest rate reduces investment spending, which is second shift #2. This causes a decrease in aggregate demand, which cuts real output and the price level.

The Independent Bank of Michigan turned down a manufacturer seeking a business loan. Other businesses could only get loans at very high interest rates. As a result, they had to cut costs, sell assets, and—most important—cancel projects. Investments in equipment or buildings that would have been made don't get made. The manufacturers of that equipment cut their production, too. The construction firms that would have built the buildings lay off their employees.

The Federal Reserve tried to reduce the real interest rate by expanding the money supply. Lower interest rates should encourage borrowing, increasing investment spending (and consumer spending on "big ticket" items). That's second shift #2, in the other direction, shown in Figure 3-12. In a sense, the Fed was battling the banks' reluctance to lend by filling their vaults with cash.

For a long time the U.S. has been importing more goods from the rest of the world than it has been exporting to the rest of the world. That means Americans are supplying a lot of dollars into exchange markets, trying to buy foreign currencies, so they can buy foreign goods. And it means foreigners are demanding fewer dollars, because they do not want to buy as many U.S. goods. Increasing supply and decreasing demand produces a decline in the exchange value of the dollar. The exchange value of the dollar fell from 2001 to the middle of 2008.

But then the world fell into recession, and there was a crisis in world financial markets. Lots of lenders all over the world had lent money in the U.S. housing market, and now those loans were not being repaid. Lending and investment fell everywhere. That reduced aggregate demand all over the world. The rest of the world went into recession.

Lower world incomes meant less demand for U.S. exports, and this contributed to a decline in U.S. aggregate demand in the goods market (Figure 3-4). Then international investors became scared about lending in the rest of the world, so they sought out the world's safest investment: U.S. Treasury bonds. They would keep their money safe by lending it to the U.S. government. Economist Cline called it "a huge safe haven effect."

To lend to the U.S. government, international investors had to have dollars. The demand for the dollar increased because of world-wide investor anxiety. The exchange value of the dollar increased. This created another reason why U.S. exports went down. The higher exchange value of the dollar made U.S. exports more costly to the rest of the world. This is second shift #4, shown in Figure 3-15. A change in the exchange market influences the goods market.

The Federal Reserve managed to reduce real interest rates in 2008 and 2009, making them lower than in many other countries. After the panic subsided, investors began to look for other places to lend their funds with higher interest rates than in the U.S. The demand for the dollar subsided and the exchange value of the dollar fell. That's second shift #5, shown in Figure 3-16. That might help U.S. exports, eventually, through second shift #4. In fact, this is a second channel through which monetary policy might work. Lower interest rates encourage more investment spending (second shift #2). Lower interest rates likely also reduce the value of the dollar (second shift #5) and by making exports cheaper, increase exports and increase aggregate demand (second shift #4).

The Congressional Budget Office's analysis of the 2009 stimulus bill projected that output growth would be higher in the first six years, but slightly *lower* after that. The analysis assumed that the budget deficits and borrowing would continue at high levels. Once the economy nears potential, the government borrowing displaces borrowing by private firms—by making interest rates higher. As the economy expands and deficits continue, second shift #3 increases money demand. That increases the real interest rate, which keeps investment lower than it could be, through second shift #2. Crowding out is diagrammed in Figure 3-14. Higher interest rates crowd out private investment and, ultimately, the economy will grow more slowly. But that's not a problem during a recession. Businesses want to borrow so little that there is plenty of money for the Federal government to borrow.

Terms in this Chapter, in order of appearance
The Three Market Model
The goods market
Aggregate demand
Aggregate supply
The money market
Demand for money; money demand
Supply of money; money supply
The exchange market
Demand for the dollar
Supply of the dollar
The Federal Reserve
Monetary policy
Buy American goods
Lend to Americans
Invest in American assets
Safe haven
Potential output
Natural rate of unemployment
Second shifts
Second shift #1: aggregate demand to aggregate supply
John Maynard Keynes
Milton Friedman
Second shift #2: money market to goods market
Counter-cyclical policy
Pro-cyclical policy
Second shift #3: goods market to money market
Crowding out
Second shift #4: exchange market to goods market
Second shift #5: money market to exchange market
Second shift (a): goods market to exchange market
Second shift (b): exchange market to money market
Fixed exchange rates

Notes
The story of John Maynard Keynes is told by Heilbroner in chapter 9 of his wonderful book.

John Maynard Keynes' first bestselling book was *The Economic Consequences of the Peace,* a vigorous criticism of the Versailles treaty after World War I. The economic conditions imposed on Germany were unworkable, he wrote. The European economy would not recover from the war. People would starve. And worse. "For starvation, which brings to some lethargy and a helpless despair, drives other temperaments to the nervous instability of hysteria and to a mad despair. And these in their distress may overturn the remnants of organization, and submerge civilization itself. . . ." It was published in December 1919. Corporal Hitler had joined the German Workers Party just three months before.

In the cover story of the issue with Keynes on the cover, *Time* quoted Milton Friedman saying "We are all Keynesians now." Friedman dashed off a letter to the editor in protest. The rest of the quote (which *Time* left out) was ". . . and none of us are Keynesians." He meant that in thirty years macroeconomics had built ideas on the foundation of the *General Theory* which had never occurred to Keynes.

Milton Friedman's speech to the American Economic Association was printed in the *American Economic Review* in 1968. Like Keynes, Friedman anticipated an awful lot of bad stuff that eventually came to pass, in the 1970's.

It took some time, but macroeconomics came to accept Friedman's ideas. We can see it in the textbooks. Paul Samuelson was the leading Keynesian economist of the day, and in some ways Friedman's great rival. Samuelson's introductory textbook was a best seller. The 1967 edition says that there is a tradeoff between inflation and unemployment that policymakers can use. The 1980 edition says that the tradeoff is less pronounced in the long run. The 1985 edition says there is no permanent tradeoff. Friedman's idea had won.

Ben Bernanke offers an appreciation of Friedman's contributions in a speech he gave in 2003. That's before he became chairman of the Federal Reserve—though he was a leading candidate, even then.

Sources
Bernanke, Ben S. 2003. "The influence of Milton Friedman's Monetary Framework on Contemporary Monetary Theory and Practice." Remarks at the Federal Reserve Bank of Dallas Conference on the Legacy of Milton and Rose Friedman's *Free to Choose*, Dallas, Texas, October 24.

Congressional Budget Office. 2009. *Estimated Macroeconomic Impacts of the American Recovery and Reinvestment Act of 2009*. Washington, D.C.: CBO (March 2). [www.cbo.gov/ftpdocs/100xx/doc10008/03-02-Macro_Effects_of_ARRA.pdf]

Friedman, Milton. 1968. "The Role of Monetary Policy" *American Economic Review* 58 (March): 1-17.

Heilbroner, Robert L. 1972. *The Worldly Philosophers*. (4th Edition) New York: Simon and Schuster.

News Articles
Andrews, Edmund L. "Fed Plans to Inject Another $1 Trillion to Aid the Economy," New York Times, March 19, 2009.

Cave, Damien. "In Florida, Despair and Foreclosures," *New York Times*, February 8, 2009.

Goodman, Peter S. "A Rising Dollar Lifts the U.S. but Adds to the Crisis Abroad," *New York Times*, March 9, 2009.

Goodman, Peter S. "Printing Money – and Its Price," New York Times, December 28, 2008.

Healy, Jack and Vikas Bajaj. "Cost of Borrowing Zooms Up for Corporations," *New York Times*, January 19, 2009.

Lipton, Eric and Ron Nixon. "In Michigan, Bank Lends Little of Its Bailout Funds," *New York Times,* January 14, 2009.

Chapter 4
The Yellow Brick Road

MacroPolicy Now: China, the Yuan and Us

"China's economy is starting to slow, after two years of torrid growth achieved following the global downturn," reported the *New York Times* on May 30, 2011. Of course, "slow" for China would be extremely rapid for the United States. China's economy had been growing at ten percent per year or more since 2008. Now it was expected to slow to eight percent per year.

The slowdown was intentional policy, an attempt to bring down inflation. Inflation ran above 5 percent in April, and economists thought that China's inflation index understated price rises. Inflation may be double the official rate in reality.

Inflation often accompanies rapid growth, but China's inflation has another cause as well. China keeps the exchange value of its currency, called the yuan or renminbi, artificially low. This makes Chinese exports cheaper, encouraging export growth. Exports have been a major factor in overall economic growth.

As the *Times* reported on May 11, "A cornerstone of that export success has been the huge intervention in currency markets. The People's Bank of China issued yuan to buy an average of $15 billion a week worth of dollars and other currencies during the first quarter, pushing its foreign exchange reserves over $3 trillion for the first time." China buys dollars in exchange markets, which increases the value of the dollar and holds down the value of the yuan.

China invests these dollars throughout the world, but particularly in U.S. Treasury bonds. In effect, China buys U.S. dollars, then lends them back to the U.S. government.

China's currency policy is criticized by U.S. policy makers and business executives. They argue that the yuan's "valuation gives Chinese exporters an unfair advantage over their U.S. counterparts by making Chinese goods inexpensive overseas." Inexpensive Chinese goods have meant fewer manufacturing jobs in the U.S.

Buying dollars with yuan puts more currency in the hands of Chinese businesses and consumers. The resulting increase in spending fuels inflation. The most direct measure that China could take against inflation would be to allow the yuan to rise in value. Not only would this reduce the amount of yuan being printed, but a higher yuan would make imports from the rest of the world cheaper. That would help bring down inflation too.

Between June 2010 and April 2011 the yuan rose in value by five percent, its fastest appreciation in years. Analysts speculated that it was "a sign that the authorities might be using the appreciation as a weapon against inflation."

The *Times* reported that "printing fewer yuan to buy dollars would be the most direct step that China could undertake to fight inflation, Western and Chinese economists say. But policy

makers have feared that doing so would let the renminbi rise too quickly and cause layoffs at export factories."

This meant, the *Times* noted, that "Chinese policy makers now face a delicate balancing act. They must try to divine how much more currency appreciation the country's highly successful export industry can withstand, before the stronger yuan makes Chinese goods less competitive on the global market."

Mark Twain said "History doesn't repeat itself, but it rhymes." In some ways, 2011 rhymes with the 1890's. Then, the U.S. had borrowed a lot of money from Great Britain. Now, the U.S. has borrowed a lot of money from China. Then, lending from Great Britain kept U.S. interest rates down. Now, lending from China helps keep U.S. interest rates low. Then, fear that the value of the dollar would fall caused a withdrawal of investment from the U.S., plunging the nation into recession. Now—well, let's hope not. . . .

The Production Possibility Frontier and the American Civil War
It was 1861. Abraham Lincoln was the new President of the United States, but the United States was breaking up. The southern states were seceding over the issue of slavery. Sustaining the union would require civil war, and that, Treasury Secretary Salmon P. Chase told the cabinet, would require "the expenditure of millions."

The spending was for weapons, of course, and food for the soldiers, and much more. Civil War historian James McPherson provides a partial list of items supplied by the Union army's Quartermaster Bureau: "uniforms, overcoats, shoes, knapsacks, haversacks, canteens, mess gear, blankets, tents, camp equipage, barracks, horses, mules, forage, harnesses, horseshoes and portable blacksmith shops, supply wagons, ships when the army could be supplied by water, coal or wood to fuel them, and supply depots for storage and distribution." McPherson estimates that an army of 100,000 soldiers needed 2,500 supply wagons, 35,000 animals, and 600 tons of supplies every day.

Where were all the soldiers and supplies to come from? The people living in the Union would have to provide. Men who had been farmers and factory workers would now be soldiers. Horses that had pulled plows would now pull supply wagons. Textile mills that had made dresses would now make uniforms. Fewer plowshares, more swords: the Union would shift its resources from the production of civilian goods to the production of military goods.

A simple economic model can help organize our thinking about this shift. Imagine a nation with resources like labor, land and capital (machinery). The nation's technology is used to assemble these resources into civilian and military goods. The more labor, land and capital a nation has, and the better its technology, the more goods it can produce.

The nation decides how many civilian goods and how many military goods it wants, and then devotes its resources to the task.

But there are limits. Combinations of civilian and military goods are limited by the resources and technology available for the job. The maximum combinations of goods that can be produced when all resources are in use are called the *production possibility frontier (PPF)*.

> **The production possibility frontier shows the maximum combinations of goods that can be produced by a nation's resources and technology.**

We've seen this idea before. In Chapter 3 we called it *potential output*. What's the difference? In the goods market, potential output is the level of real output that can be sustained when resources are fully employed. The production possibility frontier shows the combinations of two goods that an economy can sustain when resources are fully employed. Potential output is made up of the real values of lots of goods and services. The production possibility frontier divides potential output in two and shows the choices a nation makes between them.

The goods market assumes just one product. The production possibility frontier shows two. For understanding some issues, that makes all the difference.

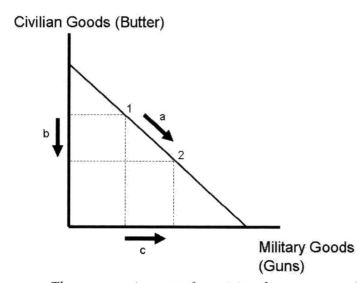

Civilian Goods (Butter)

Military Goods (Guns)

Figure 4-1. The Simplest Frontier. A production possibility frontier. The downward sloping line shows the combinations of butter and guns that can be produced with the nation's resources. The nation may choose to produce more butter and fewer guns (point 1), or less butter and more guns (point 2). The movement (a) from 1 to 2 requires switching resources from the production of butter to the production of guns. The opportunity cost of acquiring the extra guns (c) is the butter given up (b).

A production possibility frontier is pictured in Figure 4-1. The quantities of military goods that can be produced are shown on the horizontal axis. The quantities of civilian goods are shown on the vertical axis. The downward sloping line shows the maximum combinations of goods that the nation's resources and technology allow. Combinations to the right of this line are impossible. The nation does not have enough resources or good enough technology to produce so much. Combinations to the left of the line are possible, but represent unused or *unemployed resources*. More could be produced if all resources were employed. (The same unemployment idea is shown in the goods market when equilibrium output is to the left of potential output.)

In a sense, it's the simplest possible macroeconomic model. A nation uses all of its resources to produce goods. The quantity and quality of the resources determine how many goods can be produced. The nation must choose how much of each good to produce and allocates resources to the production of each based on that choice. The model is simple, but it serves nicely to organize and illustrate our thinking about resources, production, and choices. And it provides a picture of a basic economic idea, *opportunity cost*.

Opportunity cost is the next best use of resources we give up when we make a choice. It applies to our personal lives. If I choose to spend my time taking a nap, I give up spending my time perfecting my lecture notes. If you choose to spend your money on a CD, you give up spending it on a pizza supreme. It applies to business decisions. If a farmer uses her land to grow corn, she gives up what could be earned growing beans. If a retailer uses his shelf space to stock corn flakes, he gives up what could be earned stocking raisin bran.

The choices are how to spend or use resources: time, money, land, retail space. Choosing to use resources in one way means giving up the opportunity to use them in another. The benefits you could have had using your time for lecture preparation or your money for pizza measure the cost of your choice. That CD cost you one very tasty pizza supreme.

The definition measures opportunity cost with the "next best" use of resources given up. Presumably everyone devotes their resources to their best possible use. There are usually many other possibilities. Which one is *the* opportunity cost? It's the second best use of resources.

When you choose to attend college, you give up other uses of your (or your parents') tuition money. But opportunity cost tells us that you are also spending your time, and (to "coin" a phrase) time is money. You could be working, full-time, at a job. Perhaps some of your friends from high school made this choice. While

> *Opportunity cost is the next best use of resources we give up when we make a choice.*

you live the life of the impoverished student, your employed friends are buying cars and clothes and kitchen appliances with the money they earn. The opportunity cost of going to college is the tuition plus the wages you are giving up. (Sounds like an expensive choice. It's likely to pay off, though. Probably you'll recoup that cost, and then some, within a few years of graduation. The pay of college graduates is about double the pay of high school graduates, on average.)

The production possibility frontier illustrates opportunity cost from a nation's point of view. A nation may switch its resources from butter to gun production. Land used for grazing cows is paved over for a factory parking lot. People who worked in the dairy get jobs in the factory. Steel that would have made milking machines now makes factory equipment. In diagram 4-1, production shifts from 1 to 2, and more guns are obtained. What is the opportunity cost of these guns? The butter given up. The extra "c" guns are paid for with the loss of "b" butter. That means that the *slope of the production possibility frontier* measures the opportunity cost. Guns are more costly if the slope is steeper. Butter is less costly, in guns given up, with a steeper slope.

These are just the sort of choices a nation must make when it goes to war, choices Abraham Lincoln had to make in 1861. For example, on April 19 of that year he declared a blockade of southern ports. The navy had only 42 ships all told, and most of them were cruising in foreign waters. So, Gustavus Fox, the Assistant Secretary of the Navy, bought or chartered dozens of merchant ships, armed them with cannons, manned them with Navy sailors, and assigned them to the blockade. By the end of the year 260 ships were on duty off the southern coast. But that meant the ships were no longer available to carry civilian goods. Exporters had to turn to foreign-owned vessels for shipping, or they had to sell their goods domestically, for less money.

The south also faced the opportunity cost problem, but because its economy had fewer resources to spare, the choices were often grim. Men volunteered or were drafted into the army. Since 84% of the south's free labor worked in agriculture, these men came mainly from farms. Crop yields declined. The opportunity cost of a bigger army was less food.

Sometimes there is hardship behind the geometry in a production possibility frontier. A Mississippi soldier overstayed his furlough in December 1861 and wrote to his governor to explain. "Poor men have been compelled to leave the army to come home to provide for their families," he wrote. "We are poor men and are willing to defend our country but our families come first."

Specialized Resources
The production possibility frontier can be made more descriptive of the real choices nations make if we recognize that not all resources are alike. Resources are *specialized*: some are more suited for butter production; some are more suited for guns. As an example, suppose the only resource that matters is labor, and suppose there are three kinds of workers: farm, town, and city. Farm workers are experts at milking cows, town workers are competent, andcity workers don't know one end of the cow from the other.

Suppose that before the war all of these workers are engaged in the civilian economy, producing butter. The city workers don't produce much butter, but the nation had no use for military goods in peacetime. When war comes, though, who should Mr. Lincoln allocate from butter production to gun production? The city workers, of course. The extra guns will cost very little in lost butter, because these workers weren't suited to butter production in the first place. In a production possibility frontier diagram, figure 4-2, the move from 1 to 2 means the extra guns (d) come at a small cost (a).

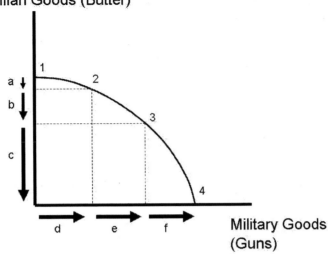

Civilian Goods (Butter)

Military Goods (Guns)

Figure 4-2. Specialized resources. Some resources are better suited to civilian production, some to military production. Starting from 1, the first resources moved to military production are those least suited to civilian production. Lost civilian production (a) is small. The move from 2 to 3 requires that resources more suited to civilian production be used for military goods. The cost (b) is higher. The cost of the last move, from 3 to 4, is even higher (c), because these are the resources most suited for producing civilian goods. The cost of producing additional goods rises. This is an illustration of increasing costs—the same reason that supply curves slope upward.

If it's a big war, and more resources must be shifted to military goods, town workers are the next to go. They're pretty good at butter production, so the added guns (e) come at a higher cost (b). The production possibility frontier slopes downward faster from 2 to 3 than it did from 1 to 2.

If it's total war, perhaps all resources are shifted to guns, including farm workers. Lots of butter is given up (c) to get added guns (f), because farm workers are very good butter producers. The production possibility frontier slopes downward especially steeply from 3 to 4.

When resources are specialized the production possibility frontier is not a straight line. It is bowed outward. Since the slope of the line measures opportunity costs, the frontier tells us that the cost of added guns gets higher when more resources are shifted to gun production. At first guns come cheaply—little butter is lost. At the last, guns are very expensive. Much butter must be sacrificed. This is sometimes called *the principle of increasing costs.*

Real world resources are specialized, and both the Union and the Confederacy recognized this when they passed their conscription or draft laws. The Confederacy enacted a conscription law in 1862, the Union in 1863. To decide which men to draft into the army, both sides considered opportunity costs. Both laws allowed draftees to buy their way out of service, by hiring a substitute to go instead. According to historian James McPherson, "This practice was based on an assumption that the talents of men who could afford substitutes might be of more value on the home front, organizing and producing the materiel of war, than in the army." The south added additional exemptions for men employed as railroad workers, miners, hospital workers, clergymen, teachers, and in other occupations. The opportunity cost in lost output by drafting such men was thought to be too great.

The price of a substitute was set at $300 in the north. That was almost a year's wages for an unskilled worker. "Three hundred dollars or your life," said newspaper headlines. "Rich man's war, poor man's fight," was the saying in the south. But a large number of working men as well as professional men managed to come up with the price of a substitute. In some communities the local governments paid for substitutes out of property taxes. Factories and railroads would sometimes pay substitutes in order to keep their workers. Men could buy $300 insurance policies for a few dollars a month, with payment made if they were drafted.

Paying a substitute for military service had a long tradition in the United States—it had been used during the revolution, too. In the Civil War it was controversial. Eventually the south abolished the substitution practice, and the north restricted it. Partly this was because of fraud. Some poor men became richer by selling themselves as substitutes, deserting, then selling themselves again, and again. Mostly, though, substitution was ended because people saw it as unfair.

Allowing draftees to pay substitutes was efficient. It reduced the opportunity cost of mobilizing for war, by exempting men who were especially productive civilians. But many saw it as unfair. The poor would be drafted; the rich would not. This illustrates another basic economic idea: there is often a tradeoff between *efficiency and equity*. Both the north and the south ultimately were willing to accept a higher opportunity cost of mobilization in order to distribute those costs more fairly.

We constantly face the efficiency-equity tradeoff in policy decisions. It's a contest between what works and what seems right; between our hard heads and our soft hearts.

> *The law of diminishing returns says that adding additional resources to production eventually produces smaller and smaller added benefits. It's the same idea as the principle of increasing costs.*

Figure 4-3 is the same as figure 4-2, but with the amounts of butter given up divided into three equal parts. Now the move from 1 to 2 adds a lot of extra guns (d) for the lost butter (a). The move from 2 to 3 adds fewer guns (e) for the lost butter (b). The move from 3 to 4 adds even fewer guns (f). The opportunity cost of guns in lost butter increases as gun output increases in figure 4-3. To say the same thing, fewer and fewer guns are produced as more and more butter is given up. Gun production is subject to *diminishing returns*. Adding additional resources to production eventually produces a smaller and smaller added benefit. This idea pops up so often that it's sometimes called the *Law of Diminishing Returns*. It's really the same thing as the principle of increasing costs.

The armies of the Civil War faced diminishing returns. The men who joined the armies at the beginning of the war were enthusiastic, perhaps naively so. They were strong and healthy too. Resources were specialized and the best soldiers joined early. By the end of the war, both armies drafted men who were less suited to soldiering. Veteran soldiers called them "off-scourings of northern slums" and "thieves, burglars, and vagabonds." While that is surely an exaggeration, the later draftees added less to the army's effectiveness. Army recruitment had reached the "point of diminishing returns."

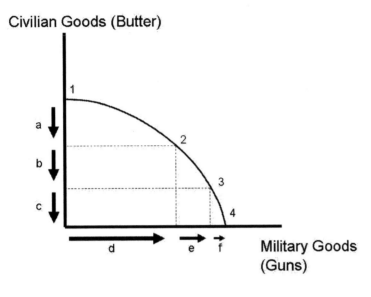

Figure 4-3.   Diminishing returns. Equal amounts of civilian goods given up (a, b, and c) yield ever less in additional military goods (d, e, and f). This is known as "diminishing returns." Note that this diagram is the same as figure 4-2, which shows "increasing costs." Same thing.

Increasing the Frontier with Resources and Technology
The drastic wartime movement along the production possibility frontier from civilian to military goods implies hardship for civilians. There are shortages of food and clothing, lack of fodder for horses, scarce medical care. That's what happened in the south. A southerner wrote in 1862, "In the name of God, I ask is this to be tolerated? Is this war to be carried on and the government upheld at the expense of the starvation of the women and children?"

Something else happened in the north. By the end of the war Union iron production was 29% higher than it had been in the previous record year of 1856, when the figure included northern and southern production. Coal production was up 21%. Traffic on the Erie Canal increased 50%. More wheat was grown in the north in 1863 than the whole country had grown in 1859. The Union not only fed itself, it increased its exports of wheat, corn, beef, and pork to Europe, where there were crop failures.

An Illinois farm writer described the nation "whitening the Northern lakes with the sails of its commerce." Abraham Lincoln declared in his state of the union address of December 1864, "The national resources, then, are unexhausted, and, as we believe, inexhaustible."

The Union increased its production and consumption of military *and* civilian goods, guns and butter. How? Through more intensive use of existing resources, the accumulation of more resources, and better technology. Again, the production possibility frontier can help organize these ideas.

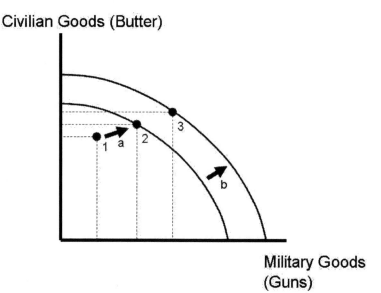

Civilian Goods (Butter)

Military Goods (Guns)

Figure 4-4. The New Frontier. After the panic of 1857, which resulted in recession, the northern economy had unemployed resources. Point 1 represents unemployed resources because it is inside the production possibility frontier. The move from 1 to 2 (a) occurs because the unemployed are again employed. Production of both butter and guns increases. Added resources—more land, labor and capital—and better technology explain the move (b) to a new higher frontier. Point 3 again shows increases in guns and butter over point 2.

The location of the production possibility frontier depends on the amount and quality of the nation's resources, land, labor, and capital. Since it's a frontier—the outer edge—all available resources are being used. The frontier also depends on the level of technology; how well the nation transforms its resources into goods.

There had been a recession before the war, known as the Panic of 1857. A recession implies unemployed resources: men and women who want to work but cannot find jobs, factories that could be producing goods but are shut down, land that could be growing crops but is lying fallow. The economy is not at the frontier, where all resources are fully employed. It is inside the frontier, where some resources are unemployed. In figure 4-4, it is at a point like 1.

The war sped recovery. Factories may have been vacant and people unemployed, but now the Union government wanted to buy anything and everything for the war effort. Business people saw their opportunity, reopened their factories and hired more workers. Existing resources were soon fully employed. In figure 4-4, the economy moved from point 1 to point 2.

The Union found more and better machinery. With so many men in uniform, farmers and factory owners adopted labor-saving technology. Farmers began using improved plows and corn planters, two-horse cultivators, and new steam-driven threshing machines. Sewing machines increased production in clothing factories. A new machine attached shoe soles to uppers faster than ever before.

The Union found more workers. Immigration continued during the war. During the five war years 800,000 immigrants arrived, mostly from England, Ireland, and Germany. Women joined the labor force, in factories and on farms. One traveler reported in 1862 seeing more women than men driving teams of horses in farm fields. *Merchant Magazine* reported in September 1863 that "At the present time so perfect is machinery that men seem to be of less necessity. Of all the labors of the field, mowing was formerly deemed to be the most arduous, and the strongest men were required for it. We have seen, within the past few weeks, a stout matron whose sons are in the army, with her team cutting hay at seventy five cents per acre, and she cut seven acres with ease in a day, riding leisurely upon her cutter."

The Union even found more land. Congress passed the homestead act in 1862, to give western land to settlers. Though its biggest impact came after the war, 25,000 settlers had claimed three million acres by 1865. And already settled land was farmed more intensively.

More capital, more labor, more land, and better technology: the Union economy boomed. The north's production possibility frontier shifted outward, shown in figure 4-4 as b. The added resources allowed the Union to produce more military goods *and* more civilian goods during the Civil War. As Lincoln said, it appeared that the nation's resources were "inexhaustible." The Confederacy could not match the Union's resources. The *expanding production possibility frontier* goes a long way toward explaining why the Union won.

Paying for the War

The American government does not have the power simply to order resources shifted from civilian to military uses. Even draftees must be paid. Instead, the Federal Treasury must buy the resources and goods it needs. For this, said Treasury Secretary Salmon P. Chase, millions of dollars in spending would be required.

The Federal government didn't have millions to spare. Most Federal government revenue derived from the tariff, the taxes on imports of foreign goods, and the sale of western lands. Tariffs and land sales could never raise the revenue needed. There was no income tax. There was no major Federal tax of any kind.

Fortunately, Union generals predicted a quick victory over the rag-tag southern army. A short war might not require big new sources of revenue. Chase proposed to borrow from financial markets about three-quarters of the amount needed for the 1861 budget. It would be easy to repay the money after the war was won.

But the southerners routed the Union army at the first Battle of Bull Run on July 22, 1861. The war would not be short. Chase realized that the Federal government's revenue needs would be much, much larger than anyone had expected.

Government has three ways to shift resources from civilian to government goods. It can impose *taxes*. Civilian taxpayers are required to turn over resources to the government, so it can provide government services. Government income increases and civilian income decreases. Government buys what civilians cannot.

Government can *borrow*. It can sell Treasury bonds to lenders on the promise to repay plus interest in the future. The government spends the borrowed funds. With so much lent to the government, civilians find it harder to borrow for their needs. Civilians must forego the buildings and equipment which they would have acquired, had they been able to borrow.

And government can *print money*. It uses the new money to offer producers higher prices for their goods than civilians can afford. This is sometimes called an *inflation tax*. The government shifts resources from the public to itself by creating money, which raises prices beyond what the public can pay.

Secretary of the Treasury Chase proposed to raise $150 million in 1861, and more later, to pay for soldiers, horses, cannons, ships, and supplies of all kinds. It was an astounding figure. The whole government budget had been $63 million in 1860. There was no income tax to raise the needed funds. There was not even an internal revenue service. Without taxes, some other way had to be found to raise the money.

> *To shift resources from the private sector to the public sector, governments can tax, borrow or print money.*

Chase traveled to New York, Boston, and Philadelphia to seek buyers for his *Treasury bonds*. The bonds would be used to borrow from banks and financiers. They would be sold to buyers for cash, on the promise to repay plus interest in a fixed amount of time. The bankers asked how the loans would be repaid, expecting to hear of a plan for broad new taxes. "Heavy taxes will excite discontent," Chase said. President Lincoln needed the support of the public in order to fight this war. Taxes would discourage support.

The bankers wouldn't have it. If there were no big new taxes, how would these loans be repaid? Chase demanded cooperation. The bankers resisted. One banker declared that if the government delayed its loan repayments, the banks would issue an ultimatum, declaring that they would not honor the government's checks. The army wouldn't be able to buy supplies.

"No!" Chase declared, "It is not the business of the Secretary of the Treasury to receive an ultimatum, but to declare one if necessary." He surveyed the room and used his trump card. Without the loan he would print money, "for it is certain that the war must go on until the rebellion is put down, if we have to put out paper until it takes a thousand dollars to buy a breakfast!"

That scared the bankers. It's easy to see why. They had lent money at interest rates of 5%, 6%, 7%. If inflation would now be 10% or 20% or 30%, the *real interest rates* they would earn would be negative. The purchasing power of the repaid loans would be less than it was when the loan was made, even with interest. The bankers' wealth would diminish. Chase got his loans, in three installments of $50 million each.

Later, back in Washington, Chase gave a dinner at Willard's Hotel to celebrate the deal. It was not very merry. A gloomy banker named Stevens told Chase that, "you have now received from the Associated Banks the vast sum of fifty millions of dollars. We all earnestly hope that this sum will be sufficient to end the war. Should it not prove to be enough, we wish to notify you that you cannot depend upon further aid."

By the end of 1861 war expenses were rising rapidly. Chase knew that American lenders had been telling the truth, they could not provide enough to the Treasury to pay for the ever-rising cost of war. He tried selling his bonds in Great Britain, but the English were angry about American tariffs and the Union blockade of southern ports. And, they weren't sure the Union would win. If it lost, would the loans be repaid? No help came from Britain.

Chase didn't really want to print money to pay war expenses. He was a "hard money" man. He thought paper money should be backed by gold stored in Treasury vaults, or even better, he thought gold coins should circulate as money. In 1861 the United States was effectively on a *gold standard*. The official, legal price of gold was $20.67, meaning that slightly less than one ounce was needed for every twenty dollars in circulation. If paper currency circulated and the nation remained on the gold standard, anyone with 20 paper dollars could drop by the Treasury and demand an ounce of gold (almost). The Treasury had to pay. That's what it meant for paper money to be "backed" by gold. But this meant that the Treasury could issue no more paper money than its gold stock would support.

In January 1862 Chase told the Congress that he had "great aversion to making anything but coin a legal tender" but the war made it "indispensably necessary that we should resort to the issue of United States notes." The legislators knew well the danger. Congressman George Pendleton of Ohio warned that "prices will be inflated, incomes will depreciate; the savings of the poor will vanish; the hoardings of the widow will melt away; bonds, mortgages, and notes—everything of fixed value—will lose their value."

Lincoln and Chase insisted, and there appeared to be no alternative. The Legal Tender Act passed the Congress, and President Lincoln signed it on February 27, 1862. The new paper money was printed with green ink, so the public called them *"greenbacks."* The Federal government did not have enough gold to back all the greenbacks it needed to print. The new law allowed it to refuse to exchange the new currency for gold. The United States was off the gold standard.

The greenbacks presented Chase with an opportunity. Lincoln had beaten him for the Republican nomination for President in 1860. He thought he could return the favor in 1864, and win the Presidency for himself. But he would have to become better known among the voters. So, when Chase selected the design for the new paper one dollar bills—the bills with widest circulation—the portrait on the bill was: Salmon P. Chase. Lincoln, the President, was relegated to the five dollar bill.

What was this new paper the Union was printing? The government had never issued so much paper money before, so some explanation was needed. On the back of Chase's portrait, the reverse side of the bill explained. It read, "This note is a legal tender for all debts public and private except duties on imports and interest on the public debt; and is receivable in payment of all loans made to the United States." It was legal money for use in transactions between buyers and sellers, employers and workers. Soldiers and defense contractors would be paid with it. But it wasn't good enough for tariffs, the taxes on imported goods. The Union wanted gold from foreign importers. And the government would pay interest to its creditors in gold, not paper, to encourage them to buy Treasury bonds.

Greenback. An 1862 one dollar bill, with the portrait of a man chasing a Presidential nomination.

The Union used its newly printed money to buy goods, bidding them away from the public. Since the government owned the printing press, there was no way for the public to outbid the government. Sellers saw the opportunity to raise their prices. "You can sell anything to the government at almost any price you've got the guts to ask" said defense contractor Jim Fisk. Everyone knew that printing greenbacks would cause inflation, and everyone was right.

Ironically, in the end the Union raised more revenue by borrowing and taxing than it did by printing money. The Treasury Department hired financier Jay Cooke to sell its bonds, and Cooke discovered that he could sell them directly to the public, as well as to bankers. Cooke sold two billion dollars worth in his war bond drives. Congress passed the Internal Revenue Act in July 1862, which created sales, inheritance and income taxes. The taxes raised $600 million, and the public continued to support the war effort.

The Union borrowed two-thirds of its revenue, and raised another fifth from taxes. That left only one-eighth for the printing press. Still, $447 million in greenbacks were printed. That was enough to double prices during five years of war, an average inflation rate of 19% per year.

In the south, the Confederacy had more trouble. It managed to raise only 7% of its spending from taxes, and issued $1.6 billion in paper money. Inflation during the war was 9,000%, which is 180% per year. Prices doubled every eight months. Breakfast never cost a thousand dollars in the north. It cost more than that in the south. Inflation that high is called *hyperinflation*. It's *always* the result of printing money. Lots and lots of money.

Wars often create inflation. Big increases in government spending are paid for with big increases in the quantity of money. "Too much money chasing too few goods" is a fine description of the source of inflation. The nation's output is limited by its resources and technology. When all the nation's labor, land and capital are in use, only so much food, clothing, guns and ships can be produced. That's potential output, the maximum amount that can be produced when all resources are employed. An economy producing on its production possibility frontier is producing its potential output. The quantity of money can grow and grow, but the nation's production has a limit. Too much money will chase too few goods.

The Equation of Exchange
We can write the relationship between money, output, and prices in an equation. Money is used for buying and selling goods and services-*90s*. The prices of all the transactions, added up, are the total value of transactions. That's a bigger number than the amount of money in circulation because each dollar is used for many transactions in a year. The average value of transactions that a dollar is used for in a year is called the *velocity of money*. Put another way, velocity is the number of times a dollar changes hands in a transaction each year.

We could calculate velocity as

$$V = T / (QM)$$

T is the value of transactions, QM is the *quantity of money*, the number of dollars in circulation, so V is the average number of times each dollar is used. Unfortunately, we don't know the number of transactions that are made each year. No one measures that number.

We do calculate the value of transactions that make up GDP, though, so we can measure the *GDP velocity of money*. That's the number of times each year a dollar is used in a GDP transaction, to buy and sell a final good or service produced that year. That lets out a lot of transactions that take place; for example, for existing houses and used cars. But we can measure GDP velocity as

$$V = GDP / (QM).$$

Remember that GDP is the product of real GDP and the price deflator. Call real gross domestic product "Q" (for quantity of output), and the price deflator "P". Then

$$V = P \times Q / (QM)$$

Multiply both sides by QM, and you get

$$(QM) \times V = P \times Q.$$

This is known as the *equation of exchange*: the quantity of money times its velocity equals the price level times real output. We'll drop the "GDP" from "GDP velocity of money," and call this "V" just velocity.

The equation of exchange is always true, of course, because velocity is calculated to make it true. It has its uses, though. For example:

- If velocity doesn't change much, an increase in the amount of money in circulation will increase nominal output, P x Q.

- If the economy is recovering towards its production possibility frontier, or the frontier itself is expanding, an increase in money might not increase the price level. Output is rising towards potential output, or potential output itself is rising. Then an increase in Q might match the rise in (QM). P might not increase.

- But if real output is at potential, and potential output isn't increasing very much, an increase in the quantity of money will increase the price level. *Too much money chasing too few goods causes inflation.*

The equation of exchange is written as QM x V = P x Q, where QM is the quantity of money, V is the velocity of money, P is the price level, and Q is the quantity of output.

These ideas are known as the *quantity theory of money*. With velocity fixed, an increase in the quantity of money increases nominal output. If real output is fixed, an increase in the quantity of money increases the price level. Inflation results from too-rapid money growth. Sometimes velocity does change, and that can mess up predictions using the quantity theory of money. Still, the equation of exchange must always be true, and that can help keep our macroeconomic models honest.

We do not have precise measures of money, velocity, and output for the Civil War period. But we do know that:

- Output in the north increased by more than output in the south;
- The quantity of money in the north increased by less than the quantity of money in the south; and
- The north saw inflation, while the south saw hyperinflation.

The table shows how the equation of exchange assembles these facts (if we assume that nothing much happened to velocity).

The equation of exchange tells us something else about war finance. Inflation is mainly due to the way military spending is paid for, not to the increase in military spending itself. If a war is financed with taxes or borrowing, money shifts from civilians to the government. Prices won't rise much if QM doesn't change. (Civilians may use their remaining dollars more quickly, so a rise in velocity may increase prices somewhat.)

Equation of Exchange	North	South
Increase in quantity of money (QM)	*Big*	*Really big*
Increase in real output (Q)	*Pretty big*	*Not much*
Resulting increase in prices (P)	*Inflation*	*Hyperinflation*

Pay for the war by printing money, though, and the big increase in QM will raise prices. That's what caused the inflation in the north and the hyperinflation in the south.

We can use the three market model and the second shifts to show what happens, too. Government purchases increase a lot. That increases output and prices, and the demand for money (second shift #3). The real interest rate would rise, except that the increase in purchases was paid for with an increase in the supply of money. The real interest rate does not increase. Since there's no interest rate rise to limit aggregate demand, output remains above potential.

Ordinarily we'd think that this would cause inflationary expectations to rise, decreasing aggregate supply. That's second shift #1. But the north saw a big increase in potential output, with added immigration, new land on the frontier, more intensive use of existing land, and lots of new machinery and technology (that's what happens in figure 4-4). So, instead, potential output rises to meet new demands. There's still inflation, but not as much as in the south, where the quantity of money rose more and potential output did not rise as much.

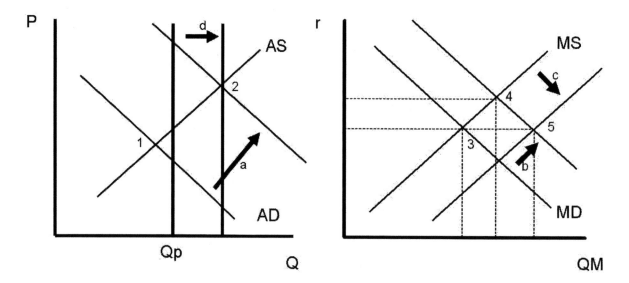

Figure 4-5. Wartime increases in government purchases cause an increase in aggregate demand (a). Output and prices rise (1 to 2). Second shift #3 means money demand increases (b). This would increase the real interest rate (3 to 4), causing crowding out through second shift #2, except the Treasury has increased the money supply (c). The real interest rate does not rise (3 to 5). Output remains above potential (2 is greater than original Qp), but new resources increase potential output (d). (We could draw an increase in AS as well, but that clutters the diagram even more.) This prevents second shift #1, holding inflation down. In the south, the rise in the money supply is greater, and there is no big increase in potential output. Second shift #1 happens in a big way. Output rises less and prices rise more.

President Lincoln had a falling out with Salmon P. Chase in 1864, and the President accepted Chase's resignation from the Treasury. But Chase was still a power in the Republican Party, so when the Chief Justice of the Supreme Court died, Lincoln appointed Chase to the job. Chase was Chief Justice until his death in 1873. In 1870 a case came before the court challenging the authority of the government to issue paper money. Chief Justice Chase led the court's majority in finding that the earlier actions of Treasury Secretary Chase were unconstitutional!

MacroPolicy Again: Hyperinflation in Zimbabwe

The government of the African nation of Zimbabwe began seizing thousands of big white-owned commercial farms in 2000 in chaotic, often violent invasions by supporters of President Robert Mugabe. Unfortunately, the farms' new owners knew little about farming. As of 2008 the big farms produced less than a tenth the corn that they did in the 1990s, according to the United Nations Food and Agriculture Organization.

In the chaos, foreign investors fled, manufacturing ground to a halt, goods and foreign currency needed to buy imports fell into short supply, and prices shot up. Then the serious problems began.

With manufacturing and farming less productive, government tax revenues fell. With prices rising, government employees demanded higher pay. President Mugabe's government began printing more Zimbabwean dollars to keep ministries functioning and to shield the salaries of key supporters — and potential enemies — against further erosion.

More and more dollars were printed. Inflation reached an annual rate of 1,281 percent by mid-2006. It hit 410,000 percent by mid-2007. Inflation was officially 231 million percent in July 2008. John Robertson, an independent economist in Zimbabwe, estimated that it had surged to eight quintillion percent — that is an eight followed by 18 zeros—by the end of the year.

The economy collapsed. Most of the nation's schools ceased to function as teachers quit showing up, because their salaries no longer covered the cost of the bus fare to work. Hospital workers faced the same situation, and many hospitals shut down. Cities couldn't buy the chemicals to treat the water, and taps ran dry. Late in 2008 a cholera epidemic began. With no sanitation and no hospital care, people died by the thousands.

President Mugabe finally was forced to accept a power-sharing arrangement with opposition leaders. A new finance minister took control of the central bank, and he let the Zimbabwean dollar die in early 2009. People used United States dollars and South African rand instead. Goods began to flow into the country and food staples cost less.

Professor Jeffrey Sachs, of Columbia University, listed the great hyperinflations in history: Germany in the 1920s, Greece and Hungary in the 1940s, and Yugoslavia in 1993. Add Zimbabwe to the list.

We know what causes hyperinflation: way too much money chasing too few goods. Only governments print money, so only governments can cause hyperinflation. But why would a government do such a thing?

One reason is lack of tax revenue. The Confederacy's founding idea was to have a weak central government, which could not impose its will on the individual states (and so not abolish slavery). That made hard for the central government to impose taxes, however.

> *Hyperinflation can occur only if the government prints vast amounts of currency.*

Another reason is a policy objective more important than economic stability. The Confederacy needed to win the war to survive. It had no well-developed banking system from which to borrow money, and foreign bankers wouldn't lend for fear of not being repaid if the south lost the war. Printing money was the only alternative.

Zimbabwe provides a modern example. The botched land reform devastated agriculture. Fearful investors withdrew and manufacturing collapsed. Tax revenues diminished, and to maintain itself in power the government had to print money to pay its supporters, the police, and the military.

I'm a hundred-trillionaire (Zimbabwean). Towards the end of the hyperinflation in Zimbabwe the central bank printed $100 trillion bills. They exchanged for less than one U.S. dollar.

This presents a third reason for hyperinflation: a government that lacks legitimacy. President Mugabe hadn't been elected in a free and fair election. He could not impose taxes and expect them to be paid. His government had to maintain itself by force, and that meant keeping its supporters happy. So the central bank printed money to fund the pay of government employees and the equipment of the police and army.

Just a glance at the equation of exchange shows what had to happen. Here it is, to glance at:

(QM) x V = P x Q.

With output (Q) down and the quantity of money (QM) up, prices (P) had to rise. As prices began to rise, those government salaries had to be increased to keep up. That created bigger deficits and required printing even more money. Hyperinflation was the result.

Hyperinflations usually end with currency reform, and Zimbabwe saw two such reforms in 2008 and 2009. The first reform simply lopped ten digits off prices and currency denominations. That made it easier to make change, but since the government kept printing money, it did not stop inflation.

The second reform killed the Zimbabwean currency. The government quit printing it. Other nations' currencies circulated instead. Since the government cannot print U.S. dollars or South African rand, the increase in the money supply stopped, and eventually so did inflation.

Deflation and Resumption of the Gold Standard

The United States had left the gold standard and inflation was the result. So, after the Civil War, it became the government's policy to get back to the gold standard. This would link the money supply to the stock of gold, which was largely beyond the government's control. The government would not be able to create inflation by printing a lot of greenbacks. Just as important, gold was the standard of international commerce. The United States was a developing country which needed investment from overseas, particularly Great Britain, the world's biggest, richest economy. Any nation that was not on gold would find it hard to attract British investors.

This was the general point of view at the end of the Civil War in 1865. Resume the gold standard at the old gold price of $20.67 per ounce. The policy became known as *Resumption*. Resumption could not be done right away. The market price of gold was by then about double the old standard of $20.67, as a result of all that inflation. Suppose the government had declared that it would trade nearly an ounce of gold for every $20 greenback. The Treasury would have been stampeded by people wanting to buy gold at the Treasury for $20 an ounce, to sell in the market for $40. The Treasury would pay out gold by the wagon-load, and within days (hours?) the Treasury's stock of gold would be gone. It would have to "close the gold window," and that meant no gold standard.

The market price of gold had to be brought back down to $20.67. (Somehow, they never considered resuming the gold standard at $40 an ounce.) That required deflation, to bring the price of gold, and everything else, back down to where it was at the start of the war.

> *Between 1865 and 1879 the government restricted the growth of the money supply. As output expanded the price level fell, and so did the price of gold. The gold standard was resumed in 1879.*

At first they tried this. The Treasury ran a surplus, bringing in more revenue than it spent. It retired greenbacks as they were paid in taxes, taking them out of circulation. With less money in circulation, prices fell. There was too little money chasing too many goods.

But this hurt! No longer could manufacturers sell anything and everything to the Federal government. The war was over. Government wasn't buying from factories, it was collecting greenbacks in taxes to destroy them, not spend them. Farmers saw their incomes from the sale of corn, hogs, and other commodities fall. Business investment spending on factories and equipment declined. Factories closed. Workers could not find work, and their consumption spending on food, clothing, and household goods decreased. The economy fell into a deep recession. The price level fell fast.

This was too much to take. The government modified its policy. It decided not to retire greenbacks, but instead to restrict money supply growth and allow the economy to "grow into its monetary coat." Output would grow faster than the money supply. *Deflation* would happen gradually. It took longer, through the rest of the 1860's and the 1870's, but it was easier on the nation's economy. By 1879 the price level was back to where it had been in 1860, and the price of gold was back down near $20. *Resumption* was achieved. The nation resumed the gold standard in 1879.

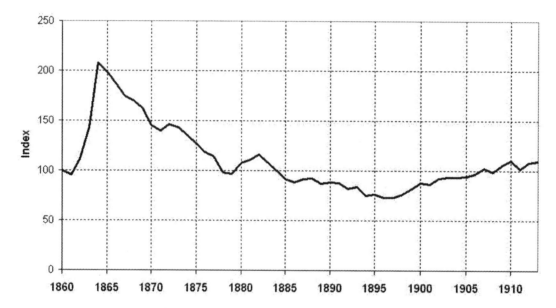

Figure 4-6. Wholesale Price Index, 1860-1914. The price index doubled from 1860 to 1864. It returned to its 1860 level by 1879, making resumption possible. Deflation continued from 1882 through 1896, sparking the bimetallism debate. Increasing gold supplies increased the price index after 1896.

Industrial Revolution and Continued Deflation
But prices kept falling. Deflation continued. On the gold standard, the money supply rises or falls with the stock of gold. The stock of gold increased when it was mined and sold to the Treasury. It also increased when U.S. exports of goods to other countries exceeded U.S. imports of goods from other countries. Foreigners paid for U.S. exports with gold, and Americans paid for U.S. imports with gold.   If exports were more than imports, the amount of gold held in the U.S. would increase. Gold was not being mined very rapidly, and U.S. imports matched U.S. exports. The money supply grew slowly.

> *During the 1880's and 1890's, the industrial revolution increased output, but the gold standard restricted growth of the money supply. The result was deflation, a continuous fall in prices and wages.*

The economy's capacity to produce—its potential output—was growing fast. Immigration was increasing the *labor* supply. The amount of *land* in cultivation was growing as the nation pushed its frontier westward. High levels of investment were increasing the stock of machinery or *capital*. The industrial revolution created new *technologies* that made this added labor, land, and machinery ever more productive.

Immigration was increasing the labor supply. Between 1870 and 1900 more than twelve million people immigrated to the United States. The nation's population almost doubled, from 40 million to 76 million. The number of people in the labor force more than doubled.

The amount of land being used for production increased. In 1870 there were 408 million acres in farms. By 1900 the number was 841 million. The number of farms more than doubled. So did the acres of harvested corn.

Perhaps most important, there was more machinery, and it used better technology. Steamships replaced sailing ships. It took 14 days to sail from New York to London in a clipper ship in 1850. In 1901 a steamship crossed the ocean in eight days. And the steamships improved. Older steamships required 2,200 tons of coal to carry 800 tons of freight. With more efficient marine engines, the ratio was reversed: 800 tons of coal could carry 2,200 tons of freight.

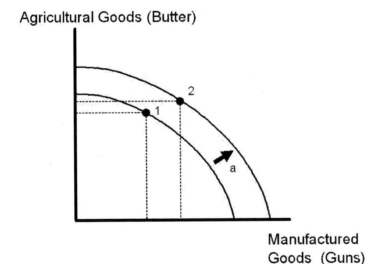

Agricultural Goods (Butter)

Manufactured Goods (Guns)

Figure 4-7. More of everything. Added resources—land, labor, and capital—and better technology-expand the production possibility frontier (a). The nation can produce and consume more of both butter and guns (1 to 2).

In 1870 railroads operated 53,000 miles of track. In 1900 it was 198,000. And the track was better. Steel rails replaced iron rails, and steel rails could carry ten times the tonnage before they wore out. The engines improved. Locomotives doubled in pulling power from 1870 to 1900. Freight car size increased 60%.

Blast furnaces for refining iron became more efficient. Experiments found that increasing the temperature and volume of the blast could double the production of pig iron. Steel became more plentiful. Steel mills produced 77 thousand tons in 1870 and 11.2 million tons in 1900.

Farm productivity improved. New planters, harvesters, and threshing machines cut the time required for farm work. In 1840 it took 25 hours to harvest an acre of corn. In 1900 it took 16. The McCormick Company introduced another innovation: installment credit. Farmers could buy their machinery on credit and repay with the proceeds of the harvest.

We've seen three ways to think about what was happening. Let's use them.

The United States was adding resources: more labor, more productive land, more machinery. It was improving its technology, combining these resources in better ways to produce more. The production possibility frontier was expanding.

Labor, land, machinery, and technology increased and improved. We can add a fifth factor that probably increased the PPF: *political stability*. The Civil War was over. The nation and the world now knew that the United States would remain one country. Investment in long-lived equipment and infrastructure, like railroads and blast furnaces, increased as political risks fell. War would not destroy these assets, and their products could be sold and shipped across state boundaries without interference. Businesses could be more certain that their investments would be profitable. So, they undertook more investments. The nation's stock of machinery grew faster.

An expanding production possibility frontier implies a rise in potential output, and an increase in aggregate supply. If aggregate demand doesn't keep up, this will reduce the price level, which is deflation.

Figure 4-7 shows an expanding PPF. Here guns and butter stand for manufactured and agricultural goods. As resources increase and technology improves, the frontier moves outward. If it fully employs its resources and technology, the nation can have more of both agricultural and manufactured goods. The nation must choose how much of each.

Figure 4-8 shows increases in potential output in the goods market. Potential output increases with more resources and better technology. After that happens, the old equilibrium (point 1 on figure 4-8) has output less than potential. Resources are unemployed. In chapter 4 we described what happens next. Second shift #1 kicks in. Workers reluctantly accept lower wages for their work. Mine owners reluctantly accept lower prices for their minerals. Farmers reluctantly accept lower prices for their produce. Aggregate supply increases until output equals potential. The price level falls. That's deflation.

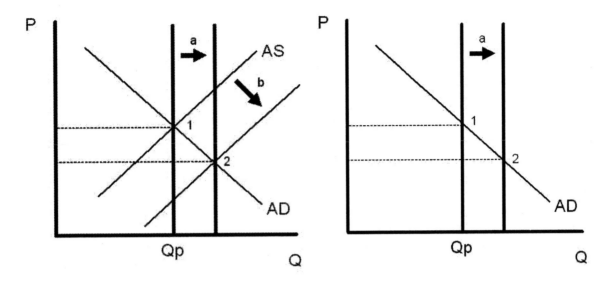

Figure 4-8. De-cluttering the graph. Added resources and better technology increase potential output (a). Output at equilibrium 1 is then less than potential. Resource prices, including wages, fall, and aggregate supply increases (b). We call that second shift #1. At the new equilibrium (2), output is at potential, and the price level is lower. Since second shift #1 assures that aggregate supply will shift from equilibrium 1 to 2 (eventually), we can "de-clutter" the goods market graph by showing only potential output. The decline in the price level (1 to 2) stands out.

In figure 4-8, the price level falls because aggregate supply increases and aggregate demand does not. Of course, aggregate demand was increasing, too, as more people earned and spent more income and businesses increased investment spending. With the money supply growing slowly, though, real interest rates remained too high to allow aggregate demand to keep up with aggregate supply. So the price level fell.

It's easy to use the equation of exchange to show why there was deflation. The equation is

$$(QM) \times V = P \times Q,$$

where QM is the quantity of money, V is the velocity of money, P is the price level and Q is real output. QM was growing slowly, Q was growing rapidly. If V wasn't changing, the price level P had to fall. The long deflation was caused by "too little money chasing too many goods," just the opposite of inflation.

Graphs and equations help explain. But what was happening? How did people produce more goods? Why did businesses lower their prices?

Consider the technological improvement in steamships. With the time required for the New York to London voyage just about cut in half, the same ships and sailors could make twice as many trips. Perhaps the number of voyages would double. So could the number of passengers carried, or the volume of freight delivered. Better technology produced more goods and services.

Or, with sailing time cut in half, perhaps the same passengers and freight would be carried by half the ships and sailors. Maybe half the sailors would be fired. Difficult for them, of course, but they were now available to work in other industries—on those new miles of railroad track or in those expanding steel mills. Better technology freed up resources for more production.

Added voyages meant added capacity. To fill their holds with freight and their berths with paying passengers, steamship companies found that they had to reduce freight rates and fares. Shipping costs were down, because to transport the same cargo, fewer ships were needed (because each made more trips), fewer sailors were needed, and less fuel was needed. Competition among steamship companies meant that these lower costs were passed on to customers in lower fares. Better technology and rising output meant falling prices.

More output meant lower prices, but lower prices meant more output, too. With fares lower, more immigrants could afford to come to the United States. And with the journey shorter, contagious diseases like cholera had less time to incubate. Death rates on steamships were one-tenth the rate on sailing ships. Better shipping technology meant that the labor supply could expand even faster.

Advancing technology reduced prices and improved quality. That was good for consumers. But some shopkeepers and craftsmen faced a new problem. Advances in technology were making the world a more competitive place. Before the Civil War, frontier blacksmiths, millers and cobblers would make their nails, bread and shoes and sell them locally. Often there were few other craftsmen in the area, so they could charge high prices (or barter for greater amounts of goods).

But as the railroads expanded every craftsman could ship goods over greater distances. The number of traveling salesman increased four-fold during the 1870's. And customers could travel too. If the local craftsman's prices were too high or his goods were too shoddy, a customer could travel to the county seat, or even the state capital, to find better. Each blacksmith, miller and cobbler found himself competing with other craftsmen for hundreds of miles around. The competition reduced prices and improved quality. That was great for customers. It was hard on the craftsmen.

Lenders, Debtors and Bimetallism
Farming was the dominant business in the south and west. The long deflation was a special concern for farmers. Most were debtors, borrowing for land, seed and equipment. Loans were usually paid back on a fixed payment schedule, so much owed each year. Farmers paid out of the income they earned from selling their crops and livestock. As

prices fell, the amount earned on sales of farm commodities fell, yet the debt payments stayed the same. It became harder and harder to earn enough to repay this debt.

Most lenders were located in the east, and deflation concerned lenders, too. They liked it. The money repaid by debtors was worth more each year as prices fell, since it could buy more goods and services.

Farmers and miners had another complaint. Resumption of the gold standard created fixed exchange rates with other gold standard countries. Great Britain had the world's dominant economy, and their currency was (and is) pounds. The Bank of England set the official price of gold for England's currency at 4.26 pounds per ounce of gold. The U.S. official price was $20.67 per ounce. So, 4.26 pounds effectively traded for $20.67, which is $4.85 for one pound, or one dollar for about one-fifth of a pound. Back in 1865, with gold selling for $40 an ounce in the U.S., the exchange rate had been one dollar for one tenth of a pound. Back then, $100 of American corn or wheat cost a British importer 10 pounds (at one dollar per one-tenth pound). Now that same $100 of corn cost the importer 20 pounds. American exports were more expensive for British people to buy.

In the eyes of western farmers, this exchange rate made the prices of their commodities too expensive in export markets. They wanted a lower value of the dollar, like it had been before resumption. This would make exports cheaper and increase demand for their goods. Eastern manufacturers were less concerned about the exchange rate. They were concerned about competing imports from European factories, but they were protected by high tariffs on these imports.

The deflation set up a conflict between regions (east versus south and west), between cultures (urban versus rural), and between classes (lenders versus debtors). Western, rural farmers opposed deflation and fixed exchange rates; eastern urban bankers and manufacturers favored deflation and fixed exchange rates.

The westerners knew what to do about the problem. Since the source of deflation was a money supply growing too slowly, somehow the money supply must be made to grow faster. Prior to resumption in 1879, they proposed staying off the gold standard and printing more greenbacks. There was a political movement in the 1870s called the *Greenback Party* that advocated this policy. It attracted many followers, but did not become powerful enough to stop resumption of the gold standard.

After resumption became a fact, the west turned to a different policy, called *bimetallism*. They proposed to base the money supply on both gold and silver. There had been a huge silver discovery in Nevada, so the supply of silver was growing faster than the supply of gold. A money supply based on both silver and gold would grow faster, and deflation would stop.

The "sound money men," as the gold supporters called themselves, opposed bimetallism as fiercely as its proponents supported it. Gold supporters said the U.S. had to stick with the gold standard because that was the standard of international trade and finance. Gold and its fixed exchange rates would aid economic development. In the United States, as in most developing nations, a lot of the investment funds that finance new factories, equipment, and infrastructure came from foreign investors. In the 19th century, these investors were European, principally British.

> *In the 1880's and 1890's westerners, farmers and debtors supported bimetallism, which would base the money supply on gold and silver. They wanted more rapid money growth to end the long deflation.*

Investors liked the fixed exchange rates that the gold standard required. It meant that the profits from investments in the U.S. could be exchanged at $4.85 per pound, and that this could be predicted years in advance. If the U.S. was not on gold, the value of the dollar would probably fall, and U.S. profits would be worth less in pounds. A million dollars in America is 206,000 pounds at $4.85. If the exchange rate rose to (say) $5.85 per pound (meaning the dollar is worth less relative to the pound), a million dollars is only 171,000 pounds. Exchange fluctuations could wipe out investor profits. A country not on the gold standard would see less foreign investment and would develop more slowly.

The bimetallists had some successes. In 1878 Congress passed the Bland-Allison Act, which required the Treasury to buy a limited amount of silver each month. When the Treasury bought silver, it paid with paper money or gold or silver coins. The money supply would increase. In 1890 Congress passed the Sherman Silver Purchase Act, which more than doubled the amount of silver the Treasury had to buy.

The Depression of the 1890's

Now came the crisis, both economic and political. The Sherman Silver Purchase Act caught the attention of international investors. The act required a lot of silver to be purchased, and its passage seemed to show the increasing power of the bimetallists. International investors began to suspect that the U.S. would leave the gold standard. This would cause the dollar to lose value relative to the pound. Investors feared for the value of their wealth and profits. They began to sell their American assets for dollars. They would take these dollars to the Treasury and exchange them for gold at $20.67 per ounce. Then they would ship the gold back home. International investment left the U.S. so fast that they called it *"hot money."*

The international demand for the dollar decreased, but the exchange rate was fixed. An excess supply of dollars was the result. Lots of people wanted to exchange their dollars for gold, but few people wanted to exchange their gold for dollars. So gold flowed out of the Treasury, and out of the country.

Silver certificate. It says "This certifies that there has been deposited in the Treasury of the United States of America one silver dollar payable to the bearer on demand."

The money supply was backed by gold, so with less gold in the Treasury, the money supply fell. This increased real interest rates, and reduced investment spending. Aggregate demand decreased. The drop in investment was big, and the effect on output and unemployment was big and long-lasting. The economy dropped into recession. Values on the stock market fell, and in 1893, the market crashed. The recession became a depression.

Here's an opportunity to work the model, complete with second shifts. Start with all three markets in equilibrium, with output equal to potential in the goods market, and the equilibrium exchange rate equal to the gold standard's fixed rate. Then comes the "*shock*." That's something outside the model that changes the equilibrium in one of the markets. If you know what the shock is, you know where to start.

Back in the 1890's, the shock was the decision by lots of international investors to pull their money out of the United States. These decisions had a political cause—the fear of bimetallist power. Expectations in the exchange market changed, the demand for the dollar decreased, and the supply of the dollar increased.

With fixed exchange rates, though, nothing else in the model seems to change. Second shift #4, for example, shows how change in the exchange rate affects aggregate demand in the goods market by changing imports and exports. But with exchange rates unchanged, second shift #4 never gets started.

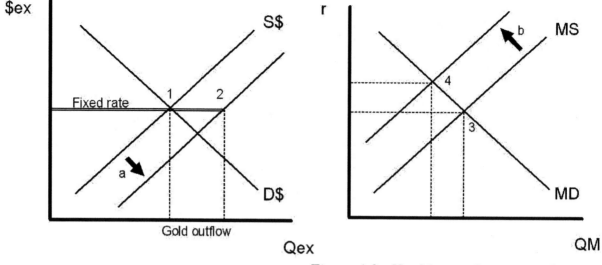

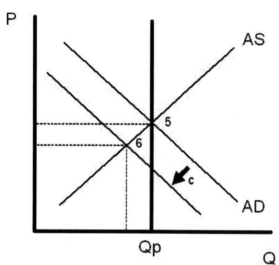

Figure 4-9. Hot Money. International investors sell their U.S. assets for dollars. The supply of dollars on the exchange market increases (a). The gold standard keeps the exchange rate fixed. At that rate, gold flows out of the country (1 to 2). On a gold standard, a decline in the stock of gold reduces the money supply (b), which increases the real interest rate (3 to 4). That's second shift (b), which can be important when exchange rates are fixed. The higher interest rate reduces investment spending, reducing aggregate demand (c), output, and the price level. That's second shift #2.

Recession and deflation result (5 to 6).

What we need is second shift (b), which shows how changes in the exchange market affect the money market. It's the shift used in special cases where exchange rates are fixed, like during the 1890's when most of the world was on the gold standard. There's an excess supply of dollars in the exchange market. Since lots of people can't trade their dollars directly for pounds at the fixed exchange rate, they exchange the dollars for gold instead and ship it out of the county.

The money supply is based on gold. With less gold in the Treasury vault, the money supply decreases in the money market. That drives up the real interest rate, which leads us to second shift #2. A higher real interest rate reduces investment spending. Fewer investment projects are profitable if businesses must pay more to borrow money.

Aggregate demand decreases. That reduces output below potential, which is a recession, and reduces the price level, which is deflation.

Grover Cleveland was elected President for a second time in 1892. Despite his party's support for bimetallism, Cleveland was a gold supporter, a "Gold Democrat," a "sound money man." In 1893 he called a special session of Congress to force repeal of the Sherman Silver Purchase Act. He played what we now call "political hardball." Any Democratic Senator or Representative who

> *In the 1890's fear that the U.S. would leave the gold standard caused international investors to leave the U.S. This increased real interest rates, reduced aggregate demand, and caused a depression.*

voted for silver would be denied patronage, meaning none of their local party loyalists would be appointed postmaster or given other Federal jobs. The arm-twisting worked. The Sherman act was repealed.

A brief economic recovery began in 1894, but confidence remained shaky. By 1896 the economy again had turned downward. It was a Presidential election year, and the Republican Party nominated William McKinley, who supported the gold standard. The conflict between the President and the Congress had split the Democratic Party into gold and silver camps. By the convention it was evident that the silver Democrats were powerful enough to challenge President Cleveland's leadership.

The silver Democrats had the upper hand in the early sessions of the convention. They succeeded in pushing through a resolution condemning their own party's President. Still in doubt was whether there would be a pro-silver plank in the party platform, and whether the party's nominee would be a silver or gold Democrat.

William Jennings Bryan was a 36-year-old two-term Congressman from Nebraska who had decided not to run again in 1894. He'd been chosen to close the platform debate for the pro-silver faction because of his skill as a speaker—they called him the "Boy Orator of the Platte." He felt the tension in the pit of his stomach. This would be the speech of his life. A friend passed him a note, "This is a great opportunity." He scribbled a response, "You will not be disappointed."

The pro-gold speaker hammered the silverites without mercy, and Bryan sensed his supporters growing restless and angry. Finally the speaker was done. Bryan sprang from his chair and took the steps to the podium two at a time. Then he stood at the rostrum, head back, right arm thrust above his head, for a full minute as the roaring crowd became quiet.

"I would be presumptuous indeed," he began, his voice rolling to the back of the hall, "to present myself against the distinguished gentlemen to whom you have listened." But, he declared, "The humblest citizen in all the land, when clad in the armor of a righteous cause, is stronger than all the hosts of error." The silverites in the crowd rose together to shout their approval, then sat silent to listen again. Bryan thought of a trained choir.

He pointed at the gold supporters. "When you come before us and tell us that we are about to disturb your business interests, we reply that you have disturbed our business interests by your course."

"The man who is employed for wages is as much a business man as his employer; the attorney in a country town is as much a business man as the corporation counsel in a great metropolis; the merchant at the crossroads store is as much a business man as the merchant of New York; the farmer who goes forth in the morning and toils all day—who begins in the spring and toils all summer—and by the application of brain and muscle to the natural resources of the country creates wealth, is as much a business man as the man who goes upon the board of trade and bets upon the price of grain. . . . We come to speak for this broader class of business men."

The silver delegates shouted and cheered. They were with him. As he came to his conclusion he brought his hands to his head with spread fingers, "You shall not press down upon the brow of labor this crown of thorns!" Then, flinging his arms wide, "You shall not crucify mankind upon a cross of gold!"

The crowd was silent, transfixed, as he backed away from the rostrum and lowered his arms. The silence, Bryan remembered, was "really painful." A whoop from the Georgia delegation broke the spell. The Coliseum erupted. They carried him from the podium on their shoulders.

The next day the Democrats nominated William Jennings Bryan for president. The silver cause had found its champion.

Bryan ran one of the first modern Presidential campaigns. He toured the country by train, giving versions of his *Cross of Gold speech* at hundreds of rallies. McKinley ran a traditional "front porch" campaign. He stayed home in Ohio, and friendly railroad owners chartered trains to bring his supporters to him. He spoke to them from his front porch.

William McKinley was elected President in 1896, with 51% of the vote. His election helped restore the confidence of international investors in the maintenance of the U.S. gold standard, and recovery began in 1897. It had been a terrible economic downturn, one of the worst in U.S. history after the Depression of the 1930s.

Late in President McKinley's first term the Congress passed the Gold Standard Act, which declared the gold dollar to be the nation's monetary standard. When Bryan lost to McKinley again in 1900, the silver issue was dead. What killed it, though, was not so much politics as economics. The bimetallists got what they wanted, and the gold standard delivered it.

In the mid-1890s world gold production increased. There were new gold strikes in Alaska and South Africa, and a new technology, the cyanide process, for extracting gold from ore. After decades of slow growth, the gold supply began to rise more rapidly. The money supply increased and the price level began to rise. Mild inflation continued for the next 15 years.

William Jennings Bryan himself gave bimetallism's eulogy, in a 1906 speech.

> The unlooked-for and unprecedented increase in the production of gold has brought victory to both the advocates of gold and the advocates of bimetallism—the former keeping the gold standard which they wanted and the latter securing the larger volume of money for which they contended.

MacroPolicy Now: China, the Yuan and Us

Consider the world from the point of view of the Chinese Communist Party. The Party is unelected and depends for its legitimacy on a "social contract" between the party and the people. The people will leave the politics to the party, as long as the party keeps the economy growing, so the people can have jobs. And the economy has been growing at eight to ten percent a year in most years since 1978. This rapid growth rate in a country with 1.3 billion people has made China a world economic power.

Millions of people each year migrate from the interior of China to the coasts, where incomes are much higher. The coasts are where trade takes place, and incomes there are driven largely by manufacturing for exports. The Party fears that if the exchange value of China's currency, the yuan (also called the renminbi), were to increase, China's exports would become more expensive and export growth would slow. Not enough jobs would be created for the millions of migrants, and this would cause unrest.

So, it is in the Party's interest to keep the value of the Chinese currency low, especially relative to the dollar, since the U.S. is the major market for China's exports. China's rapidly growing economy has been producing a lot of goods that U.S. consumers want to buy. Americans supply dollars in foreign exchange markets to buy yuan to use to buy goods from China. China doesn't buy as many goods from the U.S., so their demand for dollars is less. The relative rise in the supply of dollars ought to reduce the exchange value of the dollar, and the rising demand for yuan ought to increase the exchange value of the yuan. But this is just what China's leaders want to prevent.

How does China keep the yuan from rising and the dollar from falling? They buy dollars. China's government creates more yuan and enters exchange markets to buy dollars. This increases the demand for the dollar, and so helps keep the value of the dollar high and the value of the yuan low.

China doesn't keep all those dollars it buys in a vault in Beijing. Instead, it lends them back to Americans, mostly by buying U.S. Treasury bonds. Treasury bonds are promises by the U.S. government to repay an amount borrowed, plus interest. They're used to borrow for Federal government spending beyond tax revenues, to cover the Federal budget deficit. China and other international lenders have purchased the bulk of the Treasury bonds issued since 2005.

The dollars that China buys flow back to the United States when China buys Treasury bonds. This increases the U.S. money supply and holds down U.S. interest rates. In effect, because China finances the U.S. budget deficit, Americans don't have to. That leaves American lenders more to lend at lower interest rates. The low interest rates supported investment spending and aggregate demand in the United States during the 2001-2007 expansion. That's second shift #2. All that added lending may have helped inflate the speculative bubble in housing prices, too. The bursting of that bubble helped cause the Great Recession.

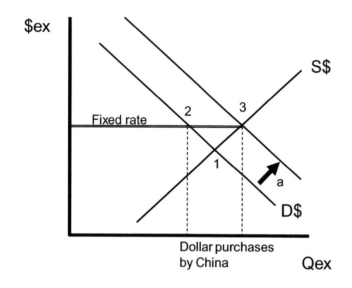

Figure 4-10. Soaking Up Dollars. Americans supply dollars to buy China's currency, the yuan, in order to buy China's goods. This should reduce the exchange value of the dollar (1). But China buys dollars, increasing the demand in exchange markets (a). This supports the dollar at a fixed rate. At the fixed rate the market demands dollars at (2). To maintain the fixed rate, China must buy dollars equal to the amount 2-3.

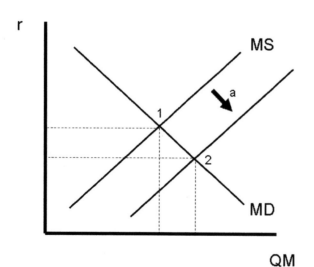

Figure 4-11. China Lends, So We Don't Have To. China buys Treasury bonds, which increases the supply of dollars the U.S. lenders can lend (a). This reduces the real interest rate in the U.S. (1 to 2), which supports investment spending and aggregate demand. That's second shift (b).

Lower interest rates are an advantage for the U.S., but China's policy has its costs, too. A higher exchange value of the dollar reduces U.S. exports and increases imports. That's second shift #4. With Chinese imports into the U.S. cheaper, U.S. manufacturers find it hard to compete. One reason why U.S. manufacturing employment has fallen in the last decade is because Americans are buying more from China, and one reason they're buying more is that China keeps its currency undervalued. That's why the Bush administration tried, and Obama administration is trying, to persuade China to allow the yuan to appreciate and the dollar to depreciate.

The policy has its costs for China, too. It must create more yuan to buy dollars. Too much money chasing too few goods causes inflation, and sure enough, inflation is an increasing problem for China. Prices had risen at least 5% in the year up to May 2011, and the official price index probably understates the true inflation rate.

China is fighting inflation by trying to restrict aggregate demand—that is, by reducing spending. Their central bank is using various measures to restrict lending by banks. Less lending to businesses and consumers means less spending on new construction or new cars. But economists and Chinese policymakers recognize that the most direct way to fight inflation is to allow the exchange value of the yuan to rise, and the value of the dollar to fall.

A rising yuan would have two effects. First, fewer dollars would be purchased in exchange markets, so fewer yuan would be printed. There would be fewer yuan chasing Chinese goods. Second, a "stronger" yuan would make the prices of imported goods cheaper to Chinese buyers. Those lower prices would reduce China's inflation rate. Competition with imported goods would encourage China's businesses to keep their own prices down, too.

So, the article says, China's policymakers are faced with a dilemma. If they allow the yuan to rise to fight inflation, their exports become more expensive and job growth may slow down. That could create unrest. If they continue to hold the value of the yuan down, job growth continues, but inflation increases. That could create unrest too.

Why include a discussion of China, the U.S. and the yuan in a chapter about the Depression of the 1890's? Consider this: Suppose China decides to allow the yuan to rise, to fight inflation. Or, suppose China decides it has bought enough Treasury bonds, or that Treasury bonds are not the secure investment they once were. China withdraws its lending to the U.S. and starts selling its dollar assets.

What do the three-market model graphs of this problem look like, you ask? Just like Figure 4-9, which showed the causes and results of hot money in the 1890's. Gold no longer plays a role—now the dollar acts as the world's currency. Other than that, the graphs in Figure 4-9 describe the risk a drop in Chinese bond purchases to the U.S. economy now.

China buys fewer dollars, and sells them instead. The demand for the dollar drops, and the supply increases (which is shown in Figure 4-9). China doesn't buy U.S. Treasury bonds, so Americans would have to buy them instead. The U.S. money supply decreases (second shift a), and that increases real interest rates. With Americans buying Treasury bonds, there is less lending for everything else. U.S. interest rates rise. Aggregate demand falls (second shift #2), and that reduces output.

This would be a serious problem if it happened fast. If investors and speculators fled the U.S. dollar—if it really was another episode of "hot money"—interest rates might spike upward, and the world would experience another financial crisis.

If the value of the yuan rises slowly and the value of the dollar falls slowly, the increase in U.S. exports could increase aggregate demand (second shift #4) just as fast as the rise in U.S. interest rates could decrease it. A gradual increase in the value of the yuan probably would be best for all concerned. The U.S. wants the value of the dollar to fall against the yuan—but not too fast!

Terms in this Chapter, in order of appearance
Production possibility frontier (PPF)
Unemployed resources
Opportunity cost
Slope of the production possibility frontier
Specialized resources
Efficiency and equity
Principle of increasing costs
Law of diminishing returns
Expanding production possibility frontier
Tax
Borrow
Print money
Inflation tax
Treasury bonds
Gold standard
Greenbacks
Hyperinflation
Transactions
Velocity of money
Quantity of money
GDP velocity of money
Equation of exchange
Quantity theory of money
Deflation
Resumption
Labor

Land
Capital
Technology
Political stability
Greenback Party
Bimetallism
Hot money
Shock
Cross of Gold speech
Yuan or renminbi

Notes
You can compare the incomes of high school and college graduates in the Bureau of Census' *2011 Statistical Abstract*, Table 691. See www.census.gov/compendia/statab . The median household income of a high school graduate is $39,962. The median household income of a college graduate is $78,290. Believe me, odds are you're doing the right thing coming to college.

The story of Salmon Chase's efforts to extract loans from the New York bankers is told in Niven (pp. 264-67). The magnificent "thousand dollar breakfast" quote is on p. 266.

McPherson's Quartermaster list is on page 325 of his book, *Battle Cry of Freedom.*

Blue (1987, pp. 143-152) and Timberlake (1993, pp. 84-86) describe the problems of Civil War finance. Blue provides the quotes from Salmon P. Chase on the expenditure of millions (p. 136), on heavy taxes (p. 144), on the price of breakfast (p. 146), and on resorting to United States notes (p. 151). Blue (pp. 302-306) covers Chief Justice Chase's decision in the legal tender case.

McPherson (p.313-14) tells of Gustavus Fox's efforts to create a Navy big enough to blockade the south. McPherson writes of the military draft in the south (pp. 430-433) and in the Union (600-605). He quotes veteran troops' opinions of later draftees on page 606. The southern starvation quote also is from McPherson (p. 440), as are descriptions of wartime prosperity in the north (pp. 816-18). Catton describes the wartime boom in the northern economy (pp. 159-164). The "stout matron" quote from *Merchant Magazine* appears in Wagner, et. al. (p. 676). McPherson quotes Congressman Pendleton on paper money (p. 446).

Catton writes of Jay Cooke's war bond drives (p. 164). The proportions of taxes, borrowing and money printing for the Union come from McPherson (p. 447). McPherson gives the Confederate inflation rate, and the tax and printing amounts for the Confederacy are cited in Wagner (p. 669).

The description of Bryan's Cross of Gold speech is based on Bryan's memoir (1925, pp. 103-116) and Coletta (1964, pp. 137-142). Has there ever been a better speech about monetary policy?

My primary general sources for gold and silver monetary policy in the late 19th century are Friedman and Schwartz (1963) and Timberlake (1993). Timberlake (1993, pp. 88-91) discusses the immediate post-war policy of currency contraction (pp. 88-91). Friedman and Schwartz cover the politics of resumption and the greenback period to 1879 (pp. 44-50). Friedman and Schwartz's chapter on "Silver Politics and the Secular Decline in Prices" is excellent on the events leading up to the 1890s crisis (pp. 89-134). Timberlake's chapter on "The Fall of Silver" covers the repeal of the Sherman Silver Purchase Act in detail (pp. 166-182).

Lebergott describes the advances in steamship technology (pp. 347-349), the impact of railroads (p. 282), technological advance in steel production (p. 348), and in farming (p. 300). He also makes a persuasive argument for the positive effect of political stability on investment (pp. 350-351). Finally, he describes the increased competition which farmers and craft workers faced during the industrial revolution (p. 281).

Frieden (1997) thinks that the desire for a lower value of the dollar in foreign exchange markets was more a motivation for bimetallists than debt relief. Simon (1960) describes the movement of gold out of the U.S. in the weeks after Bryan's nomination. Bordo and Rockoff (1996) find that nations that successfully maintained the gold standard did better with international investors.

Milton Friedman--the most prominent conservative economist of our time--estimates that the U.S. economy would have been better off under bimetallism if maintained in the 1870s, but that by 1896 it was too late (Friedman, 1990a, 1990b).

The 1906 quote from Bryan is in Cherny (1985, pp. 104-106).

You can find some good discussions of China's policies in Sachs (2005, pp. 148-69) and Kynge (2007).

Sources

Bordo, Michael D. and Hugh Rockoff. 1996. "The Gold Standard as a 'Good Housekeeping Seal of Approval.'" *Journal of Economic History* 56:2 (June): 389-428.

Bryan, William J. and Mary Baird Bryan. 1925. *The Memoirs of William Jennings Bryan.* Chicago: The John C. Winston Company.

Catton, Bruce. 1985. *The Civil War.* New York: Houghton Mifflin Company.

Cherny, Robert W. 1985. *A Righteous Cause: The Life of William Jennings Bryan.* Boston: Little, Brown and Co.

Colette, Paolo. E. 1964. *William Jennings Bryan: I. Political Evangelist, 1860-1908.* Lincoln, Nebraska: University of Nebraska Press.

Frieden, Jeffry A. 1997. "Monetary Populism in Nineteenth Century America: An Open Economy Interpretation." *Journal of Economic History* 57:2 (June): 367-395.

Friedman, Milton and Anna Jacobson Schwartz. 1963. *A Monetary History of the United States, 1867-1960.* Princeton, New Jersey: Princeton University Press.

Friedman, Milton. 1990a. "Bimetallism Revisited." *Journal of Economic Perspectives* 4:4 (Fall): 1159-1194.

Kynge, James. 2007. *China Shakes the World.* Boston: Houghton Mifflin Company.

Lebergott, Stanley. 1984. *The Americans: An Economic Record.* New York: W. W. Norton and Company.

McPherson, James M. 1988. *The Battle Cry of Freedom.* New York: Oxford University Press.

Niven, John. 1995. *Salmon P. Chase: A Biography.* New York: Oxford University Press.

Sachs, Jeffrey D. 2005. *The End of Poverty.* New York: Penguin Books.

Simon, Matthew. 1960. "The Hot Money Movement and the Private Exchange Pool Proposal of 1896." *Journal of Economic History* 20:1 (March): 31-50.

Timberlake, Richard H. 1993. *Monetary Policy in the United States: An Intellectual and Institutional History.* Chicago: University of Chicago Press.

Wagner, Margaret E., Gary W. Gallagher and Paul Finkelman (eds.). *Civil War Desk Reference.* New York: Simon and Schuster, 2002.

News Articles

Bradsher, Keith. "China's Economy Slows, but Inflation Still Looms," *New York Times*, May 30, 2011.

Bradsher, Keith. "China's Economy Slows Slightly, but Inflation Remains a Worry," New York Times, May 11, 2011.

Dugger, Celia. "Cholera Epidemic Sweeping Across Crumbling Zimbabwe," *New York Times*, December 12, 2008.

Dugger, Celia. "Fragile Signs of Hope Emerging in the Gloom of Mugabe's Rule," *New York Times*, March 20, 2009.

Dugger, Celia. "Life in Zimbabwe: Wait for Useless Money," *New York Times*, October 2, 2008.Schneider, Howard. " China's $3 trillion dilemma: What to do with all that cash?" *Washington Post*, April 19, 2011.

Wassener, Bettina. "Chinese Currency Rises Above Key Level," *New York Times*, April 29, 2011.

Wines, Michael. "As Inflation Soars, Zimbabwe Economy Plunges*," New York Times,* February 7, 2007.

Wines, Michael. "Caps on Prices Only Deepen Zimbabweans' Misery," New York Times, August 2, 2007.

Wines, Michael. "Freeze on Wages Is Latest Step to Stanch Inflation in Zimbabwe," New York Times, September 1, 2007.

Wines, Michael. "Zimbabwe's Prices Rise 900%, Turning Staples Into Luxuries," *New York Times*, May 2, 2006.

Chapter 5
The Founding of the Fed

MacroPolicy Now: Contagious Fear

"Euro Crisis Looms," shouted a *New York Times* headline on May 25, 2011. It was just the latest in a series of financial crises that began afflicting world economies in 2007. This time, the article reported, lenders were becoming pessimistic about the prospects that Greece and Portugal could pay the interest on the money they had borrowed by selling bonds. Banks in France and Germany held vast amounts of the bonds from the problem countries. If the countries defaulted—failed to pay interest and principle on time—or if the payments were "restructured"—reduced and delayed—the bonds would be worth less (if not actually worthless).

That would reduce the wealth of the banks and other lenders all over the world who held these bonds. American banks hadn't lent much to Greece. But they were closely intertwined with many big European banks, which in turn had large investments in the weaker European nations. Policymakers feared "contagion," which meant that the problems in small countries like Greece could cause investors to stop lending in bigger countries like Spain and Italy.If Greece and Portugal failed to pay on its loans, Spain and Italy might not be able to pay on theirs. Lenders in France, Germany, and the United States would be strapped for cash themselves and might not be able to pay their own creditors. And they would surely cut back on new loans, trying to build reserves, just in case.

We know it can happen, because it had happened before. Just recently, in 2008.

Lehman Brothers was a 158-year-old Wall Street investment bank. Large businesses and investors would deposit their money with Lehman, which would make loans and buy assets, and earn large returns. By the middle of the 2000's it was earning profits hand-over-fist as a major player in the market for prime and subprime mortgages.

When the housing boom collapsed, however, the mortgages that Lehman had purchased began to default. Since these investments weren't paying off, their value dropped, and the firm wound up owing more to its depositors than its assets were worth. On Monday, September 15, 2008, Lehman Brothers filed for bankruptcy.

This was a major problem for those who had funds deposited with the investment bank, or counted Lehman Brothers stock among their assets. On Tuesday, a money market fund known as the Reserve Primary Fund revealed that it had "broken the buck" and would pay investors no more than 97 cents per dollar of deposits. The Reserve Primary Fund had lent $785 million to Lehman Brothers. Now that loan was worth little or nothing. The fund lacked the assets to pay out the full amount that their depositors expected.

If the Reserve Primary Fund could break the buck, so could others. Fear is contagious. Big institutional investors like pension funds and college endowments began pulling money out of money funds on the day Lehman went under. The next day individual investors joined the stampede. In what experts call a "flight to safety," investors were taking money out of money market funds, stocks, and bonds, and buying the safest investments in the world: Treasury securities. The interest rate earned on loans to the U.S. government dropped to near zero. People didn't expect a return on their money; they just wanted to keep it safe.

If money market funds couldn't keep their deposits, then they couldn't make loans. The loans, known as commercial paper, were made to big corporations like I.B.M. and Microsoft, and to smaller businesses, too. Suddenly it was hard for businesses to get commercial loans to stock inventories, pay vendors and creditors, or meet payrolls.

Hard Rock Park in Myrtle Beach, South Carolina, featured attractions like "Led Zeppelin: the Ride." Its owners declared bankruptcy because of their inability to refinance a $15 million revolving line of credit. "Due to the frozen credit markets," wrote Steven Goodwin, the company's chief executive and chief financial officer, the company "was unable to increase the size of the revolving facility as planned." Essentially, the park operator ran out of money and couldn't borrow more.

In 2008 the disaster on Wall Street was visited on Main Street. Would contagious fear do the same in 2011?

History rhymes. The panic in 2008 looks a lot like the panic of 1907. In 2008 banks and other lenders poured money into risky investments. In 1907 banks and other lenders poured money into risky investments. In 2008 financial firms were so intertwined that the failure of one caused the failure of others. It happened in 1907 too. And in 2008 the troubles in financial markets spilled over into the economy, causing unemployment and bankruptcy. Ditto back then. There's one advantage to looking back to the Panic of 1907. We know what happened next. . . .

The nation was prosperous. The "Great Depression" of the 1890s was fading from memory, as was the long price deflation. Output was growing, unemployment was down. The economic thinkers of the day called the decade between the mid-1890s and the mid-19-aughts "the most unexampled prosperity in our history."

San Francisco shared in the boom. With its superb natural harbor and easy access to inland farms and mines, it had a population of 350,000 by 1900. It had grown ten-fold in the previous half-century, and was the ninth largest city in the country, by far the largest west of the Mississippi River. International trade helped drive the city's growth. Most western grain exports were financed by San Francisco banks. Great Britain was a particularly important trading partner, and many British banks maintained branch offices in San Francisco.

Then, at 5:13 a.m. on Wednesday, April 18, a shift in a three hundred mile section of the San Andreas Fault in northern California caused a devastating earthquake. Recent estimates put the earthquake's magnitude at just less than eight on the Richter scale. The ground shook violently for almost a minute. When it was done, thousands of buildings had been damaged and 800 people were dead.

Then the fire started. The city was build of wood—lumber was the cheapest, most plentiful building material—and the quake had destroyed the water mains. The chief engineer of the fire department had been mortally injured in the quake, leaving the department without experienced leadership. The fire burned for four days and destroyed almost five square miles of the city. More than 2,000 people died in the fire, and more than half the city's population was left homeless. Damage was estimated at half a billion dollars, which was nearly two percent of United States Gross Domestic Product.

Seismographs around the world felt the force of the 1906 earthquake. The world also felt its economic effects.

Great Britain was the world's dominant economy in 1906. British insurance companies provided a large amount of the fire insurance for San Francisco. They were avalanched with insurance claims. At first the insurance companies resisted, asserting that the buildings were destroyed by the quake, not the fire, so the insurers were not liable. The prospects of bad publicity and legal actions before San Francisco juries convinced the insurers to pay. British insurers eventually paid about $50 million in claims.

San Francisco property owners wanted payment in dollars, of course, so British insurance companies tried to trade their pounds for dollars. Dollars were soon in short supply. So the British traded their pounds for gold, put it on ships and transported it across the Atlantic, where it was exchanged for dollars at the U.S. Treasury.

Great Britain was on the gold standard (as were all developed countries), which meant that the country's money supply was based on its stock of gold. Britain's central bank, the Bank of England, became concerned about the effect of this gold drain on the nation's money supply. So, in the fall of 1906 they increased interest rates and encouraged British banks to stop lending to U.S. borrowers. These policies worked. Gold began to flow out of the United States to Great Britain; the U.S. gold stock decreased by ten percent.

The United States had no central bank to counter this gold flow, so the U.S. money supply began to shrink. This increased interest rates. In addition, businesses were unable to borrow from British lenders, so they turned to American banks. The higher demand for loans increased interest rates some more. Higher interest rates reduced investment spending. Real GDP growth slowed to a stop by mid-1907.

The nation was edging into recession by the autumn of 1907. To see how this recession turned to panic, we need to know something about how banks work.

At the financial center of the growing economy were the very big, very profitable New York banks. Then, as now, the banks received *deposits* from people and businesses. They earned profits by lending these deposits for investments. Borrowers used the loans to build homes, to build new factories and buy equipment, sometimes for speculation in land or stocks. People and businesses paid back these loans, plus interest, out of their profits and incomes. Banks paid interest to their depositors with these repayments, and what remained was profit.

Of course, once in a while a depositor wanted his or her money back. Banks kept *reserves* to meet these *withdrawals*. Not all deposits were loaned. Some portion was kept in cash in the vault, or in really *liquid* assets that could be sold for cash fast. These reserves were almost always enough to meet the daily demands of depositors. Most days, the difference between the amount people withdrew and the amount they deposited was pretty small, and often the amount deposited was more than the amount withdrawn.

Almost always. *Most* days.

Sometimes people and businesses would begin to worry that the bank didn't have the funds to pay back their deposits. Sometimes they worried so much that they showed up at the door demanding to withdraw all their funds. That's called a *bank run*. Sometimes, so many people showed up that the bank ran out of reserves, and couldn't pay all the depositors in the line. The bank would have to sell its assets, fast, and if the prices it received were too low, it wouldn't have enough to pay its depositors. The bank would fail. Even worse, sometimes this happened to many banks all over the country all at once.

Banks very sensibly would respond by trying to increase their reserves. If they had enough reserves on hand when a bank run started, depositors would see that they could get their money, so their worries would fade. Keeping more reserves meant making fewer loans. Fewer loans meant less investment spending. Output would fall and employment would decline. That's what happened in the Panic of 1907.

Agriculture was once much more important in the United States economy than it is today. The Census of 1900 reported that 36% of Americans workers were employed on farms (it's less than 2% today). Each fall when the grain was harvested it would be transported from the west where it was grown, to the east where most people lived, and where it could be exported to Europe. Buyers of grain would withdraw their funds from banks to pay farmers. Shippers would withdraw their funds from banks to pay railroads. Railroads would withdraw their funds from banks to pay employees. Banks had to build their reserves in order to pay all these withdrawals.

This meant that each fall, money was "tight." Loans from banks were hard to come by, because banks needed all their reserves and then some for the harvest-time withdrawals. With less money available for lending, interest rates would increase. With fewer loans, home or factory construction declined, and construction workers would be laid off. Most years the economy muddled through this seasonal money predicament.

In the fall of 1907, though, money was already tight. The money supply was dropping as gold flowed to Britain. British lenders were still refusing to lend to Americans. The usual harvest season demand for money was in full swing. In normal years, what happened next might not have been a problem. In 1907, it was.

F. Augustus Heinze was a millionaire copper magnate from Montana. In October 1907 Heinze and a partner tried to corner the stock of a large copper company. Cornering the stock of a company meant buying so much of it that one could charge anyone who wanted to buy its stock a very high price. On October 16, 1907, Heinze's attempt to corner the copper stock failed. He had paid high prices to acquire a great deal of copper stock, but couldn't buy enough to dictate the price himself. He now had a huge number of shares, most worth less than he had paid for them.

Some of the money for Heinze's venture came from a lender called the Knickerbocker Trust. At the time trusts were like banks, only newer. They had grown to be important lenders only in the previous decade, and bank regulations had not yet caught up with them. They kept smaller reserves than banks, paid higher interest rates on deposits, and made loans that were more risky.

> *The San Francisco earthquake, harvest season withdrawals and a failed stock speculation helped cause the Panic of 1907.*
> *Banking troubles caused a drop in lending to businesses, and a recession resulted.*

The Knickerbocker Trust Company's depositors saw Heinze's failure, and realized that a lot of his lost money was in fact their money loaned to him by Knickerbocker. They suspected that the Trust was in trouble, and so decided to withdraw their deposits. A run on the Knickerbocker Trust began on October 18.

The nation's most important banker, J. Pierpont Morgan, recognized the danger and organized a fund to lend to troubled trusts. The trusts would use the loans to pay their depositors. Depositors would find that they could withdraw their money with no problem, their panic would subside and the run would end. But which trusts deserved to be saved? Not the Knickerbocker, Morgan decided. They'd made too many bad loans. On the morning of October 22 the trust paid out its remaining $8 million in reserves, then closed its doors. It had failed.

Banks all over New York—and all over the country—watched with apprehension. Panics like this could spread nationwide.

And sure enough, the panic didn't end with Knickerbocker. Attention turned to the Trust Company of America, another trust whose directors were associated with Heinze. A newspaper article in the *New York Times* comparing the two Trusts may have created anxiety.

It was evident on Tuesday, October 22, that the Trust Company was facing a run. Morgan sent Ben Strong, a young up-and-coming banker, to examine the company's books. He worked through the night, and in the morning he reported to Morgan. The old man had just one question. "Are they solvent?" Strong said their reserves were almost gone. Morgan already knew that. He'd heard from the bank's director, that they had barely a million dollars left, and that it wouldn't last the day. "Are they solvent?" he asked again. Strong said their assets were intact, more or less. Most of the loans they'd made were good; they just couldn't be sold for cash fast enough.

"Should we see them through?" Morgan asked. Strong said yes. "This is the place to stop the trouble, then," J. Pierpont Morgan said.

When they opened Wednesday morning Trust Company directors found a line of their depositors snaking out into Wall Street. Every last one wanted to withdraw funds. It was clear that the Trust would fail without help. By 2:15 in the afternoon the trust's reserves were down to $180,000. Receiving word from Morgan, Trust Company officers carried boxes of securities to his office, as collateral for a loan. Morgan deposited three million dollars in cash with the Trust. The Trust met the demands of its depositors, and word that Morgan was lending helped calm fears. The Trust Company of America survived.

Then the trouble switched to the stock market. Banks and Trusts lent money to stock investors, to buy shares. The shares acted as collateral on the loans. If the lender wanted its money back, the stock could be sold and the loan paid off. Ordinarily this was a very liquid sort of loan, because stocks could be sold for cash quickly in the stock market. Loans for things like houses, land and factories were much less liquid, because it took time to find buyers and negotiate prices in order to sell them.

Lenders thought it was prudent to build up their reserves, to have enough to pay depositors in case there was a bank run. To build up their reserves, banks and trusts demanded repayment of their most liquid loans, those to stock market investors. The trouble was, lots of banks were trying to build reserves, so lots of investors tried to sell shares to repay loans. Not many investors were buying. Stock prices began to fall. As they did, the prices investors got for their shares weren't enough to allow them to repay their loans. Banks that thought they had lent money on the good collateral of stock shares found that the collateral wasn't so good, after all. Prices fell so much that the head of the stock exchange considered closing it.

Had investors been able to borrow funds from other sources, they could have paid off their loans without selling shares. This would slow the decline in stock prices. But British banks weren't lending, and it was October, harvest time. Money was tight. Again J.P. Morgan stepped in. On Thursday, October 24 he organized a group of bankers who pledged $24 million in stock market loans. On Friday he found another $10 million. The panic subsided, and the exchange remained open.

Probably the panic would have been worse had Morgan not acted. But the damage was done. Trusts and banks lend each other money, and have deposits with each other.

People do business with more than one bank. If one bank fails, other banks may lose their deposits or not have their loans repaid. If borrowers have their loans called by one bank in trouble, they may withdraw their funds from another bank. Financial difficulties and bank runs can spread like a disease. So economists call it *contagion*.

Seeing the problems in New York, banks around the country began building up their reserves. Many of them had deposits with the New York banks, and tried to withdraw them. Depositors around the country began withdrawing funds, too. Finally banks "suspended payments", meaning they refused to pay out cash to depositors, while continuing to clear checks and accept deposits.

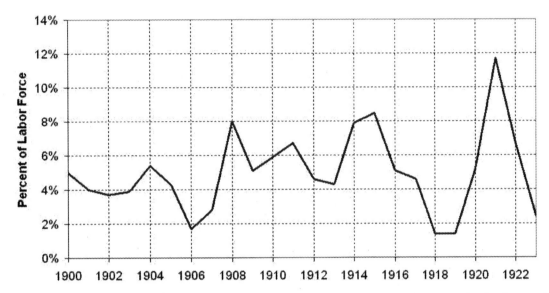

Figure 5-1. Unemployment Rate, 1900-1923. Prosperity in the "aughts" drove the unemployment rate below 2%, but the Panic of 1907 increased it to 8% in 1908. The rate was back below 2% in 1918 and 1919. The deep recession in 1920-21 increased it almost to 12%, the highest rate of the century other than the Great Depression.

Investment spending was already down, because interest rates were high and loans were hard to get. Now, with the shortage of cash, shopping became more difficult, and sales fell. Factories laid off workers, who also stopped buying. Unemployment increased more. Output fell 8% in 1908, unemployment increased from 3% of the labor force in 1907 to 8% in 1908. Prices fell 4%. It became one of the sharpest recessions in U.S. history. Mercifully, it was short. The Bank of England reversed its lending restrictions, and the underlying economy was in good shape. Recovery began by the end of 1908.

Money and Banks
The panic of 1907 decreased the nation's money supply, beyond the gold outflows to Britain. To see why, we need to know about something called the *multiple expansion of bank deposits*. Or, in the case of a panic, the multiple *contraction* of bank deposits.

Consider Table 5-1. Suppose $1,000 in cash is deposited in a bank. Suppose that it is the bank's policy to keep 20% of deposits in reserve—to handle withdrawals—and to lend 80% in mortgage loans or business loans. Of that $1,000 deposit, the bank will reserve $200 and lend $800.

Who borrowed the $800? Perhaps a shopkeeper wanting to buy one of those new-fangled Model T automobiles. He pays the Ford dealer, and the dealer deposits the $800 in his own bank. That's a new deposit for his bank, which now reserves 20%, and lends 80%. The bank keeps $160 in new reserves and lends $640. The borrower spends the $640, perhaps on a trip to Chicago to watch the Cubs in the World Series, and the ticket seller deposits the $640 in his bank. The process continues. The total deposits created are much more than the initial deposit.

Table 5-1

Deposits	Reserves (20%)	Loans (80%)
$1,000	$200	$800
$800	$160	$640
$640	$128	$512
$512	$102	$410
$410	$82	$328
. . .		
Eventual Totals		
$5,000	$1,000	$4,000

How much more? As the table shows, if the process continued down to fractions of pennies, the total added deposits would be $5,000. We know this because the *money multiplier* shows the total new deposits generated by added reserves. The money multiplier is calculated as

Money multiplier = 1 / rr

where "rr" is the reserve ratio. When the reserve ratio is 0.2 (20%), the money multiplier is 5, and an initial $1,000 deposit creates $5,000 in total deposits. When the reserve ratio is 0.1 (10%), the initial $1,000 deposit creates $10,000 in total deposits.

Bank reserves plus the money in circulation outside of banks are known as the *monetary base*. The money multiplier times the monetary base is the total money supply. So the money supply has two components: the monetary base, made up of bank reserves and circulating money, and the money multiplier, which depends on the share of deposits that banks reserve. Or, in other words, the money multiplier depends on the banks' willingness to lend.

> *The monetary base is reserves in banks plus currency in circulation. The money multiplier depends on banks' willingness to lend. The product of the two is the money supply.*

This means that the reserve ratio will help determine the quantity of money. If banks reserve more, the quantity of money will be less. If banks reserve less, the quantity of money will be more. Another way to think of the money multiplier is the relationship between the monetary base and money created. The money multiplier shows the quantity of money that the monetary base will support.

Table 5-2

Deposits	Reserves (50%)	Loans (50%)
$1,000	$500	$500
$500	$250	$250
$250	$125	$125
$125	$63	$63
$63	$31	$31
...		
Eventual Totals		
$2,000	$1,000	$1,000

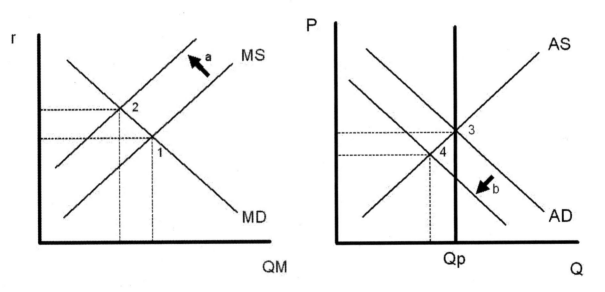

Figure 5-2. Panic in 1907. Gold flows from the U.S. to Britain, and banks increase their reserves to head off bank runs. Both the gold stock and the money multiplier decline, which reduces the money supply (a). The real interest rate increases (1 to 2). Second shift #2 reduces investment spending, and so decreases aggregate demand (b). Output and the price level fall (3 to 4). That's recession and deflation. Morgan hoped to head off bank runs with emergency loans, so banks wouldn't have to increase reserves. This would have reduced the size of the MS shift (a).

What happened during the Panic of 1907? Banks began reserving more of their deposits, for fear of bank runs. The reserve ratio increased, so the money multiplier decreased. If the reserve ratio is (say) 50% instead of 20%, the loan numbers are lower, so the deposits are lower too. In total, the same $1,000 monetary base would support only $2,000 in money supply. Because banks got scared, the money supply got smaller. Compare the deposit numbers in Table 5-2 to those in Table 5-1. When banks reserve 50% instead of 20%, a lot less in deposits are created. When the reserve ratio goes up, the money supply contracts.

Banks reserve more and lend less. This reduces the money multiplier and the money supply. The real interest rate rises, loans are harder to come by, and investment spending falls (that's second shift #2). This reduces aggregate demand, which reduces output. A recession results.

The Federal Reserve

The nation had been prosperous. Within two years it was prosperous again. It seemed that the panic and recession had been unnecessary, caused by a one-time disaster out west, the actions of the British central bank, and the ambitions of a few New York speculators. It spread because of contagion in the banking system, made worse because it was harvest time and money was tight. If the consequences of those actions had been nipped in the bud—as Morgan tried but only partially succeeding in doing—and if the banking system had been less vulnerable to panic, perhaps the recession could have been avoided. Congress began to consider reform.

The outlines of what was needed were clear. Somehow, the money supply had to be made *elastic*. This meant that when the demand for currency increased, as it did during disasters and during harvest every fall, additional currency could be supplied without forcing banks to build reserves, call in loans and restrict investment. In addition, the banking system needed a source of emergency reserves. Some agency needed to do what J.P. Morgan had done—lend emergency cash to banks with good loans as collateral—only on a bigger scale and in the public interest. The banking system needed a *lender of last resort*, to lend to banks when no one else was lending.

There may have been consensus on what to accomplish, but *how* to accomplish it was another matter. Bankers, and many of their Republican allies, had long advocated the creation of a central bank. They looked to the tradition of Alexander Hamilton, who had created a central bank in the nation's early days. A central bank would be a "banker's bank," one which could increase and decrease the supply of money when needed, and provide banks with reserves in emergencies. There would be one big bank in New York or Washington, like the Bank of England in London. Only a big bank would have reserves enough for the nation's whole banking system. It would be owned and controlled by bankers, because only they had the expertise. It would *not* be controlled by political leaders, for fear that interest rates would become the tool of the political parties in every election year.

Most Democrats opposed the creation of a central bank. This was a long party tradition, going back to Andrew Jackson in the 1830s. Jackson had engineered the destruction of the early U.S. central bank. It was a newer party tradition, too. The old silver Democrats remembered the bankers as their gold-standard opponents during the long deflation.

Democrats feared that a central bank would be run as a monopoly for the benefit of bankers. The central bank would cooperate with bankers to keep interest rates high, and sometimes even *cause* panics. Many thought that panics were profitable for bankers. They earned high interest on the emergency loans they issued. J.P. Morgan probably did make a profit with his actions to stop the bank runs and stock panic in 1907.

On May 30, 1908, the Congress passed and President Teddy Roosevelt signed the Aldrich-Vreeland Act, named after Nelson Aldrich from the Senate and Edward Vreeland from the House. The new law included some temporary measures to try to halt panics, and it set up a National Monetary Commission to study the issue of currency reform and banking regulation. The Commission worked for four years and issued a report in 1912. The report became the basis for a reform debate in 1913. The debate resulted in legislation that established the *Federal Reserve.*

The debate took place under political conditions that had not existed for more than half a century. The Democrats had gained power in the 1912 elections. Democrat Woodrow Wilson had been elected President, and both houses of Congress had Democratic majorities. The Democrats would write the reform legislation, and they were not going to create a central bank if they could help it. (Incidentally, President Wilson appointed old William Jennings Bryan Secretary of State and young Franklin D. Roosevelt Assistant Secretary of the Navy. Both the history and future of macroeconomic policy were part of his administration.)

> **The Federal Reserve became the U.S. central bank with the power to influence interest rates using monetary policy. It was established in 1913.**

Legislators proposed a solution for keeping monopoly power out of the hands of a central bank: create not one bank, but many. How many? Democrats wanted a lot, perhaps one in each state, while Republicans wanted not more than three or four. Eventually Congress compromised at 12 regional banks. The thought was that with 12, every banker in the country would be a night's train ride from a regional bank. If he needed cash, he could carry a bundle of securities on a train ride to his regional bank, get a loan, and send a telegram before his bank opened the next day telling his depositors that they need not panic.

Even the Democrats thought that the 12 regional banks needed some central coordination. Sometimes, for example, the reserves of one regional bank might not be enough to stop a panic, and a central body could direct other regional banks to help. Supporters of a central bank hoped this body would become a central bank, opponents feared that it would. The compromise was a board in Washington, known as the Federal Reserve Board, with limited power over the actions of the regional banks. The Secretary of the Treasury was made chair of the Reserve Board, so someone directly responsible to the President would have a say in policy decisions.

Since legislators thought they were creating something that was *not* a central bank, little attention was given to the goals of Federal Reserve *monetary policy*. What criteria should the Fed use in setting interest rates, influencing the quantity of money, or deciding which banks deserved loans? Questions that would concern the Fed in coming years were not the subject of much debate.

There was another reason for the lack of policy guidance. Many on all sides of the debate thought that monetary policy would be automatic. First, the nation would remain on the gold standard. The Federal Reserve Act said explicitly that the gold standard was not to be repealed, even though the Act established a new institution with money-creating powers. Gold would provide a ceiling on the amount of money the Fed could issue. There had to be a gold reserve of 40%, meaning that the Treasury had to have in its vaults 40 cents in gold for every one Federal Reserve note. The Fed's new currency would be elastic underneath this ceiling.

Second, it was thought that under the gold standard ceiling, the increase and decrease in the money supply would be determined by the course of business. When business activity increased, businesses would borrow from banks on pledges to repay from the sales of newly produced goods and services. Bank reserves would decline. The banks would then borrow from the Fed, using as collateral the pledged repayment of the loans they had made to businesses. The Fed would charge an interest rate for their lending, known as the *discount rate*.

The discount rate could be used as a tool of monetary policy. If the Fed raises its discount rate, banks would be discouraged from borrowing. They would have less to lend to their customers and would raise their own interest rates. If the Fed cuts its discount rate, banks would be encouraged to borrow more. They would have more to lend and would reduce their own interest rates. But the discount rate was not viewed as a policy tool at first.

The money supply would expand automatically as business needs expanded. When the need for funds was less, banks would redeem their loans from the Fed. The money supply would contract. This was known as the "real bills" doctrine, because the Fed was supposed to lend only to banks that had as collateral loans (*bills*) made for the production and distribution of *real* goods and services (not on loans for stock or real estate speculation).

> *The Fed can influence interest rates using its discount rate, which is the rate at which it lends to banks. The discount rate influences the interest rates that banks charge their customers.*

This is why no one thought to give the Fed much guidance about its monetary policy goals. The Fed, they thought, was not a central bank, and not in the business of monetary policy. The gold standard established the general level of the money supply. The issue and retirement of Federal Reserve notes through Fed lending provided the seasonal and emergency adjustments. It was expected to operate automatically, like a public utility.

President Woodrow Wilson signed the Federal Reserve Act on December 23, 1913. Within a year, the world for which the Federal Reserve was created was gone.

World War I

The Great War that we now call World War I began in Europe in August, 1914. The United States was determined to stay neutral. Neutral, but not out of it. As a rapidly growing industrial power with close trade ties to the combatants, the United States had to be affected by a big war. England and France looked to the United States for war material and food. Other countries looked to the U.S. for the goods they had been importing from England, France and Germany. U.S. exports increased beyond imports. Some exports were paid for with gold, so gold receipts exceeded gold payments. Gold flowed into the U.S.

The U.S. had been in recession in 1914. This meant that there was extra capacity—unused factories, unemployed workers—that allowed an increase in output and exports as the money supply increased. There was not much inflation at first. Once the economy reached capacity, though, the gold inflows and rising money supply fueled inflation. The inflation rate jumped from one percent in 1915 to almost eight percent in 1916.

The inflation was the result of the normal workings of the gold standard (in abnormal times). The U.S. was exporting much more than it was importing, so gold inflows created inflation. Rising U.S. prices would make U.S. goods less attractive. Ordinarily, this would have discouraged other countries from importing from the U.S., and encouraged Americans to import from other countries (at their lower prices). Falling exports and rising imports would have balanced trade and stopped the gold inflow.

A Federal Reserve Note from 1918. Treasury Secretary Carter Glass had the good taste not to use a picture of himself on the one dollar bill. Each regional bank issued currency with its name prominently displayed.

But like the U.S. in the Civil War, during the Great War Great Britain and France left the gold standard. They experienced more inflation than the U.S., despite the outflow of gold. And, combatant nations were willing to pay any price to import what they needed. The increase in the U.S. price level did not slow U.S. exports. Inflation continued.

The United States declared war on Germany on April 6, 1917. No more gold flowed into the United States from England and France. The U.S. provided its new allies with credits to finance needed war materials, to be repaid after the war. The U.S. began importing more materials, so gold began flowing out of the country. Eventually exports of gold were restricted.

The U.S. government built an army, and spending on soldiers' pay and on military equipment increased a lot. Though the income tax had been invented only a few years before, less than one-third of this new spending was paid for with taxes. Instead, as during the Civil War, the war effort was financed by borrowing and money creation. Not Treasury greenbacks this time, but Federal Reserve notes. As during the Civil War, this caused inflation. The inflation rate topped 17% in 1917 and 1918.

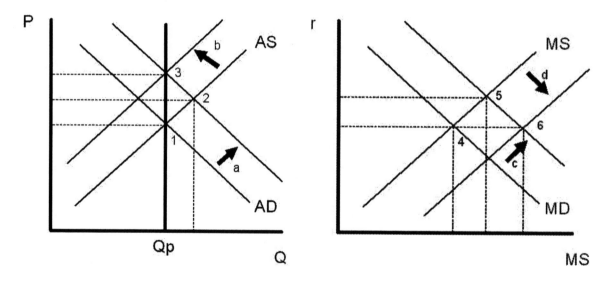

Figure 5-3. Paying for World War I. The war increases government military purchases, which increases aggregate demand (a). Output and prices rise (1 to 2). This increases money demand (c), because of second shift #3, which would raise the interest rate (4 to 5) and restrain aggregate demand through second shift #2 (back from 2 towards 1). But the Fed expands the money supply (d), in order to keep interest rates low (6). With interest rates remaining low, the shift from 2 back towards 1 does not happen. Output is beyond potential (2). As wages and resource costs rise, aggregate supply decreases (b). That's second shift #1. In the end, the higher money supply results in higher prices at the original level of output (3).

The financial arrangements were more sophisticated than they had been fifty years before. The government borrowed from the public to pay for war expenses, by selling war bonds. Banks would borrow money from the Fed to lend for bond purchases, and to buy them themselves. To make this pay, the Treasury had to pay an interest rate on its borrowing that was higher than the Fed's discount rate. It was the Fed's patriotic duty, the Treasury said, to keep the discount rate low. If the Fed kept interest rates low, it would cost the Treasury less to borrow all that money for the war effort.

The Fed kept interest rates low during the war. This caused inflation. The increase in military purchases increases aggregate demand. Soldiers are employed and paid, factories gear up to produce munitions. Output and income increase. This raises money demand through second shift #3, since more money is needed to handle the added transactions that the war and higher incomes create. To keep interest rates low with rising money demand, the Fed must increase the money supply. Federal Reserve notes made their first appearance as circulating currency.

The rise in the money supply "accommodates" inflation. Inflation cannot be sustained without a money supply increase. If rising aggregate demand pushes output beyond potential, eventually wages and other resource costs will rise. Second shift #1 sets in. Producing output will become more costly, so aggregate supply will decrease. This creates more inflation. Ultimately, the higher money supply is translated into higher prices, with no change in total output.

> *Counter-cyclical policy tries to stabilize the economy, decreasing spending when inflation threatens and increasing spending when recession is a problem. Pro-cyclical policy makes each problem worse, destabilizing the economy.*

This was a *pro-cyclical* policy. Aggregate demand expands and the Fed reduces interest rates, which increases aggregate demand even more. A *counter-cyclical* policy would require the opposite, to battle inflation by trying to restrain aggregate demand. The money supply would be decreased, causing higher interest rates. Investment spending would decline and the growth of aggregate demand would slow. In wartime, the nation had other priorities.

Post –War Inflation and Recession

The war was won, the Armistice signed in November 1918. In 1919 government spending on soldiers and equipment fell drastically. After a brief downturn, though, the economy boomed. Consumers wanted to spend their war-time savings on consumer goods. Businesses wanted to meet these demands and those of the war damaged nations for U.S. exports. Businesses financed production by borrowing from banks, and the banks borrowed (and borrowed and borrowed) from the Federal Reserve.

The last "Victory Loan" bond drive had ended in May 1919, but the Fed kept the discount rate low. In those early days there was no tradition against continuous borrowing from the Fed, so banks kept borrowing. They lent their funds at a high interest rate, and replenished their reserves with funds borrowed from the Fed at the lower discount rate.

All this borrowing increased the money supply, and increased aggregate demand. Inflation continued in double-digits.

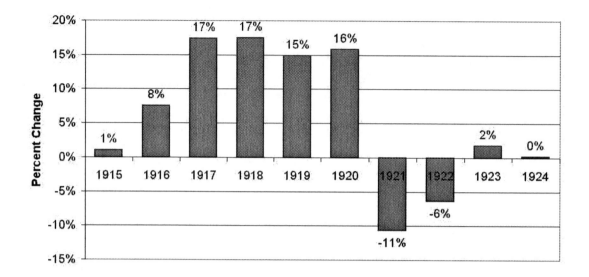

Figure 5-4. Consumer Price Inflation, 1915-1924. World War I resulted in double-digit inflation, which lasted for two years after the end of the war. The sharp 1920-21 recession resulted in deflation. The 11% deflation in 1921 was the sharpest single year drop in prices during the century.

Now began the first debate that included the new Federal Reserve. Some regional bank leaders saw the inflation, the borrowing and the increasing money supply and advocated an increase in the discount rate. A higher discount rate would make borrowing from the Fed more expensive, so banks would borrow less. Ben Strong, J.P. Morgan's old protégé and now the head of the New York Federal Reserve Bank, began to worry about inflation early in 1919. By August he was praying to be "released from this government borrowing bondage [to be] able to deal with money rates on sound lines." He wanted the discount rate ("money rates") raised to battle inflation, not limited by the needs of the Treasury to borrow. Strong wanted a counter-cyclical monetary policy.

Strong was the most forceful personality in the Federal Reserve System, but the authority belonged to Carter Glass. In the early days of the Fed the Secretary of the Treasury was also chair of the Federal Reserve Board. Carter Glass was the Treasury Secretary, so he naturally opposed an increase in the discount rate. His main concern was the cost of the government's borrowing and war time debt. The higher were interest rates on Treasury borrowing, the more costly this debt would be. Strong threatened to raise the New York Fed's discount rate without the approval of Washington. Glass threatened to have President Wilson dismiss him from his post. Throughout most of 1919, Carter Glass got his way.

This was an argument about policy, but also about power. Strong represented New York, Glass represented Washington. Strong was, to his supporters, the spokesman for banker expertise and sound money. To his detractors, he was the tool of the Wall Street money trust. Glass was, to his supporters, the spokesman of the people and a patriot trying to keep war costs down. To his detractors, he was the symbol of crass political influence on economic policy.

Strong had contracted tuberculosis in 1916 and never really recovered. On doctor's orders he left on a world-wide rest tour in December 1919. The New York Fed's interim leaders carried on Strong's fight. In January 1920 they recommended another increase in the discount rate, this time to 5 1/2%. They were astonished when Secretary Glass demanded a rate increase to 6%! A new problem had appeared. The government was required to have 40 cents in gold for every one dollar in paper notes. This was the gold standard ceiling on the Fed's actions. All that bank borrowing at the discount rate was increasing the stock of Federal Reserve notes. The ratio of notes to gold had been near 50 cents per dollar at the start of 1919. Now it was down to 43 cents, and falling.

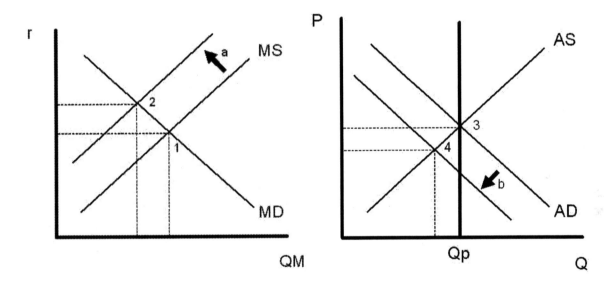

Figure 5-5. Irony. These are the same diagrams as Figure 5-2, only this time the Federal Reserve is reducing the money supply (a), causing an increase in the real interest rate (1 to 2). The higher interest rate reduces investment spending, which reduces aggregate demand (b). That's second shift #2. The Fed held the discount rate too high for too long, and aggregate demand dropped below potential output (3 to 4). Recession and deflation result. Eventually, wages and other resources costs fall and aggregate supply increases, returning output to potential at a lower price level. That's second shift #1, not shown on the diagram.

Glass said that something had to be done, or the U.S. would have to leave the gold standard. A rise in the discount rate would stop bank borrowing, so new Federal Reserve note issues would slow. And, with interest rates higher, international investors would see the U.S. as a good place to keep their wealth. Gold would flow in. The discount rate was raised the next day. The 1 1/4 percent increase remains the biggest single-day discount rate hike in Fed history.

The impact was sudden, and huge. Banks stopped borrowing from the Fed and stopped lending to businesses and consumers. Consumption and investment spending dropped. Inflation stopped. A recession began. By mid-year the downturn accelerated, becoming one of the sharpest in U.S. history. Unemployment jumped from 1.4% in 1919 to 11.7% in 1921. Prices fell almost 11% in 1921, the largest single year decline in the history of the Consumer Price Index.

Ironically, the diagram that describes the Panic of 1907 is the same as the diagram that describes the Fed's 1920 policy (compare Figures 5-2 and 5-5). A dramatic decline in the money supply raises interest rates and triggers a recession.

In 1907 the recession created the Fed. In 1920, the Fed created the recession. This monetary policy business was going to be tricky.

The Roaring Twenties and Open Market Operations
The 1920s roared. The economy recovered quickly from the very sharp 1920-21 recession. From that point through 1929, the decade saw only two mild recessions. Output grew an average of 6.1% per year above inflation from 1921 to 1929, the highest decade-long peacetime rate in the twentieth century. Unemployment and inflation stayed low. Technological improvements increased productivity.

The lives of ordinary people changed more in the 1920's than ever before. Automobiles became commonplace. A Ford Model T cost the average worker two years' pay before the War; by the end of the '20's a Model A cost only three months pay. With the new installment buying plans, owning a car was even easier. Electricity brought light to cities (though not to most rural areas). By the end of the decade 70% of factories were powered by electricity. Families gathered around that technological marvel, radio, to listen to their favorite network programs. Radio had barely existed before 1920. Movies provided another new form of entertainment, and by the end of the decade they talked. Lindberg flew the Atlantic to point out the possibilities of air travel.

"The man who builds a factory builds a temple," said President Calvin Coolidge. "The man who works there worships there." "Everybody ought to be rich," said John Raskob of General Motors in the *Ladies Home Journal*.

It seemed that there wasn't much reason for the Federal Government to make economic policy. President Coolidge did as little as possible. He said "If the Federal Government should go out of existence, the common run of people would not detect the difference in the affairs of their daily life for a considerable length of time." A White House usher said that no President ever slept as much as Coolidge.

Over at the Federal Reserve, policymakers weren't asleep. But with no financial panic to fight, and no war to finance, what was to be the Fed's mission? During the 1920s they

133

worked one out: stabilize the domestic economy, and maintain balance in international trade.

To accomplish these goals, the Federal Reserve had discovered a new policy tool. The regional banks would sometimes buy Treasury securities, the bonds issued by the Federal government to borrow when spending was more than tax revenues. The Federal Reserve banks would buy these assets, using the interest earnings on the bonds to cover their expenses like employee payrolls.

The Fed soon noticed that buying these bonds had an economic effect. It increased the money supply. When the Fed buys bonds, it creates new money to pay for them. This money finds its way into bank reserves, allowing banks to lend more. Added lending means more investment in buildings and equipment by businesses, more purchases of homes and cars by families. Banks attract new borrowers by reducing interest rates. On the other hand, selling bonds for money soaks up bank reserves. Banks pay for bonds with money, so they have less available for lending. They raise interest rates, and this reduces investment and purchases. By 1923, the Fed had learned that these *open market operations*—the buying and selling of government bonds—could influence interest rates, the money supply, and ultimately economic activity. The Federal Reserve Board in Washington established an Open Market Investment Committee, made up of board members and regional bank officials, to coordinate bond sales and purchases among the regional banks.

In 1913, just ten years before, the Fed had been created to be anything but a central bank. It was to be an association of regional banks to provide for harvest-time increases in the money supply, and to be an emergency lender, a lender of last resort. Its operations were to be virtually automatic. Now it had a national and international policy mission, with policy established by a committee in Washington, and the tools to influence economic activity at will.

> **The Fed can influence interest rates using open market operations. Buying and selling of Treasury bonds influence bank reserves, which influences interest rates.**

The Fed's first opportunity to use its new open market tool came in 1923. The economy had grown very rapidly for two years. Now inflation appeared to be a threat. The Fed responded by selling government securities. The banks used their reserves to buy these securities, and so had less to lend to businesses and consumers. They raised interest rates. Businesses invested less, consumers spent less, and the economy slowed. Growth dropped from 12% per year in 1923 to near zero in 1924, a mild recession. The Fed reversed course and bought securities in 1924. Banks had more funds to lend, spending increased, and growth resumed at a more moderate pace. Mission accomplished: domestic growth and prices were stabilized.

Trouble for the Gold Standard

The United States was on a *gold standard*, though in the first half of the 1920s much of the rest of the world was not. The major powers had left gold during the Great War. Only in 1925 did Great Britain resume the gold standard; France waited until 1928.

Resuming the gold standard was thought desirable by most of the world's central banks. It was the system that had facilitated a great expansion of trade and development for decades before the Great War. It was a system that discouraged inflation, because nations could only issue currency backed by a gold reserve. It was a system that encouraged saving and investment, because people could be confident that the value of their currency would stay the same, year after year. It encouraged trade, because exporters and importers could count on fixed exchange rates.

The gold standard was also a system that balanced trade between nations. It was supposed to work like this. Each nation set its currency value based on gold. The United States Treasury pledged to exchange one ounce of gold with anyone for $20.67. Great Britain pledged to exchange one ounce of gold for about four and a quarter pounds. The exchange rate between dollars and pounds was determined by these fixed gold prices at $4.86 per pound. This had been the dollar-pound exchange rate for as long as anyone could remember.

Britain had been damaged by the Great War, while the U.S. had continued to grow. Where before the war British manufactured goods seemed a bargain at the traditional exchange rate, after the warU.S. goods looked attractive. Britain imported more from the U.S., and exported less, a trade deficit. The U.S. exported more, and imported less, a trade surplus.

> *The gold standard played a role in balancing trade. A trade deficit caused a decline in incomes, which reduced a nation's imports, and it caused a decline in prices, which made its exports more attractive. Falling imports and rising exports eventually would balance trade.*

When it worked properly, the gold standard would correct these imbalances. Britain would pay for the excess of imports over exports by shipping gold to the U.S. With less gold in Britain and more in the U.S., the amount of money in circulation in Britain would fall, and the amount in circulation in the U.S. would rise. Incomes and prices would fall in Britain, enough, perhaps, to be called a recession. Incomes and prices would rise in the U.S., an expansion with inflation. With lower incomes the British people would buy fewer U.S. goods. With higher incomes the American people would buy more British goods. With British prices falling and U.S. prices rising, British goods would be more attractive than U.S. goods, so consumers in both countries would buy more British goods and fewer U.S. goods. This is just what was needed to close the trade imbalance. Once the value of imports and exports were equal, gold would stop flowing, and prices and incomes would stabilize.

But the international economy had changed. It wasn't just the war. The U.S. had been developing rapidly for decades, more rapidly than Britain. It was time for a permanently lower value of the pound. That would have made British goods relatively cheaper, and so would have helped British exports.

Winston Churchill had his doubts. He was the Chancellor of the Exchequer, the British equivalent of Treasury secretary. The British were running a trade deficit with the United States. That meant British prices were too high. The gold standard would force them lower, but that could mean a long recession for Britain. The head of the Bank of England, Montagu Norman, told him that gold was the standard of civilization. He wrote, "the gold standard is the best 'governor' that can be devised for a world that is still human rather than divine." He meant that government policymaking was fallible, so it was better to make monetary decisions by rule. Reluctantly, Churchill decided for gold, at $4.86 per pound, in March 1925.

With the pound overvalued, British exports were too expensive for Americans, while U.S. imports were cheap for the British. British imports from America were more than British exports to America. Britain ran a trade deficit with the U.S., year after year. Gold flowed out of Britain as the gold standard mechanism tried to adjust.

Gold was flowing into the U.S., and for the gold standard to work U.S. prices needed to rise. That would make U.S. exports less attractive, and help close the trade imbalance with Britain. To preserve the workings of the gold standard, the Federal Reserve had to allow inflation. The Federal Reserve wanted to stabilize international trade. But it wanted to stabilize domestic prices too. The domestic and international policy goals were in conflict.

The Fed pursued the domestic goal. Throughout the 1920s, when gold flowed into the U.S. and inflation threatened, the Fed sold bonds and increased the discount rate to make sure that the money supply did not increase. This was called *sterilizing gold.* The inflation necessary for balancing trade did not occur. Between 1922 and 1929, the U.S. price level was almost unchanged.

This was bad for Britain. U.S. inflation should have made U.S. goods more expensive, causing the British to buy fewer U.S. goods and the Americans to switch to less expensive British goods. The Fed stopped the U.S. inflation, so gold kept flowing from Britain to the U.S. British price and income levels kept falling. If U.S. prices and incomes were not going to adjust upward, British prices and incomes had to adjust downward even more. When the Fed sterilized gold, it made the recession in Great Britain worse.

Great Britain needed a gold reserve to back up its promise to provide an ounce of gold for anyone with four and a quarter pounds. As gold flowed out, this reserve got smaller and smaller. Ultimately, if the gold flow was not stopped, its gold reserve would be depleted, and Britain could not remain on the gold standard. So the Bank of England had to keep interest rates high, hoping that this would make Britain an attractive place for international investors to keep their gold. British prices were falling, so real interest rates were higher still. High interest rates choked off investment, which made the recession worse. By the end of the 1920's Great Britain had suffered a decade of stagnation, and its gold reserves were low.

Sometimes, the Federal Reserve saw the need to cut interest rates and expand the money supply. The U.S. had a large enough gold reserve to pursue such policies. This happened twice in the 1920s, during the two mild recessions of 1923-24 and 1926-27. In each case the Fed justified these moves for both domestic and international reasons. Expansionary policy would fight recession at home. Expansionary policy would help Great Britain maintain its gold reserve. Benjamin Strong, still the head of the New York Fed, was particularly adamant about the Fed's responsibility to the international gold standard. In 1927 it was he who persuaded the Reserve Board in Washington to expand the money supply and cut interest rates. But once the recessions were over, the Fed backed off its expansionary policies. Domestic policy needs trumped international concerns. The Fed's commitment to the gold standard was limited.

The Federal Reserve and Policy
The Fed failed to raise the discount rate in time to head off post-war inflation in 1919. This is seen as the Federal Reserve's first big policy mistake. Then they raised the rate too much, and plunged the economy into recession. They kept rates too high too long. This was a second policy failure.

The Fed helped engineer a decade of growth and stable prices with its new policy tool, open market operations. But it did not accept responsibility for maintaining the international gold standard. Instead it sterilized gold to prevent inflation.

This new institution, the Federal Reserve, was only 16 years old by 1929. It had some successes, but its failures stemmed in part from its inadequate design. This would have tragic consequences.

- The Federal Reserve was to become a central bank, yet was not created to be one. It had no policy guidance from legislation. What was it supposed to do? This confusion of goals would be a continuing problem.
- There was no experience with central banking in the United States. All they had was theory—much of it from the Bank of England's experience—and Carter Glass belittled Ben Strong's "copybook texts."
- The Fed's lines of authority were confused. The New York Fed was one power center, the Federal Reserve Board another, the regional bank presidents a third, and the Secretary of the Treasury still another. In a crisis, who was responsible for policy?
- Monetary policy was to work automatically, but the inflation of 1919 showed that the real bills doctrine was unworkable in practice. An expanding inflationary economy would increase the demand for reserves, which if supplied would cause the economy to expand and inflate more. It was pro-cyclical policy, not counter-cyclical stabilization policy. It would add to instability.

- Policies to stabilize the U.S. economy often conflicted with what was needed to operate the international gold standard. This put the traditional method of balancing trade under stress.
- Since policy would not be automatic, it depended on policy makers, all of them human beings. As human beings, they were subject to political pressures, jealousy, power struggles, uncertainty, lack of information, and lack of will. The experiment in direct human guidance of monetary policy was just beginning. Would it succeed?

MacroPolicy Now: Contagious Fear

In 2008 and 2009 we became used to the phrase, "it's the worst since the Great Depression." Many analysts and pundits compared the financial market crisis, the bank runs, and the asset market crashes to the events of the 1930's.

But the Panic of 2008 had a lot in common with the Panic of 1907, too. Consider the parallels.

In 1907 a stock speculator named Augustus Heinze borrowed lots of money from some trust companies, which were largely unregulated financial institutions, but lost his speculative gamble. His assets were worth less than he owed.

In the 2000's the Lehman Brothers investment bank, and many, many other financial institutions, made enormous investments in "mortgage derivatives," which were largely unregulated assets based on prime and subprime home mortgages. When the housing market crashed, these assets were worth less.

In 1907, Heinze's main creditor, the Knickerbocker Trust, was insolvent as a result of its bad loans for his stock speculation. It owed more to its depositors and creditors than its assets were worth. When word got out a bank run developed, and the Trust could not pay its depositors what they were owed. The Trust failed. Contagion developed, as fear of default spread from one institution to another.

In 2008, Lehman Brothers became insolvent, as its investments in mortgage derivatives were worth less than it owed its depositors. Lehman Brothers failed. The Reserve Primary Fund, a money market fund, lost money it had lent to Lehman Brothers. It "broke the buck," paying out less than the full amount its customers had deposited. Contagion developed. Many money market funds experienced bank runs.

In 1907, banks all over the country held on to their deposits, and refused to make loans. Interest rates increased, investment dropped, and the nation fell into recession.

In 2008, money market funds and then many more lenders held on to their money, and refused to make loans. Businesses that depended on short-term business loans couldn't get them, and some went bankrupt. What had been a mild recession turned into a steep drop, as real gross domestic product fell at an annual rate of 7% in the fourth quarter of 2008, and another 5% in the first quarter of 2009.

Even some of the names were the same in the two panics. In 1907 J.P. Morgan, the man, stepped in to rescue the Trust Company of America, and then supported the stock market. In 2008 J.P. Morgan-Chase, the bank, purchased the troubled investment bank Bear Stearns, rescuing its depositors and creditors. But in 1907 J.P. himself had refused to rescue the Knickerbocker Trust. In 2008 J.P. Morgan-Chase asked Lehman Brothers to put up more collateral for money it had borrowed, which Lehman couldn't do. That pushed the bank closer to bankruptcy.

The Federal Reserve and the Treasury also played the Morgan role in 2008. They decided that Lehman Brothers was not worth saving (as Morgan had let the Knickerbocker Trust go), but then supported several other big financial institutions, as Morgan did.

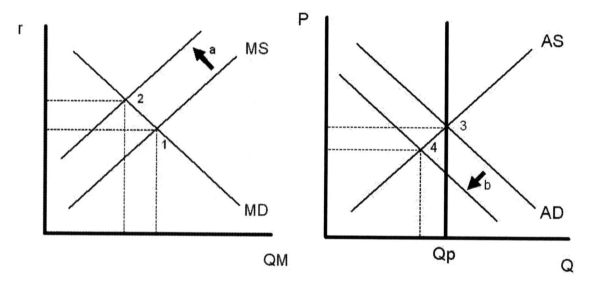

Figure 5-6. One-hundred and one years later. These are the same diagrams as Figures 5-2 and 5-5. (Three times! Must be important.) Banks become pessimistic and increase their reserves, which reduces the money multiplier. This decreases the money supply (a), causing an increase in the real interest rate (1 to 2). The higher interest rate reduces investment spending, which reduces aggregate demand (b). That's second shift #2. Output drops below potential (3 to 4), resulting in a recession.

In the three market model, the graphs for 1907 and 2008 are exactly the same. Fear of bank runs, pessimism about how much their own assets were worth, and uncertainty about who was a worthy borrower caused banks and other lenders to increase their reserves. This reduced the multiple expansions of bank deposits, making the money multiplier smaller. In the money market, the money supply decreased and the real interest rate increased. Second shift #2 causes a change in the goods market. With the real interest rate higher and loans scarce, businesses borrow less. This reduces investment spending, and it reduces aggregate demand. Output falls below potential— and we're in a recession. These two diagrams are the three-market model's representation of the effects of financial crisis on output and prices—the effect of Wall Street on Main Street.

Huge efforts by the Federal Reserve in 2008 and 2009 stopped the panic and halted the fall in the money supply. In mid-2009 the economy began to recover, though output was still far below potential as of 2011.

But financial markets still faced problems in mid-2011. The recession had created a crisis for the government of Greece. Revenues were down and the country borrowed to finance a large deficit (some of which was left over from the 2004 Athens Olympics). It was clear that Greece couldn't pay all that interest, meaning it would default on its bonds. Portugal was in similar straits. Spain and Italy were having trouble, too.
Banks that had lent to these countries worried that their bonds would be worth less. Would they have enough to meet their depositors' demands? Would other banks lend to them if they needed to borrow? If they again cut their lending the recovery in Europe would falter. U.S. banks owned Spanish and Italian bonds, too, and had connections to European banks as borrowers and lenders. They too were concerned.

In Spring 2010, and again in Spring 2011, the European Union came up with rescue packages for the troubled countries. Perhaps it would be enough to head off another panic. If not, the contagion could spread, and the economic recovery could turn again to recession.

Terms in this Chapter, in order of appearance
Deposits
Reserves
Withdrawals
Liquid assets
Bank run
Contagion
Multiple expansion of bank deposits
Multiple contraction of bank depsits
Money multiplier
Monetary base
Elastic currency
Lender of last resort
Federal Reserve
Monetary policy
Discount rate
Pro-cyclical policy
Counter-cyclical policy
Gold standard
Sterilizing gold

Notes

The description of the scene in J. P. Morgan's office in October 1907 is from Strouse's biography of Morgan (1999, p. 574-578). Columbia University economist R.A. Seligman called the decade up to 1907 a time of "unexampled prosperity" (quoted in Degen, 1987, p.15).

Odell and Weidenmeir (2002) tell the story of the international economic effects of the San Francisco earthquake. Earthquake details come from the U.S. Geological Survey website, and the Virtual Museum of the City of San Francisco websites.

The Panic of 1907 is probably the second most important U.S. economic crisis of the 20th Century, after the Great Depression of the 1930s, because it led directly to the creation of the Federal Reserve system. Perhaps for this reason there is more written about the panic than about most downturns. The story is told in Tallman and Moen (1990) and Moen and Tallman (1992), who focus on the role of the Trusts. Morgan's part is told in Strouse's biography (1999, pp. 573-596). Friedman and Schwartz (1963, pp. 156-168) and Degen (1987, pp. 11-16) provide overviews of economic events.
Timberlake (1993, pp. 214-234) discusses the debate over the Federal Reserve Act in detail.

The "Great War" is World War I, but it wasn't called by that name, of course, until World War II. Friedman and Schwartz (1963, pp. 196-221) describe the situation before and after the U.S. declaration of war. Chandler's biography of Benjamin Strong (1958, pp. 99-134) is also useful, as is Degen (1987, pp. 30-36).

The boom and bust of 1919-1921 are described in Friedman and Schwartz (1960, pp. 221-239), Degen (1960, pp. 36-40) and Chandler (1958, pp. 135-187). The story of the struggle between Strong and Carter Glass is told in Chandler (1958), especially in a letter Glass wrote a decade later (pp. 164-65) describing the events. A true politician, Glass describes Strong as "then a stranger but since my warm friend." Friedman and Schwartz, and Degen, conclude that the discount rate should have been raised sooner and cut sooner in 1919-1921. They speculate that the recession would have been milder *without* the existence of the Fed.

Good descriptions of the Roaring '20s can be found in Galbraith (1954), Schlesinger (1956), and Kennedy (1999). Calvin Coolidge is quoted in Schlesinger (p. 57), John Raskob in Galbraith (p. 57).

The Fed's discovery and use of open market operations are covered in Timberlake (1993, pp. 261-63), Friedman and Schwartz (1963, pp. 240-98) and Degen (1987, pp. 41-60). The policy of gold sterilization is also covered by Friedman and Schwartz, and Degen, as well as Eichengreen (1992) and Crabbe (1989).

Ahamed (2009, pp.224-240) tells the story of the British debate about returning to the gold standard.

Sources

Ahamed, Liaquat. *Lords of Finance: The Bankers Who Broke the World.* New York: Penguin Books, 2009.

Bruner, Robert F. and Sean D. Carr. 2007. *The Panic of 1907.* Hoboken, New Jersey: John Wiley and Sons.

Chandler, Lester V. 1958. *Benjamin Strong, Central Banker.* Washington, D.C.: The Brookings Institution.

Crabbe, Leland. 1989. The International Gold Standard and U.S. Monetary Policy from World War I to the New Deal. *Federal Reserve Bulletin* 75 (6) (June): 423-440.

Degen, Robert A. 1987. *The American Monetary System.* Lexington, Massachusetts: D.C. Heath and Company, Lexington Books.

Eichengreen, Barry. 1992. *Golden Fetters: The Gold Standard and the Great Depression 1919-1939.* New York: Oxford University Press.

Friedman, Milton and Anna Jacobson Schwartz. 1963. *A Monetary History of the United States, 1867-1960.* Princeton, New Jersey: Princeton University Press.

Manchester, William. 1974. *The Glory and the Dream.* New York: Bantam Books.
Moen, Jon and Ellis W. Tallman. 1992. "The Bank Panic of 1907: The Role of Trust Companies." *Journal of Economic History* 52:3 (September): 611-630.

Odell, Kerry A. and Marc D. Weidenmier. 2002. Real Shock, Monetary Aftershock: The San Francisco Earthquake and the Panic of 1907. National Bureau of Economic Research Working Paper 9176 (September).

Schlesinger, Arthur M., Jr. 1956. *The Crisis of the Old Order.* Boston: Houghton Mifflin Company.

Strouse, Jean. 1999. *Morgan.* New York: Random House.

Tallman, Ellis W. and Jon R. Moen. 1990. Lessons from the Panic of 1907. *Atlanta Federal Reserve Bank Economic Review* (May/June): 2-13.

Timberlake, Richard H. 1993. *Monetary Policy in the United States: An Intellectual and Institutional History.* Chicago: University of Chicago Press.

United States Geological Survey. 2006. the Great 1906 San Francisco Earthquake. Website: http://quake.wr.usgs.gov/info/1906.

Virtual Museum of the City of San Francisco. 2006. The Great Fire and Earthquake. Website: http://www.sfmuseum.org/1906/06.html.

Wheelock, David C. 1992. "Monetary Policy in the Great Depression: What the Fed Did, and Why." *Federal Reserve Bank of St. Louis Review* 74 (2) (March/April): 3-28.

News Articles
de la Merced, Michael J. "Companies Under Pressure," *New York Times*, September 26, 2008.

Erlanger, Steven and Liz Alderman. "Euro Crisis Looms for Group of 8," New York Times, May 25, 2011.

Nocera, Joe. "As Credit Crisis Spiraled, Alarm Led to Action," *New York Times*, October 2, 2008.

Story, Louise and Ben White. "The Road to Lehman's Failure Was Littered with Lost Chances," *New York Times,* October 6, 2008.

Schwartz, Nelson D. and Eric Dash. "Fears Intensify That Euro Crisis Could Snowball." New York Times, May 16, 2010.

Thomas, Landon Jr.. "In Europe, Rifts Widen Over Greece," New York Times, May 23, 2011.

Chapter 6
Money and the Great Depression

Macroeconomic Policy Now: We Won't Do It Again

When Ben Bernanke was a graduate student at the Massachusetts Institute of Technology, reported the *New York Times* in May 2010, his advisor urged him to read "The Great Contraction, 1929-1933." In that book Milton Friedman and Anna Schwartz blamed the Federal Reserve's failure to expand the money supply for the Depression's severity and duration. The book ignited a passion. "I guess I am a Depression buff, the way some people are Civil War buffs," Mr. Bernanke said.

Years later at a party to honor the 90th birthday of Professor Friedman, Bernanke, by then a governor of the Federal Reserve, brought up the mistakes the Fed made that helped cause the Depression. "We did it," he said. "We won't do it again."

Then, Bernanke became chairman of the Federal Reserve in 2006 and faced the most severe financial crisis since the Great Depression.

He was slow to get started. His first two years were dotted with missteps. He memorably and erroneously described the subprime mortgage mess as "contained" and underestimated the depths of the housing crisis and how intertwined it had become with complex Wall Street trading.

As the crisis accelerated, the Fed lent $29 billion to engineer Bear Stearns' sale in March 2008 to JPMorgan Chase. The Fed seized the mortgage behemoths Fannie Mae and Freddie Mac the following August. Then, in September, after a desperate search for a buyer, the Treasury and the Fed let Lehman Brothers go bankrupt.

Lehman's bankruptcy triggered a world financial crisis and the Fed responded with gigantic Band-Aids. It helped broker Merrill Lynch's sale to Bank of America; it swooped in with $85 billion in a rescue of the insurance giant A.I.G., and it supported Treasury Secretary Paulson's plea to Congress for a $700 billion bank bailout.

Only then did the Fed seem to get its footing. Bernanke aggressively dropped interest rates and deployed an alphabet soup of lending programs. It spent 2009 acquiring mortgage bonds, Treasury securities, and debts owed by Fannie and Freddie, while also conducting "stress tests" of the largest financial institutions.

Economists look back on the Federal Reserve's policies after 1929 and blame them for making the Great Depression worse. How do economists see Bernanke's performance? Some see his failure to anticipate the nature and severity of the financial crisis as an unforgivable lapse. Others say there was no one better equipped, once the crisis began, to respond with the force and imagination he deployed to prevent an economic apocalypse.

> Ironically, Anna Schwartz, whose work had so influenced the young Mr. Bernanke, called on President Obama to replace him when his first term as chairman was up.
>
> But in August 2009 the President decided to reappoint Bernanke to a second term. "The President thinks that Ben's done a great job as Fed chairman," said a spokesman. "He has helped the economy through one of the worst experiences since the Great Depression and he has essentially been pulling the economy back from the brink of what would have been the second Great Depression."

Wait a minute. Wasn't the Fed designed to <u>prevent</u> financial crises that could cause recessions and depressions? And now we say that the Fed <u>caused</u> the Great Depression? How did that happen? Here's the story. . . .

The Stock Market Boom

Perhaps it was the optimism of the day (everyone ought to be rich!). Perhaps it was the excitement over new technologies like radio, or the new mass consumer market that installment credit was creating. Perhaps it was the Fed's low interest rates in 1927. But whatever the reason, more and more people began to buy stock, and values on the New York Stock Exchange began to rise.

A share of *stock* is a share of ownership in a company. It entitles the owner to vote for company directors. It also entitles the owner to a share in the company's profits, which are called *dividends*. If you own a share of Microsoft stock, you are a part-owner of Microsoft, just like Bill Gates (though he owns a tad more of the company than you do). If Microsoft earns profits, they "declare a dividend," a dollar amount per share, and part of those profits are paid to stockholders.

> *A share of stock is a share in the ownership of a company. It entitles the owner to a share of the company's profits. If a company is expected to be more profitable, more people demand its shares, and the stock's price rises.*

If people expect a company to become more profitable, they'll want to own shares of the company's stock, to share in those higher profits. The demand for shares increases and the price of the stock rises. That means that people can earn income from the dividends paid on their shares, and profits from the rise in the value of the company's shares, if they decide to sell. If a company is expected to become more profitable, the value of its stock will rise. That's why stock values are thought to be measures of the prospects of a company.

Companies often start out owned by its founders. "Taking the company public" means to sell off a portion of the company to stock buyers in order to raise money for new investment in facilities, equipment or technology (or to turn the value of the company into more liquid wealth for its founders). An *initial public offering* (IPO) is the original sale of stock by a company to raise such funds.

Most sales of stock are not IPO's, though. Shares are bought and sold among secondary buyers, who are looking for a share of the company's profits or hoping to benefit from a rise in the stock's value. All that secondary buying and selling helps companies raise money with their IPO's, though. An investor is more likely to buy a share of a company if he knows that the share can be sold in the stock market at any time. The investor's money is not tied up forever.

When the economy is doing well, lots of companies become more profitable, and lots of stock values will rise. We measure changes in stock market prices with *stock price indexes*, the most famous of which is the *Dow Jones Industrial Average*. It's actually just an index of the stock prices of thirty important industrial companies. That means it's like the Consumer Price Index, only it measures the prices of stocks instead of consumer goods and services. Back in January 1929, the Dow Jones Industrial Average included General Motors, Sears, Nash Motors, Radio Corporation of America (that's RCA), Woolworth, and General Electric. The list of thirty changes now and then as the fortunes of companies rise and fall. These days the Index includes the stock prices of Microsoft, Exxon-Mobil, Wal-Mart, Disney and (still) General Electric. There are other stock price indexes that include more companies, such as the Standard and Poors 500 and the Wilshire 5,000, but the Dow Jones Industrial Average is the most famous.

If enough people expect stock values to rise and demand shares for that reason, stock values *will* rise. Sometimes investors get so excited about a booming economy and the rising stock values that they pay little attention to the potential profitability of the companies. Stock values can rise beyond any reasonable expectations for future profits. The stock market experiences a *speculative bubble*. This is what happened on the stock market at the end of the 1920's. The Dow Jones Industrial Average increased by 50% in 1928. That means an investment of $1,000 in the 30 stocks on January 1 would be worth $1,500 by December 31.

A large part of the demand for stocks was financed by borrowed money. Banks, and then other companies, began lending their reserves to people who wanted to buy stocks. Borrowing to buy assets like stocks can multiply profits. That's known as *leverage*. Suppose, for example, that an investor has $1,000 of her own money, which is called *equity*. She could invest it in the stock market, and if the market rises by, say, 10% over a year, she could sell for $1,100. She's made $100, a 10% return on her equity. Nice, but not too exciting.

Suppose instead that she borrows $9,000, and uses the loan and her $1,000 in equity to buy $10,000 in stock. Again, the stock market rises by 10%. Now her stock is worth $11,000. She still owes $9,000, but the value of her equity has doubled from $1,000 to $2,000. That's a 100% return on equity. She's doubled her money in a year. That's exciting. And if she'd borrowed $99,000, and bought $100,000 in stock, a 10% market rise would increase her equity to $11,000. That's a 1000% return on equity. That's very, very exciting.

Fueled by leverage, stock prices were running, then leaping and galloping upward in 1928.

The Federal Reserve had begun out of the financial panic of 1907. Now in 1928 many at the Fed saw the great bull market as a speculative bubble. They feared that stock prices would be bid upward beyond what company profits would justify. The inevitable crash would bankrupt people, companies and banks, and, perhaps, send the economy into sharp recession, just as in 1907. The speculation had to be stopped.

Power at the Fed was divided between the Federal Reserve Board in Washington and the regional banks, principally the New York Regional Bank still headed by Benjamin Strong. Strong wanted to stop speculation by raising the discount rate. With interest rates higher, banks would borrow less from the Fed, interest rates would rise, speculators would borrow less from the banks, the demand for stocks would diminish, and stock prices would fall. Strong and his colleagues favored a sharp rise in the discount rate that would be sure to prick the speculative bubble before it inflated too much.

The Board in Washington disagreed. Higher interest rates, they argued, might choke off speculation, but they would also reduce productive investment. The Board favored "moral suasion," which meant pressuring banks not to lend for speculative purposes, but only for productive purposes. Strong disagreed with this approach. He argued that Fed officials could not know how the funds that banks borrowed would be used.

The debate continued throughout 1928 and into 1929, but neither side prevailed. A compromise policy was adopted instead. The Reserve banks tried moral suasion, and increased the discount rate, but not sharply. Neither policy was effective in stopping speculation. The boom continued. Stock prices rose another 30% by the end of August 1929.

But the interest rate increases did slow down the economy. Higher interest rates caused consumers to buy fewer houses and cars, and caused businesses to invest less in plant and equipment. The diversion of funds into the stock market also reduced funds available for investment in factories and equipment.

The excitement about the growing economy had affected businesses, too. They had invested in new buildings and equipment, stocked more inventories, and built more houses expecting that consumers would buy them out of their growing incomes. They overdid it. Unsold inventories began to accumulate, so businesses cancelled orders for new goods until they were sold. Factories laid off workers. This is known as an *inventory recession*, and it's a common reason that recessions start. A recession did begin. The economy peaked in August 1929.

The Stock Market Crash
The stock boom continued until the end of the summer. Then, in September, stock prices stopped their steep climb. One day they would be down, another day up, then down

again. Was the market simply "taking a breather," making ready for another climb, as it had in June and July the year before? Or was this the end of the boom? The answer came in October.

With the perfect knowledge of hindsight, we know that the high point of the Dow Jones Industrial Average came on September 3, 1929, at 381 (oh for a time machine!). It fell, gradually, through September and into October.

To this day no one knows what in particular caused the crash. We now know that stocks were overvalued. The Dow Jones Industrial Average would not reach its 1929 peak again until *1954*. We know that the economy had turned to recession, that business profits were declining, and that the Fed's monetary policy was contractionary. All of these factors could cause a fall in stock prices. But we don't know why thousands of optimistic buyers so suddenly turned into pessimistic sellers, and why it happened in the last two weeks of October.

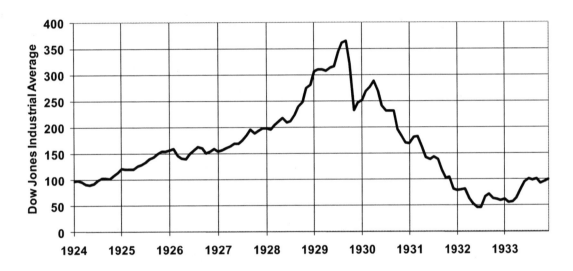

Figure 6-1. The Dow Jones Industrial Average, monthly, 1924-1933. The Dow Jones Industrial Average is a price index of the stocks of 30 important companies. Its value doubled from 1924 to 1928, then rose from 200 to 300—50%--in 1928 alone. Its monthly value peaked in September 1929. The crash in October and November 1929 cut the Average by about a third. By mid-1932 the Average was less than 50, a decline of almost 90%.

But it did. On October 24, Black Thursday, the panic began. Bankers offered "organized support," again operating out of J.P. Morgan's office (he was the son of old J.P. of 1907). Markets calmed somewhat on Friday and the half-day session on Saturday. But on Monday the market dropped again, and on October 29, Black Tuesday, it collapsed. That day sixteen million shares were sold, an enormous volume in the days of pen and paper, not to be reached again for decades. The stock ticker was overwhelmed, falling two hours behind, leaving investors around the country uninformed about prices, but fearing the worst. This added to the panic. The Dow Jones Industrial Average lost 30% of its value in just one week.

Now leverage worked in reverse. Invest $1,000 in equity in stocks, and a 10% decline loses $100. Our investor has $900 in equity left. Borrow $9,000 to buy $10,000 in stock, and a 10% decline leaves the investor with $9,000. That's what she owes to the lender. Her equity is wiped out, a 100% loss. And the investor that borrowed $99,000 now has stocks worth only $90,000. She owes more than her assets are worth. Now the bank that made the loan is in trouble. It now has a loan worth less than what it owes its depositors.

The value of the stocks served as collateral for the loan. If the bank loaned $99,000, and the stocks were worth $100,000, the bank felt secure. If necessary, the borrower could sell the stocks, or the bank could sell them, and recoup the loan. When stock values fell, though, a bank would feel insecure. It would demand that the borrower put up more collateral. This is known as a *margin call*. Buying on the margin was buying with borrowed money. The "call" was a note a bank would send to a borrower, asking for more collateral.

When margin calls went out, somehow the borrowers had to get cash or stocks for more collateral. This might mean trying to borrow more money somewhere else, but who would lend? Probably it meant selling stocks to raise cash, and using the cash as collateral. But with that increased selling, and with no one buying, stock values fell even more.

The crash and continuing volatility of stock prices challenged peoples' assumptions about the future. Increasingly through the roaring '20's people decided that the economy had entered a new era. Irving Fisher, the most respected American economist of the day, had said (three days before the crash!) that "stock prices have reached what looks like a

> *The stock market crash caused uncertainty and reduced household wealth. Both caused consumers and businesses to reduce spending, which reduced equilibrium output.*

permanently high plateau." Now the upward march had stopped. What did it mean? Economic forecasts were all over the map. Some predicted resumed growth, others continued decline. Most admitted to uncertainty.

Not knowing what to expect, businesses postponed investment. Why build a new factory now if it was not clear whether the new production could be sold to consumers? Why not wait and see what happens? Investment projects were postponed. Construction workers weren't hired. Factories that would have manufactured new equipment shut down instead. *Expectations* turned pessimistic, and this reduced investment spending.

Not knowing what to expect, consumers postponed big purchases. Why borrow to buy that new car, that new house, when you might soon be laid off from your job? Why not make do with the old for a few months to see what would happen?

Peoples' willingness to buy consumer goods depends in part on how wealthy they are. With a big portfolio of stocks, people buy more and bigger cars and houses. Their savings goals for retirement or education have been met by rising stock prices, so they can make car or house payments by saving less. If they lose a job for a time, the wealth will support their payments. With the crash, much wealth disappeared. Within three years the Dow Jones Industrial Average lost 87% of its value. A thousand dollars invested in September 1929 was worth about $100 by mid-1932. Now people needed to save more to regain financial security. Saving more meant spending less. The decline in wealth helped cause a decline in consumer spending. This is known (not too cleverly) as the *wealth effect*.

With greater uncertainty and lower wealth, the end of 1929 saw a big drop in consumer spending and in business investment spending. The recession that had begun in mid-1929 took a turn for the worse. The unemployment rate rose from 3.2% in 1929 to 8.7% in 1930. By mid-1930 the recession looked to be as bad as the severe downturns in 1907-08 and 1920-21.

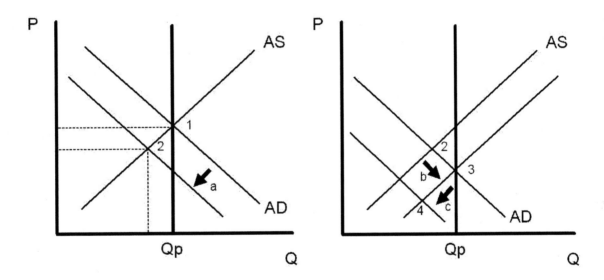

Figure 6-2. Great Depression. The Fed rate hike and excess inventory accumulation reduce investment spending and aggregate demand (a), reducing the price level and output (1 to 2). With output below potential, wages and other resource costs should fall, increasing aggregate supply (b), and restoring output to potential at a lower price level (2 to 3), through second shift #1. But then came the crash, with its wealth effect on consumers and then (we will see) more Fed rate hikes, bank failures, and a tax hike. Aggregate demand takes a second hit, decreasing again before aggregate supply can move to restore potential output. Aggregate demand got hit again and again from 1929 to 1933.

The Fed had increased interest rates to try to slow down stock speculation. That reduced investment spending. Firms continued to expect growing sales for a time, but saw unsold inventories accumulate. They cut back on inventory investment in response. The decline in investment spending reduced aggregate demand.

The stock market crashed. Now consumers had less wealth and had to start saving more. Consumption spending fell. Both consumers and businesses became uncertain (if not pessimistic) about the future of the economy. They cut back on spending until prospects became clear. This also reduced aggregate demand.

The large decline in aggregate demand dropped output below potential. Why, one might wonder, didn't wages and resource costs fall, causing aggregate supply to increase? Why didn't second shift #1 correct the problem of recession? This would have returned output to potential at a lower price level.

Many of the economists of the day expected this to happen. They recommended that the government not take any action to fight the gathering Depression, but to simply wait for price and wage adjustment to bring recovery. But wages and prices did fall, a lot, and the Depression got worse. It may be that the stock market crash produced an added shock to aggregate demand before the wage and cost adjustment allowed output to recover. And the crash was just the first of many such shocks to aggregate demand. Perhaps aggregate supply just couldn't catch up.

The Banking System Collapse
Farmers had not shared in the prosperity in the roaring twenties. The agricultural economy had been in recession through most of the decade. The reason was easy to see. During the Great War the farms of Europe could not export, so consumers everywhere looked to American farmers to fill the gap. Commodity prices rose, and farmers increased output. After the war European farms were back in business. Especially after the recession of 1920-21, commodity prices fell and stayed low.

Agriculture's problems in the 1920's had a more serious result for the economy. Most banks in the United States were small. National branch banking was prohibited, so each bank was an institution on its own, lending to local borrowers. Banks in rural areas, of course, lent mostly to farmers. During the prosperous war years, farmers expanded their operations, borrowing to buy new land and pay for new equipment. In the 1920's, as farm prices dropped, farmers were hard put to keep up with their loan payments. Many small, rural banks saw too many of their borrowers default on their loans. These defaults were not offset by good loans in other industries because virtually all of the rural banks' loans were to farmers. While the 1920's roared in the cities, hundreds of rural banks failed each year.

In the Fall of 1930, with business conditions even worse, rural banks started failing in greater numbers. Fear became contagious. Depositors listened for the slightest rumor that their bank was in trouble, then rushed to withdraw their funds. This time, fear spread from the country to the city, and on December 11 a large commercial bank in New York City succumbed to a bank run and closed its doors. The bank's name, unfortunately, was "Bank of the United States." It was just a privately-owned bank, but with a name like that it sounded like an agency of the government. News that the Bank of the United States had failed caused a further blow to confidence. In March 1931 a new, bigger wave of failures began.

What was a bank run like? Consider the story of the First National Bank of Ogden, Utah, owned by a banker named Marriner Eccles. The First National was a small bank. The big bank in town was the Ogden State Bank. By mid-summer 1931 this old, respected bank had seen so many loan defaults that it was insolvent. Rumor spread among the other bankers in Ogden one weekend that it would not open its doors on Monday.

That worried Marriner Eccles. His bank's assets were sound. That didn't matter. If Ogden's leading bank went under, depositors all over town would panic. They would rush to withdraw their funds from First National. Eccles had reserves enough to meet normal withdrawals, even heavier than normal withdrawals. But there weren't enough to handle an all-out bank run.

He called his employees in early that Monday morning and told them they would face a panicked crowd. "If you want to keep this bank open," he said, "you must do your part. Go about your business as though nothing unusual was happening. Smile, talk about the weather, be pleasant, show no signs of panic." No teller should step away from his window, not even for lunch. Sandwiches would be brought in. "If any teller's or clerk's window in this bank closes even for a short time, that will stir up more panic."

But cheerfulness was not Eccles' only strategy. All withdrawals would be paid, but he told his tellers, "you are going to pay them very slowly." Check the signatures of even the most familiar customers. Pay out in small bills. Count slowly. "Our object is to pay out a minimum today."

The bank's doors opened and the crowd rushed in. People were tense, afraid that when they reached the front of the line, there would be no money left.

Despite his tellers' efforts, Eccles could see that his reserves wouldn't last the day. So he called the Salt Lake City Federal Reserve Bank, and soon an armored car arrived. The crowd parted to allow the guards to carry sacks of cash to the vault. Eccles spotted Morgan Craft, deputy manager of the Federal Reserve Bank, who had come along for the ride. Eccles grabbed his arm and pulled him through the crowd. He leapt onto the counter.

"Just a minute!" he cried, to quiet the crowd. "It appears we are having some difficulty handling our depositors with the speed to which you are accustomed. . . . I just wanted to tell you that instead of closing at the usual hour of three o'clock, we have decided to stay open just as long as there is anyone who wants to withdraw his deposit or to make one. . . . We have just brought up from Salt Lake City a large amount of currency that will take care of all your requirements. There is plenty more where that came from. And if you don't believe me, I have here Mr. Morgan Craft, one of the officers of the Federal Reserve Bank." Eccles pulled Craft up onto the counter.

Craft came through. "I just want to verify what Mr. Eccles has told you," he shouted. "I want to assure you that we have brought up a lot of currency and there is plenty more where that came from." There was—though it didn't necessarily belong to Eccles' bank. Craft wisely omitted that detail. Payments continued into the evening.

Finally the last customer left the bank and Eccles closed the doors. He gathered his exhausted workers in the lobby. "Now listen," he told them, "Tomorrow there will be the makings of another crush, and we are going to meet it by doing the opposite of what we did today. Instead of opening at ten, we are going to open at eight. Nobody is going to have to wait outside of the bank to start any sort of line. When people come in here, pay them very fast. . . . Don't let any line form. It will mean a continuation of the panic."

> *When a bank failed, households lost their checking and savings deposits, or saw them tied up in court. Households cut their spending. Businesses had to find new lenders for business loans. This was hard to do with business conditions so bad, and many businesses failed for lack of loans.*

It worked. Lots of money was paid out on Tuesday, but no lines formed. Customers walking by the bank saw business as usual, and kept on walking. Eccles' bank had survived the run.

But in 1931 banks everywhere were in trouble. Incomes were falling, unemployment was rising. Business sales dried up, farm prices fell. Farmers and business people who had been prosperous and reliable during the 1920's were now unable to repay their bank loans. Such loans had to be "written off." They were no longer paying assets of the banks. Many banks found that they didn't have enough assets to meet the demands of their depositors. They shut their doors.

As always during banking crises, banks tried to build up reserves and people became reluctant to make deposits. Both actions reduce the availability of loans and cause interest rates to rise. Investment and durable goods purchases fall. With bank failures this widespread, there are other effects. Pessimism replaced uncertainty, causing people and firms to permanently cancel purchases. When a bank failed people lost their savings, or their savings were tied up in court for months or years, as a judge decided who would be paid how much out of the bank's remaining assets. This caused another wealth effect reduction in spending. When a bank failed, its small business borrowers had to look elsewhere. This meant reestablishing relationships with new bankers. Business was bad, so it might be tough to convince a new banker that your firm was a good risk. That meant delays in getting new loans, if loans could be had at all. Investment and employment in small business declined. In 1931 the unemployment rate rose to 15.9%.

The Fed's (Non-) Response

What did the Federal Reserve do? What did the nation's lender of last resort, the institution designed to prevent bank failures, the hand at the tiller of monetary policy, do about the worst economic disaster in American history?

Nothing.

Occasionally an alert Fed official like Mr. Craft in Ogden would loan a bank some money. But for the most part the Fed stood by. It reduced the discount rate slowly, grudgingly. It refused to buy bonds in open market operations in substantial amounts. It denied loans to banks seeking to calm bank runs by paying depositors. The Fed stood by as one-third of all banks failed. The Fed watched the money supply fall month after month, year after year.

Immediately after the stock market crash, the New York Federal Reserve bought a large amount of government bonds, injecting cash into the banking system. The Reserve Board in Washington didn't like the New York Fed's independence and made them stop their purchases.

Why could the powerful New York branch not persuade the Board of its position? Perhaps the main reason: Benjamin Strong was dead. Strong had been the most powerful, most knowledgeable, most articulate central banker in the United States. He died on October 16, 1928, of complications from tuberculosis. His death left the Federal Reserve without leadership. Some think that had he lived, the Fed would have pursued more appropriate policies, and the Great Depression avoided.

Strong's former assistant, George Harrison, was now in charge at the New York Fed. Often in 1930 and 1931 he would take the train to Washington to argue for discount rate cuts or open market purchases. Occasionally he succeeded; more often he was voted down. The task became harder in May 1930 when the Fed's open market policy body expanded from five to 12 members. Now all the reserve banks were represented with an equal vote. Harrison had the disadvantage of being new, and as Strong's protégé, he had "inherited all the antagonisms that poor Ben left behind him," said an observer. The regional banks weren't going to let the New York Fed dominate policy. In June they voted down Harrison's proposal for a modest weekly open market purchase.

> *The Fed failed to protect the banking system from bank runs. Banks increased reserves as a result, which reduced the money multiplier. The Fed failed to increase the monetary base to compensate, so the money supply fell and real interest rates rose.*

Harrison argued that the recession appeared to be serious, and that the Fed's tight money policy since 1928 had contributed to it. Banks were not making funds available for long term business investments in plant and equipment. The Fed's open market bond purchases would make these funds available.

Chicago's James McDougal argued back. Funds were not scarce, they were abundant, McDougal said. Interest rates were falling, not rising, and that implied that banks had more funds than they could profitably lend. Open market purchases now would only encourage more speculation in other commodities.

George Norris from Philadelphia held to the real bills view of policy. The Fed should make funds available when the demand for credit was expanding. "We have been putting out credit in a period of depression when it was not needed and could not be used, and will have to withdraw credit when it is wanted and can be used." According to Norris, the money from bond purchases was sitting in bank reserves, un-loaned.

Others argued that a downturn was necessary for the future health of the economy. A recession was needed to *liquidate* the assets of speculators and poorly managed businesses. Let them sell their assets to those who could manage them better, at lower, more reasonable prices, and the economy could begin to grow again. To delay the liquidation with open market purchases was to delay recovery.

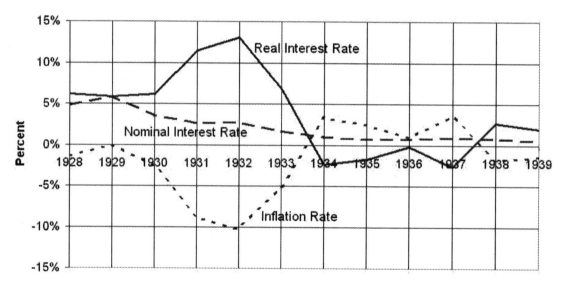

Figure 6-3. Real Interest Rate, 1928-1939. The nominal interest rate is the one year commercial rate charged by banks. The real interest rate can be calculated as the nominal interest rate less the inflation rate. In 1931 and 1932, the nominal rate had fallen, but prices were falling faster. Subtracting the negative price change from the nominal rate gives double-digit real interest rates in 1931 and 1932. The real interest rate has never been higher since.

Harrison failed to persuade his colleagues to expand the money supply. We now know that he was right and they were wrong. Interest rates seemed low because the *demand* for money was low, as a result of falling incomes and prices. And *real* interest rates actually were high. Prices were falling, and that meant the money paid back to banks was worth far more than when it was borrowed. High real interest rates in the face of low money demand could only mean very low money supply. Banks were building up reserves because they were scared of bank runs, not because no one wanted to borrow. That reduced the money multiplier. The Fed failed to increase the monetary base to compensate, and the money supply fell.

The real bills doctrine implied that the money supply should expand when money demand increased, and the supply should fall when money demand fell. That implies a pro-cyclical monetary policy, meaning the economy should be stimulated when it is expanding and slowed when it is declining. This creates greater instability. Now we think monetary policy should be counter-cyclical.

The most famous "liquidationist" was Treasury Secretary Andrew Mellon. President Herbert Hoover recalled Mellon's advice: "liquidate labor, liquidate stocks, liquidate farmers, liquidate real estate.... it will purge the rottenness out of the system. High costs of living and high living will come down. People will work harder, live a more moral life. Values will be adjusted and enterprising people will pick up from less competent people." Less competent people would sell to more competent people, and businesses would be run better. The trouble was, in the Great Depression even well-run businesses were failing.

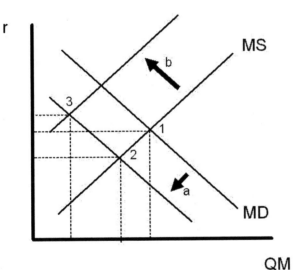

Figure 6-4. Harrison and his critics. Money demand decreased with the decline in income and prices (a). Harrison's critics thought this explained seemingly low interest rates and the decline in the quantity of money (1 to 2). In fact, money supply fell a lot because banks were holding extra reserves, which reduced the money multiplier (b). The quantity of money was lower, but <u>real</u> interest rates were higher (3).

The End of the Gold Standard
Harrison continued to suggest expansionary policy but was unable to persuade the other banks. Then on September 19, 1931, even he changed his mind. On that day Great Britain left the gold standard.

The trouble started in May 1931 with a run on the largest bank in Austria, the Credit-Anstalt. The crisis spread to Germany and investors withdrew gold from both nations. The financial dislocations left over from World War I made problems worse. Germany owed enormous war reparations payments to France and Britain; France and Britain owed enormous war debts to the United States. In June 1931 President Hoover proposed that these international payments be suspended so that Germany could keep more of its gold reserves. This was a bold move by Hoover, made contrary to the opinions of most Americans, who wanted the war debts repaid. France resisted as well, fearing that German reparations would be cancelled permanently. After three weeks of negotiations, agreement was reached. It was too late. Germany left the gold standard.

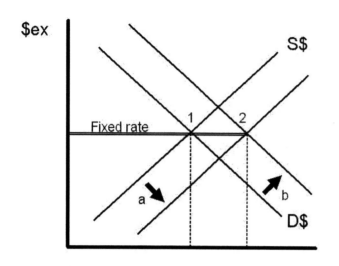

Figure 6-5. Defending the Gold Standard. International investors try to sell their dollars before the dollar is devalued. The supply of dollars in currency markets increases (a). At the fixed exchange rate, there is a surplus of dollars (1 to 2). Unable to trade their dollars for other currencies, investors demand gold in exchange for dollars from the Treasury. Gold drains away. The Fed increases interest rates to make lending in the U.S. more attractive, which increases the demand for dollars (b). That's second shift #5. Equilibrium is restored at the fixed exchange rate.

With Austria and Germany down, investors wondered about Great Britain. Britain had been having trade difficulties ever since returning to gold in 1925. Investors began to withdraw gold. With gold reserves already low, this new drain was too much. On September 19 Great Britain left the gold standard. The value of the pound depreciated against foreign currencies. This meant that the pound could be exchanged for fewer dollars, francs, or marks than before. Investors who held funds in pounds suffered a loss in wealth.

International investors now focused on the United States. Would the U.S. be next? Would wealth kept in dollars lose value if the U.S. left the gold standard? Since Britain had already left gold, and the pound had already devalued, it seemed safer to keep funds in pounds rather than in dollars. Within days after Britain left gold, investors began withdrawing funds from U.S. banks and from the U.S. itself. The United States lost 15% of its gold supply in only six weeks.

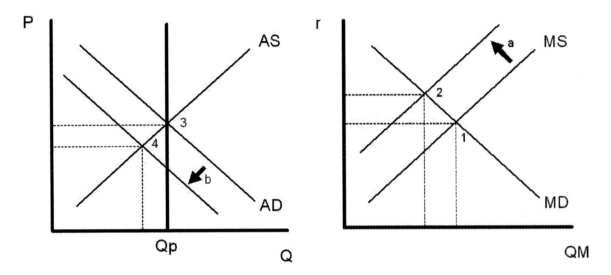

Figure 6-6. Failed Fed. Banks reserved more, the money multiplier fell, and the Fed did not respond. Then the Fed intentionally increased rates to defend the gold standard. The money supply decreased some more (a). This increased the real interest rate (1 to 2), which decreased investment spending, and so decreased aggregate demand (b), through second shift #2. Output and the price level fell (3 to 4). Had the Fed increased the monetary base—bank reserves—to offset the money multiplier drop, the money supply might have increased and real interest rates would have been lower. The Great Depression might not have been so great.

The New York Fed was charged with international policy. George Harrison knew what to do (and Benjamin Strong probably would have agreed). The classic response to a gold drain was to raise interest rates, so that keeping funds in the country was more attractive to investors. Higher interest rates meant a greater return on funds kept in dollars. On October 8 the Fed raised its discount rate a point to 2.5%, and a week later to 3.5%. It was the largest increase over so brief a period in the Fed's history, before or since.
The Fed chose to defend the dying international gold standard at the cost of higher interest rates, less investment and more contraction at home. The recession turned into depression, and the depression became Great.

The Tax Increase of 1932
International investors withdrew their funds from the U.S. after Britain left gold. Banks were failing left and right. The Fed would not lend to banks in trouble, nor would it buy enough bonds to expand the money supply. All of these events reduced the availability of loanable funds to businesses. This hampered their ability to spend for investment in factories, office buildings, and equipment. The problem was a great concern to President Hoover. In his December 1931 state of the union address he called "credit paralysis" one of the "outstanding obstacles to recovery." And he had an idea about what to do about the problem.

Herbert Hoover proposed a tax increase.

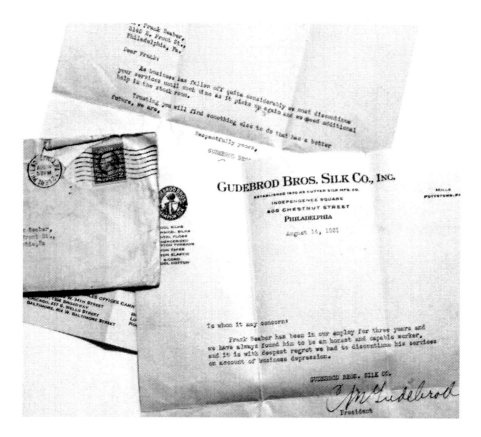

A letter to Mr. Frank Beaber, from his employer, Gudebrod Bros. Silk Co.,, dated August 14, 1931. "Dear Frank," it reads. "As business has fallen off quite considerably we must discontinue your services until such time as it picks up again and we need additional help in the stock room. Trusting you will find something else to do that has a better future, we are Respectfully yours." They enclosed a letter of recommendation. It reads, "Frank Beaber has been in our employ for three years and we have always found him to be an honest and capable worker, and it is with deepest regret we had to discontinue his services on account of business depression."

Many elected officials knew that raising taxes during a Depression was a bad idea. "It would appear to me impossible to increase taxes during the present depressed conditions," said Senator Reed Smoot of Utah. A tax hike would reduce the income consumers had to spend, and reduce the return that businesses would receive on investments in factories and equipment. Those were secondary problems, Hoover thought. In his December speech he explained

> Our first step toward recovery is to reestablish confidence and thus restore the flow of credit which is the very basis of our economic life. The first requirement of confidence and of economy recovery is financial stability of the United States Government.

The government was running a huge deficit. Income tax revenue had dropped with falling incomes and rising unemployment. The government had to borrow to fill the gap between revenues and spending. The money the government borrowed, Hoover thought, was money that was denied to private industry. To allow businesses to increase investment spending, the government's budget had to be balanced, and that meant taxes had to be increased.

> **The Hoover tax increase of 1932 was designed to encourage investment spending, but it cut consumption and investment spending instead, making the Great Depression worse.**

Congress was persuaded, despite the fact that 1932 was an election year. President Hoover signed the tax increase into law on June 6, 1932. It was a truly enormous tax hike. The top tax rate increased from 25% to 63% of income. For taxpayers with incomes under $8,000—which was most of them—the rate increase from one and a half percent to 4%. The deduction for a married couple was reduced from $3,500 to $2,500, which meant that millions of lower income people had to start paying. The tax on corporations was increased from 12% to 13.75% of profits. Estate and gift taxes were raised as well. Revenues jumped in 1933 and the deficit got smaller, but the budget was not balanced.

President Hoover pushed for higher taxes to balance the budget and encourage investment spending. He got little argument from either politicians or economists about his reasoning. But the tax hike is now seen as a huge mistake. It took spending out of the economy when it was most needed. It did little to free up funds for businesses to invest, even if they had been inclined to do so. In 1932 the unemployment rate climbed to 23.6%. Almost one out of every four workers was without a job.

What Caused the Great Depression?
What caused the Great Depression? Let's use the three-market model with second shifts to sort out the causes. Here again is the table of second shifts, for reference.

Table 6-1. Second Shifts Used in the Three-Market Model

From:	To Goods Market	To Money Market	To Exchange Market
Goods Market	**1. Goods to Goods**	**3. Goods to Money**	*(a) Goods to Exchange*
Money Market	**2. Money to Goods**		**5. Money to Exchange**
Exchange Market	**4. Exchange to Goods**	*(b) Exchange to Money*	

To start the analysis, we need to identify the "shock" that changes demand or supply in one of the markets. We've already seen that the shock that kicked off the depression of the 1890's was the panic among international investors over bimetallism.

Economists are divided into three main camps about the shocks that caused the Great Depression, one for each market.

Maybe the Great Depression was caused by a shock in the goods market. Businesses were too optimistic about future sales, and when these sales didn't pan out, inventories accumulated and they cut back on new investment spending. Then the stock market crashed. The negative wealth effect and increased uncertainty reduced consumption and investment spending. Then the Hoover administration increased taxes. This reduced consumption spending some more. Aggregate demand fell, and so did output and the price level.

Maybe the Great Depression was caused by a shock in the money market. The Fed reduced the money supply in 1928 and 1929, to increase the real interest rate, trying to stop stock speculation. The Fed failed to increase the money supply sufficiently after that, allowing the real interest rate to rise some more. And the Fed failed to act as a lender of last resort. Banks failed, and others increased their reserves and cut their lending. The money multiplier dropped, the Fed did not increase the monetary base to compensate, and the money supply fell further. Through second shift #2, the higher real interest rate reduced aggregate demand. This reduced output and the price level.

Maybe the Great Depression was caused by a shock in the exchange market. Great Britain left gold, and international investors figured the United States was next. They began to exchange their dollars for gold, draining gold from the Treasury. This reduced the money supply through second shift (b). The Fed responded by raising interest rates and keeping them high for the next two years. This was an effort to use second shift #5 to shore up the demand for the dollar. But second shift #2 meant that the higher real interest rate reduced investment spending. This reduced output and the price level.

Why wasn't the problem corrected by a fall in the price level, causing an increase in aggregate supply (second shift #1)? Prices and wages fell a lot during the Depression, but apparently not enough to bring output back to potential. Perhaps aggregate supply couldn't "catch up." Each shock caused a drop in input costs, but before this could increase output, another shock came along to decrease aggregate demand some more.

Or, perhaps falling prices are a problem as well as a possible solution to depression. The costs of inputs fall. If they fall to a new lower level and stay there, businesses will recognize a bargain

> *Shocks to each of the three markets helped cause the Great Depression. The recession, the stock market crash and the tax hike reduced spending in the goods market. Bank runs and failed monetary policy caused real intereset rate hikes in the money market. The collapse of the gold standard caused the Fed to raise interest rates and keep them high.*

and start hiring workers and buying equipment. Output will rise. But if they fall and keep falling, businesses may decide to wait—next week workers and equipment will be even cheaper. Further, if a business borrows money to buy land, buildings or equipment, falling costs would make the asset worth less than the amount owed on the loan. If sales didn't keep up, the business would not be able to repay the loan by selling the land, building or equipment. It would default.

The goods market shock was the explanation for the Great Depression that emerged from the work of John Maynard Keynes and the Keynesians at the end of the 1930's. Keynes and his followers focused on declines in spending by consumers and businesses. Prices couldn't fall fast enough to keep output at potential. The result was a surplus of goods beyond what people could buy and a surplus of workers beyond what businesses could employ.

Plenty of economists lay responsibility for the Great Depression at the Fed's door, which is what the money market shock implies. The Fed was loosely organized, its power dispersed among the twelve regional banks. It lacked leadership, especially with Benjamin Strong dead. Its thinking was confused, and this promoted pro-cyclical policy. It failed to act as a lender of last resort. Had the Fed done what it was supposed to do, the Great Depression might have been avoided.

You can think really big thoughts about the exchange market shock. World War I had weakened Great Britain, and growth in the United States had made it the world's dominant economy. But Britain wouldn't accept the end of its hegemony; theyheld to the traditional pound-dollar exchange rate. And the United States wouldn't accept the responsibilities of global economic leadership, refusing to allow the inflation that would make the gold standard work. The result was the collapse of the international economic order that the gold standard represented. Then the Fed raised interest rates to defend the dollar and left them high for two years. Perhaps this great shift in the locus of world economic power caused the Great Depression.

Which shock is *the* cause of the Great Depression? Maybe we don't have to choose. The Great Depression may have been the result of all of these shocks, coming one after another. The stock market crash, the banking crises, the collapse of gold, and the policy failures by themselves may have caused a recession, maybe a bad recession. But perhaps a Great Depression required all of them, altogether.

Fear Itself: The Last Bank Run, 1933
In 1932, after three years of worsening Depression, the nation held an election. Franklin Roosevelt defeated Herbert Hoover in a landslide. Rightly or wrongly, the voters blamed Hoover for the economic disaster. Unfortunately, in 1933 the new president would not be inaugurated until March. The 20th Amendment to the Constitution had passed, making January 20 inauguration day, but it would not take effect until 1936. This one last time, there would be four months with a lame duck president. This time, it mattered.

The last bank run began in February, 1933. People in big cities and small towns all over the nation lined up with bags and suitcases to cart their money away. One by one, then by dozens and hundreds, banks closed, their reserves gone. The governor of Michigan declared a bank holiday, closing all the banks in his state. By the end of the month governors in 31 more states had done the same. The economic life of the nation slowed to a crawl.

President Hoover pleaded with the Federal Reserve for action. The Fed offered excuses. Hoover pleaded with Roosevelt, the President-elect, to bolster confidence by revealing his intentions, or joining with Hoover in joint policy statements. Roosevelt refused. He would not be tarred with Hoover's unpopularity, nor drawn in as a supporter of Hoover's policies. Roosevelt waited, and so did the nation.

On inauguration day, Saturday, March 4, 1933, the new President Franklin Roosevelt finally took the oath of office and declared that "the only thing we have to fear is fear itself." He was right—fear had caused the banks' collapse. People were afraid that their banks would fail, and they would lose their checking and savings deposits. So they tried to withdraw their money, in such large numbers that this caused thousands of banks to close. Fear was itself dangerous.

Listen to the Radio. At the Roosevelt Memorial in Washington D.C., a statue of a man listening to the radio. President Franklin Roosevelt explained the bank holiday and the legislation to deal with banking problems in his first "fireside chat" radio broadcast in March 1933.

After the speech, in the White House and the Treasury, members of the old Hoover administration and new Roosevelt administration worked desperately to craft a solution to the banking crisis. On Sunday Roosevelt used war-time powers to order all banks in the country officially closed—they called it a *bank holiday*—then called for a special session of Congress.

By the morning of Thursday, March 9, the administration had cobbled together an Emergency Banking Act. There was no time to print copies for the House of Representatives to consider, so at one o'clock that afternoon, House Banking Chairman Henry Steagall rolled up a newspaper, waved it over his head and shouted "Here's the bill. Let's pass it!" After 38 minutes of debate they did. The Senate passed it later that day. At 8:36 in the evening, President Roosevelt signed it into law. The first banks would reopen on Monday, March 13.

On Sunday night Roosevelt spoke directly to Americans on the radio, in his first "fireside chat." He explained what his government had been doing over the previous week. He said, "It needs no prophet to tell you that when the people find that they can get their money—that they can get it when they want it for all legitimate purposes—the phantom of fear will soon be laid. People will again be glad to have their money where it will be safely taken care of and where they can use it conveniently at any time. I can assure you, my friends, that it is safer to keep your money in a reopened bank than under the mattress."

It was. When the banks reopened, deposits exceeded withdrawals. The banking system revived. The last run was over.

The Functions of Money

For almost two weeks the nation lived without banks. Money became scarce. Some of the nation's currency was locked in bank vaults, unavailable with the banks closed. Many people hoarded what cash they had, for emergencies. That took it out of circulation. It was hard to cash a check, because merchants didn't know when or if banks would reopen. People with charge accounts at stores were in luck, but almost no one had credit cards. Without dollars and cents to make purchases, people had to improvise. They called it a "bank holiday," and, somehow, it put many people in a holiday mood.

We take money for granted. It's something we live with without thinking much about it, like air or gravity. If money disappeared, though, perhaps we'd start to consider just what money is.

> Salt Lake City, Utah, March 7. Two pairs of silk hose, two tubes of tooth paste, a man's hat and a pair of trousers were among the "fare" accepted by a local transportation company from passengers who lacked cash. The trousers, the manager hastens to assure those viewing the exhibit, were the extra pair.

Sometimes we think of money as the same thing as wealth or income. It's not. Suppose people owned wealth, and earned income, but there was no money with which to store the wealth or exchange the income. People would resort to *barter*, the direct exchange of goods for goods. That's what happened in March 1933.

> Oklahoma City, Oklahoma, March 7. Pigs, chickens, eggs and vegetables will be accepted as payment during the bank holiday, a hotel here announced today. "We'll take anything we can use in the coffee shop," said the manager. A pig was accepted in the first barter.

What makes barter difficult? It requires a *double coincidence of wants*. To make an exchange, each person must have what the other wants. A farmer has a pig, and wants to stay at a hotel. The hotel has a vacancy, and needs bacon for the coffee shop. An exchange is made. But suppose the potential customer was an encyclopedia salesman. The hotel would not likely accept World Book volume Aardvark to Aztec in exchange for a room. No exchange is made, even if the book is worth as much as the pig.

> ***Money acts as a medium of exchange, a unit of account, and a store of value. It allows people to specialize in what they do best, so it's a technology that increases the output of goods and services.***

This is not a problem with money, because money is universally wanted. The salesman has money, the hotel wants it. The coffee shop has money, the hog farmer wants it. The salesman pays money for the room; the hotel pays money for the pig. In effect, a room has been exchanged for a pig, but with money in between. That's why money is called a *medium of exchange*. It comes between goods for goods transactions, and makes them easier.

Why is money universally wanted?

> Chicago, March 10. Scrip in the form of "company checks" and "pay roll drafts" was the most prevalent medium of exchange as Chicago business firms prepared yesterday to meet their second weekly pay roll under the continued bank moratorium. Confidence in the security of the individual firm is the basis on which merchants are honoring the scrip, which has no legal foundation.
>
> The Western Electric company established a scrip system by allowing employees to deposit their pay checks in a department created for the bank holiday emergency. Here the checks are broken up into $5 and $10 pay roll drafts on the company. Neighborhood merchants are honoring the drafts for the 9,500 employees, and are giving merchandise certificates as change.

Scrip was paper money printed by anyone but the Federal government. A big employer like Western Electric could pay its workers with printed paper, and the workers would accept it in exchange for their labor. Why? Because they knew that the local merchants would accept the scrip in exchange for merchandise. And why would the merchants accept this scrip? Because they knew that Western Electric was a reliable business that would honor its scrip, exchanging it for money when it became available (or exchanging it for telephones, which Western Electric manufactured).

Money works because of this *network of trust*. Everyone who accepts money does so because he or she believes that everyone else will accept money. Workers would not accept scrip as wages if they found that local stores rejected it as payment for merchandise. Workers who tried to shop outside the neighborhood where Western Electric was trusted would find that their scrip was mere paper.

Consider the problem of Francis Saitta, a lawyer from Brooklyn.

> New York, March 4. When he learned of the bank holiday he congratulated himself on having taken two $100 bills as a fee on Friday evening. He attempted to cash the bills at the Fulton Savings Bank, the County Treasurer's office and a leading Brooklyn restaurant. There were no takers. Finally he obtained two $50 bills for one of the notes at a postal savings bank. Going to a cigar store where he is known, he ordered $1 worth of cigars and proffered a $50 bill.

> "Just give us an I.O.U., Mr. Saitta," said the clerk. Mr. Saitta has the cigars— which he did not want—and the $200.

Merchants were hoarding their small bills and change. Mr. Saitta's hundred dollar bills had effectively ceased to be money. No one would accept them in exchange for merchandise. Had he known, he most likely would not have accepted them himself. Ironically, these hundred dollar bills, with all the "legal foundation" one could ask, did not act as money. Western Electric scrip, with no legal foundation at all, did act as money. Legal standing helps build a network of trust. But it doesn't guarantee it.

There's another problem with barter. The Golden Gloves boxing tournament in New York City hired an appraiser to stand at the gate. The ticket price was fifty cents, but anything worth that amount was accepted: hot dogs, noodles, spark plugs, canned goods, potatoes, and foot balm were all accepted in exchange for a ticket.

> Lewiston, Montana, March 7. The Lewiston Democrat-News announced that, until April 1, the following subscription rates will be in effect: One year, ten bushels of wheat; two years, 18 bushels; three years, 26 bushels.

> North St. Paul, Minnesota, March 7. Foodstuffs of a value of 50 cents were accepted tonight as admission prices for a high school basketball tournament.

How many hot dogs is a boxing ticket worth? How many pigs does it take for a week's stay at a hotel? Is a pair of pants good for a one way bus ride, or a round trip? With barter, people must keep in mind the values of every good or service in terms of every other good or service. If there are two goods, there is one rate of exchange to know (two hot dogs = one ticket). If there are three goods, there are three rates of exchange (hot dogs and tickets, tickets and noodles, noodles and hot dogs). If there are 100 goods, there are 4,950 rates of exchange. There are thousands of goods.

One way to solve this problem is to hire an expert. The boxing promoter hired an appraiser to judge the value of everything patrons offered. That slowed down the process of selling tickets, though, making for long lines, probably cutting down on attendance. The newspaper thought of another solution in Montana. If everyone has access to the same product, like wheat, prices can be quoted in that product. That simplifies matters, unless the subscriber raises corn.

Money solves this problem, because it is a *unit of account*. The prices of all products are measured in money. The number of prices merely equals the number of products. People know the relative value of goods and services by comparing their prices, measured in money. That's what they did in North St. Paul. They measured the value of foodstuffs in money, to determine how much was needed for a ticket. Money was used to measure value, even when the money itself wasn't used in the exchange.

Some people have an advantage in barter.

> Miami Florida, March 5. The Brooklyn Dodgers, training here in this winter playground, today found their official till totaled exactly $5.85. Manager Max Carey shot 18 holes of golf on the Miami-Biltmore course today and paid off his caddy with an autographed baseball.

> New York, March 4. Take the plight of Irving Leibowitz, president of a watch company, who had an engagement to go horseback riding. He had the horse and the crop, but no riding boots and no money. He resorted to barter, finally exchanging a watch for a pair of boots.

Some goods are almost universally wanted. Doctors and farmers do alright with barter, because medical care and food are almost as universally wanted as money. (If money disappeared today, computer experts could probably be added to the list of fortunate occupations.) There's always a baseball fan wanting an autograph from the Dodger manager. Everyone can use a watch. But barter is time consuming. Mr. Leibowitz *finally* made a barter deal. With money, he could have spent more time on his horse.

A watch manufacturer has another advantage. His product can be a *store of value*. If he has a thousand watches in his warehouse, he knows that he can buy food, pay the rent, and go horseback riding in the future. Even if the stable owner already has a watch, he or she might take another because it will hold its value. A watch is a way to save wealth for future purchases. The Dodger manager is less fortunate. Fame is fleeting, and if the Dodgers have a losing season, perhaps even a baseball fan won't want his autograph. The manager can't be too sure that his closet full of signed baseballs will buy anything in the future.

Money solves this problem, too. Money is a store of value. It can be kept and exchanged for products in the future. Barring too much inflation, it holds its value.

Back in 1933, economic activity began to shrink without money. Broadway theaters were among the first to feel the pinch. People still wanted to see shows, and they had enough income to do so. They just had no way to pay for the tickets. The presence of money increases economic activity. Its absence decreases it. In a sense, money is a technology that facilitates exchanges, just like EBay on the web.

Money facilitates exchanges, and that facilitates *specialization*. The need for a double coincidence of wants makes barter a risky business. If Mr. Saitta, the lawyer, can't find someone who needs legal advice in exchange for lunch, he goes hungry. So he dare not specialize exclusively in legal work, even if that is the very best thing he does. He must be part farmer, to make sure he is fed, part tailor, to make sure he is clothed, part carpenter, to make sure he is housed. He must do these things even if he is not very good at them. He gives up doing what he does best to do things he doesn't do well. Society gives up high quality legal services and gets low quality carpentry.

Money is a universally wanted medium of exchange. People can specialize in the things they do best. Good lawyers produce more legal advice, good farmers produce more food, and good carpenters produce more houses. Money allows more output to be produced from a nation's resources. Money not only facilitates more exchanges, it facilitates more production.

Deposit Insurance
Banks began to reopen on March 13. Bank runs did not resume. People seemed to have lost their fear. Deposits exceeded withdrawals.

The banking bill was just the first of a flurry of acts during what is now called "The Hundred Days." Some were temporary measures. Others had their time upon the policy scene, then disappeared. But some permanently changed the way the nation did business.

Closing banks was a temporary, and unsatisfactory, solution to the bank run problem. Policymakers now looked for a more permanent solution. They found it in *deposit insurance*. Deposit insurance meant that when a bank failed, its depositors would not lose the money in their checking or savings accounts. They would be repaid from a federally supported insurance fund, created by contributions from all insured banks.

Deposit insurance means bank failures do not cost people their checking and savings accounts. It eliminates the reason for bank runs. This allows banks to keep lower reserves and charge lower interest rates.

Between 1896 and 1933, 150 bills had been introduced to insure or guarantee bank deposits. The measures had always been defeated at the Federal level, but eight states had adopted such plans (the Great Plains states from Texas to North Dakota, plus Washington State). Under the stress of the bank failures of the 1920s and the banking panics of the Great Depression, all of these plans had failed. Their insurance funds had run out of money.

In 1933 Congressman Henry Steagall of Alabama again proposed deposit insurance. The Depression bank runs had given Steagall and his supporters powerful arguments. They pointed out that the fear of bank runs caused bankers to restrict lending, in an attempt to build reserves. This reduced investment. They pointed out that bank failures caused people to lose their savings, which reduced consumption. And, they pointed out the sheer injustice of a family losing the savings of years due to a bank failure. Deposit insurance would solve these problems, they declared. Bank runs would not occur, because depositors would not fear losing their money if a bank closed. This would free banks to keep lower reserves and lend more. Bank failures would not reduce consumption, because the insurance fund would repay depositor losses. Justice would be served because families would not lose their savings when their bank closed.

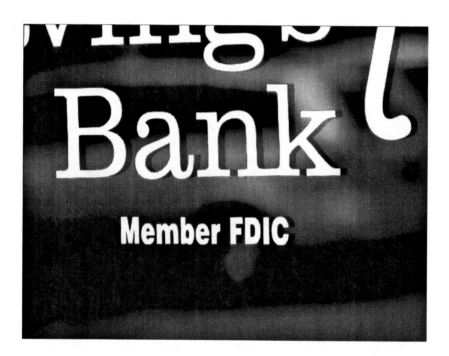

Posted in the window. Banks post the phrase "Member FDIC" in their windows to assure their depositors that their money is protected by the Federal Deposit Insurance Corporation. Should the bank face financial troubles, there's no reason to withdraw deposits. Deposit insurance means customers will be paid by the insurance fund if the bank fails.

Its opponents pointed out that deposit insurance had failed in every one of the states that had adopted such schemes. Supporters responded that the state failures happened because the western states did not have diversified economies. Too many of their small banks loaned exclusively to farmers. When the farm economy suffered, so many banks failed that state insurance funds gave out. With a national insurance program, the fund contributions would come from banks that loaned to all industries. A slump in a particular industry or region would not deplete the fund.

Why not strengthen banks rather than insure them? bankers asked. They opposed deposit insurance and supported instead nationwide branch banking. Rural banks failed because they did not have diversified loans. The bankers argued that if rural banks were instead branches of big city banks, the rural bank would benefit from the diversified portfolio of loans to all industries (as well as more competent management). No longer would country banks fail simply because of a downturn in the farm economy because all their loans were to farmers. They pointed to Canada, which had ten national banks with 3,000 branches, and no bank failures—not one—during the Depression.

Senator Carter Glass supported national branch banking. He had been an originator of the Federal Reserve bill as a Congressman from Virginia in 1913 and had been Woodrow Wilson's Secretary of the Treasury. Now he was back in Congress as a Virginia Senator. Glass proposed a bill to permit branch banking early in 1933. Senator Huey Long of Louisiana opposed it. The self-declared advocate of the little man, Long was suspicious of the concentrated power big national banks might have. When the Glass bill came up for debate, Long filibustered for ten days. The bill died.

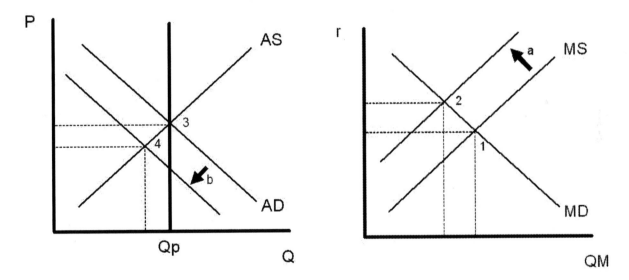

Figure 6-7. Bank Runs. Bankers fear bank runs, so they build their reserves and lend less. This reduces the money multiplier, and reduces the money supply (a). The real interest rate increases (1 to 2). This reduces investment spending, and aggregate demand (b), through second shift #2. The decline in output (3 to 4) contributes to the depression. With deposit insurance, depositors have no reason to engage in bank runs, so banks do not build excess reserves. The money supply decrease (a) never happens.

Opponents of deposit insurance were ready with more arguments. If contributions to the insurance fund were based on a percentage of deposits, most of the fund would come from big city banks in the Northeast and Midwest. Most of the failures since the Great War had been in small rural banks in the south and west. Under an insurance scheme, these failed banks would receive the payments from the fund. It wasn't fair to force big banks to subsidize small banks, city banks to subsidize country banks, the northeast and midwest to subsidize the south and west. Especially, they said, it wasn't fair for successful banks to be forced to subsidize failed banks.

Deposit insurance also would promote bad banking practices, opponents claimed. Banks that took big risks sometimes made big profits. They might offer high interest rates on deposits, hoping to attract depositors from their competitors.   They might lend to speculative real estate or mining ventures, hoping for big returns. Often enough, big risks made for big losses. Banks didn't operate this way because people would not deposit their money in a bank that took big risks. Depositors had to monitor the practices of their banks, for fear that the bank would fail and they'd lose their money, and this prevented risky practices. If deposits were insured, this incentive for people to monitor their banks would disappear. Banks could take risks without fear of losing depositors. Prudent banking practice would become impossible, because customers would flock to the banks that offered outrageously high interest rates. Deposit insurance, its opponents said, would ruin bank management, create even more bank failures, and ultimately cost depositors and taxpayers very large sums in insurance payments.

Moral hazard occurs when protecting people from risk causes them to take more risks.

This is an argument known to economists as *moral hazard*. Sometimes, adopting policies to reduce the consequences of risk causes people to take more risks. Well-paved roads may make people drive too fast.   Flood insurance may encourage people to build on the flood plain.   A well-run fire department may cause people to be careless about fire. Here, deposit insurance may make bank customers ignore risky bank practices. The result of moral hazard could be more accidents, more flooded homes, more fires, and more bank failures.

Supporters of insurance responded to this problem by placing an upper limit on the amount of deposits to be insured. The original ceiling was $2,500—an individual's deposits up to this amount were guaranteed, but deposits beyond this amount were not. Because most depositors had small amounts of money, under this ceiling 97% of all *depositors* were fully insured. But because big depositors made up a large share of total bank deposits, only 27% of total bank *deposits* would be insured. This meant that large depositors would still have an incentive to monitor bank management. Supporters argued that only big depositors were able to do such monitoring, anyway.

Deposit insurance was instantly successful, beyond the expectations of supporters and opponents. More than one thousand banks had failed in each year from 1930 to 1933— 4,000 failed in 1933 alone. In 1934, *nine* banks failed. For the next 50 years, the annual number of failures was less than 100; in most of those years, less than ten. By 1935, even the bankers had come around to support the idea.

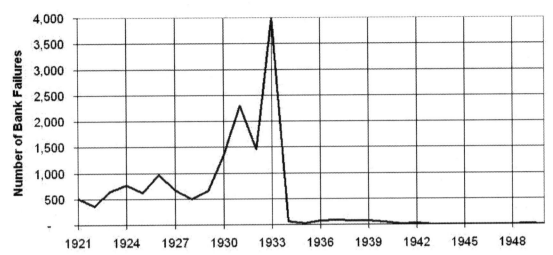

Figure 6-8. Number of bank failures, 1921-1950. Throughout most of the 1920's between 500 and 1000 banks failed every year. The figure topped 2,000 in 1931 and peaked at 4,000 in 1933. With the introduction of deposit insurance in 1934, the number of failures dropped to near zero.

The United States Leaves Gold

Almost as an afterthought, the United States left the gold standard, with a whimper, not a bang. There was no single, economy-quaking announcement, as in Great Britain in 1931. Instead, the Roosevelt administration chipped away at the standard with a series of acts. The Federal Reserve was allowed to use both gold and government bonds as a currency reserve, meaning gold hardly limited the money supply at all. It was then made illegal for U.S. citizens to own gold for monetary purposes. Private citizens were required to turn over to the government all gold not used in industry or jewelry (they were allowed to keep their gold dental fillings, too).

In effect, the Treasury no longer pledged to U.S. residents that it would exchange dollars for gold. Finally, the official price of gold was increased from $20.67 to $35 per ounce for international trade purposes, a devaluation of the dollar in foreign exchange. Gold still played a role in international trade, but by the end of 1933, the U.S. money supply was no longer backed by gold, nor was the size of the money supply influenced by gold in any significant sense. From then until now, U.S. money has been *fiat currency*, money by government decree.

MacroPolicy Now: We Won't Do It Again

As a Princeton economics professor Ben Bernanke made a career studying Federal Reserve policy during the Great Depression. He concluded, as have many others, that the mistakes in Fed policy turned a nasty recession into a full blown ten-year Great Depression. As a member of the Federal Reserve Board, he vowed "we won't do it again."

The recession that became the Great Depression began in August, 1929. The 2007-2009 "Great Recession" began in December 2007. At this writing that's 40 months ago. Let's compare what the Federal Reserve did in the first 40 months of the Great Depression, to what Ben Bernanke's Fed has done in the 40 months since December 2007.

In August 1929 the discount rate was 5%. In December 1932, 40 months later, it was 3.5%. The Fed cut the discount rate one-and-a-half points. Actually, it had been increased from 2.5% in October 1931 when Great Britain had left the gold standard.

Now the Fed's main policy indicator is the federal funds rate. In December 2007 the federal funds rate was 4.2%. It had already been cut by a point since July. By April 2010 the federal funds rate less than 0.2%. It had been near-zero since December 2008. The Fed cut the federal funds rate by more than four percentage points.

Remember that the *monetary base* is the sum of currency in circulation and bank reserves. Fed policy directly affects bank reserves. The Fed uses open market operations to buy bonds from banks for money, and that money becomes bank reserves. Changes in reserves tell us about Fed policy. In August 1929 the monetary base was $6.1 billion; in December 1932 it was $6.7 billion. That's a 10% increase.

There's been lots of economic growth and a whole lot of inflation since 1929, so the monetary base is much larger now. In December 2007 the monetary base was $847 billion. In April 2011, it was $2,532 billion (that's two-and-a-half trillion dollars). That's a 199% increase.

The money supply can be measured by the currency held by the public, plus their deposits in checking accounts. This measure is known as "M-1". In August 1929 the money supply was $26.5 billion. In December 1932 it was $20.3 billion. The money supply had *dropped* by 23%.

The money supply in December 2007 was $1,374 billion; in April 2011 it was $1,901 billion. That's a 38% increase.

Notice that in both periods, the monetary base increased more than the money supply. Remember that the money supply is the monetary base times the *money multiplier*. And also remember that, when banks get scared that their loans won't be paid or their depositors will withdraw their money, they increase their reserves and cut their lending, and the money multiplier decreases. During 1929-32, the monetary base increased a little

173

and the money supply decreased. During 2007-11, the monetary base increased a lot and the money supply increased a little. In both cases, the money multiplier was falling. Banks were scared.

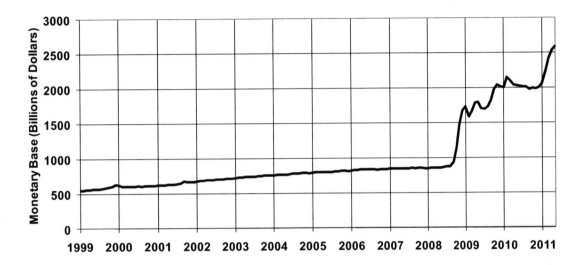

Figure 6-9. Monetary Base. The Fed responded in a huge way to the Panic of 2008. By January 2009 the monetary based had doubled from its mid-2008 level. As of May 2011 is had tripled.

They were so scared during the peak of the financial crisis of 2008 that for a time monetary policy didn't work. Banks kept as reserves most of the money the Fed created. The Fed stuffed bank vaults full of money, but lending didn't increase. In August, September and October, 2008, the Fed reduced the federal funds rate by a full point. But the rate at which banks lend to businesses short-term went *up*. Banks weren't lending, no matter what the Fed was doing. This is one version of a situation is called a *liquidity trap*, and monetary policy is not effective.

Still, in the Great Depression the money multiplier was falling. The Fed did not use its tools to increase the monetary base enough to keep the money supply from falling. The falling money supply caused high real interest rates, which choked off investment spending. In the Great Recession the money multiplier was falling. The Fed used its tools (and invented new ones) to engineer a massive increase in the monetary base. The money supply increased, and real interest rates (after a brief spike upward) remained low. Investment fell, but has begun to recover.

The Federal Reserve cut its interest rate more in the Great Recession than it did in the Great Depression. It increased the monetary base much more in the more recent crisis. It allowed the money supply to drop in 1929-31, while the money supply increased in 2007-11.

We don't have monthly unemployment or inflation rates for the earlier period, but the unemployment rate for the year 1929 was 3.2%. It was 15.9% in 1932, and rising. The unemployment rate in December 2007 was 5.0%. It was up to 9.1% in May 2011, and (in most months) falling. The Great Recession was bad. But the Great Depression was a whole lot worse.

The Fed has received (and probably deserves) criticism for failing to regulate the mortgage market and failing to recognize the scope of the disaster early on. But pretty clearly, compared to the Fed of 1929, Bernanke's Fed didn't "do it again."

Terms in this Chapter, in order of appearance
Stock
Dividends
Initial public offering
Stock price index
Dow Jones Industrial Average
Speculative bubble
Leverage
Equity
Inventory Recession
Stock market crash
Margin call
Expectations
Wealth effect
Liquidate
John Maynard Keynes
Tax increase
Bank holiday
Barter
Double coincidence of wants
Medium of exchange
Scrip
Network of trust
Unit of account
Store of value
Specialization
Deposit Insurance
Moral hazard
Fiat currency
Monetary base
Money multiplier

Notes
Good descriptions of the Roaring '20s can be found in Galbraith (1954), Schlesinger (1956), and Kennedy (1999). Calvin Coolidge is quoted in Schlesinger (p. 57), John Raskob in Galbraith (p. 57), Irving Fisher in Galbraith (p. 75), who notes correctly that

Fisher made a great many lasting contributions to economics. His reputation should not rest on his infamous stock market prediction.

You still can't beat Galbraith's (1954) description of the stock market crash for sheer drama. Galbraith notes that in the visitor's gallery of the New York Stock Exchange on Black Thursday was none other than Winston Churchill, former Chancellor of the Exchequer. Churchill had linked the pound to gold in 1925, one step on the road to the Great Depression. , Galbraith writes, "Now Churchill, it could be imagined, was viewing his awful handiwork" (p. 105). That takes some pretty vivid imagining.

Romer (1993) offers a good overview of the Depression, and takes the view that declines in consumption and investment were a major cause.

The description of Marriner Eccles heading off a bank run, doing Jimmy Stewart for real (in *It's a Wonderful Life*) is from Hyman (pp. 78-81).

The classic analysis of the Fed's (lack of) actions during the Great Depression is by Friedman and Schwartz (Chapter 7, "The Great Contraction"). Especially useful are the details of the arguments between George Harrison and his opponents (pp. 363-380). It was these authors who nailed down the fact that the Fed's policy in 1929-33 was contractionary. Degen, Romer, and just about everyone since 1963 has something to say about the Fed's culpability. Wheelock (1992) discusses several explanations for why the Fed acted as it did. The "antagonisms" quote about Harrison is from Ahamed (p. 319).

At a party celebrating Milton Friedman's 90th birthday, Benjamin Bernanke, then a Federal Reserve governor, accepted the blame for the Great Depression on behalf of the Fed. "Regarding the Great Depression," he said to Professor Friedman, "You're right, we did it. We're very sorry. But thanks to you, we won't do it again."

Eichengreen (1992), Temin (1989) and Bernanke (1994) are excellent sources showing how the gold standard contributed to the Depression. Stein (1996, pp. 26-38) tells the story of President Hoover's 1932 tax increase. The Tax Foundation (1994, pp. 98-109) provides data on federal tax rates before and after 1932.

The figures on the monetary base came from the St. Louis Federal Reserve's "FRED" website (https://research.stlouisfed.org/fred2), a great place to find economic data. That's where the more recent money supply data came from too. The 1929-31 money supply data comes from Friedman and Schwartz (1963), Appendix A.

There are a great many descriptions of Franklin Roosevelt's inaugural and Henry Steagall's famous rolled up newspaper. from the description here is based on Kennedy (1999, pp. 131-137).

Humor writer Dave Barry got it exactly right when he explained money in his book, *Dave Barry's Money Secrets* (2006, pp. 10-11).

If our money is just pieces of paper, backed by nothing, why is it valuable? The answer is: *Because we all believe it's valuable.*

Really, that's pretty much it. Remember the part in *Peter Pan* where we clap to prove that we believe in fairies, and we save Tinker Bell? That's our monetary system! It's the Tinker Bell system! We see everybody *else* running around after these pieces of paper, and we figure, *Hey, these pieces of paper must be valuable.* That's why if you exchanged your house for, say, a pile of acorns, everybody would think you're insane; whereas if you exchange your house for a pile of dollars, everybody thinks you're rational, because you get . . . pieces of paper! The special kind, with the big hovering eyeball!

Manchester (1974, p. 78) provides examples of how people dealt with the bank holiday. The Federal Deposit Insurance Corporation has published a nice history of itself (1998). Flood (1992) and Friedman and Schwartz (pp. 434-442) offer the details of the debate on deposit insurance.

Sources

Ahamed, Liaquat. *Lords of Finance: The Bankers Who Broke the World.* New York: Penguin Books, 2009.

Barry, Dave. 2006. *Dave Barry's Money Secrets.* New York: Three Rivers Press.

Bernanke, Ben S. 1994. "The Macroeconomics of the Great Depression: A Comparative Approach." NBER Working Paper No. 4814. Cambridge, Massachusetts: National Bureau of Economic Research.

Degen, Robert A. 1987. *The American Monetary System.* Lexington, Massachusetts: D.C. Heath and Company, Lexington Books.

Eichengreen, Barry. 1992. *Golden Fetters: The Gold Standard and the Great Depression 1919-1939.* New York: Oxford University Press.

Federal Deposit Insurance Corporation. 1998. *A Brief History of Deposit Insurance in the United States.* Washington, D.C.: FDIC.

Flood, Mark D. 1992. The Great Deposit Insurance Debate. *Federal Reserve Bank of St. Louis Review* 74 (4) (July/August): 51-77.

Friedman, Milton and Anna Jacobson Schwartz. 1963. *A Monetary History of the United States, 1867-1960.* Princeton, New Jersey: Princeton University Press.

Galbraith, John Kenneth. 1954. *The Great Crash 1929.* Boston: Houghton Mifflin Company (3rd edition, 1972).

Hyman, Sidney. 1976. *Marriner S. Eccles: Private Entrepreneur and Public Servant.* Stanford, California: Stanford University Press.

Kennedy, David M. 1999. *Freedom From Fear: The American People in Depression and War, 1929-1945.* New York: Oxford University Press.

Manchester, William. 1974. *The Glory and the Dream.* New York: Bantam Books.
Romer, Christina. 1993. "The Nation in Depression." *Journal of Economic Perspectives* 7 (2) (Spring): 19-40.

Schlesinger, Arthur M., Jr. 1956. *The Crisis of the Old Order.* Boston: Houghton Mifflin Company.

Stein, Herbert. 1996. *The Fiscal Revolution in America.* (2nd Revised Edition) Washington, D.C.: AEI Press.

Tax Foundation. 1994. *Facts and Figures on Government Finance.* Washington, D.C.: Tax Foundation.

Temin, Peter. 1989. *Lessons from the Great Depression.* Cambridge, Massachusetts: MIT Press.

Timberlake, Richard H. 1993. *Monetary Policy in the United States: An Intellectual and Institutional History.* Chicago: University of Chicago Press.

Wheelock, David C. 1992. "Monetary Policy in the Great Depression: What the Fed Did, and Why." *Federal Reserve Bank of St. Louis Review* 74 (2) (March/April): 3-28.

News Articles
Andrews, Edmund L. "Obama to Nominate Bernanke to Continue Role as Fed Chief," *New York Times*, August 25, 2009.

Baker, Peter. "A Professor and a Banker Bury Old Dogma on Markets," *New York Times*, September 21, 2008.

Chan, Sewell. "Is Ben Bernanke Having Fun Yet?" *New York Times*, May 14, 2010.

Chapter 7
Fiscal Policy and Automatic Stabilizers

MacroPolicy Now: Stimulus in the Great Recession

The Great Recession began in December 2007. In response, Congress passed and President George W. Bush signed an income tax cut, which took effect in the Spring of 2008. Taxpayers received $600 per adult and $300 per child.

Some people spent the windfall. A freelance writer named Rudy Adler created a website, HowISpentMyStimulus.com, asking people to post what they did with the money. "I'm goin' to Disneyworld," wrote a woman in Sioux Falls, South Dakota. A man in Johnson City, Texas, said he would send his Labrador retriever puppy to hunting dog school. A Houston couple lost their whole rebate gambling in Las Vegas. Diana Donahoo of Hampton, Virginia, posted a photo of a diamond-studded engagement ring on her finger, paid for by her sweetie's tax rebate.

But not all of the rebates added to spending. Guillermo Gonzalez, a wine salesman in Miami, received his rebate via direct deposit. He was behind on his mortgage payment, so with a click of the mouse, he sent the whole rebate to the mortgage company. "They think they give you a check to go out and spend some money, but it's not enough," he said. "The way the economy is going, people are too scared to spend."

The effects of the tax cut faded, then the financial crisis made the Great Recession worse in the Fall of 2008. In response, in February 2009, Congress passed and President Obama signed a stimulus bill worth $787 billion in added spending and tax cuts. The bill provided tax cuts to families and businesses, aid to state and local governments, and direct spending on "shovel ready" infrastructure projects. Separate bills extended unemployment insurance benefits.

Perhaps the best-known economic research firms are IHS Global Insight, Macroeconomic Advisers and Moody's Economy.com. These are non-partisan "economists for hire," who serve Wall Street and governments alike. (The state of Indiana uses estimates from Global Insight in its revenue forecasts.) They all estimate that the bill has shaved almost two percentage points off the unemployment rate. The non-partisan Congressional Budget Office considers these estimates to be conservative. Yet the stimulus bill is not seen as a success by many people.

The reasons for the stimulus's middling popularity aren't a mystery. The unemployment rate remained near 9 percent by summer 2011, and many families were struggling. Saying that things could have been even worse doesn't exactly inspire. Liberals didn't like the stimulus because they wished it were bigger. Republicans didn't like it because it required more Federal debt. The Obama administration hurt the bill's popularity by

---

---

making too rosy an economic forecast upon taking office. In addition, the introduction of the most visible parts of the program — spending on roads, buildings and the like — was a bit sluggish.

New attempts to stimulate the economy were made in December 2010. Existing tax breaks were extended, and a one-year cut in the Social Security payroll tax was enacted. In 2011 rising gasoline prices soaked up much of the spending from this tax break, and the effects of the 2009 stimulus package were fading. By April 2011 the recovery seemed to falter. There were few calls for additional stimulus, however.

It's almost standard procedure now, to use expansionary fiscal policy when the economy is in recession, or when output is less than potential. Republican President Bush offered tax cuts. Democratic President Obama offered tax cuts and added government spending. The first big use of expansionary fiscal policy—in the form of spending increases— occurred in the 1930's. What was done then can still teach us about fiscal policy issues now . . . .

Real People in the Great Depression

It was 1933. The unemployment rate was nearly 25%. Real GDP had fallen 29% from its 1929 peak. Prices had been falling 7% a year for four years. Nine thousand banks had failed. The data tell the story of the Great Depression. But numbers can be cold. Consider instead a story that journalist Russell Baker tells in his memoir, *Growing Up*.

Russell Baker was a child during the Great Depression. His father had died, and his widowed mother Elizabeth had moved with him and his sister from Morrisonville, Virginia to Newark, New Jersey, to live with her brother until she could find a job. She had been a school teacher in Virginia, but Newark didn't think much of her Virginia qualifications, and anyway the school districts weren't hiring. In 1931, there were no jobs to be had.

Her hopes came to rest on a Danish immigrant named Oluf. He was a successful man, a baker who had graduated to traveling salesman, selling margarine to bakeries in the northeast. He had borrowed to buy three houses in Pennsylvania, which he rented to tenants. He was a jovial man who considered himself a developing American success story. Elizabeth loved him.

He wrote her letters from the road, which she saved her whole life. The letters were written in his Danish-English, and always ended "with love to you and the Children from Oluf." Things began to go wrong for Oluf in 1932.

> May 9, 1932
> Dear Elizabeth: Today I have been together with our Manager all day, and he told me that it look like I will have to go June first. Business is so bad and getting worse for us, he let four salesmen go here May first so now there is only seven left. Last year there was seventheen.

He tried his contacts with bakers up and down the coast, with no luck. He went back to Pennsylvania, to tend to his real estate.

August 11, 1932
I being to think I was going to sell a House this morning, but the Party diddent have any mony, now I have three Houses empty, nothing coming in, and Taxes to be paid, well it will come out OK, I hope so, I always tell People not to worrie, so I won't eather. . . .

He had to borrow more money, for upkeep on the houses.

November 11, 1932
Butter Prices are down where they were a year ago, and till they go back up rown 30 cents pr lbs, they never will hire me to demonstrate Margarine, now I am down and out again, and I don't like to keep on borrowing Money from the Banks, because I got to paid it back sometimes sooner or later.

He kept trying.

November 25, 1932
I vill bet you I spendt over five Dollars on Stemps, sending letters to every one of this Bakers, who offered me jobs with big mony when I was traveling, but only one of them answered, no there was two, one in Newark and one in Boston, but they said they diddent have anything just now, the rest of them wouldent even spend a two cent Stamps on me, and they all were my Friends. . . .

> **Margarine is a substitute for butter. With butter prices low, no one was buying margarine, so no one would hire Oluf to sell it.**

He had a job prospect at a bakery in Baltimore, and Elizabeth advised him not to settle for too little pay.

February 1933
Thanks very much for you Advice, but Elizabeth the War is over with, and good times is over with, them days we did seat a Price on ourself, but to day we just take what we can get and must be satisfact—am I not right?

The bakery told him no. He was having trouble paying the taxes and mortgage on his houses. They hadn't seen each other in months.

April 14, 1933
I talk to the Caschier in our Bank to day, asking him to lett me have 1500 Dollars, he said, not now, but come in here middle of next month, I think then you can

have it, ef I do I will come to you, ef I could have got it to day, I would have been down with you tomorrow night . . . .

Then, suddenly, on April 24, he wrote "Dear Elizabeth, Thanks for you letter I received to day, I am sorry, but Please don't write me any more." She wrote back right away, and received a reply, "the City took everything I hat for Taxes, so I am down and out, that is why I don't want you to write me any more. . . ."

She wrote again anyway, and again, and finally, one last reply.

> May 19, 1933
> I was hope someday to come to know you, by getting a job down there, but now I never can come down, I am like I told you before, lost. . . . So I am asking you to stop writing to me, because I am not interested in anything any more, love to you all from Oluf.

Above All, Try Something

On that desperate day in March 1933, when President Roosevelt took the oath and said there was nothing to fear but fear, many people must have thought, "yes, but what will you *do*?" Roosevelt hadn't really said during the campaign, and he wasn't saying now. He was elected, not so much for a set of policies, but for an *attitude*. He'd said it in a speech in the spring of the campaign, at Oglethorpe University in Georgia:

> The country needs and, unless I mistake its temper, the country demands bold, persistent experimentation. It is common sense to take a method and try it: If it fails, admit it frankly and try another. But above all, try something. The millions who are in want will not stand by silently forever while the things to satisfy their needs are within easy reach.

"Bold, persistent experimentation" is the phrase most remembered from this speech, but another phrase, "above all, try something," may have been a better gauge of his thinking.

The country may not have known what Roosevelt's policies would be, but those policies had a name: the *New Deal*. In a speech accepting the Democratic nomination for president in July 1932, Roosevelt declared, "I pledge you, I pledge myself to a new deal for the American people". The press picked up the phrase "new deal," and that's what they called collection of policies that the administration hoped would end the Depression. The members of the administration were called "New Dealers." Eventually even Roosevelt began using the term.

No one knew for sure what had caused the Great Depression, or why it was lasting so long, or what to do about it. Economic theory seemed to have nothing to contribute. According to demand and supply analysis, the Depression would solve itself. Were people unemployed? Then wages would fall until the number of workers demanded equaled the number wanting work. Were businesses having trouble selling goods? Then prices would fall until the amount of goods for sale equaled the amount people wanted to buy. Were businesses refusing to invest in new plant and equipment? Then interest rates would fall until money was cheap enough to encourage borrowing for investment.

Economic theory had one message for government: hands off! The market mechanism would correct the problem, through changes in prices, wages and interest rates. The *liquidationists* thought that a recession might even do the economy some good, by making people work harder and save more, and by bankrupting inefficient businesses, so their resources would pass to more efficient hands.

But wages had fallen, and still unemployment rose. Prices had fallen, and still goods remained on the shelves. Interest rates had fallen (in nominal terms, not in real terms), and still businesses would not invest. Economics still had no message other than "wait."

What about monetary policy? The policy failures of the Fed in 1929-33 had a curious side effect. Many inside and outside of the Federal Reserve thought that Fed policy had been expansionary. Hadn't they reduced the discount rate? Hadn't they made some open market bond purchases, including a really big one in 1932? They decided that since the Fed had tried but failed to stop the Depression, monetary policy was ineffective. Reducing interest rates could not stop an economic downturn. Only in the 1950s and 1960s did researchers look again to find that the Fed had allowed the money supply to fall by about a third. Most now think that expansionary monetary policy could have been effective, if only the Fed had tried it.

Whether it wasn't tried, or whether it didn't work, monetary policy wasn't doing the job. So Roosevelt looked to another solution: *fiscal policy*. Fiscal is an adjective meaning "having to do with government taxes and budgets." The problem during a recession or depression is lack of demand. Businesses can produce more goods and services and employ more workers doing it, but consumers do not have the means or the desire to buy these products.

> **Fiscal policy tries to stabilize the economy with changes in the Federal government's budget. Changes in government spending and taxes influence spending, and so change aggregate demand.**

With fiscal policy, government can step in and fill the void. Government can cut taxes. This would give consumers greater *after-tax income*, which they could use to buy more goods and services. Businesses would then have reason to produce. They would open their factories and hire more workers. With sales rising, they would have greater reason to invest in plant and equipment, anticipating greater demand in the future.

Government can increase *transfer payments*. Transfers are payments of income by the government to households. Examples are unemployment insurance, social security, welfare, and veterans' pensions. Again, with more income, people would buy more goods and firms would produce more goods, hiring more workers and increasing investment.

Government can increase its *purchases*, buying directly the goods and services produced by businesses. Government can hire more employees to do useful things (or not-so-useful things). The employees can build dams, roads, post offices, aircraft carriers, pyramids. They can rake leaves. They can dig holes and fill them in again. The businesses that supply the materials like bricks, steel, lumber or asphalt would have a reason to produce, hire workers, and make investments. So would the businesses that supply equipment, like earth movers and cranes, shovels and rakes, furniture and appliances.

Deficit Spending or a Balanced Budget

Of course, during a recession or depression government tax revenue goes down. People pay a share of their incomes to income taxes, but with all that unemployment, there are fewer incomes to tax. Federal government budget deficits usually get bigger during a recession (or surpluses turn into deficits), which means that the revenue it collects is not enough to pay for its spending. During a recession, revenues drop and spending does not. The government borrows the difference by selling Treasury bonds. Investors lend the government money in exchange for bonds, which are promises to repay plus interest after a period of time. These are the very bonds that the Federal Reserve buys and sells in open market operations.

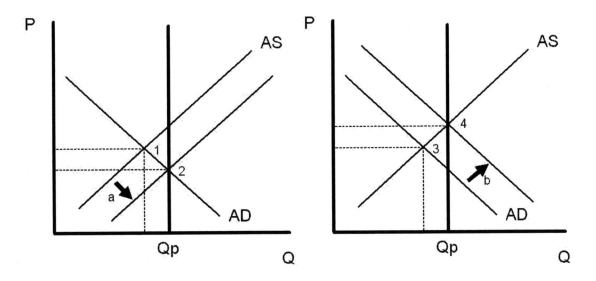

Figure 7-1. Hands Off, Hands On. An economy in Depression produces less than potential output (1 or 3). The traditional "hands-off" policy waits for wages and other resource costs to fall, increasing aggregate supply (a). Potential output is achieved (1 to 2), along with some deflation. It's a policy of waiting for second shift #1 to fix the problem. An expansionary fiscal policy—deficit spending—increases aggregate demand (b), achieving potential output (3 to 4), along with some inflation. The supply shift (a) is usually slower and more painful than the demand shift (b).

To use fiscal policy to fight a recession or depression, then, the government must be willing to make its deficit bigger. Raise spending on transfers and purchases, cut taxes, and it will be spending that much more than it takes in. This is called *deficit spending*.

It was a solution, but it was radical thinking in 1933. One such thinker was a Utah banker and businessman named Marriner Eccles. Banks won't finance new factories, he told a gathering of teachers on October 27, "when half of our productive property is idle for lack of consumption and a large percentage of our business properties are vacant, for the want of paying tenants." Banks couldn't engineer recovery, but the government could. "The only escape from a depression must be by increased spending. We must depend upon the government to save what we have of a price, profit, and credit system."

Some members of the Roosevelt administration liked what they heard and offered Eccles a job in Washington as Treasury Secretary Henry Morgenthau's special assistant for housing finance. Eccles became one of the administration's most outspoken advocates of *counter-cyclical fiscal policy*—using taxes and the budget to combat the Depression. But Eccles' allies in the administration warned him, "We are all for your thesis. But how are you going to get around Lew Douglas over in the Bureau of the Budget," who was "holding Roosevelt fast to a budget-balancing policy?"

> *To stimulate the economy during a recession or depression, the government must spend more and tax less. This usually creates a budget deficit, so it's known as deficit spending.*

The Director of the Budget, Lewis Douglas, was the administration's chief advocate of a balanced budget. In trying to "hold Roosevelt fast" to the idea, Douglas had an advantage. President Roosevelt wanted a balanced budget. He had criticized the Hoover administration's budget deficits during the 1932 campaign. Lewis Douglas regarded deficits as a great evil and was happy to accept the post of Director of the Budget when it was offered. Such a powerful position could be used to fight for balanced budgets.

Deficits required government borrowing, Douglas explained. Treasury bonds would be sold to the public, and the money the bond buyers lent to the government would be used to pay for spending above tax revenue. Some of these bonds would be bought by the public out of their savings. But, Douglas argued, big and continuing deficits would require a large number of bonds. The public couldn't buy them all, so they would have to be sold to the Federal Reserve. The Fed would buy them through open market operations. In other words, the Fed would pay by printing money. The large quantity of added money would create inflation.

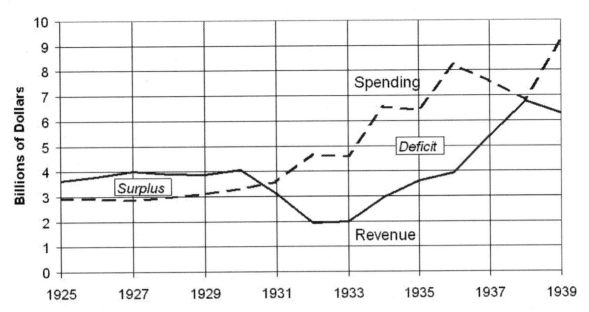

Figure 7-2. The Federal Budget. Federal revenue exceeded spending from 1925 to 1930. That's a budget surplus. Then revenue dropped with the Depression, causing a budget deficit. Revenue didn't drop from 1932 to 1933, probably because of the Hoover tax hike. Revenue began to recover after 1933, but by then the Roosevelt administration was increasing spending. The spending cuts in 1937 and 1938 nearly balanced the budget, but also helped cause a recession within the Depression.

Inflation was Douglas' worst nightmare. He contended that the Communists in Russia and the Nazis in Germany had come to power after inflation had ruined their economies. It would happen in the United States, too. "Great inflations have been followed by revolutions," he said, "The sheer weight of the economic and social forces will compel a dictatorship." Inflationary policies, he once said, would mean "the end of western civilization."

With the Great Depression at its worst, the pressure to "try something" soon overwhelmed any effort to avoid deficits. Congress pushed President Roosevelt to increase spending on construction projects, and he reluctantly signed a bill creating the Public Works Administration (PWA). The $3.3 billion in borrowed funds were meant for big projects, like hydroelectric dams, sewer systems, major highways and bridges, apartment houses. Big projects required a great deal of planning, and Harold Ickes, the Secretary of the Interior and PWA administrator, cautioned that it would be two years before any real construction began. Only $110 million of the $3.3 billion was spent in 1933. Lewis Douglas objected to the expense anyway.

Others in the administration objected to the PWA's cautious pace. Harry Hopkins had been director of relief for New York State when Roosevelt had been governor. Hopkins worried about how the millions of unemployed people would live and eat, and especially how they would survive through the winter of 1933-34. In the fall of 1933 Hopkins approached the President with an idea for a temporary employment program to provide paychecks for millions of people. Roosevelt agreed, and they decided to use some of the unspent PWA funds. Even Ickes saw the need and didn't object (as long as it was temporary). They named the new agency the Civil Works Administration (CWA).

Where Ickes was slow and cautious, Hopkins was fast. The CWA was created on November 9, 1933, and by mid-January 1934 more than four million people were employed on CWA projects. How could this be done? The projects were small—road maintenance, refurbishing existing schools and hospitals, even installing outhouses for farm families—but that meant that they could be started quickly. Hopkins got tools from army warehouses and used the Veterans Administration to distribute paychecks. In its five month existence, the CWA spent more than $800 million on work-relief, completing 180,000 projects.

Roosevelt was urged to continue the CWA. But it was expensive, and Lewis Douglas continued to hammer home the necessity to balance the budget. The program was canceled in March 1934. Hopkins loyally shut it down.

Douglas was gratified by this victory, but he was disturbed by the administration's inclination towards public works spending. The PWA would soon begin to spend in earnest. Hopkins' influence was clearly growing. Roosevelt tried to reassure Douglas that his views were important. But by August 1934, Douglas could stand no longer to be associated with what he saw as the administration's errors. He took a train to the Roosevelt's home in Hyde Park, New York, and resigned in protest.

Employment Programs

Now the tide in the Roosevelt administration seemed to turn. The most potent advocate for balanced budgets was gone. Two weeks later, President Roosevelt asked Marriner Eccles—the outspoken advocate of deficit spending—to become the new head of the Federal Reserve Board. Two weeks after that, in the mid-term Congressional elections (when the President's party usually loses seats), the Democrats won nine new seats in the House and ten in the Senate. They now had enormous majorities in both houses of Congress.

The voters seemed to have put a seal of approval on the administration's policies. Harry Hopkins saw his chance. "Boys—this is our hour!" he declared to his staff. "We've got to get everything we want—a works program, social security, wages and hours, everything—now or never. Get your minds at work on developing a complete ticket to provide security for all the folks of this country up and down and across the board."

Hopkins' had in mind a public works program much bigger and longer lasting than the CWA. His staff worked up a plan, the President agreed, and on April 5, 1935 the Emergency Relief Appropriation Act had passed Congress and was on the President's desk. (But the President wasn't at his desk. He was vacationing on Vincent Astor's yacht. The bill was brought to Florida and he signed it when the boat docked.)

Hopkins' new agency was called the Works Progress Administration (WPA). After a year it employed 3 million people; during its life, 8.5 million. Its employees built half a million miles of highway, nearly a hundred thousand bridges, and eight thousand parks. It was also criticized for creating make-work and for being used by Democratic Party bosses for political patronage. Harold Ickes' Public Works Administration (PWA) also received new funds, and his meticulous administration kept the PWA from much controversy.   Though slow to get started, eventually the PWA built such big projects as LaGuardia Airport in New York City, the San Francisco-Oakland Bay Bridge, and the aircraft carriers *Yorktown* and *Enterprise*.

Doubleday Field in Cooperstown, New York. Harry Hopkins had his fingers in everything.

Ickes did not accept the WPA as he had the CWA in 1934. He was furious at Hopkins for choosing the name WPA, so like that of his own agency, convinced it was a deliberate attempt to confuse the public. The WPA was supposed to engage in smaller projects which employed large numbers of people, while the PWA was devoted to bigger projects requiring long term planning and heavy equipment. In practice, though, the lines dividing these projects were fuzzy, and Ickes accused Hopkins of treading on his territory, as well as his budget. The two men engaged in a public feud so nasty that it made Ickes paranoid and gave Hopkins an ulcer.

Big government construction projects may take years to plan, so they won't add to spending right away. Small projects add to spending faster, but may not result in facilities of lasting use.

Ickes' big projects didn't increase aggregate demand much at first because they took so long to plan. Hopkins' projects increased aggregate demand right away. But in the longer run, Ickes' projects probably affected aggregate *supply* more than Hopkins' projects did. The dams reduced electricity costs; the highways and airports reduced transportation costs. These lower resource costs meant increases in aggregate supply and potential output. We're still getting good use out of Laguardia Airport and the San

Francisco-Oakland Bay bridge. In the long run Ickes' projects increased output more. But as Hopkins once said, "people don't eat in the long run, they eat every day."

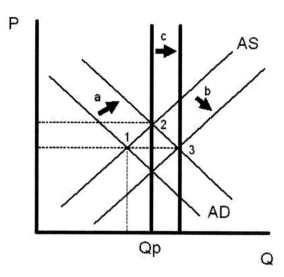

Figure 7-3. Hopkins vs. Ickes. Start with output below potential (1), a depression. Hopkins' rapid spending on small projects increased aggregate demand fast (a). Ickes' projects required more planning, so they affected aggregate demand more slowly. The shift from 1 to 2 would take years. But, after those years, the added infrastructure would reduce resource costs, increasing aggregate supply (b) and potential output (c). Output winds up bigger, and prices lower (3).

There would have to be big deficits if fiscal policy was to be used to bring the economy out of depression. Unlike Douglas, Marriner Eccles-the new head of the Federal Reserve Board-feared that the Federal Reserve would *not* buy the Treasury bonds when the government ran a deficit. The deficits would be big, and if banks had to buy the bonds, they would have little left over for private lending. That would reduce private investment spending even as government spending increased. (This idea is the combination of second shifts #3 and #2, known as "crowding out.")

So, Eccles thought, the Fed would have to buy the bonds. Yes, this would increase the supply of money, and yes, this would create inflation. After years of deflation, the United States needed some inflation, he thought. "We are talking about the fear of inflation or reflation, when, as a matter of fact, that is what we want," he told a Congressional committee.

Eccles feared that the Fed couldn't be counted on to buy all those bonds. Open market operations were controlled by a large committee dominated by the regional banks. There was no assurance that the Fed would even consider cooperating with the administration's fiscal policy. When Roosevelt asked Eccles to become the head of the Federal Reserve, Eccles said he'd take the job only if the Federal Reserve's structure was reformed.

> *Deficit spending requires borrowing, which could increase real interest rates. If the Fed increases the money supply, interest rates won't increase, but inflation might.*

Roosevelt agreed, and Eccles' ideas became the banking bill of 1935. The bill's most important feature was that it reorganized the Federal Open Market Committee, making the Chairman of the Federal Reserve Board its head, and limiting participation by the regional banks. Power over monetary policy would be concentrated in Washington, D.C.

The bill passed and President Roosevelt signed it on August 24, 1935. The Federal Reserve was reborn, in essentially the form we know today.

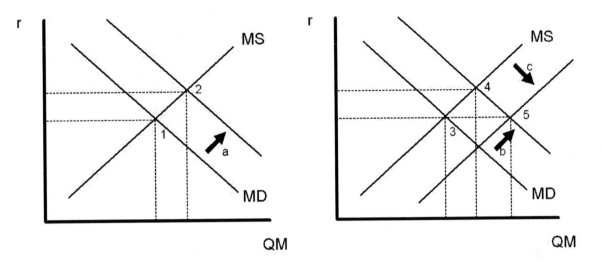

Figure 7-4. Eccles vs. Douglas. Deficit spending as in 7-1(b) would increase income and prices, and the demand for money (a). That's second shift #3. This would raise interest rates (1 to 2) and, Eccles feared, reduce investment spending (second shift #2), which would offset some of the increase in aggregate demand. Douglas' solution to this problem was to balance the budget, so that money demand would not increase. Eventually declining resource costs and rising business confidence would increase output (second shift #1). Eccles' solution to rising money demand (b) was to increase the money supply (c) so that the increase in the interest rate (3 to 4) wouldn't happen (5). Deficit spending would increase aggregate demand, and investment spending would not decrease. Douglas feared the inflation that an increase in the money supply would bring.

The National Recovery Administration

Eccles, Douglas, Ickes, and Hopkins disagreed, but they had one thing in common: they were all concerned about demand. Each in his own way wanted to increase the willingness and ability of consumers and businesses to buy the things that industry could produce. Douglas wanted to create conditions for businesses to demand more materials and labor. Eccles, Ickes, and Hopkins each promoted government spending on public works. But this was just one strand of thinking in the Roosevelt administration. The President had pledged to "try something," and with the National Recovery Administration (NRA), he tried something big.

What was the cause of the downward spiral of prices and wages? Some in the administration answered, "cut-throat competition." The problem, said former brigadier general Hugh Johnson, who headed the NRA, was "the murderous doctrine of savage and wolfish competition, looking to dog-eat-dog and devil take the hindmost." A business would cut its prices in its desperation to sell what it could produce. Its competitors would have no choice but to cut their prices, too. Lower prices meant less revenue, so businesses had to lay off employees or cut their wages. Fewer employees with lower wages could not buy what business produced.

Oluf, from Russell Baker's memoir, would have seen the fall of butter prices as responsible for his unemployment. The (too) simple solution, then, was to stop prices from falling. That's what the NRA was for.

The NRA's idea was to get businesses in each industry to agree with one another not to cut prices. They would do this by establishing industry codes, which would limit the amount each firm would produce. Without "overproduction," prices and wages could be stabilized.

For a year and a half starting in mid-1933 General Hugh Johnson ran a vigorous campaign to encourage businesses to sign on to industry codes and persuade consumers to shop at businesses that adhered to a code. A business could display a poster in its window, showing a blue eagle and the slogan "We Do Our Part," to let customers know that they followed an NRA industry code. It was hoped that customers patriotically would shop at stores displaying the blue eagle, even if their prices were higher because of the codes.

Blue Eagle. The National Recovery Administration's logo, placed in shop windows of businesses that had signed on.

The Depression problem was that the quantity of goods that consumers demanded was less than the quantity that business could supply. It was "underconsumption" said supporters of deficit spending, who said "let's increase demand." It was "overproduction" said supporters of the NRA, who said "let's decrease supply." The NRA enabled businesses to form government-sponsored cartels, to restrict production and fix prices. Labor was included. To decrease its supply, the NRA's legislation encouraged businesses to restrict workers to a 40-hour week and to end child labor. To support the price of labor—wages—the NRA encouraged workers to form unions. And it enacted a minimum wage.

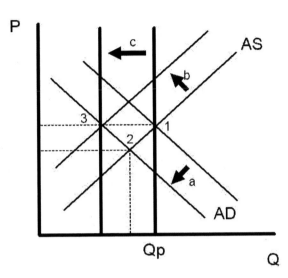

Figure 7-5. NRA. The decline in aggregate demand (a) reduces prices (1 to 2). It's a depression. Eventually second shift #1 would cause wages and resources prices to fall, too, increasing aggregate supply, as in figure 7-1(a). To stop the deflation, the NRA restricted supply by allowing businesses to form cartels and workers to form unions. Aggregate supply decreases (b). Prices are higher, but output is even lower (3). If the NRA supply restrictions become permanent, potential output would decline as well (c).

If it worked, the NRA would stabilize prices and wages, perhaps even reduce unemployment—but at a lower level of national output than could be achieved with competitive production. It didn't work. General Johnson was a flamboyant promoter of the NRA, but he was an erratic administrator, and his ultimate problem (unknown at the time) was that the idea at its core was flawed. Yes, restricting output could raise prices, but wouldn't it be better if price increases were the result of added demand and *increased* output?

> **The National Recovery Administration allowed businesses to form cartels. This would raise prices by restricting aggregate supply. It was found to be unconstitutional in 1935.**

Roosevelt became disenchanted with Johnson and fired him in October 1934. In May 1935 the Supreme Court mercifully (and unanimously) declared the whole thing unconstitutional.

People still favored the abolition of child labor and limits on working hours. Some restrictions on aggregate supply are made for social, cultural, or humanitarian reasons—the public is willing to "pay" with lower output to have them. (Abolition of child labor, though, probably increases potential output in the long run. If they're not in the factories, the kids are in school. This results in a more educated labor force that adds to productivity.) Limits on working hours and child labor, the minimum wage and the right to organize unions were re-authorized in later legislation, which the Supreme Court upheld.

"Above all, try something." Spend more or spend less. Run a deficit or balance the budget. Have a public works program that spends quickly on small projects, or have one that spends slowly on large projects. Promote inflation or avoid inflation. Increase demand or decrease supply. What was missing was the guidance of an economic theory that explained what was wrong and what could be done about it. So, the administration tried lots of different ideas, some at cross-purposes.

John Maynard Keynes

An economic theory was at hand. John Maynard Keynes supplied the theory in a book he published in 1936, *The General Theory of Employment, Interest and Money*. It was probably the most influential book about economics written in the twentieth century, and it became the basis for what we now call "macroeconomics."

Keynes was an economist at Cambridge University in England. He was well-known among British policymakers (though he was out of favor at the time). He was respected on Wall Street as the head of an insurance company and as a successful currency speculator. He was a friend of the English literary elite and was married to a Russian ballerina.

> *Economist John Maynard Keynes published the General Theory of Employment, Interest and Money in 1936. The book marked the beginning of what we now call macroeconomics.*

Though the Roosevelt administration's policies have been called *Keynesian*, Keynes never had much direct influence on the President. Several of Roosevelt's advisors had heard of Keynes, and a few knew him. They introduced the economist to the President on May 28, 1934. John Maynard Keynes talked for an hour with President Franklin Roosevelt.

We have a good idea about what Keynes must have said. He had addressed an open letter to the President five months before, on December 31, 1933, offering his views on what Roosevelt should do:

> An increase of output cannot occur unless by the operation of one or other of three factors. Individuals must be induced to spend more out of their existing incomes, or the business world must be induced, either by increased confidence in the prospects or by a lower rate of interest, to create additional current incomes in the hands of their employees, which is what happens when [investment] is being increased; or public authority must be called in aid to create additional current incomes through the expenditure of borrowed or printed money.

In bad times, he said, individuals and businesses can't be counted on. Only government expenditures will help. The administration had failed to increase deficit spending enough. The continuing Depression was the predictable result. He couldn't blame the administration "for being cautious and careful" with its spending. "But the risks of less speed must be weighed against those of more haste." What was needed was a large increase in deficit spending, with "preference given to those which can be made to mature quickly on a large scale. . . . The object is to start the ball rolling."

After the meeting Keynes told a friend "I had a grand talk and liked him immensely." But he also said he had "supposed the President was more literate, economically speaking." Roosevelt hadn't appeared to follow all that Keynes had said. The President told Labor Secretary Frances Perkins, "I saw your friend Keynes. He left a whole rigmarole of figures. He must be a mathematician rather than a political economist."

Keynes dropped by Perkins' office after the meeting and explained that a dollar spent on relief by the government was a dollar given to the grocer, by the grocer to the wholesaler, and by the wholesaler to the farmer. With one dollar paid out for relief or public works or anything else, you have created four dollars' worth of national income. Perkins wished he had been as concrete when talking to the President, instead of "treating him as though he belonged to the higher echelons of economic knowledge."

Keynes' ideas began to make inroads once the *General Theory* was published. To the some, it was a revelation. Young economists, who had grown up during the Depression chafed under what they saw as their elders' stale old ideas, embraced Keynes' revolutionary theory. Paul Samuelson, who would later be the first American to win the Nobel Prize in economics, described the reaction of young graduate students: "Bliss was it in that dawn to be alive, but to be young was very heaven!" Now the Depression could be explained. Now the battle of ideas could be joined. The theory recommending "do nothing" was met with an equally sophisticated theory that said "do something."

The Roosevelt Recession
In 1937 the new theory had something new to explain: a severe recession in the midst of the Depression—a "Roosevelt recession." After four years of expansion the economy had still not reached its 1929 level. The unemployment rate had dropped, but it was still 14%. Starting in 1937 unemployment began rising again to 19% of the labor force in 1938. Output began falling. Business investment dropped off and the stock market gave back much of what it had gained since 1933.

What had caused the recession? Production had run ahead of consumption, causing inventories to accumulate. Business cut back production and employment while waiting for those inventories to sell. Business leaders claimed that the administration's aggressive policies—profits taxes, regulation, encouragement of labor unions—were discouraging business investment. Roosevelt took up this theme himself, accusing businesses of a deliberate "capital strike" designed to discredit his policies.

The Federal Reserve surveyed the scene in late 1936 and decided (somehow) that the threat of *inflation* was the economy's chief problem. Prices had been rising since 1933. The Fed took the opportunity to use a new policy tool that it had been granted by the 1935 banking bill: setting reserve requirements. Banks keep a fraction of their deposits in reserve so they can meet customer demands for withdrawals. The Fed now had the power to set a minimum percentage of deposits that had to be kept in reserve. The percentage is called the *required reserve ratio*. Lower the required reserve ratio, and banks could lend more of their deposits. Interest rates would fall and investment would increase. Raise the required reserve ratio, and banks could lend less. Interest rates would rise and investment would decrease.

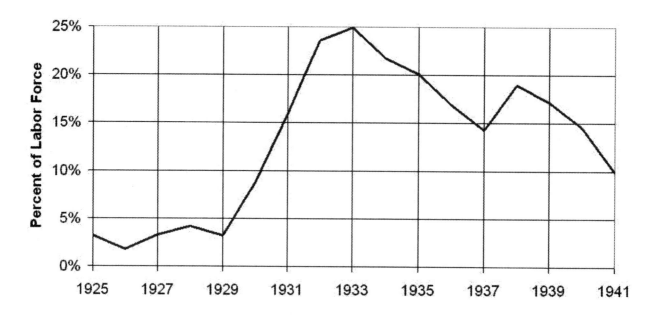

Figure 7-6. Unemployment Rate, 1925-1941. The unemployment rate peaked at just under 25% in 1933, then fell during the next four years of the New Deal. During the recession within the Depression, in 1938 the rate jumped to 19%. It dipped under 10% in 1941, for the first time in a decade.

Between August 1936 and May 1937, the Fed nearly doubled reserve requirements, from 13% of deposits to 25%. Banks had been holding excess reserves above the minimum required by the Fed. Banks did this probably because it had been only four years since the bank runs had ended, because they still had dim expectations about the ability of borrowers to repay, and because the demand for loans by businesses was still relatively small. The Fed thought that banks would not respond by increasing their reserves very much when the required ratio went up because many already held enough reserves to meet the new higher ratio.

> **The required reserve ratio is a Federal Reserve policy tool that fixes the minimum percentage of deposits that banks must hold in reserve.**

The Fed was wrong. Banks increased their reserves so they could continue to have an excess beyond the new higher requirements. They cut back their lending, and business investment fell. Marriner Eccles had gone along with the required reserve increase. But with the sharp recession erasing the gains of the previous four years, he argued for rescinding the ratio increases, or at least using open market operations to buy a large quantity of bonds, to try to increase lending again. George Harrison, still at the New York Bank, argued against this, and he carried the day. Ironic, because the arguments he used were the same as had thwarted his own expansionary ideas back in 1930.

Fiscal policy was making mischief as well. In 1936 the Federal government made a large bonus payment to veterans of the Great War. These were transfer payments, adding directly to the incomes of consumers. In 1937, no such bonus was scheduled. Spending on transfer payments dropped. In 1937, social security taxes were collected for the first time. Very few benefits were paid, however, so the initial effect of this new program was the large tax increase. Higher taxes subtracted from the incomes of consumers.

Roosevelt had nearly achieved a balanced budget in 1938 and didn't want to give it up. He resisted added spending for relief and public works. But in the Spring Harry Hopkins and his staff produced a memo which described what was needed. Gross Domestic Product needed to be $88 billion to achieve full employment. It was now $56 billion, $32 billion short. The memo said "if money invested or spent turns over two or three times a year, it would require between 7 and 10 billion dollars per year of additional investment or spending, public or private, to get reasonable full employment." Hopkins was arguing for the *multiplier effect*. If the Federal government (or a private business) spends a thousand dollars on road construction, say, that thousand dollars became paychecks for workers and equipment suppliers. They would spend their new income on food and clothing and housing and appliances, causing each of these industries to increase production and employment. The incomes of *these* employees would rise, and they would spend more, too.

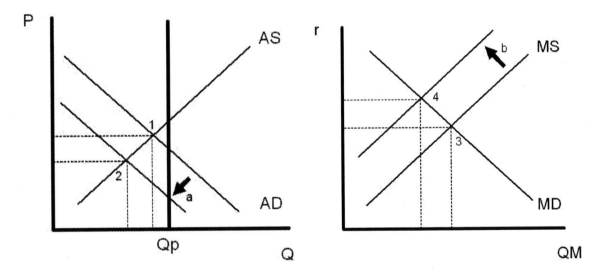

Figure 7-7. Roosevelt Recession. The economy is already below potential (1). Then government spending falls and taxes rise, which reduces aggregate demand (a). The Fed increases reserve requirements, which reduces the money multiplier and the money supply (b). Interest rates rise (3 to 4), so second shift #2 reduces investment spending and aggregate demand (a again). The result is a recession in the midst of the Depression (1 to 2).

The Consumption Function and the Income Multiplier

John Maynard Keynes took an entire section of the *General Theory* to describe how changes in income affect consumption. We can capture his ideas in an equation, called the *consumption function*, which is

$$C = A + b (Y - T + R).$$

The "C" stands for consumption spending—spending by households on food, clothing, washing machines, plumber's services and the like. The terms to the right of the equals sign show what determines consumption spending. It's an equation in three parts.

In parentheses is "$Y - T + R$." Y stands for income. When people have more income, they consume more goods and services. Most goods and services are "normal," after all, meaning the demand for them increases with income. An increase in income increases consumption. But the equation recognizes that people can't spend the income listed at the top of their pay checks. First they must pay taxes. That's what "T" stands for, the taxes paid out of income. Taxes are subtracted from income, and the result is (surprise!) after-tax income. That leaves "R", which stands for transfer payments (since we've already used "T" for taxes). Transfer payments are income taxed away from one group and paid to another, like social security, Medicare and Medicaid, welfare, unemployment insurance and veteran's benefits. That gets added to the income people earn. The result is "after-tax-and-transfer-income," which is a mouthful, so we call it *disposable income*.

Disposable income can be disposed of in two ways: it can be spent on consumption, or it can be saved. The coefficient "b" shows how much of each extra dollar of disposable income is consumed. It's called the *marginal propensity to consume (MPC)*, and its value is between zero and one. It's "marginal" because it measures how *changes* in one thing affect

> *The consumption function shows how added income affects consumer spending. The income multiplier shows how much added output is created by additional spending.*

changes in the other (we say it's the effect "at the margin"). An MPC of 0.5, for example, means that someone with an extra $1,000 in disposable income spends an extra $500 and saves the rest. An MPC of 0.8 means $800 of an extra $1,000 is consumed.

What if income was zero? Would people stop consuming everything? Not if they could help it—spending on food, clothing, and shelter would continue, somehow. That's what the "A" represents. It's called *autonomous consumption* because it is independent of current disposable income. People manage to consume even when income is zero by drawing on savings or wealth, borrowing, or relying on family or charity (we've already included options like welfare or unemployment insurance in transfers, R). People with more wealth or savings, or with a greater ability to borrow, have larger autonomous consumption.

With the consumption function in hand, we can figure out how to measure the multiplier effect. Start with our old friend,

$$Y = C + I + G + X - M,$$

and substitute the consumption function for "C" to get

$$Y = [A + b(Y - T + R)] + I + G + X - M.$$

Use a little algebra (remember algebra?) to group the "Y" terms on the left, factor out the Y and divide both sides by what's left, and you'll get

$$Y = [1 / (1 - b)] \times [A - bT + bR + I + G + X - M].$$

The bracketed term to the right is the sum things that add to spending—autonomous consumption, taxes and transfers, investment, government purchases, exports and imports. The bracketed term on the left is the *income multiplier*. When investment or government purchases or autonomous consumption change, the effect on income (and output) is that spending change times the multiplier,

$$1 / (1 - b).$$

The multiplier depends on the marginal propensity to consume. The bigger the MPC, the bigger the multiplier. If consumers spend 75 cents of each extra dollar, the multiplier is $1 / (1 - 0.75) = 1 / 0.25 = 4$. With this multiplier, an increase in government purchases (G) of \$1,000 increases income or output (Y) by \$4,000. It happens just like Keynes told Francis Perkins. A thousand dollars spent on public works becomes income for a construction worker. She spends \$750 on groceries, and that \$750 becomes income for the grocer. The grocer spends 75 cents of each extra dollar, too, which is \$562.50, which becomes someone else's income. This process continues until we're down to fractions of pennies. The total of the initial \$1,000, and all the subsequent income, will be \$4,000. When the whole economy is aggregated, output and income are the same, so the income multiplier is also an output multiplier. It shows how much GDP will increase with an initial increase in spending.

Harry Hopkins probably hadn't read the *General Theory*, but some of his advisors had. Now they said that if this multiplier was 3 (meaning the MPC was 0.67), an increase in spending of about \$10 billion would create enough added production to fill the gap between current GDP and full employment. Hopkins knew neither Roosevelt nor Congress would support that much added spending, so he set his sights lower at \$3 billion. The bill passed in June, 1938.

Unemployment Insurance
When Franklin Roosevelt was elected President in 1932, he asked Frances Perkins to head the Department of Labor. Perkins had worked as his industrial commissioner when he was Governor of New York, and she was a long-time activist on labor issues.

She told him she'd take the job if he would support her policy ideas. It was a long list. Prohibit child labor. Enact a minimum wage. Even upgrade the unemployment numbers produced by the Bureau of Labor Statistics. Maybe most important, she'd work for unemployment insurance and old age pensions. Roosevelt agreed with her goals. But he was an agreeable man, so she pressed him. "Are you sure you want these things done? Because you don't want me for Secretary of Labor if you don't," she said. He agreed to back her, and she took the job. She was the first woman cabinet secretary.

The new administration spent 1933 dealing with emergencies. But now, in June 1934, the President told his labor secretary that the time had come for unemployment insurance and old age pensions. She would chair the cabinet committee to come up with a bill, because, he said, "You care about this thing. You will drive it through." There might be good reasons to wait, Perkins said, again trying to make sure of his support. "We have to get it started or it never will start," Roosevelt declared.

Perkins became chair of a group called the Committee on Economic Security. Unemployment was the nation's most immediate problem, so they spent much of their time debating unemployment insurance. The Labor Department's economists told them that, had unemployment insurance existed in the prosperous 1920s, contributions would have exceeded benefit payments in most years. By 1929 a reserve fund of about two billion dollars would have accumulated. It would have been exhausted rapidly when unemployment surged in 1930. But it would have helped unemployed workers early in the depression.

More than this, the economists said, "it would have had a most pronounced stabilizing effect at a very crucial time." The added spending by unemployed people would have supported greater production of goods and services. Unemployment insurance would not only provide support to people in need, it would reduce the total number of unemployed people by giving businesses a reason to produce goods and employ workers.

When unemployment increases, the unemployed apply for benefits, and transfer payments (R in the consumption function) increase. Business payrolls are smaller, so unemployment insurance taxes (T) decrease. When unemployment decreases, the reverse happens; transfers decline and taxes increase. The whole process works automatically. No need for Congress to recognize a recession, debate and pass legislation, and only then start spending, perhaps too late. Instead, when a recession starts and unemployment rises, benefit payments go up because the unemployed themselves apply for benefits. Unemployment insurance is an *automatic fiscal stabilizer*.

It's "automatic" because no new act of Congress is required. Taxes and benefits vary automatically with the number of employed and unemployed people. It's "fiscal" because it deals with the government's budget, taxing and spending. And it's a "stabilizer" because it adjusts aggregate demand to offset recession and inflation.

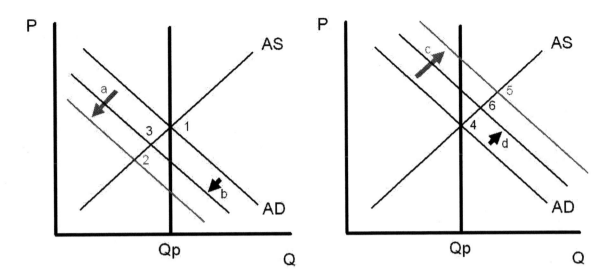

Figure 7-8. It's Automatic. A recession starts, and aggregate demand falls (a), reducing output (1 to 2). But, right away, unemployment insurance benefits increase and taxes fall. These make the fall in aggregate demand smaller (b) and the drop in output smaller (1 to 3). Likewise, when aggregate demand expands beyond potential (c), prices rise (4 to 5). But unemployment insurance benefits fall, and taxes increase, so aggregate demand doesn't increase as much (d), and neither do prices (4 to 6).

Suppose business profit expectations become pessimistic, and investment spending falls. Aggregate demand declines and output falls below potential. That's a recession. Unemployment will increase. But with unemployment insurance, the newly unemployed apply for insurance benefits, and these benefits are paid. New transfer payments add to disposable income, and this increases consumption spending, partially offsetting the aggregate demand decline. Taxes don't show up in the investment function in our model, but with payroll taxes lower firms have more left over for investment spending. That adds to aggregate demand too.

> **Unemployment insurance is an automatic fiscal stabilizer. When recessions occur, spending increases and taxes decline without the need for new legislation.**

On the other hand, suppose business profit expectations become optimistic. Investment spending rises, aggregate demand increases, and output rises above potential. It's an expansion, and it's inflationary. Unemployment will decrease; payrolls will increase. Unemployment insurance transfers decline and taxes rise. Both of these changes partially offset the increase in aggregate demand.

With an automatic stabilizer such as unemployment insurance, the fluctuations in aggregate demand are smaller. Equilibrium output remains closer to potential. Recessions are milder, and inflation is less severe.

Old-Age Pensions

Francis Townsend was a doctor who found himself unemployed at age 66 in 1933. On September 30, 1933 his local Long Beach newspaper published a letter he had written describing a plan to pay aged people a generous monthly pension, paid for with a kind of national sales tax. Within a few weeks an entire page of the newspaper every day was devoted to letters debating the *Townsend Plan*. People would come by his house looking for further details. By the end of November the doctor decided to devote himself full time to his Plan. In just one year, by the Fall of 1934, there were 5,000 Townsend clubs nationwide. Townsend incorporated under the name "Old Age Revolving Pensions, Ltd.," and coined the slogan "age for leisure, youth for work."

Under the Townsend Plan, each person 60 years old and older would receive a pension of $200 a month, so long as he or she did not work, and spent the whole amount during the month. Removing the aged from the work force would reduce unemployment, said Dr. Townsend. Requiring that the money be spent during the month would increase consumption, giving business a reason to produce and create jobs.

The pensions would be paid for with a 2% transactions tax, which was a national tax on every sale, business to business or business to consumer. The plan was "revolving" because the added spending by the aged would increase the number and value of these transactions, increasing tax receipts to pay the pensions.

We know now that the Plan could not have worked. The added transfer payments would have increased consumption, but the added taxes would have discouraged almost as much spending as the pensions created. The transactions tax had a low rate, but taxing every transaction meant that raw materials, parts, and goods sold through many stages of production would be taxed each time. The total tax passed to the consumer would be much higher than 2%.

And a pension of $200 per month was astoundingly generous. Adjusting for inflation, in 1934 $200 could buy what $3,357 bought in 2011. By comparison, the average monthly Social Security payment for a retiree in December 2010 was about $1,175. Townsend's promise (adjusted for inflation) is almost triple what we pay to retirees. Further, with 12 million Americans 60 years old or older in 1934, a monthly income of $200 would have meant annual pension payments of about $29 billion. Gross Domestic Product for the whole United States in 1934 was $66 billion, which meant that 44% of GDP would be funneled through this government program to make payments to 9% of the population. (To be fair, national income figures were not yet widely available. Townsend probably didn't know the size of U.S. GDP.)

The Townsend Plan was introduced in Congress in January 1935. Dr. Townsend himself came to Washington to testify. Both Democrats and Republicans subjected the doctor to relentless questioning until he admitted that he had no idea how much revenue his 2% transactions tax would raise. Congressional support for the Townsend Plan faded. (Faded slowly. As late as 1949 its supporters in the House of Representatives numbered almost 200.)

The Big Bill

Frances Perkins would write later that "one hardly realizes nowadays how strong was the sentiment in favor of the Townsend Plan . . . The pressure from its advocates was intense." We have to have old age pensions, Roosevelt told Perkins, "Congress can't stand the pressure of the Townsend Plan unless we have a real old-age insurance system."

Few people had their own pensions in 1934. Older people kept working until they died. If they couldn't work and had no families to support them (or, during the Depression, had families who could not support them) they depended on charities or the local poor relief agencies (many also out of money during the 1930s). The government estimated that half of all people over age 65 were on relief.

President Roosevelt was adamant about one point: there must be a pension fund. Funding payments to older people out of current revenues was welfare—the dole. "Mustn't have a dole," Roosevelt said, time and again. Perkins and Hopkins tried to point out the many problems with a pension fund scheme.

They told him that millions of retired people were in desperate need now, in 1934. They needed pensions, but they never would get a chance to contribute to a reserve fund. Put another way, an insurance scheme would start with a huge unfunded liability. Payments would be owed to currently retired folks, but there was no reserve fund of invested premiums to pay them.

They told him that building a reserve fund meant collecting taxes now, but paying benefits later. A tax hike in the midst of the Depression would cut consumer spending and make things worse. Demand would fall, jobs would be lost. "We can't help that," the President said.

Then there was a technical problem. How would the reserve fund be invested? A private pension fund would invest in stocks and corporate bonds, Treasury bonds and municipal bonds. Investment money would accumulate in each worker's account, and that money would be paid to the worker in retirement. But just about everyone would pay into the Federal pension fund. It would grow to enormous size. If the government invested this fund in private stocks and bonds, it would soon own a large share of private industry. Frances Perkins' Department of Labor might own a majority interest in General Motors. Roosevelt might have laughed at that idea. He knew it wouldn't fly in Congress. Even his supporters might call that socialism. A solution was to invest the fund only in the government's Treasury bonds. But there weren't enough Treasury bonds in existence for the fund to buy, once it got big.

Roosevelt would not be persuaded. The pension plan had to be based on worker contributions. "I guess you're right on the economics," he would say later, "but those taxes were never a problem of economics. They are politics all the way through. We put those payroll contributions there so as to give the contributors a legal, moral, and political right to collect their pensions and their unemployment benefits. With those taxes in there, no damn politician can ever scrap my social security program."

Roosevelt remained opposed to a *pay-as-you-go system*, with pensions paid out of current revenues. He insisted that payments be out of a large accumulated pension fund. And it had to grow big enough to meet demands for benefits far into the future. "It is almost dishonest to build up an accumulated deficit for the Congress of the United States to meet in 1965," he said. "We can't do that. We can't sell the United States short in 1965 any more than in 1935."

The bill was introduced in Congress in January 1935 by Senator Robert Wagner and Representative David Lewis, long-time supporters of social insurance. It included unemployment insurance, social security old-age pensions, and (for good measure) the first major Federal welfare program, known as Aid to Dependent Children. With reason, they called it *The Big Bill*.

The debate was fierce. Unemployment insurance would encourage people to loaf, its opponents said. Old-age pensions would keep them from saving. "Isn't this socialism?" demanded Senator Gore of Oklahoma. "Oh, no," Secretary Perkins replied. "Isn't this a teeny-weeny bit of Socialism?" the Senator asked, sarcastically.

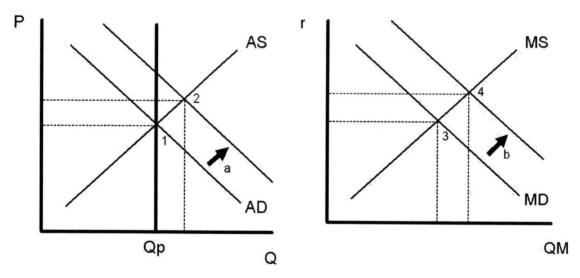

Figure 7-9. Lost saving. The prospect of social security payments probably reduces the incentive to save. This increases consumption spending and puts upward pressure on aggregate demand (a). Prices are higher, so second shift #3 makes money demand higher (b), meaning interest rates are higher (3 to 4). That reduces investment spending through second shift #2 (not shown). With less investment, the stock of capital goods increases more slowly, so potential output grows more slowly in the long run. It's our old friend "crowding out" again.

Maybe people would loaf, maybe they wouldn't, but unemployment insurance probably does allow people to search for work for longer periods. Frictional unemployment—"search" unemployment—is probably higher because of unemployment insurance. But possibly the longer search makes for better matches between employee and job, which may increase productivity.

And old-age pensions probably do decrease saving. Since people know that Social Security will pay for some of their retirement expenses, they have less incentive to save for retirement. People feel free to consume more and save less out of disposable income. The marginal propensity to consume (MPC, b in the consumption function) is higher because the program exists. This increases aggregate demand, prices, and money demand. The higher interest rate means lower investment, and lower investment translates into slower growth of potential output in the long run. Consumption probably is a larger share of GDP, and investment is a smaller share, because of Social Security.

But the Big Bill was conservative compared to the Townsend Plan, and the public clearly wanted Congress to do something. It passed, and Roosevelt signed it on August 14, 1935. The question of constitutionality loomed. The Supreme Court had thrown out the National Recovery Administration, and other New Deal legislation besides. The case wound its way through the courts, reaching the Supreme Court in 1937. On May 24 old age pensions and unemployment insurance were found to be constitutional.

> *The "Big Bill" containing unemployment insurance, Federal welfare and Social Security became law in 1935. In a sense, it marks the beginning of the U.S. social safety net, or the U.S. welfare state.*

Unemployment insurance taxes were first collected in 1936. By July 1937 every state had an unemployment insurance program. During World War II unemployment was very low, so few benefits were paid. Tax payments accumulated in the unemployment insurance funds. With the first post-war recession, in 1948-49, benefit payments surged and tax collections dropped. The program has performed this stabilizing role in every recession since.

Abandoning the Social Security Reserve Fund
Working people began paying social security taxes on January 1, 1937. Within months the Roosevelt recession began. So, before the first benefit check was cut, Social Security was reformed. The first payments were moved from 1942 to 1940. The first increase in the tax rate was postponed. Scheduled benefit payments were increased. Provision was made for widows and orphans to receive survivor's benefits. The reforms increased benefits and cut taxes to such a degree that the pension's reserve fund would not accumulate *at all*. A small contingency fund would be kept to insure prompt payment of benefits. Social security became a pure pay-as-you-go system after all, with the taxes collected from workers paid out almost immediately to current retirees.

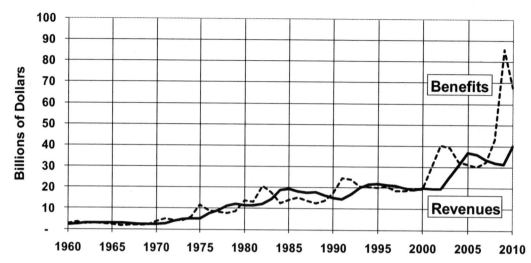

Figure 7-10. Unemployment Insurance, 1960-2010. The program acts as an automatic stabilizer. Benefit payments rise above revenue collections during recessions, as in 1970, 1975, 1982, 1991, 2001 and (by a whole lot) in 2008-09. Benefits payments drop below revenue collections during expansions, as during 1963-69, 1976-79, 1984-1989, 1994-1998 and 2004-2007.

Ida May Fuller was a mild and practical gray-haired woman, a Sunday school teacher, who lived in Ludlow, Vermont. She worked most of her life as a legal secretary and never married. She turned 65 in October, 1939, and while on an errand in Rutland she dropped by the government office to ask about benefits. She remembered "It wasn't that I expected anything, mind you, but I knew I'd been paying for something called Social Security and I wanted to ask the people in Rutland about it." She'd been paying into the system, of course, only since 1937. Her payments over those three years *totaled* $24.75.

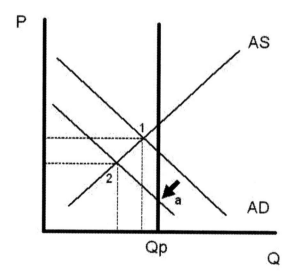

Figure 7-11. The economy was already below potential output in 1937, when Social Security taxes were increased. The policy at the time was to build a trust fund, by collecting taxes for several years before paying benefits. A tax increase without a benefit increase reduced aggregate demand (a), helping to interrupt the recovery from the Depression (1 to 2). This was one of the main arguments against building a trust fund.

She retired at the end of 1939, and one day during the first week of February 1940 she received Social Security benefit check 00-000-01, for $22.54. It wasn't a lot—she'd been earning about $75 a month at the law firm. It supplemented income she had from some stocks she owned and on an apartment she rented out (no pension from her employer, though). By the first week of March, 1940, when her second check arrived, Ms. Fuller had received more in benefits than she had paid in payroll taxes. Since she lived to be 100 years old, during her retirement she received many times the value of her tax payments.

> *Social Security was purely a "pay-as-you-go" system until the 1980's. Benefits to retirees were paid out of taxes from working people. No trust fund accumulated.*

This was possible because Social Security had become a pay-as-you-go system. Ms. Fuller was not paid out of a reserve fund with her name on it, built from the premiums she paid during her working years. That was impossible, because the program hadn't existed for most of her working years. Instead, her benefits came from the taxes paid by people working in 1940 and after. No reserve fund accumulated.

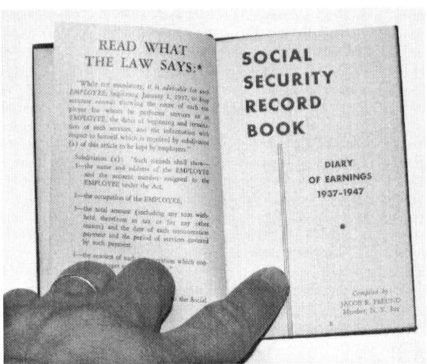

Now the government does it. A notebook printed in 1936 to be used to keep track of earnings for ten years. Social Security benefits were and are based in part on total earnings.

Social Security Finance, Past and Future

The story of the first 40 years of Social Security was one of expansion. Benefits were increased to keep up with inflation. At first this required Congress to pass a law raising benefit payments. The first was passed in 1950, and it increased benefits 77%, to offset the big inflation associated with World War II. Congress acted to raise benefits nine more times through 1973. By the beginning of the 1970's, however, inflation looked like a permanent part of the economic landscape. So in 1972 Congress created an annual *cost of living adjustment (COLA)*. The automatic adjustments started in 1975, and since then each year benefits have increased automatically by the amount of inflation, as measured by the percentage increase in the Consumer Price Index.

The social security program was expanded to include more workers. In 1950 farm workers and domestic servants were included. In 1954 the system added self-employed professionals and farmers, in 1967 ministers became eligible, and in the 1980's government employees. Today virtually everyone is covered.

New kinds of coverage were added. Amendments in 1939 added coverage for widows and orphans, known as "survivors." A program of benefits for disabled workers was created in 1956. That's why Social Security is known by the acronym "OASDI," which stands for *Old Age, Survivors and Disability Insurance*. A Supplemental Security Income (SSI) program was created in 1972 to provide added benefits for retired and disabled people with low incomes. Most significantly, in 1965 Congress created a medical insurance program—*Medicare*—for people over age 65. It is now the Federal government's second largest benefits program, after Social Security. That same year *Medicaid* was created, a medical benefits program for low-income people of all ages.

Added revenues were needed to cover these new benefits. Throughout this period payroll taxes were increased in two ways: by raising the tax rate, and by increasing the amount of income subject to the tax. The tax rate started at one percent of worker pay up to $3,000. The employer also paid one percent. Today the rate is 6.2% for Social Security, and another 1.45% for Medicare. The income limit rises automatically each year—it was $106,800 in 2011—and Medicare has no income limit. Employers pay at the same rates.

For forty years the revenues collected each year from the payroll tax were enough to pay the benefits owed to retired people, disabled people and surviving families. But cracks in the system began to appear in the mid-1970s. It became evident that revenues would not cover promised benefits forever, and that the small reserve fund might not support benefit payments for much longer at all.

The problem resulted from the *baby boom*. All of U.S. history fertility rates had fallen. Each successive generation of families had fewer children, on average. But in 1946 newly-returned soldiers made up for their years away and the number of births increased. This would have been an amusing historical footnote, except that the number of births kept increasing for the next decade, and remained above historic trends into the 1960's. The explanation had to be more than just returning soldiers. The parents of the boomers were the children of the Depression. Perhaps the economy of the 1950s and 1960s so exceeded their expectations that they felt free to have larger families. Whatever the cause, though, the boom faded after 1964, succeeded by a "baby bust" or "birth dearth."

The baby boom threatens the Social Security program. The boomers began to retire in 2008. (Kathleen Casey-Kirschling, known as the first boomer because she was born at one minute after midnight on January 1, 1946, applied for benefits on October 15, 2007.)

By the second decade of the new century enormous numbers of new retirees will be owed benefits each year. Under the pay-as-you-go system, these benefits would be paid from the taxes of current workers. But these workers are the product of the birth dearth. There aren't very many of them. In 2011 there were 2.9 workers for every retiree; by 2036 there would be only 2.1. There would not be enough payroll taxes from so few working people, at current tax rates, to pay benefits to all those boomer retirees, at current benefit levels. The system was in trouble.

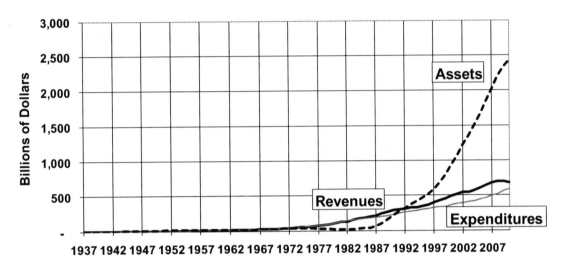

Figure 7-12. Social Security Finances, 1937-2010. A very dull graph until the mid-80's. Revenues came in, an equal amount of expenditures went out, and the trust fund (assets) never increased. Assets dip in the late 1970's, a sign of the problems stagflation created. In 1983 taxes were increased while benefits were not. Revenues have exceeded spending since then, and the trust fund is nearly 2.5 trillion dollars.

The Reagan Administration took a stab at solving the problem in 1983, setting up a National Commission on Social Security Reform, chaired by an economist named Alan Greenspan. Some of its proposals were enacted into law in 1983. The changes moved some planned tax increases forward and made some Social Security benefits taxable for upper income retirees. It required coverage of Federal, state and local government employees, which provided an immediate boost to tax revenues. It also increased the retirement age from 65 to 67 as of 2027. These changes eased the immediate funding crisis. No benefit payments were ever missed.

The most significant change, though, was the creation of a true Social Security pension fund. Tax rates were raised above the amount required to pay current benefits. The reserve fund began to grow in size. As of 2010, it amounts to nearly $2.5 *trillion* dollars. That's a lot of money. It's not enough.

Social Security needs to be reformed, but reform is very difficult. Retired people protest loudly when benefit cuts are proposed (and they vote in ever-increasing numbers). Working people protest when tax increases are proposed. Reforms run smack into

President Roosevelt's "legal, moral and political right." With reason, Social Security is called the "third rail of American politics." Touch it and you die.

At the beginning of his second term, President George W. Bush tried to make Social Security a major policy focus. The President's proposals failed to find support in Congress, even when his own party had the majority. President Bush did not try again, and President Obama has not yet made a reform attempt.

As a result of the baby boom, there will be more retirees than workers can support at current benefit levels and tax rates. The trust fund will cover the difference until 2036. After that, only three-quarters of benefits can be paid, unless a policy solution is found.

In April, 2005, President Bush visited the Treasury Department's Bureau of the Public Debt in Parkersburg, West Virginia, to have his picture taken with a filing cabinet. The cabinet contained the Treasury bonds in which the Social Security trust fund is invested. He said later, "You see, a lot of people in America think there's a trust, in this sense: that we take your money through payroll taxes and then we hold it for you, and then when you retire, we give it back to you. But that's not the way it works. There is no 'trust fund,' just I.O.U.'s that I saw firsthand, that future generations will pay—will pay for either in higher taxes or reduced benefits or cuts to other critical government programs."

Just what is the trust fund? Does it exist? In a legal and accounting sense, of course it does. That filing cabinet in West Virginia contains $2.5 trillion in Treasury bonds, the only investment allowed for the trust fund. That's why it is often said that social security taxes are lent right back to the Federal government. The money is invested in Treasury bonds, which cover the government's spending beyond its revenues. The reason only Treasury bonds are allowed was understood way back in the 1930's. If $2.5 trillion was invested in stocks, the government would be a major owner of American industry. There's no support for an idea like that.

Perhaps we can understand the meaning of the trust fund by thinking about two dates: 2014 and 2036. The Great Recession has reduced Social Security tax revenues, so the system began paying out more in benefits than it collects in taxes as of 2010. This deficit will shrink as the economy recovers. Essentially, though, Social Security will operate as it always has. Payroll taxes will be collected. The revenue will be used to pay current beneficiaries. Any surplus will add to the trust fund, used to purchase Treasury bonds.

After 2014 (say the actuaries) payroll tax revenue will not be enough to support promised benefit payments, and the current deficit will begin to grow. The Social Security administration will cover this deficit and make the full benefit payments by drawing on the trust fund. They will open that filing cabinet in West Virginia and take out Treasury bonds and present them to the Treasury for repayment. As President Bush noted, the Treasury (and Congress and the President) will meet this obligation by either borrowing from the bond market, cutting other government spending, or raising taxes. The Treasury bonds are "just I.O.U.'s", but they are I.O.U.'s from the U.S. Treasury, which has never failed to repay a loan. The Treasury will have a legal and moral obligation to pay.

In 2036 the filing cabinet will be empty. The reserve fund will be exhausted. With fewer workers supporting each beneficiary, current payroll taxes will support only three-quarters of promised benefits. Beneficiaries will have no legal claim on Treasury revenues without the Treasury bonds in the trust fund. The Social Security Administration may ask Congress and the President to continue to pay benefits, doing the same things they did when there was a trust fund: borrowing, cutting other spending, or raising taxes. But the "moral authority" of the trust fund bonds will be gone.

We can use our macroeconomic tools to cut through the accounting and actuarial mysteries, to see what's really happening.

We've promised retired people more benefits than can be supported by the tax rates we've promised working people. One solution is to increase the incomes of workers. Then the tax rates would produce more revenue, perhaps enough to pay the promised benefits.

How can we increase incomes by 2036? Remember that potential output is just aggregate supply in the long run. Aggregate supply can increase if there are more resources or better technology. More resources can be had if we increase investment in plant and equipment and research and development. We can make potential output grow faster in the future if we increase the share of investment spending in GDP now.

Suppose we find a way to get households to save more and consume less, that is, to reduce their marginal propensity to consume. Aggregate demand will decrease, but in the long run second shift #1 will return the economy to potential output, at a lower price level. With prices down, people demand less money for transactions. That reduces the real interest rate. With the interest rate lower, firms invest more. Consumption is lower, investment is higher, so more plant and equipment accumulates, and technology advances faster. Potential output grows faster.

That's exactly what the trust fund was meant to accomplish. Starting in 1983, payroll taxes were increased and benefits were not. In the consumption function, that's an increase in T:

$$C = A + b\,(Y - T + R).$$

An increase in taxes reduces consumption and aggregate demand, as in Figure 7-13. Price inflation and interest rates were less than they would have been without the tax hike. Investment was more, and so GDP has grown faster than it would have. The accumulation of the trust fund, in the macroeconomic model, represents an increase in saving and investment.

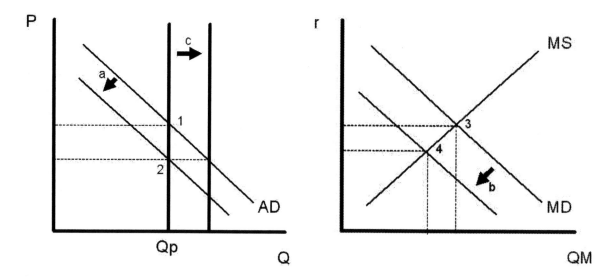

Figure 7-13. Fix it by '36. Payroll taxes rise. That reduces consumption, and so reduces aggregate demand (a). Second shift #1 adjusts output to potential after a while (that's why we've drawn the diagram without aggregate supply). The price level falls (1 to 2). A lower price level means less money demand (b), from second shift #3, which reduces interest rates (3 to 4). Lower interest rates mean more investment spending. The equilibrium at (2) has less consumption (because of higher saving) and more investment (because of lower interest rates) than at (1). With more investment the capital stock grows faster, which means potential output grows faster (c). Higher potential output means there are more goods and services to divide between working people and retired people by 2036. The is the opposite of "crowding out." Call it "crowding in."

Unfortunately, that reform didn't go far enough to solve the 2036 problem.

One solution to the Social Security funding problem, then, is to increase payroll taxes and/or cut benefits now. With T bigger and R smaller, consumption spending will decrease, and the resulting lower interest rates will produce more investment and faster potential output growth. But we don't have to restrict ourselves to payroll taxes and Social Security benefits. Any tax increase or transfer payment reduction will reduce consumption. A reduction in government purchases (G) will reduce aggregate demand as well. Raising taxes and cutting spending means reducing the Federal budget deficit. We can help solve the Social Security funding problem by balancing the budget (or even better, running a surplus).

The problem is to build more plant and equipment to increase real GDP growth, so that by 2036 GDP will be large enough to satisfy promises to working people and retired people. Accumulating enough new capital stock to increase GDP requires time. That means that it would be better for the President and Congress to agree on a Social Security solution sooner rather than later.

MacroPolicy Now: Stimulus in the Great Recession

The tax cut in 2008 and the stimulus bill in 2009 were efforts by the President and Congress to increase aggregate demand, and so increase output and employment. It was *discretionary counter-cyclical fiscal policy.* "Discretionary" because it required a special act of Congress. "Counter-cyclical" because it was intended to offset (or "counter") the decreases in spending that were causing the recession and slow recovery. "Fiscal" because that's the word we use to describe policy dealing with taxes and spending, the government's budget.

The intent of the tax cut was to increase consumer spending. Some people did exactly as expected, spending their refunds on vacations, engagement rings, canine hunting lessons. Dog trainers and jewelers will employ more people to produce the extra products that people demand. The new income these added employees earn will in turn be spent, and the effect of the tax cut will multiply through the economy. The income multiplier will increase the effect of the tax cut on aggregate demand and output.

I Knew Those Kids Would Come in Handy. The author's 2008 stimulus payment, otherwise known as the tax rebate. That's $1,800: $600 for the author, $600 for the spouse, and $300 for each of two kids. We spent it more than once, though in the aggregate, the MPC can't be greater than one.

The equation for the multiplier is

$$1 / (1 - \text{MPC})$$

where the MPC is the marginal propensity to consume ("b" in the equations above). The multiplier is bigger if the MPC is bigger. That's why the behavior of people like Mr. Gonzalez is a problem for counter-cyclical policy. If people save their tax refunds, they're not spending. If people pay down debt, they're paying for purchases they've already made. The MPC for the added after-tax income will be smaller. That will make the multiplier smaller, and that means the tax cuts have a smaller effect on aggregate demand.

The Congressional Budget Office is the non-partisan research arm of the U.S. Congress. They reviewed the evidence on the effects of the 2008 tax cut in a June 2009 publication. Based on survey data of individual households, they found that consumers spent about 19 percent of their rebates in the quarter they were received, and about 33 percent overall. That would imply a multiplier of about 1.5 (= 1 / [1 - .33]).

The total 2009 tax rebate was about $95 billion. With a multiplier of 1.5, it would have increased real GDP by $143 billion. That amounts to an additional one percent of GDP for 2008.

In the article, Mr. Gonzalez may have hit on a problem with tax cuts as an expansionary policy. "The way the economy is going, people are too scared to spend." We're trying to use tax cuts to increase spending during recession—at the very moment when people's marginal propensities to consume are lowest. One solution to this problem, though, could be to direct tax cuts to low income people. The CBO's review also found that households with low income or few assets tended to spend more of their rebates, and save less. Low income people tend to have higher marginal propensities to consume. They need the extra income for necessities.

In May 2011 the Congressional Budget Office estimated the effects of the American Recovery and Reinvestment Act (ARRA), the stimulus bill passed in February 2009. ARRA provided spending increases and tax cuts totaling $830 billion (a re-estimate from the original $787 billion). About 20 percent of the impact occurred in the first 6 months of the program, and another half took place in fiscal 2010 (October 2009 to September 2010). Most of the rest of the impact was effective by June 2011.

Its peak effect was in 2010, when half of the $830 billion in spending and tax cuts took place. That's $415 billion. CBO estimates that GDP was 1.5 percent to 4.2 percent higher as a result. Given the size of GDP, that amounts to $220 to $615 billion, which amounts to a multiplier between 0.5 to 1.5.

A look at the multiplier equation begs the question: how could the multiplier be less than one? If the marginal propensity to consumer is zero, the multiplier equation produces one. The answer is crowding out. Added Federal spending replaces some private activity. This might take place through increases in money demand and the real interest rate. But the CBO notes that the Fed held interest rates low throughout 2010. Another kind of crowding out has to do with resources. It may be that Federal spending on road construction, for example, diverted construction equipment from private sector uses. Federal construction may have replaced private construction.

We used this idea before, for potential output. Scarce resources limit the amount that output can increase. Of course, in 2010 equilibrium output was well below potential output, so there must have been unemployed resources that the government could employ. But did the unemployed resources match what the government wanted to buy? Perhaps factory workers were unemployed, while the government was looking for construction workers. Construction workers would then be pulled from private projects, while factory workers remained unemployed.

The CBO used different multipliers for different parts of the ARRA. Direct purchases of goods and services by the Federal, state, and local government had the highest multipliers, estimated at 1.0 to 2.5. Transfer payments to low income people had the next highest multipliers, at 0.8 to 2.1. Temporary tax cuts for high income people had lower multipliers, 0.2 to 0.6.

The point of the stimulus was to increase spending; the more spending increased, the higher is the multiplier.

Direct government spending appears to have the biggest bang for the buck. But as Hopkins and Ickes knew, it takes time to start spending on such projects, even if they are "shovel ready." One complaint about the 2009 stimulus bill was how slow the spending on roads and buildings was to get started.

Increases in transfer payments—like unemployment insurance—also may provide a big bang. Lower income people spend most of what they receive in transfers. Their marginal propensities to consume are high. Tax cuts for upper income people are less likely to increase spending. Upper income people save more. Their MPC's are lower. Temporary tax cuts are less effective than permanent tax cuts. If people know that a tax cut is not a permanent addition to after-tax income, they are more likely to save. People are more likely to save a windfall if they think it won't last.

ARRA was winding down as of the spring of 2011. CBO's estimated impact on GDP in 2011 is only half what it was in 2010. The economy appeared to falter in May. But Congress and the President had moved on to discussions of cutting the Federal budget deficit. Additional stimulus appeared unlikely.

Terms in this Chapter, in order of appearance
The New Deal
Liquidationists
Fiscal policy
After-tax income
Transfer payments
Government purchases
Deficit spending
Counter-cyclical fiscal policy
John Maynard Keynes
The General Theory of Employment, Interest and Money
Keynesian policies
Roosevelt recession
Required reserve ratio
Multiplier effect
Consumption function
Disposable income
Marginal propensity to consume (MPC)
Autonomous consumption
Income multiplier
Automatic fiscal stabilizer
The Townsend Plan
Pay-as-you-go system
The Big Bill
Unemployment insurance
Social Security
Trust fund
Cost of living adjustment (COLA)
Old age, survivors and disability insurance (OASDI)
Medicare
Medicaid
Baby boom
Discretionary counter-cyclical fiscal policy
Pro-cyclical fiscal policy

Notes
Russell Baker (1982, pp. 76-89) tells the story of Elizabeth and Oluf.

Eccles' memoir is a source for details on his career and his thinking, though supplemental sources like Kettl, Stein and Friedman and Schwartz are needed to temper some of Eccles' special pleading, especially on the recession of 1937-38. The story of the banking bill of 1935 is told by Eccles (pp. 200-229), Kettl (pp. 48-52), and Davis (pp. 537-541).

Lewis Douglas' laid out his ideas in a series of lectures at Harvard University in 1935, published in Douglas. The third lecture, "Dictatorship and Fiscal Policy," expresses his concerns about deficit spending, inflation and revolution. The quote about the end of western civilization is in Kennedy (p. 143). Douglas' relationship with Roosevelt and his effect on policy are taken from Perkins (p. 270), Eccles (pp. 96-97, 133-34), and Schlesinger (pp. 10-11, 290-91).

The New Deal spending programs of Ickes and Hopkins are discussed in Kennedy and Davis. Hopkins' temporary CWA program is described by Davis (pp. 307-314) and Kennedy (175-76). Davis relates the story of signing the bill on Vincent Astor's yacht (p. 467). Information about Ickes' PWA is from Kennedy (p. 152, 178, 252). Hopkins' WPA is discussed in Kennedy (pp. 252-53). The bitter conflict between Ickes and Hopkins is in Davis (pp. 470-71), and it is he who says Ickes became paranoid and Hopkins developed an ulcer.

Kennedy (pp. 177-89, p. 328) tells the story of the NRA.

The story of Keynes' meeting with Roosevelt is told in Moggridge (p. 582), Perkins (pp. 225-226), Davis (pp. 319-21) and Stein (149-51). Perkins has the quotes from Keynes about Roosevelt and from Roosevelt about Keynes. Moggridge has another from Keynes. One of Stein's themes is to what degree Keynes' ideas influenced New Deal policy (especially pp. 131-168). Keynes' 1933 letter to Roosevelt is in Keynes' *Collected Works*, volume 21, pp. 289-97 (Moggridge, editor). Stein (p. 162) gives the "young was very heaven" quote from Samuelson. It was originally written by the English poet Keats after he read Homer for the first time.

The monetary policies leading up to the recession of 1937-38 are discussed in Friedman and Schwartz (pp. 523-528). The fiscal policies are discussed in Stein (pp. 98-110). Keynes' discussion of the multiplier and the marginal propensity to consume are in the *General Theory*, pp. 113-131. That's a tough read, though.

Roosevelt's speeches and fireside chats are available on a website, the New Deal Network, at newdeal.feri.org (no "www").

The discussion Frances Perkins had with Roosevelt when she was appointed Secretary of Labor is described in her memoir (pp. 150-152) and in Martin (pp. 238-241).

Estimates on the accumulated reserve of an unemployment insurance program in the 1920's are from the Report of the Committee on Economic Security (1935), on the Social Security Administration's website. Perkins' comments on stabilization are from her memoir (p. 285). Davis has a good description of the arguments over unemployment insurance (pp. 450-51).

Perkins (pp. 282-85) and Kennedy (pp. 266-68) describe Hopkins' and Perkins' arguments with FDR over old age pension contributions. Schlesinger (pp. 308-09) is the original source for the "no damn politician" quote.

Holtzman (1963) describes the origins and details of the Townsend plan. Kennedy (pp. 224-25) and Davis (pp. 401-02) describe the Townsend movement. Dewitt (2001) provides a modern economic analysis of the Plan. Perkins' take on Townsend is in her memoir (pp. 278-79 and p. 294).

Kennedy (p.268, note 30) says that FDR sometimes said 1965, sometimes 1980 as the future date when contributions would have to be supplemented by general revenues. I used the 1965 date.

The debate on social security is described by Perkins (pp.298-299) and Schlesinger (pp. 311-312). Brown (1969) and Altmeyer (pp. 88-98) describe the amendments to Social Security in 1939.

Dewitt (1996) gives details about Ida May Fuller's tax payments and benefits. Bender (1955) and the Social Security website (www.ssa.gov/history/imf.html) have brief biographies of Miss Fuller.

The Congressional Budget Office (2001 and 2009) provides summaries of Social Security's features and problems. Kollman (1996) of the Congressional Research Service put together a detailed list of changes in Social Security.

The 1977 and 1983 Social Security reforms are detailed in Kollman. The story of the Greenspan Commission is told in Kollman, Moynihan (1988, pp. 129-133) and Martin (2000, pp. 146-147). The annual Social Security Trustees report gives the accounting view of the problem. It's on the web (www.ssa.gov/OACT/TR/. The economic view of the problem is taken by Congressional Budget Office (2001).

Chimerine et. al. (1999) and U.S. Department of Labor (1986) discuss the history of unemployment insurance legislation and its stabilizing effect.

Sources

Altmeyer, Arthur J. 1966. *The Formative Years of Social Security.* Madison, Wisconsin: The University of Wisconsin Press.

Baker, Russell. 1982. *Growing Up.* New York: Congdon and Weed.

Bender, Ray. 1955. "Our First Claimant," *Oasis* 7.

Brown, J. Douglas. 1969. "The Genesis of Social Security in America." Princeton, New Jersey: Princeton University Industrial Relations Section. Available on the Social Security Administration website, www.ssa.gov/history/jdb5.html.

Chimerine, Lawrence, Theodore S. Black and Lester Coffey. 1999. "Unemployment Insurance as an Automatic Stabilizer: Evidence of Effectiveness Over Three Decades."

Unemployment Insurance Occasional Paper 99-8. Washington, D.C.: US. Department of Labor, Employment and Training Administration.

Congressional Budget Office. 2001. *Social Security: A Primer.* Washington D.C.: U.S. Government Printing Office.

Congressional Budget Office. 2009. *CBO's Long Term Projections for Social Security: 2009 Update.* Washington D.C.: U.S. Government Printing Office.

Congressional Budget Office. 2010. *Did the 2008 Tax Rebates Stimulate Short-Term Growth?* Washington D.C.: U.S. Government Printing Office.

Congressional Budget Office. 2011. *Estimated Impact of the American Recovery and Reinvestment Act on Employment and Economic Output from January 2011 Through March 2011.* Washington D.C.: U.S. Government Printing Office.

Davis, Kenneth S. 1986. *FDR: The New Deal Years, 1933-37, A History.* New York: Random House.

DeWitt, Larry. 1996. *Details of Ida May Fuller's Payroll Tax Contributions.* Research Note 3, Social Security Administration website, www.ssa.gov/history/idapayroll.html.

Dewitt, Larry. 2001. *The Townsend Plan's Pension Scheme.* Research Note 17, Social Security Administration website, www.ssa.gov/history/townsendproblems.html.

Douglas, Lewis W. 1935. *The Liberal Tradition.* New York: D. Van Norstrand Co., Inc.

Eccles, Marriner S. 1951. *Beckoning Frontiers: Public and Personal Recollections.* New York: Alfred A. Knopf.

Friedman, Milton and Anna Jacobson Schwartz. 1963. *A Monetary History of the United States, 1867-1960.* Princeton, New Jersey: Princeton University Press.

Holtzman, Abraham. 1963. *The Townsend Movement: A Political Study.* New York: Bookman Associates.

Kennedy, David M. 1999. *Freedom From Fear: The American People in Depression and War, 1929-1945.* New York: Oxford University Press.

Kettl, Donald F. 1986. *Leadership at the Fed.* New Haven: Yale University Press.

Keynes, John Maynard. 1936. *The General Theory of Employment, Interest and Money.* New York: Harcourt, Brace, Jovanovich.

Keynes, John Maynard. 1971. *The Collected Writings of John Maynard Keynes. Volume 21, Activities 1931-39.* Donald Moggridge, editor. Cambridge, U.K.: MacMillan and Cambridge University Press.

Kollman, Geoffrey. 1996. "Summary of Major Changes in the Social Security Cash Benefits Program: 1935-1996." CRS Report to Congress 94-35 EPW. Washington, D.C.: Congressional Research Service, The Library of Congress.

Martin, George. 1976. *Madam Secretary: Frances Perkins.* Boston: Houghton Mifflin Company.

Martin, Justin. 2000. *Greenspan: The Man Behind Money.* Cambridge, Massachusetts: Perseus Publishing.

Moggridge, Donald E. 1992. *Maynard Keynes, an Economist's Biography.* London: Routledge.

Moynihan, Daniel Patrick. 1988. *Came The Revolution.* New York: Harcourt, Brace, Javanovich.

Perkins, Frances. 1946. *The Roosevelt I Knew.* New York: Viking Press.

Schlesinger, Arthur M., Jr. 1958. *The Coming of the New Deal.* Boston: Houghton Mifflin.

Slemrod, Joel and Mathew D. Shapiro. "Did the 2008 Tax Rebates Stimulate Spending?" NBER Working Paper No. 14753, February 2009.

Social Security Administration. *The 2009 Annual Report of the Boar of Trustees of the Federal Old-Age and Survivors Insurance and Federal Disability Insurance Trust Funds.* May 2009. Website: www.ssa.gov/OACT/TR/.

Stein, Herbert. 1996. *The Fiscal Revolution in America (2nd Revised Edition).* Washington, D.C.: The AEI Press.

United States Department of Labor. 1986. "Fifty Years of Unemployment Insurance—A Legislative History: 1935-1985." Unemployment Insurance Occasional Paper 86-5. Washington, D.C.: U.S. Department of Labor, Employment and Training Administration.

News Articles

Goodman, Peter S. "Consumers Lean on Rebate Checks for Bills and Gas," *New York Times*, June 1, 2008.

Kornblut, Anne E. "Bush Renews Focus on His Plan for Revamping Social Security," *New York Times*, April 6, 2005.

Leonhardt, David. "Judging Stimulus by Job Data Reveals Success," New York Times, February 17, 2010.

Social Security Administration. "Nation's First Baby Boomer Files for Social Security Retirement Benefits -- Online!" *Social Security News Release*, October 15, 2007.

Chapter 8
War and Independence

MacroPolicy Now: Federal Reserve Independence

Representative Ron Paul of Texas is a long-time critic of the Federal Reserve and the author of a book titled *End the Fed*. For many years he was kept from leadership roles in the House of Representatives because of his unorthodox views. But with the Republican takeover of the House in the 2010 election, Representative Paul was appointed to head the Domestic Monetary Policy Subcommittee. One of the committee's jobs was to conduct hearings about Federal Reserve policy. Representative Paul would be questioning Fed chair Ben Bernanke.

He would also be supporting a bill to force complete audits of Fed operations, including the conduct of monetary policy. Representative Paul had pushed for this power in the financial regulation bill that passed the Congress in 2010. A very limited audit finally was included in that bill.

Supporters of the Fed's independence have argued that such an audit would subject the Fed to political pressure. It would be harder for Fed officials to take unpopular action aimed at heading off inflation. Fed officials adamantly opposed the measure, saying it would undermine the central bank's credibility as a bulwark against inflation. Fed chair Ben Bernanke wrote that "Now more than ever, America needs a strong, nonpolitical, and independent central bank with the tools to promote financial stability and to help steer our economy to recovery without inflation."

"This is a political warning shot," said Vincent R. Reinhart, a former top Fed official who is now a senior fellow at the American Enterprise Institute. "It says that Congress has a mechanism to opine about monetary policy. The fear is that every time there's a threat of higher interest rates, someone in Congress will ask for a study of the costs of higher interest rates."

Representative Paul, however, regards the Fed with disdain. If the Fed were abolished, he wrote in 2010, "the national wealth would no longer be hostage to the whims of a handful of appointed bureaucrats whose interests are equally divided between serving the banking cartel and serving the most powerful politicians in Washington." Paul would like to see a return to the gold standard.

The Federal Reserve was rarely criticized during the chairmanship of Alan Greenspan, from 1987 to 2006. This was exceptional. Another Texas Congressman, Wright Patman, grilled Fed leaders mercilessly during the 1960's. It was said that the reason Patman chose a bright red carpet for his office was to hide the blood stains after Fed chair William McChesney Martin emerged from private meetings. Patman wrote *Time* magazine in 1964, thought the Fed was too secretive, too independent, too insensitive to

221

the hopes of small borrowers, and a tool of Wall Street bankers. Patman also pushed legislation to authorized Congressional audits of Fed policy.

Should Congress have more power over the Federal Reserve? Senator Judd Gregg, Republican of New Hampshire, sounded a note of caution. "Congress has demonstrated time and again its inability to manage the nation's fiscal policy, illustrated by our staggering national debt in excess of $12 trillion. So how can anyone think that its involvement in monetary policy would be good for the country?"

But Representative Paul argued that an audit would not undermine the central bank's independence. Its main purpose was to force the Fed to be more transparent and accountable to the public. Even without legislation, Paul may have succeeded in forcing more transparency. On April 27, 2011, Fed chair Bernanke conducted the first scheduled press conference in the institution's history. Bernanke's intent, said a reporter, "is to reach the broader public, to address widespread anger over the central bank's extraordinary response to the financial crisis by building public understanding of its actions." Representative Paul and the other critics of the Fed appear to have struck a nerve.

The Fed has had independent control over monetary policy for decades. But it wasn't always so. In fact, the United States has had the argument over Fed independence before . . . .

Wartime Labor shortage

It was Columbus Day, 1942, and President Franklin Roosevelt had just completed a tour of the Midwest and West Coast, visiting defense plants and military bases. He reported what he saw to his radio audience in another of his fireside chats.

"The main thing that I observed on this trip is not exactly news," he said. "It is the plain fact that the American people are united as never before in their determination to do a job and to do it well." The United States had just begun to mobilize, he continued.

> Germany and Japan are already realizing what the inevitable result will be when the total strength of the United Nations [the name used for the U.S. and its allies] hits them. . . . In the last war, I had seen great factories; but until I saw some of the new present-day plants, I had not thoroughly visualized our American war effort.

The war effort was enormous. Fifteen million men and hundreds of thousands of women entered the armed forces, and three-quarters were sent overseas. All of these soldiers had to be paid and equipped. More than that, the United States supplied a large amount of the equipment used by Great Britain and the Soviet Union in their struggle with Germany and Japan. British convoys across the Atlantic used American-made ships. Russian soldiers defended Stalingrad in American-made boots.

Hitler had invaded France in 1940 with an army of 2,500 tanks, supported by 3,000 aircraft. By the end of the war the United States had produced 102,000 tanks and 296,000 aircraft, as well as 88,000 warships and almost 2.5 million trucks.

The Great Depression was over. All of these soldiers and all of this equipment had to be paid for; the Federal government paid. Federal spending increased from seven billion dollars in 1938 to seventy billion dollars in 1945. During World War II the United States government spent more than it had spent during the entire period from 1789 to 1940.

It was the greatest expansionary spending program in history, and it did the trick. Idle factories reopened to produce for federal contracts. Employers hired idle workers to build the weapons of war. The unemployment rate had been almost 15% in 1940—the tenth straight year above 10%. By 1944 it was 1.2%, the lowest rate of the twentieth century. The problem was no longer too many workers for the available jobs, it was too few. There was a *labor shortage*. The President told Americans about the problem.

> In order to keep stepping up our production, we have had to add millions of workers to the total labor force of the Nation. And as new factories come into operation, we must find additional millions of workers. This presents a formidable problem in the mobilization of manpower.

Federal government spending increased ten-fold during World War II. The unemployment rate dropped to its lowest level ever, 1.2% in 1944. The Great Depression was over.

A large part of this additional "manpower" was female. "I was impressed by the large proportion of women employed," Roosevelt said, "Doing skilled manual labor running machines. As time goes on, and many more of our men enter the armed forces, this proportion of women will increase." Women's labor force participation—the percentage of women old enough to work who were working for pay or looking for paid work—increased from 27% in 1940 to 35% in 1944. Five million women entered the labor force. Partly it was the attraction of a paycheck after a decade of depression. Partly it was a patriotic desire to help with the war effort. Partly it was the encouragement of the War Production Coordinating Committee's "Rosie the Riveter" campaign. Can women do the job? "We Can Do It," said Rosie's famous poster.

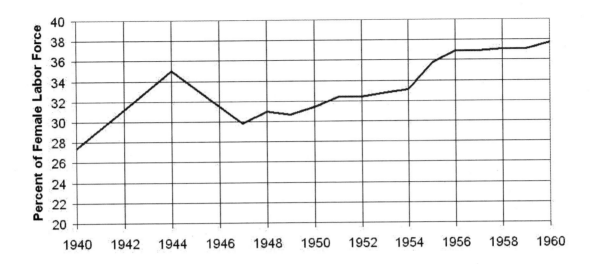

Figure 8-1. Female Labor Force Participation Rate, 1940-1960. This is the percentage of women over age 16 who were working for pay or looking for paid work. More than one-third were working at the height of World War II, a rate not matched again for a decade. Today the rate is 58%.

Roosevelt warned that old ways would have to change.

> In some communities, employers dislike to employ women. In others they are reluctant to hire Negroes. In still others, older men are not wanted. We can no longer afford to indulge such prejudices or practices.

Roosevelt had come to this opinion about black employment reluctantly. His wife, Eleanor Roosevelt, had pushed for a decade for greater opportunity for blacks. Roosevelt resisted. Whatever his personal views may have been, as President he had to get his programs through Congress. Committee chairmanships were decided by seniority, and since the Republican Party—the party of Lincoln—hardly existed in the south, Democrats were elected to term after term. Most of the Congressional committees were chaired by southern segregationists. Push too hard on race relations, Roosevelt had thought, and the New Deal would not get so much as a hearing.

Besides, the priority now was to increase production, not engage in social experiments. "Dr. New Deal has been replaced by Dr. Win-the-War," Roosevelt had told reporters. General George Marshall, Army chief of staff, had refused to order integration of the armed forces. "The Army is not a sociological laboratory," he declared. Roosevelt agreed. Now was not the time to rock the boat.

Roosevelt hadn't counted upon black labor leader A. Phillip Randolph. Randolph conceived the idea of a march on Washington, when such things simply weren't done. Other black leaders were skeptical at first, but the idea caught the imaginations of black people everywhere. What had been envisioned as a march of ten-thousand looked like it would be a march of a hundred-thousand. The date was set for July 1, 1941.

Roosevelt was appalled. This was rocking the boat and then some. The United States claimed to be supporting the fight for freedom against Nazi racism. Randolph intended to lay bare U.S. racism, right in the nation's capital. It would be a propaganda disaster.

Two weeks before the scheduled march, Randolph and Roosevelt met in the White House. "Well, Phil, what do you want me to do?" the President asked. Randolph pointed out that despite the labor shortage, many firms and labor unions were excluding blacks. He wanted a Presidential order prohibiting discrimination in defense plants. "Call off the march and we'll talk about it," Roosevelt said. Randolph calmly refused. Mayor Fiorello LaGuardia of New York City was in the room as a friend of both the President and the labor leader. He's not going to call it off, LaGuardia told Roosevelt, "I suggest we all begin to seek a formula."

A week later, on June 25, 1941, Roosevelt issued Executive Order 8802, which said "There shall be no discrimination in the employment of workers in defense industries or government because of race, creed, color or national origin." Randolph called off the march. He had demonstrated the effectiveness of mass action, and black leaders would not forget it.

Of course, racial problems were not solved by a single executive order. Millions of blacks and whites were migrating to industrial cities, and sometimes tensions mounted to violence. The worst race riot was in Detroit during the summer of 1943. Thirty four people died before Army troops could restore calm.

And the executive order didn't apply to everyone. In his fireside chat, Roosevelt told of a west coast community that had mobilized to bring in the fruit harvest, because, he said, "the usual Japanese labor was not available." Of course it wasn't: the United States government had shipped Americans of Japanese decent to camps in the desert.

Despite these deplorable events, the war had some long-term positive effects on race relations. Defense work threw blacks and whites together in new ways. Sybil Lewis offered testimony. She was a maid in Oklahoma who left for a job in a Lockheed aircraft factory in Los Angeles. She'd earned $3.50 a week as a maid. She earned $48 a week as a riveter. She'd never seen so much money at one time. Working next to her was a white woman from a cotton farm in Arkansas. She and Lewis became friends. "We learned that despite our hostilities and resentments we could open up to each other and get along," Lewis said. And with the money she earned, Lewis went to college after the war. "The war changed my life," she said.

The war changed America. There were changes in attitudes about work. Women's labor force participation dropped back near pre-war levels after the war. Most women returned to their homes. These were the mothers of the baby boom, after all. But the image of Rosie the Riveter remained. When the girls of the baby boom had grown, they had a powerful argument that women could do any work they chose.

There were changes in education. The G.I. Bill offered education benefits to returning veterans, and millions took the opportunity. Enrollment at Purdue University in Indiana, for example, increased from 3,762 in 1944 to 14,674 in 1948. Higher education would never again be the privilege of the few. Added education increased labor productivity and added to potential output growth.

There were changes in culture. Southern blacks migrated to northern cities for defense jobs. They brought their guitar-based country blues music with them. Up north they discovered electric guitars and audiences eager to dance. Within a few years this new music was on the radio. White teenagers tuned in and loved it. Alan Freed, an enterprising disk jockey in Cleveland, gave it a name: rock 'n' roll.

Wartime Inflation

The labor shortage was not the only economic problem facing the United States. In his fireside chat Roosevelt mentioned "the serious problem of the rising cost of living." Like most wars, World War II threatened to create inflation.

It was exactly the opposite problem from Depression. In Depression there was little spending, so factories cut back production, laid off workers, cut wages and prices. Now, there was a lot of spending. Factories ran round the clock and hired all available workers, and still couldn't produce enough. They bid up wages and invented new benefits, trying to attract workers from other places or industries, and they increased prices.

In part the increased employment of women and blacks would counter inflation. More goods were available to buy because so many more people were working to produce them. But mostly the added workers were in defense plants, building planes and tanks and ships. Civilian production did not increase very much. In some cases entire industries were converted to war production. Between 1942 and 1945 the Chrysler Corporation made 25,507 tanks—and no cars.

Higher taxes could counter inflation. Take a larger share of people's paychecks and they will have less to spend on consumer goods. With less spending prices wouldn't rise so much. Taxes were increased. In 1939 a family with a $5,000 income paid $48 in income taxes. In 1944 they paid $755. And the taxes were now withheld from paychecks. Before, taxpayers had to send the government a check at the end of the year. Now, the government would send the taxpayer a check if a refund was due.

> *Wartime inflation was countered by employing more labor to increase the supply of goods, by imposing higher taxes, which reduced disposable income available for spending, and with war bond drives, which increased saving and decreased spending.*

That encouraged tax compliance a lot. Still, the government did not have the nerve to raise taxes enough to pay for all the added spending. Tax revenue rose seven times, but spending rose ten times. The Federal budget deficit reached 28% of Gross Domestic Product in 1944.

War bond drives could counter inflation. Bonds were sold directly to the public, with campaigns that featured Hollywood stars and war heroes. If people lent their money to the government by buying bonds, they would be saving more and spending less. Saving did go up. Americans saved about a quarter of their after-tax incomes during the war. Part of this was due to war bonds, but much was due to the fact that there was very little to buy. There were no cars or refrigerators to be had, so people saved their money. Maybe they could buy when the war was over.

No sustained inflation is possible without an increase in the money supply. The Federal Reserve could have kept the money supply growing slowly. The big demand for funds by the government would have increased interest rates and cut back business and consumer spending. *Monetary policy* could have countered inflation.

Instead, as in World War I, the Fed agreed to hold *interest rates fixed*. The Treasury feared that the only way it would be able to sell the bonds needed to borrow billions of dollars would be to offer investors higher interest rates. That would increase the expense of borrowing. If the "disorder" of rising and falling interest rates were allowed, the Treasury might not know in advance how high their interest rates had to be. Some of the Treasury's bonds might not sell, and the war effort would be short of funds.

Buy war bonds and stamps for victory. The matchbox could have added: And to hold down inflation.

The Treasury was trying to sell lots of bonds, competing with other borrowers for the money investors had to lend. Borrowers would bid interest rates higher to attract lenders. If interest rates began to rise, the Fed would buy Treasury bonds. The money supply would rise and interest rates would fall back to fixed levels. Often the Fed would buy the bonds directly from the Treasury, in effect financing the war with newly printed dollars. This meant, though, that the Fed was not allowed to raise interest rates to combat inflation. Monetary policy was set aside for the duration of the war. The money supply increased, and inflation became a problem.

Price Controls and Rationing

So the government resorted to *price controls*. Each controlled product had a ceiling price, and it was illegal to charge more. The Office of Price Administration (OPA) enforced the controls. This kept inflation low, but it created new problems. So many people had so much new income that everything available could be sold at the controlled prices and still people would want to buy more. Factories and workers had been diverted to war production, but with prices held down there was little reason for the businesses to make more consumer goods, even if they could. The result was shortages of price-controlled goods. Gasoline, tires, meat, sugar, butter, cigarettes and many other goods were in short supply.

They weren't going to be available for the duration. "Don't you know there's a war on?" said the shopkeepers to those who complained. Shortages could be more than inconvenient. What if doctors couldn't make emergency house calls because they weren't first in line for gasoline? How could Rosie the Riveter go to work if she had to wait in line at the grocers to get food for her kids? The answer was *rationing*. Every product now had two prices—one in money, and one in ration stamps. Both were needed to buy a rationed product. Money was earned on the job, and there was more than enough money around. Ration stamps were distributed to everyone by the OPA, and they were kept scarce. Auto owners with "A cards" in their windows could buy three gallons of gasoline a week doctors got more). Controls kept the price of gasoline down. Most auto owners had money to buy as much as they needed at the controlled price—but three gallons was all they were allowed.

Price controls place legal ceilings on the prices of products. Higher incomes increased demand, which created shortages. Goods in short supply were rationed.

Price controls and rationing held down the inflation rate. From 1942 to 1945 inflation averaged only 3.4% per year. In a sense, though, inflation happened; it just took other forms. Goods were sold on the *black market* at illegal high prices to people without enough ration stamps. Businesses would make second-rate goods to hold their costs down-to get more profit under the controlled price. And in a sense, a good that is unavailable has an *infinite price*—it can't be bought for any money. None of this was recorded in price indexes.

Mr. Ernsberger's War Ration book. To buy rationed goods, he needed money and stamps.

Urban legends grew about shortages. Harry Truman was Vice President in 1945. In those days there was no official residence for the V.P. Harry and Bess and daughter Margaret lived in an apartment on Connecticut Avenue. When President Roosevelt died in April 1945, it was said that the landlord's switchboard was jammed with calls. Were people wanting to offer their advice and best wishes to the new President? No—they knew his apartment would be available, and they wanted to rent it.

The Warner Brothers Studio poked fun at the rationing system in a Bugs Bunny cartoon. The patriotic bunny battles a gremlin intent on sabotaging a bomber. In the end the plane hurtles towards earth, but stops just short of the ground, hanging in mid-air. "Sorry folks," says the gremlin, "we ran out of gas." And Bugs says "You know how it is with these A cards," pointing his carrot at the big black "A" in the window.

People told another story during the war. A prosperous-looking woman on a bus says "My husband has a better job than he ever had and he's making more money, so I hope the war lasts a long time." Another woman slaps her face. "That's for my boy who was killed at Pearl Harbor," she says. Another slap. "And this is for my boy on Bataan." The war made the United States prosperous, and people felt guilty about it. But they also worried that once the war was over the Depression would return.

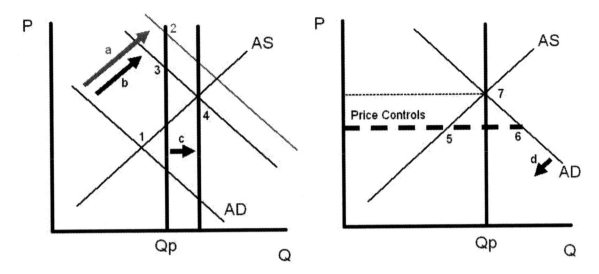

Figure 8-2. World War II inflation. The huge wartime increase in government purchases increases aggregate demand a lot (a), ending the Depression (1, less than Qp), but creating inflation, at (2) once aggregate supply shifts back with second shift #1. Taxes and bond drives reduce disposable income and the MPC, so aggregate demand does not rise as much as it could have (b), and prices rise less than they could have (3). Added female labor force participation and less discrimination against blacks increased potential output (c), which also holds inflation down (4). Price controls complete the wartime anti-inflation drive. At the below-equilibrium price level, output demanded (6) exceeds output supplied (5), a shortage. Rationing is used to divvy up the short supply among consumers. When the controls are dropped at the end of the war, prices jump (7). Pent-up consumer demand keeps aggregate demand from falling (d doesn't happen) with the fall in government purchases.

The Economic Organization of a P.O.W. Camp

Economics is not an experimental science, for the most part. Economists gather their evidence where they find it. Suppose tens of thousands of men were placed in a walled community with an adequate food supply, but nothing much to do, for two years. Would an economy develop? Would goods and services be produced and exchanged? Would money and markets be established? Of course, we're describing a prisoner of war camp. We know the answers to these questions because of one enterprising economist.

R. A. Radner was a British officer who was an economist in civilian life. He was captured in 1943 and sent to Stalag VIIA in Moosburg, Bavaria. The camp held 50,000 prisoners—British, Americans, Russians, French, Yugoslavians, and many others. When Radner was released in 1945, he wrote an article about his experience, called "The Economic Organization of a P.O.W. Camp." It's a classic.

The prisoners lived in bungalows housing 200 men. They were fed with rations from the Germans and from the contents of their Red Cross food parcels. The parcels included tinned milk, jam, butter, biscuits, bully (canned corn beef), chocolate, sugar, cigarettes, and other staples. Prisoners were not forced to work.

For Radner, the soldier-economist, this frightening and tedious incarceration was also an ideal economic experiment. If thousands of humans being were forced to live together for years, would an economy develop? The answer was yes. Radner wrote,

> One aspect of social organization is to be found in economic activity, and this, along with other manifestations of group existence, is to be found in any P.O.W. camp. True, a prisoner is not dependent on his exertions for the provision of the necessities, or even the luxuries of life, but through his economic activity, the exchange of goods and services, his standard of material comfort is considerably enhanced. And this is a serious matter to the prisoner: he is not "playing at shops. . . ."

> Everyone receives a roughly equal share of essentials; it is by trade that *individual preferences* are given expression and comfort increased. All at some time, and most people regularly, make exchanges of one sort or another.

> . . . There was a lively trade in all commodities and their relative values were well known, and expressed not in terms of one another—one didn't quote bully in terms of sugar—but in terms of cigarettes. . . . Everyone, including non-smokers, was willing to sell for cigarettes, using them to buy at another time and place. *Cigarettes* became the *normal currency*, though of course *barter* was never extinguished.

> Although cigarettes as currency exhibited certain peculiarities, they performed all the functions of a metallic currency as a *unit of account*, as a *measure of value* and as a *store of value*, and shared most of its characteristics. They were homogeneous, reasonably durable, and of convenient size for the smallest or, in packets, for the largest transactions.

> One man capitalized his knowledge of Urdu by buying meat from the Sikhs (Hindu soldiers from India, who were vegetarians) and selling butter and jam in return. . . . One trader in food and cigarettes, operating in a period of dearth, enjoyed a high reputation. His capital, carefully saved, was originally about 50 cigarettes, with which he bought rations on issue days and held them until the price rose just before the next issue. He also picked up a little by *arbitrage*; several times a day he visited every Exchange or Mart notice board and took advantage of every discrepancy between prices of goods offered and wanted. . . . By these means he kept himself smoking steadily—his profits—while his capital remained intact.

> It was this intrinsic value which gave rise to [cigarettes'] principle disadvantage as currency . . . that is, a strong demand for non-monetary purposes. Consequently our economy was repeatedly subject to *deflation* and to periods of monetary stringency. . . . Several hundred thousand cigarettes might arrive in the space of a fortnight. Prices soared, and then began to fall, slowly at first but with

increasing rapidity as stocks ran out until the next big delivery. Most of our economic troubles could be attributed to this fundamental instability.

There was a strong feeling that everything had its *"just price"* in cigarettes. . . . It can best be defined as the price usually fetched by an article in good times when cigarettes were plentiful. The "just price" changed slowly; it was unaffected by short-term variations in supply, and while opinion might be resigned to departures from the "just price", a strong feeling of resentment persisted. A more satisfactory definition of the "just price" is impossible. Everyone knew what it was, though no one could explain why it should be so.

The senior British officer attempted to fix the prices of other foodstuffs in terms of cigarettes by posting a recommended price scale. Enforcing the "just price" legally was a popular move, in part because people resented the success of traders who took advantage of ignorance and scarcity.

The onset of deflation was marked by a period of sluggish trade; prices stayed up but no one bought. Then prices fell on the black market, and the volume of trade revived in that quarter. . . . Opinion was always overruled by the hard facts of the market. . . . Prices moved with the supply of cigarettes and refused to stay fixed in accordance with a theory of ethics.

Economics has been defined as the science of distributing limited means among unlimited and competing ends. On 12th April, with the arrival of elements of the 30th U.S. Infantry Division, the ushering in of an age of plenty demonstrated the hypothesis that with infinite means economic organization and activity would be redundant as every want could be satisfied without effort.

Why do economies develop? The prison camp "experiment" offers a reason. "It is by trade that individual preferences are given expression and comfort increased," Radner wrote. The Hindu Sikhs were vegetarians, yet their Red Cross packages included tinned meat. Many western soldiers preferred the meat to butter and jam. By exchanging one item for another, each makes himself better off. Since the desire to improve one's life is practically universal, economies develop even among strangers thrown together in difficult circumstances.

In most societies the government creates money for people to use for exchanges. But the prison camp experiment shows that money is so useful that it will emerge spontaneously. Cigarettes became a medium of exchange. "Everyone, including non-smokers, was willing to sell for cigarettes, using them to buy at another time and place," Radner wrote. Prisoners would trade sugar for cigarettes, then trade cigarettes for jam. Cigarettes helped make the exchange of sugar for jam easier. The prisoner who had sugar and wanted jam did not have to search for another who had jam and wanted sugar. A *double coincidence of wants* was not needed because there was a medium of exchange.

Cigarettes were a store of value. They had to be, if they were to perform their role as medium of exchange. One sold sugar for cigarettes, and then bought jam "at another time." Cigarettes had to remain valuable over time to make exchanges possible.

Even when sugar was traded for jam directly, it was useful to have a unit of account so that the relative values of goods can be measured. Radner wrote that "relative values were well known, and expressed not in terms of one another—one didn't quote bully in terms of sugar—but in terms of cigarettes." If a packet of sugar is worth two cigarettes, and a jar of jam ten, then everyone knows that a fair trade is five sugars for one jam.

Of all the commodities in the Red Cross parcel, why did cigarettes become money? Why not jam or bread or tinned beef? Because money needs particular characteristics to be useful. Radner lists them. Money should be *homogeneous*. Every dollar is the same as another. There is no need to examine each dollar to make sure it's not actually worth $1.05. Where money is not homogeneous, exchanges become more time-consuming and contentious. Every cigarette was nearly identical.

Money should be *durable*. To be a store of value, it must last physically for the time required. Paper one dollar bills last about two years, on average. Coins can last for centuries. A number of countries, including Australia and Thailand, have experimented with plastic currency, instead of paper. Cigarettes were durable enough to serve.

Money should come in *denominations convenient* for all transactions. If only $100 bills circulated, it would be difficult to buy lunch (that was Mr. Saitta's experience in 1933—see chapter 6). If only pennies circulated, buying a car would require a dump truck full of coins. Sometimes this was a real problem for nations on the gold standard, using gold coins. At about $20 an ounce, a one dollar gold coin would weigh one-twentieth of an ounce, a very small coin too easy to lose. That's why, even on a gold standard, small change was made of cheaper metals, like silver and nickel. Single cigarettes worked for small transactions; packs of cigarettes for bigger purchases.

And, money should be useful only as money, not for other purposes. This was the principle drawback of cigarettes as money. Much of the camp's money supply would be smoked in the time between the arrival of Red Cross shipments. Money would gradually disappear. That's why dollars are useful as nothing but money. Only the very rich are ever shown lighting their cigars with flaming hundred-dollar bills. That helps keep the supply of currency stable.

The instability of the cigarette money supply was the principle macroeconomic problem of the POW economy. The equation of exchange explains the inflation and deflation that resulted from the fluctuations of the number of cigarettes in circulation. The equation is

$$(QM) \times V = P \times Q$$

where QM is the quantity of money (cigarettes in the prison camp), V is velocity, P is the price level measured in cigarettes, and Q is the quantity of goods being exchanged.

233

Radner wrote, "Several hundred thousand cigarettes might arrive in the space of a fortnight. Prices soared, and then began to fall, slowly at first but with increasing rapidity as stocks ran out, until the next big delivery." QM would jump with a new Red Cross delivery. If the quantity of goods remained the same, and velocity didn't change much, the price level had to rise. Then, gradually, QM would decline as smokers used it up. The price level would fall.

Of course, Q fluctuated too. Red Cross packages included food items as well as cigarettes. When the supply of cigarettes increased, the supply of goods did too. As cigarettes were smoked, sugar, jam and bully were eaten. If the goods supply had changed as much as the cigarette supply, the price level would not have changed. But, in addition to the Red Cross supplies, Q included daily German food rations, used boots and clothing, even services like shoe repair that prisoners performed in exchange for cigarettes. These parts of Q did not change. So prices increased when a Red Cross shipment arrived, and fell after that.

When prices are not perfectly flexible, changes in the money supply can change Q. Radner wrote, "The onset of deflation was marked by a period of sluggish trade; prices stayed up but no one bought." People formed *price expectations*—Radner calls them "just prices"—based on the prices of goods when cigarettes were plentiful. When cigarettes became scarce, people did not have enough to buy goods at the high "just" prices. People would be unwilling to sell for lower prices, at least for a while. So the number of trades declined. In the equation of exchange, QM falls, P remains stable, so Q must fall.

> *In Captain Radner's P.O.W. camp, people's fixed price expectations kept prices from falling with the decline in the money supply. As a result, for a time the quantity of trade decreased. The camp economy had a recession.*

That's exactly what happens when aggregate demand falls, before second shift #1 sets in. Prices, wages and costs do not adjust right away to the decline in spending. Businesses keep asking for higher prices, workers for higher wages. With less spending, at those higher prices fewer goods are sold. We call that a recession.

Prices, wages and costs may be slow to adjust because people's price expectations adjust slowly. Businesses have an idea of the "just price" of the goods they sell, and workers have an idea of the "just wage" for the labor they sell. Sometimes prices and wages are fixed by contract, or by law. In the camp the senior British officer tried to fix prices. In the economy unions negotiate labor contracts that fix wages for a period of years. Contracts between businesses may fix the costs of resources.

Eventually, though, prices "refused to stay fixed in accordance with a theory of ethics." In the camp, people wanted to improve their lives by exchanging goods, and were forced to buy and sell at lower prices. In the economy, unemployment and accumulating inventories force workers and firms to accept lower wages and prices. Radner wrote,

"Opinion was always overruled by the hard facts of the market." Eventually second shift #1 increases aggregate supply, reduces prices, and goods trading resumes.

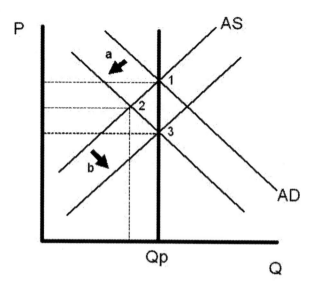

Figure 8-3. Up in Smoke. The camp's cigarette money supply declines, which reduces aggregate demand (a). Prices of goods fall some (1 to 2), but not enough to keep trading at its usual level (Qp). So trading is depressed, at 2. Eventually people reduce the prices at which they are willing to trade, and aggregate supply increases (b). Second shift #1 even happens in prison camps. The price level falls some more, and the volume of trading recovers (2 to 3).

We said that economies develop because people want to exchange goods to increase their well-being. This is true, in the presence of *scarcity*. When there are not enough goods to satisfy everyone's every desire, people must trade something of value to get something they value more. Trading starts, money develops, prices are quoted. If there is no scarcity, however, there is no reason for an economy to develop. Everyone's desires are satisfied without the need to exchange. That's what happened in April 1945 when Stalag VIIA was liberated by the U.S. infantry. Every former prisoner could have all the food, clothing—and cigarettes—he desired. Trading stopped. Cigarettes became mere commodities again.

The Treasury Takes over Monetary Policy
Added government war spending had brought unemployment down. People worried: wouldn't unemployment go back up after the war, when government spending dropped? Some economists thought so, and warned about *secular stagnation*. They thought that consumers and businesses could never spend enough to employ everyone who wanted to work.

After the war government spending did drop, a lot, but the Depression did not return. Consumers and businesses took up the slack. Many people had been unable to buy consumer goods during the Depression, and consumer goods had been unavailable in the war years. During the war people had saved a big share of their incomes. Economists called it *pent-up demand*, and now, in 1946, this demand was released. Consumers used their savings to buy the consumer goods they'd been denied so long. Businesses saw their opportunity and converted war plants or invested in new factories to produce these goods. There was no deep recession with the war's end, as there had been after World

War I. But there was inflation. Congress let the price controls expire, and prices shot up. Inflation averaged 10% a year from 1945 to 1948.

Marriner Eccles was still the chairman of the Federal Reserve. Eccles had signed on with the Roosevelt administration, as a protégé of Treasury Secretary Morgenthau, to make sure that monetary policy was consistent with New Deal deficit spending. That meant expanding the money supply so rising interest rates wouldn't choke off recovery.

Now things had changed. Roosevelt was dead, and Morgenthau had resigned. Eccles had trouble establishing a relationship with the new President, Harry Truman. Perhaps the problem was the unpleasant advice Eccles had to offer. Depression wasn't the problem anymore. Inflation was. Eccles told the President that fiscal policy had to restrain all that spending. That meant higher taxes, less government spending, budget surpluses, and a continuation of price controls. Truman didn't like it.

Eccles also wanted to raise interest rates, but here he had a problem. The new Treasury Secretary, John Snyder, insisted that interest rates remain fixed.   The huge budget deficits during the war had been paid for by borrowing. The Treasury borrowed by selling bonds to investors. The sum total of those bonds was the amount the Treasury owed to investors, known as the *national debt*. The national debt was now enormous. Some of the bonds were short term, which meant the Treasury had to pay back the bondholders in a few months or a few years. The Treasury did this by borrowing more from other investors, which was called refinancing or *rolling over* the debt.

So, every year the Treasury had to borrow billions in the bond market to refinance the part of the national debt that came due. Treasury Secretary Snyder demanded that Eccles's Federal Reserve fix interest rates low to keep borrowing costs low.   And he demanded that the Fed buy any bonds that the Treasury couldn't sell to private investors.

Eccles chafed under these demands. Interest rates needed to rise to fight inflation, he thought. The Treasury treated the Fed as if its sole responsibility was to assure a stable market for Treasury bonds, at interest rates of the Treasury's choosing. The Fed's mission was much bigger than that, Eccles thought. It should be using monetary policy to stabilize the economy, fighting recession with low interest rates and fighting inflation with high rates.

More than that, the Federal Reserve had been created as an independent agency.   With fixed rates, the Treasury controlled monetary policy and the Fed.   The Fed had to match money demand with the money supply that would fix the equilibrium interest rate at the rate chosen by the Treasury. In effect, the Treasury controlled the money supply, not the Fed.

At the core of this argument was the question of who should make monetary policy. The Federal Reserve was created as an independent agency so it could make policy decisions free from politics. Eccles accused the Treasury, and the executive branch of government, of having a "chronic bias for cheap money in all seasons." Leave it to the politicians, his thinking went, and low interest rates would create so much spending that inflation would rise and rise. Treasury Secretary Snyder found this offensive. The promotion of economic stability, he said, "cannot be carried out by an agency such as the Federal Reserve, which has no responsibility to the electorate. . . ." The nation's elected leaders should judge what was in the overall interest of the economy.

Supporters of an independent Fed pointed out that elected officials are subject to the voters. Many more voters are borrowers than are lenders. Borrowers prefer lower interest rates, and since they vote in large numbers, elected officials prefer low interest rates, too. Left to elected officials, interest rates would be too low, and that would create inflation. Critics of the Fed responded by pointing out that the Fed is the banker's bank. Banks are lenders, and lenders prefer higher interest rates. They make more profits that way. Left independent, the Fed will keep interest rates too high, so elected officials should have a say in the Fed's policies.

> *During and after World War II, the Treasury set interest rates on Treasury bonds and expected the Federal Reserve to guarantee that the bonds would sell at those rates. In effect, the Treasury controlled monetary policy.*

President Truman found Marriner Eccles annoying. The man pushed too hard for an anti-inflation fiscal policy, Truman thought, and his stand on interest rates threatened the stability of the bond market. So, in January 1948, Truman refused to reappoint Eccles as chairman of the Fed. When Eccles asked why, Truman said the reasons were best known to himself alone. Eccles's term on the Federal Reserve Board would continue for several more years, so Truman offered to appoint him as vice-chairman. Eccles accepted, and then waited for months for Truman to act. The appointment never came. Eccles finally withdrew his name from consideration, disgusted.

The new chairman was Thomas McCabe, who had been head of the Philadelphia Federal Reserve bank. McCabe was a more conciliatory man than Eccles, so it must have been a trial for McCabe to have Eccles still on the Reserve board. With Eccles free of the political restraints of chairmanship, he became even more outspoken about ending fixed rates and regaining Fed independence.

The Fed vs. the Treasury
There was actually no legal reason for the Fed to maintain fixed rates. The Fed was an independent agency and could have increased rates at any time. But it did not, for several reasons.

First, throughout most of the 1946-1950 period, the Fed wanted interest rates just a little higher than the Treasury's fixed rates. After the initial explosion with the end of price controls, inflation had been moderate. The Federal budget was in surplus, and Truman had actually asked Congress for new price controls (he was refused). There was no sharp difference of opinion with the Treasury.

Second, in 1949 the economy entered a mild recession. Now the Fed needed to reduce interest rates, and the Treasury thought that was fine. Fixed rates, it turned out, meant a ceiling on rates, not a floor. The Treasury didn't mind if refinancing the national debt cost *less*.

Third, and perhaps most important, was the power of the President. In Washington one bucks the President at one's peril, as Eccles found out. Eccles told McCabe what would likely happen if the Fed tried to raise interest rates without the Treasury's consent. The Treasury, Eccles said, "would no doubt take the issue directly to the President who, in turn, would take it to the Congress if the Open Market Committee remained adamant. There can hardly be any doubt as to what the result might be." The Fed was a creature of the Congress. The President could try to get Congress to change the rules, to make the Fed toe the line.

Eccles liked to tell a joke: A central banker in another country was asked if his bank had the right to defy the government. He replied "Yes, we value that right very greatly and wouldn't think of exercising it." Eccles said that it was not the Fed's place to "enforce its will." He hoped Congress would lend a hand.

Paul Douglas had been elected Senator from Illinois in 1948. He was well-known for his letter to President Hoover protesting the Smoot-Hawley tariffs, and his work as an economist is still remembered today (ask any economics graduate student about the "Cobb-Douglas" production function, an equation that describes how businesses combine labor and machinery to produce output). In December 1949 Douglas's subcommittee on monetary policy began hearings into the Federal Reserve-Treasury conflict, and the desirability for an independent monetary policy. Snyder, McCabe, and Eccles were called to testify.

No one likes to air their dirty laundry in public. "The Treasury has never taken an inflexible position," Treasury Secretary Snyder testified. "A splendid degree of cooperation exists between the Treasury and the Federal Reserve," asserted Fed Chairman McCabe. Senator Douglas was frustrated with these two witnesses.

He got an earful from Eccles, though. The Treasury ignores the Fed's advice, Eccles declared. "Decisions are apparently made by the Treasury largely on the basis of a general desire to get money as cheaply as possible." Fixed rates meant the Fed had no control over the money supply. The talents of the Federal Open Market Committee were wasted—it went through the motions, but policy was determined by the Treasury.

Senator Douglas's subcommittee report declared for the Fed's independence. It said, "The freedom of the Federal Reserve to restrict credit and raise interest rates for general stabilization purposes should be restored even if the cost should prove to be a significant increase in service charges on the Federal debt and a greater inconvenience to the Treasury." Douglas was a junior Senator; he in office for only a year. Yet his opinion carried weight. Knowledge is power in any group. Members of Congress can't be experts on all topics, so they rely on those who are. Douglas was an undeniable expert on monetary policy. He knew how to explain matters so his fellow legislators could understand. Support for the Fed grew in the Congress. Perhaps, Eccles thought, there was enough support in the Congress to overcome the Treasury's demands for fixed rates.

The Accord

President Truman had just arrived at his home in Independence, Missouri, for his first visit since Christmas. June 24, 1950, was hot and humid, as if summer had turned itself on with the calendar. After a home-cooked meal the President was thinking of bed. The phone rang at 9:20 p.m.. It was Secretary of State Dean Acheson. "Mr. President, I have very serious news," he said. "The North Koreans have invaded South Korea."

The Cold War was on. Mao Zedong's communists had taken over China. Joseph Stalin's Soviet Union had detonated an atomic bomb, ending the American monopoly on nuclear weapons. The United States had adopted a policy of "containment" to try to prevent any further expansion of communist influence in the world. North Korea was communist, with a large army equipped by the Soviet Union. South Korea was allied with the U.S., without much of an army at all. Truman flew back to Washington the next day and, stepping into his limousine at National Airport, told his defense secretary "By God, I am going to let them have it."

The U.S. army had been demobilized after World War II. The army was actually smaller in mid-1950 than it had been on Pearl Harbor day. To fight in Korea, military spending would have to increase. The Treasury expected its budget surpluses to turn to deficits. Deficits would be financed by borrowing. Bond issues would now be needed to support national defense-the fight against world communism-not just for national debt refinancing. The Treasury needed a stable bond market with low interest rates, and it needed the Federal Reserve to buy the bonds that investors would not.

To the Federal Reserve, though, the war meant one thing: inflation. The money supply would expand if the Fed was forced to *buy* bonds. That would be a pro-cyclical policy, a policy that would make inflation worse. It was exactly the opposite of the stabilization policy required. Now, more than ever, it was time to break with the Treasury and raise interest rates. Now, suddenly, the conflict over fixed rates really mattered.

Events seemed to confirm the Fed's worst fears. People remembered the last war, only five years before. They expected a return to shortages and rationing. Consumers reacted by buying everything in sight. Businesses reacted by ordering as much inventory as they could. Production and employment increased, but so did prices. Inflation jumped from virtually nothing in the year before June 1950, to 9% in the year after.

Eccles said "it was time the System, if it expected to survive as an agency with any independence whatsoever, should exercise some independence." In August, 1950, the Federal Open Market Committee resolved to increase interest rates beyond the fixed ceilings. They met with Treasury Secretary Snyder, not to ask permission, but to inform him of their decision. He took the news without comment. "Do you agree?" Chairman

McCabe asked him. "You've told me what you've done and there's nothing more to say," Snyder said.

But no sooner was McCabe back at the Fed building when a call came from the Treasury. "We're announcing our September and October financings immediately," Snyder said. The debt would be issued at the usual fixed interest rate. "It's in direct conflict with our announcement," McCabe later told his board members. The Fed would be announcing one interest rate, the Treasury another.

This put the Fed in quite a bind. If they sold bonds, using open market operations to raise interest rates, rates in the market would exceed those on the new bonds the Treasury was offering. Private investors could make more money buying bonds in the market than buying bonds from Treasury. So the Treasury debt issue would "fail," meaning investors would not lend money to the Federal government. If the Treasury couldn't borrow (and refused to budge on the interest they would pay), how could it pay for the war effort? In the past, when Treasury debt didn't sell, the Fed would buy it. But that meant creating more money, which would drive interest rates back down to the fixed level. Buy the Treasury's debt, and the Fed couldn't combat inflation. Let the Treasury issue fail, and be accused of hindering the battle against Communism. The Fed caved in and purchased the Treasury's debt. Emboldened, in November Secretary Snyder announced a new debt issue in December and January, again at the fixed rates.

Eccles was unhappy with this situation, but so was Treasury Secretary Snyder. Now, he realized, the Treasury was at the mercy of the Fed. Should the Fed decide not to buy its bonds, the Treasury would have no choice but to offer higher interest rates to private investors, and pay the higher borrowing costs. Snyder decided to take the matter to President Truman. There was little doubt where the President stood on the issue. Earlier that year, Truman has offered some after-dinner remarks at a Fed banquet. He'd said "Now gentlemen, you represent the greatest financial institution in the history of the world, *except the Treasury of the United States.*"

Truman sent a letter to McCabe in December, saying that "I hope the Board will realize its responsibilities and not allow the bottom to drop from under our securities. If that happens that is exactly what Mr. Stalin wants." When the FOMC didn't budge, Truman stepped up the pressure. He called McCabe to the Oval Office on January 17, 1951, and told him that a commitment to fixed rates would allow the Treasury to sell its next bond issue in the market. McCabe avoided making that commitment, but he tried to reassure the President that there was nothing to be concerned about.

The next night Secretary Snyder gave a speech in New York. The chairman of the Fed had met with the President, he said, and committed to fixed interest rates. The next morning a surprised McCabe called President Truman. He had made no such commitment, the chairman complained, and hadn't known that Snyder was going to give a speech. Truman said he hadn't known either. Eccles was infuriated. Within the week he was testifying before Congress against fixed rates.

The Federal Open Market Committee was scheduled to meet on January 31. On January 30, McCabe received a call from the White House, inviting the whole FOMC to meet with the President at 4:00 p.m. the next day. This was most unusual, McCabe told the President's appointments secretary. The Fed's policy-making body had never met with the President in all its history. But the White House announced the meeting to the newspapers, so McCabe felt he had no choice but to accept.

The members of the FOMC gathered at Fed headquarters the next morning to talk about what they should do. A board member named Vardaman said they should be "guided by whatever request was made by the President as Commander-in-Chief." New York Bank President Sproul thought they should go to Congress for new instructions. Chairman McCabe said that if the President was adamant about keeping fixed rates, they'd have no choice but to resign. The time ticked away, and they couldn't agree. It was time to go to the White House.

President Truman started the meeting with a warning. "The present emergency is the greatest this country has ever faced, including the two world wars and all the preceding wars." Then he told them a story. He'd bought war bonds in 1917, and then shipped out to France as an artillery captain. When he returned from the war the Fed had increased interest rates. Rates in the market were higher than the rates on his bonds, so he couldn't sell them for their face value. He had to take a lower price. Thousands of veterans had lost some of their savings that way, he said. That must not happen again.

McCabe could have reminded the President that the bonds sold to the public during World War II were redeemable only at the Treasury, at their face value. No returning soldier would receive less than he paid for a war bond. But the purchasing power of those savings could be eroded, if there was inflation. Fighting inflation with higher interest rates would actually protect the public's savings.

But McCabe was not one to contradict a President directly. The Fed shares your concerns, he told Truman. But economic stability was the Fed's main job. Stability in the bond market was "an extracurricular activity." Nonetheless, the Fed had performed this role for a decade, and done a good job. They all wanted to protect the credit of the United States, but public-spirited men could disagree on how that might be done. He suggested that the Fed continue to consult with the Treasury about policy, and that if they disagreed, to consult with the President.

Truman said that was entirely satisfactory, and the meeting ended with smiles and handshakes. No one brought up the conflict between the Treasury and the Fed. They'd agreed to "protect the credit of the United States." To the Treasury, that meant maintaining fixed rates, so it could sell its bonds. To the Fed, that meant raising interest rates, to prevent inflation. Each side knew that the policy of other side had not changed, even as they were shaking hands. It was, wrote economist Herbert Stein, "a masterpiece of deliberate misunderstanding."

The next day the Treasury leaked news of the meeting to the press, again implying that the Fed had agreed to fixed rates. McCabe and Sproul were meeting to figure out how to respond, when a letter arrived from Harry Truman, addressed to McCabe. "Dear Tom," it said, "I want the members of the Federal Reserve Board and the members of the Federal Open Market Committee to know how deeply I appreciate their expression of full cooperation given to me yesterday in our meeting."

> As I understand it, I have your assurance that the market on government securities will be stabilized and maintained at present levels in order to assure the successful financing requirements and to establish in the minds of the people confidence concerning government credit.

> I wish you would convey to all the members of your group my warm appreciation of their cooperative attitude.

> Sincerely,
> Harry S Truman.

It was outrageous. No one at the Fed had made any such commitment. McCabe decided that his only course was to confront the President in private, and ask him to withdraw the letter. The Federal Reserve Board members agreed that McCabe would meet with the President the next day to request that his letter be withdrawn.

But that night, as Marriner Eccles was about to leave his office, a reporter called him on the phone.

"Listen to this," the reporter said, and read him the text of President's letter.

"Where did you get that?" Eccles demanded. He thought the letter was confidential.

"The White House has just released it to the world. What have you got to say to that?"

Eccles didn't know what to say. He told the reporter he'd call him back. Now it was clear that the Treasury and the White House intended to convince the public that the Fed had agreed to hold rates constant. Then any attempt to raise interest rates to fight inflation could be portrayed as a betrayal of the Fed's word, and of the war effort. Eccles figured he had to act fast, before public opinion hardened.

Without telling anyone of his intentions, he got a hold of the Fed's confidential minutes of the meeting with the President. His secretary stayed until eleven o'clock typing copies. Then he called the reporter back. He said, in effect, that the President of the United States had lied.

The front pages of the Sunday papers on February 4 shouted the news. The minutes of the meeting showed that the Fed had not agreed to hold rates constant. The President had not even asked.   Senator Douglas issued a statement in support of the Fed.   Other Senators followed his lead. Truman and Snyder would not find support in Congress.

At a meeting of the Open Market Committee that day, some members criticized Eccles for releasing a confidential document. But Allan Sproul, head of the New York Fed, said he had "temporarily retrieved our place in the financial community and with the public."

They decided to confront the President with a letter. It amounted to the Fed's declaration of independence.

The policy of fixed rates, the letter said, meant

> . . . more and more money and cheaper and cheaper dollars. This means less and less public confidence. Mr. President, you did not ask us in our recent meeting to commit ourselves to continue on this dangerous road. Such a course would seriously weaken the financial stability of the United States. . . .

In the face of a determined Fed, and without support in Congress or the press, the Treasury surrendered. Over the next month the Treasury and the Federal Reserve worked out an agreement, known as *"The Accord."* The Fed would allow rates to rise gradually for a time, but after that it would act independently in the interest of economic stabilization. The Treasury would have to sell its bonds by offering market interest rates.

> *In 1951 the Fed and the Treasury signed "The Accord", which gave control over monetary policy to the Federal Reserve.*

Figure 8-4 illustrates the Fed's dilemma. Aggregate demand increased with the war effort. This raised money demand (b), through second shift #3. The Treasury insisted on fixed interest rates, at (3) and (5). With the war-related increase in money demand (b), this would require an increase in the money supply (c). The Fed wanted to allow rates to rise (4), to restrict the increase in aggregate demand and prevent inflation (1 to 2). They wanted to option to reduce the money supply (not shown), to raise interest rates further and restrict aggregate demand more.

At the end of February, as negotiations were wrapping up, Truman called Chairman McCabe into his office and told him that his services were no longer satisfactory. The President cannot fire the chairman of the Fed, but in the face of such Presidential disapproval McCabe felt he had to quit. The President appointed a Treasury official, William McChesney Martin, as the new chair.

Marriner Eccles resigned on July 14, 1951, after 17 years with the Federal Reserve. His career is defined by its contradictions. He was a banker who came to Washington to support the New Deal. He was the head of the monetary policy agency who thought that fiscal policy should be used to fight the Depression. He spent much of his career subordinating monetary policy to the Treasury's fiscal policy, first to finance the New

Deal, then to finance two wars. Yet his first important act was to consolidate Federal Reserve policy-making in Washington, and his last was to strike a blow for the Fed's independence. By the beginning of the 1950's, the Federal Reserve was largely what Marriner Eccles had made of it.

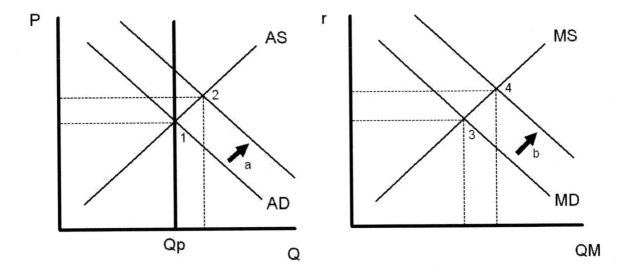

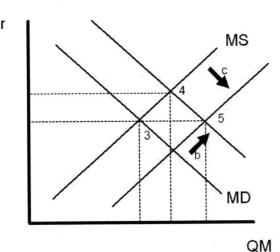

Figure 8-4. War and Inflation. War increases government purchases, and aggregate demand (a). If taxes do not rise, money demand increases with rising incomes and prices (b), through second shift #3. Interest rates threaten to rise (3 to 4). But the Fed holds interest rates constant (3 to 5) by buying Treasury bonds, which increases the money supply (c). Second shift #1 takes over in the goods market, and the price level rises (not shown). But, if taxes rise as much as spending, the aggregate demand increase (a) does not occur. Money demand does not rise, so no interest rate increase is threatened. There is no reason to increase the money supply. The price level remains constant at 1.

Korean War Inflation
World War II created a lot of inflation. The Korean War did not. The difference was fiscal and monetary policy.

During World War II taxes increased, but not nearly enough to cover the increase in Federal spending. Budget deficits rose to 28% of GDP. That increased aggregate demand, and the price level. The Federal Reserve was required to hold interest rates constant. They would buy the Treasury bonds used to finance the deficit at low, fixed interest rates. When the Fed buys bonds, the money supply increases. The increase in the money supply created inflation.

During the Korean War the Truman and Eisenhower administrations increased taxes enough to cover increased spending. Individual and corporate income taxes doubled between 1950 and 1954. No extraordinary budget deficits developed—in fact, the budget was in surplus in 1951 and balanced in1952. In wartime! With no deficit to finance, there was no need to buy Treasury bonds and no need to increase the money supply. Without an increase in the money supply, there was no sustained inflation.

That's obvious in the equation of exchange.

$$(QM) \times V = P \times Q.$$

No matter what is happening to the government's budget, if the quantity of money doesn't increase, prices won't either. If the budget deficit is financed by an increase in money, though, inflation results.

Wars create inflation, but only when budget deficits are financed by money creation. That's what happened during the Civil War, World War I, World War II, and (we will see) the Vietnam War. The Korean War is the exception that proves the rule.

Sustained inflation requires excessive money growth. For shorter periods of time, though, other factors can cause inflation. The Korean War started at the end of June, 1950. Inflation had averaged 2.9% in the previous three months. In July the inflation rate was 8.7%, in August 10.5%, in September 10.5% again. Neither Federal deficits nor rapid money growth could have caused this quick response. Instead, people and businesses remembered the World War II inflation and shortages just five years before. Many people decided they'd better buy what they wanted before goods became too expensive, or became unavailable, or were rationed. They increased their spending on goods and services. The existing quantity of money was used faster. In the equation of exchange, the price level increased because of a rise in the *velocity of money*.

The end of the fixed rate policy presented the new Federal Reserve chairman, William McChesney Martin, with a policy problem. When rates were fixed, it was obvious what the Fed should do in any situation. If the market was pushing interest rates up, the Fed bought bonds, increasing the money supply, causing interest rates to fall. If the market was pulling interest rates down, the Fed sold bonds, and interest rates would rise again. Now the Fed needed a new guiding principle.

Martin proposed one at his nomination hearing. "Our purpose is to lean against the winds of deflation or inflation, whichever way they are blowing," he said. If deflation and recession threatened, the Fed would buy bonds, cut the discount rate, reduce reserve requirements. The money supply would expand and interest rates would fall. If inflation was the problem, the Fed would contract the money supply to raise interest rates. It was a return to the idea that guided Benjamin Strong in the 1920s, but it had never been so clearly stated before. Of course, problems remained: how to decide what direction the wind was blowing, and how hard to lean.

MacroPolicy Now: Federal Reserve Independence

It's 2011, and the Federal Reserve hasn't been this unpopular in decades. The Fed may have rescued the economy from a second Great Depression, but it couldn't stop the Great Recession. And as part of its efforts, it bailed out some of the very financial institutions that were responsible for the crisis. People are angry.

So, members of Congress have pushed for legislation requiring the Fed to submit its monetary policy decisions to an audit of Congress. Supporters of the measure argue that it would make the Fed more accountable to the public. Opponents claim that it would make interest rate policy subject to election year cycles, and make it difficult for the Fed to fight inflation with interest rate hikes.

We've had this argument before. President Truman's Treasury Secretary declared that monetary policy "cannot be carried out by an agency such as the Federal Reserve, which has no responsibility to the electorate. . . ." The Fed is not accountable to the public. But Marriner Eccles claimed that a elected officials have a "chronic bias for cheap money in all seasons." Elected officials want low interest rates, even if rising inflation requires high interest rates.

Before that, when the Federal Reserve was founded, supporters of a central bank wanted a single institution based in New York or Washington, to make policy independent of politics. Those who feared that centralized power wanted many banks dispersed across the states, and a political appointee at the head of the board in Washington.

And before that, eastern bankers supported the gold standard because they preferred the resulting price stability, or even deflation. William Jennings Bryan and the western debtors favored bimetallism because it would end the deflation and perhaps create some inflation.

Who should control monetary policy is an old, old debate in the United States. Now we're having that debate again.

Different countries have organized their central banks in different ways. Some are more independent, some less. Economists Alesina and Summers (that's Lawrence Summers of the Clinton and Obama administrations) used this fact to research the relationship between central bank independence and inflation. The authors rank 16 developed country central banks from less to more independent. Sure enough, countries with less independent central banks—those more subject to pressures from elected officials— generally had higher inflation rates from 1955 to 1988.

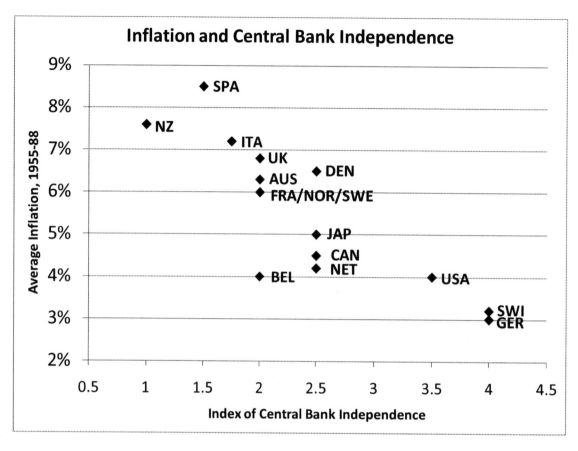

Figure 8-5. Alesina and Summers' (1993) analysis of the relationship between central bank independence and average inflation for 16 developed countries. The index of central bank independence based on legal and administrative characteristics of the banks. More independent banks are less subject to political influence from elected officials. Countries with more independent central banks have generally experienced lower inflation rates.

The latest argument about control of monetary policy has scrambled some of the traditional positions. Representative Paul opposes both "the banking cartel" and "the most powerful politicians in Washington." He favors auditing the Fed, both because the Fed bailed out some big banks, and because it increased the money supply a lot. He also favors a return to the gold standard. William Jennings Bryan shared Paul's suspicion of the big banks, but of course opposed the gold standard. Marriner Eccles wanted the Fed to have the power to fight inflation with high interest rates, but he favored an independent Fed.

Do we need a central bank? Could we return to the gold standard? There are many technical issues involved. It's unclear whether the gold standard would work if just one country adopted it, for example. But there's a more important political issue: the voters expect their elected officials to promote growth, employment and stable prices. When the economy is in recession or inflation, elected officials lose elections (as Herbert Hoover could attest). With a gold standard and no central bank, the money supply is determined by the stock of gold, which is influenced by mining and trade. The money supply cannot be used to stabilize the economy. On the gold standard, elected officials give up one of the tools that can be used to influence the economy.

Perhaps a return to gold would only be possible if the voters are willing to accept the economic results of the gold standard. But as long as the voters expect their elected officials to do something about the economy—and vote against those who don't—elected officials will probably want all the tools they can get, including monetary policy.

Terms in this Chapter, in order of appearance
Labor shortage
Taxes
War bonds
Monetary policy
Fixed interest rates
Price controls
Rationing
Black market
Infinite price
Individual preferences
Cigarettes as currency
Barter
Unit of account
Measure of value
Store of value
Deflation
Just price
Double coincidence of wants
Homogeneous
Durable money
Convenient denominations
Price expectations
Scarcity
Pent-up demand
National debt
Rolling over debt
The Accord
Velocity of money

Notes

FDR's October 12, 1942 fireside chat is available on the internet, at www.presidency.ucsb.edu/site/docs/pppusyear.php?yearindex=1942.

Manchester (289-327) and Kennedy (746-797) give histories of the home front during World War II. Stein (1994, pp. 65-70) and Friedman and Schwartz (546-591) cover the war's economic policies.

Manchester (1974, p. 296) offers the statistics on wartime equipment production. Kennedy writes of the changes brought about by the war, including women's labor force participation (pp. 776-780), and Randolph's march on Washington plans and executive order 8802 (pp. 765-768). He gives the quotes from Sybil Lewis (p. 769). Manchester tells rationing stories (pp. 293-294).

Kettl (1986, 59-62), and Friedman and Schwartz (pp. 561-563) discuss the Fed's deal with the Treasury during the war. Friedman and Schwartz discuss the ways inflation makes itself felt when there are price controls (pp. 557-558). Stein discusses war time tax policy (1994, pp.68-69).

Radner (1945) wrote the P.O.W. camp article about his own experience during the war. He must have spent a lot of time thinking about it during his years in the camp, because he had it written and published within a few months of his release.

McCullough (1992, p. 349) debunks the urban legend about Truman's apartment. Manchester (p. 289) tells the story of the women on the bus, and describes the origins of the Korean War (pp. 517-520, 532-535). McCullough (pp. 774-776) tells the story of Truman's reaction to the start of the Korean War.

The story of the fixed interest rate policy of World War II, and the struggle between the Treasury and the Fed over the Fed's independence, is told by Kettl (1986, pp. 45-81), Meltzer (2003, pp. 579-712) and Stein (1996, pp. 241-280). All the quotes in the text come from these sources. It's a dramatic story that can be told from different points of view. Kettl, for example, emphasizes the role of Marriner Eccles, while Meltzer focuses on New York Bank head Allan Sproul. I followed Kettl's approach here.

The story of Eccles' release of the confidential minutes of the meeting with President Truman is told by the man himself in Eccles (1951, pp. 486-499).

Both of Stein's books (1994, 1996) focus on the development (and breakdown) of the consensus on stabilization policy. Stein (1996) provides a detailed description of fiscal policy during the Eisenhower administration (pp. 281-371). The Eisenhower quotes come from Stein (1996, p. 367 and p. 368). Stein (1996, pp. 370-71) and Wicker (pp.180-181) tell of Richard Nixon's attempts to get Eisenhower to support a tax cut. Stein speculates that Eisenhower's tight fiscal policy cost Nixon the election in 1960.

Kettl (1986, pp. 88-91), Degen (1987, 119-126) and Friedman and Schwartz (1963, pp. 624-632) touch on monetary policy during the Eisenhower years. Kettl discusses Chairman Martin's relationship with Eisenhower.

Alesina and Summers (1993) provide research on the relationship between central bank independence and inflation.

Sources

Alesina, Alberto, and Lawrence H. Summers. 1993. "Central Bank Independence and Macroeconomic Performance: Some Comparative Evidence," *Journal of Money, Credit and Banking* 25 (May): 151-162.

Degen, Robert A. 1987. *The American Monetary System.* Lexington, Massachusetts: D.C. Heath and Company, Lexington Books.

Eccles, Marriner S.. 1951. *Beckoning Frontiers.* New York: Alfred A. Knopf.

Friedman, Milton and Anna Jacobson Schwartz. 1963. *A Monetary History of the United States, 1867-1960.* Princeton, New Jersey: Princeton University Press.

Kennedy, David M. 1999. *Freedom From Fear: The American People in Depression and War, 1929-1945.* New York: Oxford University Press.

Kettl, Donald F. 1986. *Leadership at the Fed.* New Haven: Yale University Press.

Keynes, John Maynard. 1936. *The General Theory of Employment, Interest and Money.* New York: Harcourt, Brace, Jovanovich.

Manchester, William. 1973. *The Glory and the Dream.* New York: Bantam Books.

McCullough, David. 1992. *Truman.* New York: Simon and Schuster.

Meltzer, Allan H. 2003. *A History of the Federal Reserve. Volume 1: 1913-1951.* Chicago: University of Chicago Press.

Radner, R. A. 1945. "The Economic Organization of a Prison Camp. *Economica* 12 (48) (November): 189-201.

Stein, Herbert. 1994. *Presidential Economics (3rd Revised Edition).* Washington, D.C.: The AEI Press.

Stein, Herbert. 1996. *The Fiscal Revolution in America (2nd Revised Edition).* Washington, D.C.: The AEI Press.

Wicker, Tom. 1991. *One Of Us: Richard Nixon and the American Dream.* New York: Random House.

News Articles

Applebaum, Binyamin. "Bernanke Defends Fed's Role in Running Economy, *New York Times*, April 27, 2011.

Chan, Sewell. "The Fed? Ron Paul's Not a Fan," *New York Times*, December 11, 2010.

Herszenhorn, David M. "Senate Votes Unanimously for an Audit of Fed's Actions in Financial Crisis," *New York Times*, May 12, 2010.

Irwin, Neil. "Senate bill brings new powers, new pressures for Fed," *Washington Post*, May 25, 2010.

Norris, Floyd. "Ron Paul Appears Poised to Irk the Fed Chief," *New York Times*, December 16, 2010.

Chapter 9
Trade and Tariffs

MacroPolicy Now: Greek Tragedy

The troubles in Greece came to light in October 2009, when the new Greek government announced that its predecessor had concealed a massive budget shortfall. The new government raised the country's deficit projection from 3.7 percent of GDP to a stunning 13.6 percent. Fears that Greece could not repay the debt sent interest rates on its bonds soaring.

European Union leaders and the International Monetary Fund (IMF) responded to the crisis with a 110 billion euro bailout of Greece, and soon after with a $1 trillion rescue package to support other eurozone economies.

In exchange for the loan, the IMF and European leaders demanded that the Greek impose deep government spending cuts. One out of three people is employed in the Greek civil service, which had guaranteed jobs for life.

The effects of these cuts in the midst of world recession had devastating effects on the Greek economy. At a time when other economies are beginning to grow, Greece is predicted to see a 4% drop in GDP in 2011. The unemployment rate exceeds 15 percent. Panic has hit the banking system, and Greeks are withdrawing their deposits at more and more rapid rates. Calls to suicide hotlines have doubled. "This is an explosive situation, and there could well be violence," said former economy minister Stefanos Manos.

Greece is one of the poorer countries in Europe, but it shares its currency, the euro, with its wealthier neighbors. Greece had joined the eurozone in 2000, converting from its national currency, the drachma. The relatively high value of the euro puts Greek exports increasingly out of sync with market realities, lowering the country's international competitiveness. One painful way out of this dilemma would be for Greece to engineer a continuing deflation of wages and prices. But planned deflation would require years of high unemployment.

In May 2011 a German magazine reported that Greece was considering another alternative: abandoning the euro. Greek and European officials denied the report. But no country has ever left the eurozone, and it would be a severe blow to market confidence. Fear that Greece may have to leave the euro helped cause the big withdrawals from Greek banks.

An independent drachma could depreciate against other currencies, making Greek exports cheaper, and helping the huge tourist industry. Stringent budget cuts might not be required, but default on past loans would be likely. Greece would be hard put to borrow from international lenders for many years afterwards.

In early June 2011 the European community and the IMF came through with another loan to Greece. Again, Greece was expected to accelerate its economic reform measures and cut spending. Suggestions that Greece be allowed to default on its debt were vigorously resisted by the European Central Bank. Abandoning the euro was not considered.

However, the Greek people may already be suffering from "reform fatigue." Prime Minister Papandreou has a comfortable majority in Parliament, but his popularity has been damaged by recession and rising unemployment. Protests are becoming more frequent, and now include young people as well as union members. It was unclear whether Greece could follow through with their reforms, and equally unclear whether those reforms would generate the economic growth needed to bring down unemployment.

Why are trade and finance problems like those in Greece so difficult to solve? is? Where did this International Monetary Fund come from? Can't it do something about the problem? The answers to these questions go back to decisions made during World War II. . . .

The Smoot-Hawley Tariff

"It is sometimes said," wrote economist Paul Douglas in his memoir, "that if all economists were laid end to end, they would not reach a conclusion." But that's not the case with trade, Douglas continued. "Almost unanimously, from Adam Smith on, they have favored *free trade* between localities and nations." Public opinion, however, has been decided mixed.

Tariffs are taxes on imported goods, and are the primary means for restricting trade. These taxes raise the prices of imports, making them less attractive to consumers. Instead, consumers buy the goods produced by domestic farmers and manufacturers, who employ more workers and make more profits. Tariffs help domestic businesses that compete with imports, and they help their employees. Tariffs hurt consumers and businesses that buy the higher priced goods.

> *A tariff is a tax on imported goods, designed to raise its price. Consumers switch their purchases to domestic goods, and imports are reduced. This raises employment and profits for domestic industries.*

The tariff question had been second only to silver as a hot-button issue in the 19th century. Like silver, it divided urban from rural, east from west and south. Republicans, with their electoral base in the east, supported high tariffs to protect eastern manufacturers from European imports. Democrats, with their electoral base in the south and west, supported moderate tariffs. They recognized the need for tariffs as the main source of revenue for the government, but feared the effect tariffs would have on the prices their constituents had to pay.

Since Republicans held the Presidency for most years from Lincoln to Taft (1861 to 1913), U.S. tariffs were high. When Democrat Woodrow Wilson became President in 1913, tariffs were cut substantially. The tariff reduction was made possible partly because the new income tax became the biggest source of revenue for the government. When the Republicans regained power with President Harding, however, they passed the Fordney-McCumber tariff in 1922, which sharply increased tariff rates. The average percentage tacked onto the price of imports in 1920 was16%. After the 1922 tariff, the rate was 38%. During the 1920's, falling farm incomes reduced opposition to tariffs in the south and west. Some Democrats joined Republicans in support of higher tariffs.

Herbert Hoover had pledged to help farmers by restricting imports of foreign farm products during the campaign of 1928. Farmers had traditionally been against tariffs—they wanted the manufactured goods they purchased to be cheaper—but with the collapse of farm prices after World War I, many farmers were desperate. Keeping out imported foodstuffs seemed a good way to increase demand for the products of U.S. farms.

To keep his promise, in 1929 the newly elected President got Senator Reed Smoot of Utah and Representative Willis Hawley of Oregon to sponsor a bill to raise the tariffs on imported farm products. Senator Smoot declared that the United States should have a "high degree of self-sufficiency." The United States should be "self-contained and self-sustaining" proclaimed Representative Hawley. The tariff bill became known as the *Smoot-Hawley Tariff* (though sometimes Hawley is listed first)

The tariff bill didn't pass. The farmers didn't have enough votes. Then two things happened. The Great Depression began. One policy that seemed likely to work was to restrict imports, to preserve the dwindling U.S. market for American goods. Senator Watson of Indiana said that if the tariff bill passed, "within a year from this date we shall have regained the peak of prosperity."

And, farmers formed a coalition with manufacturers. Each supported the others' higher tariffs in exchange for support of their own. The tariff bill became a big, general increase in tariff rates, rather than a farm relief bill. Some manufacturers like Henry Ford opposed higher tariffs. By the 1920's the U.S. had become an exporter of many manufactured goods, automobiles in particular. Still, in 1930 it looked like the tariff bill had a good chance of passing.

Economist Paul Douglas was aghast (the same Paul Douglas who later became a senator from Illinois). Working at Swarthmore College, on leave from the University of Chicago, Douglas joined with a Swarthmore economist Clair Wilcox to draft an appeal to President Hoover to veto the Smoot-Hawley tariff. The letter pointed out that other countries needed to sell their goods to the U.S. in order to earn the dollars to buy U.S. exports. They couldn't earn dollars if the U.S. wouldn't buy their exports. The tariffs also would provoke other countries to retaliate with tariff increases of their own. Raising tariffs to cut imports would surely lead to an offsetting reduction in U.S. exports. The tariff was self-defeating.

Douglas and Wilcox circulated their appeal. No fewer than 1,028 economists signed it. They didn't have to be laid end to end to reach that conclusion. Douglas wrote that "poor Hoover wanted to take our advice. His party was so strongly committed to protection, however, that he felt compelled to sign the bill." If the President opposed the bill, though, he made no mention of it during the June 17, 1930 signing ceremony. He used six gold pens, and handed them to Smoot and Hawley and other supporters as souvenirs.

How high did Smoot-Hawley raise tariff rates? There is some dispute. The average tariff on protected goods was 40% in 1929 and 59% in 1932. This means that, on average, the price of an imported product subject to tariffs had an extra 59% tax tacked on. This was the highest rate recorded in U.S. history. But part of this increase was due to deflation. Many tariffs were applied not as percentages, but as fixed payments per unit. For example, the tariff on peanut oil was 4 cents per pound. When the price of peanut oil fell from 12 cents a pound to 4 cents a pound from 1928 to 1930, the tariff rose from 33% of price to 100% of price. Smoot-Hawley was not responsible for much of the percentage increase in tariffs. On the other hand, to hold the tariff percentage rates constant, unit tariffs needed to *decrease*. Instead, Smoot-Hawley increased them.

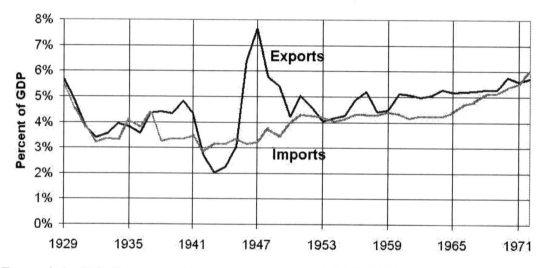

Figure 9-1. U.S. Exports and Imports as Percent of GDP, 1929-1972. Both exports and imports dropped radically from 1929 to 1932, because of the world depression and the Smoot-hawley tariff. Demand for U.S. exports was huge after World War II, while other nations had little capacity to export. The U.S. had an enormous trade surplus. The surplus got smaller and smaller during the 1950's and 1960's as the rest of the world recovered. By 1972 U.S .had a trade deficit, imports exceeded exports. But only then did the share of trade in GDP permanently reach its 1929 level.

The effect of the tariff on the economy also is disputed. It probably had a positive impact on some industries. Imports were made more expensive and spending shifted towards domestic businesses. But other nations retaliated to Smoot-Hawley with higher tariffs of there own. Canada, Spain and Switzerland increased their tariffs on American goods in direct response to Smoot-Hawley. Many other countries raised their tariffs too, but often because of their own economic downturns, not because of the higher U.S. tariffs.

U.S. imports fell, by 34% in real terms from 1929 to 1933. That's what the higher tariffs were meant to achieve. But real exports fell 46%. The U.S. trade position actually got worse in the first years after Smoot-Hawley. Both exports and imports had been nearly 6% of Gross Domestic Product in 1929. In 1933 both were near 3%. GDP had fallen, but trade had fallen faster. The volume of trade fell around the world, partly because of rising tariffs, partly because of falling incomes.

There is little doubt that the drop in trade contributed to the Depression. Still, trade was a small part of American economy. The effect of falling consumption and investment was much bigger. The Smoot-Hawley tariff didn't cause the Great Depression. But it probably made the Depression worse.

Comparative Advantage in Trade

Why are economists so unusually unanimous in opposing trade restrictions? It goes back to a British economist named *David Ricardo*. Ricardo was a successful stockbroker who took up economics after reading Adam Smith's *Wealth of Nations*. In 1817 he published his own book, *On the Principles of Political Economy and Taxation*. There he elaborated his theory of trade.

Trade is obviously beneficial in the case of *absolute advantage*. If one nation can produce coffee at low cost, and another can manufacture airplanes at low cost, it makes sense for the two nations to specialize in their low cost activities and trade. The United States imports coffee from Columbia, where it is easy to grow. It would be very expensive for the United States to try to grow coffee. Without trade, there would not be a Starbucks in every town.

Absolute advantage is the basis for only a small amount of trade, however. Most trade occurs because of a more powerful (and more difficult) idea, *comparative advantage*. What counts, Ricardo and every economist since have said, is the *relative* cost of producing products. Nations that are less efficient at producing everything can still export goods. Nations that are more efficient at producing everything can still import goods.

As an example, consider modern dentistry. A dentist is probably more skilled at cleaning teeth and at oral surgery than is the dental hygienist. Why, then, does the dentist hire the hygienist? Because the dentist is far more skilled at surgery, and only a little more skilled at teeth cleaning. The dentist has the comparative advantage in surgery, but the hygienist has the comparative advantage in cleaning teeth. The dentist's office can serve more patients (and make more money) if the hygienist cleans teeth while the dentist performs surgery.

We can use production possibility frontiers to illustrate comparative advantage and the benefits of trade. Consider two countries, called the United States and Sweden, which produce two goods, called guns and butter. Suppose the United States is more efficient at producing both. We'll use straight-line PPF's in this example, because the slopes of the two lines are then the opportunity costs of guns measured in butter, and butter measured in guns.

The PPF of the United States shows that if it devoted all its resources to butter, it could produce 30 units (30 billion pats of butter?). If it devoted all its resources to guns, it could produce 90 units (90 million guns?). The opportunity cost of an extra gun is thus 1/3 of a unit of butter. Switch resources from butter to guns, and each one butter given up yields three more guns.

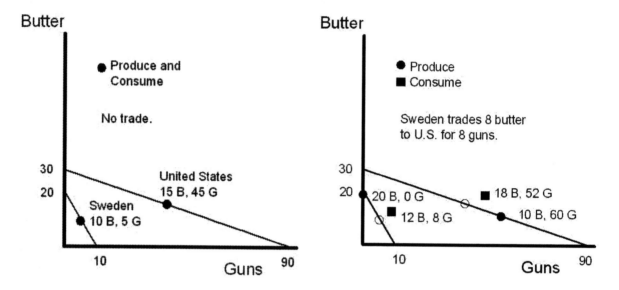

Figure 9-2. Comparative Advantage. On the left are production possibility frontiers for two countries, the United States and Sweden. The U.S. chooses to produce and consume 15 butter and 45 guns. Sweden chooses to produce and consume 10 butter and 5 guns. There is no trade. On the right, the United States shifts resources from butter production to gun production. The slope of the PPF defines the opportunity cost, which is 1/3 butter per gun. Each butter given up yields 3 more guns. The U.S. produces 10 butter and 60 guns. Sweden shifts its resources to butter production. The opportunity cost is 2 butter per gun. Each gun given up yields 2 more butter. Sweden produces 20 butter and no guns. "World" production of both guns and butter increase. The U.S. trades 8 guns to Sweden; Sweden trades 8 butter to the U.S. Each nation consumes beyond its production possibility frontier.

Sweden can't produce as much. The Swedes can churn out 20 units of butter with all their resources, or 10 units of guns. The opportunity cost of an extra gun in Sweden is 2 units of butter. Switch resources to gun production, and each unit of butter given up produces one-half extra gun.

But look: the cost of a gun in the U.S. is 1/3 of a butter. The cost of a gun in Sweden is 2 butters. Guns cost less in the U.S., relative to butter given up. And, the cost of an extra unit of butter in the U.S. is 3 guns. The cost of an extra unit of butter in Sweden is ½ of a gun. Butter costs less in Sweden, relative to guns given up.

The U.S. may be absolutely more efficient at producing both guns and butter. But the relative cost of butter in Sweden is less. Sweden and the U.S. can benefit if the Swedes export butter to the U.S., and the U.S. exports guns to Sweden.

In Figure 9-2, and in the table, suppose at the start, with no trade, both nations choose points right in the middle of their PPF's. The U.S. allocates its resources to produce and consume 15 butter units, and 45 guns. Sweden produces and consumes 10 butter units, and 5 guns.

> *Comparative advantage means that a nation can produce a product at lower cost, relative to the other products it produces. World output increases if nations specialize in the products for which they have a comparative advantage.*

Now suppose each nation decides to specialize in the product it does best, and trade. Sweden shifts its resources to butter production. They give up the five guns they used to produce, and because the opportunity cost of one gun is two butter units, they produce ten more butter units. The U.S. shifts some of its resources to gun production. They give up five butter units to get 15 more guns, since the opportunity cost of one butter is three guns.

World output has increased! Sweden gave up five guns, but the U.S. is making 15 more. The U.S. gave up five units of butter, but Sweden is making ten more. The world is producing ten more guns and five more butter units, because each nation specializes in its relatively more efficient industry.

Now they trade. The *terms of trade* must be negotiated. That's the rate at which the goods are exchanged for one another. It must be somewhere in between the two nations' opportunity costs. One gun for one butter unit works fine. Suppose the U.S. exports eight guns to Sweden in exchange for eight units of butter. The U.S. winds up consuming 18 butter units and 52 guns units; Sweden winds up consuming 12 butter units and 8 guns.

Table 12-1

	No Trade		Production w/ Trade			Consumption w/ Trade	
	Guns	Butter	Guns	Butter	Trade	Guns	Butter
United States	45	15	60	10	8 Guns	52	18
Sweden	5	10	0	20	8 Butter	8	12
World Total	50	25	60	30		60	30

These consumption amounts are beyond each nation's production possibility frontier. This leads to a conclusion that seems impossible: each nation produces on its PPF, and through trade, each nation can consume beyond its PPF. But that's what happens. Nation's specialize in their relatively most efficient industry, then trade, and each nation consumes beyond the limits of its own resources.

What made it all possible were the differences in the two nations' opportunity costs. Each is relatively more efficient at producing one of the goods. Specialization then increases world output.

So, when the Smoot-Hawley tariff reduced trade, nations could no longer specialize to the same degree in their relatively most efficient industries. They could not exploit their comparative advantages. World output diminished, and people in all nations consumed less.

Specialization can only happen if there is trade. Both nations need both goods. Without trade they will have to try to be self-sufficient in both products. Sweden would have to switch resources to guns. There will be lots of butter lost, because Swedish resources are relatively good for making butter. The United States will have to sacrifice a lot of guns to produce the butter it used to get from Sweden. Representative Willis Hawley's idea that the U.S. should be "self-contained and self-sustaining" was consistent with the pioneer spirit, but it was a recipe for less production and lower incomes.

Tariffs, Prices and Output

At first glance, though, a tariff seems like a reasonable anti-recession policy. A tariff is a tax on imported goods, intended to reduce imports. Imports are subtracted from the spending that makes up aggregate demand—recall C+I+G+X-M. If imports are reduced, consumers will spend more on domestic output, from the *import-competing* domestic businesses. Aggregate demand will increase. An increase in aggregate demand will increase output.

That's just one of the effects of a tariff, however. To buy American goods, other nations need to earn dollars, and they can only do that by exporting goods to the U.S. The less they export to the U.S., the less than can afford to import from the U.S. Furthermore, other nations may respond to a tariff with trade restrictions of their own, as they did in the case of the Smoot-Hawley tariff. The tariff reduced U.S. exports. A reduction in exports reduces aggregate demand.

Trade restrictions reduce imports, which increases aggregate demand. They reduce exports, which decreases aggregate demand. They raise input costs and reduce the level of technology employed, which reduces aggregate supply. Overall, output is lower and the price level is higher when trade is restricted.

Tariffs interfere with the most important benefit of free trade, which is the more efficient allocation of production among nations. The principle of comparative advantage means that each nation has something to contribute to world output. With trade, a nation specializes in the industries in which it is most efficient, relative to its other industries. It produces more from its resources. Trading this output in the world's markets earns it more income than it could have had without trade.

When the U.S. imported less, it switched resources to industries in which it was relatively less efficient. That means that U.S. output was produced with lower average efficiency. The same resources were used in less efficient ways, so they produced less total output. That's like a reduction in technology, and that reduces aggregate supply.

Imposing a tariff means imported equipment and materials are more expensive. And it means resources are used less efficiently. Aggregate supply is reduced, and, if the tariff is permanent, potential output is reduced too.

Netting it all out, the Smoot-Hawley tariff, like all tariffs, increased domestic demand for the output of import-competing industries (increasing aggregate demand), decreased the foreign demand for the output of exporting industries (decreasing aggregate demand), and raised resource costs and reduced average technology (decreasing aggregate supply and potential output). In the end, the tariff reduced output and raised prices.

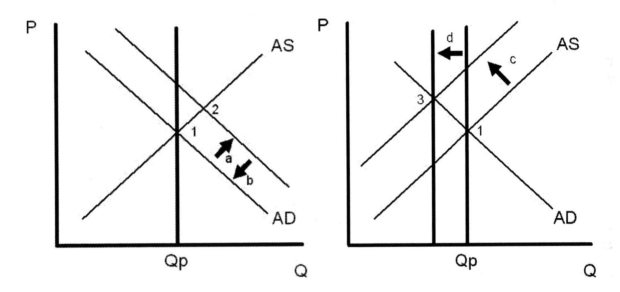

Figure 9-3. A net loser. Tariffs are increased. At first, imports fall and aggregate demand increases (a). Output and prices rise (1 to 2). But the nation's trading partners can't pay for as many exports if the nation won't buy the partners' goods. And, before long, other nations retaliate with tariff increases of their own. Exports fall, which decreases aggregate demand (b). Output and prices return to their original level (2 to 1). The nation's tariffs increase the prices of imported inputs, and shift production to less efficient industries, which is a decline in aggregate productivity. These changes reduce aggregate supply (c), and, if they persist, potential output (d). Output falls and prices rise (1 to 3).

From GATT to the WTO

The Democrats gained control of the Presidency and Congress in 1933. Historically, when that happened they would pass a reduction in U.S. import tariffs, as they had during the Woodrow Wilson administration. Democrats had opposed the Smoot-Hawley tariff.

But the Great Depression presented special problems. Most other countries had raised their tariffs too, in response to Smoot Hawley and their own economic depressions. A U.S. tariff cut might not be followed by tariff reductions in other countries, and that would put U.S. businesses at a disadvantage. In addition, President Roosevelt was only a half-hearted tariff reducer. After all, his National Recovery Administration was trying to raise prices and wages by *restricting* competition. Tariff reductions would increase competition from foreign countries. Roosevelt torpedoed an international trade conference in 1933, for fear of the competition trade might bring.

Since tariffs could not be cut unilaterally nor multilaterally (by many nations all at once), the U.S. decided to push bilateral agreements. It would negotiate tariff reductions with other countries, one country at a time. Congress approved the *Reciprocal Trade Agreement Act (RTAA)* in 1934, perhaps with the help of the Douglas-Wilcox letter. It authorized the President to negotiate bilateral agreements with other countries. Congress gave prior approval to whatever agreements the President might negotiate. The tariff reductions would not have to be ratified by Congress. It was the first time Congress had ever delegated such powers to the President. The RTAA was good for three years, after which it could be reauthorized.

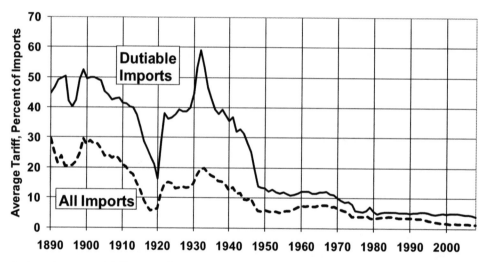

Figure 9-4. Average U.S. Tariff Rates, 1890-2008. The black line shows the average tariff collected as a percent of all imports subject to tariffs ("dutiable imports"). The dashed line shows the average tariff as a percent of all imports, including those not subject to tariffs. The two lines tell the same story. Tariffs were high at the start of the 20th century. They fell during the Wilson administration (1913-1921). The Fordney-McCumber tariff increased the rate in the 1920's, and then Smoot-Hawley raised tariffs again in 1930-31. The rate on dutiable imports reached almost 60%, the highest in U.S. history. Reciprocal agreements began to reduce tariffs during the 1930's. Then the negotiation of GATT in 1947 cut tariffs in half. Reductions from the 1960's to the 1980's came from successive rounds of GATT negotiations. In the new century tariffs are at their lowest levels in U.S. history.

By the end of the decade the U.S. had negotiated 21 bilateral agreements with its trading partners. RTAA negotiating authority was reauthorized every three years. Tariffs were reduced, but they remained as high as they had been before Smoot-Hawley. Little was changed during World War II. Then, after the war, the U.S. floated plans for a new trade body, the International Trade Organization (ITO), to help bring down tariffs farther and faster.

From April to October, 1947, representatives of 23 nations met in Geneva, Switzerland to discuss trade rules that the ITO would enforce once it was founded. The result was the *General Agreement on Tariffs and Trade*, known as *GATT*. Though it was a multilateral agreement, U.S. negotiators followed a bilateral strategy. They would pick a commodity and negotiate a tariff reduction with its biggest trading partner in that commodity. Then each would extend the lower tariffs to other countries. Because the negotiations were bilateral, they were covered under the RTAA. The President could negotiate the new tariffs on his own authority. The GATT agreement did not have to be submitted to Congress. The average U.S. tariff was cut in half.

In 1948 the United Nations sponsored a trade conference in Havana, Cuba, to hammer out a charter for the ITO. Representatives of 56 countries attended. But the U.S. Congress was reluctant to ratify yet another international organization. In 1950 the Truman administration decided not to push the treaty through. Without the United States, the ITO never got started.

The ITO was never founded, but the rules it was supposed to enforce came into being anyway. Eventually a GATT Secretariat was headquartered in Geneva to administer the rules. Nations gathered every few years to negotiate further tariff reductions and other trade rules. These gatherings were known as "*rounds*," usually named after the place where they first met. Sometimes the rounds succeeded, sometimes they did not. But tariff rates trended ever lower, and world trade increased.

The United States also undertook trade negotiations apart from the GATT framework. The *North American Free Trade Agreement (NAFTA),* for example, did away with most trade restrictions between Canada, Mexico and the United States. It passed Congress in 1993.

The last round of GATT negotiations started in Punta del Este, Uruguay, in 1986. It became known as the Uruguay Round. Trade negotiations had become more complex over the decades. In the 1940's most of the world's trade was in tangible goods like cars, machinery, or wheat. Now new products were being traded. New communications technology allowed trade in services, such as telephone answering or computer programming. Rules were needed to cover trade in services. Sometimes ideas and technologies were bought and sold over international boundaries, so rules were needed defining intellectual property rights.

In the 1940's most of the barriers to trade were tariffs, which were easily measured taxes on imports. As tariffs were reduced, however, nations found other ways to protect their industries from foreign competition. Nations could use red tape. They could require importers to obtain licenses, and then make the licensing procedures arduous to discourage imports. Nations could apply more stringent environmental regulations to imported goods than domestically produced goods. They could design their health and safety rules to discriminate against particular nations' products. Of course, some of these rules and restrictions were legitimate, designed to protect national security, the environment or consumer health. Negotiating the line between a nation's attempts to protect its security, environment or health, and its attempts to protect its domestic industries from trade, was much tougher than simply cutting a tariff rate in half.

Rules could be written and agreed to, but they were open to interpretation. How to resolve disputes between nations over trade? The Uruguay round created a new organization, the *World Trade Organization (WTO)* to resolve trade disputes. The agreement was signed in Marrakech, Morocco in April 1994. By the end of the year the U.S. Congress had agreed. In January 1995 the new trade rules came into effect, and the WTO began operation. After almost fifty years, the international trade organization envisioned at Havana in 1948 had come into being.

An early dispute illustrates the operation of the WTO, and its problems. Three weeks after the WTO set up shop, Venezuela filed a complaint against the United States. Venezuela claimed that the U.S. Clean Air Act applied stricter standards to oil imported into the United States than to oil produced in the United States. Brazil later joined the complaint. After a year of study, the WTO's Dispute Settlement Body found against the U.S. The United States appealed, and four months later the WTO's Appellate Body again found against the

> *Trade negotiations have reduced tariffs, but now must contend with new issues such as trade in services and intellectual property, and environmental and labor regulations.*

U.S. The U.S. and Venezuela took another year and a half to negotiate and implement changes in the law, but in August 1997 the dispute was settled. The U.S. brought its Clean Air rules into compliance with WTO trade rules.

Many environmental groups were appalled. As they saw it, the WTO had forced the United States to water down its environmental laws. And they were right, in the sense that imported Venezuelan oil was now not as clean-burning as it had been. They also were wrong, in the sense that the WTO would have been perfectly happy had U.S. tightened its environmental restrictions on domestic oil,, so long as the same rules applied to imported oil. One thing was clear, though: trade mattered for the environment.

Suddenly environmental concerns were a part of the trade debate. The pro-trade side pointed to what economists called the *"environmental Kuznets curve"* (named after economist Simon Kuznets, though he didn't think it up). Trade promotes development. At first, the development of basic industries increases pollution. Poor nations are more interested in income gains than pollution control, and are too poor to afford pollution abatement measures. But, as development continues, people begin to value environmental protection as much as further income gains, and can afford pollution abatement. The level of pollution begins to decline. Trade that promotes development may increase pollution at first, but over time development will reduce pollution.

Perhaps, said the environmentalists. But they pointed out that China, India, and almost all of Africa might take a long time reaching the downward part of the Kuznets curve. The world could be in for decades of increasing pollution as these regions developed. Could the world's environment survive the upward slope of the curve, long enough to reach the downward side?

Instead, environmentalists said, trade might promote a "race to the bottom," with nations competing for the world's export business by weakening their pollution rules. Businesses would invest where rules were lax, forcing other nations to relax their rules to compete for investment. Supporters of trade pointed out that the costs of pollution rules were small compared to the costs of labor and transportation, so that differences in such rules were unlikely to affect business investment.

Labor groups made similar arguments about working conditions in developing countries. Global businesses would move production to nations with the weakest standards on working hours and minimum wages. The competition for business would force all nations to weaken their standards, they feared. Supporters of trade replied that development would increase the demand for labor, which would raise wages, benefits and workplace standards.

The developing countries themselves were leery of including environmental and labor standards in trade agreements. If such standards raised their production costs, their few advantages in world trade might be erased. They suspected that developed countries wanted an excuse to protect their industries from developing nation competition, and would use environmental and labor standards as that excuse.

The next round of trade negotiations was scheduled to start with a WTO meeting in Seattle in November 1999. Delegates were met with mass protests. Environmental and labor groups combined to bring thousands of protesters to the meeting, and in some cases the protests broke out in rioting. The WTO meeting ended without an agreement. Perhaps the protests had intimidated the delegates. Perhaps the Clinton administration had pushed for the meeting prematurely, before the negotiations were far-enough advanced. Some even said that the delegates were on the verge of agreement when they had to vacate the conference hall because an optometrists' convention had scheduled the space.

After Seattle, WTO meetings were dogged by mass protests. The WTO began to schedule meetings in places that protestors couldn't reach. A 2001 meeting in Doha, Qatar—where protesters were hardly welcome—started the next round of trade negotiations.

Winners and Losers from Trade

Nations as a whole benefit from trade. But not everyone in the nation benefits. That's evident from Figure 9-2, the production possibility frontier diagram which shows each nation specializing in the product it exports. The U.S. and Sweden both consume beyond their production possibility frontiers. More goods are available at lower prices. Consumers are better off. But U.S. butter producers have seen their output and employment dwindle. Swedish gun producers have been wiped out entirely.

In the diagram, both nations continue to produce on their PPF's. That implies fully employed resources. Every unemployed Swedish gun craftsman has found a job on a dairy farm. Every bankrupt U.S. dairy farmer has gone to work in a gun factory. The shifts up and down along the PPF's mask the difficulty of these transitions. all these people probably spent some time unemployed. Communities based on traditional industries were broken up. Ways of life were lost.

Is the United States wrong to impose tariffs and quotas on imported goods? Paul Douglas's thousand economists might have answered yes. But that's a value judgment. *Economic analysis does not say that tariffs are bad policy.*

That's because the decision to impose a tariff involves comparing the value of preserving traditional industries and communities to potential increases in consumption. Some communities in our example may have depended on the traditional guns or butter industries for a hundred years. Some families have been farmers for generations. Jobs in the gun factory defined and preserved home for thousands of people.

A nation can choose to impose tariffs, for the sake of the jobs, industries, and communities the tariffs protect. Economic analysis measures the cost—the losses which tariffs impose on the economy. Let there be no doubt that there will be losses. Output will be lower, and prices will be higher, if tariffs are imposed. The nation must decide whether the benefits are worth the cost.

Great Britain's International Payments Problem

The world negotiated agreements on tariffs and trade. But another issue remained: how to pay for imports and exports? The gold standard had collapsed, and it had provided the system of exchange rates and international payments under which the world had operated for a century. What would replace it?

Events during World War II provided the answer.

At the end of 1940 Great Britain faced the threat of Nazi Germany alone. Ships, planes and munitions were vital for Britain's continued existence, but in an economic sense they were just British imports and U.S. exports. Britain bought them, the U.S. sold them. Most imports are paid for with exports. Great Britain would earn dollars by selling goods to the U.S., and would use those dollars to buy goods from the U.S. But with the war Britain was exporting almost nothing, earning few dollars. How else could it pay for U.S. goods?

They had some *exchange reserves* which were dollars earned in the past and saved. Britain had some reserves of other nations' currencies, which might be traded for dollars. Britain had some gold, which could also be exchanged for dollars at the official price of $35 dollars an ounce. British people owned some assets in the U.S.—land and buildings on American soil, stock in U.S. companies, bonds of companies and governments. These could be sold for dollars.

In ordinary times they also could have sold assets located in Great Britain to Americans, which would earn profits for U.S. investors. In ordinary times they also could have borrowed dollars from U.S. lenders. These weren't ordinary times. Business people saw added risks. Would the assets in Britain like office buildings or factories be destroyed by German bombs? If Britain was conquered, would the Nazis honor debts to Americans? Besides, "cash and carry" was official U.S. policy. No borrowing was allowed. Congress feared that if Britain became too indebted to the U.S., Americans would have too big a stake in Britain's survival, and that could draw the U.S. into the war. Some said that had happened in World War I.

Countries can pay for imports by selling exports, using reserves of foreign currency, selling assets or borrowing.

In December 1940, British exchange resources in the U.S. were almost used up. Britain had spent much of its gold stock and its currency reserves. It had sold off its American assets. It had spent five billion pounds in a year, and had only two billion left. It had already placed orders for more than that. How would Britain pay? Winston Churchill, the British prime minister, decided to write a letter to President Franklin Roosevelt.

Roosevelt had just won reelection to a third term. It had been exhausting—Wendell Wilkie had been a formidable foe--and Roosevelt treated himself to a vacation at sea. Since he was President, he had his choice of vessels. He took a two week cruise in the Caribbean aboard the Navy cruiser *Tuscaloosa*.

Presidential business goes on, even on vacation at sea. Navy sea-planes would bring the incoming mail and take the outgoing Presidential replies. On December 9, the diplomatic pouch brought a long letter from the Prime Minister Winston Churchill. It was dated December 7, 1940. In it Churchill explained Great Britain's situation.

Much of the letter was grim. "We can endure the shattering of our dwellings and the slaughter of our civilian population by indiscriminate air attacks. . . ," he wrote, but "the decision for 1941 lies upon the seas." Nazi submarines were sinking more shipping than Britain could replace. He hoped that the United States would intensify its patrol of the seas, and provide Britain ships, munitions and airplanes.

Attacks by air and sea were not the most immediate problem, though. The biggest difficulty was financial. Churchill told Roosevelt that, "Orders already placed or under negotiation . . . many times exceed the total exchange resources remaining at the disposal of Great Britain. The moment approaches when we shall no longer be able to pay cash for shipping and other supplies." Great Britain had no more dollars.

Roosevelt sat in the sun on the deck of the *Tuscaloosa*, fishing and thinking. By the end of his vacation he had an answer. He called it *Lend-Lease*. Back in Washington on December 17, he told reporters that he wanted to eliminate the dollar sign from aid to Britain, "the silly, foolish old dollar sign."

He told them, "Suppose my neighbor's home catches fire, and I have a length of garden hose four or five hundred feet away. If he can take my garden hose and connect it up with his hydrant, I may help him to put out his fire. Now, what do I do? I don't say to him before that operation, 'Neighbor, my garden hose cost me $15; you have to pay me $15 for it.' What is the transaction that goes on? I don't want $15--I want my garden hose back after the fire is over."

The U.S. would lend and lease munitions to Britain. When the war was over the British would give back what wasn't damaged, or replace what was, or work out some other compensation. The public supported the idea two to one, and by March 1941 Congress had passed the lend-lease bill. Roosevelt put Harry Hopkins in charge.

The short term problem was solved. Britain would get its equipment. But Churchill had dwelt on another problem in his letter. After Britain had won the war (Churchill didn't doubt that Britain would win) they would need to import virtually everything for reconstruction. They would have no currency reserves, and no capacity to export. How would they pay?

After all, they would still have no reserves, and with all that wartime destruction Britain would not produce much for export. British exports to the U.S. would fall short of its imports from the U.S. for years and years. If Britain couldn't buy U.S. exports, Churchill had written, it would mean "cruel privations" for the British people, and possibly "widespread unemployment" in the U.S.

Reviving trade meant reducing tariffs, but it also meant finding a way to manage international payments. Even as the bombs fell on London, the British were working on a plan for the post-war world. Back in 1940 the Nazis had declared a "New Order", an international economic plan to organize conquered Europe. The British Information Ministry wanted to respond to this propaganda with a broadcast about the benefits of free trade and the traditional *gold standard*. They asked the most famous economist in Great Britain, John Maynard Keynes, to write it.

Keynes refused. The gold standard had been a disaster for the British economy in the 1920s, Keynes told them, and efforts to support it (like the Fed's interest rate hikes) had made the Depression worse. A broadcast about a return to the old policies would likely drive public opinion into the German camp, Keynes figured. He began to think about the payments problem.

Exports and imports crossed national boundaries, but otherwise they were just the same as other goods. There were sellers, there were buyers, and there had to be a way to balance the markets so the amounts buyers wanted to buy would equal the amounts sellers wanted to sell. The gold standard provided one way. If a nation bought more imports than it sold in exports, it would use its gold stock to pay for the extra imports. The quantity of gold supporting the nation's money supply would decline, and with it the prices of the nation's goods. Other countries would find the lower prices attractive, and would begin to buy these cheaper goods. The nation's exports would rise. The falling money supply would create unemployment and declining incomes.   The nation's consumers would buy fewer imports. Exports would rise and imports would fall until they were equal. The gold standard would balance trade.

It was logical, and it had worked well from the 1870's to 1914. Then came the first war, and then the Depression. First Germany, then Britain, then the U.S. found gold draining from their Treasuries. The gold standard required that countries suffer falling prices, higher unemployment and declining incomes in such situations. Central banks were supposed to raise interest rates to help the process along. Governments were supposed to raise taxes and cut spending, too.

This was exactly the opposite of the counter-cyclical stabilization policies that Keynes advocated. In a depression governments should cut taxes and raise spending, and central banks should reduce interest rates.   The gold standard required pro-cyclical policies. Under the gold standard, fiscal and monetary policy danced to the tune of international trade. If nations wanted to pursue independent stabilization policies, the gold standard had to go. Germany, and Britain, and the United States had left the gold standard. During the 1930s most other countries followed. .

In a larger sense, it may have been democracy that finally destroyed the gold standard. As democracy gained strength in the 19th and early 20th centuries, people had a bigger say in the economic policies of their governments. When governments were run by small elites, following international rules that put people out of work was a possibility. When governments are responsible to a broad electorate, raising unemployment to balance trade was not possible. The gold standard's rules could not work if people would not accept the necessary sacrifices.

There was another way to balance exports and imports: flexible exchange rates. On a gold standard exchange rates between currencies were fixed, but without the gold standard exchange rates could vary. If people in the U.S. wanted to import goods from Britain, they would need pounds, and they would offer dollars in exchange. Likewise, the British needed dollars to buy U.S. goods. If U.S. imports from Britain exceeded U.S. exports to Britain, the number of dollars traders offered would exceed the number that traders wanted. More dollars would have to exchange for fewer pounds—the value of the dollar against the pound would fall.

That could work out just fine. If the value of the dollar fell, it took fewer pounds to buy one, and so fewer pounds to buy all those U.S. goods priced in dollars. U.S. exports then were cheaper to the British, so they would buy more. With the dollar buying fewer pounds, British imports were more expensive, so Americans would buy less. The gap between imports and exports would close. *Flexible exchange rates* could help equate imports and exports.

But Keynes and most others thought that flexible exchange rates hadn't worked very well in the 1920's and 1930's. Unstable exchange values made it hard for business people to make deals. A profitable deal this month could be unprofitable next month, if exchange rates shifted the wrong way. Currency speculators aggravated instability. If a country's exchange rate was expected to fall, speculators would sell the currency, *causing* it to fall. Often it would fall more than the import-export balance required. Sometimes exchange rates could move the wrong way, and *cause* trade imbalances. And countries that still tried to fix their exchange rates would sometimes reduce them to gain an advantage over their trading partners. Cut the value of the currency, and the nation's exports would be cheaper, undercutting competitors. Nations would engage in competitive devaluation, known as "beggar-thy-neighbor" policies.

> *The gold standard required fixed exchange rates. Balancing trade sometimes meant adopting pro-cyclical policies. Flexible exchange rates allow counter-cyclical policy, but added uncertainty to trade deals.*

Keynes wanted fixed exchange rates *and* independent stabilization policy. But this left him without a way to equate imports and exports, nor a way to equate the amounts of the various currencies demanded and supplied. Through 1940 and 1941 he worked out a plan.

Back in the United States, Roosevelt was impressed by Churchill's letter. He too was concerned about financing trade after the war. He tossed the problem to Henry Morgenthau, and the Treasury Secretary called in his right-hand man on international matters, Harry Dexter White. White was asked to prepare a memo. He wrote one the length of a book. Like Keynes, he advocated fixed exchange rates *and* independent stabilization policy.

How to Equilibrate the Exchange Market?

Great Britain had the Keynes plan. The United States had the White plan. In Fall 1943, they met to thrash out their differences. They agreed right off that exchange rates should be fixed and that nations should follow their own stabilization policies. But how then to equate imports and exports and currency flows? Especially, how could trade be adjusted when a nation imported more than it exported, when it supplied more of its currency than was demanded? There were a few possibilities, none entirely satisfactory.

- Tariffs might reduce imports until they equaled exports, and with fewer imports a nation would supply less of its currency in exchange for foreign currencies. This idea defeated the purpose of the plan, which was to increase the volume of trade.

- *Exchange controls* could be imposed. Currencies could be made non-convertible, which meant they could not be freely exchanged for other nation's currencies. This way the government could regulate just how much of its currency could be offered in exchange markets, and so could determine just how many imports its consumers could buy. Again, this interfered with the growth of trade.

- *Capital flows* could be controlled. A nation's lenders and investors could be discouraged from lending or investing in other countries. They would then supply less of the nation's currency in exchange markets. This sounded better, because at least it did not interfere with imports and exports of currently produced goods. It meant, though, that investment projects that might increase world output would not happen.

- A fund could be created that would lend to nations which were importing more than they were exporting. Each of the world's nations would contribute its currency or gold to the fund, with richer, exporting nations contributing more. If a nation imported more than it exported, and supplied more of its currency than markets demanded, it could borrow currency from the fund to buy up the excess. But how long would a nation be allowed to remain in deficit, how much could it borrow from the fund, and with what conditions?

The world would like to have: *fixed exchange rates, independent stabilization policy*, and the *free flow of capital* across national boundaries. Fixed exchange rates make business decisions more predictable. Discretionary stabilization policy lets governments respond to recessions and inflation with counter-cyclical policy. The free flow of capital increases the world's wealth by allocating resources to their most productive uses.

> *Three desirable features of an international payments system are fixed exchange rates, independent stabilization policy, and free flow of capital. One of these must be given up to equilibrate the exchange market.*

The world can only have two out of three. One of these three goals must be sacrificed to equilibrate the exchange market.

If exchange rates are fixed and trade and capital flow freely, then there cannot be discretionary stabilization policy. The foreign exchange market will have to equilibrate at the fixed exchange rates, so somehow the amounts of a nation's currency demanded and supplied must be made equal. That can only be done if income, spending and interest rates adjust as the exchange market requires, which is not necessarily as stabilization policy requires. This was how the gold standard operated before World War I.

If discretionary stabilization policy is possible and trade and capital flow freely, then there cannot be fixed exchange rates. The amounts of a nation's currency demanded and supplied will be made equal through changes in the exchange rates. Exchange rates may vary every month, week, day, hour or minute to accomplish this.

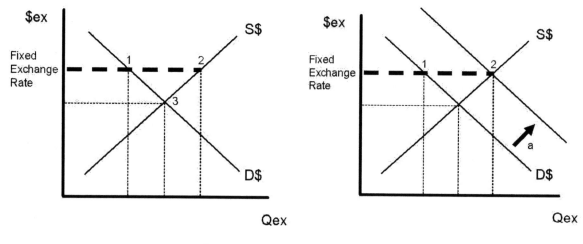

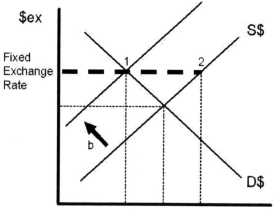

Figure 9-5. Two out of three. Here the fixed exchange rate of the dollar is above the equilibrium value. At the fixed rate, the number of dollars demanded (1) is less than the number supplied (2). There are three ways to solve this problem and equilibrate the exchange market. The U.S. could allow the dollar's value to float. It would drop to equilibrium (3), and the number of dollars demanded and supplied would be equal. But the fixed exchange rate has been sacrificed. It could raise interest rates, raise taxes and cut spending. Higher returns on lending and lower inflation would make the dollar more attractive to foreign investors (second shift #5). The demand for dollars would rise (a). But independent stabilization policy has been sacrificed. It could restrict imports and foreign transactions. If Americans don't import foreign goods or invest or lend in foreign countries, they will not supply dollars in exchange for foreign currencies. The supply of dollars will decrease (b). But free trade and the free flow of capital have been sacrificed, and the world won't produce as much as it could.

Finally, if exchange rates are fixed and discretionary stabilization policy is possible, then trade and capital cannot flow freely. Suppose the U.S. imports more than it exports. The amount of dollars supplied exceeds the amount demanded at the fixed exchange rate. To bring the equilibrium value of the dollar up, the U.S. could reduce the supply of its currency in the foreign exchange market. This could be done by restricting imports of goods with tariffs or quotas, or by restricting the convertibility of the dollar with other currencies. If Americans cannot import goods, they have no need to supply dollars in exchange for foreign currencies. Or, the U.S. could restrict the export of capital for international investment and lending. The nation could limit the amount of its currency that traders could sell in foreign exchange markets. In any case, the supply of dollars goes down, and the market equilibrates at the fixed exchange rate.

The world would like to have: fixed exchange rates, independent stabilization policy, and free trade in goods and free flow of capital across national boundaries. But equilibrating the exchange market requires either flexible exchange rates, or a stabilization policy consistent with international equilibrium, or restricted trade or capital flows. The world can have only two out of three.

The Bretton Woods Agreement

In 1943 Harry Dexter White was the principle negotiator for the United States. The U.S. was the world's biggest economy and Britain's largest creditor, so White was negotiating from strength. But across the table was the British delegation's greatest asset, John Maynard Keynes. He was Lord Keynes by now, ennobled the Baron of Tilton, a member of the House of Lords. He was the most prominent economist of his age, revered by New Dealers for providing the theoretical underpinning for stabilization policy. Among his admirers was Harry White.

"Keynes must be one of the most remarkable men that have ever lived," wrote one onlooker. "The Americans sat entranced as the God-like visitor sang and the golden light played round." Harry White was determined not to be blinded by Keynes' light, for his country's sake. So, said a witness, "White was full of vigor and manful thrust. He could be wrathful and rude. His earnestness carried him forward in a torrent of words, which sometimes outstripped his grammatical powers." One onlooker described their debates as "absolute Bedlam."

Why the strident argument? They were arguing their countries' positions. After the war everyone knew that Britain would be an importer, the U.S. an exporter. Britain would be a debtor, the U.S. a creditor. Britain had a small stock of gold, while the U.S. stock was enormous. So, Britain wanted a big international reserve fund, easy for debtors to draw upon, with a small role for gold in the system. The United States wanted a smaller reserve fund, with protections for creditors, and a larger role for gold. The U.S. was particularly concerned that it would have to provide most of the money to the fund, for all the world's debtors to draw upon. That sounded fine to the British.

There was much argument, but there was much good will on both sides. Early on White had been impressed by the similarity of Keynes' proposal to his. Keynes had said, in his maiden speech in the House of Lords, "I have not the slightest doubt in my own mind that a synthesis of the two schemes should be possible."

They compromised in the middle, though the structure of the system looked more like White's original idea than Keynes'. In negotiations, creditors have the advantage over debtors, after all. In April 1944 they issued a statement of principles. It was time to call an international conference.

When? It couldn't be in May. Some knew, most didn't, but something was coming that would keep British and American officials occupied until mid-June. It turned out to be D-Day, the invasion of Europe. It couldn't be in June. In the middle of that month was the Republican Convention, to nominate a Presidential candidate for the 1944 elections. Hold it then and the press wouldn't cover it. And it had to be before the end of July, the date of the Democratic Convention. The Democrats wanted an agreement by then so it could be part of the party platform. Early July, then: it would start on July 1.

Where? Not in Washington, not in the heat of July. A conference in July in Washington, Keynes wrote White, would be "an unfriendly act." They picked the Mount Washington luxury hotel in the mountains of New Hampshire for its cool climate. The hotel had been closed for two years due to wartime travel restrictions, but the management scrambled to get it ready. The hotel's train station gave the conference its name: Bretton Woods.

Forty-four countries sent delegations. Seven hundred delegates filled the hotel to overflowing. Harry White and John Maynard Keynes ran the show.

Wish you were here! The Mount Washington Hotel, Bretton Woods, New Hampshire, in a 1920's era postcard.

The delegates worked hard for more than two weeks. Keynes described the environment in a letter. "The pressure of work here has been quite unbelievable," he wrote. "Anything up to 200 persons in rooms with bad acoustics, shouting through microphones, many of those present with an imperfect knowledge of English."

273

I have resolutely refused to go to any committees after dinner (except once only against orders which promptly led to a heart attack, so that I suffered from guilt not less than from bodily discomfort!); whereas the others have been sitting in committees night after night up to 3:30 a.m., starting again in the committee at 9:30 a.m. next morning. How people have stood it all is a miracle. . . .

Treasury Secretary Morgenthau and his wife had particular trouble sleeping. Lord and Lady Keynes had the suite above theirs, and Mrs. Keynes was Lydia Lopokova, a Russian ballerina. The rhythmic thumps and bumps of her floor exercises kept the Morgenthaus awake at night.

At the end of the conference, Keynes, pale from his heart attack, stood to speak. He paid tribute to the Americans, especially "the indomitable will and energy, always governed by good temper and humor, of Harry White." The conference was more important than the provisions of the agreement, he said. "We have been learning to work together. If we can so continue, this nightmare, in which most of us here present have spent too much of our lives, will be over. The brotherhood of man will have become more than a phrase." The delegates sang "For He's a Jolly Good Fellow" as he left the room.

The Bretton Woods System

The final press release went out over Henry Morgenthau's name. It said, "The *International Monetary Fund* has been born." For the first time the world's nations had come together to fix the "rules of the game." What were the rules?

Exchange rates would be fixed, most of the time. Stabilization policy would be independent, most of the time. That left the problem of equilibrating trade and currency flows. This would be accomplished at first by restricting the supply of each nation's currency in exchange markets. Currencies would remain non-convertible for a time, though nations pledged to make their currencies fully convertible within a few years. Capital controls would remain in force. International lending and investing would be restrained.

Each nation was expected to set fixed exchange rates against other currencies. The U.S. dollar would be the main international currency. Nations would fix their exchange rates relative to the dollar, and hold dollars in reserve, to support their fixed exchange rates. That gave the U.S. an advantage, because it could print all the dollar reserves it wanted.   So, for

> *An international conference in 1944 established the Bretton Woods system of fixed exchange rates, and created the International Monetary Fund.*

international trade purposes, the U.S. fixed the dollar relative to gold, at $35 on ounce. That would restrict the amount of dollars that could be released into the world's trading system.

Countries were expected to "defend" their fixed exchange rates. For example, if traders wanted to buy more francs than others wanted to sell, the value of the franc would rise.

Under the rules France would sell francs at the fixed exchange rate until buyers were satisfied. If traders tried to sell more francs than others wanted to buy, the value of the franc would tend to fall. France then was expected to buy francs at the fixed rate, using their reserves of dollars or gold.

If a country's dollar or gold reserves ran short, they could borrow reserves from the International Monetary Fund (IMF). This would allow a country to maintain fixed rates if the imbalance in buying and selling was temporary. As a condition of the loan, however, the IMF might recommend higher interest rates to increase the demand for its currency, and higher taxes and less government spending, to reduce the country's imports. Stabilization policy was to be independent, up to a point.

If the imbalance was longer term—a "fundamental disequilibrium"—then the country could apply to the IMF to adjust their exchange rates. If a country bought more goods from the rest of the world than it could sell it was likely to run short of reserves. A cut in the exchange rate could make its imports more expensive, its exports cheaper, and bring trade into balance. Exchange rates were fixed, up to a point.

By the mid-1950's the IMF came into its own. France had fought several wars during the 1950s, trying to hang on to the remains of its pre-war colonial empire. It fought in Vietnam, it fought in Algeria. The military spending caused government budget deficits, which acted as expansionary fiscal policy, increasing French incomes. With higher incomes French people and businesses imported more goods. There were not enough exports to pay for these imports, so dollar reserves were used. By the mid-1950's France's reserves were getting low.

> *Under the Bretton Woods system, the International Monetary Fund would address a payments deficit with a loan of reserves, require contractionary stabilization policies, and only then authorize a devaluation of the currency.*

Then in 1956 Egypt nationalized the Suez Canal, which was a joint British-French possession. Britain and France attacked Egypt to try to get the Canal back. The U.S. refused to cooperate, and in fact an angry President Eisenhower forced Britain and France to withdraw.

The cost of the invasion was staggering. France's dollar reserves fell dangerously low, and it turned to the IMF for a loan. It came with conditions attached. Cut spending and raise taxes, demanded the IMF's experts. This would reduce French incomes, reduce their demand for imports, and so reduce the drain on their dollar reserves. The French proved unable to adopt such policies until 1958, when World War II hero Charles de Gaulle formed a government. Taxes were increased, spending was cut. Loans were granted. But the trade deficit persisted. Only then was it determined that a "fundamental disequilibrium" existed. France was allowed to devalue the franc.

The IMF had operated by its book. Offer a loan as temporary support for the fixed exchange rate. Require economic reforms to correct the underlying trade problem. If the problem appears to be long term, allow an orderly depreciation of the currency. It worked. France's trade problem disappeared. And the IMF was a major player on the world's financial stage.

Figure 9-5 above illustrates the IMF's procedures. A payments deficit exists at the fixed exchange rate (1 and 2). The nation fills in this gap with its reserves of dollars and gold. This effectively increases the demand for the currency (a), but the government does the demanding. As reserves run short, it may get a loan from the IMF. Conditions of the loan may include higher interest rates, which will increase market demand for the currency (a). Conditions may include higher taxes and lower spending, which will reduce imports and thus the supply of the nation's currency (b). If the deficit still persists, only then is devaluation allowed (3)

Trouble for the Bretton Woods System

By 1958 it appeared that the Bretton Woods system was a success. The problem caused by the American trade surplus was under control. Most of Europe made their currencies fully convertible, which allowed trading of their currencies in exchange markets. The IMF had shown that it could act in an emergency.

Then, suddenly, in what must be one of the quickest and oddest turns of economic events in the twentieth century, the United States began running a *balance of payments deficit*. Yes, it still had a trade surplus, it was still exporting more goods than it was importing. But there was also Cold War military spending abroad, economic development aid, and U.S. business investments in the rest of the world. Added together, the number of dollars available to the rest of the world was more than was needed to buy U.S. goods or assets. The dollar shortage turned into a dollar surplus.

At first this was helpful. All those extra dollars helped support a bigger volume of trade. And the rest of the world held dollars as reserves, to help them keep their exchange rates stable. But some of those dollars were presented to the U.S. Treasury in exchange for gold. At the core of the fixed exchange rate system was the United States commitment to exchange dollars for gold at $35 an ounce. The nation's enormous stock of gold began to decrease—it had fallen by only $1.7 billion from 1950 to 1957. It fell $5.1 billion from 1958 to 1960. By 1964 the number of dollars held by other countries was more than the U.S. gold stock could support. If everyone outside the U.S. who had dollars tried to exchange them for gold, the U.S. would be caught short.

What had changed? Quite simply, Europe had caught up. Their output and exports had been depressed by the war. Now, after a decade and a half of rebuilding, they were producing goods that people and businesses in the United States wanted to buy. They provided competition in markets that the U.S. had been dominating. Japan had grown even faster. Before the war it had produced cheap manufactured goods. As late as the mid-1960's, the phrase "made in Japan" could evoke laughter in children. Now it was adopting the latest technology, and exporting more than it imported. The result was called the *balance of payments problem*.

The problem at the core of the Bretton Woods system resurfaced. Exchange rates were fixed, stabilization policies were independent, and the world looked to the day that capital flows would be free. But more dollars were being supplied than were being demanded. How could the exchange market be equilibrated?

A young Canadian economist named *Robert Mundell* had given this problem a lot of thought. And why not? It was the central economic problem Canada faced in the 1950's and 1960's. Canada was closely linked to the United States. Currency, trade and investment flowed freely across its long U.S. border. But this meant, Mundell pointed out, that Canada had to choose between a fixed exchange rate and independent stabilization policy. Unlike other developed nations, Canada chose to let its exchange rate fluctuate. It kept its independent stabilization policy.

Now, increasingly, Canada's problem became the world's. The Bretton Woods system began to break down. The world had to choose two out of three: independent stabilization policy, the free flow of capital, or fixed exchange rates. It came to be called *Mundell's "unholy trinity."*

The choice between independent stabilization policy, the free flow of capital, or fixed exchange rates, is sometimes called the "unholy trinity." Economist Robert Mundell thought it up.

During the second half of the 1960s the problem got worse. The United States fought the war in Vietnam. Just like the Civil War and the World Wars, the Vietnam War was accompanied by inflation. Prices in the United States rose faster than did prices in Europe or Japan. Higher prices in the U.S. put more pressure on the Bretton Woods system.

Here's why. Suppose, for example, that "widgets" (economists' favorite imaginary goods) sell for one pound in Britain and four dollars in the United States. Suppose also that the exchange rate is $3 per one pound. An American could buy a widget in the U.S. for $4, or exchange three of those dollars for one pound and buy it in Britain. Buying in Britain is the better deal. So, lots of Americans try to exchange their dollars for pounds to buy widgets. Perhaps there aren't enough pounds to go around, so Americans start bidding up the price--$3.25 for a pound, $3.50, $3.75—until the exchange rate reaches $4 per pound. Then widgets cost the same in both countries. That's called *purchasing power parity*, and it's a way to figure out what exchange rates ought to be. Over the years, exchange rates adjust towards purchasing power parity, so that traded goods cost the same in each country.

Inflation in the U.S. was greater than it was in Europe. U.S. prices were rising faster. Purchasing power parity implied that the value of European currencies should rise relative to the dollar. But exchange rates were fixed. American inflation was too high, making it cheaper to buy goods abroad. The U.S. could have fought this problem with anti-inflation monetary and fiscal policies. But in the second half of the 1960's, President

Johnson, the Congress, the Federal Reserve (and American voters) would not support the higher taxes, reduced spending or higher interest rates required to fix the problem.

Exchange rates were fixed and stabilization policy would not bow to international needs. So the Johnson administration imposed tighter capital controls, designed to prevent U.S. investment and lending overseas. One such control was the "interest equalization tax" in 1964. This was a tax on the value of loans by Americans to foreigners. Such loans would be made if foreign interest rates were higher than U.S. rates. The tax would take away some of this extra foreign interest income, and so make the loans less attractive. Fewer dollars would flow out of the U.S. In 1965 the Johnson administration asked for voluntary restraint on foreign lending by U.S. banks. In 1968 the restraints were made mandatory.

The need to keep exchange rates fixed in the face of a balance of payments was leading to restrictions on international lending and investment. Increasingly, economists and policy makers began to consider whether fixed exchange rates were worth the trouble. Milton Friedman, an economist at the University of Chicago, first advocated flexible exchange rates in 1953, and his thinking gained influence as the problems of the 1960s mounted.

Fixed exchange rates remained an article of faith among international policymakers, though. Paul Volcker was an American Treasury official who participated in international efforts to maintain the Bretton Woods system. He wrote

> The participants saw themselves as carrying a very special and important, if arcane, responsibility to protect the stability of the international monetary system. . . . A few of them had personally participated, at least at the margins, at the Bretton Woods conference and saw themselves as disciples of the founders, who would keep their vision intact. As men with vivid memories of depression and war, they sensed the stakes were high.

Increasingly, though, the system rested on an unstated agreement among European countries *not* to demand gold for their dollars. It was tempting. If the U.S. devalued, those holding dollars would lose. Their holdings would be worth less. Those holding gold would not lose, because devaluation meant a rise in the price of gold. But everyone knew that the U.S. didn't have enough gold to redeem all the world's dollars. The first to redeem would protect the value of their reserves. The last would lose out. There was a real possibility for a run on U.S. gold, and that would bring down the Bretton Woods system. As the 1970s began, it was only a matter of time.

The End of Fixed Exchange Rates
John Connally was President Nixon's Secretary of the Treasury. He was a Texan and looked the part: big, charming, forceful. As Governor of Texas he'd been shot and wounded sitting next to President Kennedy in Dallas in 1963. He had no expertise in international monetary policy, though the Treasury staff found him a quick study. Most

important, he had no particular commitment to the Bretton Woods system. He would say to the Europeans, "The dollar may be our currency but it's your problem."

Yet at Secretary Connally's first international meeting in May 1971, he told the Europeans emphatically, "I want without any arrogance or defiance to make it abundantly clear that we are not going to devalue, we are not going to change the price of gold, we are going to control inflation. . . ." It was a strong endorsement of fixed exchange rates. Treasury Undersecretary Paul Volcker asked whether he realized that devaluation might be necessary. Connally replied "that's my unalterable position today. I don't know what it will be this summer."

That summer the U.S. trade balance turned negative for the first time, meaning that imports of goods actually exceeded exports. An influential Congressional sub-committee endorsed floating exchange rates. Small countries started asking for gold in exchange for their dollars. Some time in June or July Nixon and Connally decided to act.   If one of the big countries asked for gold, they would be refused.

It turned out to be Britain. During the week of August 9 the British asked to exchange a large quantity of dollars for gold. It was unclear to the Treasury what they wanted— actual gold or some guarantee of the dollar's value—but on Friday morning, August 13, sixteen men were called to the President's Camp David retreat in the hills of Maryland.

Speechwriter Bill Safire found himself in a Presidential limo driving out to meet the President's helicopter. One of the President's economic advisors, Herbert Stein, was with him.

"What's going on?" Safire asked Stein.

"This could be the most important weekend in the history of economics since March 4, 1933," Stein told him.

"We're closing the banks?" Safire laughed, showing an admirable knowledge of economic history.

"No," Stein replied, "but the President may close the gold window."

That meant nothing to Safire. On the helicopter to Camp David a Treasury Department lawyer asked the same question, what was happening?   "We're closing the gold window," Safire shouted over the noise. The Treasury man dropped his head into his hands. "My God," he whispered. This is big, Safire must have thought.

The top economic brains in the administration gathered at Camp David. Paul Volcker was a six foot seven inch cigar-smoking veteran of the Bretton Woods struggles, having spent the 1960's in the Treasury Department dealing with the dollar's problems. Paul McCracken and Herbert Stein were there as members of the Council of Economic Advisors. Arthur Burns was there. He was the chairman of the Federal Reserve Board,

280, and a long time Nixon advisor. And, two men soon to be notorious as Watergate conspirators were there, Bob Haldeman and John Erlichman.

The meeting, Safire would write later, was "more fun than any of the men there had ever had in their lifetimes." The accommodations were rustic, but there was tennis, skeet shooting, horseback riding, great food. The Navy attendants treated them all like admirals. And there were big decisions to make. President Nixon was intent on shaking up the economic world. He said he would "get out there so far that nobody will ever be able to say I didn't do enough."

Closing the gold window, Safire learned, meant that the U.S. dollar would no longer be exchanged for gold in international trade. The U.S. would end its commitment to the fixed value of the dollar. Without gold the world's currencies would float with market demand and supply.

Treasury Secretary Connally began by explaining the purpose of the meeting. There was no doubt that he spoke for the President, though Nixon himself didn't say much. They would take the dollar off gold. Nixon asked each man in the room for his views.

Volcker was most closely involved with supporting the Bretton Woods system. But he said "I hate to close the window. All my life I have defended exchange rates, but I think it is needed." What Volcker had in mind was negotiating a new international agreement, reforming the system with a lower value of the dollar. It could not be done with the gold window open, because currency traders and countries would anticipate devaluation, and withdraw gold. He didn't think the negotiations would take long.

Fed Chairman Burns spoke strongly against the move. The administration had decided to impose a wage and price freeze, which was a radical move in peacetime, and Burns thought this would "electrify the world." The currency markets might be so impressed by America's resolve to stop inflation that there would be no run on gold. If one developed, Burns said, the gold window could always be closed later. That didn't suit the President. If the gold window was closed in response to a run, the President would seem to be the victim of events. If it was closed in advance, he was taking control of the situation. Burns was persuaded to give his support.

Thinking back, Herbert Stein regretted that monetary policy was not discussed that weekend at Camp David. Higher interest rates were as sure a way as any to get traders to hold dollars, and as sure a way as any to hold down inflation. Volcker and Burns finally confronted this issue later at an international meeting. Burns again argued for gold and fixed exchange rates, and Volcker, exasperated, said "Arthur, if you want a par value system, you better go home right away and tighten money." Burns said "I would even do that." Yet, a week later at a press conference, Burns declared that "American monetary policy is not made in Paris; it is made in Washington." The United States, like other nations, wanted independent stabilization policy, and by the 1970's they were ready to sacrifice Bretton Woods to have it.

The economic advisors insisted that the announcement be made that Sunday night. If it was delayed until Monday, and word leaked out after the markets opened, there would be a gigantic run on the nation's gold supply. Nixon protested. A Sunday night speech would pre-empt *Bonanza*. It was the voters' favorite show.

He was persuaded. So, on Sunday night, August 15, 1971, people tuned in to see President Richard Nixon, at his desk reading a speech, instead of Hoss and Little Joe. The President spoke of changes in taxes and spending, and of the wage and price freeze. When he got to gold, he said

> I have directed Secretary Connally to suspend temporarily the convertibility of the dollar into gold or other reserve assets, except in amounts and conditions determined to be in the interest of monetary stability and in the best interests of the United States.

> Now, what is this action—which is very technical—what does it mean for you? Let me lay to rest the bugaboo of what is called devaluation. If you want to buy a foreign car or take a trip abroad, market conditions may cause your dollar to buy slightly less. But if you are among the overwhelming majority of Americans who buy American-made products in America, your dollar will be worth just as much tomorrow as it is today.

The President had written that passage in his own hand. It appealed to "buy American" sentiment. Imports would be more expensive, but they were a relatively small share of consumer purchases in 1971. Consumers who didn't buy imports would not be affected, he said. (This was not entirely true. With less price competition from imports, domestic producers would find it easier to raise prices.)

The public responded enthusiastically, and on Monday the stock market went up. That day Volcker took an air force jet to London to meet with the Europeans. He offered no new plan for international financial reform. This had been Volcker's regret about the Camp David meeting. There was no endorsement of any long term reform of the Bretton Woods system. But also, he said later, "our trading partners were not prepared to accept what we thought was required." They would need to revalue their currencies upward, reduce their restrictions on imports of U.S. goods, and help with defense costs.

> *The Nixon administration ended the Bretton Woods system of fixed exchange rates in 1971. Most of the developed world has used flexible exchange rates since then.*

Volcker's Monday meeting was just the first of many, many meetings over the following years. No long term reform agreement was ever made. Nations with trade surpluses were unwilling to sacrifice their competitive positions by accepting higher fixed values for their currencies. The United States was unwilling to re-open the gold window. By the end of 1975 the International Monetary Fund's charter was amended to permit floating exchange rates. The Fund's reason-for-being, to lend reserves in support of fixed exchange rates, had to change. Eventually, gold was "de-monetized", making it just another commodity with a price the rose and fell daily.

At the Bretton Woods conference in 1944 nations had agreed on an international monetary system. Perhaps it was made possible by the leadership of Roosevelt and Churchill, Keynes and White. Maybe it was the special wartime urgency, or the dominant position of a single country, the United States. In the very different political climate of the 1970's, this success could not be duplicated.

By the mid-1970s the Bretton Woods system was dead. The era of flexible exchange rates had begun.

The International Monetary Fund in the Asian Currency Crisis

The International Monetary Fund (IMF) had to find itself a new mission with the end of the Bretton Woods fixed exchange rate system. In the 1970's it helped channel OPEC's big oil profits to investments in the rest of the world. In the 1980's it helped resolve a Latin American debt crisis. But its main reason for being was to come to the aid of developing countries when their currency values dropped and they ran short of foreign currency reserves.

The IMF had a model of a typical country in a typical currency crisis. The crisis was triggered by the country living beyond its means. Perhaps it was running a big budget deficit, spending more on government services than it was collecting in taxes, and filling in the gap by borrowing from international lenders. Perhaps it was running a trade deficit, buying more imports than it could pay for with its exports, again covering the shortfall with borrowing. For a time international lenders will support such policies with loans. They may think the loans are being invested in industry or infrastructure that will create future exports and profits.

Then lenders get scared. Some event, some new bit of information persuades them that their loans are unlikely to be repaid, or that the exchange value of the nation's currency will drop dramatically. They attempt to sell their assets, to get out before the nationl defaults or the currency falls. No more loans are forthcoming. Sometimes this withdrawal becomes a panic. The nation finds itself unable to borrow to support its spending on programs and imports. More immediately, it is unable to borrow new money to repay old loans that have come due.

In these difficult conditions countries can appeal to the IMF. The country and the IMF negotiate a rescue plan. The IMF agrees to lend the country currency reserves—dollars, yen, euros or pounds from its stock, to meet the immediate shortfalls for spending and loan repayment. In return the country accepts a plan to force it to live within its means. Taxes are increased and spending is cut to eliminate a budget deficit. Interest rates are increased to support the value of its currency. These policies reduce the country's income, which reduces its imports. The exchange rate is allowed to fall, encouraging exports and further discouraging imports. The trade gap is closed. All of these moves are painful to the country's people (higher taxes, lost services, lower incomes, higher priced imports), and politically painful to the country's leaders. But the goal is to correct the problems that led to the crisis. International lenders will see the availability of IMF reserves, and the commitment to better policies, and stop the panic. Once the crisis is past the country's growth can resume.

That's the model. Does it work?

In the 1980s and 1990s Thailand was one of the "Asian Tigers," along with South Korea, Taiwan, Hong Kong, Indonesia, Malaysia, the Phillipines. Thailand's real GDP was growing rapidly, almost ten percent per year from 1986 to 1996. One reason was the fixed value of the Thai currency, the baht. While most of the developed world allowed the values of their currencies to fluctuate, many developing countries tried to keep their exchange rates fixed, relative to the dollar. There were a couple of reasons to do this. Thailand's growth advanced in part due to investment by Japanese automobile and electronics companies. These companies liked the fixed baht, because it eliminated their worries about unpredictable changes in the value of their investments in Thailand.

The fixed value of the baht also promoted prudent monetary policy. Again, to keep a currency's value fixed with an unrestricted flow of capital, a nation must give up an independent stabilization policy. As long as the baht was fixed in value, investors didn't have to worry that the Thai government would adopt inflationary policies which would erode the values of their loans and other assets.

The Thai central bank was responsible for keeping the value of the baht fixed. The central bank kept a reserve of foreign currencies—dollars, yen, pounds, marks—for this purpose. If the rising demand for the baht threatened to increase its value, the central bank would sell baht to the market, and build its reserves of foreign currencies. If the rising supply of baht threatened to decrease its value, the central bank would buy baht, using its reserves of foreign currencies.

This worked fine as long as the demand for and supply of foreign currencies were roughly equal. However, in 1996 the central bank found that its foreign currency reserves were shrinking. More people wanted to trade baht for dollars than the reverse. The supply of baht exceeded the demand in the exchange market.

Here's what had happened. The value of the baht was fixed to the dollar, but the dollar floated. In the mid-1990s the value of the dollar increased relative to most other currencies. Investors wanted a share of the profits from rising American productivity, and a share of the interest from rising American interest rates, so they demanded dollars. Since the baht was tied to the dollar, the baht rose in value relative to other currencies too. This made Thai exports more expensive in every country except the U.S. It made all but American imports cheaper too. Thailand's exports fell and imports rose. The trade deficit grew large.

Thailand had other problems. Thai leaders had ambitions to make the Thai capital city of Bangkok a major Asian financial center. So they gave tax breaks to foreign lenders to lend money to Thai banks. Thai banks lent the money to Thai companies. By the mid-1990's Thai banks and companies owed tens of billions of dollars to foreign lenders.

Some of this lending was influenced by Thailand's political leaders. Loans would go not to projects likely to produce quality goods that could be exported to the world, but to the pet projects of influential politicians, their families and their supporters. This problem was known as *crony capitalism*.

Thai banks also invested in huge real estate developments that were having trouble finding buyers and renters. The number of non-performing loans—loans that were not being paid back—grew ominously. Banking oversight by the Thai government was lax.

With the supply of baht growing faster than the demand for baht, the exchange value of the baht would fall. This was contrary to the fixed-baht policy, so the Thai central bank purchased the excess baht, adding to baht demand and holding its value up. To buy baht the central bank used its foreign currency reserves, earned from past exports. Now those reserves began to run short. Without reserves, the central bank could not keep the baht's value fixed.

Baht-ulism. A Thai 50 baht note issued in 1997. It was worth $2 on July 1, 1997. It was worth $1.65 on July 2.

Investors began to anticipate that the value of the baht would fall, and by the Spring of 1997 many were trying to sell their Thai assets, and exchange their baht for other currencies. The supply of the baht in exchange markets increased some more. The central bank responded by spending more of its dollar reserves to buy baht and support its value.

Finally, on July 2, with reserves almost gone, the central bank quit defending the baht. The value of the baht fell instantly, from $4 per 100 baht to $3.30 per 100 baht, an 18% fall in a single day. Put another way, the number of baht required to buy a dollar rose from 25 on July 1 to 30 on July 2. That was just the start. In September the value of 100 baht dropped under $3, in November under $2.50, and in January it dipped below $2 per 100 baht (above 50 baht per dollar). Anyone caught with Thai assets lost half their wealth in six months.

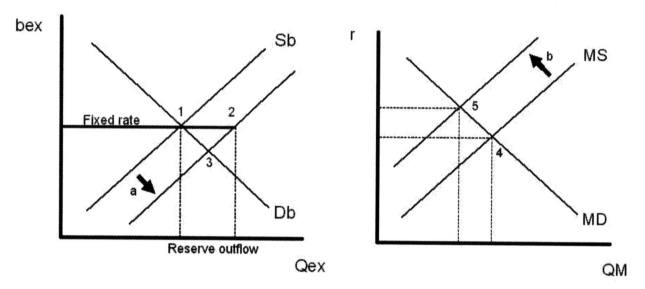

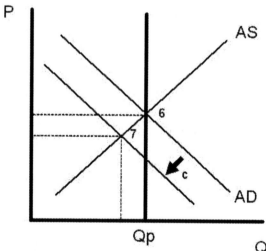

Figure 9-6. Anatomy of a Currency Crisis. Foreign investors increase the supply of baht on exchange markets (a), trying to get out of baht assets before devaluation. The Thai central bank must support the fixed exchange rate by using its foreign currency reserves to buy baht (1 to 2). Eventually the reserves run out, and it has no choice but to let the baht fall in value (3). International reserves are withdrawn from Thai banks, and banks try to replenish reserves by lending less. The Thai money supply decreases (b) and interest rates rise (4 to 5). Higher interest rates reduce investment and aggregate demand (c), which is second shift #2, leading to a recession (6 to 7).

No one would lend in Thailand, for fear of losses due to the falling baht. Companies had borrowed dollars to invest in Thailand earned profits in baht. Even if profits continued, it was more expensive to buy dollars, so it was more expensive to repay the loans. Borrowers could not repay dollar debts at the new exchange rate. Nearly all the finance companies closed. Trying to repay their foreign lenders, Thai banks called in their loans. Construction projects ground to a halt; businesses liquidated their inventories. The effects multiplied through the economy, causing layoffs and bankruptcies. Real GDP fell 11% in 1998, investment spending dropped 44%.

Thailand asked the International Monetary Fund for aid at the end of July. The IMF forced the Thai government to raise taxes and cut spending. This would reduce Thai incomes and restrain imports, eliminating the trade deficit. But Thailand's economy needed no help to restrain imports. The radical drop in GDP reduced imports so much that Thailand ran a huge trade surplus in 1998. IMF negotiators recognized their mistake once they saw the depth of the recession, but it was 1998 before Thailand was allowed to combat their downturn with counter-cyclical spending increases.

The IMF assembled $17 billion in currency loans for Thailand by mid-August. All involved hoped that international lenders would be impressed by the policy changes and reassured by the availability of currency reserves, and stop selling baht for dollars. But as part of the loan package, the Thai central bank was forced to reveal the level of its currency reserves. The reserves were much lower than lenders had guessed. Now the fear was that the IMF's loan was too small, so investors began withdrawing funds from Thailand again. The baht resumed its fall. Before long the IMF currency loan was used up. Thailand had to negotiate a second loan in November.

The IMF was accused of "bailing out" the international lenders, investors and currency speculators. Most of the money the IMF lent to Thailand quickly was paid to international lenders who were withdrawing their funds from the country. Members of the U.S. Congress called it "welfare for bankers." Meanwhile, the people of Thailand suffered economic hardships.

Thailand was one of the Asian Tigers. If one could fail, international investors thought, others can too. Withdrawals from other Asian countries began within the week. On July 11 both Indonesia and the Philippines stopped defending their fixed exchange rates. Malaysia quit defending the ringgit on July 14. By the end of July, it wasn't a Thai crisis, it was an Asian crisis.

The panic spread from country to country like a plague, which is why economists call it *contagion*. It occurred for several reasons. First, all of the Asian Tigers had large amounts of foreign debt, and none had enough foreign currency reserves to hold their currencies fixed if selling started. Second, the decline in one nation's currency, like Thailand's baht, makes Thai exports cheaper. Exports by Thailand's competitors drop, and the resulting trade deficits create downward pressure on their currencies. Third, investors who lost heavily in Thailand looked to reduce their holdings in other countries, especially in those that might have had problems in common with Thailand, like the other Tigers. Lending in all the Tigers was reduced. Japanese banks in particular cut their lending in all Asian markets after Thailand devalued.

> *A currency crisis in Thailand in 1997 caused currency crises in many other developing countries in Asia. This is called "contagion."*

The reserve outflow in 1990's Thailand also created a deep recession. But it was made shorter by the devaluation of the baht that occurred in July 1997. The reserve drain eventually stopped. Perhaps the loans from the IMF helped as well.

The value of the baht has about 2.7 dollars per 100 baht since 2001, not as high as the old fixed rate of 4 or as low as the panic rate of 2. With the baht cheaper exports began to grow again. Thailand's real GDP dropped almost 11% in 1998, but it grew 4.4% in 1999 and averaged 5% per year in the five years after that. Respectable growth, though nothing like the pace prior to the crisis.

Thailand rebounded quickly. Perhaps the IMF's policies contributed. Clear, though, the IMF did not stop the contagion from spreading to all of Asia and beyond. And millions of people in Asia suffered from a deep recession.

The International Monetary Fund in the Argentina Currency Crisis
The 1980's were bad for Argentina's economy. Six of the ten years from 1981 to 1990 saw declines in real GDP. Inflation ran between 90% and 700% per year through 1988, and then it really got going. The inflation rate in 1989 was over 3,000%. In 1990 it "moderated" to 2,000%. Recession and hyperinflation. What could be done?

Argentina came up with a novel solution: tie the Argentine currency directly to the U.S. dollar. The country would adopt a strict fixed exchange rate. In 1990 one dollar exchanged for about 9,500 australs, the Argentine currency at the time. In 1992 the government adopted a new currency, the peso, and pledged to hold the exchange rate fixed at one peso per dollar.

In effect, Argentina decided to use Mundell's trinity to restrict its own policy options, on purpose. To equilibrate the exchange market, a county must give up one out of three: fixed exchange rates, independent monetary and fiscal policy, or the free flow of capital. By fixing its exchange rate, Argentina had to give up one of the other two. It gave up independent monetary and fiscal policy.

Hyperinflation is always the result of (way) too much money chasing too few goods. It usually occurs in places that have unstable governments (like the American Confederacy or Zimbabwe). Argentina's governments tried to hold the support of favored interest groups during the 1980's by spending more than they collected in revenue. The budget deficits were financed by printing money. Now, with a fixed exchange rate, this would not be possible.

If Argentina printed money to hold real interest rates low and stimulate spending, imports would increase, which would increase the demand for foreign currencies by Argentines. This would increase the supply of the peso, offered in exchange for foreign currencies. The value of the peso would decrease. But the government had pledged to hold the exchange rate constant. It had to restrict the supply of pesos, which meant restraining aggregate demand. The money supply could not increase rapidly if the exchange rate was to be held constant.

This fixed exchange rate policy worked marvelously well for almost a decade. The economy grew 6.4% per year on average from 1991 to 1998, with only one brief recession year. Iinflation virtually disappeared. The inflation rate dropped below 5% in 1994 and stayed there until 2002.

But, unfortunately, Argentina had not solved its budget problem. The government still spent more than it took in, and borrowed to fill the gap. They weren't allowed to borrow from their central bank, since that would have increased the money supply and caused inflation. Instead, much of this borrowing came from overseas. International investors bought Argentina's treasury bonds. Argentina's debt to the rest of the world grew larger.

> *Argentina fixed the value of its peso to the dollar, to try to stop hyperinflation. It worked, but eventually a currency crisis forced the end of the policy.*

Investors expected to be repaid in their own currencies. Argentina needed to earn foreign currency, and that's done by running a trade surplus. Argentina would accept foreign currencies in exchange for its exports, and use the money to repay its debts. Of course, foreign currencies also could be used to buy imports. If Argentina imported lots of goods, there wouldn't be enough foreign currency left over to cover their debts.

Argentina did have a trade surplus in the mid-1990s. But then in the 1990's the U.S. dollar rose in value, and in 1997 it increased a lot. This happened because of the Asian currency crisis. During the panic international investors wanted to hold their wealth in low-risk U.S. Treasury bonds, and they exchanged their currencies for dollars in order to buy those bonds. The demand for the dollar increased, and its exchange value increased.

Since the peso was tied to the dollar one for one, when the dollar got stronger, so did the peso. Argentina's exports became more expensive, and imports became cheaper. Starting in 1997, the country's trade balance turned to deficit. Argentina could not earn enough foreign currency to pay back its debt.

By the end of the 1990's international investors began to wonder whether Argentina could repay. To correct its trade deficit, would Argentina abandon the fixed exchange rate and allow the peso to depreciate? If it did, any international investor holding assets in pesos would suffer losses. So, international investors became reluctant to invest in Argentina, and demanded ever higher interest rates in order to lend there. The decline in exports, the drop in international investment and the rising interest rates caused a recession.

The demand for pesos fell (no one wanted pesos to invest in Argentina), and the supply grew (investors tried to sell their holdings before devaluation). There was a growing excess supply of pesos at the fixed exchange rate. That only increased the possibility of devaluation, which fed the growing panic. The graphs in Figure 9-6 describe what happened. Just replace the "b" for "baht" with a "p" for "peso".

Like Thailand, Argentina turned to the International Monetary Fund. The IMF lent the country foreign currency to pay its debts and support the fixed exchange rate. The IMF again followed its standard model. Argentina was required to cut its government spending, reducing purchases and transfers during a recession. The recession got worse.

The IMF's efforts didn't work. The panic did not abate; international investors continued to pull out. In fact, the succession of IMF loans may have made things worse, by delaying the end of the fixed exchange rate policy. The fixed exchange rate finally was abandoned in January 2002, and the huge drop in the value of the peso caused massive bankruptcies and unemployment. Argentina had to "restructure" its debt, which meant changing the terms for repaying loans. Lenders took losses as a result.

Argentina's recession was deep and long. Real GDP fell almost 5% per year in the four years from 1998 to 2002. But once the exchange rate fell Argentine exports became cheaper, and export spending increased. With a flexible exchange rate Argentina was able to abandon pro-cyclical monetary and fiscal policies as well. Real GDP began growing rapidly in 2003, averaging 8.5% per year through 2007. The inflation rate went up, averaging 14 percent per year snce 2002. Hyperinflation has not yet returned.
The IMF applied the same policies in Thailand and Argentina. Both countries suffered recessions, but Agentina's was particularly deep. Contagion spread to the rest of Asia with the Thailand crisis. Contagion was not a problem in South America during the Agentina crisis. Thailand's economy recovered quickly, and growth has been moderate since. Argentina's recovered only when the fixed exchange rate was abandoned, and growth has been rapid since.

What policies should the IMF pursue? The evidence from the last two decades is mixed. Perhaps the IMF should force contractionary policies on countries that are already in recession, in an attempt to correct the deficit problems quickly. The aim is to reassure international investors, to stop panicked withdrawals and encourage lending. That's the standard IMF approach. Or, perhaps it should allow countries to pursue counter-cyclical policies, and once recovery is achieved, then try to correct the underlying deficit problems. That was what John Maynard Keynes had in mind when he proposed the creation of the IMF.

MacroPolicy Now: Greek Tragedy

Thailand. Argentina. Now Greece.

Greece joined the eurozone in 2000. These are a group of sixteen countries in Europe who use a common currency, the euro. The Greeks eliminated their traditional currency, the drachma, and adopted the euro, at a rate of 341 drachma per euro. Effectively, they now operate with a fixed exchange rate relative to their major trading partners in the rest of Europe.

The Greek government greatly expanded social programs beginning in the 1980's. By the 2000's the government employed one-third of the labor force, jobs were for life, and retirement before age 60 was common. Tax evasion was a problem, so the government supported its spending by borrowing. The government could not print money to support its spending. There was no Greek central bank once the euro had been adopted. The European central bank made money supply decisions, and its policies were dominated by German and French interests. Inflation was not a problem.

The deficits were financed by borrowing, mostly from European banks. The banks were willing to lend partly because a country in the eurozone was assumed to be wealthy and well-governed. In addition, the government managed to disguise the extent of its borrowing, allegedly with the help of large international banks.

In October 2009, however, Greece shocked international lenders by revealing that its deficit was actually more than triple what had been reported. Lenders feared that the interest and principle on these loans would not be repaid out of tax revenue that had been diminished by the worldwide recession. Soon Greece admitted that the debt could not be serviced.

Again, Figure 9-6 is useful in showing what happened. Investors sell their Greek assets and the supply increases (a). The overall value of the euro does fall, a little, but its value is dominated by demand for German and French goods and assets. It can't fall nearly enough to close the excess supply of euros in Greece (at 3). So investment funds continue to drain from Greece (1 to 2).

This reduces the supply of money in the money market (b). International investors are unwilling to lend, and this increases interest rates (4 to 5).

Higher interest rates reduce investment spending in the goods market, aggregate demand declines (c), and output falls (6 to 7). Greek recovery from recession can't get off the ground.

The rest of the European Union, and the International Monetary Fund, are concerned. Not just with the hardship in Greece, but with the implications of potential Greek default for the European economy. Contagion is a danger. The Greeks borrowed a lot of money. That means that European banks hold a lot of Greek bonds. Default on these bonds would reduce their value (or make them worthless). Banks that own such bonds may themselves default on what they owe other lenders, and on what they owe their depositors. These banks build , just in case, and cut their lending.
So the European Union and the IMF offered a substantial loan to Greece in 2010, then a second loan in 2011. . This money allowed Greece to meet its debt payments. But there were strings attached. Greece had to cut back on its spending, and work towards a

balanced government budget. This is the standard policy prescription of the International Monetary Fund.

Here's Mundell's unholy trilogy, again. Euros move freely among eurozone nations—that's one of the advantages of adopting the euro. It means that capital flows can't be restricted, though. And, as long as Greece uses the euro, the exchange rate cannot adjust enough to equilibrate Greece's share of the exchange market. So, independent stabilization policy must give way. Since Greece has no central bank of its own, there is no independent Greek monetary policy. Fiscal policy must be used. Spending must be cut, and taxes raised. This is pro-cyclical fiscal policy in a recession.

This could be a very long term problem. Greece's industry is simply not as efficient as Germany's. The world beats a path to Germany's door, demanding euros to buy German products. This supports the value of the euro. But that makes Greece's higher cost, lower quality products more expensive for the world to buy, because the euro's value is high. It makes tourism to Greece more expensive too. To run a trade surplus Greece must cut back its imports. Since the value of the euro is fixed, the only way to do that is to restrict Greek incomes, with higher taxes and lower government spending.

In Thailand and Argentina recovery was hastened by a devaluation of the currency. The cheaper baht and peso encouraged exports, and allowed counter-cyclical fiscal and monetary policy. With the euro, this is not an option for Greece.

Greece could encourage export by promoting "internal devaluation." The cost of its exports is the product of the exchange value of their currency, and the prices of Greek products. Since the exchange value of the euro is fixed, Greek exports can be made cheaper only with a drop in Greek prices. That's deflation. The only way to get sustained deflation is with sustained high unemployment: a long recession.

> *Greece cannot help solve its currency crisis with devaluation, as Thailand and Argentina did, because it has adopted the euro.*

Perhaps it was a mistake for Greece to adopt the euro. The euro's value will reflect the economies of Germany and France, not the needs of little Greece. As long as people want to buy products from the big European nations, exports from Greece will be expensive too.

In May 2011 a German magazine reported that Greece might abandon the euro. Both European and Greek officials denied this report. One reason: fear that Greece will leave the euro and re-adopt the drachma, may be adding to the country's problems. If Greece returned to its old currency, deposits in Greek banks would be automatically converted to drachmas, and this new currency would then depreciate relative to the euro. So, depositors are shifting their money out of Greek banks, to avoid this potential devaluation. That decreases the Greek money supply too, making Greek interest rates even higher. We saw investors flee for fear of devaluation in Thailand and Argentina too—and in the hot money episode in the U.S. in the 1890's.

It's the end of May, 2011, as I'm writing this. When you read this, perhaps we'll know more.

Terms in this Chapter, in order of appearance
Free trade
Tariffs
Smoot-Hawley tariff
David Ricardo
Absolute advantage
Comparative advantage
Terms of trade
Import-competing business
Reciprocal Trade Agreement Act (RTAA)
General Agreement on Tariffs and Trade (GATT)
Trade negotiation "rounds"
North American Free Trade Agreement (NAFTA)
World Trade Organization (WTO)
Environmental Kuznets curve
Winners and losers from trade
Exchange reserves
Lend-lease
Gold standard
Flexible exchange rates
Exchange controls
Capital flows
Fixed exchange rates
Independent stabilization policy
Free flow of capital
Bretton Woods System
International Monetary Fund
Balance of payments problem
Robert Mundell's "unholy trinity"
Purchasing power parity
Camp David meeting
The gold window
Asian currency crisis
Asian Tigers
Crony capitalism
Contagion
Argentina currency crisis
Crisis in Greece

Notes

Paul Douglas tells the story of the Douglas-Wilcox tariff appeal in his memoir (p. 71). In a 600+ page book, he devotes one paragraph to it. The man led an eventful life (we've seen him before, in chapter 8). He tells the old "end-to-end" joke on page 475.

Eichengreen (1986) and Irwin (1997) analyze the causes and effects of the Smoot-Hawley tariff. Quotes by Smoot, Hawley and Watson are from Schlesinger (1956, p. 164).

The story of NAFTA and the WTO is assembled from Lawrence (2002, pp. 294-297), Dasgupta et. al. (2002), Bhagwati (2002) and the World Trade Organization website (www.wto.org). Bhagwati notes the optometrists explanation for the failure of the WTO meeting at Seattle.

Ketchum (1989, pp. 568-571) describes Churchill's December 1940 letter to Roosevelt. The letter itself can be seen on the FDR Library website (www.fdrlibrary.marist.edu/psf/box34/a311s02.html). The text of the lend-lease press conference also is on that website (www.fdrlibrary.marist.edu/odllpc2.html).

Eichengreen (1996) and Solomon (1982) provide excellent histories of the rise and fall of Bretton Woods. Volcker and Gyohten (1992) give a first-hand account of the struggles to preserve the system during the 1960's and 1970's. Hallwood and MacDonald (2000) provide a textbook treatment.

Eichengreen (1996) describes the operation of the gold standard and the instability between the wars.

The description of the Bretton Woods conference comes mostly from Van Dormael (1978, pp. 168-223), with an assist from Moggridge (1992, pp. 721-755) and Rees (1973, pp. 221-235).

Irwin (1997), Eichengreen (1996, pp. 100-102) and Crowley (2003) describe the Reciprocal Trade Adjustment Act, the General Agreement and Tariffs and Trade and the failure to ratify the International Trade Organization.

The Suez crisis is covered by Boughton (2000, 279-81), Wicker (1991, pp. 152-54), Eichengreen (pp.112-113), and Solomon (pp. 24-25).

Frieden (2006, pp. 460-61) describes how Canada's exchange rate problem influenced Robert Mundell's work on the "unholy trinity." Mundell was awarded a Nobel Prize in Economics for his work in 1999. Later, in 2002, he appeared on *Late Night with David Letterman*, reading the "Top Ten Ways My Life Has Changed Since Winning The Nobel Prize." Number 10: "Can end almost any argument by asking, 'And did you ever win a Nobel Prize?'" Number 4: "When I call K-Rock to request Aerosmith, they play Aerosmith." Number 3: "Any meaningless crap I say, the next day it's in the *Wall Street*

Journal." That last one might well be true. Mundell's delivery was so good that Letterman had him back several times.

The Paul Volcker quote on the arcane responsibilities of international policymakers is from his memoir with Gyohten (1992, p. 29).

Wicker's biography of Richard Nixon (pp. 542-568) and Wells' biography of Arthur Burns (1994, pp. 74-77) describe Nixon's Camp David meeting. So do Volcker and Gyohten (pp. 76-80), Stein (1994, pp. 176-180) and Safire (1978, pp. 659-686). Volcker, Stein and Safire write first-hand: they were there.

DeLong and Eichengreen (pp. 218-223) and Blustein (pp. 51-83) tell the story of Thailand's baht crisis (pp. 51-83).

Sources

Bhagwati, Jagdish. 2002. "Trade Policy: Comments." Pages 333-340 in Jeffrey A. Frankel and Peter R. Orszag (eds.), *Economic Policy in the 1990's.* Cambridge, Massachusetts: MIT Press.

Blustein, Paul. 2003. *The Chastening (revised edition).* New York: PublicAffairs.

Boughton, James M. 2000. "From Suez To Tequlla: The IMF As Crisis Manager." *Economic Journal.* 110 (January): 273-291.

Crowley, Meredith A. 2003. "An Introduction to the WTO and GATT." *Economic Perspectives* 27 (Fourth Quarter) 42-57.

Dasgupta, Susmita, Benoit Laplante, Hua Wang, David Wheeler. 2002. "Confronting the Environmental Kuznets Curve." *Journal of Economic Perspectives* 16 (Winter): 147-168.

DeLong, J. Bradford and Barry Eichengreen. 2002. "Between Meltdown and Moral Hazard." Pages 191-254 in Jeffrey A. Frankel and Peter R. Orszag (eds.), *Economic Policy in the 1990's.* Cambridge, Massachusetts: MIT Press.

Douglas, Paul. 1972. *In The Fullness of Time.* New York: Harcourt, Brace Jovanovich.

Eichengreen, Barry. 1996. *Globalizing Capital.* Princeton, New Jersey: Princeton University Press.

Frieden, Jeffry A. 2006. *Global Capitalism: Its Fall and Rise in the Twentieth Century.* New York: W.W. Norton.

Hallwood, C. Paul and Ronald MacDonald. 2000. *International Money and Finance.* (3rd edition.) Malden, Massachusetts: Blackwell.

Irwin, Douglas A. 1997. "From Smoot-Hawley to Reciprocal Trade Agreements: Changing the Course of U.S. Trade Policy in the 1930's." National Bureau of Economic Research Working Paper 5895 (January). Cambridge, Massachusetts: NBER.

Ketchum, Richard M. 1989. *The Borrowed Years, 1938-1941.* New York: Random House.

Lawrence, Robert Z. 2002. "Trade Policy." Pages 277-327 in Jeffrey A. Frankel and Peter R. Orszag (eds.), *Economic Policy in the 1990's.* Cambridge, Massachusetts: MIT Press.

Moggridge, D. E. 1992. *Maynard Keynes: An Economist's Biography.* London: Routledge.

Rees, David. 1973. *Harry Dexter White.* New York: Coward, McCann and Geoghegan.

Safire, William. 1975. *Before the Fall.* New York: Ballantine Books.

Schlesinger, Arthur M., Jr. 1956. *The Crisis of the Old Order.* Boston: Houghton Mifflin Company.

Solomon, Robert. 1982. *The International Monetary System, 1945-1981.* New York: Harper and Row.

Stein, Herbert. 1994. *Presidential Economics.* (3rd edition.) Washington, D.C.: American Enterprise Institute.

United States International Trade Commission. 2004. "Value of U.S. Imports for Consumption, Duties Collected, and Ratios of Duties to Values, 1891-2004," USITC (May).

Van Dormael, Armand. 1978. *Bretton Woods: Birth of a Monetary System.* New York: Holmes and Meier.

Volcker, Paul and Toyoo Gyohten. 1992. *Changing Fortunes.* New York: Times Books.

Wells, Wyatt C. 1994. *Economist in an Uncertain World.* New York: Columbia University Press.

Wicker, Tom. 1991. *One of Us: Richard Nixon and the American Dream.* New York: Random House.

News Articles
Bilefsky, Dan. "Greeks Take to Streets in Protest of Deep Spending Cuts," New York Times, May 1, 2010.

Kahn, Joseph. "Argentina's Chaos Raises New Doubts on Monetary Fund," *New York Times*, December 22, 2001.

Thomas, Landon, Jr. "Money Troubles Take Personal Toll in Greece," New York Times, May 15, 2011.

Thomas, Landon, Jr. "New Rescue Package for Greece Takes Shape," *New York Times*, May 31, 2011.

Weisbrot, Mark. "Why Greece Should Reject the Euro," *New York Times*, May 9, 2011.

Chapter 10
The Great Inflation

MacroPolicy Now: Recovery from the Great Recession

It was spring, 2011, and the recovery was in trouble. "Hiring in the United States slowed sharply in May, suggesting the economy may be running out of steam once again," reported the *New York Times* on June 3, 2011. Economists said that job growth so far had been too slow to reverse the damage from the 2007-2009 recession. Fourteen million people were unemployed, and six million had been out of work for more than six months.

"Once again," meant that we'd been here before. A recovery had begun with the end of the recession in mid-2009, only to slow abruptly in Spring 2010. Then, the slowdown was blamed on worries over the European debt crisis. In 2011 it was blamed on higher energy prices and natural disasters, especially the earthquake in Japan.

In 2010 the economic slowdown had brought action from policymakers. Federal spending was augmented in the summer of 2010. The Federal Reserve began a second quantitative easing (called "QE2"), increasing the money supply in the hopes that still lower interest rates would stimulate borrowing and spending.

No such policies were in the offing in 2011. Policymakers were focused on concerns about the Federal budget deficit, and cited a warning by the Moody's bond rating firm about threats to the United States' credit rating. Conservatives claimed that spending programs had failed, and called instead for big cuts in federal spending and reduced regulation to stimulate corporate investment. Liberals asked for more aid to the states and more aggressive action from the Federal Reserve. Economists worried that spending cuts would weigh down the fragile recovery.

It was expected that the effects of higher oil prices and natural disasters would be temporary. Economists were hoping that the economy would soon overcome the disruption in deliveries of auto parts caused by the Japanese earthquake and tsunami. Unrest in the Middle East had caused the rise in oil prices. A settlement in Libya would boost supply. The oil producing nations in OPEC, the Organization of Petroleum Exporting Countries, were pumping beyond their quotas. But a meeting in early June ended in disarray, with no increase in production quotas.

Others were not so sure that the problems were temporary. In early June former Treasury Secretary Lawrence Summers worried that since the first quarter of 2006 U.S. real GDP growth had averaged less than one percent per year. Five years was halfway to a "lost decade," a prolonged period of slow growth and high unemployment. It had happened to Japan in the 1990's.

Summers noted the difference between this recovery and the recoveries from previous recessions. In the past, recessions were often triggered by Federal Reserve interest rate

---

297

increases, designed to bring down inflation. He wrote, "after inflation slowed, rapid recovery propelled by dramatic reductions in interest rates and a backlog of deferred investment was almost inevitable."

Not so this time. Recent expansions, he wrote, "end after a period of overconfidence drives the prices of capital assets too high and the apparent increases in wealth give rise to excessive borrowing, lending and spending." When the bubbles burst households see their wealth reduced and cut spending. Businesses have overinvested in buildings and equipment and have no need to build or buy more. Recoveries are slow and prolonged.

In 2009 economists Carmen Reinhart and Kenneth Rogoff published a book called *This Time Is Different*. The title was an ironic reference to the thinking that drives financial speculation. Is it a speculative bubble that will burst, causing a recession? No, people say every time, "this time is different." Reinhart and Rogoff studied 800 years of financial speculation and discovered that it's never different.

They also found that recoveries after financial crises tend to be slower and longer than after other recessions. In a related paper, Reinhart found housing prices took years to recover, that it took seven years on average for households and companies to reduce their debts and restore their credit. "Large destabilizing events, such as those analyzed here, evidently produce changes in the performance of key macroeconomic indicators over the longer term, well after the upheaval of the crisis is over," Ms. Reinhart wrote.

Neal Soss, chief economist at Credit Suisse, an investment bank, said "Why do the downs feel so much more threatening these days? Because economic growth should be much faster. Any little adversity feels much worse when growth is so much closer to zero." The issue: was the bad news in June a "little adversity", or a sign of a recovery that would be "slow and prolonged?"

The first "Great Recession" happened in 1981-82. It resulted from a long run-up of inflation during the 1960's and 1970's, known as the "Great Inflation." How did inflation get out of hand? Why did it lead to a long, deep recession? Perhaps our experience then could help us understand our prospects now. . . .

Eisenhower and Inflation

Dwight Eisenhower won the Presidency in 1952, the first Republican President since Herbert Hoover. Many wondered what his economic policies would be. Much had changed since Hoover. Keynesian thinking about the role of taxes and budgets in economic stability had come of age under Democratic presidents. Social Security and unemployment insurance had never been administered by Republicans. Changes in the Fed's power, and development of the new Bretton Woods international system happened on the Democrats' watch. What would the party of Hoover make of these changes?

Defense spending declined as the Korean War wound down in 1953 and 1954, and this helped send the economy into recession. It was the first downturn under a Republican

President since the start of the Depression, and so was seen as a test of the new administration's attitudes. Unlike Herbert Hoover, Dwight Eisenhower did *not* try to balance the budget with tax hikes or spending cuts. Instead, the automatic stabilizers were allowed to work—taxes declined as income dropped, unemployment insurance payments increased—causing a budget deficit. The recession proved to be mild, with the unemployment rate remaining under 6%. Republicans as well as Democrats had accepted the government's responsibility for economic stabilization.

Recessions had always been accompanied by *deflation*. When the demand for their products fell, businesses would cut prices. When unemployment increased, workers would accept lower wages. Prices had fallen during the Depression, of course, but also in the recessions of 1937-38, 1948-49 and in 1955, after the recession of 1953-54. But the recession of 1957-58 did not bring deflation. The inflation rate fell, but it never became negative.

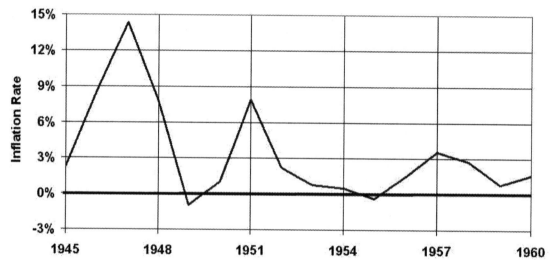

Figure 10-1. Inflation Rate, 1945-1960. Calculated as the annual percentage change in the consumer price index from the previous year. It shows the inflation associated with the end of WWII price controls (1945-48) and the one year burst of inflation during the Korean War (1951). It also shows deflation (negative inflation) during the 1949 recession, and in 1955 after the 1953-54 recession. Of concern to Eisenhower: there was no deflation with the 1957-58 recession. The rate of increase dipped, but prices kept on rising.

All the peacetime recessions and depressions up to 1955 were accompanied by deflation. At some point during or just after the recession, the price level fell. There was no deflation in any recession from then until 2009. What changed?

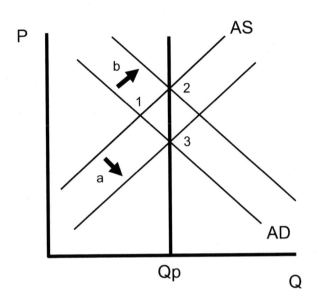

Figure 10-2. Legacy of the Big Bill? The economy starts in recession, with output less than potential (1). Second shift #1 should increase aggregate supply (a), because input costs decrease in the face of unemployment and unused capacity. The price level falls (3). The big bill of 1935 established a safety net which may delay the pain of unemployment, and so delay the aggregate supply shift (a). Meanwhile, the government more readily uses counter-cyclical fiscal and monetary policy to increase aggregate demand (b). The price level rises (2). If shift (a) is slow and shift (b) is quick, the price level may never decline.

In the goods market, when output is less than potential, we expect deflation to result from an increase in aggregate supply. Unemployment causes workers and suppliers to accept lower wages and prices, and the decline in input costs causes firms to employ and produce more output. That's second shift #1. Perhaps, since 1955, second shift #1 has been slow off the mark. Perhaps something is slowing the downward adjustment of input costs.

The "safety net"—unemployment insurance, social security and welfare—allows people to remain unemployed longer, searching for a higher wage job. This delays the aggregate supply adjustment which reduces the price level.

It's the "pain" of unemployment that convinces people to accept lower pay rather than remain unemployed. What is this pain? Watching your savings melt away. Worry about how your mortgage will be paid. Postponing your bill payments and facing down creditors. Denying your family the luxuries and then the necessities of life. In the face of these anxieties, workers might accept a job even if the wage is low.

But as of the 1950's there was unemployment insurance, Social Security and welfare. All the programs passed by the Big Bill in 1935 were operating and well-known to the public. Now the pain of unemployment could be held off for a time. Workers could wait longer for recall to their old job, or search longer for a job at a higher wage. Input costs were less likely to fall right away. Aggregate supply would increase more slowly.

The Eisenhower administration demonstrated that both parties now accepted the need for stabilization policy. Counter-cyclical fiscal and monetary policies were used to increase aggregate demand and end recessions. Aggregate demand would increase more quickly.

So, while aggregate supply was responding more slowly to recessions, aggregate demand was responding more quickly. The sluggish increase in aggregate supply, which would reduce the price level, is overwhelmed by the quick increase in aggregate demand, which increases the price level. The recession never sees deflation. Perhaps the continuous inflation from 1955 to 2008 was the result of the more elaborate *"safety net"* which protects people from some of the misfortunes of recession and the counter-cyclical efforts of government to end recessions as quickly as possible.

President Eisenhower was determined to halt this continuing inflation. He later wrote in his memoirs,

> Critics overlooked the inflationary psychology which prevailed during the mid-fifties and which I thought it necessary to defeat. . . . The administration believed that if wages and prices could increase during a recession, we could get into real inflationary trouble in time of prosperity.

As soon as the 1957-58 recession was over the President began a drive to turn the Federal government's recessionary deficit into a big budget surplus. He reduced Federal spending and resisted all calls for tax cuts.

President Eisenhower and Fed chair William McChesney Martin developed a new working relationship. Unlike Truman, Eisenhower refused to criticize the Fed publicly. Reporters would ask again and again whether he thought Fed policy was correct. Eisenhower refused comment, saying only that he endorsed Fed independence. Behind the scenes, though, Eisenhower felt free to exert pressure. When he thought interest rates were too high during the 1954 recession, he sent his Treasury Secretary to talk to Chairman Martin. Martin decided that he couldn't resist a direct plea from the White House. The Fed reduced interest rates.

The Federal Reserve also was worried that prices hadn't fallen during the 1957-58 recession. It presented the Fed with a tough policy choice. Its policy was to "lean against the wind." But which wind? If the economy could suffer from inflation and unemployment at the same time, it wasn't clear which way to lean. The Fed chose to fight inflation. Chairman Martin thought they had allowed interest rates to stay too low for too long in the 1953-54 recession. So, as soon as signs of recovery became clear, the Fed began raising interest rates. By mid-1960 the discount rate was at four percent, the highest rate in thirty years.

With Eisenhower's restrictive fiscal policy, and Martin's restrictive monetary policy, it is no surprise that the recovery from the 1957-58 recession was sluggish and short. Inflation was just 1.6% in 1960, but the unemployment rate averaged 5.5% and GDP was growing by just 2.3% per year.

301

Vice President Richard Nixon was particularly concerned about the economy's mediocre performance, since he was the Republican presidential nominee in 1960. Nixon knew that an election year recession could ruin his hopes for the Presidency. He pleaded with the President for a tax cut, to stimulate spending. Eisenhower was focused on inflation. The unemployment rate was 4.8% in February 1960. By election day in November it was up to 6.1%. Richard Nixon lost the election by 119,000 votes, two-tenths of one percent. The new President would be a Democrat, John F. Kennedy.

Kennedy's Economists

John F. Kennedy entered the Presidency with few fixed economic ideas. He had criticized the Eisenhower economic performance—three recessions in eight years—and had promised to "get this country moving again." He had little idea of how to accomplish this goal, however, and now, in January 1961, the lingering recession was his problem.

He sought advice from some of the best economists of his generation. He assigned Paul Samuelson to write a report on the economy during the November to January transition of administrations. In 1970 Samuelson became the first American winner of the Nobel Prize in Economics. On the Council of Economic Advisors was James Tobin (Nobel Prize 1981). On the Council's staff were Kenneth Arrow (Nobel Prize 1972) and Robert Solow (Nobel Prize 1987). These were Ivy League professors—Kennedy was a Harvard man. But to head up his Council of Economic Advisors, he went to the Big Ten. He appointed Walter Heller, an economist from Minnesota.

Heller and the Council decided to give the President an education in economics. Heller had a knack for clear, colorful writing, and he began sending Kennedy memos on economic topics. He sent about 300 in three years. Kennedy read them. "We had lots of evidence that he read our memoranda because he would say something in a press briefing, or in a meeting with us that he couldn't have gotten anywhere else but from our memo," Heller said later.

The press called it the "New Economics," but it was nothing new to Kennedy's economists. It was just *Keynesian economics* with enough added features that they took to calling it "neo-Keynesian," or even "the Keynesian-classical synthesis." What was new was that, for the first time, a President would propose a Keynesian fiscal policy for Keynesian reasons, using Keynesian language.

Kennedy's economists diagnosed the economy's troubles this way. The Federal budget had some automatic stabilizers. Income taxes automatically fell with incomes during recessions and unemployment insurance spending automatically increased. This helped keep recessions mild. When the economy boomed, the stabilizers helped restrain inflation. It was during recoveries that there was a problem. Taxes started rising and spending started dropping just as soon as the economy turned around. This slowed recovery and could even prevent the economy from reaching its full potential before the next recession hit.

The problem seemed to be getting worse. The 1949-53 expansion lasted 45 months, the 1954-57 expansion 39 months, the 1958-60 expansion just 24. During this first expansion the unemployment rate had dipped to 2.5%, during the second, 3.7%. In the last expansion the rate had fallen to only 5.0%, in June 1959, before turning up again. Now, at the start of the Kennedy administration in January 1961, the rate was 6.6%.

Some policy makers, like Fed Chair William Martin, thought the unemployment problem was *structural*. That meant that people were unemployed not because there were no jobs, but because they did not have the skills needed for the jobs that were open. Advances in automation were increasing the skills businesses needed in their workers. Yet nearly a million young people dropped out of high school every year. Monetary and fiscal policy could not reduce structural unemployment. Added spending could increase production and the number of job openings, but that wouldn't help unemployed people who lacked the right skills.

Heller, Tobin and the third Council member, Gardner Ackley, thought differently. Unemployment stayed high because monetary and fiscal policies were too tight. It was a *cyclical* problem. Martin, they thought, had pushed interest rates too high during the recovery, and they were still too high in the current recession. Eisenhower, they thought, was wrong to worry about inflation so soon in the recovery. Deficits during a recession and early in a recovery were to be welcomed.

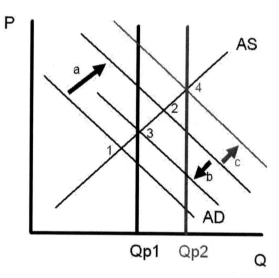

Figure 10-3. High or Low? All agree that the economy is in recession at 1. Aggregate demand is increased through stabilization policy (a), increasing output to (2). Eisenhower and Martin think that potential output is low (Qp1), because unemployment is structural. That means aggregate demand must be restrained (b) to prevent "inflationary psychology" from setting second shift #1 into motion. Output moves to (3). Kennedy and Heller think potential output is high (Qp2), because unemployment is cyclical. Aggregate demand must be increased more (c) to "get the economy moving."

Output moves to (4). If Ike is wrong and potential output is high, the economy suffers from slow growth and high unemployment. If JFK is wrong and potential output is low, the economy will experience a big rise in inflation, as aggregate supply begins to decrease with rising resource costs (second shift #1).

Expansionary policy was needed—but what kind? John Kenneth Galbraith advocated increased public spending. Galbraith was an economist and a long-time Kennedy advisor who had written a book called *The Affluent Society* in 1958. We've got lots of consumer goods, he wrote, but not enough "public goods." We drive our huge cars with their big tail fins past crumbling schools and polluted rivers. Raise Federal spending to shift the mix from private to public consumption, Galbraith said, and reduce unemployment as a side benefit. The administration tried, early on, to increase spending. Congress wouldn't have it.

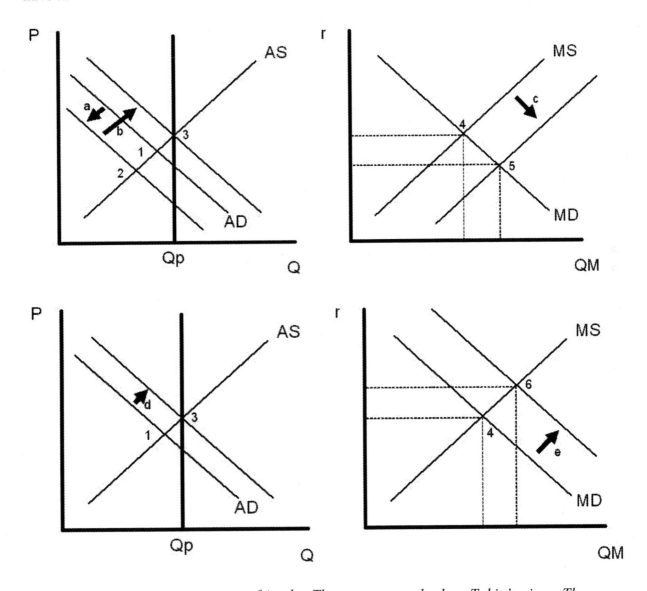

Figure 10-4. Disagreement among friends. The top two panels show Tobin's view. The economy was in recession, with output less than potential (1). He would have reduced government spending and increased the money supply. The fall in aggregate demand produced by the lower spending (a) would be more than offset by the aggregate demand increase (b) which results from the lower interest rates (5). He's counting on second shift #2. Output rises to potential (3). [Note—this would increase money demand— second shift #3-- but not enough to raise interest rates above (4).] The added investment spending increases the capital stock faster, which increases potential output faster. In the long run, output growth is greater. The bottom two panels show Heller's view. The recession is ended with a tax cut, increasing aggregate demand (d). The rise in income

increases money demand (e), through second shift #3, which increases the interest rate. Second shift #2 means investment spending will be less than in Tobin's proposal, so output will grow more slowly in the long run. Heller's proposal suffers from crowding out. Tobin's benefits from "crowding in." But recovery probably would come quicker under Heller's proposal.

James Tobin wanted a policy to promote long run growth. He was not satisfied to simply get *to* potential output, he wanted to *increase* potential, increase the number of buildings, factories and machines that the economy uses to produce output, get the Federal Reserve to cut interest rates to encourage extra business investment in plant and equipment, and run a budget surplus to retire part of the national debt. With fewer Treasury bonds available, investors have to put their money in stocks and corporate bonds. That's money for business expansion.

This idea ran smack into the balance of payments problem, however. High interest rates encouraged the demand for the dollar. Reduce them, and the United States would have to use even more of its gold and reserves to support the dollar's fixed value. This was one of the reasons Fed chair Martin held interest rates high, and it was hard to argue otherwise. Mundell's "unholy trinity" restricted discretionary monetary policy, for the sake of fixed exchange rates.

That left Walter Heller's idea: a big, permanent tax cut. Heller argued that the tax structure had been developed during World War II, when the problem was to hold down spending, to restrain inflation. But now it created *fiscal drag*, restraining recovery. Heller and his staff figured it this way. The unemployment rate in mid-1961 was about 6.5%. They estimated that it could get down to about 4% without triggering inflation. That was "full employment." Arthur Okun, a staff economist on the Council, calculated that each 1% drop in the unemployment rate produced about 3% in extra output. With tongue in cheek, they dubbed that ratio *"Okun's Law."* A 2.5% drop in unemployment, to get to 4%, meant a 7.5% increase in GDP. That was potential output, what the economy could produce without inflation, if everyone and

> *"Okun's Law" said that each 1% drop in the unemployment rate produced a 3% increase in real GDP. The Kennedy economists used this relationship to calculate the size of the tax cut needed to return to the economy to potential output.*

everything was employed. 7.5% of GDP was about $35 billion.

What did this "GDP gap" imply for a tax cut? The economists turned to the *income multiplier*, the same idea that Keynes had described to Francis Perkins almost thirty years before. If consumers spent more, businesses would produce more, they would pay more wages to more workers, and their workers would spend more, too. That would cause businesses to produce even more output. They thought the multiplier was about three: for every one dollar reduction in taxes, output would increase by three dollars. So, to close a GDP gap of $35 billion, the tax cut needed to be one-third that amount, somewhere around $10 to $12 billion dollars.

Kennedy didn't buy it. His economists were disappointed when the President-elect told them he would not increase the deficit to deal with the recession. Kennedy's margin of victory had been razor thin. He did not want business people and the Congress to label him as an irresponsible spender.

Kennedy Proposes a Tax Cut

Heller started sending his memos, but Kennedy resisted. Then, early in 1962 the recovery faltered. GDP was growing more slowly than projected, and a "Kennedy recession" seemed possible. That did it. Kennedy committed to the tax cut that summer, as an anti-recession policy. It would be introduced as legislation in January 1963.

In December 1962 Kennedy spoke to the Economic Club of New York about his tax cut. He began with a reference to the Cold War and the Cuban Missile Crisis: "Less than a month ago this Nation reminded the world that it possessed both the will and the weapons to meet any threat to the security of free men." This talk was about the economy, though. Security was strengthened ". . . by the deployment of fiscal and monetary weapons as well as by military weapons; and above all by the strength of this Nation's economy as well as by the strength of our defenses."

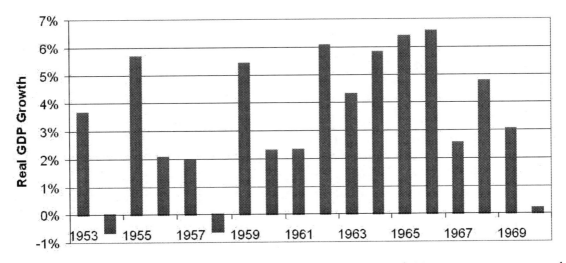

Figure 10-5. Real GDP Growth, 1953-70. Eisenhower and Martin were concerned about inflation, and so pursued policies that led to slower real growth. From 1956 to 1961 output grew less than 2.5% in 5 of 6 years. The Kennedy tax cut, Johnson Great Society programs, Vietnam War, and looser monetary policy led to more rapid growth from 1964 to 1969. But inflation increased too.

The President was "an apt pupil," Heller thought, and now it showed. "This economy is capable of producing without strain $30 to $40 billion more than we are producing today," he told his audience. There was a GDP gap. "There is no need for us to be satisfied with a rate of growth that keeps good men out of work and good capacity out of use." The gap could be closed.

And the best way to do it was

> to reduce the burden on private income and the deterrents to private initiative which are imposed by our present tax system; and this administration pledged itself last summer to an across-the-board, top-to-bottom cut in personal and corporate income taxes to be enacted and become effective in 1963.

Kennedy tossed in some of his new economic expertise. Added after-tax income would increase spending because "consumers are still spending between 92 and 94 percent of their after-tax income." One of Heller's memos had covered the marginal propensity to consume. Output would rise "several times the amount of taxes actually cut." The President had absorbed the memo on the income multiplier.

"It will not, I'm confident, revive an inflationary spiral," Kennedy said.

> If the economy today were operating close to capacity levels with little unemployment, or if a sudden change in our military requirements should cause a scramble for men and resources, then I would oppose tax reductions as irresponsible and inflationary; and I would not hesitate to recommend a tax increase, if that were necessary.

With excess capacity—the GDP gap—added spending would create greater output, not higher prices. Of course, if a big increase in military spending pushed output beyond capacity, a tax *increase* might be needed. Apparently, Vice President Lyndon Johnson wasn't listening.

The administration's people began lobbying Congress for the tax bill. They met much resistance. The "traditional budget balancers" had accepted the need for deficits in a recession. But this was different. It was a tax cut during a recovery, with a budget already in deficit. Faster growth will bring the budget into balance, said the President's lobbyists.

One of the Congressmen who had to be convinced was Wilbur Mills, chairman of the House Ways and Means Committee, where tax bills start. Walter Heller had known him for years, and took him out to lunch. Heller argued for the tax cut throughout the meal, and by the end he heard the words he wanted to hear, "Well, I'll go along with it." But then Mills added, "if you have an equal cut in expenditure." That would defeat the purpose, Heller knew. There was more work to be done.

Heller testified before the Ways and Means Committee. "How is it that you're tying to give people a tax cut, and they don't seem to want it?" asked a sympathetic Congresswoman. Heller replied off-the-cuff, "Maybe it's the Puritan ethic." "Heller denigrates the Puritan Ethic!" said the headlines the next day. And on the floor of Congress, a Congressman declared "I'd rather be a Puritan than a Heller."

The tax cut was not passed in 1963, but Kennedy sensed that he was making progress, and held out hopes for 1964.

The Great Society
President Lyndon Johnson met with Kennedy's shocked and somber advisors on the night of John Kennedy's funeral. The business of government goes on, and Heller anticipated a long effort to persuade the new President to support the tax cut. He was surprised to find Johnson already convinced that the tax cut was needed.

Johnson had decided that the painful transition to his administration would be eased if he took responsibility for Kennedy's legacy. Two days later, in a speech before a joint session of Congress, he urged them to pass the civil rights bill which Kennedy had championed. And, he said, "no act of ours could more fittingly continue the work of President Kennedy than the early passage of the tax bill for which he fought all this long year."

Johnson thought that a tax cut would be the best thing for the economy. But he had other incentives. There would be a Presidential election in less than a year. A tax cut would please the voters. Just as important, pushing a tax cut through Congress—where Kennedy's team had failed—would demonstrate that Johnson was in charge.

Johnson had been the majority leader of the Senate before becoming Vice President. He was known as a master deal-maker. Kennedy tried to get things done through education and persuasion. Johnson knew how to deal. The tax cut passed, and Johnson signed it on February 26, 1964.

It was a big tax cut, amounting to $11.5 billion dollars, compared to a total budget of just under $100 billion. The tax rate on the lowest income individuals fell from 20% to 16%, and on the highest income individuals from 91% to 70%. The corporate profits tax rate was cut from 52% to 48%.

When the tax cut took effect in July 1964, the unemployment rate was 5.2%, and the inflation rate over the previous year had been 1.3%. By the end of 1965, the unemployment rate was 4.0%. and the 12-month inflation rate was 1.9%. The tax cut seemed to have done just what Heller and company had expected: brought the economy up to capacity with unemployment at the estimated full employment level of 4.0%. But the inflation rate had risen to 1.9%. Not a big increase, but (as it turned out) it was the beginning of a trend. Still, with the economy booming and unemployment falling, Lyndon Johnson was elected in a landslide in November 1964.

Lyndon Johnson was now the elected President of the United States, and he was determined to build a legacy of his own. He had first come to Washington in the 1930s, during the late stages of the New Deal. Franklin Roosevelt was his hero. With his electoral landslide and a Congress stocked with members of his Democratic party, now was the time, he thought, to extend the New Deal. He called it the *"Great Society."*

He had coined the term in a speech in the Spring of 1964, and now he used it again and again. The Great Society would channel the nation's extraordinary prosperity to its neglected public needs. He listed his proposals in his January 1965 State of the Union speech: job training, extension of the minimum wage and unemployment compensation, high-speed railroads, a stepped up war on poverty, voting rights enforcement, immigration reform, preschool education, college scholarships, hospital care for the elderly, regional medical centers, medical research and education, services for mentally retarded, urban planning, housing programs in a new Department of Housing and Urban Development, training and equipment for police officers, new national parks and seashores, highway beautification, programs for clean air and water, pollution control research, research on distilling fresh water from the sea, establishment of a National Foundation on the Arts, and reforms of the electoral college.

With his deal-making skills, and big Democratic majorities in Congress, Johnson managed to get most of his agenda passed. His chief aide calculated that in 1965 and 1966 they had proposed 200 major pieces of legislation, and passed 181. Johnson was intensely proud of this achievement. The Great Society programs were "his babies."

The Vietnam War

North Vietnam was Communist, allied with Red China. South Vietnam was anti-Communist, allied with the United States. The two Vietnams were at war. The United States had several thousand military advisors in the south at the beginning of 1964. Lyndon Johnson was ambivalent. "I don't think it's worth fighting for and I don't think we can get out," he told an advisor, "Of course, if you start running from the Communists, they may just chase you right into your own kitchen." Most of his advisors, many left over from the Kennedy administration, urged him to commit U.S. forces to defend the South. Senator Barry Goldwater of Arizona, his opponent in the November election, advocated commitment as well. Johnson felt that he had to appear strong in the face of Communist aggression, as strong as Kennedy had been in the Cuban Missile Crisis.

Johnson hesitated for almost a year, but by July 1965 it appeared to the President and his advisors that the United States had to commit to a larger war, or get out. Weakness in the face of Communist aggression was not possible, they decided. The escalation began. By the end of 1965 the number of troops in South Vietnam approached 200,000.

The Great Society programs were expensive. The President had convinced Congress that a small deficit in the near term would eventually be balanced by revenues from rapid economic growth. Escalation in Vietnam made these calculations obsolete. Johnson feared that if the Congress knew how expensive the war would be, they would gut his Great Society programs. And, he feared, higher spending would give the Fed an excuse to raise interest rates. So for months they hid the numbers. They cancelled a meeting that was usually held to inform the Federal Reserve about the coming year's budget proposal.

William McChesney Martin had been chair of the Fed for 14 years, and he had his own sources in the Pentagon. War spending was going to increase a lot. "These things are going to go way beyond what the administration has admitted,'" he told his colleagues. At an October meeting with the President, Martin asked how much the budget would need to rise to pay for the war. "[Defense Secretary] McNamara says it very likely will be less than $5 billion for the rest of 1966," the President said. Martin had heard much higher numbers from his sources. Increased defense spending with the economy near capacity meant that business and consumer spending would have to be restrained. Interest rates would have to rise.

President Johnson's "guns and butter" policy increased Great Society social spending and escalated the Vietnam War. The increase in aggregate demand threatened to increase inflation. His economists advocated a tax increase. He refused. In 1965 the Fed increased interest rates instead.

War spending also disturbed the new head of the Council of Economic Advisors, Gardner Ackley. Ackley figured that rising revenues from the growing economy could pay for the new Great Society programs, or escalation of the war. But if the President insisted on both the war and the social programs—*guns and butter* the reporters called it—then a tax increase was needed. If taxes didn't rise, consumer, business and government spending together would outstrip the economy's ability to produce, and inflation could result. He remembered later, "we had all the evidence we needed to conclude without any question, certainly by November or early December, that a tax increase was absolutely necessary if we were going to avoid substantial inflation in 1966."

Ackley also warned the President that "monetary policy stands at the crossroads." Martin was sure to restrain spending with higher interest rates if taxes weren't raised to do the job. Sure enough, on Friday, December 3, 1965, the Fed raised the discount rate half a point.

President Johnson was furious. "It made him ill to think about those bankers collecting 12 percent interest," Ackley said. He released a mild statement to the press: "I regret, as do most Americans, any action that raises the cost of credit, particularly for homes, schools, hospitals, and factories." But he had his allies in Congress step up the pressure. Senator Proxmire demanded hearings "to determine what action must be taken to prevent this creature of Congress from endangering the nation's prosperity and from doing so in defiance of the President of the United States."

Martin could not be persuaded. At a meeting in December Johnson, Martin, Ackley and others talked about what kind of tax increase would be needed. Ackley was convinced that Johnson would ask for a tax hike in his upcoming State of the Union speech.

Johnson knew that leaders in Congress were unwilling to consider higher taxes. House Ways and Means chair Wilbur Mills told the President that such a bill wouldn't even get a hearing. Mills was against most of the Great Society programs. Cutbacks in social spending might persuade him to act, but Johnson would not sacrifice his babies.

Instead, in the January 1966 speech, Johnson asked for more Great Society programs: ending discrimination in jury selection and housing, development aid for rural areas, urban renewal, improved unemployment insurance, a higher minimum wage, a teacher corps, assistance for renters, pollution control, highway safety, consumer protection, research on a super-sonic passenger jet, and campaign finance reform. Furthermore, he declared, "This nation is mighty enough, its society is healthy enough, its people are strong enough, to pursue our goals in the rest of the world while still building a Great Society here at home." He would pursue the war and the Great Society at the same time. Guns and butter spending would continue. But he would not raise taxes.

Congress passed most of the President's social programs. The Vietnam escalation continued. By the end of 1966, there were almost 400,000 American soldiers in Vietnam. The inflation rate in 1965 had been 1.9%. By April 1966 it was 2.9%. By August, 3.5%. It had not been so high since 1958. Martin's Fed continued to tighten monetary policy, selling bonds to slow growth of the money supply and raise the federal funds rate, from 4.4% in January to 5.8% in November.

The Income Tax Surcharge

Maybe Martin was sending a message. Ackley told the President, "Perhaps it's a means of telling us that, if we do move on taxes, the Fed is ready to move on money." Raise taxes, and Martin could allow interest rates to fall. But throughout 1966 Johnson did not think the Congress or the country was ready for a tax hike. Opposition to the war was mounting. Now a push for a tax hike would not only threaten social spending, it could threaten the country's luke-warm support for the war.

Late in 1966 Johnson finally came around, persuaded by rising inflation and higher interest rates. With Martin's implied offer before him, he said in his January 1967 State of the Union address, "I recommend to the Congress a surcharge of 6 percent on both corporate and individual income taxes--to last for two years or for so long as the unusual expenditures associated with our efforts in Vietnam continue." A *tax surcharge* was a tax on a tax. Taxpayers would calculate how much income tax they owed, and then tack on an extra six percent.

Towards the end of 1966 tight money started to affect the economy. Housing construction fell sharply. In the first half of 1967 output growth slowed to a crawl. The unemployment rate edged upward from 3.6% to 4.0%. Inflation stopped rising. Johnson's advisors were now concerned that an immediate tax hike would push the economy into recession. They decided to wait until mid-year to send the tax hike proposal to Congress. The President finally submitted the tax hike proposal—now revised to a ten percent surcharge—on August 3, 1967.

The climb of inflation had stopped, and the President had come through with a tax hike recommendation. Martin kept his implied promise. The Fed reversed its open market policy in February 1967, now buying bonds to reduce the federal funds rate. In April it cut the discount rate back to four percent. Now interest rates were back where they'd been in early 1965.

The tax proposal got nowhere in Congress. Wilbur Mills, chair of the Ways and Means Committee, blocked it, and Johnson could not get him to budge. Many liberals joined the conservative Mills in opposition, seeing a vote for a tax hike as support for the war. Mills demanded big cuts in social spending as his price for allowing the tax bill out of committee. Johnson agonized, "You can't ask me to slaughter my own babies."

Meanwhile, the economy had turned. In the second half of 1967 output growth resumed. In the first half of 1968 it boomed. Inflation resumed its rise, up to 4.0% by February 1968. Martin allowed the federal funds rate to creep upward again, but did not feel he could take decisive action. He had promised Johnson not to raise rates if there was a tax hike proposal. And, he thought that tighter monetary policy would take the pressure off Congress to pass the tax hike. Raise interest rates, and Congress would think that monetary policy had done the job. Martin kept money looser than he would have in other circumstances.

Finally in 1968 the President agreed to some cuts in his Great Society programs, and Congressman Mills let the tax bill out of committee. The bill passed. As of July 1968 people saw their take home pay reduced by a ten percent addition to income tax withholding. The Fed and Johnson's advisors breathed a sigh of relief. Now spending would slow, and inflation would subside.

> *The 1968 income tax surcharge was a fiscal policy designed to decrease aggregate demand and reduce inflation. It didn't work.*

But it didn't. Consumers kept spending. Somehow, despite their reduced after-tax incomes, consumers continued to buy. The Fed actually cut the discount rate a quarter point after the tax hike took effect, expecting that now fiscal policy would carry the anti-inflation load. But inflation continued to increase, to 4.7% by the end of the year.

The economy's growth didn't slow for a year and a half after the tax hike. After a few months the Fed reversed course again and increased interest rates. Republican Richard Nixon won the Presidency, and increases in social spending subsided. With the added tax surcharge, the Federal government's budget was in surplus in 1969.

Finally, in December 1969, the nine-year-long expansion came to an end. Output declined and unemployment increased. But inflation continued to rise. It topped 6% even after a few months of recession. In most previous recessions, the price level itself had fallen. President Eisenhower had been shocked when prices had continued to increase in the 1958 recession. Now prices not only continued to increase (inflation), they *accelerated* (the rate of inflation increased).

The Phillips Curve
These events dismayed the Keynesian economists who had advised Presidents Kennedy and Johnson. Why had the tax increase not slowed consumer spending? Even more distressing, how could unemployment and inflation increase at the same time? It violated a tradeoff which the Keynesians had come to accept, called the *Phillips Curve.*

A. W. Phillips was a New Zealand econometrician (that is, an economist who uses statistical techniques with economic data). In 1958 he published an article called "The Relation Between Unemployment and the Rate of Change of Money Wage Rates in the United Kingdom, 1862-1957." It showed that for almost one hundred years in Great Britain, increases in the unemployment rate were correlated with decreases in the inflation rate (as measured by wage changes). When unemployment went up, inflation went down; when unemployment went down, inflation went up. He plotted his data on a graph, and it formed a downward-sloping curve.

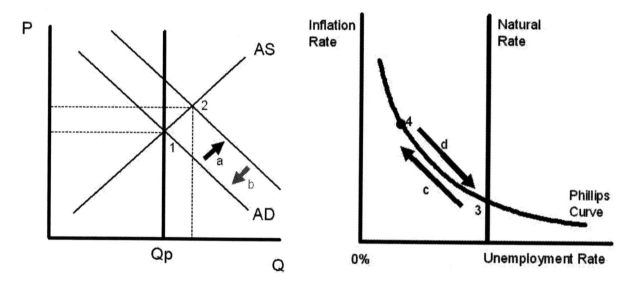

Figure 10-6. Too far. By the end of 1965 the economy was at or beyond its potential output (1), which corresponds to its "natural rate" of unemployment (3). The pursuit of the Great Society and the Vietnam War, without a tax hike or contractionary monetary policy, increased aggregate demand (a), raising prices and output (2). Likewise, the economy moved up the Phillips Curve (c) towards higher inflation and lower unemployment (4). The 1968 tax hike was expected to decrease aggregate demand (b), returning output to potential at a lower price level (1, again). It was expected to push the economy back down the Phillips Curve (d), to low inflation at the natural rate of unemployment. It didn't happen.

To Phillips it was just a regularity in economic data. To the Keynesian economists, it sang. Solow and Samuelson, two of Kennedy's advisors, wrote in 1960 that the Phillips

Curve (as they called it) was a menu of choices for policymakers. They could set fiscal and monetary policy to achieve low inflation at the cost of high unemployment, as the Eisenhower administration had done. They could set policy to achieve lower unemployment with moderate inflation, as they would advise Kennedy to do. Or, they could set policy to achieve very low unemployment and high inflation, as Lyndon Johnson did, against their advice. There was a *tradeoff* between inflation and unemployment.

> **The Phillips Curve shows the relationship between the inflation rate and the unemployment rate. It's another way to express aggregate demand and supply changes.**

Behind the Phillips Curve tradeoff was the interaction of businesses and workers in the market. If the economy was expanding, businesses would want to hire more workers to produce more goods for sale. The unemployment rate would fall. Eventually, the pool of available workers would dry up, and businesses would try to attract workers from other firms, from school or from home, with higher wages. They would pass these higher costs to consumers in higher prices. That was inflation.

Likewise, if the economy was contracting, firms would produce fewer goods and lay off workers. The unemployment rate would rise. There would be no need to increase wages, and no need to raise prices. In fact, firms might reduce prices to try to sell excess inventories. The inflation rate would fall.

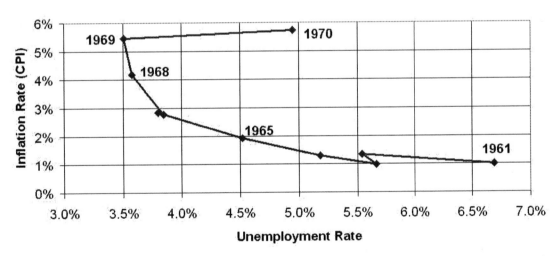

Figure 10-7. Phillips Curve, 1961-1970. The inflation rate is on the vertical axis, the unemployment rate on the horizontal axis. In 1961 unemployment was high and inflation was low. From 1961 to 1969 the economy traced a perfect Phillips Curve, with falling unemployment and rising inflation. In 1968 Johnson's economists thought the surtax would cause the economy to retrace its steps, back to the "good old days" of 1965. Instead, unemployment fell and inflation rose again in 1969, then the economy jumped off the Phillips Curve in 1970, with higher inflation <u>and</u> higher unemployment. Unemployment was about where it had been in 1964, but inflation was almost 5 percentage points higher.

"Phillips curves appeared on the backs of our envelopes," one of Kennedy's economists said later. With unemployment at 6.5% and inflation at 1% at the start of 1961, there seemed to be room to climb up the Phillips Curve, reducing unemployment without much increase in inflation. They set their target at 4% unemployment, and by the end of 1965 they had it: unemployment at 4%, with inflation still only 1.9%. Unfortunately, tax cuts and extra Federal spending kept the economy climbing. By the end of 1969 unemployment was down to 3.5% and inflation was up to 6.2%. The events of the 1960's had traced a perfect Phillips Curve. They'd simply gone too far up the curve, they thought.

The 1968 tax surcharge was meant to slow spending growth. Unemployment would rise back to 4%, and inflation would subside back to around 2%. Arthur Okun remembered thinking

> You could go down that curve just as you went up that curve. Why can't we get back to where we were in 1965, the good old days? That's exactly what we thought would happen. That's exactly what didn't happen.

Unemployment was lower and inflation higher in 1969 than it was in 1968. The economy moved up the Phillips Curve when the tax surcharge was supposed to move it down. Then unemployment and inflation were *both* higher in 1970 than in 1969. The economy had jumped off the Phillips Curve altogether. What was going on?

Milton Friedman had an answer. Friedman was an economist at the University of Chicago. He was not a Keynesian economist like Samuelson, Heller, Solow and Okun. But he did not seek to turn back the clock. In 1965 he had said, famously, "We are all Keynesians now." He meant that Keynes's focus on spending and production, and on the possibilities of stabilization policy, had become standard methods in economics. But he also said, "and none of us are Keynesians." The analysis of the economy that Keynes had launched had moved beyond Keynes's original ideas. Friedman was about to push the analysis even further.

Friedman believed that markets with flexible prices were the best way to allocate resources. So he advocated flexible exchange rates in international trade. He believed in the importance of money and monetary policy. Many Keynesians had downplayed the importance of monetary policy, until Friedman and Anna Schwartz published a mammoth volume called *A Monetary History of the United States* in 1963. The book analyzed a hundred years of U.S. economic history, showing that changes in the amount of money in circulation

> *Economist Milton Friedman pointed out that the Phillips Curve wasn't stable. Inflation would rise if people expected it, even if the unemployment rate increased. He discovered second shift #2.*

had a great deal to do with fluctuations in the economy. Friedman advocated a steady increase in the money supply as the best stabilization policy, rather than continuous adjustments as economic conditions changed. He and his followers became known as *Monetarists*.

And Milton Friedman believed in the importance of *expectations*. What consumers and businesses thought would happen was important in determining what would happen. Expectations explained why the tax surcharge hadn't slowed the economy. Spending by consumers, Friedman wrote, depended on what they thought their *permanent income* was. Consumers knew the tax surcharge was temporary, so they didn't change their long-term ideas about what they could spend. They took money out of savings, cashed in assets and borrowed, knowing that they could make up for it when taxes were cut again. Spending didn't drop much, so the tax hike didn't slow the economy. The Keynesians acted as if consumers always behaved the same way—as if the marginal propensity to consume out of income was constant. No, Friedman said, the MPC depended on expectations.

Expectations of inflation also explained why the economy had jumped off the Phillips Curve in 1970. In fact, Friedman said, the whole Phillips Curve had shifted upward and outward, because people had come to expect inflation. Amazingly, he explained this in a speech to the American Economic Association in December 1967, two years *before* the event.

"There is wide agreement about the major goals of economic policy: high employment, stable prices, and rapid growth," Friedman said. We are all Keynesians, after all but "there is less agreement that these goals are mutually compatible," or "about the terms at which they can and should be substituted for one another." What does the Phillips Curve look like, and can it be used to guide policy?

The Phillips Curve wasn't stable. Friedman said

> Implicitly, Phillips wrote his article for a world in which everyone anticipated that nominal prices would be stable and in which that anticipation remained unshaken and immutable whatever happened to actual prices and wages.

But in fact, inflation would create the expectation of more inflation. Businesses would expect their costs to rise, so they would raise prices. Workers would expect prices to rise, so they would demand wage hikes. The economy could slow and unemployment increase, but people would, for a time, continue to expect inflation. The same unemployment rate could correspond to lots of different inflation rates, depending on inflationary expectations. Since inflationary expectations were higher in 1970 than they had been in 1965 (after five years of inflationary experience), the economy could not slide back down the Phillips Curve. In 1970, 5% unemployment would correspond not to 2% inflation, as in 1965, but to 6% inflation. The Phillips Curve had shifted.

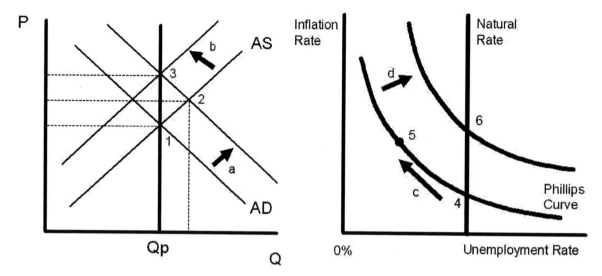

Figure 10-8. The same idea expressed two ways. The economy starts at potential output (1), with the unemployment rate at the natural rate (4). Something increases aggregate demand, like an increase in transfers or government purchases. This increases aggregate demand (a) and runs the economy up the Phillips Curve (c). Prices are higher and output is beyond potential (2), and inflation is higher and unemployment is less than the natural rate (5). Now expectations adjust. They raise resource costs, decreasing aggregate supply (b)—second shift #1. The same shift worsens the Phillips Curve tradeoff (d). In the end, output is back at potential, with a higher price level (3); unemployment is back at the natural rate, with a higher inflation rate (6). In our terminology, Milton Friedman discovered second shift #1.

There was a further implication, Friedman said. "There is always a temporary trade-off between inflation and unemployment; there is no permanent trade-off." If was not possible for policymakers to set the unemployment rate permanently below the *natural rate of unemployment*, which was the rate that existed when the economy was at full capacity. If policymakers tried to hold the unemployment rate below the natural rate (as they did in 1966-69), eventually market forces would push the economy back to the natural rate, but with a higher inflation rate. The Phillips Curve was not a menu of policy choices, it merely measured temporary fluctuations at a particular level of inflationary expectations.

"We may have banked too heavily on the stability of the Phillips curve," Kennedy's economists wrote later. Friedman's *"expectations augmented Phillips Curve"* became (and remains) the standard way to look at the inflation-unemployment tradeoff.

Friedman's analysis had one more unfortunate, and ominous, implication. Once inflation got going, it was not possible to slow the economy a little to bring it back down, as the stable Phillips Curve implied. If expectations of inflation were high enough, only a long, deep recession would work. Policymakers spent much of the 1970's looking for an alternative to that recession. They didn't find one.

Price Controls

Arthur Burns was the new chair of the Federal Reserve. He was not a follower of Milton Friedman (Friedman, in fact, had been his student). He was not a monetarist; he did not think that inflation was mostly the result of too-rapid growth in the money supply, or that tight monetary policy was the main tool to be used to bring inflation down. Instead, he thought that big corporations and big labor unions had a great deal of power to raise prices and wages. This power had to be restrained by government, and this required an *incomes policy*, a government mechanism to restrain price and wage increases.

Mandatory price controls had not been used since the Korean War, but the government had had something like an incomes policy throughout the Eisenhower, Kennedy and Johnson years. Kennedy's economists had established "guideposts" for corporate price increases and union wage contracts. Wages were not supposed to rise more than the increase in productivity. That would mean that businesses could pay for wage hikes out of increased output, without having to raise prices. The guideposts were enforced by "jawboning," which meant that the President would press union leaders to hold down their wage demands and press corporations to hold down price increases.

> *"Incomes Policies" are attempts to restrain wage and price increases through persuasion or legal controls. Price controls are a kind of incomes policy.*

The guidepost policy had faded during the Johnson years, though. With government and private spending rising so fast, companies could raise their profits with price increases, and nothing the President said could stop them. Likewise, with employment prospects so rosy, unions demanded wage hikes beyond the guideposts, whatever the President said.

Richard Nixon resisted price controls at first. As a young man he had actually worked as a low-level official for the Office of Price Administration, the agency in charge of price controls and rationing during World War II. He came away from that experience disillusioned with government's attempt to micro-manage the economy.

Through the summer of 1971 both unemployment and inflation remained unacceptably high. Democrats in Congress demanded price controls, but now many business people agreed. Businesses wanted help in resisting union wage demands. Meanwhile, the nation's balance of payments problem threatened the Bretton Woods fixed exchange rate system. The 1972 Presidential election loomed. Richard Nixon decided to go for a dramatic policy change, a "long bomb." He called his advisors to a meeting at Camp David on August 13, 1971.

Looking back after almost forty years, the most important decision made at the Camp David meeting was to close the gold window. This ended the fixed exchange rate system that had existed since the Bretton Woods conference in 1944. Most of the developed world has been using flexible exchange rates since. At the time, though, it was wage and price controls that created the sensation.

In his speech on Sunday night, August 15, 1971, President Nixon said

> The time has come for decisive action—action that will break the vicious circle of spiraling prices and costs. I am today ordering a freeze on all prices and wages throughout the United States for a period of 90 days.

Prices would be frozen for ninety days. It was hoped that three months of zero inflation would reduce inflationary expectations. Then controls would gradually be lifted in a second phase. If expectations stayed low, inflation would be lower with no cost in unemployment.

The President set up a policy-making body, the Cost of Living Council, headed by Donald Rumsfeld and his deputy, Dick Cheney. Day to day decisions were made by a Price Commission, which eventually employed 700 people. This was much, much smaller than World War II's OPA, but perhaps bigger than the President envisioned.

Inflation was low during the freeze, about 1%. It had been 6% in the three months before August. In November the Price Commission began to administer Phase II, which was a program of gradual decontrol. Phase II may have had some success: in the year before the freeze, inflation had been 4.6%; in the first year of Phase II, it was 3.7%.

As Nixon's free market economists feared, however, the controls created difficulties.

- A trucker had concluded a contract for higher wages with his drivers before the freeze. He had not yet re-negotiated his price with his only customer, a grocery chain, when the freeze was imposed. He asked for an exception to the freeze, claiming he'd go broke paying high wages while charging low prices. The Internal Revenue Service investigated his case and agreed that he probably would go broke. It was early in the freeze, though, and the Cost of Living Council wanted to appear tough. They ruled against the trucker.

- The hay crop was big one year during the price controls. Farmers needed more steel wire to tie up the hay bales. Ordinarily, the price of wire would have risen, signaling steel companies to shift production from other products to wire. But the price could not rise under the controls, and a wire *shortage* developed. A large part of the hay harvest was left in the fields. That, in turn, meant a smaller supply of animal feed, and of beef, than the nation could have had.

- After a while, labor union leaders refused to cooperate with the Price Commission. If it was clear to the union members that their wage increases were set in Washington, they reasoned, what was the justification for having a union, and paying union dues?

- After a while, it became clear that a much larger bureaucracy would be needed to enforce the controls. Most businesses cooperated with the 90-day freeze, but as Phase II wore on lawyers began to search for and find loopholes to evade the controls. The Price Commission would need to match these lawyers with their own if the controls were to continue.

Perhaps most important, the Nixon administration fell into a trap that they'd sworn to avoid. The danger was that with price controls in place, policymakers would feel free to attack unemployment with expansionary fiscal and monetary policies. This added demand would put pressure on the controls system—more employed people working at higher incomes would demand more goods, but with fixed prices businesses would have less incentive to produce more. Shortages would result. This had been the result of many price control episodes around the world, as Nixon's economists knew well.

The Federal Reserve had increased interest rates through most of 1971. Now the Fed began a rapid increase of the money supply. Interest rates fell in the first part of 1972. The economy began to grow faster. GDP increased 4.6%, and the unemployment rate fell to 4.9% by January 1973.

> *The 1971 price controls may have held inflation down for a brief time, but they created shortages. Eventually their effectiveness wore off.*

Arthur Burns' decision to expand in 1972 has been a source of controversy ever since. Richard Nixon won reelection in November 1972 by a landslide. Part of the reason was the favorable economy. Later, in July 1974, as the Watergate scandal reached its peak, an article appeared in *Fortune* magazine accusing Burns of deliberately increasing money growth to aid Nixon's reelection. The writer, Sanford Rose, reported that at an Open Market Committee meeting in late 1971 or early 1972 the committee members appeared to favor tighter money. Burns left the room, then returned to say "I have just talked to the White House." The intimidated committee accepted Burns' position for expansion.

Nixon had appointed Burns to be chair of the Fed with the expectation that he would be loyal. The President had joked "I respect his independence. However, I hope that independently he will conclude that my views are the ones that should be followed." Nixon had in the past told Burns just what kind of monetary policy he wanted. "Err toward inflation," he had insisted in a December 1970 meeting. Burns said that Nixon so often insisted on particular monetary policies that it is possible he made some decisions with a "political tinge."

In 1971 the President became so frustrated with Burns' independence that he had one of his famous dirty tricksters, Charles Colson, circulate a lie about the chairman. Colson told the press that Burns was asking for an increase in his salary while seeking to hold down wage hikes for American workers. But when asked by a reporter, Nixon defended Burns. Burns was grateful to the President for this support. Years later, after Colson became a Christian evangelist, he confessed to the trick and—on his knees—asked for Burns' and God's forgiveness. "He got mine," Burns said.

Everyone at the Fed denied the *Fortune* article report. It contained "not one grain of truth," Burns said. Still, politically motivated or not, in fact monetary policy was expansionary in 1972. The resulting rapid increase in spending torpedoed the strategy behind the wage and price controls. The controls were supposed to reduce inflationary expectations. But as prices pushed against their controlled ceilings, people began to expect that inflation would explode once the controls were eliminated. As 1972 turned into 1973, it was clear that the price control program was in trouble.

OPEC and Oil Prices

The Suez crisis of 1956-57 had closed the Suez Canal. This had reduced the supply of oil and increased its price. When the canal opened again, the price began to fall. This distressed the oil producing counties of the Middle East, in part because oil revenues funded a large part of their government budgets. So, in 1960, these countries and Venezuela combined to form *OPEC*, the *Organization of Petroleum Exporting Countries*. OPEC's main goal, at the start, was to negotiate better terms with the big oil companies. The oil companies had the upper hand because their contracts had been signed during the time when the Middle Eastern countries were colonies of Britain and France. Middle Eastern nationalism was on the rise, especially after the 1967 war between Arab countries and Israel.

The demand for oil was also rising. When the 1967 Six-Day war cut exports for a time, it began to dawn on OPEC that the supply of oil was limited. The developed world's ever-increasing thirst for oil might be used to OPEC's advantage. Then, in 1973, Israel again fought a war with Arab countries. The United States and other western nations supported Israel. OPEC responded by imposing an oil embargo on the United States, cutting off oil exports to the U.S. in October 1973. The price of crude oil nearly tripled; the average price of a gallon of gasoline increased from 36 cents in 1972 to 57 cents by 1975, coincidently a 57% hike.

OPEC was now a *cartel*. A cartel is an organization of countries or firms in a particular industry, which tries to manipulate supply to influence the good's market price. If enough of an industry's output is controlled by the cartel, it can reduce the supply of the

> *The Organization of Petroleum Exporting Countries (OPEC) is a cartel which restricts the supply of oil in order to raise its price.*

good, driving the price up. A cartel can analyze its industry's costs and the demand for its product to adjust supply to make its profits as high as possible. Each member is assigned a share of the restricted output to produce, and thus a share of overall revenue. A cartel's problem is to keep its members in line. It is always profitable for any one member to exceed its output quota—to sell more at the higher price created by the restricted supply. If a large number of cartel members exceed their quotas, though, the overall supply rises enough to reduce the price, and the cartel fails to keep profits high.

OPEC wasn't failing now, and Americans were shocked. The price of gasoline had been stable for many years, near 35 cents a gallon. Now the price was climbing to unimagined heights. Just as bad, there were gasoline shortages. Drivers couldn't be sure that their gas station would have gasoline when they needed it. So, when the station had gasoline to sell, cars lined up for blocks to buy it. The expectation of shortages aggravated the shortages.

Oil supplies had been interrupted before, during the Suez crisis and the Six-Day War, without gasoline shortages. This time, though, there were price controls. The rise in the price of gasoline was restricted by President Nixon's controls. The Cost of Living Council tried to avoid shortages by creating a complex set of rules for price changes. Imported oil could rise in price, domestic oil could not. To encourage more drilling, oil from new wells could rise in price, but oil from existing wells could not. The different oil companies had access to differing amounts of imported, domestic, old and new oil, so more rules were put in place to try to equalize oil company costs.

By the second half of 1973 GDP growth was slowing. By mid-1974 the unemployment rate began rising. Inflation had begun rising at the start of 1973. In 1974 it topped 10%-- double digit inflation. A new term was coined: *stagflation*, for stagnation and inflation at the same time.

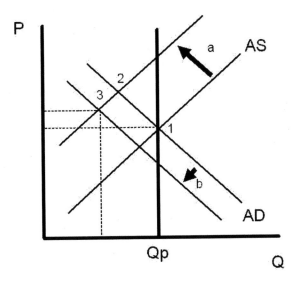

Figure 10-9. Worst of both worlds. A sharp increase in the price of oil increases resource costs. Aggregate supply decreases (a). Stagflation results, a rise in the price level (inflation) and a fall in output (recession) (2). The increased value of oil imports reduces aggregate demand (b), making the recession worse, but not enough to halt inflation (3).

Richard Nixon resigned on August 9, 1974, and Gerald Ford became President. That month the unemployment rate was 5.5%, the inflation rate was 11%. The new President called an Inflation Summit in September, and heard testimony from business people, labor leaders, economists and many others. Then, on October 8, he addressed a joint session of Congress.

The President had decided to adopt policies that people called "the old time religion." Ford asked Congress to limit the coming year's spending, and to enact a five percent tax surcharge on businesses and upper-income taxpayers. These moves would reduce the spending of government, businesses and consumers. He asked consumers to conserve gasoline and food, the goods that had seen the biggest price hikes.

What is most remembered from this speech, however, is his proposal for a big public effort to fight inflation. As the President reached into this pocket, he said

> There will be no big Federal bureaucracy set up for this crash program. Through the courtesy of such volunteers from the communication and media fields, a very simple enlistment form will appear in many of tomorrow's newspapers along with the symbol of this new mobilization, which I am wearing on my lapel.

President Ford brought from his pocket a red button, and hooked it to his jacket. He continued

> It bears the single word WIN. I think that tells it all. I will call upon every American to join in this massive mobilization and stick with it until we do win as a nation and as a people.

"Whip Inflation Now" (WIN) was an incomes policy promoted by President Ford to restrain inflation through voluntary actions by consumers and businesses. It didn't work.

"WIN" stood for "whip inflation now." A few weeks later, he and Mrs. Ford signed a pledge at a White House ceremony. It read, "I pledge to my fellow citizens that I will buy, when possible, only those products and services priced at or below present levels. I also promise to conserve energy and I urge others to sign this pledge."

Whip Inflation Now. Was it nonsense? Or a worthwhile ingenious nostrum.

In his speech Ford had rejected what he called a "politically tempting" return to mandatory price controls. He said that Americans knew the problems they create "from recent experience." A purely voluntary program would not create such problems. But it wasn't a solution either. The WIN buttons and consumer pledges were mostly ignored and widely ridiculed. The effort faded by the end of the year.

So did the "old time religion." The unemployment rate had been edging upward in 1974, but in 1975 it soared. In May 1975 it hit 9%, the highest rate since the Great Depression. The target of policy switched from inflation to unemployment. At the Fed, Arthur Burns had been raising interest rates through most of 1974. Now in 1975 the discount rate was cut almost three points. President Ford reversed course on taxes, and asked Congress for a tax cut.

Double-Digit Inflation

The legacy of the Watergate scandal and stagflation worked against President Ford in the 1976 election. He lost to the former governor of Georgia, Jimmy Carter. Carter remembered later that inflation barely had been mentioned during the campaign. Inflation, Carter said, "was not a burning issue. The only thing was, what are we going to do about jobs." The inflation rate had fallen after the 1973-75 recession, from 13% in October 1974 to 5% in January 1977. Unemployment, on the other hand, was still 7.5%.

So, the new president proposed fiscal policies to stimulate the economy. He proposed a tax rebate for 1977, with a program of spending for public employment to follow in 1978. Congress resisted the tax cuts, and when the economy began to grow more rapidly Carter dropped the tax rebate idea. The jobs program passed, and eventually hundreds of thousands of employees were added to state and local government payrolls, through the *Comprehensive Employment Training Act (CETA)*.

The unemployment rate dropped smartly in 1977 and into 1978, dipping below 6% by summer. Carter's economists had hoped that the economy could approach capacity without adding much to inflation. Instead, the inflation rate began to rise as soon as the new administration took office. By mid-1978 prices were rising by 7.5% per year. Inflation replaced unemployment as the primary economic issue.

The chairman of the Federal Reserve was still Arthur Burns. President Carter respected the independence of the Fed, but he and his team had a hard time getting along with Chairman Burns. In March 1978 his second term was up, and the president appointed a new Fed chair, G. William Miller. Miller was a businessman, the chairman of the board of the Textron Corporation. He tossed out Professor Burns' academic procedures for more businesslike management, even bringing a three-minute egg timer to Open Market Committee meetings, to stop members from making long speeches.

Before the year was out, however, confidence in Miller's management of Fed policy had faded. Yes, the Fed had increased the discount rate six times in 1978, normally a sign that the Fed was trying to restrain spending. But inflation was rising even faster. By October the influential business magazine *Fortune* ran an article titled "Why the Fed is a Flop at Managing Money." It pointed out that "what actually affects the behavior of business and consumers is the *real rate of interest*—the nominal rate minus the expected rate of inflation." In 1974, for example, the Fed jacked up interest rates to 12 percent. But lenders anticipated an inflation rate of more than 10 percent, so "business had every incentive to keep borrowing at what, in many cases, amounted to a zero real rate of interest."

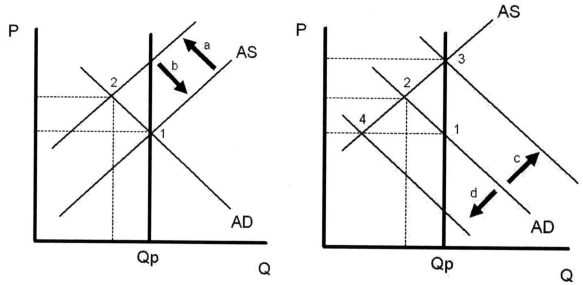

Figure 10-10. Accommodate or not? An oil shock reduces aggregate supply (a), causing inflation and recession (1 to 2). The Federal Reserve has a choice. It can fight recession by increasing the money supply. Interest rates fall and investment increases, increasing aggregate demand (c). The recession ends quickly, but there is even more inflation (2 to 3). It can fight inflation by decreasing the money supply. Interest rates rise and investment decreases, reducing aggregate demand (d). Inflation is brought under control, at the cost of a deeper recession (2 to 4). The price level ends up above (1) only when the Fed increases the money supply. A third choice is to make no policy change. Left alone, with output less than potential, workers and suppliers will accept lower wages and prices (or smaller wage and price increases). Second shift #1 means aggregate supply will increase, eventually (b). The price level falls back to (1), with oil prices up and other prices down. This requires a lengthy period of unemployment, however.

In March 1978, at the end of Burns' term, the federal funds rate was 6.8%, while inflation had averaged 6.6% over the previous 12 months. The real rate was near zero. By the end of Miller's tenure in August 1979, the federal funds rate was up to 10.9%, but inflation was 11.8%. The real interest rate was negative—in effect, lenders were paying borrowers to use their money. For five years, from mid-1974 to mid-1979, the real federal funds rate was negative more often than not. Inflation raced higher, and the Fed followed meekly with interest rate hikes that didn't quite keep up. The Fed, it was said, was always *behind the curve.*

> ***In the second half of the 1970's the Federal Reserve increased interest rates, but inflation rose just as much. Real interest rates were negative. The Fed's inflation-fighting policy was "behind the curve."***

Fortune called Miller "a fainthearted inflation fighter," and this view seemed to be borne out when in November the Open Market Committee voted to increase the discount rate. Miller voted against the increase. No one at the Fed could remember a chairman being outvoted on the committee. When inflation topped double-digits early in 1979, Carter's economic team started to worry about the Fed's ineffective policy. The Secretary of the Treasury, Michael Blumenthal, and the head of the Council of Economic Advisors, Charles Schultz, began to campaign for tighter money. They made speeches and they leaked complaints to the press. Again, no one could remember a time when the President's people wanted the Fed to *raise* interest rates, while the Fed resisted. The *Wall Street Journal* called it a "world turned upside down."

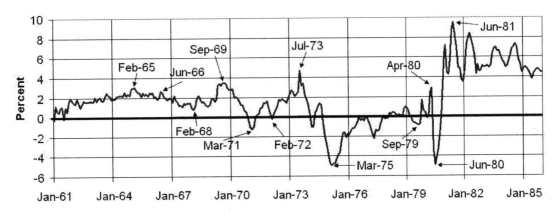

Figure 10-11. Real federal funds rate, monthly, 1961-1985. Calculated as the actual federal funds rate minus the percent change in the Consumer Price Index over the previous 12 months. According to this indicator, monetary policy became tighter from 1961 to 1965. It remained relatively tight through June 1966, then became looser for two years. These two years were a key to the beginning of the Great Inflation. The Fed finally tightened in 1969, then loosened to battle a recession. The sharp dip in the rate in February 1972 is seen by some as evidence for Fed Chair Burns' support of President Nixon's re-election. The rate fell a lot by March 1975 to combat the mid-decade recession. Then, however, it remained negative for four years, meaning inflation was rising faster than the federal funds rate. The Fed was "behind the curve." The rate became positive as Volcker took office at the end of 1979, but dipped sharply with the 1980 recession. Finally, by early 1981, the federal funds rate was jacked up far beyond the inflation rate and remained high. The resulting recession finally beat inflation.

Chairman Miller just laughed. It was a waste of time, he said. President Carter supported an independent Fed, "he's told me so repeatedly." And Miller was right. The President was angry when he realized what his economic team was doing. Schultz remembered later, "we got a very nasty note from the President at one time, in effect saying, lay off."

The price of oil had faded as an issue by the end of 1978. The Organization of Petroleum Exporting Countries (OPEC) cartel managed crude oil prices, and they stayed between $10 and $15 a barrel. The price of gasoline remained around 60 cents a gallon from 1975 to 1978. This was much higher than it had been before 1973, but the public and industry adjusted. Conservation measures were taken. Sales of fuel efficient cars from Japan began to grow.

A 1972 Honda Civic. Honda first exported cars to the U.S. in 1969, and introduced the Civic in 1972. When gasoline prices nearly doubled in 1973, and doubled again in 1979, Americans looked for fuel efficient small cars. Nearly a million Civics were sold from 1973 to 1979.

Then came three events: President Carter negotiated a peace treaty between Israel and Egypt in 1978, called the Camp David Accord. This angered the other Arab nations in the Middle East. Then, Iranian fundamentalists overthrew the Shah of Iran, and the Ayatollah Khomeini assumed power. Iran's oil exports fell during the chaos. Then, in 1980, Iraq invaded Iran, beginning a war that was to last for eight years. Now neither Iraq nor Iran was exporting crude oil, and with two of its members at war, OPEC decision-making was paralyzed.

Prices were first driven up by the drop in supply after the Iranian revolution. Uncertainty about future Iranian supplies caused buyers to stockpile crude oil, increasing demand. Prices rose further. Some Saudi Arabian leaders sought to increase their production enough to offset the price rise. But Arab nations were angry over the Camp David Accord, and the Saudis felt that they had to maintain solidarity with their neighbors. When the Iran-Iraq war started, supply dropped again, and prices rose further. Again OPEC might have increased production to hold prices down, but the organization was so split that it could come to no agreement.

The price of crude oil jumped from $15 a barrel in January 1979 to almost $40 in April 1980. The price of gasoline rose 65 cents a gallon in 1978 to $1.35 a gallon in 1981. The oil and gasoline price controls were still in effect—no one had had the nerve to rescind them in the midst of rising inflation—so again there were shortages and gas lines. Some state governments imposed rationing schemes.

Paul Volcker at the Fed

In the summer of 1979 President Carter retreated to Camp David to consult with experts about the economy. The President came down from the mountain and on July 15 gave his famous "malaise" speech. "The erosion of our confidence in the future is threatening to destroy the social and the political fabric of America," he said. Then he fired his Treasury Secretary, and replaced him with William Miller, who had been appointed chair of the Federal Reserve only 16 months before. That left a hole at the Fed. The President needed a new Fed chair. The new chair had to be someone willing to fight inflation, to somehow push the Fed ahead of the curve. The very mention of his name should restore respect for the Fed.

One name kept surfacing: Paul Volcker, then head of the New York Federal Reserve Bank. He was a balding cigar-smoking six-foot-eight graduate of Princeton (yes, he was on the basketball team). He had been a figure in the world of monetary policy and international finance for two decades. He had been at Treasury in the sixties, desperately trying to defend the Bretton Woods fixed exchange rate system. He had been at Richard Nixon's 1971 Camp David meeting, when the system came crashing down. He was now the head of the New York Federal Reserve Bank, in the heart of the nation's financial district. He was known to be an inflation "hawk."

Volcker was surprised to get the call, and he went down to Washington without expectations. He walked into the Oval Office and sprawled on a couch. He puffed on his cigar and started talking. "Mr. President," he said, "You must understand my concern about the importance of an independent central bank and the need for tighter money—tighter than Bill Miller wants."

Some of Carter's advisors were horrified that Volcker was being considered. The President's Georgia banker friend Bert Lance called an aide. "I want you to tell him something for me. He should not appoint Paul Volcker. If he appoints Volcker, he will be mortgaging his reelection to the Federal Reserve." But Jimmy Carter appointed Paul Volcker chair of the Federal Reserve, and Volcker took office in August 1979.

Within a week he persuaded the Open Market Committee to raise interest rates. The vote in the committee was 4 to 3 in favor of the rate hike. Volcker knew he had the votes to raise rates some more, but the markets saw the close vote as a sign that the Fed would not be tightening again. Perversely, the rate hike probably increased inflationary expectations. It was time, Volcker thought, to find a new policy to "shake up" inflationary psychology.

In making monetary policy, the Fed could target either the money supply or the interest rate. To target the interest rate, the Fed adjusted the supply of money to meet the amount of money demanded. To target the money supply, the interest rate would rise or fall to equate the supply to the amount demanded. The Fed had always targeted interest rates in the past.

Milton Friedman advocated targeting money. In his deep study of the history of money, he found that the Federal Reserve often misinterpreted economic conditions. The Fed would start cutting interest rates too late, just as a recession was turning to recovery. The extra spending would merely promote inflation. The Fed would start raising interest rates too late, just as an expansion was turning to recession. That made recessions worse. The Fed tended to slam on the brakes too hard to stop inflation, stomp on the gas too hard to stop recession. "Stabilization" policy was really just the opposite, pro-cyclical policy that made matters worse.

Better, Friedman said, for the Fed to follow a policy of stable money supply growth. Pick a growth rate near the average rate of growth in GDP, and stick to it through good times and bad. There then would be no sustained inflation, and at least the Fed would not contribute to recessions. The policy was called *monetarism*.

It was Friedman who brought the equation of exchange (and, with velocity fixed, the quantity theory of money) back to economics. His policy prescription is obvious from the equation of exchange,

$$(QM) \times V = P \times Q.$$

Added resources and advancing technology are always increasing potential output. That's Q in the quantity theory of money. If velocity doesn't change, the price level can be held stable by increasing the quantity of money in line with output. So, said Friedman, the Fed should set the growth rate of money equal to the long run growth rate of GDP.

The Fed had always targeted interest rates. It was a "psychological trap," Volcker thought. No one knew for sure how high the federal funds rate had to be. Volcker wrote later

> [It is] a psychological fact of life that the risks almost always seem greater in raising interest rates than in lowering them. After all, no one likes to risk recession, and that is when the political flak ordinarily hits. The corollary is that there is a tendency to make moves, and especially moves to tighten money, only in small increments to "test the waters." That may be all fine and prudent when the prices and expectations are relatively stable. But in the midst of accelerating inflation, what the Fed might think of as prudent probing looked to the rest of the world like ineffectual baby steps.

It was a recipe to put the Fed "behind the curve," Volcker thought, always "reacting too slowly and too mildly only after the evidence was abundantly clear, which by definition was too late." *Targeting the money supply*, on the other hand, offered the Fed several advantages.

There was a tactical advantage. The Fed did not know how high to raise the federal funds rate to fight inflation. It had a better idea about how much the money supply had to grow to keep inflation low. They would set money supply growth, and interest rates would rise just a much as the markets required.

> *The Fed can conduct monetary policy by targeting the interest rate, or by targeting the quantity of money. In 1979 the Fed began targeting the quantity of money, restricting its growth, and interest rates soared.*

There was a political advantage. "It was a camouflage for raising interest rates," said Open Market Committee member Nancy Teeters. The Fed would come under strong attack if it simply announced the very high interest rates required to do the job. Instead they would set money supply growth at a reasonable level, and the markets would increase interest rates.

And, Volcker hoped, there might be a psychological advantage. "People don't need an advanced course in economics to understand that inflation has something to do with too much money," Volcker thought. Announce a money growth target loud and clear—so loud and clear that the Fed could not back off—and the Fed's credibility might be restored. People would understand what the Fed was doing and why, and they would believe the Fed would follow through. Their expectations of future inflation would drop. "We would have a chance of affecting ordinary people's behavior," Volcker thought.

Chairman Volcker called a secret meeting of the Open Market Committee on Saturday, October 6, 1979. Volcker described his idea, and warned committee members that interest rates would be more volatile, and would likely rise a lot. The Committee supported him. Some of the members were eager to go ahead.

That Saturday night Volcker announced their decisions. He announced changes in all three of the Fed's tools, all at once. The *discount rate* would rise by another point. There would be new higher *reserve requirements* on commercial bank deposits. And, most important, the monetarist approach to *open market operations* would be adopted. The money supply would be targeted, and interest rates would rise as they would.

And they did. When the markets opened on Monday, October 8, the federal funds rate was 11.6%. By the end of the day the rate was 13.9%. In two weeks it was 17.6%. But it wasn't a steady rise. The next day the rate dropped to 15.7%, it was 10.9% on November 7, 14.2% on December 10. The federal funds rate was higher and more volatile, just as Volcker had warned. Other interest rates followed suit. The home mortgage rate averaged 11.3% in September. By April it was 16.3%. The monthly payments on a new 30-year mortgage rose by 40%.

Interest rates rose higher than Volcker had thought they would, yet the inflation rate did not come down. It was 12.2% in September 1979, 14.8% in April 1980. This was partly the result of rising oil prices, but the hoped-for psychological impact on inflationary expectations never appeared. "We soon learned that any dreams we might have had of changing public expectations by the force of our own convictions were just that—dreams," Volcker said.

Credit Controls and Recession

President Carter refused to criticize Volcker's policies. The Carter administration was working on its own anti-inflation policies, and they needed the Fed's cooperation. They would attempt to reduce both public and private spending. The President planned to submit a new budget to Congress with significant spending cuts. The budget would be close to balanced in fiscal 1981. Carter intended to reduce private spending with a new energy tax. And, he would impose *credit controls*. A law passed in 1969 allowed the President to authorize the Federal Reserve to restrict borrowing by consumers.

Volcker was against credit controls, but he felt he had to support the President. Carter had refrained from criticizing high interest rates, and was about to propose spending cuts, as Volcker had urged. In return, he was asking that the Fed respect his judgment that credit controls were needed, both to restrain spending and convey a sense of urgency to the public. "I found it impossible to resist," he said later. The controls were mostly symbolic, anyway. They did not apply to mortgage or auto loans. It was effectively "a tax on credit cards."

President Carter announced the new policies the afternoon of March 14, 1980. The response was extraordinary. Charles Schultze described it later.

> What happened was absolutely fascinating. We got the steepest decline in GNP in one quarter in our history, I would guess. Something nobody could ever figure out in advance. The American people felt guilty about using credit, I'm convinced, and as soon as the President said something about credit, they didn't bother to read the regulations, or what they meant. They were actually very mild, but the public just stopped using credit. We had merchants calling in to complain that all their customers thought that the President declared consumer credit illegal, immoral, unpatriotic. There were huge temporary drops in appliance sales. It had an incredible impact on real demand.

Some consumers cut up their credit cards and mailed them to the White House with letters saying "Mr. President, we will cooperate." Real GDP dropped at an annual rate of almost 8% in the second quarter of 1980. It was the second worst quarter for GDP in the second half of the twentieth century. The economy plunged into recession.

It made a mess of the Fed's new monetary policy. Consumers stopped spending, using their bank balances to pay off their credit card debt instead. Bank balances declined, and since such balances are a big part of the money supply, so did the measure of the quantity of money which the Fed was trying to hold steady. Now, instead of having to restrain money growth, the Fed had to push it up. It bought Treasury bonds to increase bank reserves. The federal funds rate dropped from 17.6% in April to 9% in July. The Fed quietly ended the consumer credit controls that summer.

Consumer guilt wore off quickly, and the decline in interest rates made buying more attractive. By August the economy was growing just as fast as it had declined. It had been a short, sharp recession. Too short, as it turned out, to reduce inflation much. The inflation rate remained above 12% for the rest of the year.

By late summer the Fed realized that the recession was over. Inflation had not been smashed, or even dented. But by now the Presidential election campaign was on in earnest. Frederick Schultz, vice chair of Fed, said that "our attitude toward the election is that we'd like to dig a foxhole and crawl in until it's over." This was especially true after the accusations that Arthur Burns had pumped up the money supply to aid Richard Nixon's reelection in 1972. The federal funds rate crept upward during the campaign, but only to 12.8% by October. The real federal funds rate was just about zero.

Jimmy Carter was fighting for his political life against the Republican nominee, Ronald Reagan. In the twentieth century only Herbert Hoover ran for reelection in a tougher economic environment. Yet, said Charles Schultze, "Jimmy Carter would never have let us attack the Fed strongly in the last days of the campaign." Carter himself slipped just once, a month before election day, saying "I think they put too [many] of their eggs in the money supply basket." Pretty mild from a desperate President! Ronald Reagan was elected in November.

The Great Recession of 1981-82
"It was in a way a mostly wasted year restoring credibility in the attack on inflation," Volcker recalled later about 1980. But now that the election was out of the way, he and the Fed resolved to renew the attack. The federal funds rate was 12.8% in October, with a real rate near zero. By January, as Ronald Reagan gave his inaugural address, the federal funds rate was 18.9%, and the real rate was about 7%. The federal funds rate would remain above ten percent for the next year and a half.

The recovery ended after only one year. This new recession would be sharp, but not short. It is marked from July 1981 to November 1982. At 16 months it was the longest recession since the Great Depression (to that time). It was a "double-dip," a second recession almost on top of a first. The economy was in recession for 22 of 34 months from 1980 through 1982.

The unemployment rate remained above 10% for ten straight months in 1982 and 1983, topping out at 10.8% in December 1982. It was, again, the highest unemployment rate since the Depression. Unemployment in the Midwestern "rust belt" soared. The unemployment rate topped 10% for 27 straight months in Indiana, peaking at 12.4%.

The home mortgage interest rate hit 18.5% in October 1981. People built and bought many fewer houses. "For a while my office was deluged with sawed-off wooden two-by-fours in a campaign organized by homebuilders to lower interest rates and stimulate their business," Volcker remembered. Farmers blockaded Fed headquarters with their tractors for a day to protest high interest rates.

The Reagan administration supported the Fed's tight money policy. Many Reagan economic officials were monetarists themselves, who applauded the Fed's conversion to their way of thinking. Non-monetarists recognized that the administration's big tax cuts could require strong efforts to restrain inflation. David Stockman, the budget director, told his colleagues that the Fed was "the critical linchpin of the whole program."

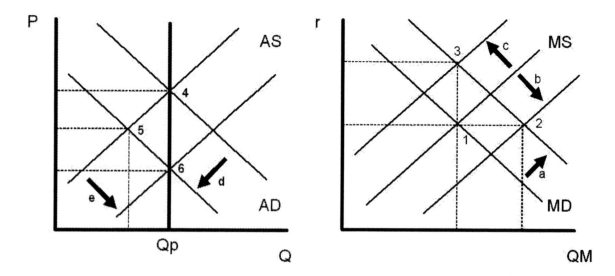

Figure 10-12. Volcker. Money demand rises fast because of continuing inflation (a). The Fed under Burns and Miller accommodated inflation by raising the money supply (b) to hold real interest rates down (2). As Fed Chair, Paul Volcker reduced the growth of the money supply. Here the quantity of money (QM) is held constant at points 1 and 3 by a reduction in the money supply (c). Interest rates rise as the demand for money requires (3). Second shift #2 reduced investment spending, and aggregate demand (d). Output fell below potential, a recession (4 to 5). The long, deep recession eventually convinced workers and suppliers to moderate their inflationary expectations, until they were willing to accept lower wages and prices for the sake of employment and sales. That's second shift #1. Aggregate supply increased (e), ending the recession and reducing inflation (shown here as a fall in the price level, 5 to 6).

As the economy sank deeper, however, a few cracks in administration support appeared. A Treasury official declared that "the administration had no idea that the Federal Reserve was about to slam on the brakes and throw us all through the windshield." Members of

Congress joined in the criticism. Representative Henry Reuss, chair of the Joint Economic Committee, threatened "political dismemberment of the Federal Reserve System." Democrat James Wright and Republican Jack Kemp both called for Volcker's resignation. Senator Edward Kennedy suggested a return to credit controls. Representative Kemp suggested a return to the gold standard.

Two things saved Paul Volcker's policy. President Ronald Reagan never wavered in his support for the Fed's independence. And, most important, Volcker's strategy was working. Inflation remained above 10% through the end of 1981. Then it started to drop. In January 1982 it was 8.4%. By July, 6.4%. And in December, 3.8%. The inflation rate had not been so low since January 1973.

> *The Great Recession of 1981-82 was the result of the Federal Reserve's efforts to bring down inflation. It worked, but at great cost in high unemployment and lost output.*

By mid-1982 Volcker thought it was time to ease off the monetary brakes. On October 7, 1982, the Open Market Committee voted to reduce interest rates, and Volcker announced that the Fed would "de-emphasize" the money supply targeting approach to policy.

Money supply targeting was abandoned partly because it turned out to be hard to measure the money supply week to week and month to month. It was abandoned partly because the Fed wanted more flexibility in policy making. And it was abandoned partly because the fight against inflation had been won. The monetarist approach served an important purpose, providing political cover when interest rates had to be raised to record heights. But Volcker was never a committed monetarist, and he thought that following such a rigid rule would sometimes lead to unacceptable policies.

Milton Friedman and the monetarists predicted that the end of targeting would mean a return to inflation. It didn't. The Fed had discovered its anti-inflation mission, and gained anti-inflation credibility. Since 1982 the annual inflation rate has topped 5% only once.

What Caused the Great Inflation?
By 1985 the Great Inflation was over, but at great cost in unemployment and lost output. To avoid a reoccurrence, we need to know: what caused the Great Inflation?

Sustained inflation is impossible without a too-rapid rise in the money supply, beyond growth in potential output. Inflation is caused by too much money chasing too few goods, just as much in the 1960's as in the 1860's.

But this is too simple an answer. Why did inflation-fighters like Fed chairs William McChesney Martin and Arthur Burns allow the money supply to rise so fast? Martin, for one, held inflation in check during the 1950's. The Kennedy administration thought he kept money too tight. Why the change during the '60's?

The answer lies in the problems and priorities that the President, the Federal budget, and the rest of the economy present to the Fed. In the 1950's the Truman administration paid for the Korean War with taxes. Military spending rose but consumer spending fell. The Fed did not have to make a choice between allowing inflation or risking recession.

In the 1950's President Eisenhower was very concerned about inflation. He was willing to run a budget surplus to try to restrain it. Chairman Martin was encouraged to follow suit with tight money, and he did. Here the Fed did risk recession to restrain inflation, but it had a popular President as a supportive partner.

In the 1960's, though, the Johnson administration followed through with the Kennedy tax cuts, then increased spending on war and social programs. The budget fell into deficit. This increased government and consumer spending, after output had reached potential. The Fed now had a choice: allow the expansion to continue at the risk of inflation, or raise interest rates to restrain spending and risk recession. Martin chose to raise interest rates in 1966. Growth slowed, unemployment edged upward, and inflation stopped rising.

But unlike Eisenhower, Lyndon Johnson did not see inflation as problem number one. Where Eisenhower sought a budget surplus, Johnson accepted a budget deficit. Fed chair Martin and Johnson's economists pressed him to raise taxes to restrain spending, but Johnson's political instincts told him that a tax hike would threaten his social programs and support for the Vietnam War. Martin made an implicit deal with Johnson, to cut interest rates if he would support a tax hike. Johnson announced his support in early 1967, but the tax was not enacted until mid-1968, and did not turn out to be effective in restraining spending. Meanwhile, Martin kept interest rates too low. Inflation increased.

Then came the oil shocks in 1973-74 and 1979-80. Stagflation was the result. Again, the Fed was faced with a difficult choice. It could have resisted inflation by reducing money supply growth, but this would have made the recession worse. It could have resisted recession by increasing money supply growth, but this would have made inflation worse. For the most part, the Fed chose to fight recession. Inflation got worse.

The Fed fell "behind the curve" in the second half of the 1970's. Yes, it increased interest rates to try to restrain inflation, but the inflation rate was rising faster. *Real* interest rates remained very low. By the end of the decade even the President's Secretary of the Treasury was lobbying the Fed to raise rates faster, surely the only such period in history.

The Fed doesn't increase the money supply too rapidly without a reason. In the 1950's there was no reason to do so. In the 1960's and 1970's there was. Tax cuts, war spending, spending on social programs, Federal budget deficits, oil shocks, Presidential pressure *and* the Fed's accommodating response caused the Great Inflation.

What stopped the Great Inflation? Not incomes policies, price controls, nor "WIN" campaigns. Recessions bring down inflation. This probably was clear to policymakers in the 1970's. The 1970 recession brought the inflation rate down from 5.7% to 3.2%. The 1973-75 recession brought in the inflation rate down from 11.0% to 5.8%. But in both cases policymakers responded to recession with expansionary fiscal and monetary policies, and inflation soon returned.

In the Great Recession of 1981-82, the Federal Reserve did not attack rising unemployment with expansionary monetary policy. Instead, it held real interest rates high throughout the first half of the 1980's. The inflation rate fell from 13.5% to 3.2%, and remained under 5% until 1990. The lesson: to beat inflation, have a recession. To beat the Great Inflation, have a Great Recession.

MacroPolicy Now: Two Great Recessions

We called the long, deep recession of 1981-82 "The Great Recession." It was the worst downturn since the Great Depression. We called the long deep recession of 2007-09 "The Great Recession." Perhaps it was the worst downturn since the Great Depression. It was definitely the worst since 1981-82.

How do the two Great Recessions compare?

They are very different. Let's mark the peaks of each expansion, which are the starts of each recession. The peak at the start of the first Great Recession was July 1981; the peak at the start of the second Great Recession was December 2007. In 1981 the core inflation rate for the previous 12 months was 11.1% and the unemployment rate was 7.2%. In 2007 the core inflation rate was 2.4% and the unemployment rate was 5.0%.

The unemployment rate was too high in 1981 (there had been a recession in 1980), but inflation was seen as the primary problem. A reason for the inflation had been the Federal Reserve's unwillingness to raise interest rates enough to get "ahead of the curve." The real federal funds rate the year before, in July 1980, had been -3.3%. The inflation rate exceeded the federal funds rate. In effect, lenders were paying borrowers to borrow their money. This was an incentive to borrow and spend. Real interest rates had been negative for several years, and this had contributed to the Great Inflation.

In the year before the recession began, the Fed radically increased the real federal funds rate. It rose from -3.3% to 9.7% in June 1981. This spectacular increase choked off borrowing and spending, reduced aggregate demand, and caused a deep recession. The point was to reduce inflation. It worked. By November 1984, 40 months from the peak, the inflation rate was down to 4.8% and it was still falling.

Inflation was not a problem in December 2007, and neither was unemployment. The problem was the bursting of the housing bubble, and, in another year, the financial panic of 2008. The Fed responded with reductions in the real federal funds rate, from 2.6% in December 2006, one year before the peak, to -1.6% in December 2008, one year after the peak.

In 1981-82 the Fed caused the recession. In 2007-09 the Fed fought the recession.

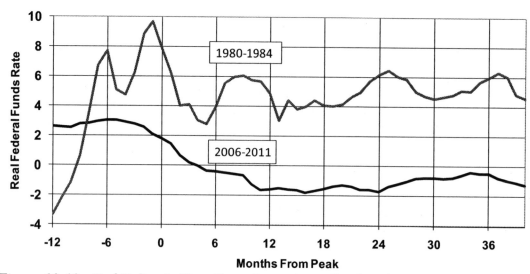

Figure 10-13. Fed Policy in Two Great Recessions. Real Federal Funds Rate, monthly, July 1980-December 1984 and December 2006 to April 2011. The month marked zero is the month of the business cycle peak, that is, the beginning of the recession. The dates are July 1981 and December 2007. The year before the peak is shown, as are the 40 months after the peak. The Fed increased the real federal funds rate radically before the 1981-82 recession, from about -3% to nearly 10%. In 1981-82 the Fed was holding the economy back to fight inflation. In 2007-09 the Fed was trying to stimulate the economy, to lessen the effects of recession.

How do the recoveries compare? Again, they are very different. Let's look 40 months after each peak. That's November 1984, and April 2011. In 1984 the unemployment rate had dropped to 7.2% from a peak of 10.8%, a 3.6 point drop. (That helped President Reagan get re-elected that month.) In 2011 the unemployment rate was 9.0 down from a peak of 10.1%, a 1.1 point drop. Real GDP had grown 5.6% over the previous year by the fourth quarter of 1984. In the year to the first quarter of 2011, it had grown 2.3%.

Forty months after the peak, the economy had taken off from the 1981-82 recession. The recovery was still "iffy" in 2011.

Perhaps the reasons for the slow recovery by 2011 were temporary, soon to be reversed. Oil prices were a greater problem in 2011 than in 1984. The real price of crude oil (in 1982-84 dollars) was $26 in November 1984. It had been falling since 1980. The price was $49 in April 2011. It had been rising since 2009. Since most crude oil is imported, the increase in the cost of oil means an increase in spending on imports, which subtracts from aggregate demand. Oil is an important input to the production of almost everything (think of energy, chemicals, plastics, fertilizer and the transportation of any product to market). Rising costs cut business profits and reduced the incentive for new hiring.

Was this a temporary problem? Just three years before, in 2008, oil prices had spiked upward, only to drop just as fast in 2009. And, in May, oil prices did take a sudden plunge before stabilizing, still at high levels. If the crisis in Libya reached a settlement, or if OPEC decided to increase production, the price of oil could plunge again. On the other hand, rapid growth in the developing world, especially China, may represent a permanent increase in oil demand and prices.

The March 11, 2011 earthquake and tsunami in Japan, and the subsequent radiation problems in many nuclear power plants, reduced production of auto parts and other supplies from Japanese factories. American auto companies had trouble getting parts, and this slowed production and inhibited hiring. Ironically, American auto companies were affected just as much as Japanese companies. Mazda's factories recovered quickly. The Ford Focus was in short supply because its transmission came from a damaged Japanese factory.

Parts are inputs to production, and a scarcity of parts represents a supply shock. The recovery in 1984 faced no similar problem. This probably is a temporary problem, since Japanese factories will resume production or companies will find alternate sources of supply.

But as Summers, and Reinhart and Rogoff noted, recovery from financial crises usually takes longer than other recoveries. The 2007-09 recession was caused by a financial crisis. The 1981-82 recession was not.

We can see the difference in financial indicators. Consumer debt as a percentage of income was 16.2% in the fourth quarter of 1984, and rising. Consumers and lenders felt confident enough to lend and borrow, and this increased spending. The percentage was 16.6% in the fourth quarter of 2010, and falling. Consumers were decreasing their borrowing. Perhaps they were not yet confident enough in their job prospects to increase their borrowing. Perhaps lenders were not yet confident enough in the prospects for repayment to increase their lending.

A crash in the housing market kicked off the 2007-09 recession. Housing starts in November 1984 were 1.7 million at an annual rate. That was double the low point of the recession. Housing starts in April 2011 were 523 thousand, near the low-point of the recession. Housing construction remained in deep trouble. The typical home sold in 4.7 months in November 1984. It took 8.8 months in April 2011. It was tough to sell a house—so there was not much reason to build more.

The Fed fought the recession in 2007-09. Its massive increase in the monetary base probably prevented a much deeper financial crisis. But its second round of "quantitative easing," QE2, seems to have been less successful. The program is ending as of summer 2011.

Could it be that Fed policy is more successful bringing down growth, as it did in 1981-82, than it is in supporting growth, as was tried after 2007-09? If interest rates are high

338

enough, they can cut off borrowing and spending, no matter how optimistic consumers and businesses might be. But nominal interest rates can only approach zero, and real interest rates can only be negative if inflation is high. In 2001, it's not that high. If consumers and businesses are pessimistic, if they have debts to repay and excess inventories to sell off, it's possible that interest rates cannot be set low enough to encourage much spending.

We may be in for a long, slow recovery.

Terms in this Chapter, in order of appearance
The Great Inflation
Deflation
Safety net
Keynesian economics
Structural unemployment
Cyclical unemployment
James Tobin
Fiscal drag
Okun's Law
Income multiplier
Kennedy tax cut
The Great Society
The Vietnam War
Guns and butter
Tax surcharge
The Phillips Curve
Inflation-unemployment tradeoff
Monetarists
Expectations
Permanent income
Inflationary expectations
Natural rate of unemployment
Expectations augmented Phillips Curve
Incomes policy
Price controls
Shortages
Organization of Petroleum Exporting Countries (OPEC)
Cartel
Stagflation
Whip Inflation Now (WIN)
Double-digit inflation
Comprehensive Employment Training Act (CETA)
Real interest rate
Behind the curve
Paul Volcker

Monetarism
Discount rate
Reserve requirements
Open market operations
Money supply targeting
Credit controls
The Great Recession, 1981-82
Monetary base
Japanese deflation

Notes

The story of Martin, Johnson and the December 1965 discount rate hike is told in Hargrove and Morley (1984, pp. 248-249), Kettl (1986, p.104) and Califano (2000, pp. 106-109).

Two of Kennedy's economists, Solow and Tobin (1988, p.6), say that Kennedy had no fixed economic ideas when he took office. Heller describes the economic education of President Kennedy in Hargrove and Morley (p.175). Kettl (p. 98), Solow and Tobin (pp. 8-9) and Hargrove and Morley (p.168) describe Heller's and Martin's views of the structural vs. cyclical unemployment question. Stein (1996, pp. 379-384), Heller's piece in Hargrove and Morley (p. 196) and Solow and Tobin (pp. 10-11) catalogue Galbraith, Tobin and Heller's views on expansionary policy.

The GDP gap, Okun's Law, multiplier calculation is based on a 1961 essay by the Council of Economic Advisors, published in Tobin and Weidenbaum (1988, pp. 29, 58-59). Prior to about 1990, policy debates like this used Gross National Product (GNP), not Gross Domestic Product (GDP). I've used GDP throughout this book, for consistency.

Kennedy's speech to the Economic Club of New York is available on the internet at www.presidency.ucsb.edu/site/docs/pppusyear.php?yearindex=1962. Heller tells the story of lobbying for the Kennedy tax cut, describes Kennedy's strategy of persuasion in Hargrove and Morley (pp. 205-209). Hargrove and Morley (pp. 169) describe Kennedy's interest in poverty.

Heller (Hargrove and Morley, pp.209-211) talked about the transition to the Johnson administration, and his negotiations with Senator Byrd. Heller also describes Johnson's skills at making deals (p. 181). President Johnson's speeches are available on the web at www.presidency.ucsb.edu/site/docs/index_pppus.php. Dallek (1998, p. 72) offers the "pee one drop" quote.

Joseph Califano's memoir of his years on Johnson's staff is an excellent source of policy details. He calculates that the administration passed 181 of 200 bills in 1965 and 1966 (Califano 2000, p. 149). Gardner Ackley notes that the Great Society programs were Johnson's babies (Hargrove and Morley, p. 247)

Ackley in Hargrove and Morley (pp. 247-249), Okun in Hargrove and Morley (pp. 293-95), Kettl (pp. 103-105) and Califano (pp. 106-109) tell the story of Fed chair Martin's response to the added spending required by Vietnam in 1965. Ackley describes Johnson's reaction to the Fed's tight monetary policy (pp. 232-238). Kettl describes the dance between Johnson and Martin over the tax surcharge and looser monetary policy (pp.107-109). Arthur Okun in Hargrove and Morley (pp. 305-306) and Califano (pp. 284-288) discuss the legislative battle to pass the tax surcharge.

Okun in Hargrove and Morley (pp. 306-308) talks about the failure of the tax surcharge to restrain growth or inflation. Solow and Tobin (p.15) report that the Kennedy-Johnson economists were using the Phillips Curve. Milton Friedman's speech to the AEA convention is in Friedman (1968).

The story of Volcker's appointment and his new policies is told by the man himself in Volcker's memoir with Toyoo Gyohten (1992, pp. 163-170), in Mussa (1994, pp. 95-97) and in Biven (2002, 237-244).

Stein (1994, pp. 139-143) and McCracken in Hargrove and Morley (1984, pp. 340-344) describe policy at the beginning of the Nixon administration. McCracken in Hargrove and Morley (p. 345) mentions Nixon's interest in a dramatic "long bomb" policy change. Stein (pp. 104-105) and Heller and Ackley in Hargrove and Morley (pp. 166-168, pp. 259-263) describe price guideposts during the Kennedy and Johnson years. Arthur Burns' support for wage and price controls is described by Kettl (pp. 122-123), in Stein's piece in Hargrove and Morley (pp. 376-378) and by Stein (1994, pp. 154-156). Wells (1994, p. 57) reports that Milton Friedman felt betrayed.

Wicker (1991, pp. 552-560), Stein (1994, pp. 166-168, 176-187), McCracken in Hargrove and Morley (pp. 344-57), Stein in Hargove and Morley (pp. 390-401), and Safire (1975, pp. 659-686) tell the story of the wage and price controls and its problems. The story of the baling wire is from Sterba (1973).

Sources for Burns' alleged support of Nixon's reelection through loose monetary policy in 1972 are the original Rose article (1974), Wicker (pp. 563-564), and Kettl (p. 116). The Charles Colson dirty trick story is told in detail in Safire (pp. 634-641), and in Wicker (pp. 563-64), Wells (1994, pp. 100-101), and Kettl (pp. 113-114).

Skeet (1988) provides a history of OPEC. The formation of OPEC is covered on pages 15-34, the first oil crisis on pages 99-123, and the second oil crisis on pages 157-177. Stein (pp. 190-193) and Stein in Hargrove and Morley (pp. 403-405) describe the interaction of the oil embargo and the price controls. Stein (p.186) gives Nixon's frozen river quote.

Stein (pp. 213-216) describes Ford's economic policies, including the WIN buttons. Greenspan in Hargrove and Morley (pp. 440-458) discusses his time at Ford's economic advisor. Ford's speeches are available on the internet, at http://www.presidency.ucsb.edu/site/docs/index_pppus.php.

Biven (2002) provides an excellent study of Jimmy Carter's economic policies. He mentions Carter's recollection that inflation had not been a 1976 campaign issue (p.85). Biven (pp. 69-83) and Hargrove and Morley (pp. 476-481) discuss the Carter stimulus package of 1977.

Kettl covers the Miller Fed and mentions Miller's egg timer (p. 169). The October 1978 *Fortune* article was by Arthur Burns' old nemesis Sanford Rose. The phrase "behind the curve" to describe Fed policy in the late 1970s appears in many sources, such as Mussa (p. 92) and Volcker and Gyohten (pp. 165-166). Kettl (pp. 169-170) and Hargrove and Morley (p. 485-486) tell the story of the administration's campaign for higher rates, and Carter's angry reaction.

Kettl sketches Volcker's biography (pp. 172-73). Volcker's quotes on the psychological trap and being behind the curve are from Volcker and Gyohten (p.166). Mussa (pp. 96-97) catalogues the tactical, political and psychological advantages of targeting money growth. The Teeters quote is in Kettl (p.177). Volcker's "dreams" quote is from Volcker and Gyohten (p. 170).

Carter's support of the Fed's independence comes from Biven (p. 244-45) and Volcker and Gyohten (p.169). Schultze's disagreement with the monetarist approach but agreement with high interest rates are in Hargrove and Morley (p. 486) and Volcker and Gyohten (p. 168-169). Volcker describes why he felt he had to support Carter's credit controls in Volcker and Gyohten (pp. 171-172). He called them a tax on credit cards in Volcker (p. 147). Schultze's description of the response to credit controls is from Hargrove and Morley (p. 494). The story about the cut-up credit cards is in Volcker and Gyohten (p. 173).

Charles Schultz is quoted in Mussa (p. 103). The Schultze quote on criticizing the Fed during the campaign is in Hargrove and Morley (p. 499). Kettl has the quote from Carter, (p. 179), and interprets it as a stronger statement than it seems to this author. Volcker called 1980 a wasted year in the inflation fight in Volcker (1994, p. 148). He remembers the two-by-fours in Volcker and Gyohten (p. 176). Kettl mentions both the homebuilder and farmer protests (p. 187). The criticisms of the Fed from the Reagan administration and Congress are from Kettl (pp. 180-181). Kettl describes the decision to back away from money targeting (pp.183-184).

Sources
Biven, W. Carl. 2002. *Jimmy Carter's Economy: Policy in an Age of Limits.* Chapel Hill, N.C.: University of North Carolina Press.

Califano, Joseph A., Jr. 2000. *The Triumph and Tragedy of Lyndon Johnson.* College Station, Texas: Texas A&M University Press.

Dallek, Robert. 1998. *Flawed Giant: Lyndon Johnson and his Times, 1961-1973.* New York: Oxford University Press.

Friedman, Milton. 1968. "The Role of Monetary Policy" *American Economic Review* 58 (March): 1-17.

Hargrove, Erwin C. and Samuel A. Morley (eds.). 1984. *The President and the Council of Economic Advisors: Interviews with CEA Chairmen.* Boulder, Colorado: Westview Press.

Kettl, Donald F. 1986. *Leadership at the Fed.* New Haven: Yale University Press.

Mussa, Michael. 1994. "Monetary Policy," Pages 81-145 in Martin Feldstein, *American Economic Policy in the 1980s.* Chicago: University of Chicago Press.

Reinhart, Carmen M. and Kenneth Rogoff. *This Time Is Different: Eight Centuries of Financial Folly.* Princeton, New Jersey: Princeton University Press, 2009.

Rose, Sanford. 1974. "The Agony of the Federal Reserve," *Fortune* 90 (July): 91-93.

Rose, Sanford. 1978. "Why the Fed is a Flop at Managing Money." *Fortune* 98 (October): 53-68.

Safire, William. 1975. *Before the Fall.* New York: Ballantine Books.

Schlesinger, Arthur M. 1965. *A Thousand Days.* Boston: Little, Brown and Co.

Skeet, Ian. 1988. *OPEC: Twenty-Five Years of Prices and Politics.* Cambridge, U.K.: Cambridge University Press.

Solow, Robert M. and James Tobin. 1988. "Introduction: The Kennedy Economic Reports." Pages 3-16 in James Tobin and Murray Weidenbaum, *Two Revolutions in Economic Policy.* Cambridge, Massachusetts: The MIT Press.

Stein, Herbert. 1994. *Presidential Economics (3rd Revised Edition).* Washington, D.C.: The AEI Press.

Stein, Herbert. 1996. *The Fiscal Revolution in America (2nd Revised Edition).* Washington, D.C.: The AEI Press.

Volcker, Paul A. 1994. "Monetary Policy." Pages 145-151 in Martin Feldstein, *American Economic Policy in the 1980s.* Chicago: University of Chicago Press.

Volcker, Paul A. and Toyoo Gyohten. 1992. *Changing Fortunes.* New York: Times Books.

Wells, Wyatt C. 1994. *An Economist in an Uncertain World: Arthur F. Burns and the Federal Reserve, 1970-1978.* New York: Columbia University Press.

Wicker, Tom. 1991. *One of Us: Richard Nixon and the American Dream.* New York: Random House.

News Articles
Chan, Sewell. "Bankers Told Recovery May Be Slow," *New York Times*, August 28, 2010.

Krauss, Clifford. "Spilt by infighting, OPEC Keeps a Cap on Oil," *New York Times*, June 8, 2011.

Rampell, Catherine. "Hiring in U.S. Slowed in May With 54,000 Jobs Added," *New York Times*, June 3, 2011.

Summers, Lawrence. "How to Avoid a Lost Decade," *Washington Post*, June 12, 2011.

Chapter 11
Deficits

MacroPolicy Now: Deficits and Debt

In Washington D.C., a city full of pompous politicians and bombastic bureaucrats, Van Zeck quietly runs one of the government's truly indispensable operations. He is not a policy maker. He does not decide how much to borrow. He just makes sure the money is borrowed, in a regular and predictable way, at the lowest possible cost to the government over time.

In 2010 alone, Mr. Zeck auctioned off approximately $8 trillion of Treasury securities, to replace maturing debt and to meet new borrowing needs. That's an average of more than $400,000 every second.

The Federal government runs a deficit when its spending exceeds its revenues. It borrows the difference. The Congressional Budget Office estimates that the deficit will be $1.5 trillion in 2011, about 9.8% of GDP. Recent deficits relative to the economy's size have been the highest since World War II. The Federal debt is the accumulated borrowing since the nation's founding, less the few surpluses it has run. Since the deficits are so large, the debt is accumulating rapidly. Under the president's budget the federal debt held by the public will grow rapidly compared with the size of the economy -- rising to 69% of gross domestic product in 2011 and 75% in 2015, from 53% in 2009.

Federal Reserve Chair Ben Bernanke has weighed in on the deficit. "Policy makers urgently need to put the federal governments' finances on a sustainable trajectory," he said in June 2011. He cautioned that large spending cuts should not be imposed immediately, but that a plan could produce immediate benefits "by leading to lower long-term interest rates and increased consumer and business confidence."

At an earlier hearing, Bernanke pointed out that huge long-term deficits could not be sustained. "In order to maintain a stable ratio of debt-to-G.D.P., you need to have a deficit that's 2 ½, 3 percent at the most," he said referring to the gross domestic product. Future deficits, which government agencies estimate at from 4 percent to 7 percent of G.D.P., are unsustainable, Mr. Bernanke said.

This implies that actually balancing the budget is not needed. Because of technological progress, population growth and inflation, the nation's income and tax base grows over time. If the government's debts grow at or below that pace, paying interest on the debt will not become a major problem. That means the government can run budget deficits in perpetuity, as long as they are not too large. A deficit of less than 3 percent of GDP will

not increase the debt relative to GDP. Bigger deficits—like those projected for the coming decade—will increase the debt ratio.

Bigger deficits could result in higher interest rates. Donald L. Kohn, vice chairman of the Federal Reserve, said: "Unless the trajectory is changed, the competition for savings between the government, on the one hand, and households and businesses, on the other, could be significant as households and businesses begin to borrow and spend in the recovery, putting upward pressure on interest rates."

Instead of interest rate increases, big deficits could result in inflation. Thomas M. Hoenig, president of the Federal Reserve Bank of Kansas City, warned that in the worst case, the Fed could face pressure to inflate the nation's way out of its indebtedness. "It seems inevitable that a government turns to its central bank to bridge budget shortfalls, with the result being too-rapid money creation and eventually, but not immediately, high inflation. Such outcomes require either a cooperative central bank or an infringement on its independence."

The Standard and Poors bond rating agency fired a warning shot across the government's bow in April 2011. The agency lowered its outlook on the United States bond rating to negative. They didn't reduce the actual bond rating, which remained at AAA, the highest possible rating indicating the least-risky debt. It was a warning that without policy change, that AAA rating could be in danger. Treasury bond interest rates spiked immediately after the announcement.

In May and June, though, Treasury interest rates dropped to near record lows. The Federal government has had no trouble selling its bonds. Federal officials have been pleasantly surprised to see the demand for Treasury securities keep pace with the growing supply. Invariably, they get "coverage," meaning that the bids exceed the amount of securities being offered — a great relief to federal money managers.

Foreign investors have generally shown a strong appetite for federal debt. China, the largest foreign holder of Treasury securities, sent a chill through credit markets early in 2010 when its prime minister said he was "a little bit worried" about China's investments in the United States. The Treasury secretary, Timothy F. Geithner, quickly assured the Chinese that their assets were "very safe" here.

With rising deficits, Treasury auctions have become larger and more frequent. The auction calendar is extremely crowded. On almost every work day, the Treasury is announcing, conducting or settling auctions. When Mr. Zeck tells people he works at the Bureau of the Public Debt, he said, they often quip, "You will have work forever."

In 2011, the Federal government's budget deficit is huge. It's expected to remain huge for some time to come. The national debt will increase, a lot. Is this a problem? Maybe, if it increases interest rates or causes inflation. We've run big deficits before. Here's what happened back then. . . .

The Laffer Curve

According to legend, it began on a napkin. On December 4, 1974, at the Two Continents restaurant in Washington, D.C., economist Arthur Laffer had dinner with two companions. They were Jude Wanniski, an editor at the *Wall Street Journal*, and Dick Cheney, a member of the Ford administration. Talk turned to the budget problems faced by the new administration. The budget was in deficit, and Wanniski and Cheney supposed that a tax increase would be needed.

A tax increase can *reduce* tax revenue, Laffer told them. Cheney and Wanniski were mystified. Laffer grabbed a cocktail napkin and sketched a diagram. He drew a vertical axis and labeled it "Income tax revenue." He drew a horizontal axis and labeled it "income tax rate," and he drew a half-moon shaped curve.

How much revenue would the government raise if the tax rate was zero? he asked. Nothing, was the answer. How much revenue would be raised if the tax rate was 100%? After a pause, Laffer told them, also nothing. If government took all the earnings from working or saving or investment, then no one would have any reason to work or save or invest. The *tax base* would be zero. As the tax rate rises from zero, at first revenue increases. But after a while, people stop working as much, and higher tax rates will bring in less revenue.

> *The Laffer Curve shows the relationship between tax rates and tax revenues. Revenue is zero when the tax rate is zero and when it is 100%. This means that, when tax rates are very high, a decrease in the tax rate could increase revenues.*

It was a revelation to Jude Wanniski. Taxes affected the behavior of businesses and employees. If taxes were lower workers would supply more hours of work. Businesses would supply more goods and services. As he stared at this *Laffer Curve*, Wanniski realized something else: if taxes were high, a tax cut could stimulate so much new output, income and wealth that tax revenue could *increase*.

Taxes didn't just affect spending, the demand for goods. They affected the supply of work and savings too. It looked like a new kind of economics: *supply-side economics*.

Back in New York Wanniski persuaded the *Wall Street Journal* editors to adopt the supply-side idea in their editorials about tax policy. He wrote a book called *The Way the World Works* extolling the Laffer curve. He and Laffer explained the idea to the new Congressman from Buffalo, a former NFL quarterback named Jack Kemp. Kemp was so impressed that he and Delaware Senator William Roth wrote a tax bill to reduce tax rates by 10% a year three years in a row, a 30% cut altogether. By 1978 Kemp-Roth tax cut was part of the Republican platform in the Congressional elections.

Ronald Reagan had been a well-known actor, and was the former Governor of California. He had been a New Deal Democrat until the end of the 1940's (he'd voted for Truman in 1948), but his concern about the threat of communism made him turn to the right. He entered politics as a Republican. Reagan made his first political splash in a speech endorsing conservative Republican Barry Goldwater for the 1964 presidential nomination. He ran for the Republican nomination himself in 1968, and again in 1976, nearly taking the nomination from President Gerald Ford.

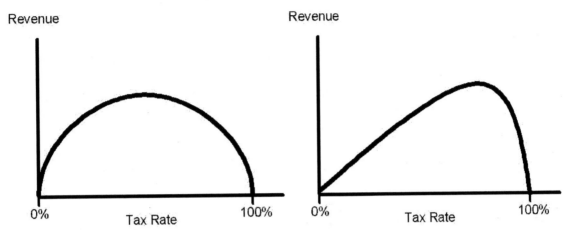

Figure 11-1. Two Laffer Curves. Revenue is on the vertical axis, the income tax rate is on the horizontal axis. The Laffer Curve was often pictured as at left, with the peak near the 50% tax rate. There is a large section of the curve to the right of the peak where reductions in the tax rate will increase revenue. However, for most taxes and most taxpayers, the response of hours worked to the income tax rate was relatively small. The Laffer Curve actually looked as it does at right, with a peak nearer to 100%, and little room for tax cuts to increase revenue.

Now, in 1980, he was running for the nomination again. He was 69 years old, so this was his last chance. His chief opponent, George H. W. Bush, unexpectedly won the Iowa caucus in January. The New Hampshire primary was next. It would make or break Reagan's candidacy.

Reagan's campaign managers set up a seminar on national issues for their candidate, to prepare him for the crucial primary. Among the instructors were Arthur Laffer, Jude Wanniski and Congressman Jack Kemp. They told him about the Laffer curve. He understood instantly.

"I came into the big money making pictures during World War II," he told them. The tax rate in the top bracket was raised to 90% during the war. Those with the highest incomes kept only a dime of every extra dollar they earned. "You could only make four pictures and then you were in the top bracket," Reagan said, "so we all quit working after four pictures and went off to the country." Had the tax rate been lower, he would have made more movies. Lower tax rates meant more work, higher incomes, and, plausibly, more tax payments and revenue.

Reagan had endorsed the Kemp-Roth tax cuts in 1978, but to the supply-siders he had seemed a luke-warm supporter. Now the Reagan campaign emphasized tax cuts as the centerpiece of their policy proposals. George Bush called it "voo-doo economics." But it persuaded the voters. Reagan won in New Hampshire, and two months later a victory in Illinois clinched the nomination. Ronald Reagan won the Presidency in November.

The Reagan Tax Cut
Donald Regan, the new Secretary of the Treasury, discovered that the new President was both hard and easy to read. He was hard, because he wouldn't tell his aides what he wanted done. Regan wrote later, "In the four years that I served as Secretary of the Treasury I never saw President Reagan alone and never discussed economic philosophy or fiscal or monetary policy with him one-on-one." But the President was easy to read, too, once his aides figured out his style. "The President seemed to believe that his public statements were all the guidance his private advisors required," Regan wrote. "Ronald Reagan's campaign promises *were* his policy."

What had the new President promised?

- Inflation would be brought down. Reagan had been influenced by the monetarism of Milton Friedman. The economy could be stabilized and inflation kept under control with slow and steady growth in the money supply. The President would consistently support the Federal Reserve's efforts to reduce inflation, even at the cost of a deep recession.

- Defense spending would increase. "Defense is not a budget issue," the President said, "You spend what you need." The President thought a big buildup was needed after years of post-Vietnam neglect. The Soviet Union was still a big threat, Reagan thought.

- Taxes would be cut. Reagan favored two existing tax proposals. One was the Kemp-Roth tax cut bill, which would reduce income taxes on individuals by 30% over three years. The other was a bill to allow businesses to depreciate their facilities and equipment more rapidly for tax purposes. This would reduce taxes on businesses, and make it cheaper to invest in plant and equipment.

- The budget would be balanced. As a candidate Reagan had repeatedly criticized Carter administration budget deficits. And Republicans had always been for balanced budgets.

More generally, the President thought that free markets could promote the efficient use of resources and technical innovation. "Free" meant free of government regulation or interference. In this the Reagan administration was part of a world-wide trend toward greater reliance on markets. The Carter administration had deregulated trucking and air travel. Margaret Thatcher's new government in Great Britain was moving in this direction. Amazingly, so was China's communist government under its new premier, Deng Xiaoping.

Reagan depended on his aides to invent and implement policies to bring these promises about. He would use the symbolic powers of his office to ensure their success. He used these powers, Treasury Secretary Regan said, with "astonishing skill." The new administration decided to launch their economic package in a speech to Congress, scheduled for February 18, 1980.

This was a problem for David Stockman, the new budget director. The President had promised lower inflation, higher defense spending, a tax cut, and a balanced budget. The problem, Stockman knew, was that these campaign promises were mutually incompatible. Stockman had been a Congressman until the President had picked him to head the Office of Management and Budget (OMB). He was known for his encyclopedic knowledge of the Federal budget. He needed that knowledge now.

One of Stockman's problems was the economic forecast. He had to know how fast the economy would grow and how high inflation would be, in order to project tax revenues. Only then would he know how big the spending cuts had to be in order to balance the budget.

The forecast became a battleground. The supply-siders thought that tax cuts would create a lot of economic growth. They championed *real* GDP growth projections of 5% to 6%. Growth had averaged 3% during the 1970s. The monetarists held out for the lowest possible growth in *nominal* GDP, about 7%. That's what would result if the money supply grew at a slow, steady pace. If real GDP grew 5%, and nominal GDP grew 7%, then inflation had to be about 2%. As of February 1981 the inflation rate was 11%.

Murray Weidenbaum was named chair of the Council of Economic Advisors, and came to the forecast debate late. He was an easygoing man, but when he saw this inflation prediction he roared, "Nobody is going to predict two percent inflation on my watch! We'll be the laughingstock of the world!" The forecast debate was back to square one.

The President would speak in less than two weeks, and Stockman was desperate for a forecast, any forecast. Finally they made a deal. Weidenbaum would accept substantial real growth, if the others would agree to his higher inflation figure. That meant growth of 5.2%, inflation of 7.7%, for nominal growth of 13%. "What model did this come out of, Murray?" asked another forecaster, sarcastically. Weidenbaum slapped his belly. "It came right out of here. My visceral computer." When the forecast was published, critics called it the "rosy scenario."

Even with growth and inflation so high, Stockman still needed large spending cuts to show a balanced budget. He set 1984 as the target date. In that year spending, before cuts, was projected to exceed revenues by $118 billion. Stockman had identified $74 billion in proposed cuts. The remaining $44 billion looked to some like a deficit. Instead, it was marked with what they called the "magic asterisk," and labeled "future savings to be proposed." These concerned Stockman and many others, because they represented cuts that would be politically more difficult to get. But a projected deficit would threaten support for the Kemp-Roth tax cuts, so the asterisk stayed.

On February 18, President Reagan announced his economic program in a speech to a joint session of Congress. He proposed a litany of spending to be cut: federal aid to education, subsidies to arts and humanities, the synthetic fuels program, funds for local economic development, trade adjustment assistance, grants to states and local governments, postal subsidies, and NASA space programs. Eligibility rules would be tightened for Medicaid, food stamps, welfare, and the school lunch program.

He cited the Soviet military threat to justify a defense buildup. Then, he made the Kemp-Roth tax cut his own. What was needed, he said, was

> a tax program which provides incentive to increase productivity for both workers and industry. Our proposal is for a 10-percent across-the-board cut every year for 3 years in the tax rates for all individual income taxpayers, making a total cut in the tax rates of 30 percent.

The question now was whether the program could be pushed through Congress. The administration started with the spending cuts, in the Senate. The Republicans had the majority there. There were protests from some Senators who worried that the asterisk budget cuts would not come about, leaving the budget with a substantial deficit. When votes were on the line, though, they were with their new President. The spending cuts passed.

Democrats still controlled the House, and so held all tax and budget committee chairs. It was here that Reagan's "astonishing skill" in using his office came into play. The Democrats floated a compromise proposal. "I'm convinced," Reagan said, "that the American people strongly support my program and don't want it watered down." There would be no compromise. Each representative was either with the President or against him. When the President survived an assassination attempt on March 30, public support grew. By the end of April the Democrats threw in the towel. Speaker Tip O'Neill said "the will of the people is to go along with the President. I've been in politics a long time. I know when you fight and when you don't." The spending cuts passed the House.

There was still the matter of the $44 billion asterisk, the added spending cuts needed for a balanced budget by 1984. Stockman had known all along that the lion's share of those cuts had to come from Social Security. He put a benefit reduction package together and ran it by the President. Reagan was enthusiastic. He had been skeptical of Social Security since the 1960s. But his White House staff feared the public's reaction, and persuaded him not to push the program. Instead it was introduced as a Health and Human Services bill. Without strong Presidential backing it never had a chance. The Senate—the Republican-controlled Senate—passed a special resolution against the plan by a 96 to nothing vote. Stockman's revolution had been derailed by the third rail of American politics, Social Security. Without the Social Security cuts, the $44 billion in savings could not be achieved. There would be a deficit in 1984.

Kemp-Roth was the next big item on the agenda. At first the Democrats pushed to reduce the size of the tax cut. The administration agreed to trim the first year's tax cut from 10% to 5%, and to delay its effective date. But when his advisors told him more compromises were needed, Ronald Reagan drew the line. He told them, "Twenty-five percent is as low as we can go. I don't want you fellas asking me to go under that figure. We'll take it to the people if we have to."

This put the Democrats in a political bind. With the President's strong support, the Republicans and their conservative Democratic allies appeared to have the votes to pass Kemp-Roth. The House Democrats had just suffered a major defeat on the budget bill, and they wanted to reassert control. They needed a tax cut bill of their own, to compete with Kemp-Roth. And so began what has been called a "one-time, sixty-day breakdown in the normal partisan checks and balances of the fiscal process," or more simply, a "feeding frenzy" and a "bidding war."

The Democrats would propose an additional cut, such as a tax cut for savers. The Republicans would adopt it too, and add another like a tax cut for small businesses, which the Democrats would then try to top. The bidding war was on. "I don't like this poker game of calling and raising," said Jim Wright, a leading House Democrat. But he added, "frankly, we'll put anything in the bill if it will buy votes."

Then, in late July, came one addition that had profound long-term effects. When there was inflation, the Federal income tax was subject to a phenomenon called *bracket creep*. The Federal income tax is progressive, which means that people with higher incomes pay a higher percentage of their incomes in taxes. This is accomplished by having income tax brackets. People with incomes in the $14,000 and $16,000 bracket paid 37% of each extra dollar in taxes; people with incomes in the $16,000 to $18,000 bracket paid 43%, and so forth. These brackets were fixed by law. As inflation increased prices it also increased pay. People were pushed into higher and higher income tax brackets. The percentage of their income paid in taxes increased, even though their pay had not increased, in real terms. Real after-tax incomes were reduced. The Federal government collected more revenue.

> *Bracket creep is the increase in tax revenues that occurs because inflation pushes incomes into ever higher tax brackets. Income tax indexing increases the brackets with inflation, which prevents bracket creep, but also slows revenue growth.*

Senator Bill Armstrong of Colorado proposed *income tax indexing*. Indexing would increase the brackets each year by the amount of inflation. With indexing inflation would not push taxpayers into higher tax rate brackets. The brackets would increase too, so the taxpayers' rates would stay the same. But this meant that inflation would no longer accelerate tax revenues. Without indexing, the rate cuts in Kemp-Roth would eventually be erased by inflation and bracket creep. Revenues would recover. With indexing, the rate cuts in Kemp-Roth would be permanent.

On July 27, President Reagan went on TV to ask for support for the Kemp-Roth version of the tax cut. The main difference between them, the President said, was that the Democrat tax cut was temporary, while the Republican cut was permanent, because of indexing. After one last round of additions (a subsidy for peanut growers to win over Georgia Democrats), Kemp-Roth passed on July 29, 1981.

On August 3 budget director David Stockman ruined a victory luncheon with the bad news. "The scent of victory is still in the air," he declared, "but I'm not going to mince words. We're heading for a crash landing on the budget. . . . It's going to be harder than hell to get to a balanced budget even by 1986."

The tax cut had been bigger than planned. The spending cuts had been smaller than planned. And, now, the administration's economists were insisting that the rosy scenario forecast be brought back to reality. There would be recession in 1982, not the 5.2% predicted growth. Inflation was falling and would be much less than the 7.7% prediction. Both these facts meant even lower Federal revenue. Revised projections had deficits growing to more than $100 billion by the middle of the decade.

"What about the revenue feedback from the tax bill?" asked one of the President's political advisors. The big tax cut, after all, was supposed to generate so much added economic activity—more work, more saving, more investment—that the lower tax rates would produce higher revenue. It was the Laffer Curve argument, the idea that had started it all.

It was not that the Laffer Curve didn't exist. Of course lower taxes increased the amount of economic activity, so that cuts from very high taxes could actually increase revenue. The question was *how much* added activity tax cuts would produce, and how high taxes were in the first place. What was the *elasticity of supply* of labor, or investment? How much would it respond to an increase in after-tax wages or returns?

As Reagan administration Treasury official (and economist) Donald Fullerton wrote, the economic response to tax rates, and the tax rates themselves, "are both low enough to suggest that broad-based cuts in labor tax rates would not increase revenues." Or, as administration economist Martin Feldstein put it, "for most taxpayers a cut in the tax on wages and salaries would increase tax revenue only if the resulting increase in labor supply was much greater than either logic or previous experience suggested was at all likely."

> *The elasticity of supply of labor shows the response of the income tax base to a tax cut. It's too small for a tax cut to increase revenues.*

The Federal budget deficit had been $74 billion in 1980, the last full year of the Carter administration. In 1982, the deficit grew to $128 billion. Both 1980 and 1982 were recession years, so deficits were to be expected. But 1986 was the fourth year of an expansion, and by then the deficit was $221 billion. At 5% of GDP, it was the largest deficit since World War II up to that time.

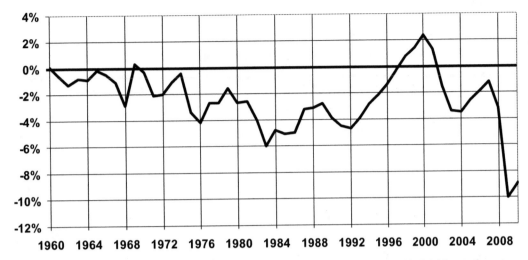

Figure 11-2. Federal budget balance as percentage of GDP, 1960-2010 and estimated 2010. The budget moves towards bigger deficits during and just after recessions, as in 1970-71, 1974-76, 1979-83, 1989-91, 2000-2003 and 2007-09. The budget moves towards surplus or to bigger surpluses during expansions, as in 1962-65, 1971-74, 1976-79, 1986-89, 1992-2000, 2003-06. In two instances, though, the budget deficit has become bigger or stayed big during expansions: during the Johnson Vietnam War-Great Society spending increase in 1965-1968, and during the Reagan tax cut-defense buildup in 1983-1986.

The tax cut had passed at the end of July. By September it was clear that deficits would grow huge, and there was talk of new taxes. Over the next five years Congress passed a series of tax increases. The President would not support an income tax rate increase, but did support elimination of many of the ornaments that had been attached to Kemp-Roth during the bidding war. The deficits changed the direction of tax policy-making. Many loopholes were closed; many favors were withdrawn in order to raise more revenue without raising rates.

Deficits and Crowding Out
Ronald Reagan did not oppose these tax increases because he really did believe in a balanced budget. At the August 3 victory luncheon he had told Stockman "we can't give up on the balanced budget. Deficit spending is how we got into this mess." Yet the President was not willing to give up any of his other promises to balance the budget. Defense spending would be increased. Tax rates would be cut. Inflation would be brought down. Balancing the budget was apparently the last of these four in importance. So budget deficits increased.

What "mess" did the budget deficit create? In the past big deficits always had increased inflation. But the experience in the 1980s showed that inflation was not a necessary result of deficits. Whether deficits produced inflation depended on the actions of the

Federal Reserve. Lower taxes increase consumer and business spending. A bigger defense budget increases spending directly. Incomes rise, and consumers need more money for transactions. Businesses want more loans to expand operations. The government must borrow more for its spending. All this pushes interest rates higher.

The deficits present the Fed with a choice. During World War II the Fed kept interest rates fixed. With the demand for money rising, this required increases in the money supply. During the Vietnam War the Fed increased interest rates in 1966, but kept them too low in 1967 and 1968. To do this they increased the money supply. Inflation increased during and after both wars. The reason was the increase in the money supply beyond the rise in the economy's capacity to produce. It was too much money chasing too few goods.

Paul Volcker could have increased money supply growth when the big deficits of the 1980s emerged. He wrote later

> Although it was never pressed, sometimes there were intimations of a deal; if the Federal Reserve would commit itself to reducing interest rates, that would provide political lubrication for some combination of spending cuts and a tax increase to cut the deficit. History taught me to be cautious about that. Once before, in the late 1960s during the debate over an income tax increase to pay for Vietnam War costs, the Fed eased in anticipation of fiscal tightening. I don't know how much the decision to ease was meant as a political gesture as well as being economically appropriate. But it had become part of Fed lore that it was all a big mistake; the tax increase never had the restraining effect anticipated, the Federal Reserve was for months politically locked into inappropriate policy, and the momentum of inflation speeded up.

Volcker would make no deal. The Fed maintained a strong anti-inflation policy. That meant no added increases in the money supply to bring down interest rates. Without rapid money growth, high inflation did not re-emerge.

The cost of the budget deficit, then, was higher interest rates. Nominal interest rates came down a lot in the first half of the 1980s, but real interest rates remained high. In other words, the interest rates that lenders charged borrowers fell, but inflation fell a lot more. Higher real rates meant that business investment spending was less than it could have been.

The government spent more on defense. Consumers spent more because taxes were lower. Overall spending was restrained (and inflation held in check) because higher interest rates kept investment spending from growing. Investment spending as a share of GDP peaked in 1984. Then it fell throughout the rest of the 1980s expansion. As Paul Volcker put it, "the environment for domestic investment was not as good as it should have been. We had the longest peacetime expansion in history, but it was not exceptional for either its increases in productivity or for new investment in plant and equipment."

This is a phenomenon known as *crowding out*. Government activity crowds out private activity, because government borrowing crowds out private borrowing.

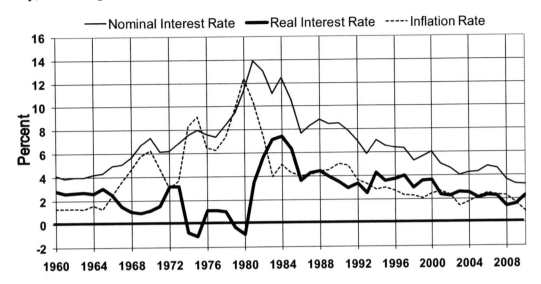

Figure 11-3. Real Interest Rate, 1960-2010. Treasury 10-year bond rate minus Consumer Price Index inflation, core rate. The real interest rate was near 3% through the 1960's, but dipped lower in the second half of that decade. During the second half of the 1970's it was lower, even negative, reflecting the Fed's accommodation of inflation. The real interest rate shot upward after 1980, because of the Fed's tight monetary policy. It remained high throughout the 1980s because of the combination of big Federal budget deficits and tight money. The real rate has fallen steadily since then, dipping to 2% during the past decade.

Martin Feldstein became head of the Council of Economic Advisors in 1982. He began speaking about the crowding out problem. "During the Fall of 1982," he wrote later, "I spent considerable time explaining publicly as well as inside the administration that the recent deficit surge was cyclical but that, as the economy recovered, we would still face a substantial structural deficit." During the recession year of 1982, a deficit was to be expected. This was not a problem—in fact, the lower taxes and added spending would help with recovery. But the deficits would remain as the economy expanded. This was a problem. With the economy at capacity, a big deficit would keep interest rates high.

Budget deficits and contractionary monetary policy in the 1980's raised real interest rates. Investment spending declined as a share of GDP. This was "crowding out."

"I explained also that a persistent structural deficit would inevitably lead to reduced investment in plant and equipment and therefore to lower levels of future real income," Feldstein wrote. That was the main problem with crowding out. Today's investment is tomorrow's capital stock. Less investment today means a smaller stock of machinery and equipment tomorrow. With fewer tools to work with, employees are less productive, and, over the years, GDP grows more slowly. Feldstein advocated bigger tax increases and bigger spending cuts to reduce the budget deficits, to the dismay of the President's political advisors.

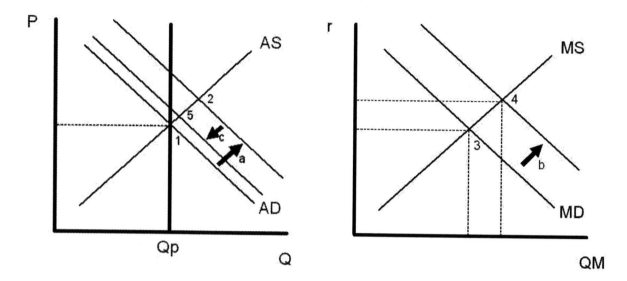

Figure 11-4. Crowding Out Investment. The Federal budget deficit increases aggregate demand (a), threatening to raise prices and output beyond potential (1 to 2). However, the resulting rise in money demand (b), from second shift #3, is met with no increase in money supply. The interest rate rises (3 to 4). This reduces investment, and lessens the increase in aggregate demand (c), though second shift #2. There is less inflation (1 to 5), so the increase in inflationary expectations is smaller. In second shift #1, aggregate supply will shift less (not shown). Investment spending bears the burden of keeping AD from rising. In the long run, with less investment spending the capital stock grows more slowly, and so does potential output. That's crowding out.

Surpluses in the 1990's, Deficits in the 2000's
After the experience of the 1980's, for a time Congress and the Presidents began to take the problem of *structural deficits* more seriously. A structural deficit is one that exists even when the economy is expanding, producing as much revenue as it can at existing tax rates. Structural deficits contrast with cyclical deficits, which occur during recessions because of temporary declines in tax revenue. If the deficit is cyclical, once the recession is over revenues rise and the budget returns to balance.

During President Reagan's second term Congress passed the *Gramm-Rudman-Hollings Act* (usually know only as Gramm-Rudman, one assumes to the dismay of Senator Hollings). This set future deficit reduction targets, to be achieved mostly by spending cuts or slower spending growth.

> *Cyclical budget deficits are caused by the declines in revenues that result from recession. Structural budget deficits remain after the economy recovers.*

But often when the targets threatened to prevent spending that Congress wanted to pass, the deficit targets were changed, or accounting gimmicks were invented to meet the targets in law but evade them in fact. Gramm-Rudman probably restrained spending to a degree, however, because evading the targets required public debate, an added political cost to increased spending. But the continuing expansion may have reduced the deficit more. By the beginning of the Bush administration in 1989, the deficit was down to $153 billion, 3% of GDP, from its peak in 1986 of $221 billion, 5% of GDP.

The 1980's expansion ended in the 1990-91 recession. With the slowing economy, the deficit began to increase again. This is the counter-cyclical, automatic stabilizing function of the budget, but in the context of the times many in Congress and the administration found it alarming. In the spring and summer of 1990 Congress and the President negotiated a deficit reduction bill. President George H.W. Bush reached an agreement with the Congress to cut spending and to raise the top income tax rate from 28% to 31%. (This move angered many of the President's supporters. They remembered his 1988 campaign pledge, "no new taxes.")

In the 1990's, the administration of President Bill Clinton also restrained spending and increased taxes, as part of its "financial markets strategy." With the Bush and Clinton tax and spending changes, and a recovery from recession, Federal budget deficits began to shrink. By 1996 the deficit was $142 billion, just under 2% of GDP. In 1998 the budget deficit turned to a *budget surplus*. For the first time in 30 years, the Federal government took in more revenue than it spent. The surpluses lasted for four years, peaking in 2000 at $189 billion, almost 2% of GDP.

This astonishing development had three causes. First, the 1990s expansion was the longest on record, lasting exactly ten years. Expansion almost always reduces the budget deficit. Income tax revenues rise, automatic stabilizer spending falls. This expansion lasted so long that it turned the deficits into surpluses.

Second, Republicans won both the House and Senate in the elections of 1994. For the rest of the decade, the Republicans controlled the Congress, the Democrats controlled the Presidency. The result was stalemate. Republicans checked the President's efforts to raise spending; the President blocked the Republican's attempts to cut taxes. Without discretionary spending hikes or new tax cuts, the budget moved towards balance.

> *Federal deficits turned to surpluses by the end of the 1990's. The reasons were the long expansion, political stalemate and a stock market boom.*

Third, there was a stock market boom in the second half of the decade. The Federal income tax applies to "capital gains," which is income that comes from the sale of stocks and other assets that increase in value. With the big rise in stock values, capital gains income increased a lot, and so did income tax revenue.

Budget deficits returned with the recession of 2001, then lasted through the 2001-2007 expansion.

The three reasons for the surplus explain the return of the deficits. First, one party (the Republicans) controlled both Houses of Congress, and the Presidency, from 2003 through 2006. President George W. Bush proposed tax cuts in 2003. Bigger budget deficits were predicted as a result, and for a time crowding out became a hot-button political issue. Administration spokesmen denied a connection between deficits and interest rates. Treasury Secretary John Snow testified that deficits posed little danger. The deficits, Snow said, "are really modest and clearly manageable and will not have any impact on long-term interest rates, which is the real concern." Former budget director Mitch Daniels referred to large deficits in the 1980's, saying "They didn't produce disaster before. They won't this time, either." The tax cuts passed.

Second, the asset boom in the 2000's was not in the stock market, but in housing. Housing prices rose to heights never seen before. This required home buyers to borrow more, and pay more mortgage interest. But home mortgage interest payments are a *deduction* from taxable income. The 2000's asset boom probably reduced Federal income tax revenue.

And third, the expansion after the 2001 recession lasted only six years. It reduced the deficit, as expansion usually do. By 2007-08 the deficit was 1.2% of GDP, down from 3.4% in 2004-05. Had the expansion continued for another two years the budget would have been balanced again. Instead, the economy fell into a new and deeper recession.

The Value of the Dollar
The combination of deficits and tight money during the 1980's meant that real interest rates in the U.S. remained high compared to interest rates around the world. International investors saw this as an opportunity to earn a higher return on their wealth. International investment in the United States increased.

To some extent this reduced the crowding out effect of high real interest rates. The U.S. was not limited to its own savings to pay for plant and equipment since it could borrow funds from abroad. Fed chair Paul Volcker wrote, "the shortage of domestic savings was compensated in substantial part by an enormous inflow of mainly borrowed capital from abroad." The amount that could be borrowed, he remembered, "turned out to be far larger than I had thought possible." Some in the Reagan administration argued against economist Martin Feldstein that crowding out was not a problem because so much could be borrowed abroad.

Feldstein agreed, in part. More foreign funds did lessen the effect of crowding out on domestic investment. But this created a new kind of crowding out. To invest or lend in the United States, foreign currencies had to be converted to dollars. The demand for dollars increased because real interest rates were higher in the U.S. than they were elsewhere. Since exchange rates were flexible, this increased the value of the dollar.

With the dollar's value higher, U.S. exports became more expensive, and U.S. imports became cheaper. So (after about a year) U.S. exports began to shrink, and U.S. imports began to expand. The *trade deficit* grew. Lower import prices helped bring inflation down, both because the prices on imports were lower, and because domestic companies that competed with imports had to keep their prices down too.

But U.S. exporters found their sales declining. For example, the American earth-moving equipment manufacturer, Caterpillar, was engaged in intense competition with its Japanese rival Komatsu in the early 1980s. The company found it impossible to reduce its costs enough to maintain its competitiveness with international buyers, in the face of the rising value of the dollar. Komatsu's equipment became cheaper, Caterpillar's more expensive to international buyers. Increasingly, Komatsu made sales and Caterpillar was shut out.

> *Federal budget deficits and tight monetary policy increased real interest rates during the 1980's. Higher interest rates increased the demand for the dollar, which increased its exchange value. This made U.S. exports more expensive, and led to a trade deficit. The budget and trade deficits were called the "twin deficits."*

Martin Feldstein supported a lower budget deficit. If this wasn't possible, though, a rising value of the dollar helped to spread the pain of crowding out more broadly. Higher interest rates increased the value of the dollar. The pain of crowding out was spread from interest rate-sensitive industries, like construction, to exchange rate-sensitive industries, like agriculture, automobiles and aircraft.

Again, some in the Reagan administration were angered by this line of thinking. Treasury Secretary Regan insisted that the rise in the value of the dollar was a tribute to the success of the administration's economic policies. International investors were demanding dollars in order to share in U.S. business opportunities and lower taxes, he claimed. Regan made his opposition to Feldstein's view plain in testimony before the Senate Budget Committee in 1984. One of the senators read him a passage from *The Economic Report of the President*, describing the link between budget deficits, high interest rates, the high value of the dollar, and the trade deficit. The senator did not give the source of the quote, and asked the Treasury Secretary what he thought. "Toss it in the waste basket," Regan growled.

In the middle of 1984 the real interest rate began to edge downward. Yet the value of the dollar continued to rise. The dollar had developed a momentum of its own. The trend to a higher dollar began as the world's investors sought to lend at high U.S. interest rates. Traders reacted to this trend by buying dollars, expecting a further increase in value. But the act of buying dollars itself increased the demand for dollars, and so increased its value. Paul Volcker wrote, "expectational and 'bandwagon' effects that occur when traders try to ride a trend can create wide currency swings far out of keeping with a reasonable balance in trading patterns." The rising value of the dollar had become a *speculative bubble* by early 1985.

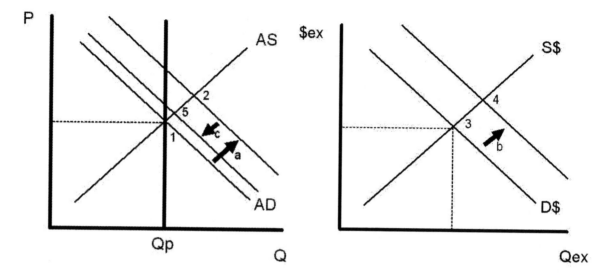

Figure 11-5. The twin deficits. There is a Federal budget deficit. This increases aggregate demand (a) and threatens inflation (1 to 2). Second shift #3 causes interest rates to rise as in figure 11-4. This attracts international investors, and second shift #5 increases their demand for dollars (b) in order to lend in the U.S. at the attractive interest rates. With more funds being lent, interest rates do not rise so much (not shown), and investment does not decline so much. But the rise in the value of the dollar (3 to 4) increases U.S. imports and decreases U.S. exports. That's second shift #4. The resulting trade deficit holds the aggregate demand increase down (c), meaning there is less inflation (5). But the budget deficit combined with tight monetary policy has caused a trade deficit.

During the first Reagan term, the administration did not try to influence the value of the dollar. But by 1984 manufacturers like Caterpillar, farm groups and labor unions were pressuring the administration to do something. Congress considered bills to force the Treasury to intervene in exchange markets. After his 1984 reelection, Ronald Reagan appointed a new Treasury Secretary, James Baker. When asked about exchange rate policy at his confirmation hearing, Baker said it was "obviously something that should be looked at." Perhaps this pricked the speculative bubble, because in February 1985 the value of the dollar began to fall.

If a rising dollar was a sign that administration policy was working, was a falling dollar a sign that it wasn't? The administration didn't see it that way. They dropped that line of argument, and this opened the way for exchange rate intervention, to try to bring the value of the dollar down further.

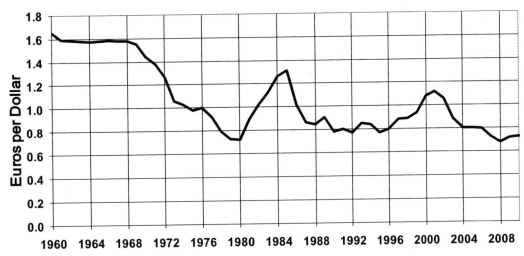

Figure 11-6. Euros per dollar, 1960-2010. Euros became Europe's currency in 1999. The euro-dollar exchange rate can be calculated from a combination of the European currencies that combined into the euro (German marks, French francs, Italian lira, etc.). Exchange rates varied little, under the Bretton Woods fixed exchange rates through the end of the 1960s. Some countries let their currencies float even before the U.S. closed the gold window in 1971. The dollar got weaker and European currencies stronger until 1980, when the rise in real interest rates made lending in the U.S. attractive. The value of the dollar in euros rose until 1985, then fell as real interest rates fell, government intervention took hold, and the speculative bubble burst. The euro remained near 0.8 for a decade after 1987. An international currency crisis and rising U.S. interest rates increased its value from 1996 to 2001. Falling U.S. interest rates and the U.S. trade deficit reduced its value until mid-2008. Then the world financial crisis increased the demand for the dollar as a "safe haven."

The Plaza Accord

The Treasury and the Federal Reserve hold reserves of foreign currencies. *Intervention* means that one or both enters the foreign exchange market and buys or sells dollars or foreign currencies in an attempt to influence exchange rates. If the dollar's value is thought to be too low, or if it is falling, the Fed or Treasury could buy dollars. Reserves of foreign currencies would be traded for dollars. This adds to the demand for dollars, which should raise the dollar's value, or stop it from falling. If the dollar is thought to be too high, or is rising in value, the Fed or Treasury could sell dollars. The added supply should depress the dollar's value, or stop it from rising.

The Treasury takes the lead in setting policy, and the New York Federal Reserve Bank acts as the Treasury's agent, doing the actual buying and selling. But both the Treasury and Federal Reserve have legal authority to intervene in foreign exchange markets. If they acted in opposite directions they could offset each others' policies, so usually each is reluctant to act unless the other agrees.

The trouble was, by the 1980's, hundreds of billions of dollars were traded in exchange markets every day. The Treasury or Federal Reserve would have to buy or sell enormous amounts of currency to affect exchange rates. Intervention is more likely to work if the treasuries and central banks of many countries act together. This is called *concerted intervention*. The problem with that, of course, is getting all sides to agree on a particular policy.

> **Governments intervene in exchange markets when they buy or sell foreign currencies to influence exchange rates.**

In 1985 the new Secretary of the Treasury, James Baker, sensed that the time was right for such an agreement. The Europeans had been complaining about the high value of the dollar for several years. While the high value made it easier for Europe to export to the U.S., it increased the prices of U.S. imports in Europe, adding to European inflation. There were rising protectionist pressures in the U.S. Congress. The high value of the dollar was increasing the volume of imports, and many in Congress were pushing for trade restrictions to protect American companies and jobs. The Reagan administration opposed trade restrictions. Its free market beliefs did not stop at the border. The Japanese also feared U.S. protectionism, and were willing to let the yen rise in value relative to the dollar to head it off.

The Plaza Hotel. Here it is in 2007. Twenty-two years before, it was the site of the G-5 meeting that signed the Plaza Accord. In 2007 it was partially converted to condominiums (starting at $1.5 million each).

Baker planned to call a meeting of the finance ministers (secretaries of the treasury) and central bank chairs of five countries: the United States, Great Britain, France, Germany and Japan. These countries were known as the group of five or G-5. They met at the Plaza Hotel on Sunday, September 22, 1985. Volcker had offered the New York Fed's headquarters building on Wall Street as a place to meet. But Baker didn't want a discreet meeting in the Fed's fortress. He wanted a flashy meeting in a posh hotel, with reporters and television cameras, so the world would take notice. Most of the groundwork had been done already, and the G-5 were in agreement. That afternoon they issued a communiqué':

> The Ministers and Governors agreed that exchange rates should play a role in adjusting external imbalances. In order to do this, exchange rates should better reflect fundamental economic conditions than has been the case. They believe that agreed policy actions must be implemented and reinforced to improve the fundamentals. Some further orderly appreciation of the main non-dollar currencies against the dollar is desirable. They stand ready to cooperate more closely to encourage this when to do so would be helpful.

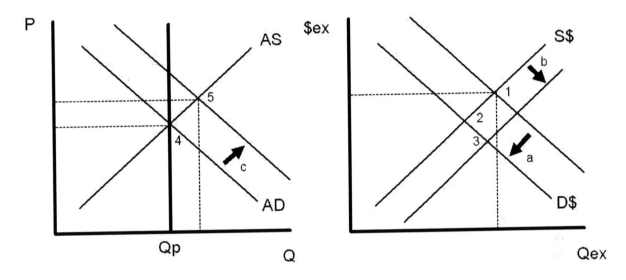

Figure 11-7. Falling value of the dollar. The speculative increases in the demand for the dollar are reversed, and the demand for the dollar falls (a). The value of the dollar falls (1 to 2). Countries try "concerted intervention", supplying dollars into currency markets. The supply of the dollar increases (b) and its value drops some more (2 to 3). The lower value of the dollar increases exports and decreases imports (second shift #4), which increases aggregate demand (c), raising output and prices (4 to 5).

The main external imbalance was the U.S. trade deficit. The big trade deficit and falling U.S. interest rates were fundamental conditions that meant the dollar's value ought to fall. Policy actions meant selling dollars, and they all agreed to cooperate. And, as Volcker said, "the words 'when to do so would be helpful' were quite rightly read to mean tomorrow." The mild-sounding statement screamed at currency traders: big increase in the supply of dollars tomorrow! The next day the dollar's value dropped 4%.

At first no intervention was needed. Market expectations drove the dollar down. Later the United States and other countries sold dollars to sustain the downward trend. The dollar dropped steadily for the next two-plus years, until by the end of 1987 its value against the German mark was down 42% from its September 1985 level, 51% from its February 1985 peak.

> *The Plaza Accord in 1985 was an agreement among the major economic powers to sell dollars in exchange markets, to bring down the value of the dollar.*

After a year U.S. exports began to grow, for the first time since 1980. Exports doubled during the next eight years, 1985-1993. The trade deficit nearly disappeared in the early 1990's.

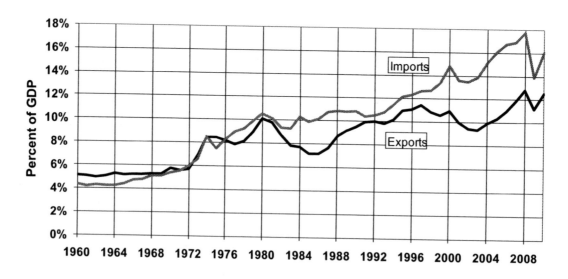

Figure 11-8. Total exports and imports as a percentage of GDP, 1960-2010. The export share doubled from 1969 to 2008; the import share tripled. The gaps between exports and imports are the trade balance. It's been negative—a trade deficit—since 1977. Crowding out explains the big gap in the mid-1980s. The gap almost closed in 1991-92, after the Plaza Accord and the fall in the dollar's exchange value. The Asian crisis started the increase in the trade deficit after 1997. The growth in the U.S. economy relative to Europe and Japan, and the too-high value of the dollar relative to the Chinese yuan and the Japanese yen, explained the biggest-ever trade deficit in the mid-2000's. The falling value of the dollar against most currencies during the 2000's finally began to close the deficit later in the decade. In 2009 trade volumes dropped because of the world recession. Since imports fell more than exports, the trade deficit got smaller.

The *Plaza Accord* marked the first time that major nations had cooperated on exchange rate policy since the end of the Bretton Woods era. The intervention was seen as a success. It seemed that the agreement had caused the dollar's value to fall. But there is some question. The dollar's value had already been falling for seven months at the time of the Plaza meeting. It decreased just a little more rapidly over the next seven months.

Real interest rates had fallen since mid-1984. It may be that the markets responded more to changing economic fundamentals than to threats of government intervention.

Deficits in the Sixties and the Eighties

Let's use the three market model with second shifts to look at the differences between policy in the 1960's and 1980's. Both decades saw big tax cuts and big defense spending increases. Both decades saw growing deficits during expansions.

Taxes were cut in 1964. Then the Vietnam War and the Great Society increased spending. The budget was nearly balanced in 1965, but by 1968 there was a deficit of almost 3% of GDP—after three years of expansion. Taxes were cut in 1983, '84 and '85. Defense spending increased. The budget was in deficit coming out of the 1981-82 recession, at almost 4% of GDP. In 1983 the deficit increased, and remained between 4.7% and 6% of GDP over the next four years—again, four years of expansion.

In the goods market, government deficits increase aggregate demand. This increases output and the price level. Consumers and businesses need more cash and money in checking accounts to handle added transactions with higher prices. Second shift #3 increases money demand.

The two decades differ in monetary policy. During the Johnson years the Federal Reserve under William McChesney Martin accommodated inflation. By February 1968 the real federal funds rate was under one percent. During the Reagan years the Federal Reserve under Paul Volcker fought inflation. The real federal funds rate remained above 4% from 1983 through 1987, topping 7% in several months.

In the money market, the Martin policy was to hold the real interest rate down as money demand increased. This required increases in the money supply. The Volcker policy was to restrict the growth in the money supply as money demand increased. This increased the real interest rate more.

> *The effect of a Federal budget deficit during an expansion depends on monetary policy. With low interest rates, it creates inflation. With high interest rates, it crowds out investment and exports.*

In the 1960's, then, real interest rates did not rise, so they did not restrain the increase in aggregate demand. There is no second shift #2, no crowding out. In the 1980's, higher real interest rates restrained the increase in aggregate demand.

Second shift #2 crowded out investment.

With no restraint from higher real interest rates in the 1960's, aggregate demand increased and output moved beyond potential. Second shift #1 set in. Input costs began to rise, inflationary expectations were established. Aggregate supply decreased and inflation increased. The restraint of higher real interest rates in the 1980's meant that output did not rise much beyond potential. Second shift #1 did not decrease aggregate supply significantly, and inflation did not increase.

In the 1960's the real interest rate was low. International investors looked elsewhere than the U.S. for high returns on their lending. Second shift #5 did not increase the demand for the dollar. In addition, the inflation in the U.S. made lower priced foreign goods more attractive to consumers, and income growth gave Americans the means to buy more foreign goods. Rising imports increased the supply of the dollar. That's second shift (a)—it comes in handy once in a while—here it reinforces the effect of second shift #5. The exchange rate was fixed under the Bretton Woods system so there was no second shift #4. Had the exchange rate not been fixed, the exchange value of the dollar would have fallen, as it did throughout the 1970's once rates became flexible. In fact, the need for a lower exchange value of the dollar helped cause the abandonment of the Bretton Woods fixed exchange rate system.

In the 1980's the real interest rate was high. International investors looked to the U.S. for high returns on their lending. Second shift #5 increased the demand for the dollar. Exchange rates were flexible, so the exchange value of the dollar increased. Through second shift #4, exports decreased and imports increased. The big budget deficits created a twin big trade deficit. Sometimes they were called the *twin deficits*.

The budget deficits were similar, but their results for the economy were quite different. During the Johnson administration inflation increased. During the Reagan administration inflation decreased. During the Johnson administration real interest rates were quite low. During the Reagan administration, real interest rates were quite high. During the Johnson administration there was downward pressure on the fixed exchange rate (though the rate remained fixed). During the Reagan administration the exchange rate increased, exports stagnated and imports soared, producing a large trade deficit. The difference was monetary policy. A Federal budget deficit will produce inflation if the Fed lets it happen. If the Fed refuses, the budget deficit crowds out investment and exports instead.

Alan Greenspan and the 1987 Stock Market Crash

Ronald Reagan had been supportive during Paul Volcker's first term as chair of the Federal Reserve, and had reappointed him to a second term. Now, however, in mid-1987, Reagan's Presidency had only a year and a half to run. There was an election coming up, and it would be very convenient for the probable Republican candidate, Vice President George Bush, if interest rates stayed low and the economy kept growing.

That made Paul Volcker a problem. As Treasury Secretary James Baker said, Volcker was "a known Democrat." More than that, Baker found Volcker aloof and disagreeable. For his part, Volcker resented Baker's attempts to stack the Federal Open Market Committee with new appointees who (Volcker feared) would be administration puppets.

Baker had a Republican candidate in mind: Alan Greenspan. Greenspan was a 61-year old economic consultant, an expert on economic data. He had headed President Ford's Council of Economic Advisors, forming a close working relationship with the President. He did yeoman service for the Reagan campaign in 1980, and for the administration as head of the Commission that brokered the Social Security reforms in 1982-83. He was well-known for an economist—he had been on the cover of *Newsweek* during the Ford administration, perhaps because he so looked the part of an economic policy maker. Said one observer, sort of like Woody Allen with math skills.

When Volcker decided not to accept reappointment, President Reagan named Alan Greenspan chair of the Federal Reserve. He took office on August 11, 1987.

Two months later the stock market crashed.

No one ever knows for sure what causes a crash. The market had been riding high. The Dow-Jones Industrial Average had passed the 2,000 mark for the first time in January 1987, and stood at a record 2,747 on August 25. But by 1987 the economic expansion was five years old, and problems seemed to be mounting. The trade deficit was huge. So was the budget deficit. Interest rates were rising again, partly because Greenspan's Federal Open Market Committee (FOMC) had just increased the discount rate half a point. A secret Fed study of the market called values "probably unsustainable." At some point, enough traders became pessimistic and began selling shares. That reduced values, and more traders decided to sell.

This time the selling was abetted by computers. The big institutional investors—pension funds, insurance companies—used *program trading*, computers programmed to protect stockholders by selling when prices fell below certain thresholds. As prices fell the programs dumped huge blocks of shares into the market. There weren't enough buyers, prices fell more, and the programs offered more shares for sale. Panicked traders ran from the floor to throw up in the rest rooms; fist fights broke out on the trading floor.

By mid-morning on Monday, October 19, the market was down 200 points. Greenspan was flying to Dallas for a speech, and was out of touch (no cell phones back then). When the plane landed Dallas Fed vice president Jim Stull met him at the gate. The first thing Greenspan asked was what had happened to the market. "Down five-oh-eight," Stull said.

Down only 5.08? Greenspan thought. "What a terrific rally!" he said, but Stull's face showed his mistake. The market was down five-hundred and eight points, 22.7% in one day. On the worst day in 1929, it had fallen 11.7%. Five-hundred billion dollars in wealth had disappeared, about the size of the GDP of France. It was (and still is) the biggest single day drop in stock market history.

The crash put the nation's economy in danger, just as in 1907 and 1929. Brokerages did much trading on borrowed funds. The shares they bought were pledged as collateral. With the big drop in prices, though, the collateral was worth less than the value of the loans. Loans could not be repaid. Commercial banks that made the loans owed payments to other banks, and to depositors. If the loans couldn't be collected, banks couldn't pay what they owed. Brokerages and banks would teeter on the brink of failure. With so much added risk all lenders would decide to build their reserves, and not make loans, for stock purchases or anything else. Without credit, houses could not be built, inventories could not be stocked, cars could not be sold. Production would fall, unemployment would increase. The nation was on the brink of financial panic and recession.

In his hotel room in Dallas that night, Greenspan took a call from Howard Baker, the President's new chief of staff. Baker had one word for Greenspan: "Help!"

"Something bothering you, Howard?" Greenspan answered. Baker told him he was alone in Washington, and he didn't know what to do. The other Baker, Treasury Secretary James, was in Sweden hunting with the King. He'd take the Concorde back the D.C. that day. Greenspan told Baker he intended to make his speech. You do that and the markets will think you're completely out of touch, Baker told him. Greenspan said he couldn't get a flight until after the speech, anyway.

"We've still got airplanes," Baker declared, and dispatched a Gulfstream military jet to Dallas, a jet with continuous secure communications. Greenspan cancelled the speech.

The conference call took place with the Chairman on the plane. They needed a statement, they decided, something clear and to the point that everyone would understand. At 8:41 a.m. on Tuesday, October 20, 1987, the Fed issued a press release over Alan Greenspan's name. It read

> The Federal Reserve, consistent with its responsibilities as the nation's central bank, affirmed today its readiness to serve as a source of liquidity to support the economic and financial system.

The Fed was willing to act as a lender of last resort. It would lend, freely, to any bank that needed money. Fed officials spent the next weeks putting out financial fires, but within a month it was over. The markets settled down, though it took 15 months to recover what had been lost on October 19. The overall economy didn't miss a beat. The unemployment rate fell six-tenths of a point in the six months after the crash. Real GDP grew 4.5% in the fourth quarter. And the movers and shakers in Washington and New York had learned something about their new central banker. "I just don't think Alan gets nervous," James Baker would say.

It was a lesson on how to handle financial market crises: flood the markets with money. There would be several opportunities to apply that lesson in the coming decades.

The Savings and Loan Crisis
Now the Fed faced a more traditional concern. As the expansion continued, the inflation rate was creeping upward. It topped 4% in mid-1988, 5% in early 1989. Greenspan and the Open Market Committee decided to raise interest rates. The first half-point increase was announced in August 1988—in the middle of the Presidential election campaign.

That was exactly what the administration had hoped to avoid by appointing Greenspan. The Chairman delivered the bad news to James Baker himself. Baker screamed at him for twenty seconds, then calmed down. The administration issued a press release supporting the move. Baker told one Fed governor that the interest rate increase was probably needed, "but your timing sucks." George H.W. Bush was elected President anyway—no thanks to Alan Greenspan. By the time the new President took office, the federal funds rate had been increased three percentage points. Inflation stopped rising. It seemed that the Fed might achieve a "soft landing"—a reduction in inflation without a recession.

Savings and Loans, also known as thrifts, were institutions that took deposits from the public and loaned money for home mortgages. They had been encouraged to develop during the Great Depression, as a way to foster home ownership. Most were small, local institutions. Until the end of the 1970's, regulations required that they lend to homeowners within a fifty-mile radius of their home offices. Competition was restricted. Neither banks nor thrifts were allowed to operate across state lines. Further, "Regulation Q" limited the interest rates banks and thrifts could pay on deposits. For decades the thrifts were profitable. Thrift managers, it was said, operated on the 3-6-3 plan: pay three percent on deposits, charge six percent on loans, and be on the golf course by 3 p.m.

But in 1979 the Volcker Fed began to raise interest rates to bring down inflation. Interest rates on Treasury bonds rose into the teens. This presented a problem for thrifts. Treasury bond interest rates were much higher than the Regulation Q interest rate limit. Thrift depositors began to withdraw their funds, to invest in Treasury bonds.

Congress recognized this problem. One solution was to do away with Regulation Q, and allow thrifts to pay competitive interest rates on their deposits. This solution created another problem. The assets of thrifts were fixed-rate, long-term mortgages. Most of these had been issued in the 1950s, '60s and '70s, when interest rates were lower. If thrifts paid competitive interest rates to depositors, and earned lower rates on their loans, they would lose money. Losses would continue until thrifts could issue enough high-interest mortgages to offset their stock of low-interest mortgages. That would take years.

Congress faced the choice: continue the interest rate ceiling and watch thrifts fail as depositors withdrew their funds, or eliminate the interest rate ceiling and watch thrifts fail as interest payments exceeded interest earnings. The compromise solution was to deregulate both sides of the ledger. In legislation in 1980 and 1982, the interest rate ceiling was phased out, and thrifts were allowed to make more consumer loans and commercial real estate loans, in addition to home mortgage loans.

The result was disaster. About one-third of all thrifts lost money during each year in the 1980s. Deregulation was not enough to save them from the interest rate trap. Thrift deposits were federally insured by the Federal Savings and Loan Insurance Corporation (FSLIC), just as bank deposits were insured by the Federal Deposit Insurance Corporation (FDIC). The FSLIC saw its reserves dwindle.

Worse, the newly deregulated thrift industry attracted speculators who gambled on high-risk high-return investments, including some notorious ventures in swampland and desert real estate. If the investments paid off, the speculators earned the profits. If the investments failed, and the thrift became insolvent, the FSLIC would bear the losses. Thrifts began failing in large numbers. There were runs on state-insured thrifts in Maryland and Ohio. Five Senators were accused of trying to keep regulators from investigating one savings and loan, in exchange for campaign contributions.

It was the nightmare result that opponents of deposit insurance had predicted back in 1933. Depositors would have no incentive to monitor the behavior of lenders, so lenders would make risky loans. When they failed, the government would have to make good on billions of dollars of depositor losses. Economists call such situations *moral hazard*. Regulations that protect people from the consequences of risky decisions, cause them to make more risky decisions. In 1989, Congress created the Resolution Trust Corporation, which paid off the depositors of failed thrifts at taxpayer expense. The total costs are disputed, but certainly ran to many hundreds of billions of dollars.

The Recession of 1990-91
The banking system also faced a crisis. In the 1970s many of the largest banks had taken deposits from newly enriched OPEC nations and invested them in development projects in Latin America. In the early 1980s Mexico threatened to default on those loans. Soon the problem spread to the rest of Latin America. The banks that had made the loans were threatened with insolvency—their assets falling short of what was owed to depositors. The Federal Reserve and U.S. Treasury assembled a rescue package for Mexico that prevented financial collapse, but many banks remained on shaky ground for the rest of the decade.

The savings and loan crisis, and the shaky condition of so many banks, led to a *credit crunch* by 1989. Banks were shoring up their reserves, and tightening their lending requirements. Loans for home construction were harder to come by, since so many savings and loans were in trouble. Loans for business expansion were scarce, too. In response, by mid-1989 the Fed reversed course, and began reducing interest rates. But the credit crunch continued, and investment spending started to fall. By the beginning of 1990 real GDP growth had dropped under 3%.

Then, on August 2, 1990, Iraq invaded Kuwait. President Bush declared that "this shall not stand," and organized an international coalition to oust the Iraqi army from Kuwait. Bombing began in January. By March, half a million U.S. troops were in Saudi Arabia. When the attack began Kuwait was liberated in four days.

But the economy went into recession. The Fed's interest rate hikes in 1988 and 1989 had slowed

> *Without a big increase in military spending, the 1990-91 Gulf War created economic uncertainty. Consumers and businesses reduced their spending, and the economy went into recession.*

growth. The credit crunch had slowed it some more. The Gulf War pushed it over the edge.

Past wars had stimulated the economy. The Gulf War did not. Big increases in military spending during the World Wars and the Vietnam War increased aggregate demand, which increased output and employment. In the Gulf War, however, there was no big increase in spending. The war was short, U.S. allies helped pay, and the Reagan administration had built up the military during the 1980s. The equipment had already been bought. There was no big military spending increase during the Gulf War.

The war affected the economy in other ways. Oil supplies were temporarily interrupted, and oil prices shot upward. More important was the effect on *expectations*. Uncertainty about the future caused households to cut back on consumption spending, and businesses to cut back on investment spending. Both fell at the end of 1990 and the start of 1991. The recession is marked as beginning in August 1990, and ending in March 1991. These are the same months that the Gulf crisis began and the Gulf War ended. Wars do not always stimulate the economy.

Greenspan and Bush

Relations between President Bush and Fed chair Alan Greenspan had gotten off to a rocky start. When the Fed continued to increase interest rates in 1989, The new budget director, Richard Darman, badgered Greenspan with memos and faxes, demanding lower interest rates. Greenspan ignored the budget director, respectfully, but the Fed started reducing rates in response to the credit crunch. Darman was encouraged—he seemed to be getting results.

But in 1990 Greenspan was slow to recognize that a recession had started. The first cut in the discount rate did not come until December 1990, five months after the recession had begun. After that, though, the Fed acted aggressively, reducing the discount rate by three and a half points over the next year and a half. The recession ended in March 1991 (though this wasn't clear at the time). The recovery was slow and uneven. It was called a *jobless recovery* because the unemployment rate continued to rise. It peaked at 7.8% in June 1992, more than a year after the recession's end.

After the Gulf War victory, President Bush's approval rating was sky high. It sank under the weight of rising unemployment. As the reelection campaign approached, the administration grew increasingly desperate for a more rapid recovery "Interest rates should be lower—now," President Bush said in his January 1991 State of the Union address.

Again the administration pressured Greenspan, at one point by trying to deny him invitations to the best Washington parties. Greenspan thought that attempts at pressure were worse than useless. The Fed needed to keep its hard-won credibility with financial markets. If the administration pressed for a rate cut, and the Fed did cut rates, Wall Street would think that monetary policy was being made for political reasons. Greenspan had once told the Senate Banking Committee that if political pressure for lower rates continued, "we will feel the necessity to do the opposite."

Bush reappointed Greenspan in 1991 despite these conflicts. The administration couldn't find another candidate, and a poll showed that 75% of Wall Street financial people supported reappointment. But relations between the two never improved. The recovery remained sluggish, and George Bush lost his bid for re-election in November 1992. In an interview in 1998 the ex-President said about Alan Greenspan,

> I think that if the interest rates had been lowered more dramatically that I would have been reelected president because the recovery that we were in would have been more visible. I reappointed him, and he disappointed me.

The Financial Markets Strategy

"It's the economy, stupid," was campaign advisor James Carville's way of reminding his candidate that economic issues would decide the 1992 election. Bill Clinton won the presidency on pledges of economic help for the middle class. There would be a middle-class tax cut, new investments in job training, investments in infrastructure, a fast-track spending program to stimulate the sluggish economy, health care reform—and a reduction in the Federal budget deficit. But as they tried to craft a tax and budget proposal out of these promises, his economic advisors realized that they didn't add up. New deputy budget director Alice Rivlin was blunt about it. She told Clinton's protesting political advisors that the campaign had fundamentally misrepresented the situation. Its statements had been "dishonest" and "untrue." The political people didn't like that at all.

Recovery from the recession had just begun, and cyclical budget deficits were large. But there was a structural deficit too. Deficits were expected to remain large, even as the economy expanded. Alan Blinder, an economist from Princeton, presented the case for deficit reduction at a meeting with the President. He realized the policy was a political loser. It required a long chain of reasoning: spending cuts lead to a smaller deficit, which leads to lower interest rates, which leads to more investment, which leads to higher productivity, which results in higher standards of living. "It doesn't fit on a bumper sticker," he told Laura Tyson, the new head of the Council of Economic Advisors. Blinder glanced at the President. Clinton looked grim.

It was possible, Blinder continued, for deficit reduction to be much less painful. The President perked up. Perhaps economic growth would increase, despite the drop in aggregate demand that the balanced budget implied. Suppose interest rates fell sooner rather than later? It could happen if the bond market believed that the President's program would discourage inflation. They would then charge a smaller "inflation premium" on their long term interest rates now. It also could happen if the Federal Reserve anticipated lower inflation, and allowed interest rates to fall. With lower interest rates, investment spending would rise. If the lower interest rates reduced the value of the dollar (that's second shift #5), U.S. exports would increase.

> **The financial markets strategy in the 1990s combined moves towards a balanced budget with lower interest rates, to encourage investment and long-term growth.**

Bill Clinton was reluctant, but he agreed. Deficit reduction was needed for the future of the economy. And, he was learning, Congress and much of the public seemed to agree. Within a week he had adopted the *financial markets strategy* as his policy. They would cut the deficit substantially, and hope for a quick fall in interest rates. They set the deficit reduction target at $500 billion over four years.

In a sense, it was a "crowding in" strategy. Balance the budget, and so reduce money demand. Interest rates would fall, with the help of a more expansionary monetary policy from the Fed. The resulting increase in investment spending would stimulate the economy, and (eventually), increase potential output. Real GDP would grow faster in the long run. It's a strategy that had been proposed before: by James Tobin, during the Kennedy administration (see Chapter 10). Now the Clinton administration put it into effect, thirty years later.

But they needed a deal from the Fed—would they reduce interest rates if there was a plan to balance the budget? The administration sent Treasury secretary Lloyd Bentson to talk to Alan Greenspan. A good choice, they thought. Bentson and Greenspan were friendly tennis opponents.

No dice. "He's not going to give us a deal," Bentsen told the President, reporting on his meeting. "There can be no quid pro quo." Greenspan would not guarantee an interest rate cut in exchange for a proposed deficit cut. The lesson of the William McChesney Martin-Lyndon Johnson deal still held sway at the Fed. Greenspan supported the policy, though, and testified in its favor in Congress, which gave Clinton's budget bill a boost.

Clinton's political advisors weren't happy with the plan. It meant they couldn't fulfill their other campaign pledges, at least not soon. It made the President uncomfortable too, even angry. "I hope you're all aware that we're all Eisenhower Republicans," he told his staff sarcastically. "We stand for lower deficits and free trade and the bond market. Isn't that great?"

The Soft Landing

President Clinton adopted his financial markets strategy in 1993. The idea was to cut the deficit, reduce Federal borrowing and so cut interest rates. The hope was that interest rates would fall in anticipation of lower future deficits. The administration was encouraged when interest rates fell through most of 1993. The mortgage rate, for example, was 8% in January, 6.8% in October.

There was no sign of rising inflation in early 1994. The inflation rate was 2.5% that January, lower than it had been a year before. Yet, thought Alan Greenspan, conditions were right.

The Fed changes interest rates to try to influence investment spending. A rule of thumb from Milton Friedman's work on monetary policy is that it takes nine months to a year for interest rate changes to have an effect. That meant that if the Fed was to head off inflation—stop it before it started—it had to anticipate conditions a year in the future. If it could do so, there was a chance for a *soft landing*. Spending growth would slow enough to stop inflation but not enough to create recession. If inflation never got started, a future recession would not be required to bring it down. Early in 1994 Greenspan decided to launch a "preemptive strike" on inflation, raising interest rates now to prevent it from ever getting started.

Greenspan paid a courtesy call on President Clinton to tell him about the new policy. Clinton's financial markets strategy depended on interest rates coming down, so Greenspan's news was tough to take. The President swallowed hard and told him "I want to keep interest rates low, but I understand what you may have to do." Privately, Clinton was angry. His economic advisors let him blow off steam, and then reminded him that public criticism of the Fed was likely to be counterproductive. The President kept quiet in public.

Between February 1994 and February 1995 the Fed increased the federal funds rate by three percentage points, in seven separate moves. To make sure everyone knew what they were doing, for the first time the Fed began announcing their federal funds rate decisions on the day they were made. Up until 1994 only the discount rate changes had been announced. The market had had to guess about federal funds rate changes, by watching the direction of interest rates day to day.

Greenspan was criticized from the right and the left. Radio commentator Rush Limbaugh called Greenspan's inflation policy "paranoia." Congressional Democrats held hearings, criticizing the preemptive strike, as well as Fed secrecy, pay raises and lack of diversity.

> *The Fed probably achieved a "soft landing" with interest rate increases in 1994-95, stopping inflation before it started, without causing a recession.*

Real GDP growth slowed in 1995, and the unemployment rate stopped falling. Over the same period, inflation remained in the 2.5% to 3% range. It was a slowdown, but it was no recession. In 1996 real GDP growth picked up, and remained over 4% in most quarters through the year 2000. The unemployment rate began falling, dropping below 5% in 1997. Inflation did not increase. In fact, it fell, in 1997 and 1998, and remained below 3% until the year 2000.

It appeared that Greenspan had pulled it off: a soft landing. Inflation was held in check without a recession. Criticism of the Chairman all but disappeared in 1996. Instead a new term was coined: the *Goldilocks economy*. It was not too hot, not too cold--just right. Bill Clinton reappointed Greenspan to a third term. His appointment passed the

Senate 91 to 7. Bill Clinton won reelection in 1996 in the midst of all this good economic news.

Productivity

Now it was 1996, and Alan Greenspan didn't think the productivity numbers were making sense. *Productivity* is the amount of output produced per unit of the economy's inputs: labor, capital and other resources. The numbers showed little or no growth in productivity. Yet, business profits were rising, while product prices were not. To increase profits, businesses could charge more for their products, or pay less to their workers. Or, they could produce products more efficiently. Since prices weren't rising, and wages weren't falling, productivity had to be increasing.

For twenty years low productivity growth had been a mystery. Between 1947 and 1973, labor productivity—output per worker—increased by 2.4% per year. Then, starting in 1974, this rate of increase dropped. From 1974 to 1995, output per worker rose only 1.1% per year. This may seem like a small drop, but it's the sort of thing that adds up over time. Had labor productivity continued to rise 2.4% per year through 1995, GDP would have been 34% larger. The average wage-earner would have had about one-third more in income.

Many reasons for the productivity slowdown were debated. None seemed to offer a complete explanation. Among the possibilities:

- Starting in the early 1970s, the huge baby boom generation began entering the labor force. With so many new workers, the labor force as a whole became less experienced. Less experienced workers are less productive.

- The big increase in energy prices starting in 1973 made large parts of the capital stock obsolete. Firms had built factories expecting continued low energy prices. The factories were most productive when they used lots of cheap energy. When energy prices increased, firms tried to operate these factories with less energy, and they were less productive.

- The 1970s and early 1980s saw big economic disruptions. Energy prices rose, inflation was high, interest rates fluctuated a lot, there were two big recessions, Bretton Woods collapsed, international competition increased. Business managers had to devote their efforts to dealing with these problems, rather than thinking up and applying new technologies that would increase productivity.

- The big budget deficits and high real interest rates of the 1980's reduced growth in investment spending. The capital stock was now smaller than it could have been. Perhaps the continued productivity slowdown was the expected result of crowding out.

- The 1970s saw an increase in new kinds of government regulation. Firms were required to devote resources to worker safety and pollution control, for example.

Billions of dollars of investment that might have gone to produce more output went instead to smokestack scrubbers to prevent air pollution. While this was a benefit to society, it was not measured as part of GDP. Measured productivity growth slowed.

A problem with these explanations was that almost all of them had been reversed by the mid-1990s. The boomers now had twenty years work experience. Energy prices had collapsed in 1986. There had been low inflation and only one short recession since the early 1980s. The budget deficit and real interest rates had come down. Regulation for pollution and worker safety hadn't lessened, but other kinds of economic regulation, which restricted competition in airlines, trucking and communications, had been abolished during the Carter and Reagan administrations. Still productivity growth lagged.

> *Productivity is the amount of output produced per unit of input, like output per worker. Productivity growth was slowed from 1973 to 1995, but picked up in the second half of the 1990's.*

Most curiously, the nation seemed to be in the midst of a technological revolution. Starting in the early 1980s, personal computers appeared on millions of employee desks, then on top of employee laps. Cell phones had been the richest of luxuries in the 1980s, but were now common. Fax machines came and went, email arrived, and then, in the 1990s, the internet began to grow by leaps and bounds. Yet productivity growth remained slow.

Pessimists thought the *information technology* (IT) revolution never would enhance productivity. IT's contribution to productivity just wasn't substantial compared to past innovations. When air travel had replaced rail, for example, a trip from New York to California had shrunk from three days to four hours—*that* was a productivity improvement. The ability to send email instead of making a phone call wasn't comparable.

Optimists pointed out that past innovations had not improved productivity right away. It had taken decades for the introduction of electricity in the 19th century to improve business operations enough to show up in productivity data. Businesses had to experiment with the new technology to discover new and better ways of producing. Businesses were experimenting with IT. Someday—soon, the optimists hoped—those experiments would pay off.

Maybe that's what was happening, Greenspan thought. If so, more rapid productivity growth would have implications for monetary policy. The unemployment rate was falling. In September 1994 it had dropped below 6%; by mid-1996 it dropped below 5.5%. The NAIRU—the *non-accelerating inflation rate of unemployment*—was thought to be about 6%. When unemployment dropped below six, the inflation rate tended to rise. With unemployment low, firms would have to jack up wages to bid employees away from one another, or to attract workers from school or home. Higher wages would be passed on in higher prices. Low unemployment led to higher inflation.

But what if productivity was accelerating? Then firms could pay higher wages, *but they would not have to raise prices*. With each worker using new technology to produce more product, higher wages could be paid out of higher sales receipts. Wages would rise, profits would rise, but prices would not. Employment could increase without price increases. And that meant the unemployment rate could fall below 6%, with no increase in inflation.

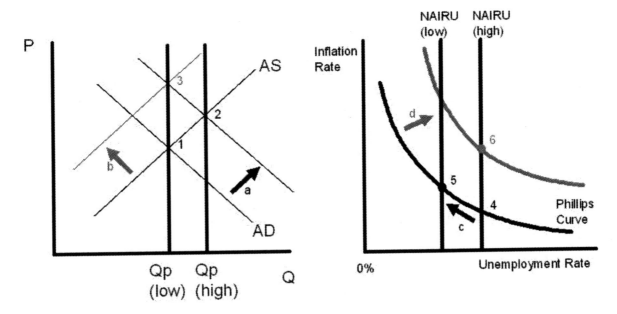

Figure 11-9. Greenspan vs. Meyer, seen two ways. These two graphs show the same ideas. Greenspan thought productivity increases had increased potential output (Qp high), while Meyer didn't think so (Qp low). If Greenspan was right, the increase in aggregate demand (a) won't lead to higher inflationary expectations (in fact, productivity growth means that aggregate supply would have increased to hold prices down, not shown here to avoid clutter). Output would be at potential (2). If Meyer was right, point 2 is beyond potential output, which will lead to rising inflationary expectations and a decrease in aggregate supply (b), which is second shift #1. Output will fall and prices will rise (3). Greenspan and Meyer discussed this issue in terms of the Phillips Curve. The NAIRU is the non-accelerating inflation rate of unemployment, which is the same idea as the natural rate of unemployment. Greenspan thought the NAIRU was low, because of productivity increases. Meyer thought it was high. That's the equivalent to the disagreement about potential output. The move up the Phillips Curve (c) is equivalent to the AD shift (a). If Greenspan is right, this low unemployment rate (5, equivalent to 2) can be sustained. If Meyer is right, the unemployment rate is below the NAIRU, and inflationary expectations will shift the Phillips Curve outward (d, equivalent to b). Inflation and unemployment will end up higher (6, just like 3).

It was a risky position for the Fed to take. If it was wrong, inflation would increase and the Fed would be behind the curve, just like in the 1970s. Greenspan decided to take the risk. Not everyone on the Federal Open Market Committee was convinced. Lawrence

Meyer, in particular, thought the productivity growth argument bordered on fantasy. Meyer was a recent Clinton appointee to the board, an economist with a national reputation for accurate forecasting. By April 1997 the unemployment rate had dropped to 5.1%. To Meyer it was a clear signal that inflation was going to rise, soon.

Greenspan persuaded the FOMC to leave the federal funds rate essentially unchanged through 1996, 1997 and into the Fall of 1998. During this time the unemployment rate fell from 5.6% to 4.5%. Real GDP kept growing, at 4-quarter rates between 3.7% and 4.8% in 1997, 1998 and 1999. But not only did inflation not increase, it continued to fall. The 12-month rate dropped under two percent in 1998.

> **More rapid productivity growth meant that the unemployment rate could fall below 6% without an increase in the inflation rate.**

By the mid-1990s the productivity data finally began to accelerate. From 1995 to 2007, growth in labor productivity averaged 2% per year, almost double the rate of 1974-95. The productivity data finally showed the effects of technological advance. And it was the best explanation around for the simultaneous drop in inflation and unemployment.

This was better than Goldilocks—just right and then some. The economy had achieved falling inflation, falling unemployment, and rapid GDP growth at the same time. Greenspan got much credit for this success, credit for *not* taking action. Interest rates were not increased, unemployment was allowed to fall and GDP to grow, because Greenspan recognized the acceleration of productivity and persuaded the FOMC to his point of view.

The Fed in the Asian Crisis
Finally, in 1998, the Fed made a change in interest rates. The federal funds rate was *cut*. The crisis in Asia threatened the U.S. expansion. In 1997 the Thai baht collapsed, and then financial contagion caused investors to withdraw from most of the Asian Tiger developing economies. The Tigers dropped into deep recessions in 1998. (The story is told in Chapter 9.)

The 1990's was the first decade after the fall of communism, and the Russian economy was having trouble adjusting. Its government ran big budget deficits, mostly because its tax collection bureaucracy was inadequate. It sold state-owned enterprises at bargain prices to political favorites. Uncompetitive businesses were subsidized. Its government and economy survived mainly on its earnings from selling oil.

With most of the Asian Tigers in recession in 1998, the demand for commodities like oil declined. The price of crude oil fell by half. That was fine for the United States, which saw gasoline prices drop to 96 cents a gallon by early 1999. It was not so fine for Russia. That's where international investors focused their concern.

The familiar events began. Investors tried to sell Russian assets. The supply of rubles outstripped the demand at the going exchange rate. The Russian central bank used its reserves to support the ruble, but their reserves ran short. And it couldn't earn enough foreign currency to pay interest to its foreign creditors. Finally, on August 17, 1998, Russia defaulted on its government bonds. Russia then restructured its debt, without the consent of its creditors, paying much lower interest over a much longer period of time.

Many of these Russian bonds had been bought on credit. Now the bonds were worth much less than the amount that had been borrowed to buy them. Traders were forced to put up more collateral for their loans. They had to sell other bonds to pledge this added collateral. The increase in the supply of these bonds reduced their price.

The Russian default led to a fall in the value of all bonds. When a large "hedge fund" called Long Term Capital Management collapsed, the bond market froze. Lots of investors wanted to sell bonds; few wanted to buy. Brokers wouldn't buy bonds from their customers for fear that they couldn't be sold again. Business firms hoping to sell bonds in order to raise funds for new investments found no buyers.

The Federal Open Market Committee held its regular meeting on September 29, and Greenspan proposed a quarter point rate cut. The FOMC agreed unanimously, but the results were disappointing. The stock market dropped 450 points (6%) over the next two days. Usually the market rose with a rate cut. Greenspan had tried to use the quarter point cut to send a message that the Fed was alert to the problem. But the message the markets received from such a small rate change was that the Fed didn't understand just how big the danger was.

FOMC member Ed Boehne checked into a Pennsylvania hotel. The clerk saw who he worked for, and said "Oh, you're from the Fed. You didn't do enough." Boehne told Greenspan, "When hotel clerks in central Pennsylvania tell you that you didn't do enough, it's time to do more."

But the next FOMC meeting wasn't scheduled for a month. Greenspan set up a conference call with the members on October 15. Then, at 3:30 in the afternoon, the Fed announced another quarter point rate cut. The press release said

> Growing caution by lenders and unsettled conditions in financial markets more generally are likely to be restraining aggregate demand in the future. Against this backdrop, further easing of the stance of monetary policy was judged to be warranted to sustain economic growth in the context of contained inflation.

It was a surprise to investors. The Fed hadn't changed rates between meetings in years. The stock market jumped more than 300 points, and continued to gain for the next week. Within three weeks the market had regained everything it had lost since the Russian default. The bond market thawed.

What had happened? Fed Governor Lawrence Meyer thought the surprise rate cut sent the message that the earlier cut had not. The Fed understood the problem and is ready to do what is needed. It provided a boost in confidence to investors. Markets began functioning again. The U.S. economy continued to expand, and by 1999 most of the developing countries were growing as well. In a sense it was another application of the lesson from 1987. In a financial panic, flood the markets with money.

The Fed responded to the 1998 Asian crisis with cuts in interest rates. This reassured investors and helped prevent panic.

But now Greenspan had another concern: the stock market. It had been rising since the 1990-91 recession, and by the mid-1990's it was rising a lot. The Dow Jones Industrial Average had dipped below 2,600 during the recession. By October 1996 it topped 6,000, more than doubling in six years. Investors were excited about technological advance (values on the NASDAQ, a stock exchange for high tech companies, were rising even faster). They were excited about the new investment opportunities presented by globalization and the collapse of Communism. But how much excitement was too much? If values moved upward beyond what firm profits and prospects justified, they could crash. The effects of the crash of 1987 had been contained. The effects of another crash might not be.

But the Fed had little influence over the stock market. It could raise interest rates, but that would slow the economy generally and might not slow the stock market. It hadn't worked in 1928-29, Greenspan knew. He decided to issue a warning. It could not be direct—the Fed had no business telling the markets what to do, Greenspan believed—so he decided to phrase it as a question in a speech he would give to the American Enterprise Institute in December. He spoke of the collapse of a real estate bubble in Japan in 1989. Then he asked, "How do we know when *irrational exuberance* has unduly escalated asset values, which then become subject to unexpected and prolonged contractions as they have in Japan over the past decade?"

Herbert Stein, a member of the audience and former head of the Council of Economic Advisors, said to himself, "good thing the markets are closed." But when the markets opened the next day, the Dow Jones Industrial Average fell only 55 points, less than one percent. It more than recovered the loss on the next trading day. "Irrational exuberance" may be the most famous two words Alan Greenspan ever said, but they had little effect on the stock market.

Stock values continued to rise rapidly, 26% in 1996, 23% in 1997, 16% in 1998, 25% in 1999. The Dow Jones Industrials topped 10,000 in March 1999, a four-fold increase in less than a decade. People began saying extraordinary things to explain why the stock market boom was not a bubble that would end in a crash. Two respected economists wrote an article and a book called *Dow 36,000*. "Stock prices could double, triple, or even quadruple tomorrow and still not be too high," they said. The headline in *The Wall Street Journal's* special millennium edition on January 1, 2000 read "So Long, Supply and Demand." "There's a new economy out there," the article began, "and it looks nothing like the old one." Of course, people had said the same kinds of things about the market in 1928 and 1929 (and would about the housing boom in the 2000's).

Two weeks later, on January 14, 2000, the Dow Jones Industrial Average closed at 11,723. It wasn't that high again for more than six years. Unlike 1929 or 1987, there is no single day that can be labeled "Black Monday" or "Black Thursday." Traders gradually began to recognize that they'd been irrationally exuberant, and began to sell more than they bought. The Dow fell 6% in 2000, and 7% in 2001. On the *NASDAQ*, the stock market home to the high tech stocks, values fell farther and faster. The NASDAQ index peaked at 5,048 on March 10, 2000. By May 10 it was down 33% to 3,384. It bottomed out on October 9, 2002, at 1,114, a 78% loss from its peak. The Dow had fallen 87% from high point to low point over 1929-32.

Suddenly it was hard to raise funds for new investment on the stock market. Investment spending began to fall. Suddenly consumers found their portfolios shrinking in value. Some hadn't realized that declines could happen. The wealth effect began working in reverse and consumer spending began to grow more slowly.

There was more.

- The same exuberance that affected the stock market had also affected investment spending, especially in high tech equipment. Businesses spent freely, but by 2000 they were finding that they had the capacity to produce more product than consumers would buy. They cut back on investment spending.
- In 1999 Greenspan and the Federal Reserve finally decided that demand had outpaced productivity growth, and that inflation was a threat. Interest rates were increased. Businesses had yet another reason to cut their investment spending.
- The Asian crisis of 1997-98 had cut demand for oil, driving down its price. In response, the Organization of Petroleum Exporting Countries had cut back on oil supplies. The average price of a gallon of gasoline had been $1.06 in 1998; by 2000 it was $1.51. Consumers had less left over to spend. Business costs increased.
- The Asian crisis had reduced U.S. export growth, and had raised the value of the dollar, making imports cheaper. The trade deficit ballooned. Lower exports and higher imports reduced spending some more.

Then came the attacks of September 11, 2001. The attacks closed U.S. financial markets for several days. They destroyed the communications equipment used by some banks to make payments. They cut airline travel and tourism. The Federal Reserve responded by flooding the markets with money (again!). Consumer and business spending dropped a lot for a couple of weeks, then resumed in October.

The 9-11 attacks were not a *cause* of the 2001 recession, for the obvious reason that the recession began in March, while the attacks were in September. Can an event in September "cause" another event the previous March? Perhaps in one sense it can. The National Bureau of Economic Research marks the beginnings and ends of recessions. In

November 2001 they announced their decision to date the start of the recession in March. But they also said "the attacks clearly deepened the contraction and may have been an important factor in turning the episode into a recession." Had the 9-11 attacks not occurred, the 2001 slowdown might not have been severe enough to be labeled as a recession. A later event can change the *perception* of an earlier event.

MacroPolicy Now: Deficits and Debt

The decade has just begun, but we can say with near certainty that Federal budget deficits will be a big issue in the 20-teens. In 2011 the deficit is huge, almost ten percent of GDP, among the largest percentages since World War II. Much of this is due to revenue shortfalls resulting from the recession. But even with recovery, Federal agencies estimate that the deficit will still be 4% to 7% of GDP by decade's end.

Such deficits are often called "unsustainable." With deficits that big, the national debt grows relative to GDP. The national debt is the sum total of all the borrowing the Federal government has done, less the amount that's been paid back. Put another way, it's the sum of the value of Treasury bonds owned by the public.

Interest must be paid on these bonds, and the interest payments are an expenditure in the Federal budget. If the debt grows, interest on the debt grows too. Revenues tend to keep pace with GDP growth. So, if the debt grows faster than GDP, the share of revenues that must be used to pay interest also grows. That means there's less left over for government purchases and transfer payments. If the debt grows faster than GDP for a long time, eventually interest payments are such a large share of revenues that essential services— like defense or environmental protection—would be compromised. That's unsustainable.

That means that smaller deficits *are* sustainable. Interest payments can rise, but if revenues rise faster, we can afford it. Put another way, the debt can rise, but if GDP rises faster, we can afford to pay the interest. According to Fed chair Bernanke, a deficit in the 2.5% to 3% range, at most, can be supported by GDP and revenue growth.

That's what happened the last time we ran up the debt. After the huge deficits of World War II the national debt rose to 120% of GDP. It then fell as a share of GDP for the next 35 years, not because the government ran huge surpluses, but because deficits were small in most years. The growth in GDP outstripped the growth in the debt.

Chairman Bernanke pointed out that the budget cannot be balanced now. The spending cuts and tax increases required would reduce aggregate demand and threaten another recession. Deficits are counter-cyclical fiscal policy in recession, and they help get recoveries going..

Once the economy recovers, though, private borrowers like businesses and consumers will be competing for loans with the Federal government. That was Fed vice-chair Kohn's concern when he said that there could be upward pressure on interest rates. On the other hand, if interest rates threaten to get too high, the Treasury may ask the Federal Reserve to buy its bonds. Buying bonds is an open market operation that increases the money supply. This would create inflation. That's the concern of Thomas Hoenig of the Kansas City Fed. For that to happen, either the Fed would have to cooperate, or it would have to be forced. That would compromise its independence.

This may be the source of Bernanke's speculation that a plan to balance the budget in the future could reduce long-term interest rates now. If lenders anticipate future inflation, they raise interest rates. If they find a plan to balance the budget credible, they may reduce their inflationary expectations, and reduce long-term rates.

On the other hand (how many hands do I get?), the Treasury bonds could be sold to foreign investors, like those from China. They would have to demand dollars on foreign currency markets in order to buy, which would push up the value of the dollar. And even China's appetite for Treasury bonds may be limited. Treasury Secretary Geithner had to reassure China that U.S. Treasury bonds were safe early in 2010.

We have seen all this before, of course.

- Suppose the Federal Reserve "accommodates" the deficits, expanding the money supply to hold down real interest rates. Then inflation is likely to increase, but crowding out will be less of a problem. That's what happened in the 1960's.

- Suppose the Federal Reserve holds money growth down, allowing real interest rates to rise. Then investment will be crowded out, long-run growth will be reduced, but inflation will not increase. That's what happened in the 1980's.

- Suppose the Federal Reserve holds money growth down, allowing real interest rates to rise, but this attracts huge inflows of international investment. Then the exchange value of the dollar will rise, exports will be crowded out, but inflation will not increase. That also happened in the 1980's.

So far, it's not a problem. Interest rates are very low. Inflation is low, and the independent Fed intends to keep it low. Domestic and international investors want to lend as much as the government wants to borrow. The exchange value of the dollar has been up and down, but each European debt crisis sends investors back to the safe haven of the dollar and Treasury bonds.

Come the recovery, though, big deficits and rising debt would be a problem. Making a plan for smaller deficits in the future would be a good idea.

Terms in this Chapter, in order of appearance
Laffer curve
Supply-side economics
Reagan tax cut
Bracket creep
Income tax indexing
Elasticity of supply
Budget deficit
Crowding out
Structural deficit
Cyclical deficit
Gramm-Rudman-Hollings Act
Budget surplus
Trade deficit
Speculative bubble
Intervention
Plaza Accord
Twin deficits
Alan Greenspan
Stock market crash of 1987
Program trading
Savings and loan crisis
Moral hazard
Jobless recovery
Financial markets strategy
Federal budget surplus
Soft landing
Goldilocks economy
Productivity
Information technology (IT)
Non-accelerating inflation rate of unemployment (NAIRU)
Asian crisis
Irrational exuberance
NASDAQ

Notes
Fullerton (1994) tells the Laffer napkin story. It's Wanniski's story—neither Laffer nor Cheney remember it.

Feldstein discusses bracket creep (pp. 4-6). Data on tax brackets are available in Edwards (1994, p. 100). Stein (1994) tells the story of Ronald Reagan's career (pp. 257-59). Stockman (1986, p. 10) quotes Reagan on the high tax rate in the top income bracket. Feldstein also mentions the frustration Reagan felt with high taxes during his movie career (p. 21).

Ronald Reagan's beliefs and policies are described in Regan (157-59), Feldstein (p. 3, pp. 20-22), and Stein (264-67). Stockman (pp. 92-97) tells the story of the Rosy Scenario forecast. Feldstein (pp. 49-50) and Fullerton (p. 179) also discuss it. Stockman quotes Weidenbaum's roar (p. 95), and tells the story of the "magic asterisk" (pp. 159-167). Stockman describes the efforts to pass the budget cuts in the Senate and House (pp. 167-177), and the battle over the Social Security cuts (pp. 181-193).

Fullerton briefly (pp. 179-182) and Stockman extensively (237-268) describe the tax bidding war of June-July 1981. By the Spring of 1981 the Kemp-Roth bill had acquired a new name, Conable-Hance. It's called Kemp-Roth throughout this text for clarity. Stockman (p.270) calls the tax cuts of June-July 1981 a breakdown in partisan checks and balances; Fullerton (p. 181) calls it a feeding frenzy and a bidding war. Stockman (p. 239) quotes Reagan drawing the line at 25%, and Wright on calling and raising (pp. 255-56). Fullerton (p. 190) says the deficits changed the direction of tax policy-making. Stockman (pp. 269-275) describes the August 3 victory luncheon.

Fullerton (p. 175) quotes himself on the Laffer Curve. Feldstein (p.24) criticizes the extreme supply side claims. Volcker and Gyohten (p. 178) describe the relatively low domestic investment during the 1980s, and (pp. 181-182) describe the fiscal-monetary policy deal that he refused to make. Feldstein (p. 53) recalls what he told his Reagan administration colleagues about crowding out, and discusses the campaign against him (p. 57). Volcker records his surprise at the amount that could be borrowed from abroad (p. 179). He describes the effects of trends on currency trading (pp. 230-31).

Gramm-Rudman is described in Feldstein (1994, pp. 61-62). The Bush and Clinton administration's budget policies are detailed in Elmendorf et. al. (2002, pp. 60-70). The crowding out debate in 2003 is from contemporary newspaper accounts.

Feldstein (pp. 66-68) offers his view on how foreign investment spread crowding out to exporting and import-competing industries. Frankel (p. 321) uses Caterpillar's example to illustrate the problems of the high valued dollar for American exporters. Both Frankel (p. 298) and Feldstein (pp. 67-68) tell the story of Regan's "toss it in the waste basket" testimony. Frankel (p. 302) quotes Baker's confirmation hearing comment. Volcker (pp. 232-235) describes the roles of the Treasury and Fed in exchange intervention. Volcker describes his discussion with Baker about the Plaza meeting in Volcker and Gyohten (p. 243).

Bob Woodward (2000) wrote a history of the Greenspan Fed, called *Maestro*, which is the source of many of the stories told here. He wrote of the argument between Laurence Meyer and Alan Greenspan (pp.183-187), and about Greenspan's suspicions about productivity (pp. 166-168, 171-174).

Woodward (2000, p. 16) has Baker's quote about Volcker as a known Democrat. Martin (2000, p. 127) compares Greenspan to Woody Allen. Martin (pp. 153-155) and Woodward (2000, pp. 15-25) tell the story of Volcker's dismissal and Greenspan's appointment.

The story of the 1987 stock market crash is pieced together from Woodward (2000, pp. 35-47), Martin (pp. 171-183) and Litan (1994, pp. 536-538). Woodward (2000, p. 53) reports James Baker's opinion of Greenspan's 1988 timing. Litan (pp. 521-536) tells the story of the Savings and Loan crisis. Woodward (2000, pp. 72-74) and Martin (pp. 188-94) look at the crisis from Greenspan's point of view. Woodward (2000, pp. 68-72) describes the effect of the Gulf War on monetary policy.

Woodward (2000, pp. 61-63, 81-83, 88-94) and Martin (196-198) report the Bush administration's efforts to influence Greenspan's policies. Woodward (2000, pp. 69-71) and Elmendorf (pp. 70-71) discuss the monetary policy response. Martin (p. 198) gives Bush's "disappointed" quote.

Woodward's book on the first years of the Clinton administration, *The Agenda* (1994), is the main source for the details on the formation of the "financial markets" strategy. The January 7 meeting is described on pages 79-94. Rivlin's "dishonest" quote is on pages 120-121. Bentson's consultation with Greenspan is on pages 101-102, and Greenspan's testimony favoring the Clinton plan is on pages 158-159. Clinton's quote about being an Eisenhower Republican is in Woodward (1994, p.185).

Mankiw offers a review of monetary policy in the 1990's (2002, pp. 19-43). Greenspan's pre-emptive strike on inflation, aiming for a soft landing, is discussed in Woodward (2000, pp. 115-124) and Martin (pp. 204-209). Blustein (2003, p. 329) is one among many who define the "Goldilocks economy."

Baily (1986) reviews the possible explanations for the productivity slowdown. Greenspan's trouble with the productivity numbers are in Woodward (2000, pp. 166-168, 171-174), as is a discussion of his debate with Laurence Meyer (pp. 183-187).

Blustein has a chapter on the Russian default (pp. 235-277). The story of Long Term Capital Management is told by Blustein (pp. 305-325) and Woodward (2000, pp. 199-208). Woodward reports on the Fed's interest rate decisions in Fall 1998 (2000, pp.203-212), and so does Blustein (pp.325-331, 349-355).

Martin (pp. 214-217) tells the story of the "irrational exuberance" speech. "Dow 36,000" is from Glassman and Hassett (1999); "So Long, Supply and Demand" is from Petzinger (2000).

The National Bureau of Economic Research puts its press releases on its website, at www.nber.org.

Sources

Baily, Martin Neil. 1986. "What Has Happened to Productivity Growth?" *Science* 234 (October 24): 443-451.

Bhagwati, Jagdish. 2002. "Trade Policy: Comments." Pages 333-340 in Jeffrey A. Frankel and Peter R. Orszag (eds.), *Economic Policy in the 1990's.* Cambridge, Massachusetts: MIT Press.

Blustein, Paul. 2003. *The Chastening (revised edition).* New York: PublicAffairs.

Congressional Budget Office. 2011. *Budget and Economic Outlook, Fiscal Years 2011 to 2021.* Washington, D.C.: Congressional Budget Office (January).

Edwards, Chris R. (ed.) 1994. *Facts and Figures on Government Finance (1994 Edition).* Washington, D.C.: Tax Foundation.

Elmendorf, Douglas W., Jeffrey B. Liebman and David W. Wilcox. 2002. "Fiscal Policy and Social Security Policy During the 1990's." Pages 61-119 in Jeffrey A. Frankel and Peter R. Orszag (eds.), *Economic Policy in the 1990's.* Cambridge, Massachusetts: MIT Press.

Feldstein, Martin. 1994. "American Economic Policy in the 1980's: A Personal View." Pages 1-79 in Martin Feldstein (ed.), *American Economic Policy in the 1980's.* Chicago: University of Chicago Press.

Frankel, Jeffrey A. 1994. "The Making of Exchange Rate Policy in the 1980's." Pages 293-341 in Martin Feldstein (ed.), *American Economic Policy in the 1980's.* Chicago: University of Chicago Press.

Friedman, Thomas. 1999. *The Lexus and the Olive Tree.* New York: Farrar, Straus and Giroux.

Fullerton, Don. 1994. "Tax Policy." Pages 165-208. in Martin Feldstein (ed.), *American Economic Policy in the 1980's.* Chicago: University of Chicago Press.

Glassman, James K. and Kevin A. Hassett. 1999. "Dow 36,000" *The Atlantic Monthly* (September): 37-58.

Litan, Robert E. 1994. "Financial Regulation" Pages 519-57 in Martin Feldstein (ed.), *American Economic Policy in the 1980's.* Chicago: University of Chicago Press.

Mankiw, N. Gregory. 2002. "Monetary Policy." Pages 19-43 in Jeffrey A. Frankel and Peter R. Orszag (eds.), *Economic Policy in the 1990's.* Cambridge, Massachusetts: MIT Press.

Martin, Justin. 2000. *Greenspan: The Man Behind Money*. Cambridge, Massachusetts: Perseus Publishing.

Petzinger, Thomas, Jr. 2000. "So Long, Supply and Demand." *Wall Street Journal* (January 1): R31.

Regan, Donald T. 1988. *For The Record*. New York: Harcourt Brace Jovanovich.

Stein, Herbert. 1994. *Presidential Economics (3rd Revised Edition)*. Washington, D.C.: The AEI Press.

Stockman, David. 1986. *The Triumph of Politics*. New York: Harper and Row.
Volcker, Paul and Toyoo Gyohten. 1992. *Changing Fortunes*. New York: Times Books.

Woodward, Bob. 1994. *The Agenda: Inside the Clinton White House*. New York: Pocket Books.

Woodward, Bob. 2000. *Maestro: Greenspan's Fed and the American Boom*. New York: Simon and Schuster.

News Articles
Andrews, Edmund L., "Greenspan Throws Cold Water on Bush Arguments for Tax Cut," *New York Times*, February 12, 2003.

Andrews, Edmund L., "U.S. Deficit Seen as Rising Fast," New York Times, March 5, 2003.

Appelbaum, Binyamin. "Fed Wants Priority Put On Deficit," *New York Times*, June 7, 2011.

Chan, Sewell. "Bernanke Expects Extended Low Rates," *New York Times*, February 25, 2010.

Chan, Sewell. "Federal Reserve Officials, Often Tight-Lipped, Openly Voice Deficit Concerns," *New York Times*, February 17, 2010.

Hauser, Christine. "S.&P. Lowers Outlook for U.S., Sending Stocks Down," New York Times, April 18, 2011.

Mankiw, N. Gregory. "What's Sustainable About This Budget?" *New York Times*, February 14, 2010.

Pear, Robert. "The Man Who Sells America's I.O.U.'s," *New York Times*, August 24, 2009.

Chapter 12
The Panic of 2008

MacroPolicy Now: Scenes from a Worldwide Collapse

Jerry Martinez, a general contractor, and his wife, Marcie, an accounts clerk, bought their house in a new San Francisco suburb for $630,000 in early 2005. By the end of 2008 it was worth about $420,000. That means they, like most of their neighbors, were "underwater" on their home. They owed more on their mortgage than their house was worth. They had an interest-only mortgage, a popular loan during the housing boom that allowed them to forgo principal payments for a time. But only for a time. In 2015, Mr. Martinez said, his monthly payments will be $12,000 a month. He laughed and shook his head at the absurdity of it. The Martinezes are learning the necessity of self-denial for themselves and their three children. No more family bowling night. No more dinners at Chili's or Applebee's. Instead, they rent movies and play board games. (But not Monopoly — its real estate theme is too much like real life.)

In that same California town, at the furniture store Cribs, Kids and Teens, Jason Heinemann says his business is also down 50 percent. He opened the store in early 2006; last month was his worst ever. "Grandparents are big buyers of kids' furniture, but when their 401(k)'s are dropping $10,000 and $20,000 a week, they don't come in," he said. Mr. Heinemann laid off his one employee. He dropped his advertising in the local newspaper and luxury magazines. And he is tightening his own belt. "I used to be a big spender," he said. "We're setting a budget for Christmas."

John Parsons was a mortgage supervisor at Washington Mutual, a bank specializing in sub-prime mortgage loans. The bank's slogan was "the power of yes." So Mr. Parsons approved mortgage loans for baby sitters claiming salaries worthy of college presidents, and schoolteachers with incomes rivaling stockbrokers'. Even by these standards, one loan stood out. The customer claimed a six-figure income—from his job as a mariachi singer. The income couldn't be verified, so Mr. Parsons had him photographed in his mariachi outfit in front of his house. With that photo in his file, the loan was approved. "I'd lie if I said every piece of documentation was properly signed and dated," said Mr. Parsons, from his California prison cell.

For a while, Japanese housewife Nakako Ishiyama made a great deal of money trading currencies, stocks and bonds over the internet. Then she started losing. "My husband was so angry at me. We had a fight right there in the bank," she says of the day she told him the extent of her losses. She blames herself. She says she read about subprime loans and wobbling American banks but couldn't imagine that such far-off happenings had anything to do with her or that she had anything to do with them. Reaching for an expression of her grandmother's, she sums up her investment experience: "Like a blind person with no fear of snakes, I have acted like a fool."

Chinese Premier Wen Jiabao was asked about his country's economic links to the United States. "We have lent a huge amount of money to the U.S.," he said, "Of course we are concerned about the safety of our assets. To be honest, I am definitely a little worried." The U.S. government planned to run huge budget deficits, trying to fight recession. What if this caused inflation, and eroded the value of American bonds? One of China's top monetary economists quoted John Maynard Keynes: "If you owe your bank manager a thousand pounds, you are at his mercy. If you owe him a million pounds, he is at your mercy."

For years investment banks had been pressuring the Securities and Exchange Commission to remove regulations that restricted the amount of debt they could take on. Remove the regulation, the bankers said, and it would free billions of dollars that were held in reserve as a cushion against investment losses. They could be invested in the fast-growing world of mortgage-backed securities, credit derivatives, and other exotic assets. Finally, one Spring afternoon in 2004, the commission members met in a basement hearing room to abolish the regulations. A lone voice dissented, Leonard Bole, a software consultant from Valparaiso, Indiana. In a letter, he said he didn't think that the banks' computer models took sufficient account of risk. Of course, the commission ignored him. "I'm a little guy in the land of giants," he said later. "I thought that the reduction in capital was rather dramatic."

The day after the collapse of the Lehman Brothers investment bank, money manager Michael Lewitt warned that there was an even bigger problem hanging over financial markets: credit default swaps. These were a form of financial insurance, where one party would insure another against a fall in asset values, in return for a fee. But, Lewitt wrote, "The insurer is required to post collateral to support its payment obligation, but in the insane credit environment that preceded the credit crisis, this collateral deposit was generally too small." The insurers had promised payments that they could not make, if asset values fell. The credit default market had grown in less than a decade from almost nothing to double the size of the whole U.S. stock market. The biggest insurance company involved in this market was American International Group, AIG. Within days AIG was begging for a Federal bailout.

For almost 25 years the economy had been remarkably stable, so much so that economists called it "The Great Moderation." But suddenly, home values began falling, banks began failing, loans became hard to come by, and the economy plunged into the deepest recession since 1982, or 1975, or maybe even 1933. How could this have happened? We can't know the complete story, since it's still going on. But here's what we do know. . . .

The Great Moderation
Economists called it the *Great Moderation*, and it lasted from the mid-1980's until 2007. There were just two short recessions, and two of the longest expansions in United States history. After the 1981-82 recession faded, the unemployment rate topped 7% in only one year, and actually dropped to 4% in 2000. Inflation topped 5% in only one year, and the rate was often less than 3%. Interest rates trended downward throughout the period.

How moderate was the Great Moderation? We can measure the variation in a series of numbers by using the *standard deviation*. This statistic is essentially the average difference between the values of a number series, and its average. The higher the standard deviation, the more variable is the series. Divide real GDP growth into three periods: 1930 to 1950, 1951 to 1982, and 1983 to 2007. The standard deviation during the first period is 9.1%, of the second, 2.7%, and of the third, 1.4%. Real GDP growth has varied up and down less as time has passed. The period of the Great Moderation saw the smallest variation.

Improved business practices undoubtedly play a role in greater stability. Businesses kept better track of their sales and inventories. Before, a business might continue to produce products for months before realizing that sales were down. Inventories of unsold goods piled up. Production had to be cut back and employees laid off until those inventories were sold. Since there were so many unsold products, the layoffs lasted a long time. But if a business realized its sales were down after just a week or two, production cuts and layoffs could be fewer and shorter.

Luck may have played a role in the Great Moderation. The first half of the twentieth century saw two world wars. Wars of that size disrupt an economy, making for very high growth rates while they're being fought, and big declines in production once they're over. The first war so weakened the gold standard that it may have been a cause of the Great Depression. The 1950 to 1982 period saw two smaller wars (in Korea and Vietnam), and two big oil shocks (in 1973 and 1979). The period since 1983 saw two even smaller wars (the Gulf and Iraq/Afghanistan), and its oil shocks were shorter. The *shocks* to the economy got smaller as the century continued. Perhaps the Great Moderation was mere luck. ("Luck" from an economic policy point of view.   The absence of wars and oil shocks may be the result of better foreign policy.)

The first half of the century saw much, much wider swings in real GDP growth, and most other indicators, than the second half of the century. It seems likely that the long-term reforms adopted during the 1930's, plus the sheer growth in the size of government, played a role in that moderation.

The Social Security program created a group of income recipients who are immune to the ups and downs of the economy. Recessions come along, and social security recipients keep on spending. The unemployment insurance program automatically cuts taxes and increases benefits when recessions hit. Deposit insurance prevents bank runs, which supports bank lending. The money supply is less variable as a result, and that means real interest rates don't spike upward during recessions. All three forms of insurance—old age, unemployment, bank—support aggregate demand during recessions.

Whatever else it may do, bigger government probably stabilizes the economy. If tax rates are higher, the income multiplier is smaller. Spending by one person becomes income for the next. After saving, and taxes, the next person spends, and that becomes income for a third person. Each successive round of spending is smaller if taxes are higher. A smaller multiplier means that shocks to spending have smaller effects on overall output.

These changes help explain the drop in economic variability after 1950. The Great Moderation got its start in the mid-80's, though. Part of the reason for the Great Moderation may have been better fiscal and monetary policy.

When Arthur Okun said "You could go down that curve just as you went up that curve" he implied that, in the 1960's, economists thought there was a permanent tradeoff between inflation and unemployment. It was thought that policymakers could choose whatever combination of inflation and unemployment they preferred. The Johnson administration's guns and butter policy, and the Federal Reserve's low interest rates, sent aggregate demand "up that curve" in the 1960's. They chose lower unemployment at the cost of higher inflation.

Then second shift #1 set in, inflationary expectations developed, and aggregate supply decreased. Now they had higher inflation without lower unemployment. There is no permanent tradeoff between the two. The erroneous idea that there was helped create the Great Inflation.

When Arthur Burns supported wage and price controls in 1971 he implied that inflation was not simply a result of too-fast growth in the money supply. Labor unions and big corporations had power over prices, which helped cause inflation, he thought. If the link between the money supply and inflation was weak, policymakers were free to use interest rates to try to influence unemployment and real GDP growth.

> *The Great Moderation lasted from the mid-1980's to 2007. There were three long expansions, two mild recessions, low inflation and falling interest rates. One reason for the moderation was counter-cyclical monetary policy.*

We now think that the money supply is the primary culprit in inflation. The erroneous idea that it was not helped create the Great Inflation.

The recession of 1981-82 brought down the inflation rate, and since then Paul Volcker, Alan Greenspan and Ben Bernanke have consistently pursued counter-cyclical monetary policy. The federal funds rate has been reduced substantially during each recession since 1983. The Fed may have been a little slow off the mark in 1990-91 (as President Bush thought), starting big rate cuts only in October 1990, after the recession began. In both the 2001 and 2007-09 recessions, though, the Fed began reducing rates *before* the recession started. The 2001 recession is marked as starting in March. The Fed began cutting rates in December 2000. The 2007-09 recession is marked as starting in December 2007. The Fed began cutting rates in August 2007.

Output is still less than potential as recoveries begin. Only after a few years of expansion is potential output attained. During the Great Moderation the Fed held rates low during the first few years after the end of each recession. The 1990-91 recession ended in March

1991; the Fed held rates low until January 1994. The 2001 recession ended in November 2001; the Fed held rates low until June 2004. The Fed would begin increasing interest rates once potential output was approached and inflation became a threat.

In addition, monetary policy responded to financial crises, with interest rate cuts during the crises of 1987, 1998 and 2008-09. And Greenspan was among the first to recognize that productivity growth would hold inflation in check in the second half of the 1990's. The Fed did not increase interest rates, even as unemployment fell below levels that, in the past, would have generated inflation.

First came the Great Depression. Then came the Great Inflation. And then, the Great Moderation. What ended the Great Moderation? The Great Recession, of course.

The Housing Bubble

For more than fifty years after World War II, home prices rose at about the same rate as inflation. Once in a while housing prices would increase faster, but always these booms would fade, home value price increases would slow, and inflation in goods and services would catch up.

Starting in 1998, however, housing prices began to rise much more rapidly than inflation. By 2001—even though it was a recession year—real home prices had topped any previous boom. By 2006 the real price of houses was nearly double its long run average.

The house price increase was a regional event. In some places house prices rose a lot. In others, not so much. From January 1998 to July 2006, home prices in Los Angeles rose 241%, in San Diego, 218%, in Miami 207%. In Cleveland, though, prices rose 36%, in Charlotte, North Carolina, 39%, in Detroit, 45%.

These differences can be explained by changes in demand and supply. The demand for houses depends on population. When population grows, more people need houses. Demand depends on income. Higher income people are more likely to be homeowners. Demand depends on household size. Given the size of the population, smaller household sizes mean more households, so more homes are needed. People borrow money to buy homes, so demand depends on the mortgage interest rate and the terms of the mortgage. Lower mortgage rates and easier terms increase demand.

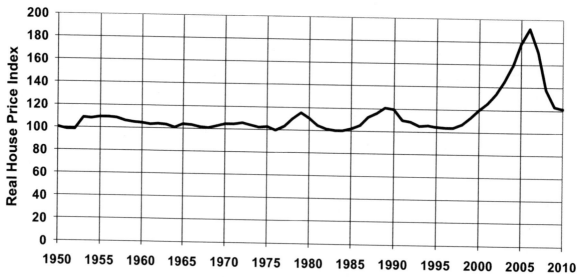

Figure 12-1. Index of real house prices, 1950-2010. Calculated with the Shiller house price index, divided by the consumer price index. The index varies between 100 and 120 for most of the 1950-1998 period. This means that housing prices rose at about the same rate as CPI inflation for almost fifty years. Occasionally house prices rose faster, as in 1976-79 and 1986-89, but in the years after that the CPI rose faster and the real index dropped back to near 100. Starting at the end of the 1990's, however, house prices rose much faster than inflation, with the index reaching nearly to 200, far higher than it had ever gone before. House prices peaked in 2006 and have fallen substantially since then. By 2010 the index was still not back to 100, however.

The supply of houses depends on input costs. What must be paid to hire construction workers, buy bricks and lumber, rent equipment? Most of all, how much does land cost? Higher input and land costs decrease supply. Legal restrictions matter too. Most communities impose zoning restrictions, limiting where houses and other structures can be built. There may also be requirements on lot size, landscaping, and other construction features. Tighter restrictions decrease supply.

Consider a state where house prices increased only a little (call it "Indiana"), and a state where house prices increased a lot (call it "California"). Figure 12-2 shows demand and supply for housing in these two states. In Indiana population rises by a small amount, and income growth lags the national average. Demand for housing rises slowly as a result. In California population grows rapidly, and so does income. Demand for housing rises a lot.

In Indiana most cities and towns are surrounded by farm land. This large supply of land is available for building, so it keeps land costs down. Indiana has relatively weak zoning restrictions as well. California cities are huge, and surrounded by already developed land. Land costs are high. Most California cities have strong zoning restrictions.

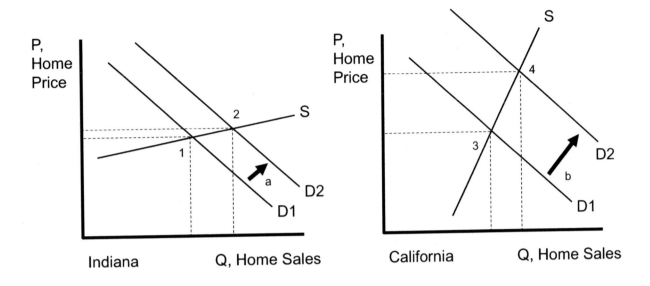

Figure 12-2. Tale of two markets. House price supply is elastic in "Indiana", because rural land is available on urban boundaries, and zoning is less restrictive. Income and population grow more slowly in Indiana, and mortgage lending standards are stricter, so housing demand rises less (a). House price supply is inelastic in "California", because the state is heavily urbanized with less rural land available, and zoning is more restrictive. Income and population grow faster in California, and mortgage lending standards are looser, so housing demand rises more (b). As a result, home prices rise less in Indiana (1 to 2), more in California (3 to 4).

Figure 12-2 shows the supply of housing in Indiana to be elastic, and the supply in California to be inelastic. In Indiana it takes only a small increase in the house price to call forth a lot of new housing, because land can be acquired so easily. But in California, land is expensive, so builders can make a profit from home construction only when price rises a lot.

In the western states and Florida, and other big cities such as New York, Boston and Washington, house prices rose rapidly due to population growth, income growth, and high cost land. These are good demand and supply reasons to expect bigger price rises. The price increases are explained, it is said, by the *fundamentals* of the market.

Sometimes, though, price rises due to fundamentals lead to price rises due to *speculation*.

House prices are subject to momentum. When prices have been rising, then tend to keep rising; when prices have been falling, they tend to keep falling. There are a couple of reasons for this momentum. First, houses are not just consumer goods, they are investments as well. They can be re-sold, usually for more than the owner paid originally. Second, it takes longer to build, buy and sell houses than most products.

When income and population increase, and land is scarce, house prices rise. Sometimes this causes people to anticipate even higher prices. The expectation of higher future prices causes demand to rise now. Consumers behave this way (buy before the price goes up). Investors behave this way too (buy low, sell high). Investment demand may cause people to buy houses that cost more than they can afford, expecting to resell at a profit.

> *The housing bubble was a huge run-up in house prices from the late-1990's to 2006. It occurred mainly on the coasts and in big cities.*

The demand increase causes the price to rise, which confirms and reinforces this expectation. At first nothing much happens to supply. Housing supply is inelastic over shorter periods of time. The added demand raises the price of the existing housing stock. Prices rise a lot.

California   Q, Home Sales

Figure 12-3. California nightmare. This diagram continues the California story from figure 12-2. The increase in demand (b in 12-2) has finally increased the number of firms in the market. Supply increases (c). This reduces the price (4 to 5), and shatters home buyers' expectations of future higher prices. Now the expectations of falling prices reduce demand (d), and may drive the price below its original level (5 to 6, with 6 less than 3 in 12-2).

But then local home builders, home builders in other communities, even business people in other industries see that extraordinary profits can be made in housing. It takes time to acquire land, get zoning and building permits, install utilities and roads, and then build the houses. But eventually supply increases, and this slows the increase in housing prices. If supply increases enough, prices may start to fall.

Households begin to notice that prices are not rising. The expectation of future price increases fades, and may change to an expectation of falling prices. That causes demand to decrease, even as supply continues to increase (those construction plans can't be cancelled right away). Prices fall a lot.

Why was the Bubble So Big?

Demand and supply, so far, may explain why housing bubbles happen, but they don't yet explain why the 1998-2006 bubble was so large. Something must have increased demand more, and for a lot longer, than any previous housing boom. Here are a few possibilities.

Capital Gains Tax Cut. During the 1996 Presidential campaign, Republican candidate Bob Dole proposed an across-the-board cut in capital gains taxes. These are taxes on increases in the values of assets, like stocks and houses, paid when the assets are sold. Dole was running against President Bill Clinton, a Democrat. Clinton's campaign felt it had to respond with a tax cut proposal of its own, but the President's economic advisors thought such a huge tax cut would undo the budget deficit reductions that had been achieved in Clinton's first term. So they responded by proposing a more modest tax cut, to eliminate the capital gains tax on most houses. The tax cut passed the Republican-controlled Congress in 1997.

The tax code now treated houses more favorably than other investments. Put your money in stocks, and any gains would be taxed when the stock was sold. Put your money in a house, and most of the gains would be tax free. This may have diverted investment funds from other assets, like stocks and bonds, into houses. The added demand would have increased prices.

Not everyone agrees that this tax change had much effect, but there is some evidence that it increased turnover in the housing market. Before the tax change, people avoided the capital gains tax by simply staying in their houses longer. After the tax change, they could sell and buy more frequently without paying taxes on the increasing value of their houses.

Monetary Policy. Alan Greenspan's Federal Reserve began cutting interest rates in January 2001, two months *before* the 2001 recession began. During the course of 2001 the federal funds rate was cut twelve times, from 6% to 1.25%. The rate remained under 2% through the end of 2004. Mortgage rates fell too, after a while, from 7% at the end of 2001 to a low of 5.2% in mid-2003. They have remained under 7% since then.

In most recessions housing construction drops a lot. Construction can be measured by "housing starts," the number of new homes that builders start each month. In the recessions in 1991, 1982, 1980, 1975 and 1970 monthly housing starts dropped below a hundred thousand. In 2001, though, housing starts remained high. The housing market sailed through the recession with hardly a pause. Starts increased from there, peaking at almost two hundred thousand per month in mid-2006.

The low interest rates in the first half of the 2000's decade were counter-cyclical policy. The economy fell into recession and output remained below potential, so lower interest rates were appropriate to increase aggregate demand. Stimulating investment in housing construction is one of the desired results of counter-cyclical monetary policy. But, perhaps, interest rates remained too low for too long. Low mortgage rates made borrowing cheaper, and increased the demand for housing. In addition, perhaps a housing slump in 2001 would have punctured the bubble before it started, reminding homebuyers and mortgage lenders that house prices could decline.

Again, not everyone agrees that the Fed held interest rates too low too long. The unemployment rate was still 5.6% in mid-2004, and the inflation rate was still under 2%, so monetary stimulus had some justification. Further, the Fed began increasing the federal funds rate in mid-2004, but long-term rates did not respond. Corporate bond rates—and home mortgage rates—fell for another year, then rose by much less than the federal funds rate increase. In testimony before Congress, Greenspan called this a "conundrum." The Fed could not increase long-term rates when it tried, so it is not clear that it could have limited mortgage lending by raising rates before 2004. The answer to *Greenspan's conundrum* was probably the enormous flow of funds from overseas. When mortgage lenders couldn't get the money from the Fed, they got it from Japan, China and Saudi Arabia.

Homeownership and Mortgage Innovation. The percentage of households who live in homes that they own—the homeownership rate—varied up and down between 64% and 66% from 1969 to 1995. Then the rate began to grow, peaking at 69% in 2005. It has since fallen to 67%. If more households own homes, and fewer rent, the demand for houses will rise, house prices will rise, and rents will fall (or rise more slowly).

The main explanation for the rise in homeownership is greater access to credit. Traditional mortgages require a down payment, have a fixed interest rate, and a fixed payment month to month, with payments over a period of thirty years. Mortgage lenders began to invent new mortgage alternatives and it became easier to get a mortgage starting in the middle-1990s. Interest-only mortgages have an initial period when monthly payments cover only the loan interest. Later, loan payments rise to cover repayment of principal. Negative amortizing mortgages start with payments less than current interest, with the difference added to principal. Again, loan payments rise later. Adjustable rate mortgages raise or lower interest rates and payments based on changes in market interest rates.

How did these mortgage innovations add to homeownership? For example, suppose a young family, just starting out, has little savings and a relatively low income now. But they have good jobs, and prospects for promotion, and in five years they will have increased their incomes and their savings. For this family, a mortgage that requires little or no down payment and has lower monthly payments for the first few years would put homeownership within reach. Mortgage payments would be lower now, higher later. Homeownership increased most for young families with higher education levels—people with low income and low savings now, but with excellent prospects for higher incomes later.

Homeownership also increased because of the rise of "subprime" mortgages. A subprime mortgage is one made to a borrower with no credit history, or who had failed to repay loans in the past, or who had low income relative to the size of the proposed mortgage payment. Traditionally such borrowers would have been denied mortgage loans, because lenders thought that there was too great a risk that the mortgage would not be repaid, and the borrower would default. Denied credit, these households would not have been able to buy homes.

Mortgage lenders began to make more subprime mortgages in the 1990's. Because the risk of default was higher, subprime borrowers were charged higher interest rates. This was called "risk-based pricing", and it was an innovation in itself. Prior to the 1990's, riskier borrowers weren't offered mortgages with higher rates. They were denied mortgages all together.

> *The main reason for the housing bubble was the increased availability of mortgage loans to buyers who would have been considered unqualified in earlier times.*

Government policies played a role in encouraging subprime lending. The Community Reinvestment Act was passed in 1977 to encourage lenders to provide loans to borrowers in lower income areas. Since many people in these areas would be regarded as poor credit risks, they would be offered subprime mortgages.

Some analysts worried that home buyers were being lured into risky mortgages against their best interests. Perhaps some were being defrauded by these mortgage deals. Federal Reserve Board member Edward Gramlich was particularly vocal. As early as December 2000 he advocated tighter regulation on subprime mortgage lenders. In 2002 he accused many lenders of charging excessive fees, and promoting mortgage refinancing in order to generate more fees. The mortgage process, he said, was "confusing, costly and far less than optimal." But the Greenspan Fed was relying on industry self-regulation, and Gramlich's warnings went unheeded.

The Secondary Mortgage Market

These factors help explain why the demand for housing rose more during 1998-2006 than it had in the past. But, as usual, the answer to one question generates another question. Where did lenders get the money to make all these additional mortgage loans?

For decades mortgage lending was done by savings and loan institutions and commercial banks. The main source of the money for making these loans was from the deposits of households in the community. Households deposited their savings in banks and received interest; banks lent this money to mortgage borrowers who paid interest. The mortgage rate was a little higher than the deposit rate, and the difference was bank profits.

The savings and loan crisis at the end of the 1980's changed these practices. Suddenly a large number of financial institutions that had made mortgages were out of business. And, lenders realized that it was risky to make a loan for thirty years at a fixed interest rate, when interest rates paid on deposits could vary up and down by a lot. What if the interest rate required to attract deposits rose higher than the interest rate being paid on all those old mortgage loans? That's what had caused the savings and loan crisis in the first place.

These problems led to an enormous expansion of the *secondary mortgage market*. Lenders would originate a loan—find the borrower, negotiate the terms, complete the paperwork and lend the money—but they would then sell the loan, or the rights to the mortgage payment, to an investor in the secondary market. The lender would receive the money from the investor, which could then be used to make another loan, and the investor would receive the mortgage payments, and bear the risk of default. The original lender would make its profits on the mortgage fees, not the mortgage payments.

The secondary mortgage market was a government invention. The Great Depression had increased foreclosures and depressed home construction. In 1938 the Federal government created the Federal National Mortgage Association (FNMA), which became known as *Fannie Mae*. It was Fannie Mae's job to borrow money from investors, buy mortgages from local lenders, and repay investors from the mortgage payments. Local lenders would gain more funds for loans, and get rid of the risk of default. This helped stimulate mortgage lending. Fannie Mae was originally a government agency, but in 1970 it became a private firm, though with a few special privileges. In 1970 a second similar company was created, the Federal Home Loan Mortgage Corporation (FHLMC), known as *Freddie Mac*.

Fannie Mae and Freddie Mac had a peculiar place in financial markets. They were private institutions, not government agencies. Yet when they borrowed money from investors, they were treated as if they were government agencies. The interest rates that they had to pay to borrow money were almost as low as those that the Treasury paid on its bonds. Investors must have expected that, even though they were private firms, should there be trouble the Federal government would come to Fannie's and Freddie's rescue (turns out they were right). The two were labeled "Government Sponsored Enterprises."

> *In the secondary mortgage market, the rights to receive mortgage payments are bundled and sold as securities to investors. The payments that lenders receive allow them to lend more for mortgages.*

Fannie Mae and Freddie Mac wouldn't buy just any loan. They would only buy loans that met certain standards that made the risk of default low. In fact, it was these standards that divided prime from subprime mortgages. A prime mortgage was one that Fannie Mae or Freddie Mac would buy. A subprime mortgage was one they would not buy. Since the number of subprime mortgages increased during the 1990's and 2000's, the share of Fannie and Freddie in the secondary mortgage market decreased. In 1989 over 90% of all mortgage loans sold in the secondary market were Fannie and Freddie's. By 2007 their share was less than half.

By 2007 private firms made up the majority of the secondary market. Some of the larger participants in the secondary market were Countrywide Financial, Lehman Brothers and Wells-Fargo. These firms would buy up mortgages and package them together in *mortgage-backed securities*, a process known as *securitization*. These new securities would be sold to investors. The mortgage payments would flow from the mortgage borrower through the financial firm to the investors.

Mortgage-backed securities would be divided into classes, or "tranches." The tranches were ranked based on their priority in claims on mortgage payments. The top, least risky tranche would have first claim on payments. The bottom, most risky tranche would have last claim on payments, and would suffer the first losses from default. That made the top tranche the least risky, so it would have the lowest interest rate. The bottom tranche would be most risky, so it would have the highest interest rate.

The tranches meant that the mortgage-backed securities had something to offer everyone. Investors who preferred low-risk assets, and were willing to accept a lower return, could buy a share of the top tranche. Investors who wanted a higher return, and were willing to accept more risk, could buy a share of the bottom tranche. Appealing to this wide range of investors increased the demand for mortgage-backed securities, allowing the financial firms to sell more securities at higher prices. And that made more money available for mortgage lending.

The volume of subprime mortgages increased in the early 2000's. By 2006 71% of mortgage-backed securities issued by private financial firms were based on subprime mortgages. In that year financial writer Roger Lowenstein had the rare privilege of watching the staff at Moody's Investors Service analyze a mortgage security. Moody's is a *credit rating service*, meaning it analyzes securities to tell investors how risky they are. Lowenstein's experience can provide us with an example of how mortgage-backed securities worked.

The financial firm wanting to issue the security was unnamed to Lowenstein, and the security was masked with the name "Subprime XYZ." It was a pool of 2,393 mortgages with a total value of $430 million. All the mortgages in the pool were subprime. The borrowers were thought to have a higher-than-usual risk of default. The original lender had provided information on the borrowers and their homes. Three-quarters of the borrowers had adjustable-rate mortgages, which had low initial interest rates which could climb fast. Almost half of the borrowers did not provide verification of their incomes. Twelve percent were for properties in Southern California, which was a risky degree of concentration in a single market (if something went wrong in that one market, the security was in trouble).

The financial firm wished to sell the rights to the pooled mortgage payments to investors. These rights were divided into twelve tranches, which Moody's would rate from least risky to most risky. The subprime mortgages themselves were obviously risky. How could they support securities rated at low risk? Because the highest-rated tranche would have first call on the mortgage payments, then the next tranche, then the next. The tranche at the bottom got the highest interest rate, but would absorb the first losses if any homeowners defaulted.

Mortgage securities like those in Subprime XYZ were just the beginning. Often they became parts of *collateralized debt obligations*, or C.D.O.'s. C.D.O.'s were constructed with tiers of mortgage securities, again rated from least to most-risky. The mortgage security was a first-order derivative, drawing directly on payments by homeowners. C.D.O.'s were second-order derivatives. They drew on income streams from combinations of mortgage securities. There were also third-order C.D.O.'s, known as C.D.O.'s squared, which were constructed from the C.D.O.'s that were constructed from mortgage securities.

Remember, the purpose of the secondary mortgage market was to make more money available for mortgage loans, to more people, at lower interest rates. Mortgage-backed securities were sold in world bond markets, purchased by people and institutions all over the world. This made it possible for anyone in the world with money to invest to lend in a local mortgage market. More money became available for mortgage lending, and that helped keep mortgage interest rates low.

The World's Money

Again, this presents another question. Why would investors in the rest of the world want to lend for U.S. mortgages? The first answer is simple: because they could get a higher return on their investments. Perhaps interest rates paid on mortgages or other assets in their own countries were low, compared to the interest rates on U.S. mortgages. In effect, mortgage-backed securities worked because interest rates differed around the world. Investors in countries with low interest rates would lend to borrowers in the U.S., where interest rates were higher. Since the mortgage-backed security interest rate would be higher than the rate in the investor's country, the investor would be satisfied. Since the mortgage-backed security interest rate would be lower than the rate in the borrower's country, the borrower would be satisfied. Both the investor and borrower were better off.

Japan. The answer to this question is more complicated when we look at individual countries. Consider Japan. By the end of the 1980's Japan was at the peak of its economic power. The familiar Japanese corporations—Sony, Toyota, Mitsubishi—where producing innovative products that the world wanted to buy. Japan ran big trade surpluses. The value of the Japanese yen had been rising since the end of fixed exchange rates, because of the increased demand for Japan's exports. After the Plaza Accord in 1985, the dollar fell against most currencies, and the yen began to rise faster.

This concerned the Bank of Japan, which is Japan's central bank. If the yen became too strong, Japanese exports would become expensive. A decline in exports would slow Japanese growth. So the Bank of Japan cut interest rates. Lower interest rates would make lending in Japan less profitable. The demand for the yen would drop (that's second shift #5), and the rise in the yen's value would slow down.

> *Interest rates were very low in Japan during the 2000's, so Japanese investors lent money for U.S. mortgages through the secondary mortgage market.*

The combination of strong economic growth and low interest rates fueled a spectacular real estate boom. For a while, it was said, the land surrounding the Imperial Palace in Tokyo was worth more than all the real estate in California. Then, of course, the bubble burst. Japanese investors lost trillions of yen as real estate values and stock values fell. Japan's economy suffered a decade of below-average growth, followed by a period of deflation. Its economy still has not fully recovered, twenty years later. The Bank of Japan was slow to respond, but by the end of the 1990's it had reduced its interest rate to near zero, trying to stimulate consumer and business spending (that's second shift #2).

Women control the family finances in Japan. There were children to educate, elderly parents to care for. Their savings were earning next to nothing at the near-zero interest rates. So they looked around for an alternative. In the early 2000's, aided by the newly available internet, they found international stocks, bonds and currencies. An astonishing amount of money flowed out of Japan looking for higher rates of return in the rest of the world. International investors would ask the question: "what are the housewives investing in these days?"

It was called the *yen carry trade*. Housewives, and professional investors and traders, would borrow at near-zero interest rates in Japan, and invest abroad. Some of the money went to nice safe U.S. Treasury bonds. But much of it sought out higher returns, in investments like mortgage-backed securities.

China. China began to abandon communism as a way to organize its economy in 1978, and turned increasingly to market organization. Chinese real gross domestic product began to grow fast, averaging 9.9% per year from 1978 to 2008 (the U.S. economy grew 3% per year during this time.). Growth fell below 8% only twice during these nearly three decades, in 1989 and 1990: the years of unrest surrounding the massacre at Tiananmen Square. The lesson was not lost on the Communist Party leaders. Keep the economy growing, or the party's hold on power could slip.

In 1994 China devalued its currency, the yuan, to 8.3 to the dollar, and kept it there for ten years. This made Chinese exports even cheaper in the United States and the rest of the world. Exports grew rapidly (that's second shift #4). A cheap yuan made imports expensive, however. And, the end of the communist economy meant the end of the "iron rice bowl": no more free medical care, support for the elderly in retirement, or subsidized housing. The Chinese people responded by spending less and saving more.

With exports cheap and little spending on imports, China ran enormous trade surpluses, especially with the United States. Ordinarily such a surplus would result in a rise in the value of the yuan and a fall in the value of the dollar. Americans would supply dollars into foreign exchange markets, trying to buy yuan, in order to buy Chinese products. The

Chinese would not demand so many dollars, since they weren't buying many American products. With dollar supply rising faster than dollar demand, the value of the dollar should have fallen.

A rising yuan would have made Chinese exports more expensive, threatening the economic growth upon which the Communist Party's position depended. So the Chinese central bank began *buying dollars* to prevent the dollar from falling and the yuan from rising. These purchases increased dollar demand and supported its value, which kept the value of the yuan low. What to do with all those dollars they had purchased? China lent them back to the United States, buying Treasury bonds and the bonds issued by Fannie Mae and Freddie Mac. By 2010 China owned more than a trillion-and-a-half dollars in American bonds.

> *To keep the value of the Chinese yuan from rising, China printed yuan and bought dollars. It invested these dollars in U.S. Treasury bonds and in the secondary mortgage market.*

Many members of the U.S. Congress were unhappy. The big increase in imports from China was part of the reason for the drop in manufacturing employment in the U.S. Some demanded that China be accused of manipulating its currency, and that high tariffs be placed on their imports. The tariffs were never enacted (though there were a few on specific products), but the U.S. began to pressure China to allow its currency to appreciate.

China's central bank agreed. All those yuan it was printing to buy up all those dollars was starting to fuel inflation. But Chinese exporters disagreed. A higher value of the yuan might curtail export growth. In mid-2005 they compromised, allowing the value of the yuan to rise in value, but slowly. The central bank still had to buy billions of dollars to keep the yuan from rising too fast, and it lent those dollars to the Treasury, Fannie and Freddie.

Leverage

A household buys a house for $200,000 cash in California. In three years it doubles in value to $400,000. The homeowner sells, and makes $200,000, a 100% return on the original $200,000 investment.

A more ambitious household buys ten houses for $2,000,000 in California, with a $200,000 cash down payment and a mortgages totaling of $1,800,000. In three years the houses double in value to $4,000,000. The homeowner sells, repays the mortgages plus interest (say $2,100,000), and has $1,900,000 left over. That's an 850% return on the original $200,000 investment.

A mortgage with a down payment is an example of *leverage*. When asset values are rising, borrowing money to invest in assets can multiply profits many times. Investors in many asset markets had to make choices like this, between earning $200,000 in three years, and earning $1.9 million in three years. A lot of investors chose the larger amount.

The leverage ratio in this example is nine to one. The household borrowed $9 for each one dollar in equity, which is the cash down payment. In financial markets during the 2000's, leverage ratios were much bigger. The Bear Stearns investment bank was leveraged at 33 to one (before it failed).

Leverage ratios for homeowners and investment banks are regulated. Homeowners were traditionally required to put 20% down on a standard thirty-year mortgage: a $200,000 house would require a $40,000 down payment. During the housing boom, these terms were relaxed. Some homeowners were allowed to purchase homes with a down payment of 5%, or 3%, or no down payment at all.

The *Securities and Exchange Commission (SEC)* is the agency charged with enforcing leverage ratios on investment banks. It was established during the New Deal to regulate the financial markets, after the stock market crash in 1929. By the early 2000's, many of these regulations were thought to be obsolete. The SEC relaxed its leverage requirements for investment banks in 2004. This allowed the banks to borrow billions of dollars for added investments in mortgage backed securities and other assets.

Credit Default Swaps

A home buyer with a small down payment will often be required to buy mortgage insurance. For a monthly payment from the home buyer, the insurance company will guarantee the bank that the mortgage will be repaid. If the home buyer fails to repay, the insurance company will repay the bank, out of its reserves.

This insurance idea, magnified billions of times, is the idea behind *credit default swaps*. An insurance company, bank, hedge fund, or private individual accepts a fee from an asset buyer, and in exchange guarantees the asset's value. If the value of the asset falls, the insurer must pay. The insurer has taken on the risk, but receives the fee.

> *Credit Default Swaps are a kind of insurance on the value of assets. The insurance company guarantees the value of an asset in exchange for a monthly fee. If the value of the asset falls, the insurance company pays.*

Credit default swaps are a recent invention. Back in 1998, specialists at the J.P. Morgan investment bank came up with the idea, and approached the American International Group (A.I.G.), a huge insurance company. J.P. Morgan proposed that A.I.G. agree to provide insurance to investors who held mortgage-backed securities, collateralized debt obligations, and other assets, in case they defaulted. A.I.G. was happy to make the deal. Most of the assets they would insure seemed safe, which meant A.I.G. would collect fees without having to pay much in claims.

Activity in the credit default swap market exploded in the 2000's. Starting from nothing in 1998, by 2001 the market was worth one trillion dollars. By 2007, it was worth $45 trillion. Part of the reason for this explosive growth was that investors could take out insurance on other people's assets. I could bet that the asset you own would default, and if it did, I'd collect from the insurance company.

Insurance is a regulated industry, and one thing the regulations address is the ability of the insurance company to pay claims. When a company agrees to insure some risk (be it the possibility that you'll wreck your car, or require hospitalization, or default on your mortgage), it is required to place money in reserve. It can draw on these reserves if claims must be paid. The credit default swaps were so new, however, that they were unregulated. No government agency attempted to guarantee that the insurers had the resources to pay claims, if there were any.

What Went Wrong

This was the situation in the mid-2000's: the economy had seen 20 years of the Great Moderation. Home prices were rising, especially in big cities and on the coasts. Private investors, and the government sponsored enterprises Fannie Mae and Feddie Mac, were buying subprime mortgages and selling them in the secondary mortgage market. Mortgage-backed securities and complex collateralized debt obligations based on subprime mortgage payments, were in heavy demand. Money flowed into the markets from Japan and China. Investment banks became highly leveraged in order to multiply their investment returns. Insurance companies offered trillions in credit default swaps, insuring mortgage-backed securities and CDO's against loss.

What could possibly go wrong?

Home Prices Fall. Home prices started falling. Sellers set high asking prices, anticipating further price increases. Eventually many homebuyers couldn't afford the buy, even with favorable mortgage terms. Houses took longer and longer to sell. Home construction started catching up with rising demand, which put downward pressure on prices.

Expectations turned in 2006. Now people expected prices to fall, not rise. People holding houses as investments tried to sell before prices dropped further. That increased the supply of houses on the market, and prices dropped some more.

Now many homeowners found themselves *underwater* or "upside-down" on their mortgages. They owed more on the mortgage than their house was worth. That means that, if they couldn't make their payments, they could not sell and pay off the loan. Default and foreclosure was the result. When home prices were rising, default was masked because the house could be sold to pay off the mortgage. That wasn't possible if the mortgage was underwater.

Subprime mortgages were most likely to wind up in foreclosure. With small (or no) down payments, these homeowners borrowed near the full value of the home. As soon as the price dropped the mortgage was underwater. With mortgage terms that included rising interest and principal payments after a few years, many homeowners found their payments impossible to make. Many had counted on refinancing or selling at ever higher prices. Now, owing more than their house was worth, they could only default.

That's the situation of the Martinez family of Mountain House, California. The value of their house had fallen by one-third, from $630,000 to $420,000. Their mortgage was underwater. They had an interest-only mortgage, which meant that they paid only the interest on the loan at first, not the principal. Eventually they would have to pay on the principal, and then their payments would rise, way beyond what the family could pay.

The lenders that made these loans, and didn't sell them in the secondary mortgage market, were the first to feel the effects. Big mortgage lenders like Countrywide Financial and Washington Mutual saw rising delinquency rates on the loans that they hadn't yet bundled and sold. Losses mounted and bankruptcy threatened. Countrywide was sold to Bank of America, and Washington Mutual to JP Morgan Chase, at steep discounts, in 2008.

> *Rising house prices had masked problems of default. As house prices fell, defaults rose, and mortgage backed securities lost value.*

Fannie and Freddie are Seized. Fannie Mae had been losing its share of the secondary mortgage market, because it would not buy subprime loans. Lenders were threatening to bypass Fannie and sell directly to investors, unless Fannie agreed to buy riskier loans. And, Congress was pressuring Fannie to make more loans available to low-income buyers. Home prices were rising much faster than incomes, legislators pointed out. It was Fannie's responsibility to keep homeownership within reach.

Daniel Mudd, Fannie Mae's chief executive, described the problem. "Fannie Mae faced the danger that the market would pass us by. We were afraid that lenders would be selling products we weren't buying and Congress would feel like we weren't fulfilling our mission. The market was changing, and it's our job to buy loans, so we had to change as well."

Mudd met with Angelo Mozilo, the head of Countrywide Financial, who threatened to end their partnership unless Fannie started buying Countrywide's riskier loans. Countywide had been selling more loans to Fannie Mae than anyone else. "You're becoming irrelevant," Mr. Mozilo said. Fannie's investors also pressured the company to buy riskier loans. Other companies were making billions in the mortgage market. Why wasn't Fannie?

So Fannie and Freddie began buying riskier loans. Between 2005 and 2007, Fannie tripled its purchases of mortgages with down payments of less than 10 percent. This may have encouraged further expansion of subprime lending. When a government sponsored enterprise bought a mortgage, it seemed to have a stamp of approval.

Sometimes warning bells would sound in Congress. Should Fannie be restricted in the kinds of loans it was buying? When that happened, Fannie and Freddie would lobby hard to keep Congress at bay. At one point they made millions of automated phone calls to voters, saying "Your congressman is trying to make mortgages more expensive. Ask him why he opposes the American dream of home ownership." Congress never acted.

As home prices began to fall and default rates rise, Fannie and Freddie found that many of the mortgages they held were not worth what they had paid for them. Both companies had guaranteed the values of the mortgages that they sold to investors. If those mortgages defaulted and the values of the mortgage-backed securities fell, Fannie and Freddie would have to make up the difference. It would cost billions, money that Fannie and Freddie didn't have.

On September 8, 2008, the U.S. government *seized* Fannie Mae and Freddie Mac, funneling several hundred billion dollars to the companies to make good on their commitments. It was feared that the failure of these two firms would paralyze the mortgage markets. After all, they still bought half the mortgages issued in the U.S. Without them, where would lenders get the money to make mortgage loans? The housing market would be paralyzed. Some had hoped that the nationalization of Fannie and Freddie would calm financial markets. It may have had the opposite effect. If Fannie Mae and Freddie Mac, the biggest mortgage buyers on Earth, could not survive this crisis, who could?

Mortgage Defaults and Bank Failures. Something odd was happening to the mortgages that provided the income for Subprime XYZ, that mortgage backed security that Moody's Investor Services had rated. Some homeowners fell behind on their mortgage payments within the first 90 days. Six percent of the mortgages were delinquent after six months. These were much higher delinquency rates than analysts had expected.

Moody's looked into the problem and was dismayed to find that some homes didn't have lawns or landscaping, or that the owner had never picked up the keys. They had never moved in. People had bought homes as speculative investments. When housing prices began to fall, they walked away from their mortgages. By the spring of 2007, 13 percent of Subprime XYZ mortgages were delinquent. By early 2008, it was 27 percent, an enormous percentage. It was happening to a lot of the mortgages issued in 2006. The 2007 mortgages did even worse.

The bonds in the lowest tranche of Subprime XYZ became worthless. They didn't earn any income. But with so many defaults, even the middle tranche bonds lost income, and the owners of the highest tranche bonds felt threatened. Now was the time for investors to sell these assets. But, if everyone tries to sell, prices fall.

Bear Stearns was an 85-year-old investment bank that had never lost money. But it was a major lender to buyers of mortgage-backed securities, and now these assets were falling in value. Realizing this, the investors in Bear Stearns—equivalent to the depositors in a community bank—began withdrawing their funds. It was a run on the bank, and investment banks are not covered by deposit insurance.

In March 2008 JP Morgan Chase bought Bear Stearns for $2 a share, which was less than 10% of the share price just two days before. The Federal Reserve and the U.S. Treasury helped negotiate the sale. The Fed provided a $30 billion loan to JP Morgan Chase to make the purchase.

Why was the government interested? Because Bear Stearns was so widely tied to other financial institutions. The bank had borrowed money to make risky investments. If it could not repay, its lenders would be in trouble, too. The government was trying to keep the crisis from spreading. It was trying to stop contagion.

> *Government-sponsored mortgage buyers Fannie Mae and Freddie Mac, and investment banks Bear Stearns and Lehman Brothers, had purchased too many mortgage-backed securities. When these securities fell in value, these institutions failed.*

Lehman Brothers was a 158-year-old investment bank. It too was a big lender for and investor in mortgage-backed securities. On September 15, 2008 it filed for bankruptcy. Its managers had searched in vain for a buyer, and had pleaded with the government for a bailout. None was forthcoming.

Why did the Fed and the Treasury assist Bear Stearns, and not Lehman Brothers? Treasury Secretary Henry Paulson claimed, "We didn't have the powers." He said that the law allowed the Federal Reserve to lend to a bank only if it had enough good assets to serve as collateral. Lehman Brothers didn't.

Others dispute this reason. Two possible buyers for Lehman Brothers walked out of meetings when the government wouldn't offer the same loans and guarantees that it had offered for Bear Stearns. And, the very next day, the government did bail out the biggest insurance company in the U.S., *American International Group, A.I.G.*

Suddenly, A.I.G. was responsible for claims on all those credit default swaps they had issued. These were insurance policies that guaranteed asset values against default. Now mortgage-backed securities were suffering losses from defaults, and any asset tied to Lehman Brothers was worth a lot less than it had been just days before. A.I.G. had not reserved enough to meet all those claims. They would be far more than A.I.G. could pay.

The day after Lehman's collapse, A.I.G. begged for help from the government. The government reversed course and came to the rescue. A.I.G. could not be allowed to fail. Had it collapsed, every asset that it insured would instantly have been worth less, because without the insurance the assets would be riskier. Since A.I.G. insured such a large amount of assets, investors, banks and businesses worldwide would have suffered losses. They may not have been able to repay their own

> *The A.I.G. insurance company made most of the credit default swap guarantees. When asset values fell, A.I.G. couldn't pay, and the government stepped in.*

debts, or meet the demands of their depositors. "The spillover effects would have been incredible," said Princeton economist Uwe Reinhardt.

The government effectively nationalized A.I.G., using government money to buy up its stock. On September 16 the government offered $85 billion; by March 2009 the figure had climbed to $180 billion. The U.S. government owned 80% of A.I.G.'s stock.

But the Lehman Brother's bankruptcy and the A.I.G. bailout sparked a world financial panic. Willem Sels, a German banker, said that "when Lehman defaulted, that is the date your money markets freaked out."

The Markets Freak Out

Lenders have choices of where to lend their money. They can play it safe, and lend to the U.S. Treasury. The interest rate the U.S. government pays may not be so high, but the money is safe. The Treasury has never defaulted, never even missed an interest payment.

Or, lenders can lend to private businesses. The interest rates businesses pay are higher, because there is a risk that the loan won't be repaid. If sales are less than expected, the business may go bankrupt, and the lender will not recover the value of the loan.

When the economy is expanding, the risk of lending to a private business is not so much greater than lending to the Treasury. The interest rates on the two kinds of loans are not much different. But when the economy is in recession, lenders get scared that private business loans won't be repaid. They decide to lend more to the government, less to private businesses. So, the government doesn't have to pay much interest to attract funds, while businesses have to pay more. This is called a *flight to safety*.

The difference between the public and private interest rates increases. This interest rate spread is a measure of how scared lenders are about the risk of lending to businesses.

During the a typical week in 2006, before the financial crisis, the interest rate on a loan to the government for three months was 4.73%, and the rate on a three month loan to a commercial business was 5.07%. These are loans that many businesses use to stock inventories or meet payrolls. In ordinary times, they always are repaid from the sales of the inventories or the work that the employees do. The spread between these two rates was 0.34%, about a third of a point.

In the week before September 15, 2008, the three month Treasury interest rate was 1.60%, and the three month commercial rate was 2.72%. The spread had widened to 1.12%. Lenders were already more nervous than usual about lending to businesses. In the week of September 15—the week of the Lehman bankruptcy and the A.I.G. bailout—the spread increased to 2.24%. By October 15 the spread was 3.73%. Lenders wouldn't lend to private businesses unless they paid a much higher interest rate than the government. And, incredibly, during three days in December the interest rate on three-month Treasury securities dropped to zero. So many people wanted to lend to the government that the Treasury didn't have to pay *any* interest. The U.S. Treasury became like a very large mattress. People put the money there for safekeeping, expecting no return at all.

Private credit markets *froze*.

Now leverage worked in reverse, magnifying losses. If a $5 million asset, purchased with one million dollars in equity and $4 million in loans, drops in value by 20%, to $4 million, the investor's equity is wiped out. If it drops more, the loan may not be repaid and the lender is in trouble. If a $5 million asset was purchased with $150,000 in equity and $4.85 million in loans, just a 3% decline in the asset will wipe out equity. That's a 32 to one debt to equity ratio—like Bear Stearns had.

When asset values drop, lenders send borrowers a *margin call*. The loan was made based on an understanding that the borrower would have a certain amount of equity as collateral for the loan. If a decline in the asset value reduces that equity, the lender asks that the borrower pledge more collateral. To do so, the borrower will have to sell some assets. The increased supply of assets in the stock and bond markets drove down their values even more. Values on the New York Stock Exchange, measured by the Dow Jones Industrial Average, fell 42% in the six months after September 15.

Meanwhile, on Main Street

Credit default swaps, mortgage-backed securities and interest rate spreads were problems for financial markets, but did they affect the real economy? The answer, of course, was yes.

Home builders saw houses on the market for months, then years, at ever falling prices. They could not know whether they would be able to sell the houses they built at a price that would cover their costs. And, banks were putting more and more foreclosed houses on the market, at cut-rate prices. Home builders quit building. Construction workers were laid off.

The value of a house is the major asset owned by most households. House values fell. People felt poorer (and they were!), so they reduced their consumption spending. Households had supported their consumption spending partly with *home equity loans*. Banks would lend based on the value of the house, above what was owed on the mortgage (that's the homeowner's equity). Now equity shrank, or became negative. Home equity loans disappeared, and consumption declined. That's the *wealth effect*.

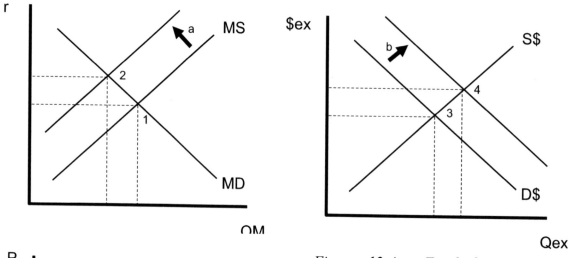

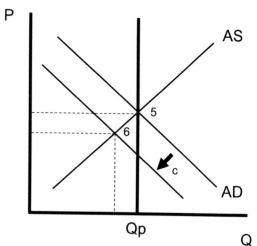

Figure 12-4. Freaked out. The collapse of financial markets causes lenders to build reserves and restrict lending. The money multiplier falls, which reduces the money supply (a). The real interest rate (on business loans) increases (1 to 2). International investors flee risk worldwide and buy U.S. Treasury securities, which increases the demand for the dollar (b). The exchange value of the dollar rises (3 to 4). Aggregate demand declines (c). This happens because collapsing home and stock values reduce household wealth, causing consumption to decline; the higher real interest rate reduces investment spending (second shift #2); and the higher exchange value of the dollar reduces exports (second shift #4). In addition, aggregate demand falls because of pessimistic expectations by businesses, which reduce investment, and falling world incomes, which reduce exports. Output falls (5 to 6), resulting in recession. The inflation rate falls, perhaps enough to create deflation.

People also own stocks and other financial assets. The values of these assets fell at the end of 2008. Those saving for college or retirement had to increase their savings efforts, which meant a decline in consumption. Retired people, living off of their savings, saw their interest and dividend income decline. Mr. Heinemann of Cribs, Kids and Teens in Mountain House, California noticed that Grandparents were no longer buying kids' furniture, because their retirement accounts were falling in value.

Businesses had to pay higher interest rates for loans, or couldn't get them at all. This made it harder to stock inventories or meet payrolls. It also meant that fewer investment projects looked profitable, so many projects were cancelled. Investment spending declined.

There was a worldwide "flight to safety." International investors looked to U.S. Treasury securities as a *safe haven* in the financial turmoil. This meant, however, that they had to obtain dollars in order to lend to the Treasury. They traded their own currencies for dollars. This increase in the demand for the dollar increased its exchange value. After dropping by almost half over seven years, suddenly the value of the dollar starting rising. It was 0.63 euros per dollar in April 2008. In December it hit 0.79, a 25% increase. U.S. exports became more expensive, and that, combined with the drop in world incomes, caused a decline in export spending. Businesses that sold in international markets cut production and laid off employees.

> *In 2008 financial markets froze as lenders increased reserves and refused to make new loans. Investors shifted funds to Treasury bonds. Loans became unavailable and interest rates were high. Falling home and asset values discouraged consumption. Investment and consumption spending fell, and the economy sank into a deep recession.*

All these effects multiplied through the economy. Mr. Heinemann in Mountain House laid off his employee. That person probably cut his or her spending. He cut his advertising in newspapers. Newspaper revenues dropped, and many were threatened with bankruptcy. He said he would spend less at Christmas. Christmas 2008 retail sales were dismal, causing more production cutbacks and layoffs.

The National Bureau of Economic Research marked the beginning of the recession in December 2007, but the first nine months were relatively mild. The unemployment rate rose from 4.9% in December 2007 to 6.2% in September 2008. Real GDP *increased* a little, by 0.8% from the third quarter of 2007 to the third quarter of 2008.

Starting in October, though, the economy dropped rapidly. Unemployment began leaping upward by three, four and five tenths each month, reaching 8.5% by March 2009. The unemployment rate was the highest since 1983. Real GDP fell at an annual rate of 6.8% in the fourth quarter, and another 4.9% in the first quarter.

Monetary Policy
The Federal Reserve began cutting its federal funds rate in September 2007, three months *before* the recession started. By December 2008 it had cut the rate to a target of zero to 0.25%. That's as low as it can go. Still, the recession got worse.

The Fed was increasing the *monetary base*, which are bank reserves plus cash in circulation. It was buying Treasury bonds from banks in exchange for money. Usually, this would cause banks to lend more. During the panic of 2008, banks reserved the money instead. They were too pessimistic about business conditions, too scared about the value of their own assets, too concerned about the possibility of depositor withdrawals, to do much lending. Higher reserves and less lending meant the *money multiplier* was declining. The money supply is the product of the monetary base and the money multiplier, so for all the Fed's efforts, the money supply didn't increase very much.

Figure 12-5 shows the Fed's difficulty. Ordinarily the federal funds rate, which the Fed controls with open market operations, is nearly the same as the 3-month commercial interest rate, which banks charge for short-term business loans. In March 2008 the two rates differed by less than one tenth of one percent. In most of the next seven months, the Fed cut the federal funds rate, but the commercial rate *went up*. By October the commercial rate was more than two percentage points higher than the federal funds rate. The Fed was buying bonds from banks, but the banks weren't lending. They were reserving the money instead. Commercial loans became scarce, and the interest rate required to get one increased.

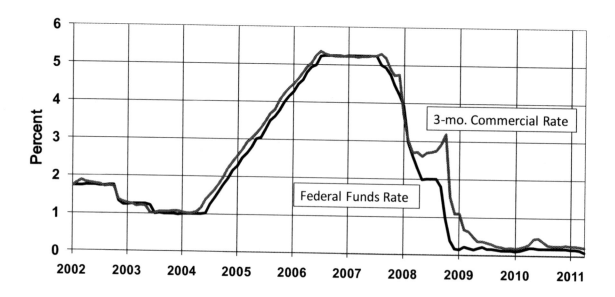

Figure 12-5. The federal funds interest rate and the 3-month commercial interest rate, monthly, 2002-2011. Usually these two interest rates move up and down together. The Fed can reduce the cost of business borrowing for inventories and payroll by reducing the federal funds rate. In mid-2008, though, the Fed cut the federal funds rate from 2.75% to 1%, and the commercial rate went up. Monetary policy wasn't working.

This is one version of an idea known as the *liquidity trap*. Interest rates were so low, and risk was so great, that banks preferred keeping their money in reserve, rather than lending it to earn interest. In a liquidity trap, monetary policy doesn't work. The central bank can increase the monetary base all it wants, and nothing happens. It's been compared to "pushing on a string." The Fed can pull the interest rate string to bring the economy down, but it can't push the interest rate string to build the economy up, if lenders won't lend.

Federal Reserve Chair Benjamin Bernanke anticipated this problem. As early as 2004 he was asking the question, what should the Fed do if the federal funds rate was zero? In a speech to the American Economic Association, Bernanke pointed out "that the public might interpret a zero instrument rate as evidence that the central bank has 'run out of ammunition.'" Bernanke invented new policy tools for the Fed, to make sure it had plenty of ammunition.

The Fed created a new way to lend directly to banks. The Fed's oldest function is as a lender of last resort. Banks have been able to borrow directly from the Fed since its founding. But by 2008, few banks took the opportunity. If a bank borrowed from the "lender of last resort," it meant that it could

> *The Federal Reserve cut its federal funds interest rate to near zero, and invented new ways to flood the markets with money.*

borrow from no one else. That might signal a bank's weakness to the markets.

William Gavin, a vice president of the St. Louis Fed, wrote that the Fed's new lending program included a "very public campaign to eliminate the 'stigma' associated with borrowing at the discount window. . . ." They called it the *Term Auction Facility*, and it was an auction of money. Banks that wanted to borrow from the Fed would bid an interest rate, with the highest bidder allowed to borrow the money. The auctions began at the end of 2007 and were stepped up in October 2008. Prior to these auctions, the Fed had only $300 million in direct loans to banks. By the end of January, 2009, the loans totaled $630 billion.

Commercial loans to businesses became scarce in 2008. The Fed responded with a new *Commercial Paper Funding Facility*. The Fed became the lender of last resort in the commercial paper market, lending directly to non-bank businesses. The intent was to back up that market, allowing banks and businesses to lend and borrow with more confidence. By the end of January 2009, the Fed had lent $316 billion to commercial businesses.

At the beginning of 2009, the Fed announced plans to buy $500 billion in mortgage-backed securities issued by Fannie Mae and Freddie Mac. The intent was to provide more funds to the mortgage market. Mortgage interest rates fell when this announcement was made, and by April the average rate on a 30-year mortgage was at its lowest level in at least forty years.

These new tools were extensions of the Fed's traditional tools. The Term Auction Facility was a new way to lend directly to banks. The Commercial Paper Funding Facility extended the Fed's direct lending to other kinds of businesses. Both of these were extensions of the Fed's traditional lending at the discount rate. The Fed's plan to buy mortgage-backed securities was an extension of its open market operations, buying bonds beyond the traditional Treasury securities.

These are a few of the Fed's new policy tools. For decades, we have spoken of the Fed's three policy tools. By May 2009 their website listed eleven.

Bailouts

It was the week of the Lehman Brothers bankruptcy, and the A.I.G. bailout. Investors were pulling money out of even the biggest, most profitable banks. Credit markets had frozen. Fed chair Bernanke and Treasury Secretary Paulson decided that it was time to act. Some aides suggested a "bank holiday", a nationwide closing of banks, as in 1933, but Bernanke and Paulson thought that would just scare people more. So, instead, they "broke the glass" on their most drastic rescue plans.

They met with Congressional leaders in a hastily called meeting to present the outline of a $700 billion plan to rescue the financial system. Bernanke told them, "If we don't do this, we may not have an economy on Monday." When the House of Representatives rejected the first version of the plan, the stock market had its worst day since the crash of 1987. Finally, on October 2, 2009, Congress passed the $700 billion *Troubled Asset Relief Program* (TARP). The money would be distributed in two $350 billion packages.

The original idea was to buy "toxic assets" from banks. Many of these were mortgage-backed securities in the lower tranches, which were taking most of the losses from mortgage defaults. Banks and other institutions that owned these assets were in financial trouble, and this was causing them to increase reserves and reduce lending. If the Treasury bought them for cash, they'd be removed from the banks' portfolios, and the banks would have the added cash to lend.

The plan didn't work. One problem was how much to pay for the toxic assets. No one would buy them, so their prices were effectively zero. But the Treasury couldn't pay a zero price—that wouldn't give added cash for banks to lend.

Instead, in November, the Treasury reversed course and decided to purchase shares in banks, another way to give them cash to lend. Nine of the largest banks in the U.S. were given $25 billion apiece, and a great many smaller banks were offered money as well. This had the side effect of making the U.S. Treasury a part owner of major U.S. banks, an astonishing move for a Republican administration. The Treasury also lent the TARP money more broadly, using the last of the original $350 billion to support U.S. auto makers General Motors and Chrysler.

Unfortunately, most reports revealed that by the end of 2008 most banks had not lent the TARP money, but had added it to their reserves. They were still too pessimistic and uncertain about their finances, and the prospects of borrowers, to release the money into the economy.

The second $350 billion would be distributed under the new Obama administration. The new Treasury Secretary, Timothy Geither, offered a plan. The details were sketchy at first (and Geither was severely criticized). By April 2009, though, the plan had taken shape. The Treasury would subsidize private investors to help them buy toxic assets. Banks would undergo "stress tests" to determine their financial health, and those that failed would have to find new investors, or come to the Treasury for more TARP funding, in exchange for a share of ownership.

Later that Spring there were some optimistic signs. The interest rate spreads had dropped back towards normal, and some banks were reporting profits. The crisis appeared to be past, at least partly because of the strenuous efforts of the Fed and the Treasury to stabilize financial markets.

But the unemployment rate continued to climb.

Fiscal Policy

In February 2009 the Obama administration's stimulus package passed the Congress. The *American Recovery and Reinvestment Act (ARRA)* as it was passed contained $787 billion in added spending and tax cuts, about two-thirds added spending, one-third tax cuts. Most of the spending would take place from the second half of 2009 to the first half of 2011.

The tax cuts would not come in the form of rebate checks, as the Bush administration tax cuts had done in 2008 (see Chapter 7). Then, households saved much of their rebate checks, or paid down debt. This time, income tax withholding rates would be reduced. Workers would see a little bit extra in their take-home pay each week or each month. These weekly amounts were small, and this part of the stimulus package was criticized as insignificant.

This may have been an application of the *permanent income* idea. Milton Friedman's theory was that consumers base their spending on their expectations of income in the long term. Short run windfalls, like tax rebates, do not cause consumers to spend much more, because they know the added income is temporary. So instead, the 2009 tax cuts reduced withholding, adding to take-home pay. The hope was that employees would see this as an addition to their permanent incomes, and so increase their spending.

Putting America to Work. A highway sign in 2010 telling us that the funding for a road construction project came from the stimulus bill, known as the American Recovery and Reinvestment Act.

Another feature of the stimulus package was *fiscal stabilization*. State and local governments must balance their budgets. They cannot run deficits like the Federal government can. This is because they cannot borrow as easily from financial markets, and because they cannot print money. When tax revenues fall in recession, state and local governments are forced to cut spending or increase tax rates. Both of these are pro-cyclical policies. If fifty states all act this way, much of the effect of the Federal government's stimulus could be erased. So, a substantial share of the stimulus bill was aid to state and local governments, to try to keep them from cutting spending or raising tax rates as much.

In May 2011 the Congressional Budget Office (CBO) estimated that, at its peak in 2010, the ARRA has increased real GDP by 1.5% to 4.2%, and had reduced the unemployment rate by 0.7 to 1.8 percentage points. This implies that, without the stimulus, the unemployment rate in 2010 would have averaged not 9.6%, but 10.3% to 11.4%. That means 1.1 to 2.8 million additional people would have been unemployed.

That was cold comfort for the 15 million people who still were unemployed in 2011, however. And as of mid-2011 most of the impact of the stimulus was over.

MacroPolicy Now: Spring 2011

Our march through policy history ends here, in Spring 2011. The beginning and ending sections of the first eleven chapters apply the economic models, and the lessons of history, to current issues. Let's bring these together in this last section.

What the Data Say
In the first quarter of 2011 real GDP grew at a 1.9% annual rate. It was the seventh straight quarter of growth—the recession was over—the the low rate of growth was a disappointment. The unemployment rate in May 2011 was 9.1%. It had increased slightly for two months. The all-items inflation rate over the twelve months to April 2011 was 3.4%. The core inflation rate was 1.5%. The all-items rate was so high because of rises in oil and gasoline prices. The core rate had fallen through December 2010, to a record low of 0.6%, but had risen in 2011.

The federal funds interest rate was near zero, and had been since December 2008. The 10-year Treasury bond rate was 3.2%, back down in May to where it had been in June 2010, after a few months of increase. The 30-year mortgage interest rate was 4.6%, little changed from a year before. A dollar exchanged for 0.7 European euros, back down to where it had been at the end of 2009.   A dollar exchanged for 6.5 Chinese yuan, having dropped slowly but steadily for a year.

These are the economic indicators we saw in Chapter 1. Now let's see what we can make of them.

GDP and Its Components. Consumers are beginning to spend on durable goods, but not much else. Real consumer spending rose only 2.7% from the first quarter of 2010 to the first quarter of 2011 (the past year). Durable spending increased 11% over that period. Auto sales are up. Consumers are gloomy: an index of consumer sentiment hasn't recovered much from its recession levels in 2009. High unemployment, falling home prices and high gasoline prices are probably the reasons. That keeps overall spending from increasing. But durable goods eventually wear out and have to be replaced. Maybe that's why durable goods spending has increased.

During the 2001-2007 expansion real consumer spending averaged 2.8% per year, not so different from 2010-11. But to climb out of the "hole" that the recession dug for the economy, consumer spending has to *accelerate*. That's not happening yet. For the recovery to really get going, we need consumers to spend more. Why? Because (all together now) consumers are more than two-thirds of the economy.

Two categories of investment are growing fast. One is inventories. Businesses cut production during the recession, and allowed their inventories of goods to diminish. Now they're restocking their shelves. The other is investment in equipment and software, which is up 14.7% in the past year. But investment in housing and business buildings was down in the past year. Housing in particular has not recovered at all from the low point of the recession. There is a glut of unsold houses depressing new construction and causing home prices to fall. Overall, investment was up 7.3% over the past year, but it still hasn't regained the level it had before the recession started. Interest rates are low, so if businesses do become more confident lending for investment is available.

Government purchases were nearly unchanged over the past year. Considering that we're supposed to be spending stimulus funds, and we're fighting a war, this was a surprising drag on GDP growth. The main culprit was state and local government, which saw a decline in purchases. State and local purchases have fallen in four of the six quarters since the end of the recession. These governments must balance their budgets, so when revenues fall, so do purchases. The ARRA stimulus package provided some aid to state and local governments, but not enough to prevent cutbacks.

Purchases are only a part of government spending, of course. We must also look at transfer payments ("R" in our model), and we might as well look at taxes ("T") while we're at it. Transfer payments are up 24% since the beginning of the recession. Tax revenues are down 10% since the beginning of the recession. Little wonder that the Federal government's deficit is so big, and that state and local governments are cutting their purchases.

Both exports and imports are growing rapidly, as trade recovers from its steep fall during the world recession. Imports grew slightly more than exports during the past year, so "net exports" fell (that's X – M), which reduced GDP growth. Consumers increased their spending on imports more than on domestic goods. The value of the dollar quit falling against the euro once the recession got going, and it's been up and down since. The value of the dollar needs to fall to make exports cheaper and imports more expensive. The dollar is falling against the Chinese yuan, but not by much.

With so many houses for sale, and so many commercial buildings available, construction investment is not likely to increase much. With the budget deficit so huge, it seems unlikely that stimulus spending will be extended. With revenues down, state and local governments are likely to cut their purchases. Exports are growing, but so are imports, so trade has not provided much of a boost. And consumers are gloomy and unlikely to resume spending unless they become more confident in the jobs, or gas prices fall.

So, where will the recovery come from? New households form as young people graduate from high school and college. The excess supply of housing will gradually be diminished, and construction may slowly resume. Businesses may continue investing in equipment. Interest rates are low. Employment is increasing, slowly, and gasoline prices are falling, slowly. These factors may increase consumer confidence, and consumers may increase their spending. Unless there are further financial crises, the value of the dollar may begin falling again. It is falling against China's yuan. This should eventually encourage exports and discourage imports. The outlook is for recovery, but it's hard to see why recovery will be very fast.

Unemployment. The unemployment rate is still 9.1% in May 2011, almost two years into the recovery. That's down from the peak rate of 10.1% in October 2009, but not by much. It takes real GDP growth of 2.5% to 3% per year to keep the unemployment rate from rising. The labor force keeps increasing, so GDP must grow to generate enough employment for the new job seekers. Real GDP growth has averaged 3.0% since the end of the recession. That's only enough to bring the unemployment rate down at a very slow pace.

It takes about 4.5% real GDP growth to bring the unemployment rate down one percentage point during a year. That's rapid growth by recent experience. Only two quarters in the whole 2000's expansion had growth rates over 4.5%, and there was no full year that approached that rate. This implies that it will take a long time for the unemployment rate to get back to 5%, where it was before the recession. If it's back at 5% by 2015, we'll consider ourselves fortunate.

This seems like a "chicken and egg" problem. Real GDP can't grow fast unless consumers spend more. Consumers won't spend unless the unemployment rate comes down. But the unemployment rate can't come down unless real GDP grows fast. That seems to imply that an economy could sink into recession and stay there.

Here's where second shift #1 comes in. Output is less than potential (we know it is, because the unemployment rate is higher than the natural rate). With so many unemployed resources, resource costs fall, aggregate supply increases, and the price level decreases. Output moves back towards potential as consumers (and others) buy more products at lower prices.

So the fall in home prices, for example, is necessary to make them affordable. If prices fall enough sales will increase and so will employment in home construction. This is why the rise in oil prices is so distressing. We need input prices to fall to increase output and employment, but the price of that one very important input is rising.

These benefits of falling prices run counter to other observations about prices, though. Sustained deflation tends to depress consumer spending, as Japan found in the 2000's. If consumers expect prices to be lower next month, they won't buy this month. If home prices are expected to fall some more, households will wait to buy. Deflation also increases the burden of debt payments, as happened in the U.S. during the 1865-1896 period. Home values make up a large share of most families' wealth. Declining home values create a negative wealth effect, which also depresses consumption.

Households face a tradeoff. Lower prices are tempting. Deflation and falling wealth are inhibiting. Perhaps what we need is for home prices to bottom out. If they are low, but not falling, households may begin to buy.

Inflation. The all-items inflation rate was 3.4% over the twelve months to April 2011. This was quite a bit higher than the core rate of 1.5% over the same period. The reason, as usual, was oil. Gasoline prices were up 37% from May 2010 to May 2011 (Chapter 2 looks at oil prices). Prices eased a bit at the end of May and in June. But the huge gyrations in oil prices make the all-items inflation rate a poor measure of underlying trends in demand and supply.

At 1.5%, the 12-month core rate was low, but it had increased by nearly a percentage point since the end of 2010. Oil price increases may be the reason for the increase, even though energy prices are not included in the core rate. With oil prices higher, so are the prices of chemicals, and plastics, and transportation to market. Rising prices for those inputs can raise the prices of lots of goods and even some services in the core rate.

Interest Rates. Households may be aided in their decisions to purchase by low interest rates. The interest rate on a 30-year, fixed rate mortgage in May 2011 was near its record low. Other interest rates, such as those on Treasury bonds and corporate bonds, are also near record lows, in both nominal and real terms.

The Federal Reserve has stepped up its purchases of Treasury bonds, and effort known as quantitative easing, part two, or "QE2". The Fed bought about $600 billion in bonds over the past year as a result of this effort. And, in fact, the average Treasury bond interest rate has been half-a-point lower over that year than it was the year before. Corporate bond rates were lower too. This effort is scheduled to end soon. Will interest rates remain low? If not, will this discourage consumer and business spending?

Exchange Rates. For most of the 2000's the exchange value of the dollar fell against the euro and most other currencies. The big trade deficits meant that more dollars were being supplied than demanded in currency exchange markets, and this drove the dollar's value down. The dollar leapt upward in the Fall of 2008 with the financial crisis. U.S. Treasury bonds remained a safe haven during economic crises, and international investors needed dollars in order to lend to the U.S. government. The demand for dollars in exchange markets drove up its value.

During the 2008 panic, the exchange value of the dollar rose from 0.63 to 0.78 euros per dollar. That's a 24% increase. Once the crisis passed, the exchange rate fell, back to 0.67 at the end of 2009. Then the first Greek crisis arrived, Europeans again fled to Treasury bonds, and the exchange value of the dollar rose to 0.82 euros per dollar in June 2010. Again that crisis subsided, 0.69 in April 2011.

But by mid-June the exchange value edged up to 0.70 euros per dollar. The current financial disquiet is not yet a panic. At this writing a second aid package for Greece is being negotiated. If the IMF and the Europeans come through with an adequate aid program, a second Greek panic may be avoided. If so, the value of the dollar will probably fall again.

Meanwhile, over the past year China has allowed the value of the yuan to rise, and the value of the dollar to fall. The dollar's value is down 5% against the yuan.

The dollar's value needs to be lower against the euro and yuan to close the remaining U.S. trade deficit. Financial panics interrupted this move against the euro; for several years the Chinese government prevented the dollar from falling against the yuan. Another Greek panic probably would make the dollar's value rise against the euro. But it is likely to continue its fall against the yuan.

That's what was happening, according to the numbers, as of Spring 2011. But what about the future? Here are four issues likely to loom large in the coming decade.

Financial Regulation

Former Federal Reserve chair Alan Greenspan testified before Congress on October 23, 2008, about the financial crisis. He said, "those of us who have looked to the self-interest of lending institutions to protect shareholder's equity (myself especially) are in a state of shocked disbelief. Such counterparty surveillance is a central pillar of our financial markets' state of balance. If it fails, as occurred this year, market stability is undermined." *Counterparty surveillance* was the incentive for each player in a deal to make sure the other players had the resources to follow through with its terms.

Greenspan had opposed regulation of the *shadow banking system*, the huge network of investors dealing in mortgage-backed securities, collateralized debt obligations, credit default swaps, and all the new financial instruments which had grown so important in the

2000's. He had thought that the self-interest of the investors would check any excessive behavior.   Surely, he thought, no one would buy an asset if its risk could not be evaluated, no one would offer or accept insurance without adequate collateral, and no one would leverage equity at thirty to one without confidence in the assets being purchased.

The events of September and October, 2008, had left Greenspan in "shocked disbelief."

On July 21, 2010, President Obama signed the Dodd-Frank financial regulation reform bill, named after Senator Christopher Dodd and Representative Barney Frank.

Here are some of the problems that helped cause the financial crisis, and the new regulations that address them.

In search of more "paper" to sell to financial markets, mortgage lenders offered loans to borrowers who were unlikely to repay.   Mortgage terms were inappropriate to the borrowers' circumstances. Regulators, who were supposed to protect consumers, didn't.

- The law will establish a new consumer financial protection agency.   The new agency would have to power to write rules for banks and other lenders, but certain types of firms (like auto dealers) are exempt.

Mortgage lenders made many subprime loans to people who were unlikely to repay, because they knew that by the time the borrowers defaulted, the mortgage would be sold to investors. Investors didn't know how risky they were, because they were so complex, because bond rating agencies mis-rated them, and because rising home values masked the potential for default.

- The law requires that firms that sell mortgage-backed securities keep at least five percent of what they issue, so that they remain subject to some of the risk.

Huge investment banks lent too much and reserved too little, so that falling asset values drove them to bankruptcy. Big insurance companies promised too much and reserved too little, so that they couldn't make promised payments when asset values fell. These firms had to be bailed out, because their failure would have had devastating effects on financial markets. The collapse of lending would have made the recession much worse.

- The law places restrictions on leverage and imposes stricter reserve requirements on the biggest financial firms.   It establishes a fund, paid for by financial firms themselves, to be used for bail outs when they are needed.

Exotic assets like collateralized debt obligations and credit default swaps were unregulated.   They were created and traded in individual deals, so the terms were not public. Little information about them was available, so neither traders nor regulators knew how much risk they posed for the financial system.

- The law requires that these assets be traded on exchanges or clearinghouses, with public disclosure and supervision by the Securities and Exchange Commission.

The law has been signed, but its implementation is behind schedule. Republicans who took over the House of Representatives in November 2010 have different ideas about financial regulation. In particular the consumer protection agency has been severely criticized, and the appointment of a director has been delayed. The financial firms are making a strong lobbying effort to lessen the severity of the regulations. The writing of many of the new regulations is behind schedule.

At this writing it is unclear how effective the Dodd-Frank legislation will be, or how long it will be before the new regulations are in use.

Unsustainable Budget Deficits

The Congressional Budget Office is the non-partisan fiscal analysis arm of the U.S. Congress. Here's what the CBO says about the long-term outlook for the Federal budget:

> Under current law, the federal budget is on an unsustainable path—meaning that federal debt will continue to grow much faster than the economy over the long run. Although great uncertainty surrounds long-term fiscal projections, rising costs for health care and the aging of the U.S. population will cause federal spending to increase rapidly under any plausible scenario for current law. Unless revenues increase just as rapidly, the rise in spending will produce growing budget deficits and accumulating debt. Keeping deficits and debt from reaching levels that would cause substantial harm to the economy would require increasing revenues significantly as a percentage of gross domestic product (GDP), decreasing projected spending sharply, or some combination of the two.

The CBO's concern is not with the size of the deficit in 2010 and 2011, even though these deficits are larger as a share of GDP than any since World War II. The deficits are appropriate counter-cyclical fiscal policy during a recession. Big deficits are appropriate for a big recession. Most of these deficits are *cyclical*, meaning they result from revenue declines due to recessionary drops in income, and spending increases due to added entitlement spending, plus stimulus spending on the TARP and ARRA programs. As the economy recovers, and actual output again approaches potential output, the deficit will decline. Revenues will recover, entitlement spending will grow more slowly, and the special programs will expire.

The CBO estimates that the deficit will be 9.8% of GDP in 2011. By the time output is back at potential, though, the deficit will still be 4% to 7% of GDP, according to CBO projections. How much depends on assumptions about tax and spending policy. This implies that there is a *structural deficit*, a deficit that exists even when the economy is doing as well as can be expected.

The reasons for this growing structural deficit are rising Social Security, Medicare and Medicaid spending (see Chapter 7). The baby boomers are retiring, so ever more people will be eligible for these entitlement programs. Health care costs are projected to grow faster than the average rate of inflation, meaning they will outpace the growth in tax revenues.

Structural deficits in the 4% to 7% range are "unsustainable," because that percentage is so much more than the likely real GDP growth rate. Since this year's deficit adds to next year's debt, a deficit that large will make the debt grow faster than GDP does. A rising debt percentage means an ever increasing share of GDP must be devoted to paying interest on the debt. That can't be sustained.

The "substantial harm" to the economy is *crowding out* (sounds like the 1980's from Chapter 11). The CBO says that "large budget deficits would reduce national saving, leading to more borrowing from abroad and less domestic investment, which in turn would depress income growth in the United States." Bigger deficits raise interest rates and reduce investment. Lower investment means a smaller growth in capital stock (buildings, machinery, technology), and so smaller growth in potential output. In addition, more borrowing from abroad would increase the exchange value of the dollar, which would reduce U.S. exports.

Economist Herbert Stein liked to say, "If something can't go on, it will stop." Here, this means that if budget deficits that big can't be sustained, then they won't continue. The concern is *how* they will stop. Will Congress and the President come up with a plan to restrain spending and raise revenues? Or will lenders quit buying Treasury bonds, forcing sudden budget adjustments, or forcing the Federal Reserve to buy the bonds, increasing the money supply and fueling inflation?

Monetary Policy

Between 2008 and 2011 the Federal Reserve tripled the size of the monetary base, trying to stabilize the financial markets and lessen the length and depth of the recession. Over that same period the money supply increased only 40%. Since the money multiplier was falling, the increase in the money supply was relatively small (that's in Chapter 6). But eventually, lenders will start lending again. The money multiplier will increase. With the monetary base that big, the money supply will increase a lot. Inflation will be a threat.

Fed chair Bernanke is aware of the problem. He said as early as January 2009, "when credit markets and the economy have begun to recover, the Federal Reserve will have to unwind its various lending programs. . . . [This] effectively constitutes a tightening of policy, the principal factor determining the timing and pace of that process will be the Committee's assessment of the condition of credit markets and the prospects for the economy." In other words, the Federal Open Market Committee will be responsible for increasing interest rates, and reducing money supply growth, to prevent inflation from rising.

The trick is timing. Reduce the monetary base and raise interest rates too fast, and the economy may fall back into recession. Leave the monetary base large, and hold interest rates low, and the economy may experience rising inflation.

Monetary economist Allan Meltzer is not so sure this can be accomplished. He doesn't doubt the Fed's knowledge or technical ability to hold inflation in check. But he wonders whether there is "a political consensus that the much larger Obama deficits will not pressure the Fed to expand reserves to buy Treasury bonds." An *independent Federal Reserve* could resist the inevitable pressures to hold interest rates down as budget deficits rise. But, Meltzer said, "under Mr. Bernanke, the Fed has sacrificed its independence and become the monetary arm of the Treasury." The Fed and the Treasury had worked together on all those financial bailouts.

Meltzer is saying that he expects a replay of the 1960's and 1970's in the coming decade. (You can see what kind of replay he expects, in Chapter 10.) He wrote, "sooner or later, we will see the Fed, under pressure from Congress, the administration and business, try to prevent interest rates from increasing. The proponents of lower rates will point to the unemployment numbers and the slow recovery. That's why the Fed must start to demonstrate the kind of courage and independence it has not recently shown."

Ben Bernanke fought hard to head off Congressional threats to the Fed's independence (find that in Chapter 8), so perhaps the Fed did not sacrifice its independence in the bailouts. But, what if: the Federal government does run huge deficits throughout the decade, and domestic and international investors demand ever higher interest rates to buy all those Treasury bonds. It could take most of the decade to bring the unemployment rate back down to 5%. Supporters of lower interest rates will have ample evidence for their view. Will the Fed come under political pressure to hold rates down by buying more Treasury bonds, increasing the money supply and generating inflation? Professor Meltzer thinks it's possible.

China and the U.S.
For a decade the people of the United States spent too much and saved too little. The people of China spent too little and saved too much. The savings from China flowed to the U.S., holding U.S. interest rates down and helping to finance the housing bubble. U.S. Treasury securities provided a safe place for China to hold their savings.

China's demand for dollars held the exchange values of the dollar high, and the exchange value of the yuan low. This promoted China's exports to the U.S. Imports from China flowed into the U.S., and their low prices helped keep U.S. inflation in check. Production for exports helped keep employment high in China. But manufacturing employment in the U.S. declined (we compared all this to hot money in the 1890's, in Chapter 4).

This too is unsustainable, so it will stop. Remembering Herb Stein's saying, what matters is *how* it will stop. It could all come crashing down. Suppose China decides that it owns enough U.S. Treasury securities. It stops lending to the U.S. The exchange value of the dollar falls, and if a panic starts, it falls fast. U.S. interest rates would rise, and in a panic, they would spike upward. U.S. financial markets freeze, investment falls, and the U.S. economy sinks into recession again (more contagion, like in Chapter 5). Fewer goods would be purchased from China, employment in China's export industries would decline, and China's growth would decline. It would be the 1997-98 Asian crisis on a larger scale (you'll find that disaster in Chapter 9).

Or maybe not. Suppose consumers in China start spending more. There is evidence pointing in this direction. Chinese factories are raising wages, partly to increase domestic consumption. Suppose China continues to allow the yuan to rise in value relative to the dollar. Increasing inflation in China can be countered when a higher value of the yuan reduces import prices. In addition, if China's government doesn't have to create so many yuan to buy so many dollars, it can reduce money supply growth to reduce inflation.

The U.S. has pressured China to consume more, and to allow the value of the yuan to rise. This may happen—slowly—in coming years. The part the U.S. must play in this adjustment is to save more. U.S. households have been saving more since the beginning of the recession. Total national saving includes government, though, and big Federal deficits mean continued borrowing. The adjustment to sustainable international finance requires a Federal budget closer to balance.

What needs to happen is for the U.S. to save more, China to spend more, the exchange value of the dollar to fall relative to the yuan, and for all of this to happen *gradually*. If it happens gradually, the falling value of the dollar will encourage U.S. exports, which could offset the decline in investment due to the higher interest rates. The U.S. would not fall into recession, and neither would China.

Moral Hazard and Stabilization Policy.
The story of American macroeconomic policy over the last century was the movement towards greater stability. At the start of the century the actions of one stock market speculator could plunge the nation into recession. But then:

- The Federal Reserve was created in 1913, to eliminate harvest season credit crunches and back-stop the banks during financial crises.

- Deposit insurance began operation in 1934, and bank runs largely disappeared as a characteristic of economic downturns.

- Unemployment insurance and social security were passed into law in 1935, providing automatic fiscal stabilizers that damped the effects of downturns on consumer spending.

- The Federal Reserve centralized its policy-making in 1935, and declared its independence from the Treasury in 1951. It adopted a policy of leaning against the wind, to adjust interest rates in to counter recession and inflation.

- Policymakers learned from a series of policy disasters in the 1960's and 1970's, that too-expansionary fiscal and monetary policy will produce inflation that can only be countered by severe recession.

- The Federal Reserve under Volcker and Greenspan discovered its mission and built its credibility, applying counter-cyclical monetary policy better than ever before.

The result was the Great Moderation, twenty-five years of economic stability.

And then the Great Moderation ended. And looking back, we also notice that amidst the moderation there were three stock market crashes (1987, 2000-01 and 2008-09), and speculative bubbles in the dollar (1980-85), tech stocks (1995-2000), housing (2000-2006) and oil (2007-08). Each of these events required policy responses.

Perhaps the Great Moderation and the frequency of bubbles and crashes are related.

When the economy is stable, people may underestimate risk. Home buyers and mortgage lenders think that home prices never fall, and so they borrow and lend more than they should. Manufacturers think that recessions will always be brief and shallow, so they invest in more plant and equipment than they should. Insurers think that claims will never need to be paid, so they keep less in reserve than they should. Investors think big companies and big countries are "too big to fail," that if there's trouble, they will be bailed out by the Fed or the Treasury. They invest in riskier ventures, knowing that their losses will be made good by the government.

It's a version of *moral hazard*. People who are protected from risk make more risky decisions. This overconfidence sometimes creates speculative bubbles, and when these bubbles pop, lenders lend less, and consumers and businesses spend less. Sometimes the crash isn't big enough to affect the economy much, and sometimes timely policy averts a recession. But sometimes, as we learned in 2008, the bubble is huge, and the reaction of lenders, consumers and businesses overwhelms the policy response.

Policy success creates stability. Stability creates risky behavior. Risky behavior creates financial booms and busts, and recessions. Better regulation might be an answer, but financial innovation always seems to outrun regulation. Perhaps that means, for all our efforts, permanent stabilization cannot be achieved.

Terms in this Chapter, in order of appearance
The Great Moderation
Standard deviation
Shocks
Housing bubble
Market fundamentals
Speculation

Capital gains tax cut
Greenspan's conundrum
Mortgage innovation
Secondary mortgage market
Fannie Mae
Freddie Mac
Mortgage-backed securities
Securitization
Credit rating service
Collateralized debt obligations
Yen carry trade
China buying dollars
Leverage
Securities and Exchange Commission
Credit default swaps
Underwater mortgages
Mortgage default
Bear Stearns
Lehman Brothers
American International Group (A.I.G.)
Flight to safety
Margin call
Home equity loans
Wealth effect
Safe haven
Monetary base
Money multiplier
Liquidity trap
Term Auction Facility
Commercial Paper Funding Facility
Bailouts
Troubled Asset Relief Program (TARP)
American Recovery and Reinvestment Act (ARRA)
Permanent income
Fiscal stabilization
Counterparty surveillance
Shadow banking system
Unsustainable budget deficits
Cyclical deficit
Structural deficit
Crowding out
Federal Reserve independence
Moral hazard

Notes

The full history of the "Panic of 2008" has yet to be written. I relied on two books in particular, which tell as much of the story as has yet occurred. They are Charles Morris, *The Two Trillion Dollar Meltdown*, which is good for details about mortgage-backed securities and other financial maneuvers, and Paul Krugman, *The Return of Depression Economics and the Crisis of 2008*, which has a nice overview of the causes of the panic. Much of the rest of the information in this chapter comes from news reports, in particular the *New York Times'* series of articles under the title "The Reckoning," which offer many of the stories told in this chapter.

The Federal Reserve sponsored a series of papers called *Synopses of Selected Research on Housing, Mortgages, and Foreclosures,* which I relied on for the description of the housing bubble's rise and fall. It's online at www.newyorkfed.org/regional/Synopses.pdf.

Robert J. Shiller's data series on house prices goes back to 1890. It's available in spreadsheet form on his website, at www.econ.yale.edu/~shiller/data.htm.

Americans were concerned about Japan's growing economic power during the 1980's. Novelist Michael Crichton wrote a thriller called *Rising Sun*, which included a Japanese plot to take over the U.S. computer industry. A political science professor even wrote a best seller called *The Coming War with Japan*. He didn't mean a trade war. Americans were particularly worried when Japanese investors bought New York's Rockefeller Center. These concerns faded fast during Japan's lost decade.

A review of the Dodd-Frank financial regulatory legislation in July 2010is available fromthe *New York Times* website, http://topics.nytimes.com/topics/reference/timestopics/subjects/c/credit_crisis/financial_r egulatory_reform/index.html?scp=1-spot&sq=financial%20regulation&st=cse ..

Information on the impact of ARRA and the long-term budget projections comes from Congressional Budget Office publications, 2010-2011.

References

Bernanke, Benjamin and Vincent R. Reinhart. 2004. "Conducting Monetary Policy at Very Low Short-Term Interest Rates," Presented at the Meetings of the American Economic Association, San Diego, California (January 3).

Congressional Budget Office. 2010. *The Long Term Budget Outlook.* Washington, D.C.: CBO (June).

Congressional Budget Office. 2011. *Budget and Economic Outlook, Fiscal Years 2011 to 2021.* Washington, D.C.: Congressional Budget Office (January).

Congressional Budget Office. 2011. *Estimated Impact of the American Recovery and Reinvestment Act on Employment and Economic Output from January 2011 Through March 2011.* Washington D.C.: U.S. Government Printing Office.

Gavin, William T. 2009. "More Money: Understanding Recent Changes in the Monetary Base," *Federal Reserve Bank of St. Louis Review* 91 (March/April).

Greenspan, Alan. 2008. "Testimony Before the Subcommittee on Government Oversight and Reform," U.S. Congress (October 23).

Krainer, John. 2008. "Recent Changes in the Homeownership Rate," in *Synopses of Selected Research on Housing, Mortgages, and Foreclosures*, New York Federal Reserve (March 17).

Krugman, Paul. 2009. *The Return of Depression Economics and the Crisis of 2008.* New York: W.W. Norton and Company.

McDonald, Daniel J. and Daniel L. Thornton. 2008. "A Primer on the Mortgage Market and Mortgage Finance," *Federal Reserve Bank of St. Louis Review* 90 (January/February): 31-45.

Morris, Charles R. 2008. *The Two Trillion Dollar Meltdown.* New York: Public Affairs.

Murphy, Edward Vincent. 2007. "Subprime Mortgages: Primer on Current Lending and Foreclosure Issues," *CRS Report to Congress*, Congressional Research Service, RL33930 (February 19).

New York Times, "Comparing the House and Senate Financial Reform Bills," Website, March 17, 2010.

Rosen, Richard J. 2007. "The Role of Securitization in Mortgage Lending," *Chicago Fed Letter* 244 (November).

Wilcox, James A. 2008. "House Price Dynamics," in *Synopses of Selected Research on Housing, Mortgages, and Foreclosures*, New York Federal Reserve (March 28).

Wilcox, James A. 2008. "Research Findings on House Prices and Fundamentals," in *Synopses of Selected Research on Housing, Mortgages, and Foreclosures*, New York Federal Reserve (March 28).

News Articles
Bajaj, Vikas and David Leonhardt. "Tax Break May Have Helped Cause Housing Bubble," *New York Times*, December 19, 2008.

Barboza, David. "Changes in China Could Raise Prices," New York Times, June 7, 2010.

Bradsher, Keith. "China Slows Purchases of U.S. and Other Bonds," *New York Times*, April 13, 2009.

Chan, Sewell. "Fed Ends Its Purchasing of Mortgage Securities," *New York Times*, March 31, 2010.

Duhigg, Charles. "Pressured to Take More Risk, Fannie Reached Tipping Point," New York Times, October 5, 2008.

Goodman, Peter S. and Gretchen Morgenson. "Saying Yes, WaMu Built Empire on Shaky Loans," *New York Times*, December 28, 2008

Labaton, Stephen. "Agency's '04 Rule Let Banks Pile Up New Debt," *New York Times*, October 3, 2008.

Landler, Mark. "Chinese Savings Helped Inflate American Bubble," *New York Times*, December 26, 2008.

Lewitt, Michael. "Wall Street's Next Big Problem," *New York Times*, September 16, 2008.

Lowenstein, Roger. "See a Bubble?" *New York Times*, June 5, 2005.

Meltzer, Allan H. "Inflation Nation," *New York Times*, May 4, 2009.

Morgenson, Gretchen. "Behind Insurer's Crisis, Blind Eye to a Web of Risk," *New York Times*, September 28, 2008.

Nocera, Joe and Edmund L. Andrews. "Struggling to Keep Up as the Crisis Raced On," New York Times, October 23, 2008.

Pilling, David. "Japan's Fearless Women Speculators," *Financial Times*, February 20, 2009.

Sorkin, Andrew Ross. "JP Morgan Pays $2 a Share for Bear Stearns," *New York Times*, March 17, 2008.

Sullivan, Patricia. "Obituary: Fed Governor Edward M. Gramlich," *Washington Post*, September 6, 2007.

Streitfield, David. "A Town Drowns in Debt as Home Values Plunge," *New York Times*, November 11, 2008.

Index